INTERNATIONAL BUSINESS ENTERPRISE

second edition

INTERNATIONAL BUSINESS ENTERPRISE

ENDEL J. KOLDE
Professor of International Business
Graduate School of Business Administration
University of Washington

PRENTICE-HALL, INC., Englewood Cliffs, New Jersey

Library of Congress Cataloging in Publication Data

Kolde, Endel Jakob
International business enterprise.

Bibliography: p.
1. International finance. 2. International business enterprises.
HG3881.K63 1973 658.1'8 78-37518
ISBN 0-13-472381-3

Printed in the United States of America

10 9 8 7 6 5

Prentice-Hall International, Inc., *London*
Prentice-Hall of Australia, Pty. Ltd., *Sydney*
Prentice-Hall of Canada, Ltd., *Toronto*
Prentice-Hall of India Private Limited, *New Delhi*
Prentice-Hall of Japan, Inc., *Tokyo*

To

Hubert, Ann-Elise, and Velle

Contents

VII

Environmental Dynamics: Modernization of Developing Areas 553

Preface

What a course in international business should cover is still a debatable issue. Like any new field, it lacks the separate lineage and heritage that define and delineate the domains of older disciplines. It also lacks the corps of scholars whose prime dedication is to defend the separate identity of the field. Only now are opportunities emerging in doctoral programs for young scholars to choose international business as their major field. It will take time before their undivided professional input will create a scholarly consensus on the focus and boundaries of the field.

In the meantime the dimensions of international business remain fluid and its coverage the subject of a dialogue among the four older fields that have contributed most to its birth: economics, finance, marketing, and management. While recognizing the need for a substantially new and different handling of international business problems, these older fields have at the same time tried to keep international business from sliding outside their own academic jurisdictions. In its efforts to subordinate the new field, each of the older ones has considered those problems its own methods would solve and has neglected the others. As a result, international business today means different things to different people. But these substantially different meanings have a common feature: Since their frames of reference are derived from just one of the older fields, they can cope only with certain problem areas of international business. Thus the content and emphasis of international business programs vary significantly from school to school. Although the different brands of international business have been on a convergent course, both educators and executives concerned with international business affairs find it hard to abandon the value scales of their previous specialties. And, thus, the dialogue must continue.

In this dialogue, however, one thing is certain: International business must be more than an appendix to any of the parent fields; it must reject a satellite status and derive its focus and perspective from the need for international business knowledge and understanding rather than from traditional monuments that antedate the birth of international business. It must be primarily concerned with problems which arise when business operations or institutions transcend national boundaries and become international and multinational in scope and character.

With this concept as a guide, the topic outline of the present volume was developed. The outline recognizes that the problems peculiar to international business, and especially the causes and sources of these problems, flow primarily from the environmental differences that business encounters in the international realm. Accordingly, the environmental structures, dynamics, and processes are emphasized. In this respect, the book goes beyond the traditional bounds of business disciplines. It does so deliberately; for if the fountainhead of the discipline's concern is the multinational environment, it will be doomed if that environment is not understood.

Another consideration in designing the coverage of this book was the audience the book is to serve. Here, too, the format and standards are yet to emerge. Different schools continue to experiment with different approaches, different courses, and different combinations of offerings and prerequisites. Any single-purpose book could, therefore, serve but a fraction of the collegiate audience. And, as books on international marketing, economics, finance, and other functional aspects multiply, the need for an overall perspective and frame of reference for the subject as a whole becomes increasingly acute.

To meet these many needs the book was designed for multiple use. This design necessitated comprehensive coverage and a large volume, which allow the user substantial flexibility. For example, the schools where international economics is not a prerequisite to international business will find relevant the concepts and techniques discussed in Parts I and II. Schools where international economics is required can proceed from the introductory chapters directly to Part III and will still find ample material for an academically solid course. Schools which require functional courses, such as international finance or international marketing, may wish to postpone assigning certain chapters in the book or to improve their functional offerings, which should follow rather than precede the broad basic exposure to international business provided in this volume. In schools with a limited number of business courses, this book can serve as a comprehensive survey of the business system and of its international context and ramifications. Finally, the liberal arts schools may find the material of the book a significant complement to, if not a substitute for, the traditional treatment of international relations because the book focuses on the factors and problems that are more decisive in the contemporary world than are the doctrines and ideologies of the past. For the business executive the usefulness of the book should be self-evident.

Writing a comprehensive textbook in a new field is a difficult task. As there are no formats to be followed, it requires much more research, learning, and originality of approach than are expected from textbook writers in established fields. To carry the research burden this author was gratified to receive financial grants from the Institute of Business and Economic Research, University of California, Berkeley, and from the Graduate School Research Fund, University of Washington. Recognition must also be given to the Nestlé Foundation and its Management Development Institute (IMEDE), Lausanne, Switzerland, under whose auspices I was able to conduct extensive field work abroad.

Among the many individuals who have significantly contributed to the preparation of the manuscript the following deserve particular mention: John Chiu from Singapore and Luc G. Willame from Brussels, who worked with me as research assistants at Berkeley; Professor Richard E. Hill from Sacramento, California, who helped to formulate the international management concepts; and Professor William G. Orthman from the University of Puget Sound, who provided much of the material on the legal environment while enrolled in the doctoral program at the University of Washington. Credit is also to Dean Kermit O. Hanson and Professor Guy G. Gordon, whose consideration and cooperation greatly facilitated the completion of the project. In conclusion I would like to thank Professor Richard N. Farmer, Chairman of the International Business Department of the Graduate School of Business of Indiana University for his helpfulness in reviewing the original manuscript.

ENDEL J. KOLDE

I

Background

The habit of going to the bottom of things usually lands a man on top.

1

The International Business System

Definitions of business are notoriously apt to delude. To some people, business is the pursuit of profits, to others it is private enterprise, and to still others it is any occupation or calling. None of these or similarly limited notions can sustain the burden to be launched in this volume. For us, business is a comprehensive concept; it includes all productive enterprises organized to supply goods and services for man's material needs. Since in this country and many others business firms are primarily in private control, it is inevitable that in talking of those countries the word "business" becomes more or less synonymous with "privately owned business." Conceptually, however, the term "business" as used in this book encompasses also enterprises owned by states, municipalities, or other public bodies. To refer to socialized industries and soviet enterprises as business may clash with ideological stereotypes or strain some latent biases. To the American tycoon it may be outrageous, to the Soviet commissar malicious, and to the Swedish neutralist slanderous. Yet it cannot be helped. For neither the advocacy of one or another type of business system nor the defense of any particular ideological dogma can enhance the search of truth about a new and little-known subject. Objective analysis demands emotional indifference.

Business, then, is modern society's means of subsistence. In industrial countries it determines not only the material standards of life but also the modes of production, consumption, work, and leisure, and to an increasing degree the influence and power structure of the society. Business has replaced the traditional elites—the landed aristocracy, the ecclesiastics, and the military—in the industrial countries and is forcing reform in the semiindustrial and even the primitive areas. Thus, business is more than the workshop of the society. Besides goods and services, it provides the stage on which most of modern life's drama is played, and besides being the main fountain of wealth and power, it is a source of both economic and social progress. Indeed, modernity in a social sense is synonymous with a business-dependent industrial society such as is found in the United States, Japan, and Western Europe.

The National Business System

A system is a set of interrelated elements. In simple systems the elements are individual components or factors which have cause-and-effect relationships to one another. In complex systems the elements are interacting subsystems, which themselves may contain several orders of subsystems as well as nonsystem components. The business system is such a complex hierarchy of subsystems of different order and character.

The components of this complex are, first, the different enterprises—both private and public—created to produce goods and services. They, in turn, consist of internal subsystems such as subsidiaries, branches, divisions, departments, cost centers, and work groups. A second category of components of the business system consists of industry associations of various kinds; they range from intraindustry trade associations (often with limited purposes) to interindustry and community-wide bodies such as Chambers of Commerce, development associations, and industrial planning boards. A third set of components comprises labor, vocational, and professional groupings, which are self-explanatory. A fourth category embraces subsystems which function simultaneously as components in the business system and in one or more of the political, legal, governmental, educational, and other social systems of the country. These elements link the business system functionally to most other important systems of the society. And through such links the interactions between the business system and the society as a whole, the inputs and the outputs, manifest themselves.

As a methodological clarification it might be added that, for any one of the subsystems in a complex hierarchy such as the international business system, the next smaller subsystems are its components and the larger systems to which it belongs constitute its environment. The impacts of the environment upon the system (effects of the system on a subsystem) are inputs, and the impacts of the system upon its environment (effects of a subsystem on the system) are its outputs, positive or negative. The impacts among the components, the interactions within the system, constitute the behavior of the system.

The International Business System

The national business systems combine into the international or multinational business system. Its components are basically of five types:

(1) the national business systems of individual countries

(2) the various intermediary institutions designed to serve as channels for interaction among them (export and import middlemen and specialized foreign trade service firms)

(3) multinational enterprises

(4) intergovernmental agencies and arrangements

(5) supranational entities and bodies

Categories (2) and (3) are peculiar to international business in the sense that they do not exist in the domestic business scene. They have evolved in response to multinational business requirements, and in the absence of such business they would at best have a tangential impact on the domestic system. As intercountry links, they transmit and often generate many of the interactions among the different national business systems. For this reason, the study of international business tends to polarize around intercountry links and to treat the internal workings of the national business systems in only a limited way.

The international business system has no fixed geographic boundaries but varies with one's objective. Unlike the national system, which, by definition, has concrete territorial scope and which, in turn, is composed of relatively easily defined subdivisions—regions, provinces, and municipalities—the international business system may be delineated in any way from only two countries up to the global totality. Between these extremes one can conceive, at least in theory, as many different systems as there are combinations of countries. In practice, the boundaries of the system should be chosen to facilitate the study or analysis of particular aspects or particular behavior. Thus, different geographical boundaries are appropriate for different purposes.

The Business System Contrasted to the Economic System

For clarity, it is important to note that the concept of the business system as used here is not synonymous with that of the economic system. As defined above, the business system embraces all of society's productive organization and its behavior. The economic system is a much narrower concept, best delineated in terms of the areas to which modern economics as a field of knowledge is confined. They are three: the theory of price (microeconomics), the measurement of the aggregate production and income of a country (macroeconomics), and more recently the development of mathematical tools to improve economic analysis. But the science of economics has very little to do with the concrete processes of producing or distributing goods, not to mention organizing and directing enterprises. In recent years attempts have been made to bring into the purview of economics organizational, technological, and behavioral problems which traditionally have been beyond its scope. However, the concerns with these and other so-called "externalities" have found expression primarily by scholars in business administration and its supporting disciplines—urban systems, management science, business and society, and industrial sociology—rather than by those in economics. It is unlikely that the concepts of economics and of the economic system will be broadened to coincide in scope with those of the business system.

Although the study of both economics and business must be based on the scientific method, the values, the criteria, and the frames of reference are different. Business is reality-centered. For it the overriding requirement is to understand, explain, and reform reality. Economics is theory-centered. Its main concern is with abstract principles and concepts, which may or may not explain reality. Since the economic system, as usually defined, is a narrower concept, it must be viewed as a special component of the business system. As a whole, it is more useful to classify economics and the economic system with other specialized disciplines, such as communication, psychology, anthropology, political science, law, and mathematics, which can all serve as tools for the study of business administration.

International Business Administration

Business administration deals with the organization, operation, and behavior of business enterprise. It has two main objectives: to explore the ideas, institutions, and processes which control and condition business activity; and to cultivate the knowledge and skills which can enhance the productive efficiency of business from both an economic and a social standpoint. Thus business administration is an unusually diverse and complex subject; indeed, it might be argued that, instead of being one discipline, business administration is a composite of many related but different subjects—production, finance, marketing, transportation, personnel, management science, operations research, etc.—which all focus on the study of business enterprise. Many other academic disciplines have similar branches or subdisciplines. Physics, for example, consists of optics, acoustics, mechanics, thermodynamics, etc.; biology of botany, zoology, bacteriology, etc. As the systematized knowledge of business administration grows and matures, its branching into subfields is likely to continue, and, as in other fields, some of these branch disciplines will become relatively, if not entirely, independent of business administration itself. Such a branching process has been the beginning of practically all the disciplines, except philosophy, that we know today. Business administration itself started as an offshoot of economics in the beginning of this century, and, because of this, it is often confused with applied economics.

None of the foregoing is meant to imply that business administration is independent of other fields. In fact, it draws on many disciplines, especially economics, social sciences, law, and quantitative methods. The degree to which these various subjects enter into business administration varies from subfield to subfield. Since the study of the environments and the functioning of enterprise in different societies involves many cross-cultural and other "nonbusiness" problems, international business is particularly dependent on the knowledge and analytical tools of other fields. The more important disciplines for international business are economics, area studies, cultural anthropology, law, political science, and social psychology. Geography, history, languages, regional science, and comparative literature also make important contributions. From the subdisciplines of business administration itself the most important areas for international business are finance, marketing, and business policy. Others such as production, industrial relations, organization theory, and social environment including government-business relations grow in importance as one's studies of international business progress.

Transferability of Knowledge

The applicability of American business learning to international and especially to foreign business situations is much more limited than is generally recognized because business administration deals to a great extent with phenomena which either are products of or are conditioned by the culture of the society involved. The business knowledge which has been developed in the United States treats many culture-determined factors as universal knowledge. This practice may be dangerously misleading in the international field for only pure theories, techniques, and principles are universal knowledge and, as such, have applicability irrespective of the cultural setting. As in other social sciences, much of business administration is not theory, technique, or principle; instead, it deals with culture-determined phenomena such as institutions, behavior, motivation, regulation, and control, which cannot be transplanted from one country to another without some adaptation.

Consider, for instance, fields such as finance, marketing, and personnel. What part of them has international applicability? Only that which is left after one plucks from them all the elements that are purely American: the laws; the public policies; the size and linguistic unity of the American market; the labor organization; the American consumer with his particular economic, social, and psychological makeup; the American ideas of competition, fair play, and acceptable conduct; the specialized services such as marketing research, advertising, labor relations, investments, and counseling.

Only after all the elements of *Americana* have been removed can one talk about the universal and thus the internationally transferable portion of business administration. Obviously, the scope of transferable knowledge varies with the intercultural heterogeneities which any particular group of countries presents. Close cultural kinship such as between Canada and the United States or Ceylon and India permits a much greater carryover of business knowledge and experience from one to the other than would be possible between Canada and Ceylon or India and the United States. The carryover varies inversely with the number of countries and cultures involved: the greater the number, the greater the intercountry differences and the smaller the body of system-wide business knowledge; and conversely the fewer the countries, the greater the chances for internal similarities as well as for adaptations.

Since neither the multiformities nor the uniformities of the international business environments follow any consistent pattern and since the fabric of cross-cultural influences continuously changes, it is futile to endeavor to distinguish the aspects of business administration which have international applicability from those which do not. Our concept of universality must be based not on a *catalogue raisonné* but on analytical comparisons of business realities at specific points in time in different countries. The elements of thought and practice which are congruent to the different environments can emerge only after the observer becomes aware of the value of comparative analysis. The lack of such awareness together with cultural inertia—having exclusively American ways of viewing and doing things—seem to be the most common obstacles keeping U.S. businessmen and scholars from a more rational and productive utilization of business administration in the international field.

Problem Areas

A general outline of the main areas with which international business must cope is in Figure 1-1. In the center lie the objectives of the enterprise (usually either profit maximization or the fulfillment of norms prescribed in a national plan). To achieve the objectives, management must formulate and implement appropriate strategies, programs, and policies. From a functional standpoint, the managerial responsibilities fall into four main categories: finance, production, marketing, and the organizational and institutional structure within which the enterprise is to function. Each of the four contains subareas, of which three main ones are shown in the figure. An explanation of how these, in turn, proliferate into clusters of component fields will occupy much of this book. However, they all represent only the internal view of an enterprise.

From the outside the company encounters both positive and negative elements which must be identified, understood, and anticipated before rational choices can be made among the alternatives available in different parts of the world. The environmental effects on business enterprise are among the most subtle and complex influences in an international context. As the scope of an enterprise transcends a single country and extends successively to more countries, the environmental diversity grows progressively in countless respects. From such diversity arise new opportunities, uncertainties, incentives, impediments, and necessities for the enterprise and its management. Multinational diversity may also transmute the previous norms, the managerial conduct, the executive action, and the corporate behavior as a whole. The multinational environment framework, within which international enterprise must function and in reference to which its administrative decisions must be made, is, therefore, of paramount importance in the study and the understanding of international business.

FIGURE 1-1

The Scope and Composition of International Business

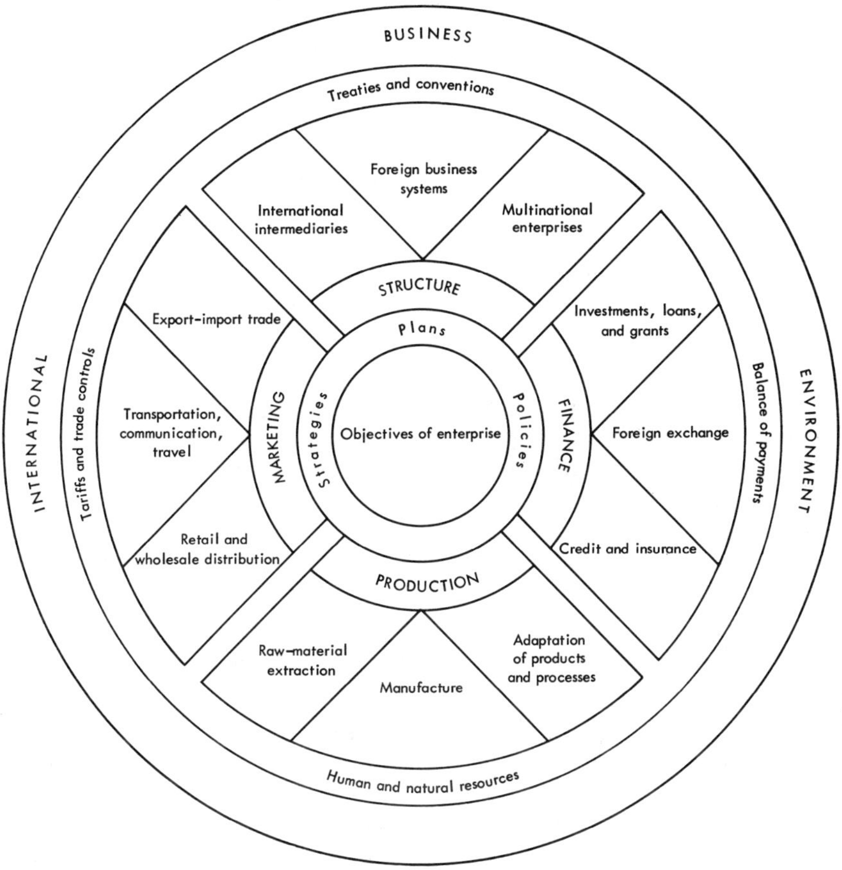

Some have argued that the need for international business as a field could be obviated if only the traditional areas of business administration would broaden their coverage to the international aspects of their respective subjects. Although the advocates of this view have been dwindling in number and the experience of multinational companies has strongly discredited this view, the point may still be worth making that no amount of "internationalization" of the specialized subfields of business administration can take the place of international business per se. Technical and functional disciplines such as finance, marketing, and production are often helpful and sometimes vital for the study of international business. But, since none of them deals with the multinational framework as such, they can neither singly nor collectively cope with the basic problems of international business administration. Not only is the sum of the parts smaller than the whole, but also many of the parts, including the most important ones, would never be included if the environmental framework of international business were not subjected to thorough analysis and study. It goes without saying that the problems peculiar to foreign societies lie far beyond the purview of the traditional subfields of business administration as we know them today and as they are taught by collegiate schools in this country.

The growth of multinational business operations and the increasing interdependence of world economies are exerting growing pressures upon business educators to go beyond the American experience. There is little doubt that sooner or later all fields of business administration will cover some international subjects. The sooner this happens the better. International business is not a substitute for but a supplement to the other fields of business administration. It is not, and should not be permitted to become, a technique-oriented or functionally confined subject. Its basic pedagogical task is to broaden the executive's perspective by giving him a wider and a structurally more flexible frame of reference and a more diversified conceptual grasp than he otherwise would possess. This knowledge will increase his powers to perceive, compare, and adapt. International work done in the base subjects such as finance, marketing, and production is a direct benefit to international business since it contributes to the total store of relevant knowledge and enables more sophisticated, higher-level treatment in the integrative and behavioral analyses which international business must pursue.

Conversely, a solid international business program benefits all other fields of business administration by providing the frame of reference in which they can more effectively pursue international objectives of their own. Thus the fear of faculties in some business schools to allocate the necessary resources to international business lest it displace some subareas is quite unfounded, except where some of the existing course offerings are outdated or otherwise unable to withstand an objective reappraisal of their educational merits in comparison with those of international business. As the problems and needs in the business world change so must the courses and research efforts of universities. Certain courses and entire subject fields may decline in importance, and they should in the interest of maximizing the return on the scarce educational resources be replaced by those of relatively greater relevance to the contemporary business scene. It is only in this context that international business represents a "threat" to some other subjects in the business school curricula. It is not alone in this role; others—operations research, simulation, computer technology, and management science—challenge the position of the older and more traditional areas of business administration. This is as it should be.

International Business, Trade, and Economics

International business is a new concept. It was first accepted as a distinct field by two or three universities in the mid-1950's. Since then it has replaced its academic predecessors—foreign trade and international economics—progressively at more and more collegiate schools of business administration. Outside the business schools, especially in the departments of economics, the older concepts continue to be used. Although the three fields—foreign trade, international economics, and international business—overlap, they are essentially different concepts.

Foreign trade is the oldest of the three. It has had several connotations in economic and business literature. For the classical and neoclassical writers it was synonymous with international economic relations. Much of this aspect of it was later transferred to international economics. In contemporary usage *foreign trade* refers to export and import activities, i.e., selling to or buying from residents of other countries. Whether we concentrate upon the theory of these activities or upon the practical operations of enterprises engaged in them, the scope of the field remains narrow.

International economics is a newer concept and covers a wider range. Although no two economists may agree on the precise delineations of international economics any more than they agree on those of economics per se, the field is essentially confined to those transactions which give rise to international financial obligations. In addition to import and export activities, international economics thus covers cultural, political, diplomatic, and all other transboundary transactions if they result in international payments.

International business, as already indicated, goes beyond both the older concepts by encompassing not only international transactions but also *institutions and organizations which cross international boundaries.* Although international economics identifies some international institutions, such as the International Monetary Fund, the World Bank, and notably cartels, it has nothing to say about multinational companies, joint ventures, foreign-based affiliates, or even the European Common Market. It is in the area of international institutions, especially in their motivation, functioning, and behavior, that international business makes its unique contribution. These entities have most of the capacity for carrying out transboundary activities and in relation to one another they produce the structural framework to which international transactions must conform.

What has been said so far refers to binational or multinational transactions and institutions. However, international business, quite unlike international economics, also embraces certain *uninational activities.* Transactions between a French subsidiary of an American company and a French firm are a simple illustration. In the same way, international business includes the study of entities which may be uninational from legal and organizational standpoints but which function primarily in the international realm, such as certain airlines, steamship companies, and export or import brokerage houses.

International Operations

The change in academic concepts from foreign trade to international economics and finally to international business was antedated by analogous changes in business practice. For many generations international business activity was confined to foreign trade. Accordingly management concepts as well as business organizations provided for an entity to perform exporting or importing functions or both: it was typical to find an export department, an import department, or a foreign trade department. Although such functionally narrow units still exist, they have been incorporated into or entirely replaced by broader entities usually called *international operations, foreign operations,* or *overseas operations.* This is not just a play on words. Indeed the words do not adequately reflect the nature and magnitude of the real changes which have occurred in the shift from foreign trade to international operations. As will be shown in Chapters 14 through 22, the new terminology hides more than it reveals. The shift involves not only organizational adjustments but also a fundamental change in the objectives of and the approaches to international business enterprise.

The Central Theme

Instead of trying to summarize these introductory notions, it might be appropriate to state the focal concern of this new field. The central objective of international business as an academic field is to study the problems which arise when business operations and organizations cross national boundaries and become multinational in structure and scope. In recent years, international expansion has become commonplace in U.S. business, making an organic aspect of management the ability to adjust the movement of men, money, materials, and information (including technology) in response to various pressures around the world. As a result, there is an increasing need to understand foreign environments, business methods, and the techniques of adapting management processes and organizational behavior to new and different conditions. The rest of the book is addressed to this growing need.

2

Global Spheres of Business Enterprise

The modern world is a variegated mosaic of nation-states. Its organization rests on the theory that each nation is the sole source of all the rights and powers to govern human affairs in its territory. It may be debatable if this theory of national sovereignty is capable of serving the contemporary man's best interests—for many ways nations are interdependent and becoming more so—yet the factual record leaves no room for doubt about the decisive importance of the nation-state in the modern world. Not only is each state a distinct national economy but also a distinct system of institutions, laws, social behaviors, and innumerable other characteristics stemming from cultural heritage, political ideology, natural resources, external influences, economic development, and many other causes.

In terms of economic development, for example, the range extends from the nations who have barely reached an agrarian feudalist economy all the way to the postindustrial economies with almost as many types and stages in between as there are countries in the world. For except in a statistical sense no two countries are really economically the same. Beside the vertical differences, there are also horizontal ones: the transition toward modernity need not and, in fact, does not proceed along a single path that all countries must travel, but there are many different paths to the same goal. Contrary to a widely held misconception, the underdeveloped countries of today will not have to go through the historic experiences of Germany or the United States any more than the United States had to follow France or China is following the U.S.S.R. Each nation forges its own economic patterns and its own path for progress.

Political, social, and cultural developments reflect similar originality in different countries. As a result the environmental framework for business, whether defined in narrow economic terms or in the broad sociocultural sense, is in countless respects unique in each country. To operate across international boundaries requires from business the ability to cope with the plurality inherent in the international environment. In a fundamental sense, this is what distinguishes international business from domestic business. More precisely, the primary distinction between an international and a domestic business lies in their environmental frameworks and in the organizational and behavioral responses that flow from these frameworks. As a company transcends a national setting, its environmental framework changes progressively in countless respects. There arise new ground rules as defined by law, custom, and culture; new values; new contradictions, interactions, and balances among external forces; and new opportunities as well as uncertainties. The wider the company's international scope, the greater the environmental diversities surrounding it. To make rational choices among the alternatives available to it in different countries, the company must be able to identify, understand, and anticipate both the negative and the positive forces of the international environment. To put it another way, rational managerial action can be taken only in the context of the environmental system within which an enterprise is to function. Whether it is legal status, ownership, organization, objectives, strategies, policies, practices, community responsibility, or the social status of executives, the criteria for it flow from the environmental setting.

In domestic business, the external factors are relatively constant for most firms. Changes are gradual and generally do not lead to any sudden differentiation among opportunities and constraints or among different industries or types of enterprise. From a comparative standpoint, then, the environmental constraints in domestic business can be considered not only as constraints but also as unifying factors common to the national business system as such rather than to management in particular. In other words, some of the environmental constraints act not as differentiating but as integrative forces in the domestic business process. Some of the integrative factors are the general world view of the people, the religious and cultural values, the social and political structures, and the basic economic organization of the national society. Since the study of business management to date has been conducted almost exclusively within the domestic setting, the effect of the environment upon managerial efficiency and business behavior is generally ignored in management theory and, for that matter, in business literature in general.

The International Environment

When an enterprise expands its operations and institutions beyond the domestic sphere, the environmental setting can no longer be regarded as a constant. Both the constraining and the liberating factors of the environment become variables both in space and in time. The constraints—social attitudes, public policies, price regulation, etc.—are no longer homogeneous constants but heterogeneous variables which increase in complexity as the firm expands its scope. Besides juxtaposing the different environmental complexes, the multinational setting is also more dynamic, partly because of the different speeds at which the various environmental parameters are changing in the different countries and partly because of the nature of the parameters themselves. And all these changes are relative since the environment in some countries in the corporate orbit remains relatively static while in others it changes; thus the overall environment of the firm is constantly variegated and the spectrum of alternatives with which management must deal is broadened correspondingly. This means that opportunity costs become more fluid and the chances for both success and failure are greatly magnified. To be able to establish its goals and strategies rationally, a multinational firm must not only understand its environmental structure but also be sensitive to the sources and forces of change that constantly transform the incentives, impediments, and rewards which define opportunities and provide the standards for managerial performance.

Which aspects of the international environment should be considered and which can be ignored remains an unanswerable question. The subjective belief of this writer is that no aspect of a society's culture is totally irrelevant to business enterprise. This is not to deny that some are more relevant than others and that the relevance of any particular factor may vary with the country or with the combination of other factors present. For example, family and kinship relations pose no significant problems to the management of a company operating in the United States, Sweden, or Switzerland and can therefore be considered irrelevant; but, if the same firm enters a country with an extended family structure such as Indonesia, Algeria, or Tasmania, the kinship relations and the attendant social and economic obligations emerge as highly relevant determinants for rational managerial action.

Because of such variability in their relevancy, no classification of environmental factors can provide a fully satisfactory model for analyzing and measuring their impact upon human enterprise. Nevertheless a logical structuring of the variables may greatly simplify the task and contribute to consistency in approach. The research to date on this immensely complex subject has been too rudimentary for one to make any firm suggestions on how the factors should or should not be treated without running the risk of obscuring instead of clarifying the relevant relationships. Professors Farmer and Richman have constructed a matrix of what they term the "critical managerial elements and external constraints."[1] Their approach is a valuable step toward a more precise method of studying the interplay between the international environment and managerial behavior.

However, until a firmer analytical base has been built through further

[1] Richard N. Farmer and B. M. Richman, *Comparative Management and Economic Progress* (Homewood, Illinois: Richard D. Irwin, Inc., 1965), pp. 37–38.

research and theorizing, interplay between the international environment and the behavior of the multinational enterprise must be conceived from its broadest perspective. There is a strong lure to short-circuit the process by going directly to the questions from which the payoff must ultimately come, that is, to the interplay itself. By doing this, one proceeds on the implicit assumption that both sides to the interplay—business enterprise and the international environment—are sufficiently well understood as separate phenomena to permit him to distinguish between what is indigenous to each and what is an impact or interaction. This is a dangerous assumption, for the study of the international business environment has just begun and even the "experts" have but crude notions of what it really entails. Before the interactions between international enterprise and its environment can be catalogued and systematized—assuming this will become possible—research efforts must focus on the international environment as such. This requires that the business scholar broaden his educational background and conceptual equipment to deal with environmental problems which in his approach to domestic business have been of little practical significance. That international executives will astutely employ any findings, factual or conceptual, which such studies produce seems safe to assume.

In Parts VI and VII the international business environment is treated from two different but complementary perspectives: one focuses on its dynamics —the sources, manifestations, and implications of change; the other on the contrasts among the different environmental systems. Thus, no comprehensive description of the international environment is attempted except for the brief exposé in the remainder of this chapter. Instead, the discussion will center on the key areas of change and contrast, which provide the most valuable information for and about international enterprise.

Environmental Systems

It is not the intention here to catalogue either the constitutional details or the specific changes that the international environment entails. Both are too numerous to count and too elusive to classify. The purposes of this endeavor are (1) to construct a structural frame and (2) to identify the principal sources—the prime movers—of global dynamics, and, thereby, to move a step closer to a conceptual scheme for the emergent multinational business system.

The global business environment defies any simple characterization. A specialized discipline such as economics or sociology could attempt in its own terms to treat it systematically, but any such attempt would, by necessity, leave vast segments of the total environmental complex unexplored. As indicated before, international enterprise cannot be compressd into disciplinary boundaries; its function and behavior pervade society as a whole. Any attempt to deal realistically with the environmental framework of international business must utilize an *interdisciplinary approach* both varied and flexible enough to deal with relevant factors regardless of their nature or academic

FIGURE 2-1

Major Divisions of the World Economic Environment

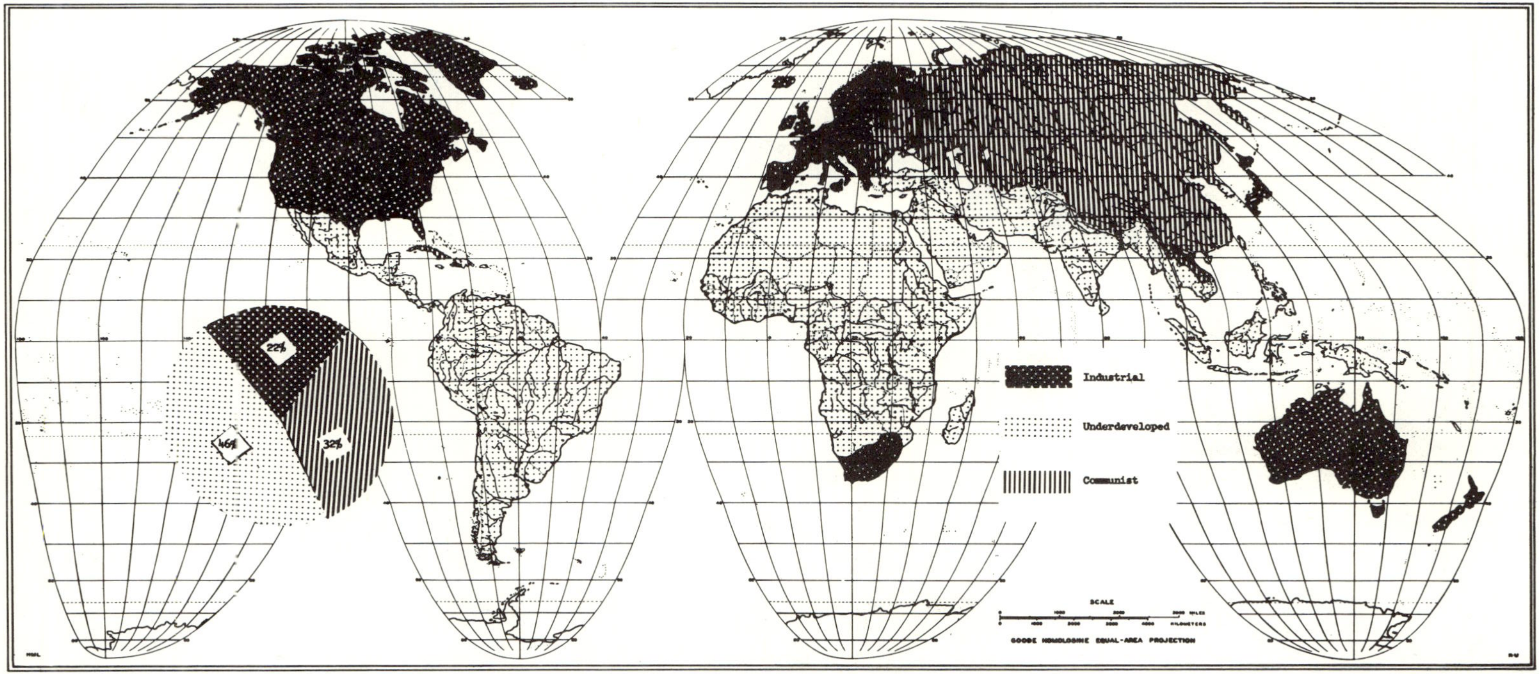

home. Such an approach also minimizes and dogmatic prejudice which the relatively narrower frame of reference of a single subject may tolerate or even foster.

Viewed from an interdisciplinary perspective, the global community consists of three environmental spheres or systems: the industrial West, the communist East, and the developing South which for purely economic purposes can be further subdivided into semideveloped and underdeveloped countries. The geographic scope and the locations of the three spheres are shown in Figure 2-1. As shown by the inserted pie chart the three business systems are vastly different in size; nearly half of mankind lives in the developing or subindustrial South, one-third in the communist East, and only slightly more than one-fifth in the industrial West. If natural growth rates are considered, the conclusion cannot be escaped that the population disparities among the three spheres are certain to grow rather than to diminish in the future. From the standpoint of economic production the industrial West accounts for approximately 60 percent, the communist East about 25 percent, and the developing South only 15 percent; hence the per capita disparities are immense. However, it should be emphasized that the three sections of global society, or the three environmental systems as they have been called here, are by no means homogeneous and harmonious blocs. To the contrary, each is full of internal differences, tensions, and even contradictions. But their internal diversities are overshadowed by the sharp contrasts among them. And, like the environmental systems, the enterprises within them have sharp contrasts in character and behavior.

The Industrial West

The industrial nations rim the North Atlantic, with Western Europe and North America being the two principal clusters. Japan, Australia, New Zealand, and the Republic of South Africa complete the industrially developed sector of the free world.

The Capitalist Model

All these are fundamentally capitalist countries with market-oriented economies. Private property, free enterprise, and open competition are the pillars of their ideological edifice. The basic regulator of the system, if not always in fact at least in theory, is the free competitive market, where a producer is judged by his ability to meet or better the performance of other producers and where the consumers must compete against each other for the optimum satisfaction of their needs. Since the producers try to maximize their profits—revenue less cost—and the consumers try to minimize their expenditures and thereby maximize the total quantity of goods and services which any given income can buy, the market mechanism tends to allocate the available resources to the uses which make the greatest contribution to human welfare as interpreted by the particular society as a whole.[2] According to the classical explanation of capitalism, the competitive market guides economic decision making throughout the society. It is a decentralized process which acts as an autonomous regulator of prices, as a guarantee that all factors of production will be paid (through wages, interest, rent, or profits) in accordance with the society's estimate of their contribution, as an incentive for increased efficiency, as a generator of a greater variety and abundance of goods and services, and as the protector of the freedom of opportunity. To put it differently, the classical capitalist system functions through the mechanism of competitive prices, which direct businessmen to those industries which are profitable. The existence of profits—the difference between the cost of production and the price which the consumers offer to pay—indicates that the utility of the product to the society is greater than its cost, and that, therefore, its production should be increased. And by reverse reasoning, the production of products for which the consumer is not willing to pay enough to cover the cost should be reduced. Since prices settle at the level where supply and demand balance, the system harmonizes the interests of the producers and the consumers. If prices rise above the balance point, producers gain an "unearned" profit and the consumers suffer a "loss," which sooner or later curtails the demand and results in a cutback of prices or a cutback of output. In the same manner, competition sets the standards for factor payments—wages, rent, and interest—in the factor markets. Thus the system generates an overall harmony which benefits all groups of the society. So much for the theoretical model.

Discrepancies between the model and reality

In reality, the capitalist model is not perfect. This is due not to its construction but to the conditions under which it has to be employed. People are not always economically motivated and often act in contradiction to the dictates of the economy. More often, the information at the disposal of the individual—either producer or consumer—is insufficient to permit a fully rational choice or decision. And, too, political, social, and moral standards are often invoked which interfere with the operation of the model. The result is a complex blend of economic, political, and social ideologies, where the individual, the community, and the public interact in a multitude of ways.

Contemporary capitalist society incorporates much of what once passed for socialism, statism, and collectivism. Although it still derives the standards for efficiency and economic performance from the classical model described

2 If the reader is not familiar with the competitive economic model, he would greatly benefit from studying some basic book on microeconomics or price theory, for nothing is more fundamental to economic science than the model of perfect competition. Not only are the other price and value models derived from it but also, and more importantly, the competitive model serves as the standard by which all others are judged.

above, it amplifies and sometimes replaces the market mechanism with social controls which centralize certain decisions in the hands of the various control agencies. Public utilities, banking, and labor legislation are cases in point.

As for its performance, modern capitalist society has given to its members all the material benefits promised by socialist leaders half a century ago. In fact, the contemporary abundance of the capitalist world makes the socialist claims of yesteryear quite modest and insignificant. As a result, democratic socialism (as distinguished from the Marxian version) has become meaningless in most industrial countries. Their focal thrust was against "private property," which is the collective term for legal claims to income from the assets that the capitalist system enables its members to hold. In their preoccupation with redistributing the benefits derived from property, the socialists overlooked the more fundamental propositions that redistribution can have lasting benefit only if the production and the growth of property are maintained at least on the previous level and that private property represents not only claims on income from assets but also a system of cues and incentives which, despite its flaws, helps to put the property to its most productive use and thereby to make the assets of the society grow.

Wherever socialist governments have introduced nationalization or other schemes of substituting socialized ownership for private enterprise, they have been compelled to imitate in complex and expensive ways those controls which private property has provided automatically. This has led to a new phenomenon: the socialist "entrepreneurs"—executives of socialized industries who have only very general directives from the government and who are expected to behave as if they were running private companies. Despite the very limited publicity given to it by socialist leaders, the socialist entrepreneur is now commonplace in all developed and many developing countries. To the disillusionment of socialist theoreticians, property as a socioeconomic institution has proven itself indestructible. Many of the goals which socialists espoused have turned out to be obtainable only through the use of private property and a free market. This non-Marxian realization seems to be gaining acceptance even in the Soviet countries. But as far as the capitalist world is concerned, nineteenth-century socialism and capitalism are both passé, only socialism more so. The modern blend, which absorbs them both, bears a far greater resemblance to the more efficient, flexible capitalist concept than to dogma-bound socialism. Whatever its proportions, the blend, which here has been called *modern capitalism,* is far more potent than either of its ideological ingredients, for it has exceeded the objectives of each.

Political and Social Characteristics of Modern Industrial Societies

Politically the industrial countries are guided by the principles of representative government, democratic processes, and the rule of law. That deviations occur and that perfection is seldom achieved do not invalidate these principles as the standards for political relations within the society. They are the ideals toward which Western civilization has struggled since antiquity and which in this century have been realized in many more ways than not.

Although the three premises themselves require no explanation for a collegiate reader, the ramifications of their implementation, especially those arising from the industrialization of the society, deserve elaboration.

The industrial societies are held together by a participant polity which expresses itself in special action structures and in elected functionaries; a great many functional organizations and special-purpose groups arise in the industrial countries. These groups play an influential and often the decisive role in the decisions made in the interest of the public. Formally, the industrial countries are either republics or constitutional monarchies; actually, they are all *polyarchies* which utilize the methods and principles of democracy but have failed to attain it in the strict sense of the term. Whether pure democracy can ever be attained cannot be debated here. The complete political equality which pure democracy prescribes is not likely to replace the ever-increasing variety of special-action organizations that advancing technology and its attendant specialization spawn in the industrial world. That is, individuals in an industrial society can often maximize their subjective goal attainment by substituting inequality for equality. All special-purpose groups help to do this to a certain degree.

Inequality is not only a functional working arrangement but also the more permanent distribution reflected in social stratification. The status or "class" of an individual in an industrial society is determined primarily by his achievement and not granted by ascription. In this respect in countries such as England, Sweden, and Japan, where aristocratic traditions have yielded to the industrial code of social stratification more slowly than elsewhere, the social structure is often blurred and inconsistent. However, the trend is unmistakable: Wherever hereditary status is not reinforced by achievement status, it is drained of substance and reduced to being a relic.

The industrial countries are open societies with strong tendencies toward mass culture. Communications, interpersonal relations, and economic activities all, to varying degrees, are organized and manipulated by different interest groups—the participant polities. Even leisure and recreation are highly organized and mobilized as mass enterprises. Fad and fashion, propagated through mass media, hammer away at objective standards and subjective tastes to coerce conformity. There is a peculiar interplay between social stratification and integration in the industrial countries. The same technique which fuses individuals into a mass may mean achievement, distinction, and status to one or a few in whose interest the mobilizing action was engineered, either by design or by coincidence.

Family and Religion

Although the place of religion in the capitalist countries is a conspicuous and honored one, its impact on the ideological environment is declining. Separated from the business and technological spheres, religion can at best influence industrial decisions by indirection, since it has been deprived of its original methods: prescribing, proscribing, and passing judgment. Also, religion lacks the aggressive dynamics upon which industrialization must feed.

Tradition-oriented and committed to ritual, religion finds itself in fierce competition with progressive, rationalist philosophies which provide the social ideology of industrial enterprise.

The relative decline of religious influence has stirred many Western industrialists and political leaders to endeavor to restore religious authority and guidance to the business system. Also, several fundamentalist movements have been inspired by the same objective. At best, these efforts have succeeded in increasing church membership and have re-emphasized its traditionally exalted position. But all the maneuvers and deliberations have failed to produce any clear definition as to what functions religion should play in modern industrial society. While the debate goes on, governmental agencies, professional groups, and other functional organizations continue displacing the clergy from the social and cultural spheres which once were its exclusive domain. Education, charity, child care, care for the aged, social welfare, disaster relief, and health programs all have been successively transferred from its domain to specialized, secular agencies. That any of these social functions will be reconsecrated to religion seems no more likely than does the resurgence of theocracy as a political system.

Familial patterns in industrial countries differ sharply from those in subindustrial societies. Even the concept is different. While in the subindustrial societies the family includes kin groups on an extended basis—second- and third-degree cousins, for example, being members of such a group—a family in the industrial world seldom exceeds the primary kin group, i.e., parents and children.

The conversion from the extended to the primary familial pattern takes place gradually in response to a country's industrialization. The higher the degree of industrialization the fewer the kin groups included in the family. And, as specialized social institutions, such as homes for the aged, social security, and pension plans become prevalent, even the primary group—parents-children-grandchildren—is subdivided.

The function of the extended family in the traditional society has been to integrate enterprise and home life; the entire family group participates not only in the social and consumptive activities but also in the production process. In the industrial society, in contrast, the economic function of the family is to separate domesticity and enterprise. The contribution of children to the productive enterprise is neither needed nor plausible. This frees them for training and preparation for the specialized industrial skills which the society demands. And marriage becomes semivocational—the woman specializes in operating an increasingly mechanized household, which permits the husband to concentrate on his business or profession. Hence, the familial pattern of industrial countries is highly compatible with their basic rationale.

Summary

In sum, modern industrial countries are characterized by a proliferation of organizations, laws, and regulations. The political structure is a polyarchy based on the principle of democracy and held together by a participant polity.

All these countries operate through representative institutions and a regime of equal rights under law. The expressive sphere of their culture tends toward industrialized enterprise along with that of economics and business. There are mass markets, mass entertainment, and mass hobbies. Family and religious life, too, have been molded to fit the industrial requirements.

The Communist East

The communist realm occupies most of the large Eurasian land mass and is geographically more cohesive than the other two business systems, Cuba being its only detached outpost. Ideologically, too, the communist realm is quite cohesive. This ideology rests on the doctrines expounded by Marx, Engels, and Lenin and is characterized by a theoretical rigidity and a monolithic "omniscience" unparalleled in the non-communist systems. Although contemporary interpretations of the ideology show some divergent tendencies, as dramatically evidenced by the Sino-Soviet rift, its basic body has not been challenged or disclaimed. The Sino-Soviet rift has been more a struggle for power and leadership in the communist movement and less a quarrel about ideology as such. There has been no attempt to debase Marxism-Leninism, but there have been attempts to challenge the position and authority of its high priests. More than any other, the communist bloc has been an ideology-conscious, ideology-directed, and ideology-dependent society.

The Soviet system emerged from the Bolshevik Revolution of 1917 and has since been recognized as being different not only from capitalism and democracy but also from Western absolutism and tsarist autocracy. Political theorists have labeled the Soviet order (along with fascism and nazism) *totalitarianism* and defined it as a system with a total concentration of power—political, economic, and cultural. The centrum of the concentration is the communist party, which prescribes a single set of all-inclusive values, preferences, and beliefs and which demands overt compliance from the entire nation. Totalitarianism, thus, is a name given to a system where a monopoly party directly administers and controls all political, economic, social, and cultural activities of the society.

The Communist Economic Model

The whole society in a communist country has a bureaucratic command structure. Every citizen is a state employee with a specialized function; his entire life is organized by and lived within the framework of state institutions governed by the communist party. In this command economy state monopoly replaces private ownership and enterprise. All land and natural resources, industrial and commercial establishments, and financial institutions belong to the state.

No individual can own any means of production or real estate. Private property rights are confined to nonproductive chattels, primarily personal effects. Neither inheritance nor personal accumulation can serve as an economic control. The market mechanism, too, is abandoned. In brief, the communist system sterilizes all capitalist society's decentralized regulators of economic activity (private enterprise, property rights, and price competition in an open market) and substitutes for them centralized, coercive planning administered by an enormous bureaucratic hierarchy and enforced by all agencies of the government, not only as the Marxist mode of production but also as an aspect of socialist justice.

Planning

Although a description of the totalitarian industrial bureaucracy would require volumes, its basic model can be explained in relatively simple terms. The economic objectives of the country are established by the highest political organ: the Central Committee of the communist party. The important or primary objectives are kept fairly limited in number for any particular planning period. Professional planners translate these objectives into specific production goals and quota allocations implemented by a gigantic state bureaucracy. The plan specifies not only the outputs for each industry and enterprise but also the inputs needed to realize these goals. All communist enterprises are compelled to behave according to the plans. None is free to choose its own objectives, not to mention its own product line, size, or location. Although all orders are not plans, all plans are legal orders which an enterprise management must obey. Thus the principal task of communist executives is to fulfill the plan.

For output, the planned quantity is interpreted as being the minimum, i.e., fulfilling means to equal or to exceed the planned quantity; but for inputs and costs, the planned quantity is the maximum, and fulfillment means staying under the planned figures. "Profits" arise from exceeding the plan (a) by producing more than than the prescribed quota at the planned input ratio, (b) by meeting the quota at a lower input ratio than planned, or (c) through a combination of the two.

Both allocation of resources and integration of the economy are, thus, carried out centrally by coercive planning and legal enforcement of the process. In this, the communist system resembles war economy: It relies on command rather than on any economic or scientific standard which could serve as a basis for decentralization of decision making. Since there is no such standard, the central command system must not only ration the inputs and outputs of the entire economic process but also make all decisions of strategy and policy for the enterprises. The main function of the enterprise executives is to implement these central decisions. Their own decision-making authority is confined to the operational and procedural aspects. This does not mean that clever managers do not try to influence policy decisions by various means, but by so doing, they are, in effect, subverting the system rather than living by its rule.

Only in the distributive phase of command-produced consumer goods is a type of market economy substituted for rationing; i.e., goods are sold to people with money to pay for them rather than distributed on a quota basis. However, prices are subject to various degrees of regulation, and the total quantity of product sold to a particular buyer is often limited.

Its inability to decentralize is a weakness of the communist economic system. The seriousness of this weakness was fully realized in 1965, when the Soviet Union abandoned a plan of economic territorialization which the Khrushchev regime had introduced in an effort to decentralize and better adapt the country's production to local needs. According to sovietologists, decentralization could offer the following improvements to the communist system: (a) decrease the complexity and the burden of planning, which is believed to be roughly "proportional to the square of the product of the number of goods and the number of economic units;[3] (b) release local initiative and ideas for innovation and modernization by removing the obstacles to them (lack of authority, finances, and equipment); and (c) create within the productive system channels for lateral communication which would be quicker and more efficient than the present vertical communication with its long channel and many intermediaries. As the 1965 experience shows, the system cannot meet these objectives without suffering, at least in the eyes of its architects, in other and more important respects. Centralism is to serve "the crucial functions of safeguarding the regime's values and of assuring balance to the economy."[4]

Political and Social Organization

A communist society is a one-party dictatorship. The party members constitute a power elite with a complex internal structure based on militaristic superior-subordinate relationships and directed by the party *aktiv,* a handful of professional "revolutionaries" who act on behalf of the entire nation; the *aktiv* differs from traditional absolutist elites in that it dominates the fate of individual citizens not only in the political sphere but also in all other aspects of life.

To transmit that power effectively, the elite tolerates no apolitical intermediaries between the party and the masses. Pre-communist social organization has been atomized, and direct access to the people has been established through a prescribed organizational structure in which all entities, regardless of function, are "activized and politized" by the party. Terror, violence, and coercion are legitimate instruments for enforcing social conformity and political integration around the overt ideology of the party. Although the extreme atrocities of the Stalinist era have been replaced with less barbaric methods in most communist countries, none has eliminated terror as a political control. Since the communist party's membership constitutes only a tiny minority of

3 Gregory Grossman, "The Structure and Organization of the Soviet Economy" in *The Development of the U.S.S.R.*, ed. Donald W. Treadgold (Seattle: University of Washington Press, 1964), p. 54.

4 Grossman, "The Structure and Organization of the Soviet Economy," p. 55.

the population, it must rely on terror to stifle individualism and social ideas that might threaten the indoctrination of the people—a basic prerequisite for transforming the party's power into effective authority.

The practical necessity to restrict the communist party's membership to a small minority was dramatically demonstrated by the Czechoslovak-Russian confrontation in 1968. Beside the removal of the democratically minded Alexander Dubcek and his "revisionist" reforms, Kremlin masters insisted on drastic reduction of the Czechoslovak communist party—from 1,700,000 members to 400,000 members. At that time the country's population was 14.3 million. According to the Soviet party's chief, Leonid Brezhnev, this was necessary (a) to slice off counterrevolutionary, meaning democratic, elements, and (b) to solidify the ranks of the socialist vanguard in Czechoslovakia.

It appears that after the first generation of communist rule, voluntary compliance with the party's objectives increases, and the need for terroristic controls diminishes correspondingly. However, since the emergence of groups having different goals from those of the party remains an ever-present danger, potential political terror must be kept in the background, to be applied whenever ideological arguments and social castigation fail.

The totalitarian political machine is always consciously mobilized to strive toward an official set of objectives. Professor Zbigniew Brzezinski puts it this way: "One of the most distinctive features of the Soviet system, and particularly of its ruling regime, is its *conscious purposefulness* [my italics]. Everything it does—in fact, its very existence—is related to a conscious striving toward an announced but not exactly defined goal. Since this action is focused necessarily on the immediate task facing the party, whether it is collectivization and class struggle or the further limitation of the individual's opportunity for personal ownership, different aspects of the ideology may be emphasized at different times. The varying emphases provide clues to the changing preoccupations of the regime."[5]

Professor Alfred Meyer has described the communist organization as a nation-corporation where the party's Central Committee "owns" the society and annihilates all ideas, associations, and activities which are not subservient to its objectives. "As a giant industrial bureaucracy, Soviet society is governed by the principle of *careerism* [my italics]; and its educational system is geared to this. Upward mobility is an accepted value. There is a good deal of room at the top. To the ambitious and talented, the U.S.S.R. is an open society. Although the existence of vested interests makes for a certain amount of corruption, there is a growing trend toward equalizing opportunities and advancement. . . . One further principle of selection for advancement is conformism. In the bureaucratic society the organization man wins over the creative, autonomous personality."[6]

Culturally, the communist world is almost evenly divided between the

[5] Quoted in Grossman, "The Structure and Organization of the Soviet Economy," p. 10.

[6] "U.S.S.R. Incorporated" in *The Development of the U.S.S.R.*, ed. Donald W. Treadgold (Seattle: University of Washington Press, 1964), p. 23.

occidental and the oriental. Although the communist leadership so far has come mostly from the Western cultures, the system itself has spread more toward the South and the East. As a result, Asians have surpassed Europeans and outnumber them by a 30-to-1 ratio in the communist citizenry at the present time. Peking's challenge to Moscow is at least in part a reflection of the shift in the ethnic and cultural balance of the communist bloc. But both in the Occident and in the Orient communism—the society of liberated, cooperative, and joyful men which Marx envisaged—has turned out to be a bureaucratic nightmare. Instead of liberating the mind of man, the Russian and Chinese revolutions have locked it into a state's prison tighter than it ever was under absolutist tyrants. And equally paradoxically, the economic ideal—"to all according to their needs, from all according to their abilities" —remains as much a hollow slogan in the communist empires as it was under the nineteenth-century monarchist empires when Marx first uttered it.

The Developing South

The subindustrial sector of the global society covers vast expanses of Africa, Central and South America, Oceania, and Southern Asia. Unlike the other two, this developing world has no basic political doctrine or economic philosophy of its own. However, as will be explained later, certain ideological contours are emerging which may provide these countries with a common philosophical base. Politically the underdeveloped world consists mostly of pseudodemocracies and outright personal dictatorships. Culturally and ethnically these countries represent the widest possible range. The cultural and social heterogeneity which in many of the developing countries was long repressed by the disproportionate influence of the European elements is now coming to the fore and inviting anxious curiosity throughout the world.

From a historical perspective the developing nations fall into two groups: the new nations which have emerged from the postwar breakup of colonial empires; and the old nations which, despite lengthy political independence, have experienced only limited industrial development and economic growth. With one or two debatable exceptions, the latter countries are in Latin America.

The New Nations

Large areas of the world that previously were subjugated to colonial rule have recently acquired political independence. Now the decolonization process has almost run its course. Just a few relatively small areas retain a subject status; and these, too, are approaching a state of self-determination. Except in the communist bloc, colonialism as a political philosophy and diplomatic objective is passé. But its economic, social, and cultural effects linger on.

The backwash of the decolonization process remains too turbulent to permit unobscured observation of the ex-colonial societies' autogenous characteristics, and it appears that the actual transformation from colony to nation is a slower and more precarious process than the achievement of juridic self-determination. What, in fact, is ascribable to the backwash effect and what is organic to the milieu of an ex-colonial country will have to remain a subject for debate and speculation until these societies have had time to develop and emerge as distinctive members of the family of nations in their own right; and the time necessary for that may be decades or generations rather than years.

A Pluralistic Society

The most distinctive feature of the ex-colonial world is its pluralistic culture. One would be hard pressed to find a segment of the globe in which more heterogeneous cultures are found. Even their physiographic settings exhibit the widest possible diversity, in which the only conceivable geographic bond among the different countries is the potential or actual complementary facets of their national endowments.

Ethnic plurality

Racially, the Caucasian Indians, the Arabs, the Negroes, and the Mongoloid peoples of Southeast Asia provide four basic stocks. In addition, there are scores of racial minorities and innumerable variations of the main racial themes. The meaning of such ethnic heterogeneity is not easy to find.

Although the racial differences have not been rationalized in terms of Euro-American attitudes, ethnic particularism and prejudice pervade nearly all aspects of human relations in the ex-colonial world. The main manifestations are these: an almost universal antagonism toward whites, which, unhappily, is growing; regional hatreds of particular immigrant nationalities, especially the Chinese and the Indians; and local animosities based on tribal and other pseudoracial prejudices. However, even if the varieties of human physique are tolerated more readily in the ex-colonial world than elsewhere, as some writers have claimed, the gain is obliterated by the religious and social disunities.

Linguistic barriers

Linguistically, the ex-colonial world is unparalleled. Even on the level of basic linguistic families it shows the greatest possible plurality. In the Far East the languages of the Sino-Tibetan family dominate; in India and Ceylon many languages belong to the Indo-European family (Hindi, Urdu, Bengali, Panjabi, Sinhalese, etc.), and the others, especially those of southern India and northern Ceylon, derive from the Dravidian family. The peoples of Oceania and the Malay Peninsula communicate in Malayo-Polynesian languages (Indonesian, Melanesian, Micronesian). In the Middle East the Altaic group, with Turkish its best-known representative, coexists with the Hamitic and Semitic languages of the Arabian peninsula and Mediterranean Africa. In the rest of Africa a variety of Negro languages, many still subliterate, are spoken.

The linguistic families represent more than just different collections of words and grammar. Each has its own communication principles, thought structures, and syntactic relationships. As such, they are cultural originals which deeply affect the outlook, attitudes, values, and behavioral characteristics of the people in their respective realms. Upon the foundation of the linguistic families rest the multitudes of actual languages with their peculiar vocabularies, pronunciations, and grammatical rules. The languages, in turn, divide into countless dialects, which in much of Africa and Asia vary from tribe to tribe and sometimes even from village to village. Consequently, the ex-colonial world, unlike Latin America or the industrial West, has no road to easy communication. Even in multilingual Europe, one finds that knowledge of his own language, be it English, Rumanian, or Russian, will cut a wide swath in learning the other languages of the continent, as nearly all of them are cognate[7] in structure and in concepts. But a knowledge of Siamese is no help in learning Hindi, Malay, or Arabic. To learn new languages in the ex-colonial countries invariably requires that one learn not only new vocabularies but also new linguistic structures and communicative ideas which are wholly dissimilar to those of his native tongue. The colonial solution was to superimpose the metropolitan country's own language to bridge the indigenous linguistic barriers. Dutch, French, English, Portuguese, and Spanish all have served in that capacity in their respective spheres. To a lesser degree the same can be said about Chinese and Japanese.

But political independence repels and inhibits the continued use of an imported language which is viewed as a vestige of the colonial past. Thus, indigenous linguistic barriers are being re-emphasized throughout the area. However, the conversion from the imported metropolitan language to a local one requires more than political freedom and desire. The lack of scientific and literary works has confronted the national authorities with the costly problem of translating and reprinting all books and educational materials available from the developed countries. The conversion cost may well turn out to be insurmountable, at least for the present generation of ex-colonial peoples. As the tempo of scientific and literary production accelerates, the rate of obsolescence in educational materials, especially in science and technology, increases accordingly. This process leaves the backward nations with a choice between scanty resources of outdated native-language materials or the relatively much more plentiful resources of up-to-date material in an exogenous language. Although the officials have without exception declared

7 All European languages, except the Finno-Ugric group—Estonian, Finnish, and Hungarian—belong to the Indo-European language family and are, therefore, very similar in their fundamental structure and word roots.

for the indigenous language, efforts to match the words with deeds have generally failed as the financial and pedagogic implications of this choice have become clearer. Moreover, young people have sensed the necessity to know a world language, and their spontaneous demand for such instruction has vastly outstripped the supply of the educational system in nearly all new countries. The urge to learn has not, however, reaffirmed allegiance to the past colonial nation in all instances. Although English and French enjoy perhaps an even stronger position in their traditional regions, other languages, such as Dutch, Portuguese, and Spanish, have lost ground to either English or French, and, to a lesser degree, also to Chinese and, more recently, to Japanese. English and French are currently the languages most widely used by the educated people in the ex-colonial countries. As the leaders of these countries become cognizant of the necessity for an international language, they may ultimately replace their present unilingual aspirations with a bilingual system in which, besides the native tongue, either English or French will be granted official currency.

Social organization

The social system which had been built during the colonial era derived its organization and especially its coordination from the political and business administrators of the colonizing country. With independence, that system collapsed, and its architects were, for the most part, buried beneath the ruins. What remained was the aboriginal substructure, mutilated to various degrees by the colonial practices. With the exception of the situation in a few large cities, the social organization almost everywhere in the ex-colonial countries is anchored in various tribal systems, with primary loyalties based on the personal relations of tribal elders to their dependents and on kinship among the latter. Upon this aboriginal structure has been superimposed, with varying degrees of success, territorial ties which often had their beginnings in religious movements, such as Buddhism, Mohammedanism, and Catholicism, but which now are compounded by political and governmental organizations. Leadership in all the new countries tends to extreme nationalism and chauvinism, which often are misinterpreted in other countries as the general attitude of the people. In truth, in few new nations have people as yet come to think of themselves as citizens with primary loyalties and responsibilities to the nation. Indeed, for many, nationhood and citizenship remain abstract ideas which are neither completely comprehensible nor reconcilable with the traditional tribal and kinship systems.

In more than one sense the old and the new social organizations and loyalty patterns are in sharp conflict. Politically, the national structure undermines the power of the chieftains and spiritual leaders on the village or community level. Socially, it weakens the kinship ties by offering opportunities for employment and security outside this structure. Economically, the governmental institutions must strive for efficiency and productivity, which not only disregard custom and traditional criteria for one's advancement in the society but also are in fundamental conflict with them. The aboriginal social organization, as said before, is a complex of imperfectly assimilated tribal elements, with the chain of authority and loyalty based on personal relationships traditionally endowed with the sanction of religion. Since its strength and stability depend solely on the regard for custom, this organization cannot absorb change without threatening its own existence. It therefore resists economic development and social progress as forces destructive to the fundamental relationships of the old society. Yet, if independent nationhood is to have substance, economic and social progress are the only vehicles which can deliver it. Hence, superstructures which are now being erected upon the traditional system generate unceasing economic pressure upon it, and the native socio-cultural order is breaking up and declining in significance. To what extent the national institutions will be able to substitute an effectively functioning, modern social organization for it remains to be seen. In many areas the breakup of the old organization produces crowds of individuals lacking social order and reacting against the society. Although more mobile and productive than they were under the old system, the structureless crowds represent a grave problem that is certain to become worse before it becomes better.

Political organization

To weld heterogeneous social elements into a nation with a common institutional structure and with national policies designed to serve the general welfare rather than the particularistic ambitions of the constituent tribes and regions, the ex-colonial new nations need strong governments. Unless the government is stronger than the strongest of the particularistic interests that it must control, it will be unable to enhance national growth and may itself promote a particularistic interest to the detriment of the weaker elements of the society.

Since none of the particularistic interests is likely to be synonymous with the national interest, and since to the vast illiterate masses general welfare and national unity are incomprehensible abstractions, democratic processes and institutions patterned on Western models cannot be expected to stand the strain which primitive pluralism imposes. Unhappily, many Western observers, including those who warmly sympathize with the aspirations of the emerging nations, misunderstand the requirements of the situation, often indulge in undeserved critcism, and advocate unworkable reforms. Heirs of the great liberal tradition of Western culture, they fail to appreciate its limitations in a vastly different social environment. Empirical evidence accumulated since the 1940's demonstrates irrefutably that in most of the new nations, Western institutional forms and governmental practices are incompatible with either strength or stability. Western institutions can fortify a social structure which is already strong, but in a feeble, disintegrated society they collapse, leaving behind anarchy and chaos.

Must the new nations, then, reject democratic principles? No, only their Western manifestations. Form does not determine function in political organization any more than in science or technology. Rather, function determines form. The test of the political structure, therefore, is its capacity to deal with the problems of the society and not its organizational design. If the problems are well understood and clearly defined, the institutions for dealing with them will emerge from the society itself. That is the basic premise of the democratic principle. Transplantation of political institutions is never a truly democratic solution to a problem except in the unlikely event that the problem and the circumstances in both countries coincide.

For most of the new nations, their independence has been too recent for a political structure to crystalize. Many of their institutions are inherited from the colonial past and must be regarded as makeshift arrangements to serve in the initial stages of their transition from being subject peoples to being independent societies. Political leadership in the new nations up to this time has been exercised primarily by revolutionaries whose claim to fame and power derives from anticolonist insurrectional activities and guerrilla warfare but whose qualifications for responsible public service and wise statesmanship remain to be tested and judged by their postrevolution performance. Because of their revolutionary background, the top governmental leaders have strong autocratic tendencies and are inclined to employ militaristic methods and practices. With only two or three exceptions, the new nations can be better described as different degrees of dictatorships than as democracies.

Brotherhood in Poverty

The unifying characteristic of the developing South is economic backwardness and widespread poverty—poverty in the absolute sense of the word, i.e., inability to secure the physical necessities of sustaining one's life. This concept should not be confused with "poverty" in the relative sense as used in reference to the less privileged groups in this country.

Detailed analysis of the economic characteristics and peculiarities of the developing countries requires several chapters and is reserved for Part VII. However, we should note from the outset that poverty is the common concern which all these peoples share and which has started to emerge unmistakably as the bond unifying and solidifying their otherwise diverse interests. The imperatives of poverty, as we will see later, dictate economic and social goals and policies which no business, local or international, can ignore.

The Convergence Hypothesis

Certain trends have given rise to the thesis that the three world spheres, which since World War I had been developing in divergent directions, are now on convergent paths. The proponents of this thesis argue that economic and business issues have acquired more political currency in the capitalist world than they had before. As a result, the political leaders in capitalist countries have started to place greater emphasis on collective than on private consumption, and government regulation of business activity as well as of consumer spending is constantly increasing. Since governmental controls are means of coercion, the basic precepts of the capitalist model—individual freedom, private enterprise, personal initiative, and market competition—are subjugated more and more to collectivist goals and values.

In the communist world, opposite tendencies can be observed. Experiments with regional and local planning, with monetary incentives for enterprises, and with market tests for certain consumer goods are indications that the totalitarian command structure is being loosened, slowly to be sure, and that the standards and criteria of the capitalist world are being interjected into the system.

In the developing countries the convergence hypothesis is expected to find its most complete realization. As these countries are bound to borrow much from both the West and the East to foster their own development, they are likely to produce a more perfect synthesis of the two systems than either of the economically more developed spheres.

Any factual proof of the convergence hypothesis must be left to future generations. Even if its proponents should be proved right, it will be within decades or generations rather than within months or years. There is virtually no risk that the three spheres will dissolve into a homogeneous system in the foreseeable future.

3

The Legal Environment of International Business

All business is conducted within a legal framework. The concept of private property—the basis for all business under a private-enterprise system—is a legal concept. The right of an individual to the exclusive possession, use, and enjoyment of property; the conditions under which title to property may be transferred from one owner to another; and the circumstances under which property may be owned by more than one person are all based on the prerogatives of the state to establish and enforce legal precepts concerning private property. From this basic right the ancillary rights of contract and inheritance are derived, and from these ancillary rights are evolved concepts concerning the media of business, such as negotiable instruments, agencies and partnerships, commercial transactions, corporations, and other forms of organization.

The Nature of the Legal Environment

The foundation of all law is the concept of sovereignty—complete jurisdiction over persons and things. In its simplest definition, sovereignty is the right to govern. It describes the supreme power which governs the body politic or society constituting the state. This power is independent of the particular form of government—totalitarian, monarchic, aristocratic, or democratic.[1]

The jurisdiction of sovereignty is primarily territorial. The laws of a

[1] *Judicial and Statutory Definitions of Words and Phrases* (St. Paul, Minnesota: West Publishing Co., 1904), VII, 6562.

state or country apply at home and not abroad. Jurisdiction of the courts extends to persons and transactions within and not beyond the borders of the country. Within these borders, however, the laws and jurisdiction of the courts apply to all—to foreigners as well as to citizens or subjects, to transients as well as to residents. The only notable exception to this rule is found in primitive countries in which the principle of extraterritoriality prevails.[2] Since World War II, however, the number of these countries has been reduced to a relatively unimportant handful.

If all business were transacted within the confines of a single country, the legal environment would be precise and definitive. Only the laws of that country would prevail. When a business entity engages in a transaction across an international boundary, however, it is operating not only within the jurisdiction of the two states in question but also, in a sense, within the purview of third and fourth states as well. In addition to the enacted domestic laws or those embodied in the legal fabric by judicial precedence, laws derived from treaty arrangements between the two states also prevail. Because of the interlocking nature of treaties and the operation of most-favored-nation clauses, treaties made with third and fourth states may also have effect. Finally, because of the comity of nations and the almost universal recognition of the binding nature of usage and customs in relations between civilized states, the observances of the entire community of nations come into play. Thus, the business entity, in entering into a transaction across an international boundary, finds itself not only in the legal domains of its own state and the second state in the transaction—not only within the purview of the municipal laws of the two states—but also within the legal purview of that body of law called *international law* or the *law of nations.*

Municipal law is the internal law of a country. It is defined as "a rule of civil conduct prescribed by the supreme power of the state, commanding what is right and what is wrong." It is "the particular law of a state or nation, as distinguished from public or international law."[3] It is called municipal rather than national law for historic reasons; namely, it predates the nation-state.

International law or the *law of nations* is "a body of rules recognized as binding on civilized independent states in their dealings with one another and with one another's subjects."[4] According to the source of its principles and rules, international law is subdivided into customary or general international law and conventional law or treaty law. The former embodies the rules which have actually been observed by independent nations in their relations with other countries long enough to become generally accepted as international rules of conduct. It is a system of jurisprudence which has

2 Edward Ewing Pratt, *Modern International Commerce* (Boston: Allyn and Bacon, Inc., 1965), p. 540.

3 *Judicial and Statutory Definitions,* V, 4628.

4 Sir Frederick Pollack, "The Sources of International Law," 2 *Columbia Law Review,* 511–12 (1902), quoted in *International Law* (2nd ed.), William W. Bishop Jr. (Boston: Little, Brown and Co., 1962), p. 33.

evolved from custom, that is, experience and necessity, and it is based upon the common consent of nations. Conventional law includes the rules governed by treaties and agreements between two or more states; they are binding only on the signatory states and not on the community of nations as a whole.

Because of multilateral treaties and the cooperation manifested by many international organizations, the scope of international law has been steadily expanding in recent years. This has given rise to the term *cooperative international law,* which refers specifically to rules for positive international collaboration on both social and economic levels. The advent of permanent international bodies, such as the United Nations, the Organization of American States, the European Economic Community, and the Central American Common Market, has given new and enhanced meaning to international legal relationships. At the same time, the municipal laws of individual nations have been expanding and evolving to meet new conditions.

This chapter identifies and describes in some detail the major areas of the complex legal framework in which international business is conducted. It also isolates the more dramatic changes that have been taking place and gives a general conceptual overview of this vast subject.

International Business and Municipal Law

The laws, rules, and regulations with which the international firm must contend vary from country to country, as each has its own municipal jurisprudence. Although the specifics may be bewildering, the underlying principles and basic rules are derived from two major bodies of judicial doctrine: the Roman or civil law and the British common law.

The sources of legal systems—the Roman law and the common law

The continental countries of Europe base their municipal law on the civil law—the old Roman law which has come down to modern jurisprudence via the Napoleonic code. Such law is enacted by the legislative entity of the state. It is codified, is construed by the courts as written, and generally is divided into private and public law with special courts for each. Although the municipal laws of the various states employing the civil code differ, the legal "climate" is similar in most civil law countries.

The term "*civil law*" has a dual meaning; in a broad sense it denotes the entire system of Roman law (the civil law system); in a narrow sense, it refers to a small part of this system, namely, the code dealing with rights, privileges, and obligations of private citizens. Examples of other codes are the commercial code, the criminal code, the labor code, and the marriage code.

In the United Kingdom and in most of the states of the British Commonwealth and former empire, municipal law is based on British common law. The common law derives not only from legislative enactment but also from a body of legal precedence handed down by the judiciary under the doctrine of *stare decisis*. "The common law of England is derived from memorial usage and custom, originating from the acts of Parliament, not recorded, or which have been destroyed or lost. . . ."[5] Its principles, rules, and maxims are developed by judicial decisions as necessities arise from time to time for legal litigation and adjudication of cases. Compared with the civil law the common law is more pragmatic and flexible; it can adapt to new conditions or new interpretations through precedent-setting decisions by courts. The civil law, on the other hand, rests on strictly defined principles and does not recognize the doctrine of *stare decisis,* except as a conjunctive device.

In many jurisdictions, especially in the United States, the common law has been modified by legislative enactment, i.e., by statutory law. The distinction is made between *code states,* those in which statutory enactment has greatly limited the basic common law doctrine, and *common law states,* those in which the old common law is still predominant. The U.S. municipal law was originally based on the common law doctrine, but through legislative and regulatory enactments a vast body of statutory law has emerged, much of which has been patterned after the codes in the Roman law.

The nature of federal systems

The United States is also an outstanding example of a country with federated jurisdiction, in which the sovereign powers of the nation are divided among the central government and the political subdivisions such as states, counties, and cities, or provinces, cantons, and districts. In federated states the business firm must comply with the laws of both the central government and the political subdivisions of the country. In the United States, for example, the rules of contract are laid down by the states; the control of fraud is also within the jurisdiction of the states; and the domestic corporations receive their corporate charters, by virtue of which they are legal entities, from the states. But the antitrust laws and the laws on bankruptcy are enacted by the federal government, and a host of federal laws and regulations governs the movement of goods and services in interstate commerce.

The division of powers among the central government and the political subdivisions varies from one federal state to another. Switzerland limits the confederation mostly to foreign relations and tariffs, leaving the cantons sovereign in other respects.[6] The Canadian confederation operates in much the same manner as the United States, the major difference being that in the United States all powers not expressly granted to the federal government are reserved to the states, whereas in Canada, under the British North America Act of 1867, all powers not expressly granted to the provincial governments are reserved to the confederation.[7] In actual practice, the Canadian provinces, with the power to legislate on property, civil rights, education, and local

5 *Judicial and Statutory Definitions,* II, 1326–27.
6 "Switzerland," *The Columbia Encyclopedia* (1963), p. 2079.
7 "Canada," *The Columbia Encyclopedia* (1963), p. 328.

affairs, perform about the same functions as the states of the United States. India's constitution is modeled somewhat on that of the United States, although the union government's control over the development of strategic and basic industries makes it one of the more powerful central governments; also, the federal coordinating function is areas reserved to the states and the many functions that are shared by the union government and the state governments give India a legal environment unique among federal systems.[8]

Theocratic legal systems

Theocratic systems are characteristic of states basing their municipal law on the *Koran*. Under Islamic principles only Moslems can be citizens, and, as a result, in earlier days Moslem states provided separate courts for Christians. The privilege of appearing before the kadi (lower level of judges) or the services of the mufti (lawyers) were denied to non-Moslems. Although in practice most Moslem countries have now separated religious law from civil law, the civil law is still strongly Islamic in character and most Moslem jurists follow the same general precepts. Reference is made to the *Koran* and the *Sunna* (the elaboration of Koranic teaching accepted by all Moslems except the Shiite sect) just as often as to the civil code. The result is a mixture of civil law and religious precepts.

Authorities on Moslem law stress the religious basis of the principles of *pacta sunt sevanda* for the Islamic people. The *Koran* demands truthfulness in obligations, and a contract is safeguarded by divine as well as by human sanctions. In some of the Moslem states, the most notable being Turkey, the civil law has completely replaced the Islamic code. Under Kemel Attaturk, the Swiss civil code and the Italian criminal code became the only law of Turkey, and all Islamic trappings were purged.[9] Few Moslem countries have gone this far. In most Moslem countries, mixed systems continue, sometimes to the bewilderment of businessmen from Western nations. The commercial code, which has come down to civil law states from Napoleon's Code de Commerce,[10] is found in some of the Islamic states, while the commercial aspects of the English common law are found in states, such as the Islamic Republic of Pakistan, which have passed through a period of British tutelage.

Laws of Sovereign States

Municipal law, the law of individual sovereign states, is thus as complex and varied as the countries in which these various systems operate. It may derive from the Roman law, the common law, or the Islamic systems; and each nation molds to suit its own needs whatever system it may have inherited. In no two countries is the legal environment identical. And these three

[8] William N. Loucks, *Comparative Economic Systems* (7th ed.) (New York: Harper & Row, Publishers, Inc., 1965), p. 655.

[9] "Islam," *The Columbia Encyclopedia,* p. 1051. Also, Wolfgang Friedmann, *The Changing Structure of International Law* (New York: Columbia University Press, 1964), p. 308.

[10] Pratt, *Modern International Commerce,* p. 540.

systems—civil, common, and Islamic law—do *not* comprise the entire list. The communist states are evolving a distinct system of jurisprudence, vestiges of the old Imperial Chinese law are found in Taiwan, and the ancient Jewish ceremonial and political law based on the *Talmud* still has a place in the legal system of Israel.

In order to do business across international lines, a firm must adapt its operations to the legal constraints and privileges of the country in which it finds itself. In adjusting to the municipal law of many nations, the firm is aided by accommodations under what is called the *comity of nations.* This is the formal expression of mutual respect accorded throughout the civilized world by the representatives of each sovereign power to those of every other in their official acts. "Its source is a sentiment of reciprocal regard, founded on identity of position and similarity of institution."[11] "Comity is not a rule of law, but it is a rule of 'practice, convenience and expediency. It is something more than mere courtesy, which implies only deference to the opinion of others, since it has a substantial value in securing uniformity of decision, and discouraging repeated litigation of the same question.' "[12]

Because of comity, foreigners engaged in trade and industry in a country usually have the same right to legal protection under the local laws as citizens or subjects of that country. However, this general rule does not always apply automatically. Reciprocity is sometimes required, exceptions are frequently made in regard to certain branches of commerce and industry, and not infrequently particular requirements apply to foreign corporations, partnerships, and individuals.[13]

Even in those areas in which domestic persons and foreigners are treated alike, there are perplexing pitfalls for the international concern. For example, in common law countries the question of whether an individual acts as a private citizen or as a businessman rarely becomes important in litigation. This question, however, is frequently raised in civil law countries. Business firms and executives in their work are required to comply with many special legal requirements normally contained in the so-called *commercial code* as distinguished from the civil code, which applies to nonbusiness personalities. These countries have two different systems of rights, privileges, duties, and obligations as far as trade and business affairs are concerned; one set of rules applies to the "professionals"—the businessmen—the other to the "amateurs" —the private citizens.

Different concepts of legal entities

There are other marked differences. Although almost every country has some kind of incorporation roughly equivalent in form and theory to incorporation in the United States, there are considerable differences between

11 *Judicial and Statutory Definitions,* II, 1280.

12 J. Brown, in Mast, Foos & Co. v. Stover Mfg. Co., 177 U.S. 485, 488, 20 S. Ct. 708, 710, 1951, cited in Manley O. Hudson, "Johnston v. Compagnie Generale Transatlantique," *Cases and Other Materials on International Law* (St. Paul, Minnesota: West Publishing Co., 1929), pp. 1012–13.

13 Pratt, *Modern International Commerce,* p. 541.

civil and common law countries in the treatment of various organizations. Many countries recognize juristic personalities, or legal entities, which are not known in the United States or in other common law countries. The ordinary partnership is treated as an entity in civil law countries. In other countries the house, the firm, or the concern is recognized as a separate unit or personality and is so regarded by the law. In common law countries, however, the members of a partnership are legally regarded as individuals. The individual partners sue and are sued, own the property, and own the debts. The partners' personal property and private affairs are not legally distinguishable from those of the firm. In civil law countries, other forms of business organization exist which have legal personalities separate and distinct from those of the individuals who own or manage the firm, just as a corporation has an entity separate and distinct from those of the individual stockholders, directors, and officers in the common law countries.

Differences in welfare and economic legislation

Differences in legal concepts among nations are particularly pronounced in the area of governmental attempts to influence economic well-being.[14] Antimonopoly legislation is a case in point. In the United States, a series of federal enactments—the Sherman Antitrust Act of 1890, the Clayton Antitrust Act of 1914, and the Robinson-Patman Act of 1936—attest to the American concern over any reduction of competition through restraint of trade. These laws have been applied not only to mergers and combines in American territory but also, at times, to activities outside the United States. In the *United States* v. *Aluminum Co. of America,* Justice Learned Hand said, in part: "It is settled law . . . that any state may impose liabilities, even upon persons not within its allegiance, for conduct outside its borders that has consequences within its borders which the state reprehends; and these liabilities other states will ordinarily recognize. . . . There may be agreements made beyond our borders not intended to affect imports which do affect them, or which affect exports." Concluding that the agreements in this case did affect imports, Justice Hand went on to say that these "agreements would clearly have been unlawful, had they been made within the United States; and it follows . . . that both were unlawful, though made abroad, if they were intended to affect imports and did affect them."[15]

In the *United States* v. *Imperial Chemical Industries, Ltd.,*[16] American and British companies were found to have divided up trade throughout the world through jointly held companies and patent agreements. The British defendant was ordered to deal with certain patent agreements made with third parties. An injunction was served in England on one of these third parties restraining the recipient from dealing with the patent rights. The writ

14 Milton Katz and Kingman Brewster, Jr., *The Law of International Transactions and Relations, Cases and Materials* (Brooklyn, New York: Foundation Press, Inc., 1960), p. 549.

15 148 Fed. 2d 416 (2d Cir. 1954), cited in Bishop, *International Law,* pp. 469–70.

16 100 Fed. Supp. 504 (S.D.N.Y. 1951), 105 Fed. Supp. 215 (1952), cited in Bishop, *International Law,* p. 470.

was served to enforce the verdict of the American court. Although affirming the decision in a subsidiary suit, the British Court of Appeal commented, "There is raised a somewhat serious question, whether the order of [the American court], in the form it takes, does not assert an extraterritorial jurisdiction which the courts of this country cannot recognize, notwithstanding any such comity."[17]

In recent years, there has been much discussion of the applicability of American antitrust laws to activities outside the United States. Clear distinction has not always been made between the expansion, set by the courts, of the applicability of American laws concerning business activities and the point at which other nations may object to such extension on the grounds of interference with their sovereignty and international rights or with those of their nationals.[18]

Overlapping and conflicting regulations for controlling welfare and economic activities are the result of differences in policy and practice, reflecting differences in tradition and ideology. Some societies, such as the American, believe in enforced competition. Others believe in the "rationalization" of price and production by private or quasigovernmental cartels.[19]

Europe has a tradition of cartels and restrictive business practices. For the most part, European laws do not subject monopolies and mergers, as such, to legal scrutiny. Such scrutiny has only emerged where business laws, less stringent than the Sherman Act and the Clayton Act, have been passed—in Britain, France, West Germany, the Netherlands, Belgium, and Spain. The West German law emphasizes the benefits of competition, and any combination that tends to limit competitive activity is suspect. The French antitrust law is concerned primarily with inflation. Accordingly it provides for sweeping action against price-fixing; there are, however, no antimonopoly provisions as such. The United Kingdom's postwar legislation is concerned only with abuses of the public interest, and only the abuse of a dominant position, not the dominant position itself, is illegal.

Some price agreements are now illegal in several of the member states of the European Economic Community. Price-fixing, resale price maintenance, and exclusive dealing arrangements are prohibited in France, and resale price maintenance is no longer protected in West Germany. In the United Kingdom, West Germany, and the Netherlands, certain restrictive agreements must be registered with national cartel offices, but the registration requirement does not imply official displeasure.[20]

Meanwhile, on the other side of the world, the *zaibatsu*—the great family trusts of Japan—having thwarted attempts of the military cliques to break them up in the 1930's and having survived similar attempts by the Allied occupation forces after World War II, appear to be bothered very little by Japan's weakly written, and even more weakly enforced, antimonopoly laws.

17 Bishop, *International Law,* p. 470.

18 Bishop, *International Law,* p. 469.

19 Katz and Brewster, *The Law of International Transactions and Relations,* p. 549.

20 *The European Markets, a Guide for Businessmen* (New York: The Chase Manhattan Bank, January 1964), p. 43.

The rise of new entities and new centers of economic power, however, have reduced somewhat the control over Japan's economic life enjoyed by the *zaibatsu*.[21] On the other hand, foreign firms operating in Japan are confronted with both formal legal restraints and informal administrative and procedural difficulties to prevent their acquiring a dominant position in any major Japanese industry.

Uniformity in fundamental principles of law

This brief glance at some of the antimonopoly positions of various countries illustrates why the businessman contemplating entry into international business sometimes feels faced with interminably complicated legal harassment. Fortunately for the foreign trader and for the international business firm, several circumstances mitigate these difficulties.

Despite the apparent differences, there is a substantial degree of uniformity in the fundamental principles of law throughout the world. Both common law and civil law, for example, usually allow the parties to a contract the utmost freedom. Similarly, the law of agency is very much alike in all civilized countries. The general rule applying to the passing of title is that title passes where and when the parties to the transfer of the merchandise agree that it should pass.[22]

Despite the similarities in legal principles and business usage, however, rapid developments in all countries make it mandatory for the management of an international business to keep abreast of many changes. The interaction between social change and legal change is varied and complex. Especially in social welfare and economic activities, as has been noted in antimonopoly legislation, such changes are different from country to country and vary from period to period. They are considerably influenced by the cultural and economic traditions of the country as well as by the country's constitutional structure. In adapting to social change, the courts perform an important function of legal reform and development. This is true not only in the common law systems but also in civil law countries, where substantial changes are frequently accomplished by judicial interpretation of statutes. Under any system, however, a persistent demand for social change will eventually make itself sufficiently felt to find its way into legislation.[23]

International Law

The nature of international law has long been the subject of considerable controversy among legal scholars. In Green Haywood Hackworth's *Digest of International Law* it is stated that the question of "whether international law

[21] The leading *zaibatsu* are Mitsui, Mitsubishi, Sumitomo, and Yasuda. *The Columbia Encyclopedia*, pp. 2377–78.

[22] Pratt, *Modern International Commerce*, p. 538ff.

[23] Friedmann, *The Changing Structure of International Law*, p. 117.

is law in a strictly *legal* or Austinian sense depends upon the meaning attributed to the word *law*."[24] W. E. Hall, in his *Treatise on International Law,* states, "International law does not conform to the most perfect type of law."[25] Katz and Brewster point out in *The Law of International Transactions and Relations* that the scholarly use of phrases such as *international legal order, international community,* or *international society* does not mean that they exist in fact. "The terms may conceal wistful assumptions, born of yearning for world order and economic development. It is, of course, beyond question that there are an immense number and variety of conditions and events that transcend national boundaries and in the aggregate make up international life. From the mere existence of international life, however, it does not automatically follow that international life contains elements which justify considering it an international 'society or legal order'."[26]

There is no question that treaties between nations establish enforceable law. The contention is made, however, that because treaties are compacts between independent nations, a treaty depends for its enforcement on the interest and honor of the governments which are parties to it. If the provisions are not fulfilled, the infraction becomes the subject of international negotiations and reclamations and in the end may be enforced by war. "It is obvious that with all this the courts can give no redress. But a treaty may also contain provisions which confer certain rights upon the citizens or subjects of one of the nations. . . which partake of the nature of municipal law, and which are capable of enforcement as between private parties in the courts of the country."[27] This implication that treaties can influence municipal law, however, does not in itself necessarily prove the existence of international law.

The right to make treaties that are binding on the citizens of the contracting state and enforceable in the courts of that state is recognized as one of the prerogatives of sovereignty. In the United States this prerogative is recognized in the Constitution, which states that "all treaties made, or which shall be made, under the authority of the United States, shall be (along with the Constitution itself and the laws made thereunder) the supreme law of the land."[28] The Permanent Court of International Justice has in recent years repeatedly propounded the principle that not the municipal law of a country but the international law determines the rights and privileges of the country in its international relations, and, therefore, the legality of its conduct must be judged on the basis of the latter if the two conflict.

Treaties as a Source of Municipal Law

The argument is sometimes made that treaties are a source of law only to the extent that their provisions become *ipso facto* a part of the municipal law of the contracting powers. In what is called *private international law*

24 Quoted in Bishop, *International Law,* p. 12.
25 Quoted in Bishop, *International Law,* p. 12.
26 Quoted in Bishop, *International Law,* p. 1.
27 *Judicial and Statutory Definitions,* VIII, 7086.
28 Art. 6, § 2.

(that part of international law which governs the actions of private organizations, firms, and persons), so this argument goes, legal authority and enforcement derive not from the treaty itself but from the law of the land—stated implicitly as in the U.S. Constitution or recognized as a prerogative of sovereignty in states generally—whether stated in statutes or established by domestic juristic interpretation. To the extent that treaties are the law of the land, treaty provisions entered into by the sovereign power are binding on citizens or subjects. Treaties are, in effect, one of the accepted ways in which states enact municipal law, but the sole source of the authority of such treaties is the recognition the state extends them. In other words, the source of law is the sovereign state and not some internationally recognized higher authority. According to this view, wherever private law exists there is an enforceable law, the source of which is the enforcing agency.

Customary International Law

The United States generally recognized accepted practices as the basis for international law until fairly recent times. It regarded international law as a body of rules which independent states *had accepted as binding* in their dealings with one another and with one another's residents. This body of rules consisted of "a system of jurisprudence which, for the most part, has evolved out of the experience and necessities of situations that have arisen from time to time."[29] This position, which envisaged international law, sometimes called *customary international law,* as growing out of recognized custom and usage between states, together with conventional international law growing out of the network of existing treaties and international agreements, became the generally accepted basis on which a theory of international justice was erected in the period between the two world wars.

Public and Private International Law

A more recent complication has arisen from the distinction between public and private international law. Conceptually, *public international law* is that portion of the law of nations which governs the conduct of the nation itself as a unit or entity in its relations with other nations. Except as agreed to by treaty or convention, a sovereign nation can neither be made a party to any action brought before an international tribunal nor be made a party, without its consent, to actions brought before a municipal national court. *Private international law* is that portion of international law which governs the actions of private organizations, firms, and persons and which is within the purview of municipal national courts.

29 Bishop, *International Law,* p. 3.

The distinction between public and private international law has become blurred by the emergence of a variety of semiautonomous enterprises either partially or fully owned by various public bodies (government-owned airlines, shipping lines, oil companies, steel mills). Whether international transactions among entities of this kind are subject to public or to private international law remains an open question. The other side of the coin is represented by "quasidiplomatic" functions, which private corporations have in a number of instances been asked to fulfill. Their international transactions are often a mixture of business and political affairs and may be carried out in partnership with the government.

The result is an increasing strain on the principle that sovereignty precludes a foreign government's being subjected to the jurisdiction of a municipal court of another country. One government after another has engaged in commercial transactions with international ramifications, and more and more private firms, such as construction companies, survey teams, and technical consultants, have become involved in public and quasipublic contractual international activities; and this trend is not limited to what are generally regarded to be socialist or semisocialist countries. The U.S. government has been in the forefront, and probably more American private firms than those of any other nation are engaged abroad in public or semipublic projects.

The changing realities have outrun the legal adaptations. The problem of where the line is to be drawn is complicated by the fact that almost all aspects of public international law—sovereign immunity, neutrality, the comity of nations, and the jurisdiction of various municipal and international tribunals—are involved. This entire question is in a state of flux, and undoubtedly jurists will be hammering out a new basis for the distinction between public and private jurisdiction for some years to come.

In the meantime, business firms contemplating entering into commercial arrangements with governmental agencies and government-owned or partially owned entities must wrestle with the problem of whether the doctrine of sovereign immunity will prevent them from litigating or arbitrating disputes. Some countries, for example, Italy, have rejected the doctrine of immunity for government-created entities engaged in commercial activities. In the United Kingdom and the United States, the trend is away from the recognition of sovereign immunity in business transactions, but formidable authority still supports the principle.[30]

Thus, the distinction between public international law, which applies to sovereign governments, and private law, which applies to private individuals and entities, is breaking down. This has particular significance in treaty or conventional international law.

30 Walter Sterling Surrey, ed., and Crawford Shaw, asst. ed., *A Lawyer's Guide to International Business Transactions* (Philadelphia, Pennsylvania: Joint Committee on Continuing Legal Education of the American Law Institute and the American Bar Association, 1963), pp. 989–90.

Treaties and Conventions

Great weight is now being placed on agreements and declarations, especially those which are multilateral. Although treaties and conventions are binding only on the parties involved, acts of international congresses or conferences which have been held to solve problems of universal concern and from which have emerged agreements permitting adhesion by powers not originally parties to the proceedings go far in establishing the elusive legitimacy so long sought for international law.

When several of the great powers have accepted certain rules as binding to their international conduct, other countries tend to attribute very great significance to them even though they have never expressly consented to them. For this reason international jurists put special emphasis on multilateral treaty arrangements as a basis for international law. Particularly in private international law, which comes within the jurisdiction of municipal (national) courts, multinational agreements—and especially those agreed to with near or complete unanimity—create international law of such concerted sanction as to make academic any question as to whether it is the community of nations or national sovereignty which gives the law its force.

Among such multilateral agreements are those setting up the specialized agencies under the general supervision of the Economic and Social Council of the United Nations. There are now 13 of these, some of which existed before the United Nations itself or even before the League of Nations.[31] The Universal Postal Union, with headquarters at Bern, Switzerland, is a good example of the international scope of such agencies. Established in 1875 with the adoption of the Universal Postal Convention, the union came under the jurisdiction of the United Nations in 1947 and by 1962 had 114 members. It has a governing body, the Universal Postal Congress, which usually meets every five years. The Congress reviews and considers the activities of an Executive and Liaison Committee of 19 members elected on a geographical basis. Members of the union comprise a unified postal territory with easy international mail exchange. Accounts are cleared through the International Bureau.

Another of these United Nations agencies, the International Telecommunication Union, with headquarters in Geneva, was created in 1934 and

[31] Among them are: the Universal Postal Union; the International Telecommunication Union; the International Civil Aviation Organization; the World Meteorological Organization; the Food and Agricultural Organization; the International Monetary Fund; the International Bank for Reconstruction and Development; the United Nations Educational, Scientific, and Cultural Organization; the International Finance Corporation; the Intergovernmental Maritime Consultative Organization; and the International Development Association. See George E. Taylor and Ben Cashman, *The New United Nations* (Washington, D.C.: American Enterprise Institute for Public Policy Research, 1965), p. 76.

by 1962 had 109 full members and five associate members. The union today functions under the International Telecommunication Convention, which was adopted in 1947 and went into effect in 1949. The organization allocates radio frequencies and perfects communications in rescue operations. A plenipotentiary conference at which all members are represented normally meets once in five years. The conference elects an administrative council of 25 members to carry out its provisions.

What is characteristic of such bodies, in addition to the almost universal scope of their jurisdiction, is their permanent nature. Both the Universal Postal Union and the International Telecommunication Union maintain permanent offices, convene at regular intervals, pass regulations which the members are in large measure precommitted to accept, and take on many aspects of supranational governments in specialized fields. The agreements reached as they relate to private persons are respected and enforced—directly or indirectly—by the municipal courts of the member states.

Those agreements which are effectively treaties automatically become the law of the land in the United States and in a number of other countries. In the United Kingdom and much of the British Commonwealth accommodating legislation is necessary to give treaty law effect in the courts, but such legislation differs only slightly from the ratifying procedures of the American system. As a result of such agreements, the operator of a radio station in one country may be ordered to cease and desist from encroaching upon the allocated frequencies of a station in another country; and the priorities which are accorded to the mails by common carriers may not be set up to favor those destined for a particular country.

Similarly other international organizations, with permanent offices and staffs and regular convening of members in representative bodies, set rules for the operation of aircraft and for the rates that airlines may charge on international flights; enforce sanitary restrictions for international shipments via plane, ship, rail, and truck; and prohibit international commerce in certain activities deemed internationally criminal, such as traffic in women and children and traffic in human slaves.

Some permanent mechanisms, such as the General Agreement on Tariffs and Trade, apply only to member states although a vast majority of the civilized nations of the world are members. Others, such as the Paris Declaration on Privateering, are observed almost universally although put into effect by a minority of the national states now in existence. Still others, such as the Treaty of Rome, which established the European Economic Community, are regional or limited in jurisdiction although far reaching in the scope with which they affect the member states.

In relation to these multinational treaty arrangements, international law takes on new meaning and power. Radio and television signals do not respect man-made boundaries; wavelengths and frequencies are regulated internationally or not at all. Similarly, sputniks and other orbiting space satellites have made a dead letter of the legal fiction that national jurisdiction follows boundaries that extend outward from an angle at the center of the earth to the vertex of the heavens, just as the advent of the airplane made a shambles of the same concept as it applied to municipal laws of trespass.

Other changes are making themselves felt. The sheer size of international investments and the increased recognition of the interdependence of nations are bringing enhanced awareness of the part international law must play. The changing nature of the international firm itself is bringing new concepts and reevaluation of old concepts to the attention of courts and jurists.

If international society "still remains primitive in the degree of submission of national sovereignty to a supranational rule of law," says Friedmann, "it is highly developed and articulate in other respects. Modern international society is, after all, compound of nations which dispose of the most modern and sophisticated media of communication, including legal communication. In this respect, contemporary international society in no way corresponds to the feudal society preceding the establishment of centralized national states many centuries ago. It does not have to rely on the slow growth of custom, or on the cumbrous diplomatic machinery of the time of Grotius, or even of the nineteenth century. Any problem of territorial waters, fisheries rights, exploitation of continental shelves or the protection of foreign investment is made the subject of continuous discussion and articulation, by draft conventions, conferences, resolutions and the like."[32]

From this vast network of quasigovernmental, supranational activity a new body of private international law is emerging. In the realm of public international law, society is taking only halting steps toward substituting a rule of law for a rule of force. But the advent of the European Common Market and the European Free Trade Association; the rise of smoothly functioning multinational organizations such as the International Telecommunication Union, the International Civil Aviation Organization, and the Intergovernmental Maritime Consultative Organization; and the development of sophisticated international corporations willing and able to adapt to the cultures and practices of the countries in which they find themselves are having their effects on international jurisprudence. These developments bring the hope that in the economic sphere, at least, the rapid emergence of more universally recognized and perhaps codified international laws with specific procedures for litigation and sanctions for enforcement is not too far distant.

32 *The Changing Structure of International Law,* p. 119.

II

International Trade

Of all the problems we call "economic," few have so baffled the expert and the nonexpert alike as those that involve the relations between nation-states. Indeed, one might even go so far as to say that economics, as a "science," got its start from efforts to explain how gold and goods traveled from nation to nation, working their various effects on the countries they left and those they entered.

Robert L. Heilbroner

4

The Resource Base of International Business

Natural resources may be defined as all the physiographic phenomena which can satisfy human needs. This capacity may be readily apparent, as with water and timber, or it may be hidden behind a series of technical changes performed before the capacity can be released, as with bauxite or iron ore. From the standpoint of need, a particular product such as apples or fish may be obtained directly from a particular resource, while others such as cameras and ballistic missiles require an intricate process of adaptation and combination of elements derived from a number of different resources. How much human effort is required to make a resource usable depends not only on the properties of the resource itself but also on the quality standards which govern the use for which it is intended. Both the resources and the consumption standards vary with time and place.

Types of Natural Resources

For economic purposes natural resources may be grouped into these classifications: agricultural, forest, industrial materials, energy, and locational. From agricultural resources, which are a combination of arable land and climate, are derived the foodstuffs, rubber, and natural fibers which provide the basis for food-processing, textile, clothing, and rubber industries. Forest resources supply lumber for woodworking, pulp, paper, container, and building-construction industries. Industrial materials resources include metallic and nonmetallic minerals usable as raw materials or as catalytic agents in various manufacturing industries; the principal derivations from these resources include ferrous and nonferrous metals, ceramic materials, and chemical compounds. Energy resources comprise oil, natural gas, coal, hydroelectric power, and fissionable materials; they provide the motive power for all industries except manual ones and thus play a fundamental role in industrial production and economic growth. Locational resources can be defined only in relative terms, since they are the advantages a particular site may offer when compared with others. Three locational relationships are relevant to enterprises engaged in international business: the relation to other resources, the relation to markets, and the relation to trade routes.

Industry Location

Which of these locational relationships constitutes a resource for a particular business enterprise depends upon the industry to which the enterprise belongs.

Resource-oriented industries

That extractive industries must be located where the resources are is self-evident. But many manufacturing industries also are attracted to resource locations. This is true where the cost of transporting raw materials or fuels is greater than the cost of distributing the finished goods or where there are organizational advantages in having the extractive and manufacturing phases integrated. Examples of resource-oriented industries include lumber milling, fruit and vegetable canning, pottery and most other ceramic manufacturing, cotton ginning, industrial chemicals processing, and pulp production. In some of these the raw material used loses much weight in the production process, which significantly affects the cost of transportation.

Market-oriented industries

The success of certain industries depends on quick and easy access to the market. These industries fall into four principal categories. First, manufacturers of products which gain weight or bulk in the production process. Beer, soft drinks, ink, automobiles, and upholstered furniture are products of this type. Second, manufacturers of perishable goods such as bakery products, fresh milk, flowers, and ice. Third, providers of various consumer services—laundry, cinema, appliance repair, and the like. Fourth, for many industries, including trade and business service activities, freight carriers, custom brokerage houses, export promotion firms, etc., location on an international trade route represents the market and as such offers a special advantage over other locations.

Neutral industries

The economics of certain industries are relatively unaffected by the location of natural resources or markets. Known popularly as the *footloose industries,* they primarily involve products for which the transportation cost is insignificant compared with other costs. To this group belongs a multitude of items of high value, such as watches, cigarette lighters, cameras, and various novelties. Some of the largest products, both in physical size and in sales volume, also belong to the neutral group: aircraft, cement, shoes, ready-to-wear items, and books. A location close to the market thus becomes as much a resource for these industries as are raw materials and power.

Community locational advantages

In a broader sense location is an advantage not only to companies but also to entire communities. This is particularly true for major world ports. For example, much of the shipping, handling, warehousing, financing, marine insuring, and marketing activities in New York are based upon the movement of goods from the Midwest to foreign countries or from abroad to the inland areas. The employment, payrolls, and business incomes attributable to locational advantages are no less real than are those attributable to other resource advantages. Other ports, such as San Francisco, Seattle, New Orleans, and Vancouver, B.C., derive a high percentage of their employment and income from their location. How great a resource location is for a community depends on the hinterland which it serves. Location is decisive for export and import firms, ocean carriers, and for certain service enterprises (customhouse brokers, freight forwarders, etc.) and is considerably important for manufacturers depending on frequent export or import shipments.

International Differences in the Resource Base

Natural resources

Although in modern industrial society the connections between resources and industries may be diffuse and obscure, they are nevertheless real. Since no productive activity is conceivable apart from resources, and since every industry is engaged in productive activity, it is a truism that all business activities are directly or indirectly based upon natural resources. This does not imply that natural resources are the all-decisive factor, but simply that they are an absolute precondition for industrial and agricultural production and, therefore, for all other business activity. In other words, natural resources are a necessary but not a sufficient condition for productive activity. The mere existence of resources does not guarantee production, for it takes other factors such as labor, capital, and management to activate them. Yet, unless the resources are there, there is nothing to be activated. Consequently, the resource base of a country or region indicates the productive activity the area can support; and differences in resource endowments tend to be reflected not only in the business activities of different countries but also in their export and import trade.

Differences in international resource bases are of three types: differences in the variety of resources, e.g., the kinds of resources found in a country; differences in the quantity of resources, e.g., the amount of available acreage, the size of ore deposits, or the kilowatt capacity of hydroelectric sites; and differences in the quality of resources, e.g., the fertility of land, the purity of ore, or the cost of building a dam. The first type is the most decisive for international trade, since these differences are absolute. A country which possesses no iron-ore deposits must import either the ore to make steel or the steel products; it has no other alternative. Conversely, only a country which possesses iron-ore deposits can serve as a supply source for other countries. There is the tendency, therefore, for the composition of the resource base to be repeated in the commodity composition of a country's exports and for the gaps in the resource base to coincide very nearly with the import mix.

The differences in the quantity and the quality of resources can be—to an extent—mutually offsetting: a small high-grade (high-metallic-content) ore deposit in one country may be the economic equivalent of a large deposit of low-grade ore in another. But such compensations are rare. More commonly the differences in quantity and quality are compounded, and their effect upon trade is magnified. Since countries also vary in size, their productive potentialities vary in a great many ways, with the consequence that each country is unique in some respects, most countries in most respects, and some countries in all respects. Their business enterprise, production, and trade reflect the same diversity, and from this diversity spring the possibilities for mutually beneficial exchange as well as the incentives for foreign investments in different or better resources.

Human resources

The productive potentialities of different countries depend not only on their natural resources but also on their human resources. Here again, the international distribution is uneven, both in quantity and in quality. Some countries such as China and India have enough people to populate a continent; others such as Norway and Iceland do not have enough for a good-sized city. The differences are even greater in the qualitative aspects, though they may not be so easily observable. Longevity, education, industrial skills, understanding of arts and sciences, and productivity-oriented values—just to name the key dimensions of the qualitative aspect—range widely in the populations of the most advanced industrial nations down to those of primitive, tribal communities. Their respective capabilities to activate and to enjoy whatever natural resources they possess must, therefore, vary accordingly. These variations, too, affect the nature of indigenous enterprise and the opportunities for exogenous exchange.

Cultural resources

Although relations between the cultural resources and the productive alternatives for business enterprise are more difficult to discern, they are nonetheless of basic importance. Cultural heritage, social structure, and fundamental philosophy of life provide criteria and guides for individual as well as for collective conduct in any particular society. Related to these elements are tastes, aspirations, ideals, and other determinants of motivation for action and inaction, for work and leisure, and for production and consumption. Through the consumption criteria the cultural environment defines much of the demand for goods and services as well as the directions and trends in the growth and development of human resources, that is, in the employment of the available manpower and its productive capabilities.

In combination, the cultural, human, and physical resources form myriad patterns of productive advantages and disadvantages from which the fundamental incentives for international business spring.

Conflicting Ideas on Resources

The relative importance of the different resources defies concrete measurement. Theoretical concepts recognize the necessity of all three categories but conflict sharply regarding their relative roles. North American economists have generally de-emphasized the contribution of natural resources and have endeavored to explain industrial and other business achievements primarily in terms of human and environmental forces. The extreme flank of this school dismisses the whole question, arguing, "If natural resources are important, why did the American Indians fail to achieve significant economic progress, and why did things change after the European colonization of the continent?" This argument obviously lacks analytical merit. If the Indian had reached the same technological level the colonizing white man had inherited from his ancestors in Europe, or if the Indian were left alone to find his own way to modernity, he might not only have equaled but also possibly surpassed the white man's achievement. Since history cannot disclose the alternatives, there is no way of knowing what the evolution of Indian civilization would have been without intrusion.

Asiatic theoreticians, with support from many others, have taken the opposite position. They maintain that the natural-resource base is the prime determinant of the industrial and economic potential of each nation. As historical proof of their position, they point to the economic success of Europe, the United States, and the Soviet Union—all of which possessed a great abundance and diversity of natural resources at the time of their rapid growth. However, the argument seems less convincing in reference to some Latin American countries.

Most European economists take an intermediate position in this theoretical dialogue. They attribute more or less equal importance to both natural and human resources and are positive about the role of the cultural environment.

The three positions reflect quite accurately the critical problems of the different areas. In the United States and Canada, where natural resources have abounded until very recently and have never been a real obstacle for business enterprise, economic study and conceptualization have focused upon the human resource, from which much industrial conflict and tension have arisen. In Asia the critical problem has been the scarcity of arable land and of most other natural resources. Accordingly, the intellectuals' attention has been attracted to the diminishing ratio of resources to population. In Europe the population-to-land ratio is also very high. But this was not the case when its original industrialization took place a century and a half ago; at that time the population was a fraction of what it is now, so the ratio was much lower. Moreover, since no other area had any significant industrial capacity in those days, Europe was free to draw not only on its own unusually rich natural endowment but also on that of the rest of the world. More recently, especially since World War II, Europe's access to overseas resources has been severely curtailed through the disintegration of colonial relationships, and its internal resources have been increasingly drained. Consequently, there has been more realization of the critical role which natural resources must play. In the United States, too, the orthodox concept seems to be undergoing revision as shortages of certain industrially strategic materials are indicated by long-range projections of supply and demand.

The Dynamics of Resources

When progress was slow and changes in the business world were gradual, economic doctrines on resources—as on other aspects of business enterprise—served as useful simplifications of an otherwise inexplicable reality. The value of such doctrinaire positions has declined as contemporary society has rapidly changed on all conceivable fronts.

The static concept

In earlier periods natural resources were visualized as a given fund, or a fixed inventory, which a nation had been provided with either by geological developments in its particular location or by Providence. The depletable resources such as minerals would be exhausted sooner or later, and society's long-range hopes had to be pinned on the renewable variety of resources such as arable land, forests, animal life, and water power. This was essentially a static concept. It still lingers but fails to describe the rapidly changing conditions of contemporary reality.

The dynamic concept

Natural resources were previously defined here as those aspects of the physiographic environment which have the capacity to satisfy human needs. This capacity is not synonymous with the absolute potential of the environment; rather, it is a function of the scientific knowledge and the technological capabilities which a society at any particular time possesses. Iron ore was useless to Stone Age aboriginals, as was uranium to preatomic generations.

As science and technology advance, man's capacity to control and utilize his natural environment is enhanced in two principal ways: synthetics are developed to supplement natural resources (synthetic fibers, rubber, drugs, etc.), or applications are discovered for previously unusable parts of the physiographic environment (making plastic out of waste, distilling sea water, etc.). In either case, scientific and technological progress converts some of the useless into the useful, thus creating new natural resources. Although it is customary to think of the new materials as synthetics or artificial products, they are, of course, derived from some natural source. What is different, for example, between a synthetic and a natural fiber is not the chemical elements from which the fibrous molecular structures are formed (the original resource) but the processes of manufacturing the desired molecular structures. If they are produced by the self-generating processes in nature, such as in plant or animal biology, the fiber is "natural"; if they are produced by technological means, the fiber is "synthetic." If the fiber were the goal, this distinction might seem justifiable. But the fiber is only a step toward the real goal, which is human satisfaction—the protection or the beauty which a garment made of the fiber is expected to provide. Thus the manufacturing process must go on to change the fiber into thread, the thread into cloth, and the cloth into a garment. In principle this is no different from the arrangement of chemical elements into molecules, molecules into compounds, and compounds into fibrous material as part of the synthetic process. Consequently, the greater length of the manufacturing process rather than the "naturalness" of the material distinguishes synthetics from what traditionally are called natural materials.

As synthetics manufacturing can either duplicate or parallel certain natural processes, it can dip deeper than conventional manufacturing for its raw materials. Thus the society both deepens and broadens the scope of natural materials which can be harnessed for economic purposes. As science and technology create new capabilities, business enterprise will push the starting point of the man-made manufacturing process closer and closer to the original elements of matter for an increasing number of materials. And the natural-resource base will continue to expand. From a technical standpoint it is therefore axiomatic that the resource bases of all countries will gain more depth and variety rather than deteriorate in the long run. Gaps and shortages will occur only to the extent that technological discoveries fail to provide alternatives to natural materials. And the number of those gaps is diminishing rapidly.

From an economic standpoint the international outlook for resources is not so sanguine. When synthetics excel, they may displace the corresponding natural materials either because of lower costs of production or because of higher quality. Although the natural material is still usable from a technical standpoint, it may thus become obsolete from business and economic standpoints. Such degeneration of old resources progressively removes them from the realm of economic usefulness.

Thus in the long run the economically usable resources of a nation are not accurately described as a fixed inventory or a fund. Rather, they represent a complex variable continuously changing in size, diversity, and composition through the ingress and egress of different aspects of the physiographic environment. In the short run, however, the fixed-fund concept is still a helpful guide, especially for explaining the current possibilities for trade and payments among different countries. In investment analysis, reliance on the conventional concept is much more precarious. In some industries technological change is rapid; in others it is slow. In some industries technology has stabilized on a certain plateau, and only a major breakthrough can bring any substantial change; in others no point or plane of stabilization is in view. The rightness or wrongness of resource-oriented investments, therefore, must be judged in terms of the technological developments in the particular industry and in terms of the time involved.

Transformers

Science develops theoretical knowledge, which defines the probable and the possible. Technology transforms the possible into physical capabilities. The end product for science is explanation in the form of mathematical formulation or verbal discourse; the end product for technology is the transformation of the available resources into the desired goods and services. The capability to transform depends on the available instruments—installations, structures, carriers, and other machine systems—which are the physical vehicles of the process. They are, therefore, the focal concern of technology. Collectively, the vehicles of transformation may be called *transformers*. In traditional economic analysis the assumption is made that transformers represent a constant capacity in the same way that resources represent a fixed natural inventory. The acceleration of technological change has made the weakness of this assumption glaringly apparent. Not only are the transformers changing, but also they have become the most decisive variables in the relative potentialities of different nations.

It is useful to think of transformers in three functional categories: energy transformers, material transformers, and space transformers. To the first category belong the various prime movers: engines, dynamos, and atomic reactors; they govern a country's capacity to do productive work. The material transformers embrace the great variety of machine tools, structures, and installations designed to change the physical and chemical configuration of different materials; they determine which inputs, including work energy, can be transformed into outputs and how efficiently. The space transformers comprise trains, planes, conveyor belts, cranes, and other transporting and communications systems which determine the extent to which and the speed with which materials, ideas, and information can be moved about within a business system.

Each type of transformer plays a primary role in a country's productive capabilities and not only can offset a disadvantage but also can change a disadvantage to an advantage in the original resource endowment. A new theory propounded by Kelso and Adler is that, in modern times, the transformers have become the most decisive of all productive factors and that their significance will be even greater in the future. Correspondingly, the significance of the human resources and the natural resources will decline. If substantiated, this theory would require a complete revision of traditional economic thinking and would focus international comparative studies upon the amount, nature, and distribution of the transformers in different countries.

Resource Incentive for International Business

The discussion to this point has centered on the character and causes of differences in production potentialities which underlie international business relations. This section reverses the proposition and examines the effect of international business upon resource utilization and productive efficiency. The exercise which follows demonstrates that such a theoretical relationship exists. To minimize the numerical complications only two countries and two commodities are considered. Obviously, both variables could be multiplied without disturbing the central concept. The exercise is based on these suppositions:

— Countries Delta and Theta both possess land resources suitable for the production of oranges and olives.

— These land resources are interchangeable between the two commodities, but their productivity (the input-output ratio) varies with the degree of substitution as shown in Table 4-1.

— All suitable land resources are utilized to produce the quantities in Table 4-1.

— Both nations have centrally planned economies in which consumption and production volumes are determined by the plan.

— The consumption requirements are planned as follows:

Product	*Delta*	*Theta*
Oranges	21	15
Olives	7	7

Under the given conditions both countries can meet their respective consumption requirements with their own resources providing they select the correct alternative from the production-possibilities schedule in Table 4-1. For Delta the right combination is *D*, and for Theta it is *F*. With these combinations, the output in each country precisely matches the planned requirements. All suitable land resources are then employed, and all needs are satisfied from domestic production; the situation is in internal balance. The policy of self-sufficiency works well in both countries, or so it seems.

Suppose now that the production planners set out to maximize the output from the resource input. In Delta they find that by shifting 1 unit of land from oranges to olive culture (by going from combination *D* to *E*), a 2000-bushel decline will occur in oranges picked with a 3000-bushel increase in olive output; hence, there is a net gain of 1000 bushels in total harvest. If

TABLE 4-1

Production Alternatives with a Fixed Resource Input (in 1000 bushels)

Delta				*Theta*			
Combination	*Oranges*	*Olives*	*Total Product*	*Combination*	*Oranges*	*Olives*	*Total Product*
A	25	0	25	*A*	24	0	24
B	24	2	26	*B*	23	2	25
C	23	4	27	*C*	22	4	26
D	21	7	28	*D*	20	5	25
E	19	10	29	*E*	18	6	24
F	18	14	32	*F*	15	7	22
G	13	16	29	*G*	12	8	20
H	10	17	27	*H*	9	9	18
I	7	18	25	*I*	6	10	16
J	4	19	23	*J*	3	11	14
K	0	20	20	*K*	0	12	12

Delta shifted still another unit of land and adopted combination *F*, the country would lose 1000 bushels of oranges but gain 4000 bushels of olives. Since this land allocation would maximize the total harvest, planners in Delta would not contemplate any further shifts. However, they cannot actually make the shift to combination *F* because it fails to meet the consumption requirements of the country; they would be producing too little of one and too much of the other product.

Induced by the potential gain of 4000 bushels in total output, Delta planners now seek possibilities for trading their potential surpluses with other countries. In Theta they should find an interested party, for Theta's planners are faced with an analogous prospect. If they shift their land allocation from combination *F* to *C*, their country would enjoy a gain in total output of 4000 bushels while the total resource input would remain unchanged. But, as in Delta, this optimum total cannot materialize because of insufficient quantities of both products to satisfy the consumption requirements of the country.

If the planners of both countries now work out a program for production and trade with plans to exchange the surplus olives of Delta for the surplus oranges of Theta on a bushel-for-bushel basis, they find that the following situation will hold:

	Delta		*Theta*	
		Domestic Potential		
	Oranges	*Olives*	*Oranges*	*Olives*
Consumption requirements	21	7	15	7
Output	18	14	22	4
Balance	3	+7	+7	−3

	International Trade Potential			
	Oranges	*Olives*	*Oranges*	*Olives*
Imports	3	—	—	3
Exports	—	3	3	—
Actual consumption (equal to requirements)	21	7	15	7
Net gain	—	4	4	—

Through international trade both nations gain in *real* terms by shifting their production schedules to maximize output, by maintaining resource input unchanged, and by satisfying domestic consumption requirements as before. The gains, in the form of 4000 bushels of olives for Delta and 4000 bushels of oranges for Theta, can now be traded for some other products in third countries, and thus consumption can be enriched further through international trade; or, alternatively, the land required for surplus outputs of olives and oranges can now be converted to some other use: industrial sites, residential development, or recreational areas. Note that none of these possibilities existed before the two countries entered into trade.

The process which took place in the above exercise is presented graphically in Figure 4-1. It not only summarizes how the land resources were released through trade in this specific illustration but also underscores the interdependence of resource productivity or yield and international trade. This relationship has been neglected in American economics, and very little actual research and factual information pertain to it. This is a serious omission.

In the communist orbit as well as in the developing countries great stress is placed on resource productivity and on the minimization of resource inputs to obtain the desired production and consumption objectives. The Soviet Academy of Sciences announced in May 1965 that geographic research in that country is being focused on the resource problem, especially that of maximizing resource yields. Both economic and physical geography divisions will concentrate on this objective. (It might be added that in the Soviet classification

FIGURE 4-1

Minimum Resource Inputs to Meet Fixed Output Targets with and without Trade

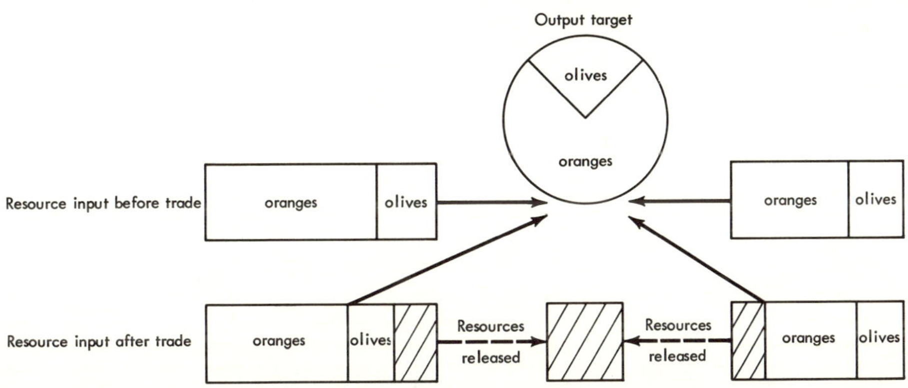

of knowledge, geography covers a broader and more influential segment than it does in this country.)

In India, China, and Japan systematic empirical and theoretical efforts are made to shed new light on maximizing resource yields. Despite rapid progress in the development of synthetics, or perhaps because of it, the Western countries will have to join in this effort to find a more rational basis than they now have for analyzing and appraising the increasing numbers of resource alternatives created by technological advances, especially by various new transformers.

5

Economics of International Trade

Business activities and institutions transcend national boundaries for economic reasons and for managerial reasons. This division does not imply mutual exclusivity. The two categories have considerable substantive overlap, and no sharp line can be drawn between them. Rather, the demarcation is a broad zone intermeshed on one side with the economic and on the other with the managerial. The categorization is essential not so much for classifying information as for establishing the point of view and the frame of reference for analysis and interpretation.

Economic explanations utilize the problem settings and the analytical tools of economic theory; managerial explanations focus upon the behavior and the success of business enterprise. Neither per se is more scientific than the other. However, the former deals primarily with theoretical concepts, principles, and models, de-emphasizing facts and evading complex realities by simplified assumptions. The latter deals primarily with facts and relationships of the actual entrepreneurial situations; it, too, utilizes theoretical concepts, principles, and models but only as a means of analyzing and dissecting reality and not as systems or objectives in themselves.

In this chapter the economic-theoretical concepts are reviewed; the managerial reasons will be discussed in Chapter 10. As indicated earlier, the economist's view of international business is a narrow one; it conceives export and import trade as the main body of international economic relations and reluctantly admits that international investments and other nontrade business transactions may also exceed national boundaries. In addition, it has nothing at all to say about the organization and functioning of multinational enterprises. Hence, the economic-theoretical concepts provide a better explanation of international trade and payments than of multinational companies and their operations.

The Theory of Trade

In economics, international trade is explained by the *law of comparative advantage.* This theory postulates that internal cost ratios vary among products in different countries, giving rise to different price structures, that is, different relative values of any particular product in terms of other products. The different cost ratios and price structures create relative advantages and disadvantages. These in turn induce countries to specialize in the production of certain products which they will export and to divert their resources from others which they will import.

International barter

To make the central idea of this doctrine more explicit, assume that we are dealing with two countries *X* and *Y*, both producing cotton and wool but with different per unit costs of production as reflected in the required factor inputs below:

	Required Factor Inputs Per Unit (Bale) of Output		
Country	*Cotton*	*Wool*	*Internal Price (Factor Input Ratio)*
X	5	10	1 bale of cotton = $\frac{1}{2}$ bale of wool or 1 unit of wool = 2 bales of cotton
Y	10	15	1 bale of cotton = $\frac{2}{3}$ bale of wool or 1 bale of wool = $1\frac{1}{2}$ bales of cotton

Clearly, *X* is the more efficient producer of both products, since its inputs are lower than the corresponding inputs required in *Y* to achieve the same output.

Is mutually beneficial trade possible between *X* and *Y* under such conditions? Or, to put the question differently: Can trade contribute to the welfare of either country without hurting the other? On the surface, the answer seems to be negative, for how could a high-cost country such as *Y* benefit from trading with a low-cost country such as *X*? How could trade take place at all under these circumstances? Yet, this common-sense reaction proves fallacious under theoretical scrutiny. The relative domestic costs, which are assumed to reflect internal prices, are 1 bale of wool to 2 bales of cotton in *X*, and 1 bale of wool to $1\frac{1}{2}$ bales of cotton in *Y*. Hence, the internal cost and price structures are different in the two countries. If, now, the merchants in *X* and *Y* start trading, this is what would happen:

Country X		Country Y
A. Merchant in this country acquires 30 bales of cotton at a cost of 15 bales of wool		
Exports 30 bales of cotton	⟶	30 bales of cotton traded here at local prices bring
Imports 20 bales of wool	⟵	20 bales of wool
Result: gain 5 bales (20—15)		
B.		Merchant in this country acquires 20 bales of wool at a cost of 30 bales of cotton
20 bales of wool traded here at local prices bring	⟵	Exports 20 bales of wool
40 bales of cotton	⟶	Imports 40 bales of cotton
		Result: gain 10 bales (40—30)

If the merchants reverse their positions—those in *X* try to export wool and import cotton, and those in *Y* try to export cotton and import wool—the results would be reversed and both would suffer a loss. This the reader can easily test by referring to the above exercise. The secret of the success or failure of the merchants, the focal point of the theory of comparative advantage, lies in the difference between relative home prices in the two countries, i.e., 1 to 2 in *X* and 1 to $1\frac{1}{2}$ in *Y*. As long as a bale of wool can be changed for a greater quantity of cotton abroad than in *Y*, it will pay to export it regardless of domestic resource input and cost; and, as long as a bale of wool can be acquired from abroad by people in *X* by giving up a smaller amount of cotton than they would have to on the home market, it will pay to import it despite the lower factor inputs required at home. The absolute cost levels have no influence on this theory.[1]

Notice that if the relative price ratios stay 1 to 2 and 1 to $1\frac{1}{2}$, respectively, trade between *X* and *Y* could go on endlessly as a chain reaction. The merchants in *X*, for instance, could not only export cotton and trade it for wool but also exchange the imported wool for a still larger amount of cotton, export it, and get a yet larger quantity of wool to bring back, continuing this circular profit-making ad infinitum. In the real world the opportunities are curtailed by transportation costs, which may neutralize the advantage. Also, the actual commodities number in the thousands instead of being only the two used in expounding the theory, and even the two commodities would normally represent a number of types and grades, which would make chain-reaction trading more difficult. Yet these objections do not invalidate the principle involved. Merchandising firms which have the ability to uncover and to capitalize on relative price differentials in different countries make the big profits in international trade. Indeed, trade profits arise from little else.

1 Some economists argue that it is the comparative cost rather than the comparative price which determines the possibility for gainful trade. This argument requires several complicating assumptions which are difficult to defend in reality and add little to the basic concept.

But the relative price differentials are seldom static; they change in response to trade flows as well as to changes in factor costs. In the *X* and *Y* example, once trade between the two countries starts, the supply-and-demand conditions in both will be altered, and the likelihood of reallocation of factor inputs from wool to cotton in *X* and from cotton to wool in *Y* is strong. If this reallocation does not affect factor prices (wages, rents, and interests), *X* will specialize completely in producing cotton and *Y* in producing wool. And, each will buy from the other the needed quantity of the abandoned commodity.

It is more realistic, however, to assume that after the start of trade, domestic price relationships will change, and the possibilities for gain from trade will diminish with further conversion from one product to the other. At the point where relative price ratios in both countries become identical, for instance 1 to 2 and 1 to 2, no mutually gainful trade whatsoever could take place between them.

Trade under money prices

To this point the discussion has been in terms of real as distinguished from money prices. This was done to focus the analysis on the fundamental point of the theory. This section demonstrates the validity of the principle if money prices are use.

Assume that the domestic prices are as follows:

	Cotton	*Wool*	*Ratio*
Country *X*	10 pesos	20 pesos	1 : 2
Country *Y*	50 rupees	75 rupees	1 : 1½

Assume further that there has been no trade between the two countries to this point, and consequently no peso-rupee exchange rate exists. When trade starts, the following situation arises:

Country X		*Country Y*
A. Exports 30 bales of cotton at a cost of 300 pesos	→	Sells 30 bales of cotton for 1500 rupees; buys with proceeds
Sells 20 bales of wool for 400 pesos, a profit of 100 pesos	←	20 bales of wool (1500: 75)
B. Sells 20 bales of wool for 400 pesos; buys with proceeds	←	Exports 20 bales of wool at a cost of 1500 rupees
40 bales of cotton	→	Sells 40 bales of cotton for 2000 rupees, a profit of 500 rupees

International trade has produced the same advantages as it did in the barter situation. And, in all other respects, the same comments and qualifications apply.

To move another step closer to reality, replace the no-exchange-rate assumption with that of a pre-existing exchange rate, 1 peso = 4.5 rupees. How would the comparative advantage in the previous illustration be affected?

Country X		Country Y
A. Exports 30 bales of cotton at a cost of 300 pesos	→	Sells 30 bales of cotton for 1500 rupees; exchanges proceeds into pesos
333 pesos, a profit of 33 pesos	←	Obtains 333 pesos
B. Sells 20 bales of wool for 400 pesos; exchanges proceeds into rupees	←	Exports 20 bales of wool at a cost of 1500 rupees
Obtains 1800 rupees	→	1800 rupees, a profit of 300 rupees

As these transactions show, the advantage still exists. The figures, converted to a per-unit basis, show that the advantage for *X* is 1.11 pesos per bale of cotton exported and for *Y* 15 rupees per bale of wool exported. But when the exchange rate changes, the per-unit export advantages have to change also. Take, for instance, the exchange rate 1 peso = 6 rupees. If trade is attempted now, the results are quite different. (See below.)

Country X		Country Y
A1. Exports 1 bale of cotton at a cost of 10 pesos	→	Sells 1 bale of cotton for 50 rupees
Obtains 8.33 pesos, a loss of 1.67 pesos	←	Exchanges 50 rupees (50 : 6)
A2. Exports 1 bale of wool at a cost of 20 pesos	→	Sells 1 bale of wool for 75 rupees
Obtains 12.5 pesos, a loss of 7.5 pesos	←	Exchanges 75 rupees (75 : 6)
B1. Sells 1 bale of wool for 20 pesos	←	Exports 1 bale of wool at a cost of 75 rupees
Exchanges pesos (20 × 6)	→	Obtains 120 rupees, a profit of 45 rupees
B2. Sells 1 bale of cotton for 10 pesos	←	Exports 1 bale of cotton at a cost of 50 rupees
Exchanges pesos (10 × 6)	→	Obtains 60 rupees, a profit of 10 rupees

Obviously trade could not take place under these exchange rates, as *X* can sell neither product without suffering a loss, and *Y* can profit on both. The shift of the exchange rate from 1 peso = 4.5 rupees to 1 peso = 6 rupees has destroyed all comparative advantages which *X* previously had and has simultaneously conferred upon *Y* an absolute advantage in both products. Consequently, the relative values of the two currencies, as expressed in their exchange rate, can either create or negate the prerequisites for profitable international trade. But to what extent? The answer can be found by establishing the international price ratios for both products. Cotton costs 10 pesos in *X* and 50 rupees in *Y*, hence the ratio is 10:50 or 1:5; wool costs 20 pesos in *X* and 75 rupees in *Y*, giving a ratio 20:75 or approximately 1:4. These ratios set the upper and lower limits for the exchange rate. As the exchange rate fluctuates, it shifts the advantages more toward the country whose currency depreciates and away from the country whose currency appreciates. On the limits, one of the countries will break even and the other will derive all the advantage from the trade. Beyond the limit, as shown above, the comparative advantages disappear, and trade must stop, since one of the countries cannot export and thus cannot earn the other's currency to pay for any imports.

Multiproduct trade

If, however, we also assume that the bilateral trade between *X* and *Y* involves a variety of commodities, the last conclusion must be modified—namely, trade may continue in spite of the exchange rate's having moved beyond the price ratios of these two particular products and in spite of one country's having gained all the advantages while the other is burdened with all the disadvantages as far as cotton and wool are concerned. The limits in a multiproduct trade relationship will be set by the price relationships of the products at the two extremes: the product in which *X* enjoys the greatest comparative advantage or least comparative disadvantage and that in which *Y* enjoys the greatest comparative advantage or the least disadvantage. Unless cotton and wool, used in the above illustrations, happen to be the two items, the range for the exchange rate of pesos and rupees will be wider than the 1:5 and 1:4 ratios.[2] Under those circumstances trade in wool and cotton need not stop when the exchange rate reaches, for example, 1:6, as long as this ratio lies between the limits set by the two extreme ratios of the commodity mix. The theoretical consequence of this is that people in *X* will not only continue importing wool from *Y* but also start importing cotton simply because both imports cost less than their domestic counterparts. As these imports increase they are likely to make the rupee a more sought-after currency and to augment the supply of pesos, with the result that the exchange rate may start shifting back toward the range where the original comparative advantages are restored, and two-way, mutually beneficial trade will follow. But it should be underscored that as long as the exchange rate 1:6 is maintained, either by trade in other products or by an artificial control measure, the one-way flow of cotton and wool from *Y* to *X* will continue and may ultimately lead to the complete disappearance of these industries in *X*.

Multilateral trade

If the trade is multilateral instead of between two countries, the interpretation of comparative advantage is greatly obscured. The substitution of a multiproduct mix for two-product trade already raises some difficult questions and necessitates exceptions to the principle as indicated in the preceding section. But if the multiproduct mix is placed into a multilateral context,[3] hopes for any concrete application of the theory vanish almost entirely. At best one can endeavor to construct international advantage patterns as general guides, but so far such attempts have failed to bear any practical fruit. Future developments in computer technology may enable us to use the concept for analyzing concrete problems. For the time being, however, the concept must

[2] The reader may wish to experiment with the rate 1 peso = 3 rupees to test the validity of this statement in reference to the lower limit.

[3] Some economists, anxious to salvage the cherished theory, suggest that we combine all other countries into one group, "the rest of the world," and proceed as if there are only us and them. The trouble with this suggestion is that nobody knows how to trade with the whole world at the same time, as the world consists of many very different and very disintegrated sovereign nations.

remain in the realm of pure theory. This does not mean that it can be discarded by international executives and practicing economists, for it is a logical explanation of relationships and tendencies, and, although not usable as an instrument of analysis, it provides a frame of reference for and a way of thinking about the underlying tendencies of international trade. The next section will clarify and reinforce this opinion.

An Integrative Approach to the Theory of Trade

The different theoretical ideas discussed in the preceding sections, together with the opportunity-cost concept of resource-productivity maximization, can be synthesized into an integrated theory of trade, which follows. The formulation of the integrated theory depends on the behavior of opportunity cost under varying inputs and outputs—that is, when it is constant, when it is decreasing, and when it is increasing.

Trade under Constant Opportunity Cost

Constant opportunity costs exist when any unit of input produces a constant increment in output regardless of the levels of resource utilization and total output volume. Such a situation is illustrated by the figures in Table 5-1. In *X* every unit of wool displaces 2 units of cotton, and in *Y* every unit of wool displaces 1.5 units of cotton; in reverse, the relationships are 1 to 0.5 and 1 to 0.67, respectively. The ratios remain constant on all points of the production-possibilities scale.

TABLE 5-1

Production Possibilities with Constant Opportunity Costs

X		*Y*	
Cotton	*Wool*	*Cotton*	*Wool*
240	0	240	0
180	30	180	40
120	60	120	80
60	90	60	120
0	120	0	160

For greater precision these relationships may be portrayed graphically. In Figure 5-1, line *X* represents the production schedule for country *X* in the form of a function or input-output transformation curve between cotton and wool. If this is a competitive market where costs and prices are synonymous, the line also reflects the relative internal prices in country *X*. If all resources in *X* were devoted to cotton production, its aggregate output would reach 240 bales a year; if all resources were shifted to wool production, the aggregate quantity would be 120 bales. Between these limits *X* can produce any desired combination located on the transformation function.

Line *Y* depicts the quantitative relationships applicable to country *Y*. Since its resources are better suited to wool production, the line slopes more toward the wool axis. If all resources were employed in wool production, the total output would be 160 bales; if all were transferred to cotton, the total output would be 240 bales. Between these two outputs the country can choose any combination on its transformation function (or its relative cost and price curve).

In the absence of trade, wool will be exchanged for cotton at the rate of 1 to 2 in *X* and 1 to 1.5 in *Y*, just as in our original illustration. These prices are graphically measured by the slopes of the respective transformation curves and could be expressed in linear equations. When the slopes are different, the internal price structures are different in the two countries, and a comparative advantage exists for mutually beneficial trade; when the slopes are the same—the two lines parallel—an absolute advantage exists; and when they are coincident, no advantage to either party exists.

When the transformation function of *Y* is superimposed upon that of *X* in the same chart, the comparative advantage geometrically is the area between

FIGURE 5-1

Trade under Constant Opportunity Costs: Country *X* (scale in tens)

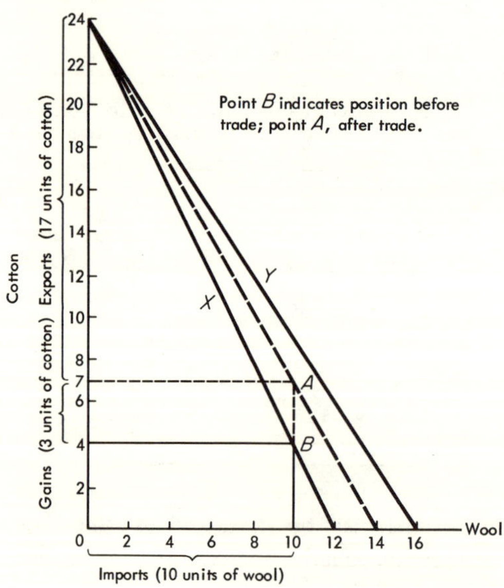

the two lines. The terms of trade—that is, the unit price of one country's exports relative to the unit price of its imports—can move within this region but cannot go outside the limits set by the two lines. That is, trade is beneficial to X as long as it can export cotton at any unit price exceeding the domestic acquisition cost, which is $\frac{1}{2}$ unit of wool, but Y can reciprocate only as long as it can export wool to X at some price which is higher than the cost ($1\frac{1}{2}$ units of cotton) in its domestic market. The relative position of country Y is depicted in Figure 5-2. To show its comparative-advantage region the scale for X's transformation curve has been adjusted so that both curves have a common origin on the wool axis.

FIGURE 5-2

Trade under Constant Opportunity Costs: Country *Y* (scale in tens)

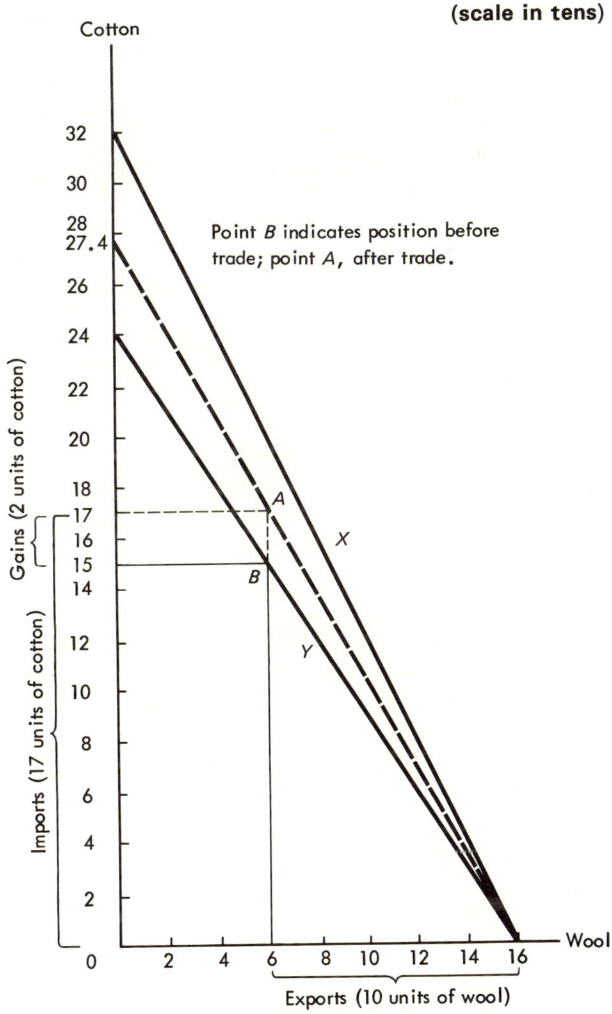

Measurement of gains

To determine the gains from trade, the pretrade consumption level must be established. Any point on the respective country's production-possibilities line can be chosen. For illustration assume that before trade the following situation pertains:

Country	*Cotton*	*Wool*
X	40	100
Y	150	60
	190	160

Since both countries are self-sufficient, their consumption and production figures are identical.

When trade opens, *X* finds it profitable to export cotton, in which it has a comparative advantage, and import wool, in which it has a comparative disadvantage; *Y* is in the opposite position. This sets the processes of specialization in motion: In *X* resources are gradually converted from wool to cotton production, and in *Y* from cotton to wool production. Since the transformation ratios in both countries are constant, these shifts do not destroy the respective comparative advantages, and the specialization process continues until all resources in *X* are devoted to cotton production and all those in *Y* to wool production. When this point of complete international specialization of production is reached, total wool production remains 160 units, but total cotton output has increased from 190 to 240 units. Hence, there is an overall gain from trade of 50 units of cotton.

How this gain is distributed between the two countries depends on where the terms of trade settle. The theory does not provide any formulas for establishing that point. It depends on several composite variables such as the degree

TABLE 5-2

Gains from Trade under Constant Opportunity Cost

Item	*X*		*Y*	
	Cotton	*Wool*	*Cotton*	*Wool*
Before trade:				
Production	40	100	150	60
Consumption	40	100	150	60
After trade:				
Production	240	—	—	160
Consumption	70	100	170	60
Exports	170	—	—	100
Imports	—	100	170	—
Gains from trade	30	—	20	—

to which either country needs the product of the other (elasticities of demand), the relative sizes of the two countries, and their international financial relations. In Figures 5-1 and 5-2 the assumption is made that these forces balance along the dotted line, approximately halfway between the two transformation functions, which represents the terms of trade after specialization. Of the total gain of 50 units of cotton, 30 units then would accrue to *X* and 20 units to *Y*, as shown in the respective charts. For numerical comparison the exercise is also summarized in Table 5-2.

Trade under Decreasing Opportunity Cost

Line *Y* in Figure 5-3 represents a production transformation function between cotton and wool on which the shift of resources from one to the other results in the progressively increasing output of the other. The line is based on Table 5-3. Assume that before trade starts the country's consumption necessitates a resource allocation at point Y_B, that is, 7 units of cotton and 8 units of wool. Should an opportunity now present itself for exporting wool and importing cotton at terms more favorable than the domestic price ratio of 20 units of cotton = 30 units of wool, the country would rapidly shift its resources out of cotton production and devote them exclusively to wool production. The incentive for this shift would be the increasing return that substituting wool production for cotton production yields. Even if the international exchange ratio coincided with the internal price line, the country would still gain from trade by moving its "consumption boundary" to its new "production boundary" at point Y_A, where consumption equals 11 units of cotton and 13 units of wool. This situation is summarized in Table 5-4.

TABLE 5-3

Production Alternatives under Decreasing Opportunity Cost: Country *Y*

Commodity \ Combination	*A*	*C*	*D*	*E*	*F*	*H*	*K*
Cotton	20	14	11	7	6	3	0
Wool	0	2	4	8	10	18	30
Total product	20	16	15	15	16	21	30

Note that the opposite shift (from wool to cotton) is equally possible under these circumstances. If, for example, the initial advantage in trade had favored the importation of wool and the exportation of cotton, the country would have had a progressively increasing incentive to specialize completely in cotton production and to abandon wool entirely. At point Y_B in the figure, the relationship between the two commodities reverses; consequently, in the region to the left of this point cotton production has a decreasing opportunity

FIGURE 5-3

Trade under Decreasing Opportunity Costs: Country *Y*

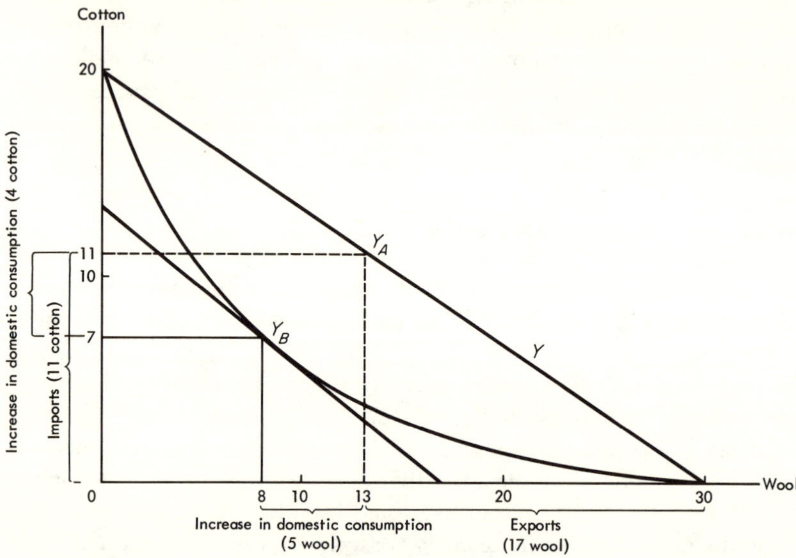

TABLE 5-4

Gains from Trade under Decreasing Opportunity Cost: Country *Y*

	Cotton	*Wool*
Before trade:		
Requirements	7	8
Production	7	8
After trade:		
Production	0	30
Exports	0	17
Imports	11	0
Actual consumption	11	13
Gains from increasing returns	4	5

cost (increasing return), and in the region to the right of this point wool production has a decreasing opportunity cost. At point Y_B the internal economy is in unstable balance in the sense that a price increase of wool in terms of cotton will cause producers to shift out of cotton, and conversely a price increase of cotton in terms of wool will encourage the opposite shift; both processes once set in motion will gain momentum. Which product will become dominant under such cost assumptions depends entirely on external influences, such as trade with other countries and in other commodities; these influences determine the exchange rates and world prices which define the initial comparative advantage for the country's international trade.

Trade Under Increasing Opportunity Cost

When increasing opportunity costs exist, the shift of resources from one product to another requires a progressively greater sacrifice, and the incremental returns become correspondingly smaller. Figure 5-4 depicts such a

FIGURE 5-4

Trade under Increasing Opportunity Costs

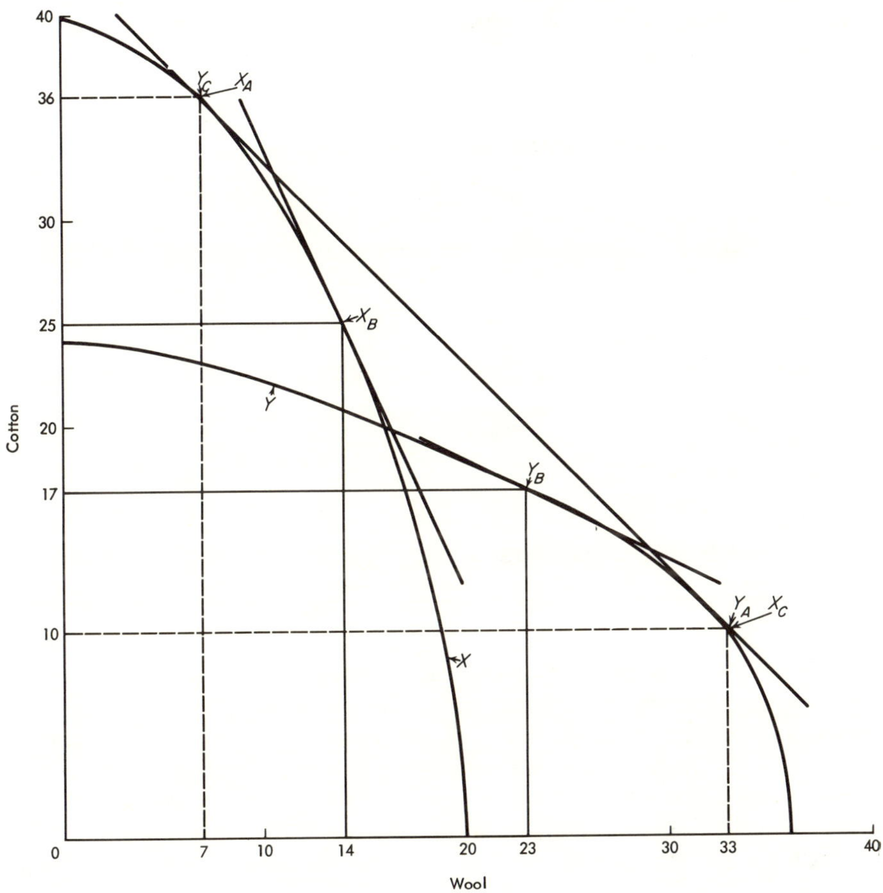

situation. The convexities of the transformation functions X and Y reflect the differences of successive cost increments or the rate of change in the substitution ratio between the two products in each country.

Assume that before trade X is producing 25 units of cotton and 14 units of wool at point X_B. Its domestic price ratio is 2 cotton: 1 wool, as the tangent to the transformation function at that point indicates. Similarly, Y produces 17 units of cotton and 23 units of wool to satisfy its pretrade consumption requirements. Its internal price relationship is 1 cotton: 2 wool, as the tangential slope at point Y_B shows.

When trade between the two countries develops, specialization will follow, but only to the point where the internal price relations become identical; any further shift of resources from wool to cotton in X or from cotton to wool in Y would obviously be undesirable, as it would cause a decrement in total consumption. Since the internal price relations are expressed by lines tangential to the respective production function, the points at which the two countries have identical prices must have the same tangent. Consequently, production will shift to X_A and Y_A, where outputs are 36 units of cotton and 7 units of wool for X and 10 units of cotton and 33 units of wool for Y. Table 5-5 summarizes the entire process.

TABLE 5-5

Gains from Trade under Increasing Opportunity Costs

	X		*Y*	
	Cotton	*Wool*	*Cotton*	*Wool*
Before trade:				
Production	25	14	17	23
Consumption	25	14	17	23
After trade:				
Production	36	7	10	33
Consumption	10	33	36	7
Balance of trade:				
Exports	26	—	—	25
Imports	—	25	26	—
Gains from trade	−15	19	19	−15

But what about the fact that the price lines for both countries coincide in Figure 5-4 after trade? Does this not destroy the comparative advantages and thereby remove all incentive for further trade, Economic theory is hazy on this point. In the static sense of the comparative-advantage theory the answer is yes. But, as indicated before, much international trade stems from an absolute advantage such as the presence of a particular resource, human skill, or industry in one country and the absence of the same in another. Thus from a broader perspective the answer is no. Comparative advantage should not be looked upon as a static condition but as a dynamic force for adjustment and change toward the optimum position, where the total output of both countries is maximized. When the optimum is reached, the force does not disappear but continues as a deterrent for deviations from this position. Since any other than the optimum combination of production alternatives causes a decrease in output or consumption, deviations from the optimum are synonymous with comparative disadvantage for either country. To rephrase, as a dynamic force comparative advantage works not only to maximize the gains or advantages but also to minimize the losses or disadvantages for a country.

6

National Control of International Trade Relations

Truisms are usually of no value in learning something new. But in this case a truism will help us to establish the starting line and to delineate one extremity of the area to be analyzed. The truism is that international trade must have its origin in the rise of the nation state; if there were no nations, there could be no international activity, trade or nontrade.

The Nation-State Concept

But what does the concept of a nation-state entail? Its foundation is political sovereignty: the society's being a source of its own political power, and an absence of any external authority of force that could control or interfere in the exercise of this power. As a pure concept, the nation-state demands absolute sovereignty; it is an exclusive idea. To maintain its sovereignty, in fact, its governmental system, the sole generator of political power and social control and fully independent from external interferences, the nation-state must protect itself against external intrusions, whatever their nature. For this it needs international (political) boundaries to define the territorial scope of its own sovereign jurisdiction, and the nonjurisdiction of all other nation-states, or perhaps more correctly, to tell the outside world to stay out.

But demarcation lines are not enough. If the sovereignty of a nation-state is to remain unadulterated it must surround itself with peripheral barriers that will guarantee that no transboundary contacts could occur outside the discretionary tolerance of the agencies or organs of the sovereignty.

While in the current political context this may seem like a description of a totalitarian state, the point here has nothing to do with the *internal* political system. In concept any nation state is absolutist in its *external* relations. That the communist countries have employed this concept much more literally than the noncommunist countries is quite irrelevant for our purposes here. Those interested in this matter may find a plausible explanation in the communists' emphasis on doctrine in all aspects of life and especially in their totalitarian system, which can function and preserve itself only if operated as a closed system.

Returning to the point of issue, let us reiterate that the peripheral barriers of the nation-state must be absolute if it is to avoid external interferences. In its pure and complete form the nation-state is a closed system. Thus, to attain and maintain maximum sovereignty, to become and remain completely unaffected by external influence, the nation-state must have no international trade. Its political ideal of complete independence can be assured only by one economic policy: complete *self-sufficiency.*

But this policy collides head on with the theory of trade. Complete self-sufficiency, as we saw in the previous chapter, would deny the nation the opportunities for specialization, increased resource productivity, and greater real income which free trade can offer. The gains from trade foregone would thus measure the cost to the country of its absolute national sovereignty. This cost no nation can afford. Neither of the two conceptual ideals: political sovereignty or free trade, has proven attainable for the nation-state. Rather than forming separate policy targets, they serve by necessity as the limits of the continuum for national regulation of international trade. In a graphic sketch a nation's policy range might be construed as this:

FREE TRADE	CONTINUUM OF	SELF-SUFFICIENCY
complete interdependence among nations	←POLICY OPTIONS→	complete independence of each country

Any shift toward one ideal will always exact a cost in terms of the other. The nation cannot attain both ideals simultaneously. All it can do is to search for the point in the continuum which serves best the total national interest as perceived by the nation itself. There is no objective measure what the total national interest is or ought to be; it is determined by the political process by each independent country for itself. Considering their ideological priorities and economic necessities, different nations assign different values to independence and interdependence. Therefore, the policy continuum is not a straight line axis with objectively measurable trade-off costs, but an infinite variety of curved paths. Each country moves in its own particular path. For most the path is parabolic with the costs approaching infinity as the country gets close to either ideal. Neither the left nor the right limit of the continuum is, therefore, attainable; neither the pure economist nor the pure nationalist can ever reign supreme in a nation-state. It must always be something for both.

Self-sufficiency was attempted by the U.S.S.R. and China as inevitable corollaries to their nationalist isolation. Despite their command economies, closed borders, and inhuman sacrifices, complete self-sufficiency was not attainable. They are now slowly revising their goals. No other nation has ever come even near to real self-sufficiency.

The free-trade ideal, on the other hand, had never been tested as a complete system in the industrial world until the creation of the European Economic Community in 1957. Although limited in scope, this experiment is hoped to yield many new insights into international relations. Especially interesting will be to find out if it is possible for a member nation to remain a nation in any real sense after it has relinquished all control over transboundary business activity. That the outward shell of sovereignty can be maintained under such circumstances is illustrated by the instance of Andorra, Liechtenstein, Luxembourg and other "postage-stamp nations." But are they nation-states? Not really. They are remnants of an earlier era. Their substantive independence is also debatable. Perhaps they are too small? Perhaps indeed. But until any evidence to the contrary can be found, we have no choice but to proceed on the assumption that some form of control over transboundary activities is an integral part of the nation-state system of the contemporary world.

The Political Process

The regulation of international trade is primarily a political process. It revolves around the noneconomic as well as the economic factors involved. Neither the perspective nor the problem setting of economics, therefore, can produce an undistorted reflection of its essential nature.

A political process is a pragmatic process: the art of the possible, the road of least social resistance, and the compromise of conflicting interests. Its course is determined more by facts and conditions than theories or systems. And the products of the political process, to use a sportsman's analogy, are rules rather than plays, referees rather than performers, and positions rather than baskets, runs, or victories. More precisely, the political process yields political results—laws, procedures, and hierarchies of power. Its instrumentation is legalistic and its orientation social.

Therefore, we land on firmer ground if we seek to understand international trade controls not merely as elements of economics, but also as instruments of political governance.

Instruments of Trade Policy

If the nation-state system of political organization were invented today, the system of transboundary trade controls which would be its most logical accompaniment would need only three moving parts: quotas, monetary restrictions, and technical or administrative procedures. From the standpoint of control the export and import quotas are the most direct and efficient tools.

In size they can be varied from zero (complete embargo) to infinity (free trade), and in coverage from a single article to the entire national product.

Currency controls would provide an indirect and more diffusive alternative, while the technical procedures would be an unavoidable administrative corollary to the other two, i.e., any set of controls necessitates certain administrative techniques and processes which in themselves become resistances to trade in that they require skill and competence from traders which raises the cost of transboundary transactions.

But the nation-state system is not a contemporary invention. It predates our modern notions of systems analysis, concepts of control, and theories of trade. It was not designed as a logical system, but was shaped more by historic accidents and whimsical tyrants than by logical reason and intellectual insight. Taxation of transboundary movements was the favorite tool of the early rulers. As the result, tariffs have up to now provided the most important instrument for foreign trade policy. All the instruments: tariffs, quantitative trade restrictions, and foreign exchange regulations, are legal enactments. They are tools for exerting a nation's policy vis-à-vis the rest of the world.

The subject of foreign exchange will get considerable attention in later chapters. We shall defer that discussion for the moment. In this chapter we will examine the more technical aspects of tariffs. The actual trade policy of the United States and the respective roles of different policy instruments in its formulation will be the subject for the next chapter.

Tariffs

A tariff is a tax levied on transboundary movements of goods and services. It is the oldest form of taxation in use by modern nations. The practice of imposing tariffs is believed to have originated on the island of Tariffa, off the Iberian peninsula; from its name came the now international word *tariff*.

An international cargo can be taxed by the country from which it leaves, by the countries through which it must move to reach its destination, and by the country into which it enters. Accordingly tariffs are classified as export, transit, and import duties.

In the contemporary world tariffs are synonymous with import tariffs. Export and transit tariffs have been abolished by all major trading nations. Several developing countries continue assessing export tariffs and/or transit tariffs, not as instruments of trade controls, but as sources of public revenue which their meager tax base necessitates. The effect of these on world trade is quite negligible, and for our purposes they can be safely overlooked. For the United States tariffs have always been a major issue. In fact, the issue predates the nation. In the colonial days the dispute between the British Crown and the colonies about the tariffs levied on American cargoes culminated in the Boston Tea Party and provided much fuel for the independence movement.

When independence was subsequently won, the importance of the tariff issue was underscored by the constitutional provision which prohibits export tariffs in this country. Import tariffs, however, were left in the hands of Congress to be used in the best interest of the then infant nation. And, over the years, tariffs have been a persistent election issue and a principal instrument of foreign policy.

Theoretical Relationships

The theoretical effects of a tariff are best shown by graphic analysis. For simplicity, it is assumed here that transportation costs are negligible and that there are no government controls or any other artificial restrictions to prevent the quantities which are exported and imported to respond to prices and costs. It is further assumed that only two countries and a single commodity are involved. Such a situation is presented in Figure 6-1.

In the absence of tariffs, the exporting country will sell to the importing country a quantity which equalizes prices in both countries; in the graph the common price is p_1. At this price the total demand and supply in the exporting country are equalized at the volume q_1; the demand is determined from d_1 (domestic consumption) and e_1 (export sales), and the output is determined by the supply schedule S. In the importing country, the demand and supply are equated at v_1; the supply is made up of S_1 (domestic output) and i_1 (imports), and the demand is determined by schedule $\mathfrak{D}$. Hence $d_1 + e_1 = q_1$, $s_1 + i_1 = v_1$, and $e_1 = i_1$. If now an import tariff t is imposed on the movement of the commodity, the price in the importing country rises, as the importers are trying to pass on the tariff to the consumer. But, since all consumers are not willing to pay a price higher than p_1, the demand for the commodity shrinks and only a smaller volume v_2 can now be sold. The shrinkage of demand in the importing country leaves a surplus in the exporting country and intensifies competition among suppliers. As a result the price declines to the point where the quantity offered equals the quantity demanded; i.e., where $d_2 + e_2$ equals the supply (that is, from q_1 to q_2). Under these supply and demand conditions, depicted in Figure 6-1, the effects of tariff t will be to raise the price in the importing country from p_1 to p_2 and to lower the price in the exporting country from p_1 to p_3: the difference between the new prices will be equal to the tariff t. At the new prices the quantity of exports will have declined from e_1 to e_2 and the volume of imports declined correspondingly from i_1 to i_2; $e_2 = i_2$ and $p_2 = p_3 - t$.

How the tariff effect will be distributed between any two countries depends on the relative slopes of their supply and demand schedules. If, for instance, the demand curve of the importing country were flatter in the above illustration, a price lower than p_2 would be necessary to balance supply and demand; this change would mean that a greater part of the price effect would have to be borne by the exporting country and p_3, too, would have to be lower than now shown. The reverse would hold, for example, if the supply curve in

FIGURE 6-1

Effects of Tariffs

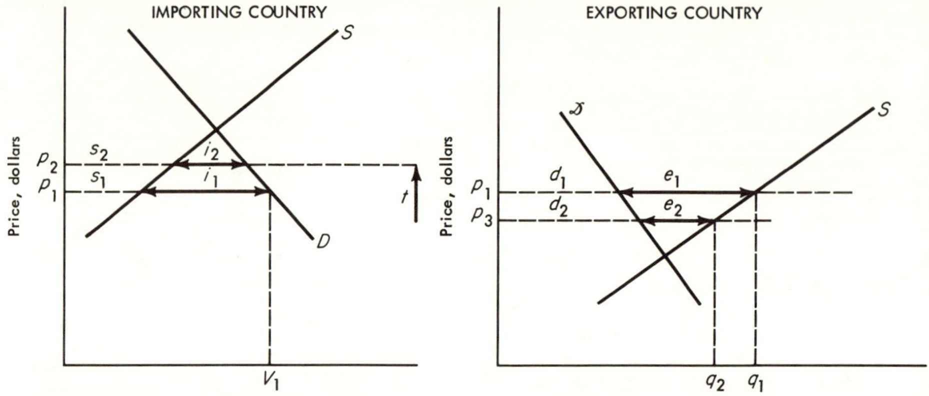

the exporting country were steeper. The reader who wishes to carry this reasoning to its ultimate numerical conclusions is advised to use the formulas of elasticity, which can be found in any good text on price theory.

The essence of the relationship can be summarized in two conclusions: the imposition of a tariff by one country affects both countries of a trading relationship by creating a price spread equal to the amount of the tariff between them; and the burden of the price spread falls primarily on the country which has the steepest supply and demand curves for the commodity involved.

Unilateral perspective

In practice trade relations are usually multilateral and the two-country assumption used above seldom holds. In a multilateral context, the total effect of a tariff becomes diffused and difficult to ascertain. Although this effect does not change the nature of the relationships, it distributes the results among a greater number of countries and makes them difficult to trace. Therefore, the arguments and reasoning employed in connection with actual tariff-policy formulation are normally centered on the effects in the importing country itself rather than on those in the international trading community as a whole.

Viewed from such a unilateral perspective, the price effect of an import tariff can be (a) no effect, (b) a price rise lower than the tariff (c) a price rise equal to the tariff, or (d) a price rise greater than the tariff. The (b) case is the typical one and fits well the discussion above. The no-effect situation exists whenever the exporting country is willing to lower its export prices by an amount equal to the tariff and thus neutralize its effect upon the importing country's demand. This is usually the case when the exporting country has idle production capacity, has surplus stocks on hand, or is afraid to lose the import country's market to a competitor. Another no-effect situation exists when the duty is imposed on a product which the country is both importing and exporting. To illustrate, suppose the United States imposed an import tariff of 50 cents per bushel on wheat in the hope of raising the domestic price. What would the effect be? Since large quantities of U.S. wheat are exported, any price rise which might initially follow the tariff would quickly be drowned out by exporters, who would immediately divert their entire supplies to the domestic market as soon as the U.S. price rose above the world price. Thus, at best, any price rise that might occur would be short lived. However, the tariff would still affect the quantities traded, and both imports and exports of the United States would decline.

A price rise equal to the tariff is theoretically possible only when the pretariff price differential between the two countries is either larger than or equal to the duty, or when prices are set in ignorance of the true supply and demand relationships. Both these situations do occur.

A price rise greater than the duty may occur when the imported article moves through a chain of middlemen after being cleared through the customs. Each middleman adds his markup based on the landed cost. The figures below illustrate such a situation:

	No Tariff	*25 percent Ad Valorem Tariff*
Importer's C.I.F. price	$5.00	$5.00
Duty		1.25
Landed cost	5.00	6.25
Importer's markup (40 percent)	2.00	2.50
Total cost to retailer	7.00	8.75
Retailer's markup (40 percent)	2.80	3.50
Price to consumer	9.80	12.25

Hence a tariff of $1.25 has led to a price rise of $2.45.

Nominal vs. Effective Tariff Rates

How much protection to any particular industry against import competition a tariff provides is not readily reflected by the actual rates charged on a product by the customs; it depends also on the relationship of this rate to the duty rates of its ingredients. Consider, for example, a finished product which is subject to an *ad valorem* rate of 15 percent. Suppose that the product is a Scandinavian-style desk and that its value has been derived 40 percent from raw material—Asian teakwood—and 60 percent from manufacturing. If the U. S. would assess a 15 percent duty on raw teakwood, the effective protection of the American furniture industry would, in fact, be the same as the numerical or nominal rate, that is, 15 percent. But if the U. S. imposes no duty whatsoever on teakwood, the entire weight of duty on the finished desk will fall on the manufacturing share of its value, giving an effective rate of protection to American furniture manufacturers not 15 percent but $15 \div 0.6 = 25$ percent. Consequently, domestic manufacturers' costs of converting teakwood into Scandinavian-style tables can exceed 25 percent of that of its foreign competitors before any real import competition can occur. The effective protection is 10 percent greater than the nominal protection by official numerical rates.

Since most countries' tariff rates rise with the degree of finality of a product—raw materials have the lowest, semi-manufactured medium, and finished goods the highest duty rates—the effective protection provided to the domestic manufacturers tends to exceed the level of the nominal rates of duty. The difference between the two depends on the relationship which the rates on raw materials and other inputs bear to the rates on finished goods. This can be concretely illustrated by broadening our example of the teak desk above to four countries, all of which depend on imported teak. Suppose we have these data:

Costs:

Cost of teakwood at world market price	$400
Value added in manufacturing	600
Value of desk (free of duty)	$1,000

Ad valorem import duty rates:

Country	*Teak Lumber*	*Desks*
A	0	20
B	10	20
C	20	20
D	30	20

Effective protection

Country	*Dollar Equivalent*	*Effective Rate*
A	$200	$\frac{200}{600} = 33.3\%$
B	$200 − 40 = 160	$\frac{160}{600} = 26.7\%$
C	$200 − 80 = 120	$\frac{120}{600} = 20.0\%$
D	$200 − 120 = 80	$\frac{80}{600} = 13.3\%$

Although all four countries have the same *ad valorem* rates of duty on finished desks, the protection provided to domestic furniture manufacturers varies from 13.3 to 33.3 due to differences in raw material duties. We must, therefore, conclude that the actual protectiveness of a country's import tariffs to any particular industry or economic sector is not accurately reflected in the height of nominal duty rates but is affected also by any differences in the structure of the rates as between the industry's input and output goods.

Attitudes toward Tariffs

In business the attitudes toward tariffs vary with their effect upon the particular industry. For industries which depend on foreign materials or finished goods, import tariffs mean higher costs of doing business. Under competitive conditions the tariff cost cuts directly into the industry's profit margin; under monopolistic competition it forces higher prices and a consequent reduction in the volume of sales. Import-dependent industries, therefore, are strongly opposed to tariffs and support trade liberalization policies.

On the opposite side are industries whose products must compete against imports. For them import tariffs are a protective wall that reduces competition and raises the profit margin for the industry. The higher the tariffs, the smaller the foreign competition. The import-competing industries, therefore, are the strongest advocates of high tariffs. They engage in intensive lobbying in support of protectionist measures and policies. From their aggressive behavior comes the erroneous public belief that the business community as a whole seeks high, protectionist tariffs.

Industries that are neither import-dependent nor import-competing have no direct stake in tariffs. They constitute, so to speak, an *indifference zone* between the other two groups. However, indirectly they may be influenced by either side. For example, a company whose customers are import competing will tend to take a protectionist stand; conversely, another whose customers are mainly import dependent will lean toward free trade as a matter of solidarity. Schematically, the attitudes of business toward tariffs might be depicted as in Figure 6-2.

FIGURE 6-2

Attitudes toward Tariffs

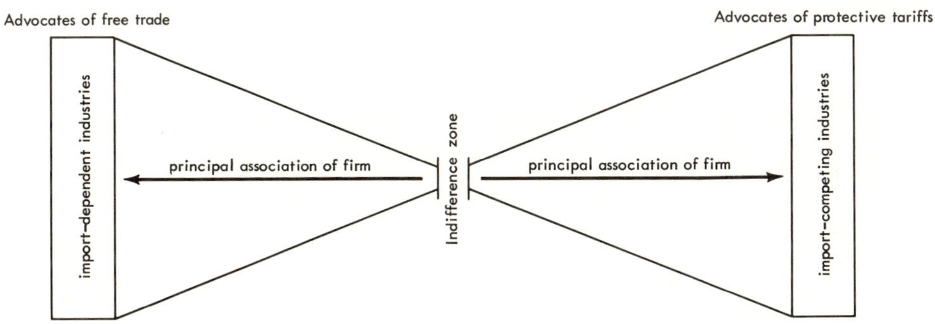

Consumer

For the consumer, tariffs mean higher prices. Yet, the consumer's influence on tariff policy is small. Public attitudes toward tariffs are usually vague and seldom motivated by the economic self-interest of the individual. This is true partly because foreign trade is a complex matter much of which the consuming public does not comprehend, and partly because those who do comprehend have professional or business interests which normally are more decisive for their attitude than their consumer interest is. A businessman whose profits depend on tariff protection is not likely to favor tariff cuts for his or any other products although his consumption expenditures might be reduced by a cut. Thus, the consumer interest, though universal, is a secondary interest which motivates very few to action. Also, consumers are too diffused and unorganized to have any significant influence on a country's tariff. A recent study found: "Americans who are interested, aware, and have an opinion of the subject, have switched from protectionist doctrine to what appears to be a predominant support for the liberal position."[1] But the report states that "unless the issue as a whole becomes a matter of increased popular concern . . . the potential support [for liberalization] resting in the citizen body may be entirely offset by the political activity of relatively small groups, with particular and immediate stakes in the issue."[2]

Government

For governments, tariffs are a source of revenue and an instrument of control and direction for the nation's international economic relations. In the advanced countries the revenue aspect is usually subordinated to the regulatory aspect. However, the use of import tariffs by any government involves discrimination against those whose consumption requirements are better met by foreign than domestic goods; they are also a discrimination against the foreign producers and marketers as compared to their domestic counterparts: tariffs shield domestic business against foreign competition. The use of import tariffs implies the assumption that foreign competition is not only different from domestic competition but also inadmissable in the national interest. That takes us back to political priorities and self-interest of different groups.

Issues of Tariff Policy

Since tariffs affect different groups of the population in different ways, tariff policy is always a controversial subject. In terms of concrete specifics, the arguments in the controversy range over a wide spectrum; in principle, they reduce to six primary issues: employment, wage standard, infant industry, economic growth, use of a scientific tariff, and national security.

[1] R. A. Bauer, Ide Sola Pocel, and L. A. Dexter, *American Business and Policy* (New York: Atherton Press, 1963), p. 104.

[2] Bauer, Pocel, and Dexter, *American Business and Policy,* p. 104.

Employment

The employment issue goes back to the depression of the 1930's. The central thesis here is that all imports have a certain labor content which displaces domestic labor and contributes to unemployment in the importing country; therefore, the objective of tariff policy should be to minimize imports of all products that could be produced by domestic workers. This means high tariffs for the great majority of industries.

In certain instances this argument may be valid, but only to a point. Domestic employment can benefit only if the demand for the protected article is highly inelastic; that is, if the rise in price which the tariff will cause will not destroy its effective demand. Otherwise, there will be little, if any, gain in employment and a loss to the great majority of consumers who are deprived of the product by the higher, after-tariff price. In addition, if a country's imports are curtailed, its exports, too, tend to decline, as other countries' abilities to buy from it are reduced by an amount equivalent to the value of the imports which were eliminated by the tariff. Or, the other countries often retaliate with high tariffs of their own. Whichever the case, the resultant reduction in exports will create unemployment in the export industries. Thus, from the national standpoint the real question is: Which of the two opposing effects of an import tariff is greater—the gain of employment in import-competing industries or the loss of employment in the export industries? If the two are equal, the tariff will not contribute to total employment but will merely redistribute it between the two types of industries. As workers may not readily shift from the stagnating export industries to the newly protected industries, a structural dislocation in the labor force may result with unemployment in one and overemployment in the other. If the loss of exports is greater than the reduction of imports, the whole argument collapses completely. However, since tariff advocates are normally concerned with their own particular labor union, community, or industry rather than with the nation as a whole, they often see in this argument an instrument for pursuing their own purpose.

Wage Standard

The wage-standard argument is propagated by labor groups in the industrial, high-income countries. It contends that a country with high wages must have a protective tariff against imports from low-wage countries to prevent its own wage standards from deteriorating and ultimately falling to the level of the poorer nations. A free-trade policy is claimed to pauperize domestic workers.

The argument can be either true or false depending upon the actual circumstances. More often it is false, because it rests on the assumption that differences in wage rates represent identical differences in the cost of production. This is the case only if the productivity of labor is identical in both countries. But if the productivity differs, the wage rates alone reveal nothing, for the cost of labor is not equivalent to the hourly or weekly wage rate but to the total wage bill that a product must bear. This bill is determined by the hourly wage rate times the number of hours of work required to produce a product. Suppose that an American worker is paid $3 per hour and that ten hours of work is required to make a particular article; the cost of the labor then is $30. Suppose further that the wage rate in Algeria is $0.50 per hour and that it takes 90 man-hours to produce the same product; the Algerian cost of labor thus is $45, or 50 percent higher than the American cost despite the fact that its wage rates are six times lower. This is not an exaggerated illustration. Many U.S. industries have, in fact, vastly higher productivity per man-hour than producers in less developed countries have. The other industrial nations are in a similar position. The principal reasons for the superior productivity are greater capital investment in the plant and equipment, superior technology, and better preparation of the worker himself—his investment in education. Any one or all three of these factors may affect productivity significantly. Since the conditions vary from industry to industry, the vulnerability to foreign low-wage competition varies accordingly. As a rule the older industries with relatively stagnant technology, such as textiles, shipbuilding, and glass, are least able to compensate for relatively higher wage rates by correspondingly higher productivity. In the more dynamic fields the wage rate has no significance for tariff policy.

Infant Industry

Since 1791, when Alexander Hamilton wrote his *Report on Manufactures,* the thesis that new industries require protection against foreign competition in their early years has been widely accepted as a justification for high tariffs. According to this thesis certain industries in a country cannot develop because of competition from already established producers in other countries even though, once developed, they will have a comparative advantage.

The argument rests on a reasonably sound theoretical base. With a small demand and limited capital resources, an infant industry is bound to have higher per-unit costs than an already established competitor operating at or near the optimum on the cost curve, as in Figure 6-3. If not protected, the infant industry has no chance to reach optimum capacity, since the foreign industry can undersell it and the only customers it will have are those willing, for patriotic or other noneconomic motives, to pay a higher price. Also, the established foreign industry can perpetuate the advantage by continued improvement of techniques, product quality, and marketing methods. As a result, the country's resources remain idle and its industrialization is retarded. Given tariff protection, the new industry is encouraged, and, as it grows in size and strength, the tariff barriers can be reduced and finally at its maturity completely removed.

For obvious reasons the infant-industry theory appeals strongly to industrially underdeveloped countries. Like the United States in the eighteenth and nineteenth centuries, the devloping nations of Asia, Africa, and Latin America in the present time are avid supporters of it. In the developed countries, its backers are primarily small businesses.

If one could predict with certainty which industries, if started and given tariff protection, would ultimately reach an efficiency comparable to or greater than that of their foreign competitors, the infant-industry thesis would provide a sound basis for tariff policy. But the policy makers can only hope and guess. They have no sure way of forecasting the relative success of different industries. Hence, they run the risk of protecting the wrong industry—one which never will reach competitive maturity and which will always remain dependent on tariff protection. Such misallocation of resources not only defeats the purpose of the tariff but also retards the development of other industries which might have put the resources to more efficient use.

Another problem of applying the infant-industry theory is the practical difficulty of removing the tariffs as the industry matures. Once enacted they are forgotten and stay on the books like any other tariff.

Economic Growth

In the industrial countries where the infant-industry argument has become progressively less convincing, protectionists have shifted their emphasis to economic growth. They reason that, given tariff protection, any import-competing industry will grow. Its growth will create new demands for goods

FIGURE 6-3

Per-Unit Cost for Infant and Established Firms

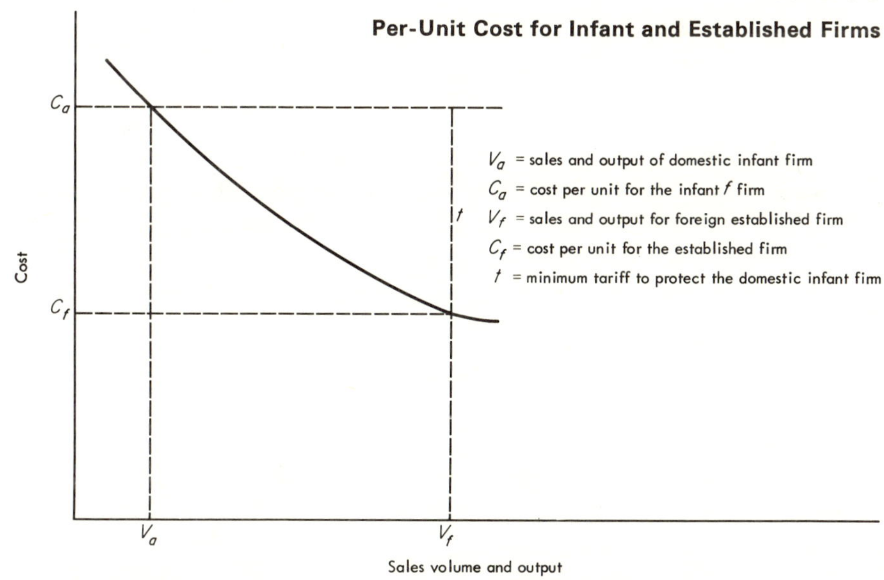

and services from other industries which thus will also grow and give rise to still other new demands. Consequently, the expansion of industry will multiply and lead to economic growth on a broad front and to the enlargement of the domestic market.

There are two objections to this view. First, if a country has full employment the tariff will not contribute to growth but will draw resources away from nonprotected industries and give them to protected industries. To the extent to which they may be employed less efficiently in the protected industry, there may be an actual retardation of growth. Second, any reduction of exports which the tariff may cause by cutting imports will tend to counteract any growth that the protected industry may enjoy. The only situation where this argument can prevail is when there is chronic unemployment in a country whose import and export flows are independent of each other.

Scientific Tariff

Of great appeal to the economic layman is the so-called *scientific tariff*—a levy designed to equalize the cost of imports with that of domestic products. Such a tariff would vary from shipment to shipment depending upon the cost differential. This tariff was termed *scientific* because its early proponents believed that, by equalizing the cost, an objective, unbiased standard rather than political self-interest would determine if and how much of a tariff were to be levied. Also, the method was believed to enhance competition and fairness for all concerned. But the advocates of this view did not understand that, by equalizing costs arbitrarily, one renders the principle of comparative advantage inoperative and destroys the theoretical basis for international trade.

National Security

Since certain industries are important for national defense, it is argued that they should be protected against foreign competition to ensure that the country has an endogenous capacity to provide strategic goods and does not have to depend on foreign suppliers in case of war. The cost of production and other economic considerations, according to this argument, should be subordinated to the defense objective; if the militarily strategic industries cannot meet import competition, they should be built and maintained in the shelter of protective tariffs.

Being a political argument, it defies any conclusive economic analysis. In the United States, it has been used with consistent success by watch manufacturers, the maritime industries, and a number of producers of military supplies. For small countries whose military needs are limited, a tariff policy based on this argument would be suicidal in today's world of weapons systems, atomic bombs, and supersonic aircraft—all of which demand mammoth investment in plant and equipment.

Tariff Administration

A country must have an administrative system to implement its tariff policies. It is this system more than the policy issues or the policies themselves that managers of international trade activities must understand and cope with in their daily operations.

Classification of Duties

Regular duties

Duty rates are based on either the physical unit or the monetary value of the imported article. If stated in a fixed amount per physical unit, such as a piece, a dozen, a barrel, a meter, a ton, or a square foot, it is referred to as a *specific duty*—specific in that the total duty obligation is unaffected by the price or other costs of the imported cargo. If stated as a percentage of the value of the imported product, it is known as an *ad valorem duty*. In this case the total duty obligation varies with the price and quality of the imported cargo and bears no relation to the physical quantity imported. Quite frequently the two techniques are combined by superimposing on a specific duty an ad valorem rate; for example, $3 a pair plus 10 percent ad valorem. They are called *compound duties*.

A specific duty is retrogressive; it taxes cheaper commodities more heavily than higher grade goods. And, when prices rise, the effect of a specific duty declines progressively, reducing its significance both as a cost factor and as a protective device. Under declining prices its impact is magnified automatically for all concerned. In contrast, an ad valorem duty maintains a fixed relationship to the value of the cargo under both stable and variable prices and its effect upon the importer and his domestic competition remains unchanged; one remains constant in amount but varies in significance, and the other varies in amount but remains constant in significance. Since all countries have suffered from inflation, which erodes any tariff policy based on specific duties, a general tendency in recent years has been to emphasize the ad valorem and compound rates at the expense of the specific duty.

Corrective duties

Most countries have various duties designed to cope with possible malpractices of participants in the export-import process. The most typical among these are *antidumping duties*. They are assessed on goods which are imported at a price lower than the price at which they are sold in the country of origin (exclusive of transportation costs). Such pricing practice is motivated sporadically by excess inventories or by the availability of other distress goods which are dumped on a foreign market at low prices to keep the domestic price structure intact. Sometimes exports below normal prices are used to soften competition in a particular country. Known as predatory dumping, that practice aims at gaining monopolistic control of the particular market and thereafter profiting from substantially higher prices, which could go unchallenged. Still another incentive for dumping may be a high domestic price, possibly protected by import duties, which enables the manufacturer to charge all his fixed costs to domestic sales and export the product at prices based on variable costs alone.

Whatever the incentive for it, dumping may seriously undermine price stability and cause injury to industry in the recipient country. To prevent this, antidumping duties are used. Normally, they amount to the difference between the dumping price and the regular price. Thus they nullify any profits from the dumping attempt.

Countervailing duties are a similar device. They are imposed on imports which have been subsidized by governmental or other sources in the exporting country. For example, a British manufacturer whose product costs £25 may be paid a governmental subsidy of 20 percent to enable it to undersell local competition in Belgium. Receiving £5 from the government for each unit it exports, the British company can thus market the product at the equivalent of £20 instead of £25 on the Belgian market. The British government would pay the subsidy because it lacks any other products that could be used to pay for British imports from Belgium or because it wants to bolster exports in general to earn foreign exchange.

The amount of the countervailing duty may be equal to the foreign subsidy or exceed it by a certain penalty to suppress the subsidization practice. When the subsidized product is also marketed in the country of origin, either antidumping duties or countervailing duties can be applied. But when the product is differentiated, application of the antidumping duties becomes difficult or impossible, and the only remedy to correct any underpricing of imports is the use of countervailing duties. In the United States, antidumping duties can be applied only if injury to domestic industry has been established; the legislation on countervailing duties has no such requirement.

Penalty duties include a variety of levies and charges which customs authorities are authorized to assess in cases of faulty documentation of cargo, noncompliance with customs procedures, attempted smuggling, or some other infraction of the import regulations. Depending on the infraction, the penalty rates range from a few percent increase of the regular rate to several times the regular rate and may include confiscation.

Classification of Goods

Since the number of articles which move in international commerce is very large and constantly changing because of new inventions, no tariff schedule can list all products individually; instead, they are classified by one method or another into a hierarchy of groups and subgroups called *positions* for which different duty rates are established.

In spite of the great need for comparability, no common system of classifying imports for duty purposes has so far been universally adopted. However, two international systems in recent years have been accepted by a majority of nations. In 1950 the United Nations Standard International Trade Classification (SITC) was published and recommended for world-wide use. In 1955 the Brussels Tariff Nomenclature (BTN) was adopted by most European countries. Originally, the SITC system was based on the economic classifications (use categories) of goods. Subsequently, it was revised to allow some classification by material. In its revised form it has more main sections, each subdivided into divisions, groups, subgroups, and items.[3] The main sections are these:

Section	*Heading*
0	Food and live animals
1	Beverages and tobacco
2	Crude materials, inedible
3	Mineral fuels, lubricants, and related materials
4	Animal and vegetable oils and fats
5	Chemicals
6	Manufactured goods classified chiefly by material
7	Machinery and transport equipment
8	Miscellaneous manufactured articles
9	Other

The BTN system classifies the goods according to the nature of the material of which they are made. It consists of 21 sections:

Section	*Heading*
I	Live animals; animal products
II	Vegetable products
III	Animal and vegetable fats and oils
IV	Prepared foodstuffs, beverages, spirits, and vinegar; tobacco
V	Mineral products
VI	Products of the chemical and allied industries
VII	Artificial resins and plastic materials; rubber
VIII	Hides, skins, and articles thereof
IX	Wood and articles of wood; cork
X	Paper-making material; paper and paperboard and articles thereof
XI	Textiles and textile articles
XII	Footwear, headgear, umbrellas, . . . fans
XIII	Articles of stone, of plastic, of cement, of asbestos, of mica, and of similar materials; ceramic products; glass and glassware
XIV	Pearls, precious and semiprecious stones, precious metals, and articles thereof; imitation jewelry; coin
XV	Base metals and articles of base metals

[3] See United Nations, *Standard International Trade Classifications, Revised,* Statistical Papers, Series M, No. 34 (New York, 1961).

XVI	Machinery and mechanical appliances; electrical equipment; parts thereof
XVII	Vehicles, aircraft, and parts thereof; vessels
XVIII	Optical, cinematographic, surgical, scientific, musical, and acoustical instruments and apparatus including precision instruments and watch-makers' wares
XIX	Arms and ammunition
XX	Miscellaneous manufactured articles
XXI	Works of art, collectors' pieces, and antiques

The SITC was rejected by the European countries because it was considered more suitable for underdeveloped areas than for industrial economies; its lack of precision in definitions and inadequate number of positions for manufactured goods were the main drawbacks. In 1959, after consultations with the Brussels group, the SITC was revised and an item-to-item correspondence scheme between the two systems worked out. This is useful not only for comparative analysis of the tariffs but also for collective statistical information in relative detail on flows among all countries which have adopted either SITC or BTN.

The United States has so far retained its old classification system. For the purposes of trade statistics an attempt was made to conform to SITC in 1963, but this experiment was abandoned a year later for reasons which remain obscure. Great Britain and Canada both have their own classifications, which also are different from the two international systems. Thus, comparison among the major trading groups remains impaired by the lack of uniform customs classifications.

Tactical Aspects of Tariffs

Tariffs are devices for discriminating among goods according to the country of origin. The discrimination has two levels. The first makes a sharp distinction between the domestic and the foreign origin of products; and the second, among the different foreign origins. The first-level discrimination is inherent in all tariff systems; the second level depends on the type of tariff system.[4]

As devices for international discrimination, tariffs can serve certain tactical objectives such as retaliation against another country's restrictive practices, compelling some other country to negotiate, or, as shown above, to deal with dumping, export subsidization, or other malpractices of international trade. To be effective in such ways, the basic duty rates must be relatively high, for low rates would leave little room for tactical maneuvers. This concept is as old as commercial treaties and has until very recently been in widespread use throughout the world. Currently, however, it is being de-emphasized.

[4] In the nineteenth century some countries had different tariff rates for all countries with no general tariff column at all. This exclusive, preferential system is now defunct.

The Most-Favored-Nations Treatment

International commitments relating to customs duties may relate to absolute standards—i.e., to cutting the existing rate or to refraining from increasing it—or they may be formulated in terms of relative standards which specify that one party will not discriminate against the other compared to any third country. The relative commitments are much more general in trade agreements than are the absolute concessions. And it is through the relative commitments that the absolute concessions gain widespread use.

The relative commitments are based on the most-favored-nation (m.f.n.) principle, which provides that a country will not impose higher restrictions on imports from the other country than those it imposes on imports coming from any third country. Thus the m.f.n. clause guarantees that the only discrimination that the contracting country's imports will be subjected to is that between the domestic and the foreign products and that no other foreign products will be accorded a more favorable treatment. Over time, the country granting m.f.n. treatment will thus tend to treat all imports alike. This says nothing about the absolute standards. All imports may be treated very badly or very well. But in the long run the use of the m.f.n. clause leads toward a general liberalization of trade. Negotiations between any pair of countries on any specific product or rate of duty will be shared with all others, making it generalized. Since the m.f.n. principle has been applied also to invisible tariffs, such as import licenses, quotas, carriers, various legal restrictions, and bureaucratic procedures, it has played a very decisive role in reducing trade barriers.

National Treatment

The national-treatment principle requires that the same treatment be accorded to foreign products, investments, vessels, entrepreneurs, or any aspect of commercial relations as is applied to the domestic counterparts in like situations. It recognizes no distinction between foreign and domestic. Thus the national-treatment principle attacks any international discrimination.

Despite overt support by many, very few countries have applied this principle to things other than the treatment of ocean carriers (docking charges, tonnage dues, dry-dock privileges, and so on). The only significant exceptions here are the European and Central American common markets, whose members are the first to adopt the national treatment as their basic policy vis-à-vis other member countries. They require that all deviations from the national-treatment principle be handled on an exception basis and as such require thorough scrutiny and special justification. Outside the common-market schemes, the national-treatment principle is not likely to find any acceptance, as most national governments are eager to maintain control over international business relations and will, therefore, resist abandoning the tools which enable them to discriminate between the domestic and the foreign. However, in specific applications the national-treatment principle can be expected to gain ground at the expense of the m.f.n. theory.

Customs Valuation

Application of ad valorem and compound rates requires concrete standards for determining the value from which the duty is to be computed. These standards are not universal but vary from country to country. Several attempts have been made to establish internationally uniform criteria for customs valuation. None has been fully successful. The broadest support was given to the General Agreement on Tariffs and Trade (GATT), to which most non-communist countries belong, which sets forth the principle that the value for customs purposes should be the price at which the imported goods are sold in the ordinary course of trade under competitive conditions. The practical effect of this agreement on customs valuation has been negligible, partly because the parties to the agreement reserved the right to continue any value criteria, either consistent or inconsistent with the principle, which were contained in their customs laws at the time they signed the agreement.

The U. S. Tariff Commission recently completed a study of customs valuations in a number of countries.[5] The following discussion is based on that study.

The U.S. Customs Valuation

Since 1958 the United States has been using four sets of valuation standards, which are stated in sections 402 and 402a of the Tariff Act. They are:

(1) Export value—the price at the point of exportation (F.A.S. value) in the country of origin based on usual wholesale quantities for the product; it makes allowance for export discounts and includes export packing and other costs of making the goods ready for export shipment.

(2) U.S. value—the wholesale price of the imported or a like production in the United States less normal markups, commissions, cost of transportation and insurance, and import duties.

(3) Constructed value—the total cost of materials and manufacturing of the product in the country of origin plus the normal costs incidental to export preparation.

(4) American selling price—the U.S. wholesale price of an American product similar to the imported article.

These four criteria apply to all products which have not been specifically listed as exceptions. The *export value* is the primary standard; all ad valorem duties are to be collected on this basis if the value can be reliably determined. If the export value cannot be determined, the U.S. value will be used; if this

[5] U.S. Tariff Commission, *Customs Valuations.* TC Publication 180 (Washington, D.C.: U.S. Government Printing Office, July 1966).

too is unavailable, the duty will be based on the constructed value. The American selling-price standard applies to a few specifically designated lines of goods which include benzenoid chemicals, canned clams and related products, rubber-soled shoes, and wool knit gloves.

Section 402b

Section 402b contains the pre-1958 valuation system. It was not completely discontinued, however, when the new system discussed above was legitimized and still applies to products listed in the so-called *final list.*[6] Its principal difference from the new system lies in the use of a dual primary standard.

Foreign Value or Export Value, Whichever is Higher. Foreign value is defined as the price at which the imported product is freely offered for sale in wholesale quantities in the exporting country. The definition of export value is the same as that in the new system. The practical effect of this dual standard is that the duty is higher because export discounts are used or for other reasons the export price is lower than the foreign wholesale rather than the invoice value. Thus, an importer may be obligated to pay a higher percentage of his invoice price than the actual rate of duty. If the importer, for instance, was fortunate to buy for $80 per unit German cameras which normally are exported from Germany at $100, and the duty rates were 25 percent, the customs would assess $25, not $20, per camera regardless of what the invoice and shipping documents showed.

This old system was retained for certain products because protectionist members of Congress feared that the elimination of the dual standard would lead to a significant de facto tariff reduction for certain products. Accordingly the Secretary of the Treasury was instructed to ascertain for which products the reduction would exceed 5 percent; those were placed on the final list and have to be valued under the old system. The other standards in the old system are practically the same as those in the new.

Brussels Convention on the Valuation of Goods for Customs Purposes

The Brussels Convention was signed in 1950 by ten countries: Belgium, Denmark, France, Italy, Luxembourg, the Netherlands, Norway, Sweden, Germany, and the United Kingdom. It thus represents a major step toward international standards of valuation. All the signatory countries have fully implemented the convention and are now using identical standards.

The Brussels definition identifies customs value as the *normal price,* i.e., the price the imported goods would command at the time the import duty becomes payable on a sale in the open market between buyer and seller independent of each other for delivery at the place of importation. This price must include all expenses incidental to that sale and delivery of the goods to that

6 A list published by the Secretary of the Treasury in 1958 pursuant to Section 6 of the Customs Simplification Act of 1966.

place, including nonrecoverable duties and taxes applicable outside the country of importation. When the invoice price is not the sole consideration given by the buyer or when that price does not reflect all the rights conveyed in connection with the sale (such as the right to patents or trademarks), such values are to be added to the value of the goods for customs purposes.

7

United States Commercial Policy

Commercial policy is the composite of official attitudes and formal actions, including laws, which form the objectives and rules for a nation's international trade relations. As such, commercial policy is a complex subject. It is not something that any one official, any one government, or even any one country alone can make. The formulation of commercial policy is an ongoing process. Many divergent interests of the country itself as well as its interactions with other countries participate in this process. The policy is never complete, nor fully articulated. Its formation, elucidation, and interpretation are ongoing processes that require a historic perspective to be understood. We shall, therefore, focus our attention on the historic processes rather than the specific composite of trade controls in any particular point in time. In commercial policy, only the past can explain the present.

Protectionist Tradition

At no time in its history has the United States engaged in free trade. The first Congress passed an import tax in 1789, and some tariff legislation has been in effect ever since. The first tariff was recommended to Congress by Alexander Hamilton, then Secretary of the Treasury, as a method of raising federal funds. The members of that Congress, however, recognized that the interests of their constituents were at stake and proceeded to place the burden of the tariff on those imports which were most competitive with domestic production.

From that time, United States tariff policy has been based upon the same two criteria: protection of domestic industry and gain of revenue. The burden of the tariff has always been placed on those goods which compete with domestic production, while those commodities which are used as inputs in domestic manufacture have had very low assessed duties.

Tariff Legislation

The basic tariff law of the United States was a product of depression protectionism. When the overheated American economy collapsed in 1929, a crisis of unprecedented severity swept the globe. Frantic efforts were made everywhere to cope with the massive unemployment, shrinking incomes, and hungry people. Among the many measures born in the turmoil of the depression was the 1930 Tariff Act which, though greatly amended, is still the tariff law of the United States. Popularly known as the Smoot-Hawley Tariff, this law can claim the notorious distinction of having been the most protectionist measure ever enacted by American Congress.

The act was passed in the tragicomic belief that by stopping imports, the demand for American-made goods would increase (as the unsatisfied import demand would be shifted to domestic goods) and, as a result, production and employment in the country would go up. Anybody interested in historic research will find the newspaper columns and speeches of U.S. politicians of that year a most amusing commentary to economic witchcraft. The Smoot-Hawley bill was intended to be a magic potion, a panacea to cure all the ills that had afflicted the depression-ridden economy. In reality, it was a cataclysmic rupture that set off a tidal wave of protectionist hysteria throughout the world. Its destructive effects were three-dimensional: it spread, deepened, and prolonged the depression.

What the lawmakers had overlooked in enacting the protectionist measure were the responses it would elicit from other nations and how these, in turn, would change the actual international trade relations and policies. That this had been a colossal blunder became clear almost instantly after the act had been signed. Thirty-four countries launched formal protests, and most of the rest joined them in quick retaliation. The most significant counteraction was British enactment of a high tariff law in 1931, followed by the Ottawa Agreement in 1932, which established a discriminatory high tariff against all nonmembers of the British Commonwealth. Import quotas, exchange contracts, and administrative directives spread rapidly all around the world to reinforce the rising tariff walls and to intensify the protectionist race. As a consequence, world trade declined and the United States share in it plummeted 30 percent. World economy sank from a depression to a coma with no equal in modern history.

Trade war

The rash of countermeasures taken by countries all around the world signaled the start of a protectionist trade war.

In a protectionist war there are no winners, only losers. But some are greater losers than others. The greatest loser of all is the country that has the largest surplus in its balance of trade, for if the war is fought to its bitter end, that surplus will be wiped out. At the same time the surplus country's ability to fight back (to destroy other countries' exports) is limited to its own total imports which must be much smaller than its total exports. It so happened that the United States possessed the largest export surplus in the world when the battle began. Thus it stood to lose more on the export side than it ever could hope to win on the import side.

Hence, the Smoot-Hawley tariff had put this country into a most precarious position. When its disastrous consequences started to materialize on a global scale, action had to be taken to prevent this fatal process from running its full course. A crucial turning point had been reached. A new direction had to be found and a new international trade policy initiated. It is this turn of events that marks the beginning of the evolution of international trade policy that regulated world trade relations until our present difficulty.

The Reciprocal Trade Agreements Program

Having so decisively contributed to the calamity of the early 1930's, the United States recognized that it had to show new initiative, to implement a positive program that would stop the protectionist trend and provide a basis for trade liberalization. Such a program was put forth in 1934 in the form of the first reciprocal trade agreement act.

The aim of the act was to bring about international negotiations to reduce tariffs. This law was necessary because in the American system of government, tariff-making powers are reserved exclusively to Congress; the President and his cabinet have no jurisdiction over tariff-making. Therefore to enable the President to negotiate and to make binding international agreements on tariffs, it was necessary that Congress delegate to him the power to do so. The Reciprocal Trade Agreement Act of 1934 thus started a process of delegating to the United States President some of the congressional powers of tariff-making, for a certain period of time—a process that each subsequent trade agreements act carried on until the last such act expired in the summer of 1967. Consequently, it was a 33-year sequence.

The Reciprocal Trade Agreements Acts did not rescind or replace the 1930 Tariff Act; they were really a new and unique technique of amending it. All prior tariff acts had been changed in the usual way or rescinded outright when a new tariff law was passed. But not in 1934. The 1930 Smoot-Hawley Act remained and continues to be the basic tariff law of the United States. And superimposed on it have been the Reciprocal Trade Agreements Acts, each for its own short duration and special mix of provisions authorizing the President to take certain actions at his own discretion or by following procedures stated in the act. The legal essence of these acts was to sanction in advance all the actions and international agreements which the President consummates within the defined limits of the act. Any international agreement signed by the President under the act thus becomes automatically a congressional commitment and enters into force. But notice that the Reciprocal Trade Agreements Acts compelled no one to do anything—they were only enabling acts.

Bilateralism

The inherent peril of the historic method of research is the temptation to study any past phenomenon in the context of contemporary environment. Nothing could create more monstrous distortions of truth or lead to more fictitious conclusions by laboriously wasted scholarship. To avoid committing this cardinal error, we must digress from our main theme to examine the relevant aspects of the international environment of time when the reciprocal trade agreements program was initiated. For that was the environment in which it was to function and which conditioned its course.

That was a bilateralist system. As its name implies it was a system of two's where each country negotiated with only one other country at a time and entered into a separate bilateral arrangement—trade and payments agreement or commercial treaty—with each foreign nation. Being a product of separate negotiation, each bilateral arrangement was in some or most respects different from all others.

Hence, under the bilateralist system the rules and conditions of international trade varied not only from country to country but also within the same country since it had different agreements with each of its trading partners. That this must have resulted in a bewildering number of different rules and regulations of trade is an algebraic inevitability.

International Discrimination

Why then did bilateralism gain dominance in the interwar period, and why does it continue to be advocated by policy makers of certain countries? Because it is inherently a system of international commercial discrimination and as such holds the lure of enabling an anxious government or an ambitious official to take shortcuts in improving the relative trading fortunes of its own and perhaps a select few other countries at the expense of the rest of the world. Specifically, the objectives of bilateral trade and payments arrangements may include any number of the following: to improve terms of trade, to stabilize export markets and prices, to assure import sources for strategically important goods, to obtain foreign loans and advantageous credit terms, to assist in expanding and redirecting trade, to diversify the industrial base and trade mix, and to carry out national economic development plans which, especially in developing countries, often depend on foreign credits and imported goods and services. Thus, on the surface at least the bilateral relations seem to serve most commendable national objectives. But experience shows that this is seldom the case. Based on a political bargain, the bilateralist game often ends up as a power play where the relative size and industrial strength of the partners become decisive. Any disparity in the power base tends to be reflected in the distribution of any gains that the trade might have produced. This problem is succinctly ellucidated by Swidrowski:

> While bilateral payments arrangements assumed large proportions prior to and after World War II, since then their importance in world trade has been gradually reduced. While it still plays a role, bilateralism in payments and trade no longer interferes as extensively as it once did with the mechanism of a free exchange of goods and services and the movement of capital. Because bilateralism still plays some role in the system of international settlements and trade, it is worthwhile to take a critical look at it; even if we cannot altogether avoid the repetition in the future of mistakes committed in the past, at least we can appraise these errors.
>
> One of the most common difficulties has been that the arrangements have been used by strong partners to the detriment of weak ones, particularly through accumulating debit balances on bilateral accounts. Such tactics may, unfortunately, be carried a long way; in extreme instances, an economically powerful country can gradually obtain extensive control over a weak partner. The first step may be to insulate this weak partner from a world market by raising the prices of its raw materials or agricultural products purchased through bilateral channels, thus leading the weaker country to devote its resources to producing certain products on a greater scale at higher costs. Such a step might well seem to be advantageous to the weaker country in the short run, as its terms of trade would be improved and production and employment would be expanded. But as soon as a strong partner becomes a major factor in the entire export strategy of a weak partner, it can increase the prices of its own exports to that partner, and gradually even the nominal terms of trade are likely to become less advantageous to a weak partner. Once the economy of a weak bilateral country becomes tied to that of a strong bilateral country, the position cannot be easily reversed. The situation may be even worse if a strong partner should also use its political as well as its economic power to influence the policies of its weak partner. This is not a theoretical problem; the recent and less recent history of bilateral arrangements provides interesting examples. History also shows that the weak partners were seldom able to overcome the economic influence attained by their strong partners.[1]

In business, due to the bureaucratic complexity of transboundary transactions, management of international trade became a "technical profession." Ordinary marketing personnel was usually not able to cope with the legalistic-technical aspects of international transactions. Special training and consider-

[1] Jozef Swidrowski, "Bilateralism in Payments and Trade," *Finance and Development,* Vol. 8, No. 1 (1971), p. 19.

able practical apprenticeship were required before one could acquire the necessary experience to competently handle foreign trade transactions.

The overall character of the bilateralist system may be summed up by saying that it was a disruptive and corruptive system which bred international commercial discrimination, undermined fair and open negotiations and agreements, and greatly complicated foreign trade practices. It is this system that the reciprocal trade agreements program had to change if its objective of general tariff reduction was to be achieved by all countries.

Toward Multilateralism

Although the reciprocal trade agreements acts had been designed from the beginning to promote multilateral trade relations, the bilateralist system, aided by war conditions, did not yield its grip until the General Agreement on Tariffs and Trade (GATT) was signed by one country after another in the late 1940's and early 1950's. This was an epoch-making document.

It was multilateral agreement to make multilateralism the cardinal principle of international trade relations. This was to be brought about in two principal ways:

a. By providing an open forum for simultaneous trade negotiations to all member countries (this is where the name GATT round originates), the opportunity was created for all countries to participate on an equal basis in negotiations and to gain access to any deliberations of other members. The open forum could be used not only for negotiation of tariff matters but also to air any grievances that any member country might have against any other, such as mistreatment of its goods or carriers, commercial discrimination, unfair competition, or any other international misbehavior.

b. The second key provision of the General Agreement was to outlaw international commercial discrimination outright. Any member country is required to treat *all* other members as equals and is entitled to the same consideration. All forms of favoritism or disfavoritism are violations of the GATT principle. Thus, any particular product should be treated the same by the importing country regardless where its origin is if the producing country is also a member of GATT.

The practical vehicle of implementing the nondiscriminatory provision was the *most favored nations* principle which was made a universal requirement for all tariff adjustments within the GATT framework.

The general adoption of the m.f.n. provided new impetus and new force to the policy of trade liberalization through tariff reductions. This was evidenced by substantial tariff cuts by all 22 countries who were the original signatories to GATT, and by the fact that many others elected to sign the agreement.

Noninjury Principle

The reciprocal trade agreements acts were based on two principles:

a. reciprocity in trade liberalization, especially in tariff reduction, i.e., if one country removed some trade barriers, it was entitled to similar concessions from the country or countries benefiting from this action; it was hoped that the reciprocity requirement would set in motion the process of general trade liberalization among all trading nations.

b. prevention of injury to domestic industry, known as the noninjury principle. This meant that tariff cuts should not be made when they would lead to such increase in imports as would be harmful to the import-competing domestic industry. It also meant that any tariff concessions had to be limited in magnitude so as to avoid going below the point where actual injury to the domestic industry could result.

The noninjury principle was harnessed for the dual task of predefining what tariff concessions could be contemplated by this country and of adjudicating claims for protection against existing import competition. For the implementation of these dual aims, the so-called *peril-point* and *escape-clause* mechanism was designed and perfected in the course of the Reciprocal Trade Agreements Program.

Peril point

Under the peril-point provision of the previous Trade Agreements Acts, the President was required to furnish the Tariff Commission with a list of all products on which any tariff negotiations were contemplated and to ask the Commission to ascertain what concessions could be offered to other countries without threatening injury to American business. By holding hearings and conducting statistical studies, the Commission was directed to make precise determinations for each item on the President's list of the point below which the respective tariff could not be cut without injury to domestic producers.

Since the most active participants in the Commission hearings were the industries lobbying for the greatest possible protection, the peril points were, as a rule, set so high that little room was left for effective tariff reductions. This fact was most forcefully underscored when in the 1961 GATT meeting the EEC countries proposed a 20 percent across-the-board tariff reduction which the United States could not reciprocate. For any lesser member of the organization this lack of ability to practice what it had so loudly preached would have been a major scandal. But the international embarrassment had a most salutary domestic effect, namely, it helped on the one hand to burst the bubble that U.S. propaganda had created about its leadership in trade liberalization, and on the other hand to shatter the sanctity of the noninjury principle; this latter result opened up new approaches to the problem of import competition, and the consequences were far-reaching.

In the 1962 Act the precise-peril point no longer exists. A remnant of the peril-point concept was retained, more to appease the protectionist hard core than for any practical application. The repeal of the peril point removed the rigidity which had immobilized U.S. tariff negotiations in the past. It also removed the ax of the escape clause from over the other countries' heads, as the next section will explain.

Escape clause

The Trade Agreements Extension Act of 1951 enacted escape-clause provisions under which any company or industry which felt that it had suffered serious setbacks because of increased competition from imports occasioned by Trade Agreements negotiation could appeal to the Tariff Commission for tariff relief. If the Commission found that injury had been caused or threatened, it was required to make specific recommendations to the President regarding necessary tariff or quota relief to remedy the damage. Such tariff relief could go as high as 150 percent of the duty rates in effect on July 1, 1934, i.e., to the orginal ultraprotective rates of the Hawley-Smoot Act. If the President rejected the findings of the Tariff Commission, he was obliged to show cause in a report to Congress. Congress could, by a two-thirds vote of both houses, overturn the President's action or inaction and require that the Tariff Commission's recommendations be put into effect. This made the noninjury protection absolute. All U.S. trade agreements had to include the clause giving the U.S. the right to unilaterally withdraw the concessions it granted in an agreement to other countries (through GATT or otherwise) if found subsequently that the peril-point provision had been violated. Suppose for the purpose of illustration that, based on such an official trade agreement an industry in country X could project a substantial volume of exports to the United States and that to meet that demand it must make large investments in new production capacity. A year or two later when the new factories have been completed and their output starts flowing to the American market, the affected U.S. industry claims injury and demands a new peril-point investigation. Suppose further that the concessions granted to country X two years earlier do indeed violate the peril-point criterion. The consequence then would be for the Tariff Commission to recommend that the President invoke the escape clause of the trade agreement with X and nullify the concessions. The mere possibility of this happening placed U.S. intentions in doubt abroad and tended to serve as an invisible tariff against imports.

Precisely how great the restrictive effect of this procedure was cannot be measured. There can be, however, no doubt that the factual record of revocations would greatly understate this effect since a significant portion—probably a preponderance—of foreign firms must have refrained from the potentially disastrous venture of testing the firmness of the concessions granted by the U.S. trade agreements. It was a safer and more reasonable alternative to exclude any concessions from their planning and growth strategies and view the concessions as speculative opportunities that may or may not stand an actual market test.

The Policy Crisis of the 1950's

The peril point and escape clause not only symbolized the schizophrenic dilemma of the American position, but also blocked the passage for tariff reduction in an increasing number of commodity classifications, the peril point setting an absolute floor, and the escape clause creating the uncertainty that kept both negotiators and traders guessing as to what was or was not permissible under the U.S. law. Naturally, the principle of reciprocity could have only limited application under those circumstances and the intergovernmental policy dialogue on trade matters was diverted from substantive issues, i.e., actual liberalization of trade in the commodity categories which had the greatest potential for increased trade, to formalistic machinations and propaganda maneuvers, often crowned by illusionary liberalization measures such as tariff cuts on overprotected products of peripheral significance. Clearly, then, the international trade policy had been sidetracked from its original goal of trade liberalization through tariff reduction into a lateral motion that was dissipating its energies in propagandistic assertions and gimmicky manipulations reminiscent of the international money muddle of the last few years.

The Impact of the European Common Market

A new thrust forward came from the creation of the EEC in 1958. While the GATT program had been losing momentum, six European nations concluded a customs union and embarked upon a program of complete economic and social integration of their countries. This provided the prospect for a mass market and ultimately a mammoth economy comparable to that of the United States.

The new union provided two kinds of incentives to the outside world for a broader trade liberalization. First, there was immediate danger of the trade diversion from nonmember countries to the member countries since the internal import duties were to disappear while a uniform external tariff was to be imposed. Second, there was a longer range prospect for mass marketing and mass production that had never existed outside the United States. Both of these were realities which, to the American businessman, spoke louder than any theories or concepts.

Thus, the business community in the United States as well as other nonmember countries began to demand concrete steps for obtaining an easy access to the European market. Riding on the crest of this ground swell, President John F. Kennedy boldly put forward his trade program, which Congress enacted as the 1962 Trade Expansion Act.

Trade Expansion Policy

The Trade Expansion Act of 1962 was the twelfth extension of the Trade Agreements program. Its purpose was to provide the President with all necessary powers to bargain with the European Common Market. Many observers feel that this act was the most important piece of legislation enacted under the Kennedy administration. The move was felt to be crucial for the United States because it was believed that the trading power and productive capacity of the nations of the Common Market would increase to an extent that would seriously challenge the U.S. position in world economy. American business was anxious to gain easy access to this large integrated market. Mutual tariff reduction seemed the way to get that access.

Key Provisions

The new law gave the President three important tools for trade liberalization: tariff relief, across-the-board negotiations, and a trade adjustment program. All of these had certain features designed to directly engage the EEC.

Tariff. The tariff reduction power included not only manufactured but also agricultural goods. Fifty-percent rate reductions from the then existing levels plus elimination of the so-called nuisance tariffs—five percent or lower —were authorized. These were sweeping powers.

Negotiation. The traditional "item-by-item" negotiation requirement was abolished and the President empowered to decide how wide a range of products any particular tariff negotiation should cover—a single product, an industry, or "across-the-board," i.e., the whole economy. This allowed for vastly increased efficiency of negotiation as well as a more comprehensive application of tariff concessions.

Foreign Competition. The most radical departure from the previous policy was contained in the provisions dealing with injury to American business from import competition, known as the trade adjustment program.

In his message to Congress on January 25, 1962, President Kennedy made the following statement concerning the proposed Trade Expansion Act:

> Once given a fair and equal opportunity to compete in overseas markets and once subject to healthy competition from overseas manufacturers for our own markets, American management and labor will have additional reason to maintain competitive costs and prices, modernize their plants, and increase their productivity. The discipline of the world marketplace is an excellent measure of efficiency and a force for stability. To try to shield American industry from the discipline of foreign competition would isolate our domestic price level from world prices, encourage domestic inflation, reduce our exports still further, and invite less desirable governmental solutions.

Accordingly, the law that President Kennedy proposed had no need for the peril-point and escape-clause provisions to assure protection to high-cost domestic industries. As a result of intense agitation of the protectionist forces in Congress a greatly weakened escape-clause provision was included before the law was finally passed. It can be invoked only if *direct causal relationship* can be proven between tariff concessions and an industry's profits. Covariation of the two no longer is sufficient grounds for escape-clause relief. And even more importantly both the President and the applicant are provided for by the adjustment alternative.

The important consequence of deflating the escape-clause provision was that it substantially reduced the threat to the outside world of escape-clause action which could nullify prior concessions made by the United States and could cause ruin to foreign companies and industries which took seriously the U.S. government's trade agreements and built or expanded their capacity to serve the American market. If it subsequently turned out that American industry brought escape-clause action and won, their access to the U.S. market was terminated. For firms of small countries, where alternative markets for large-scale export production do not exist, the escape-clause actions were catastrophes. However, the escape-clause and peril-point provisions had become the source of so much consternation and notoriety in larger countries also that serious negotiations with the EEC on a general tariff reduction would have been inconceivable without the revisions which the 1962 Act embodies.

Trade-adjustment program

The trade expansion policy regarded increased foreign competition in the domestic market as a necessary part of trade liberalization. To remove obstacles to U.S. exports abroad, this country had to remove obstacles to other countries' exports at home. Repeal of the peril-point provision was certain to adversely affect some high-cost domestic industries if the import restrictions were reduced.

To help them adjust to the more competitive conditions without sharp income and unemployment losses, the new law made available governmental adjustment assistance including: low-interest loans for working capital; technical assistance, particularly in research and development; the whole range of managerial consultant services and any other means which would raise the efficiency of an import-competing company. Thus, the expansion act still distinguishes between foreign and domestic competition. If despite the adjustment assistance competitive costs cannot be achieved, the employees in the high-cost firm can receive funds from the Federal government for retraining and relocation to gain employment in more competitive companies. This helps to shift the resources to more efficient uses. Consequently, the trade adjustment program helps to reduce economic immobility and to increase incomes as it opens the way for tariff reduction. All that is in sharp contrast with the peril-point concept under which high-cost domestic industry would be perpetually shielded by tariffs against international competition.

The Kennedy Round

Although embodying bold ideas, the Trade Agreements Act, like all other trade agreements acts, was only an enabling legislation which had no direct effect on tariffs. To actually reduce the tariff barriers, the provisions of the act first had to be subjected to international negotiations involving issues of reciprocity, measurement of concessions, pressures from the affected sectors of society, and national economic interests of the participating nations; second, the results of the negotiation—expressed in concrete schedules—had to be formalized in binding trade agreements.

Officially recorded as the Sixth Round of Negotiations by the Contracting Parties of GATT, the international proceedings to implement the 1962 Trade Expansion Act are generally known as the Kennedy Round. Although the entire GATT membership was involved, the dialogue was mostly between the United States and the EEC.

The results of these marathon negotiations were most dramatic. The final accord provided 33 to 50 percent across-the-board tariff reductions on over 5000 different product categories, and so represented a historic achievement in multilateral trade liberalization. It thus signifies, as President Kennedy had predicted, a turning point in U.S. foreign-trade policy and opens new horizons for trade expansion throughout the world.

The Issues

The major issues which occupied the negotiators fell into three main categories: industrial tariffs, agricultural protection, and nontariff obstacles to trade. Relations with developing countries rose during the negotiations as a significant secondary issue. It arose because of the inability of developing countries to offer reciprocal concessions, their need for industrialization, and their weak export position. It was resolved by an agreement to make all the liberalization measures which the industrial powers adopted available also to the developing nations on a nonreciprocal basis.

Industrial Tariff

In this area the most absorbing problem was the tariff disparity which arose from the fact that the U.S. tariffs varied in a very wide range (some products having very high, others very low rates), while the EEC rates were relatively uniform, most falling into a narrow, 10 to 20 percent, range. Because of the different rate structures, any across-the-board tariff cut could have had a different effect on each party. For example, suppose the United States maintained a 66 percent import duty on product *X* while that of the Common Market was 18 percent. A 50 percent across-the-board reduction would leave the U.S. level still prohibitively higher than the EEC tariff was at the start and thus would mean no real concession whatsoever. The EEC, therefore, demanded an alignment of tariff structures, i.e., a cutting down of the high peaks before any across-the-board reduction was attempted. However, the United States strongly resisted this demand and the negotiations remained deadlocked for several months. It was finally agreed that, where large disparities existed, the reductions by the EEC could be smaller than those of the United States.

Agricultural Tariff

The Common Market is the world's biggest importer of agricultural products and the best agricultural customer of the United States. Therefore, agricultural duties were a central issue of the Kennedy Round. The United States was very interested in lowering EEC tariffs on farm commodities to aid American producers and to reduce its balance-of-payments deficit. The Common Market, on the other hand, was determined to increase its own agricultural production and to reduce its dependence on external sources for food.

The agricultural policy of the Common Market can affect the U.S. interests in two ways. First, there is a direct effect on U.S. exports of agricultural products to the Common Market; and second, there is an indirect effect that is equally important—if the Common Market is to be a highly protected agricultural area, exporting countries will suffer and their ability to continue importing U.S. manufactured goods will decline. Therefore, it is of vital interest to the United States and most of the developing countries to obtain free access to the EEC's agricultural market. Unfortunately, the United States has not been prepared to open its own market for agricultural imports but has tried to maintain a highly protective farm program since the 1930's. To understand this problem, it is necessary to state briefly the basic farm policy of both parties.

The U.S. farm policy

The United States has encountered one of the most stubborn problems of governmental policy in attempting to reconcile its domestic farm program with its declared purpose of promoting expanding opportunities for international trade. The main purpose of the U.S. farm program was to lift and stabilize farmers' incomes on a par with nonfarm incomes through measures that in recent years have increasingly led to the use of import quotas, export subsidies, and increased tariff protection in the form of import fees.

Through a series of legislative acts after 1930, the United States has provided six general methods for governmental intervention on behalf of agriculture:

(1) establishment of limitations on acreage

(2) establishment of limitations on amounts permitted to be marketed without penalty

(3) enforcement of producer agreements regulating marketing

(4) subsidization of exports through direct payments

(5) direct governmental support of market prices by means of CCC (Commodity Credit Corporation) purchases or nonrecourse loans

(6) imposition of quota restrictions and fees to block import competition[2]

By the mid-1950's most agricultural commodities for which the domestic support program was in effect had been made subject to import quotas or fees. Since these restrictions violated the rules of GATT, a general review of the problem was made in 1955. Despite strong protests from other countries, the United States was able to obtain a waiver because of its superior bargaining power, and its restrictive farm program thus was "legitimized" ex post facto.

The Common Market agricultural policy

The basic objective of the Common Market agricultural policy is "to create a stable market to guarantee a fair income for farmers and reasonable prices for consumers."[3] The measures used in the program include a variable levy system, stabilized prices, export subsidies, regulated competition, and financial support. To accomplish this aim the program abolishes all member states' restrictions on agricultural trade, allowing the commodities to be bought and sold freely throughout the Community. Prices used in administering the common farm policy are defined below.

Target or guide price—the base price determined in the principal consumption center which has the least adequate local supply in the Community of the commodity involved, that is, at the point where the price has normally been the highest.

Intervention or support price—the price set by the EEC Commission at which the EEC Guidance and Guarantee Fund is obliged to buy from farmers. This price constitutes the guaranteed minimum selling price. It is normally 5 to 10 percent below the target price.

Free-at-frontier price—the price of imports delivered to a port of entry with all charges paid except customs duties, that is, the world price at the gates of the EEC.

Threshold or sluice-gate price—the price used as the basis for calculating the levy on imports from outside the Community. It is established by deducting from the target price the cost of distribution, mainly transportation, from a principal port of importation to the marketing center that was used in fixing the target price.

In this structure the actual market price is allowed to fluctuate around the target price, which is to remain unchanged for any marketing year. If the

[2] John M. Leddy, "United States Commercial Policy and the Domestic Farm Program," in *Studies in United States Commercial Policy,* ed. W. B. Kelley (Chapel Hill, North Carolina: University of North Carolina Press, 1963), p. 179.

[3] "A Common Agricultural Policy," *Common Market,* I, No. 3 (January 1961), 47.

market price rises above the target price, imports will be encouraged since the levy will still remain the same—the difference between the free-at-frontier price and the sluice-gate price—which enables importers to earn a higher profit as long as the world price remains constant or increases less than the EEC market price.

If the market price falls below the target price, imports will be suppressed, since the import levy will now cut into importers' earnings or compel overseas suppliers to accept lower prices. This is, of course, not true if world prices decline as much or more than the EEC market price. Consequently, the agricultural imports into the EEC in any particular marketing year depend principally upon the relative movements of the internal market price and the world price. In a longer run, however, the EEC Commission can manipulate the degree of protectiveness by adjusting the threshold price in relation to the target price and thereby either increasing or decreasing the import levy. During 1966 the various agricultural programs were consolidated into a cohesive system which meant the completion of a common agriculture policy, three years ahead of the timetable provided in the Treaty of Rome. Despite intensive pressures from the U.S. delegation, no significant change in this policy (system) resulted from the Kennedy Round.

Nontariffs

During the Kennedy Round negotiations the issue of nontariff distortions of trade rose again and again. Import quotas, export subsidies, taxes, customs valuation, administrative procedures, labeling and marking requirements, health and safety regulations, dumping and antidumping practices, buy-national laws, and other forms of regulatory restraints on international trade were found to be in much greater use by many countries than before. This discovery, while shocking to many, significantly contributed to a better understanding of the actual trade barriers as well as the failings of the reciprocal trade agreements program. To this point attention at international trade negotiations had been narrowly fixed on tariffs; now the nontariffs were also placed under critical scrutiny. As each side sought maximum concessions, it attacked those nontariffs in which the opposition was more vulnerable than the party itself.

Charges against the United States

The main charges against the United States were these three:

(1) Customs Valuation. The U.S. system of customs valuation was criticized as more complicated, confusing, and unfair than that used by European countries which have adopted the Brussels Convention (see Chapter 28). The application of the American Selling Price (ASP) as the basis for assessing ad valorem duties caused the greatest controversy. Under this criterion U.S.

customs can refuse to accept an invoice price or the actual wholesale price of an exporting country and use the ASP instead. It has been applied to organic chemicals, rubber-soled shoes, woolen gloves, and a few other articles. Involving the largest amount of trade, the chemicals group was the principal battleground. Since the American price for these products is typically much higher, sometimes five or six times their invoice value, the application of ASP raises the import price considerably. The system also contradicts GATT provisions (Article VII) which prohibit importing countries from using domestic prices for duty purposes.

Since the 1962 Trade Expansion Act contained no provision for reforming the system of customs valuation, the U.S. trade delegation lacked the authority to make any definite concessions in the ASP issue. Furthermore, the political pressure which the American chemical industry generated through intensive lobbying against any change compelled the delegation to pursue a generally conservative course.

The outcome was a two-package agreement for the chemical sector. The *first package* included the following unconditional obligations: U.S. reductions of tariffs by 50 percent on items carrying duties over 8 percent and by 20 percent on those below 8 percent. These cuts applied to 95 percent of U.S. chemical imports and averaged 43 percent. Most of these imports had originated in the EEC, Britain, Japan, and Switzerland. The reciprocal concessions made by these four areas averaged only 26 percent, but they covered a volume of $900 million of chemical imports coming from the United States. The U.S. concessions covered only $325 million of imports from the four other chemical producers. The *second package* provided for the eventuality of Congress' eliminating the ASP system. If that happened the U.S. rates would first be converted from the ASP basis to their equivalents in protection but would be expressed in terms of regular valuation, i.e., the foreign export value basis. Then these converted rates would be reduced in stages by 50 percent or to an ultimate duty of 20 percent, whichever would be lower. A tariff ceiling of 20 percent ad valorem would thus be set. The overall reduction on U.S. tariffs would thus amount to 48 percent. Foreign reciprocity for these concessions would bring their total average tariff cuts to 46 percent for the EEC and 47 percent for the others. In addition, Belgium, France, and Italy would modify their road-use taxes, which discriminate against American-size automobiles, and Switzerland would lift its embargo against canned fruits preserved in corn syrup.

(2) Antidumping Act. The EEC delegation proposed that a common procedure for antidumping measures be worked out on the basis of the GATT principles. This met with serious difficulty, partly because of the varied practices in use, and particularly because of the U.S. Antidumping Act, which allows the administration to charge an additional (antidumping) duty on any imports that satisfy its definition of dumping. The threat of the antidumping duty was alleged to restrain many European exporters from trying to enter the U.S. market. They considered particularly harmful the power of U.S. customs to suspend valuation of imports whenever dumping was suspected, even when

no proof of injury was submitted. The inquiries and investigations that must follow such suspension were considered a serious obstacle to trade. No European country has a similar procedure.

(3) Buy-American Act. This Act requires all U.S. government agencies to patronize American suppliers in preference to foreign sources. Only after the acquisition costs show a differential greater than 6 to 12 percent (depending on unemployment in the area concerned) can import procurement be legitimately undertaken. For orders relating to national defense, the preference was raised to 50 percent in 1962. Up to the early 1960's, this Act applied only to goods to be consumed in the United States. But more recently the Defense Department has extended it also to purchases to be used abroad. Since the preference margin was raised, European industry has reportedly given up quoting on U.S. contracts.

U.S. Charges against European Countries

In its counteroffensive, the United States claimed that the EEC and its supporters maintain four types of nontariff obstacles and demanded this elimination:

(1) Quota Restrictions. In the early postwar years, when Europe had serious payments problems, import quotas became commonplace. Many of these had continued in force, although the payments problem had long disappeared. At the time of the negotiations, most of the major trading countries such as France, Germany, Great Britain, Italy, and Japan had numerous import quotas in force. (Japan had license requirements for 154 products.)

In this area the U.S. delegation directed its severest criticism against Great Britain, which had established absolute prohibition against U.S. coal imports. Coal also figured significantly in the debate with several other countries.

Although the U.S. case was well documented in the field of manufactured products, it quickly disintegrated when the consideration was extended to oil and dairy products, on which the United States has maintained a rigid system of import quotas.

(2) Arbitrary and Undisclosed Procedures. The strongest U.S. complaint was against arbitrariness and the lack of disclosed procedures in European governmental practices affecting international trade. This charge embraced such questions as bidding on foreign governments' purchase contracts by U.S. firms, the use of executive measures in such areas as antidumping, "buy at home," and customs clearance, where the United States has always relied on the legislative process. In essence this was a defense of the American system of doing things, which had been severely criticized by the Europeans.

(3) Taxation. The third chapter of American complaints dealt with fiscal matters. It criticized the "value-added" taxes and turnover taxes used in the

EEC and demanded a change in the practice of taxing automobiles in Austria, Belgium, France, and Italy on cylinder capacity or horsepower instead of on the price of the vehicle. Since most American cars are considerably bigger than European makes, they are thus severely penalized by such taxes even though they may be considerably cheaper to buy.

(4) Health Regulations. The proceedings of the Kennedy Round showed that nearly all countries employ health regulations which, when strictly applied, can form serious obstacles to trade. For example, France prohibits entry of citrus fruits which are chemically colored or preserved with diphenyl, as is done in the United States. Some others restrict importation of chickens and other animal products from countries where certain chemical substances like antimony or hormones are used in feeding. The United States has a number of laws setting up strict requirements as to purity, quality, and labeling of food products, drugs, textiles, and various other consumer goods. All of these have allegedly been used by the authorities to discriminate against foreign suppliers.

New Focus

The evidence now available points up the fact that while tariff has occupied the stage for international trade negotiations under the reciprocal agreements program and in the GATT forums, nontariff restrictions were quietly harnessed by individual countries to neutralize tariff concessions made in the trade agreements. Schematically, the situation might be depicted as in the figure below.

After 33 years of tariffs reduction and especially after the Kennedy Round reduction has become effective, tariffs will remain but will be a rela-

FIGURE 7-1

Perceived and Actual Trade Liberalization

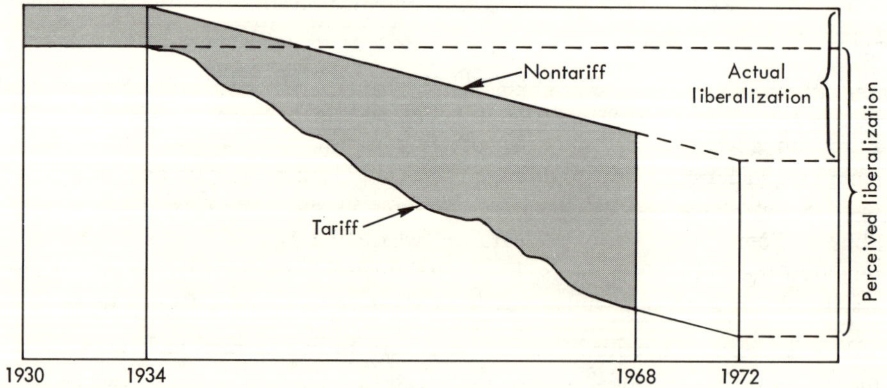

tively minor hurdle to trade. The nontariff barriers, on the other hand, have become increasingly formidable both in relative and absolute terms. It is, therefore, self-deception to equate tariff reductions with trade liberalizations as we have done in the past. To have trade liberalization, all barriers—tariffs and nontariffs—must be eliminated. As the tariff problem has, by and large, been solved, it is imperative to shift the focus now against the nontariffs—the invisibles which often can be more destructive to trade than the visible tariffs. To do this, new concepts and new instruments of trade legislation and commercial diplomacy are needed. The Kennedy Round talks have given us a beginning in this respect but the main job remains yet to be done.

Protectionist Resurgence

By all indications this will be a precarious task. Not only is every effort to dismantle the nontariffs met with savage resistance by various self-interest groups, but an almost global offensive is currently being waged by protectionist forces to raise the existing nontariffs and to introduce nontariffs to many new sectors of the business system.

Hardly had the cheers over the successful completion of the Kennedy Round subsided before the protectionist forces mounted their furious counter-offensive. This was particularly pronounced in the United States. The old protectionist elements, including glass, watches, and textiles, found reinforcement in such powerful industries as steel, machine tools, electronics, and chemicals. A rash of new bills and amendments to those already pending were introduced in the United States Congress by both Democrats and Republicans demanding quotas, licenses, and similar devices which were designed to nullify the gains achieved by the Kennedy Round. Together there were over one thousand bills for special protection introduced between 1967 and 1972. If all these bills were enacted by Congress, there would be rigid limitations on about 50 percent of United States total imports, and from 85 to 90 percent on dutiable imports.

This offensive reaction of the protectionist elements, while not unanticipated, has been surprising because of its vigor and power. The free-trade forces have, so far, had to fight a holding action to prevent the gains of the Kennedy Round from being annihilated. They hope that this delaying tactic will enable a new initiative for trade liberalization, not only in the United States but also in other countries where similar protection pressures are felt. But this hope is far from becoming reality at this time.

Post-Kennedy Round trade policy in the United States has taken on a more and more conservative tone—one of defensiveness and holding on. The Nixon administration has held to the belief that the key to U.S. foreign trade relations is keeping domestic inflation in check. While this would improve the country's trade balance, it cannot be a substitute for trade policy in any real sense.

Appendix to Chapter 7

Chronology of U.S. Tariff Legislation Since World War I

1918–34 After World War I, political isolationism and economic nationalism generate pressures for a protectionist commercial policy. The United States becomes a creditor nation but does not lower tariffs to let foreign countries earn dollars to service debts.

The tariff of 1922 is designed to protect farmers and to help the chemical industry and other "war babies."

The United States adopts an unconditional most-favored-nation (m.f.n.) policy in 1923.

The world slides toward depression, and the United States enacts the Hawley-Smoot Tariff with high levels of protection.

Foreign governments retaliate; world trade drops but U.S. trade drops even faster.

1934–62 The Trade Agreements Act of 1934 amends the Hawley-Smoot Tariff and shifts the leading role in tariff-setting from Congress to the President on a temporary basis.

From the beginning of the era of reciprocal agreements under the Trade Agreements Act, the guiding philosophy is to increase exports and ensure "no injury" to U.S. business.

The Trade Agreements Act changes the U.S. tariff from its historical position of being a single-column tariff to being a maximum-minimum tariff.

The United States negotiates 31 trade agreements with other governments from 1934 through 1945. In each case, the United States generalizes its own concessions to most other trading countries under the m.f.n. clause.

Following World War II, the United States holds tariffs down, whereas, after every other major war, tariffs had risen.

The fourth extension of the Trade Agreements Act in 1945 gives the President power to negotiate further reductions of up to 50 percent of the rates in effect at the outset of 1945.

The United States kills the formation of the International Trade Organization but joins in the formation of GATT.

Early postwar tariff cuts matter the most, as the U.S. tariff hardly changes during the 1950's. American negotiators at GATT conferences are hobbled by amendments to the Trade Agreements Act (RTA).

In 1951 Congress writes an escape clause into the RTA, formalizing the procedures established in 1947. This clause retains for the United States the right, under stipulated circumstances, to withdraw or modify any concession that might be granted through GATT.

A peril-point provision in the RTA, first introduced in 1948, directs the President to list the products on which he plans to make concessions at GATT meetings so that the Tariff Commission can decide what duties are needed to prevent injury to U.S. business. The President can ignore the commission's findings but has to defend his actions to Congress.

In 1955 and 1958 Congress broadens the escape clause and makes it more difficult for the President to reject the Tariff Commission's recommendations.

In 1955 the National Security Amendment is added to the RTA to erect another barrier against import competition. In the following years, however, the amendment is invoked only once—to place quotas on imports of petroleum.

The 1955 extension of the RTA gives the President authority to reduce duties through negotiation up to 15 percent of previous rates and up to 50 percent on all rates higher than 50 percent.

The formation of the European Economic Community and the restoration of convertibility of the European currencies leave tariffs a major barrier to trade.

A 20 percent reciprocal reduction of tariffs is negotiated between the EEC and the U.S. in which 18 other countries join in 1961–62 GATT Conference.

1962–67 The United States enters a new tariff era. The Trade Expansion Act of 1962 grants substantial authority to the President to negotiate reductions in all tariffs (up to 50 percent of the 1962 level on all items and up to

TABLE 7-1

Major Tariff Acts and General Level of U.S. Tariff, 1909–72

Act	*Period used to determine general level*	*Equivalent ad valorem rate, ratio of duties to: Dutiable imports*	*Total imports*
Payne–Aldrich Tariff (1909)	1910–21	41	19(1)
Underwood Tariff (1913)	1914–21	27	9
Fordney–McCumber Tariff (1922)	1923–30	39	14
Hawley–Smoot Tariff (1930)	1930–33	53	18
Trade Agreements Act (1934)	1934–37	41	17
Extension of Trade Agreements Act			
1937	1938–40	38	14
1940	1940–43	34	12
1943	1944–45	30	9
1945	1945–47	28	9
1948	1948	13	6
1949	1949–51	13	6
1951	1952–53	12	5
1954	1954	12	6
1955	1955–57	12	6
1958	1958–62	12	7(2)
Trade Expansision Act, 1962	1963	115	7

Sources: (1) Calculated from Historical Statistics of the United States, Colonial Times to 1957, Table Series U 15–20 (Washington, D.C.; U.S. Government Printing Office, 1964). (2) Statistical Abstract of the United States, 1964, Table 1234 (Washington, D.C.: U.S. Government Printing Office, 1964).

80 percent on articles in any category where the United States and the EEC together account for 80 percent or more of the aggregated world export value).

The Trade Expansion Act also marks the first move away from the trade-hampering no-injury rule with the inclusion of provisions for adjustment assistance for workers and businesses in place of tariff protection.

1967 to this writing (1972) Presidents Johnson and Nixon failed to get Congress to enact any new trade liberalization measures. Some one thousand bills seeking nontariff protection for special industries are introduced under intensive pressure from business lobbies. The goal of national trade policy seems to be adrift.

8

East-West Trade Relations

In sharp contrast to their political influence and military power, the communist bloc countries have made but modest contributions to world trade. Their peripheral status is attributable to several factors. Emphasis on self-sufficiency, bilateral trade balancing, and preference on intrabloc dealings are voluntary strategies which have held down the volume of trade with the non-communist world. Foreign import restrictions, especially anticommunist discrimination, lack of marketing knowhow, and poor product quality have placed involuntary constraints on their ability to export to the West. Without exports, importation from the West has been impeded by lack of foreign exchange. The inflow of Western imports has further been restrained by the Soviet organization of foreign trade under which export and import activities are exclusively assigned to special government-owned trading monopolies. Western sellers can, therefore, compete only up to the border, but can never deal directly with the consumer or even the domestic distributor of a communist country. Given the state trading monopolies, penetration of the communist markets in a direct sense of the term by Western exporters would be unthinkable even if the regulatory barriers were relaxed. But since the trading monopolies in the Soviet system are in reality nothing but the operating arms of the Foreign Trade Ministry, they can be expected to be fully responsive to any changes in the governmental trade policies and regulations. The key to any increased trade with the West is clearly the governmental policy as far as the Soviets are concerned.

From the U.S. side the same is true. Trade with the Soviet countries has been subject to strongest national regulation which has in many ways excluded the communist markets from normal business considerations.

Both sides are now reassessing their mutually inimical policy positions. The exact size of economic gains from trade to each side that has been lost is a matter of speculation. But considering the industrial capacities, economic diversities, and national incomes, say just of the U.S.S.R. and the U.S. alone, suggest that the ultimate potentialities for East-West trade are enormous by any standard. Realization of this fact has started to reach wide-enough circles to provide a counterweight against rigidly frozen policies of the cold-war era. Unfreezing of these policies is now in process on both sides. Hence there is a very high probability for a change toward vastly increased economic interaction between the East and West.

Political Impediments

Western governments and, in particular, the United States, have accused the Socialist countries of using foreign trade as a tool to obtain political objectives. It is claimed that economic profit or gain is sacrificed to political interests. For example, in 1954 the Soviet Union agreed to purchase the entire Italian almond crop after the United States announced import restrictions. In 1948 the Soviet Union, despite domestic shortages, exported wheat to France and Italy to strengthen the two respective communist parties. The Soviet Union began purchasing Icelandic fish after Great Britain cut off her fish imports from Iceland. Exports to the Soviet Union have grown from two percent to 60 percent of Cuba's total foreign trade. More general examples of the mixing of politics with trade might be the size of intrabloc trading among COMECON members despite incomparably better alternatives outside the bloc. Politically motivated trading ventures such as these are not accidental. In the words of a Soviet expert, "Foreign trade policy of the U.S.S.R. is an integral part of its foreign policy. The unity of political and economic administration in the sphere of foreign trade is attributable to the fact that political, economic, and organizational problems are closely interwoven in the Soviet economy. . . a political approach is necessary in preparing and concluding commercial treaties, trade agreements, protocols, and other documents."[1]

Thus, the argument that the centrally planned economic policies of the east bloc countries are particularly amenable for use in achieving political objectives is not unfounded. But to infer from this that economic considerations are completely irrelevant in communist foreign trade, as the popular view in the West tends to depict it, is to badly distort the actual situation. Even a cursory study of the communist trade record and literature reveals that in all soviet countries foreign trade is basically a *complement to domestic economics* of the nation's economic plan. Its function is to supply the material

[1] P. A. Cherviakov. *Organizatsoya i Tekhnica Vorishnei Torgovli SSR* (Moscow: 1962).

needs of which domestic capacity is lacking or inadequate and to generate the foreign exchange with which to pay for the foreign purchases. These are economic objectives, and they are pursued primarily by economic means. Occasional misuse of trade by the totalitarian government cannot transform its real nature. Indeed, such misuse of trade tends to produce its own antidotes, which by suffocating the normal trade exacts a punitive price from the country. The U.S. trade policy toward the communist bloc glaringly underscores this truth. Though an excessive overreaction and perhaps in part also ideologically messianic, it has confounded business firms and governments alike throughout the world.

American Trade Policy toward Communist Nations

While protesting the east bloc's economic foreign policies, the United States and, to a lesser extent, Western Europe, have pursued much the same type of policy. Trade with the East has been tied with politics. A number of legal restrictions have been imposed that severely curtail U.S. companies' ability to trade with the east bloc nations.

1. *The Export Control Act* of 1949 is the main law regulating United States export trade. In it Congress declares that the policy of the United States is to use export controls to the extent necessary to protect the domestic economy from any excessive drain of scarce materials and to reduce the inflationary impact of abnormal foreign demand; *to further the foreign policy of the United States* and aid in fulfilling its international responsibilities; and *to exercise the necessary vigilance over exports from the standpoint of their significance to the national security.* Under this law, the United States government barred all exports and imports to Communist China and Manchuria, North Korea, North Vietnam, Inner Mongolia, and Cuba (except that food and medicine could be exported to Cuba); barred also the export of arms, strategic and critical materials—but not other items—to the Soviet Union, Outer Mongolia, and most of the communist countries of Eastern Europe (with the restriction being slightly less on Poland and Romania): to place no restrictions on exports to noncommunist nations and Yugoslavia. This law is enforced by the U.S. Department of Commerce through a system of export licenses.

2. *The Mutual Defense Assistance Control Act* (Battle Act) of 1957 embargoes the exports of arms, ammunition, atomic materials, petroleum, and several other products. Any country disregarding the U.S. embargo may be denied U.S. economic and military aid.

3. *Export-Import Bank Act* forbids banks to guarantee, insure, extend credit or participate when (a) the purchase or lease of a product is by a communist nation and when the product is for the principal use of a communist nation although negotiated by a third country.

4. *The Johnson Act* prohibits private firms from engaging in credit transactions with foreign governments who are in default in payment to the U.S. unless such countries are members of the International Monetary Fund, or the World Bank. Since the U.S.S.R. has not liquidated its war debts to the United States and does not belong to either of the world financial organizations, it is subject to this law.
5. *Trade with the Enemy Act* requires all persons wanting to trade with communist countries to first obtain a license from the U.S. government. The same law prohibits the transfer to certain communist countries any interest in property subject to U.S. jurisdiction.
6. A number of other laws and regulations restate and further expand these restrictions. The most important additional provisions include:

6.1 The withdrawal of most-favored-nation treatment to all communist countries in 1957; Poland and Yugoslavia have since been reinstated.

6.2 Complete embargo on imports from mainland China; partially lifted by President Nixon in 1971.

6.3 Miscellaneous specific restrictions range from United States government funds not being used to purchase school laboratory equipment made in communist countries to the exclusion of Soviet turbines for the Grand Coulee hydroelectric project.

7. *The Export Administration Act* of 1969 introduces a cautious shift from restriction toward liberalization. It allows non-military goods to be decontrolled and authorizes presidential approval of Export-Import Bank's financing American sales to Soviet countries. Nearly 2000 products had been removed from the restricted list by 1972.

But at the same time the U.S. government has used indirect suasion to discourage business with the Soviet bloc. At this writing, for example, Renault of France is negotiating the construction of a truck-manufacturing plant in Russia. Initially the Soviet government had asked the Ford Motor Company to bid on the plant. This was highlighted during a well-publicized visit to the Soviet Union by Henry Ford II. However, because of United States government disapproval, the Ford Motor Company declined to bid on the project. Fiat of Italy has already built an automobile-manufacturing plant in the U.S.S.R. West European governments are now extending credits to the east bloc as long as 10 to 15 years. While the West European governments have agreed in principle on an embargo of strategic goods to the east bloc, their definition has been much narrower than that of the United States. Therefore, what is restricted from foreign commerce by one nation may be exported by another.

The Rationale of Restrictions

The United States policy of restricting trade with the Soviet bloc is based on a number of arguments. As mentioned above, the United States policy is in part a response to the perceived use of trade as a political tool by the Soviet bloc.

The United States discourages foreign trade with the east bloc because it may strengthen economically and militarily a politically hostile government, provide technical knowledge, allow the diversion of resources to military production, cause the West to become too dependent upon the Soviet bloc trade, finance Soviet bloc economic development through long-term credits, tend to weaken the Western Alliance, and help prove the superiority of communism to the Third World. And lastly, it is held that Western firms are at a disadvantage in dealing with the Socialist state trading monopolies.

But the United States efforts to prevent the communist countries from getting Western goods are not very effective, especially when it comes to things that the communists really want. The U.S. embargoes can usually be circumvented through trade with third parties. The east bloc may either import comparable goods directly from a nation which does not embargo the particular goods, or it may obtain the U.S. goods "illicitly" by dealing with an intermediary abroad.

United States policy is also based upon the assumption that the east bloc is heavily dependent upon the importing of Western technology for its economic progress. This is probably true though difficult to prove. However, if it is true, the east bloc is generally able presently to import the needed technology either through espionage or third countries. Moreover, in several fields the east bloc is achieving a degree of technological equality with the West. Certainly, Soviet progress in military aircraft, the SST program, space travel, and medicine all point to sophisticated technological development.

The basic proposition that trade with the Soviet bloc will strengthen a hostile power is political and cannot be answered in economic terms alone. But there is no longer room for doubt that the Soviet Union and the east bloc will grow militarily and economically with or without an increase in Western trade. These countries have not only shown an ability to undergo hardships imposed by import restrictions for long-run political and economic goals but also are far beyond the point in development where external supplies can decide further progress. Furthermore, the Soviet Union is perhaps the most richly endowed in natural resources of any nation. In fact, it exports to the U.S. certain metals, such as chromium, which the U.S. has placed upon its own export restriction list. It would seem that there is more to be gained than lost if the present trade restrictions will be relaxed and both the American and Soviet diplomats ceased to burden trade policies with insidious political cargo.

The Communist Foreign Trade System

All communist countries initially modeled their international economic relations after, if not under, the Soviet Union. Although subsequently each country has modified that system for its own unique reasons, in some ways, they still remain essentially the same. Differences among them relate mainly to the product composition of imports and exports rather than objectives, policies, trading organizations, and/or methods. We can, therefore, greatly simplify this discussion by ignoring the differences and assay the U.S.S.R. as the arch model for the entire bloc.

The U.S.S.R. Model

Responsibility for the conduct of foreign trade in the U.S.S.R. is divided between the Ministry of Foreign Trade, which produces the "foreign trade plan" with the foreign trade department of the Gosplan and concludes overall trade agreements, and a number of state foreign trade monopolies, largely specialized by commodities, whose functions are to deal with the country's producing and consuming enterprises and to negotiate specific contracts for purchases and sales abroad according to the Ministry's plan.[2] The task of both units is the same as that of any other economic enterprise in the East—to fulfill the plan and make profits, i.e., to do more business than planned with given resources or to fill the quota by using less resources than planned. Any particular trade monopoly is concerned only with the sale and/or purchase of goods on its own list. While it can make representations about market opportunities, it is essentially charged with exporting or importing a quantity of commodities which it is planned to do. The trade corporations operate branches in the principal cities of the communist counties and have joint or separate offices in noncommunist capitals. Financial aspects of Soviet international business are handled by Vneshtorgbank (foreign trade bank), which has correspondent relations all over the world.

Pricing in Communist Trade

The iron law of communist trade is that exports must pay for imports. Since their currencies have no recognized international value, nearly all foreign trade takes place in convertible foreign currencies or gold. To meet the import requirements which the national plan has fixed, the volume and prices of exports are to be varied so as to generate the necessary amount of foreign exchange. This is the overriding objective of pricing policy.

The export price in the Soviet realm need not bear any direct relationship to internal prices or costs. In domestic pricing the authorities pursue two objectives. First, retail prices for consumer goods are set so that the foreplanned output will be cleared, i.e., equal to available consumer spending in a particular sector; this is the nearest to supply and demand that Soviet pricing ever gets. Second, wholesale and producer prices are determined by averaging the cost of all producers over a given reference period (by necessity a past period) to which a planned markup is added. The markup is varied by authorities to make things come out "right."

Since neither of these domestic pricing policies is readily adaptable to the competitive conditions in the world markets, the Soviets rely on a negoti-

[2] The ministry works out three plans: annual, five-year, and long range.

ated price rather than a prefixed or planned price in foreign trade. The world market price, if one exists, is used as the basic standard. Otherwise either the Soviet wholesale price or the trading partner's domestic wholesale price provides the starting points of the price negotiations. The managers of the trading monopolies are required to drive hard bargains with foreign firms and are awarded special bonuses if they succeed in realizing particularly favorable prices for the Soviets.

Most exports and imports of communist countries are priced very near to the two basic standards: the world market price or the wholesale price in the country of origin. However, all are not. Nor is there any compelling reason why they should. The concentration of total control over international trade in the Foreign Trade ministry creates a supermonopoly which can manipulate export prices and products to effect results that are unthinkable under our free-enterprise system. Suppose a communist country needs an automobile plant and decides to import it as a turn-key project. Three foreign firms offer to build the plant: an American for $60 million, an Italian for $68 million, and a Swedish for $72 million. The American company is the lowest bidder. But it asks for payment in dollars or gold. The communist country's foreign exchange reserves are too small to meet these terms. If it bought the plant from the Italian or Swedish companies it could receive long-term credit or pay in kind by raw material exports. Suppose further that for a source of dollar exchange the Foreign Trade ministry finds that a U.S. airline is anxious to buy from it four supersonic aircraft, if it priced them at $15 million instead of the $16.2 million they cost to produce. By selling the four SST's at a $4.8 million loss, the Ministry saves $8 million on the turn-key project (the difference between the American and Italian offers) and records an overall *profit* of $3.2 million.

This is a potentially awesome power. The Soviets have to date used it sparingly; capitalist enterprise, where each individual firm must break even to survive, has no counterforce to neutralize this totalitarian advantage. No amount of rhetoric about the superiority of competition and the market mechanism over centrally planned economies will help, except perhaps as a tranquilizer. If the superiority of competition did not do the trick in the past when the communists were underdeveloped and weak, it is certain it will not do it in the future. How to come to grips with this disparity in pricing power is a fundamental problem to which U.S. government and business must jointly seek a solution. It would seem that certain cherished ideals of competition and antitrust in this country would have to be viewed from a new perspective before such a solution can be contemplated.

Intrabloc Trade

Once a monolithic colossus reigned from Moscow, the communist countries no longer form a solid bloc. Separatist tendencies have produced a polycentric power structure in which both Peking and Belgrad challenge the

Kremlin and many other capitals vie for greater self-assertion. The Sino-Soviet split has been the main force undermining the old order. The loosening of political control has been followed by more independent trading policies of the individual countries. China's own trade epitomizes the shuffling directions in intrabloc trade. In pre-communist days, only 5 percent of China's foreign trade was with communist countries. After the communists gained power the direction of Chinese trade was shifted toward the U.S.S.R. and other communist countries, and their share had already reached 77 percent by 1955. Since the Sino-Soviet split in 1960, the percentage dropped to the neighborhood of 25. Yugoslavia's experience is very smiliar.

In the other East-European countries, the U.S.S.R.'s dominance has weakened somewhat but still remains decisive. Through COMECON (The Council for Mutual Economic Assistance) the trade policies of Bulgaria, Czechoslovakia, East Germany, Hungary, Poland, Roumania, and the U.S.S.R. are subjected to centralized supranational coordination. This quasi-common market arrangement has been used by the U.S.S.R. to impose its own control on the trade relations of the other members. However, the resistance to this control has become increasingly apparent.

The stated goals of COMECON include: (a) increase of intrabloc trade, (b) development of more optimal allocation of resources among member countries, and (c) achievement of more equal per capita production and consumption standards in the bloc nations. As already noted, the first objective has become increasingly illusive in the last few years. As to the second objective, a violent disagreement has erupted about the type of specialization which the U.S.S.R. has sought to impose on the other members. Roumania, particularly, has protested against being forever relegated to an agrarian role that it considers less prestigious and less rewarding than industrial development. The need to work out an acceptable communist theory of international economic integration and intrabloc trade has been emphasized but remains so far unmet. That leaves political negotiations and relative power positions as the only means for settling the issues. Incomparably bigger than all the others combined, the U.S.S.R. can be assured of continued dominance of the COMECON trade.

International Industrial Cooperation

Realizing the increasing importance in world trade of multinational enterprises, the U.S.S.R. in 1966 initiated a program of industrial collaboration with capitalist countries. By 1972 eleven European countries and Japan had signed agreements; several others were exploring possibilities for joint industrial projects with the U.S.S.R. The latter's main goal is to have licensing arrangements or turn-key projects rather than permanent capitalist direct investments in its own borders. However, the projects may have a duration of ten or twenty years and a wide spectrum: the development of mineral and forest resources; building factories, pipelines, and other major facilities; or conducting research. Beyond its own territory, the U.S.S.R. wishes to participate in joint ventures both in manufacturing and marketing in the advanced countries, and to collaborate with capitalist enterprise in developmental projects in the third world.

This program opens a promising new frontier for East-West business relations. The smaller communist countries in Europe are aggressively promoting their own industrial cooperation with the West and are outdoing the U.S.S.R. by providing greater incentives and better terms to foreign firms. For them this new frontier signifies the beginning of the end of being completely dependent on the Soviet Union, or so they hope.

III

The Multinational Company

Business firms are no longer what they were. True, there are still many companies whose world is tightly boxed into national boundaries and for whom the nation remains the universe, or so their managers think. But their number is decreasing and their significance fading. Both the uninational firm and its ethnocentric management system are rapidly becoming an anachronism as we learn to understand and employ the superior power, stability, and efficiency of the multinational company.

9

Concepts and Growth of Multinational Companies

Since World War II international business relations have undergone a radical change. To trade that consisted of product flows have been added transnational movements of technology, management personnel, knowhow, and investments in operating facilities in foreign countries. As a result both the executive and the economist have been groping for a term to distinguish this broader concept from the restricted notion of international trade. An entirely suitable one has not so far been proposed.

Operations

The term *operations* acquired a special connotation after World War II, when business adopted certain techniques of analysis and planning from the military. These techniques, developed during the war by university personnel who had been drafted by the armed forces, were tentatively labeled *operations research*. It was a makeshift phrase devised under intense pressure to distinguish the totality of a military campaign from its subordinate and supporting activities. *Operations* thus came to denote the composite of all specialized functions, material, and manpower in a particular undertaking. It is in this integrative meaning that business borrowed the term: *foreign operations, international operations, overseas operations,* and more recently *multinational operations* have been alternatively adopted by different companies to identify foreign undertakings which go beyond export and import activities. Although the adjective may vary, the noun remains the same. The adoption of the operations concept was helpful in that it created a distinction between the functionally narrower idea of trade and the broader concept of an international enterprise. But it provided only a partial answer to the problem. Besides being clumsy and easily confused with the more common meanings of the word, *operations* failed to convey the idea of institutional adjustment to different national environments—an adjustment which for military purposes was either nonessential or controlled by the command but which for business enterprise plays a paramount role. Yet the term stuck and for a decade or so seemed to have gained general currency in the business world. More recently, however, the terms *enterprise* and *company* (with the adjectives of international or multinational) have been adopted to cover the general field, and *operations* has been restricted to covering the activities aspects. However, neither practice is universal. Having helped to propagate the newer trend, this author prefers *enterprise* and *corporation* to *operations.*

Definition of Multinational Enterprise

The basic notion in any definition of multinational enterprise is that of a number of affiliated business establishments which function simultaneously in different countries. Two simple models of such an enterprise are shown in Fig. 9-1. The four-country complex in the left half of the figure consists of a headquarters company and three foreign-based affiliates, each located in a different country. The four different national units of the structure function together. From the headquarters company (and country) flow direction and control, and from the affiliates products, revenues, and information.

FIGURE 9-1

Spatial Models of Multinational Enterprise

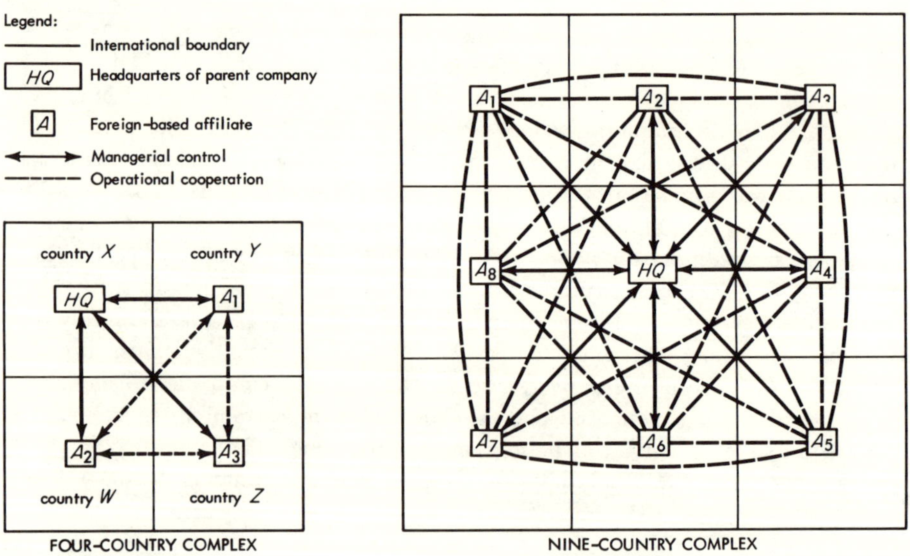

Among the affiliates there are operational interties for cooperation in planning, technical services, and intracompany trade. The nine-country complex is an analogical arrangement but has a much more intricate network of interties among its national entities. Both these models are monocentric in that all affiliates have a direct relationship to the headquarters company and equiponderant in that the affiliates are assumed to be comparable to one another in size, character, and managerial autonomy. Neither of these simplifying assumptions needs to be present in any particular multinational firm. Until the internal organization of the headquarters company and the different types of affiliates have been explored in the next chapter, the monocentric pattern with equiponderant affiliates will illustrate the basics of the spatial structure of the multinational company.

The emphasis on structure to this point should not be interpreted to imply that the multinational enterprise is only a mechanical concept. At its center lies the dynamic idea of the management process expanded to cope with the variegated forces of the multinational environment. Adaptation, assimilation, and reconciliation of conflicting forces in continuous change are, therefore, as inseparable from the multinational enterprise as are the national subunits from its organizational structure. And the structure itself is seldom static. Both the form and functions of its parts—the foreign-based affiliates—respond to new incentives and disincentives, to the growth of one affiliate and the decline of another, to legal and economic changes, and to the strategies and policies promulgated on the multinational level by the firm itself.

Foreign Investments: A Narrower Concept

Multinational enterprise is not to be confused with the orthodox notion of foreign investments, which is a much narrower concept and indeed a subordinate function to multinational enterprise. The contrast is particularly sharp with *portfolio investment,* that is, the purchase and ownership of foreign stocks and bonds for the purpose of dividend and interest payments as return on the investment. The international portfolio investor is primarily a creditor whose main concern is the placement of his capital among the existing enterprises of different countries. He does not actively participate in the management of the enterprises involved. Although he may be entitled to vote his share of stock, he normally plays a negligible role in the managerial affairs of the corporation.[1] International portfolio investments are thus on the periphery of the contemporary multinational enterprise concept. Only in the exceptional case where they provide the means for acquiring the ownership interest necessary for ultimate managerial control do portfolio investments play a direct, although temporary, role.

A direct foreign investment is the acquisition by an enterprise of specific productive capabilities abroad, such as warehouses, mining properties, assembly plants, or power stations. As such, direct investments are the vehicles for the

[1] Charles P. Kindleberger, *International Economics* (3rd ed.) (Homewood, Illinois: Richard D. Irwin, Inc., 1968), p. 404.

birth and growth of multinational enterprise. But the two can never be considered synonymous. The central concerns of the multinational enterprise are production, distribution, and other operational activities that generate outputs and profits. Investments play a role in this complex of activities but only a supporting role. Furthermore, the typical multinational company tends to minimize its international capital transfers by drawing upon indigenous resources for both equity and loanable funds where feasible and by plowing back profits to its affiliates in different countries. Regrettably, these important distinctions are not recognized in orthodox economic literature, and much confusion exists on this point. The newer and better economics texts recognize that a distinction exists but have yet to explain its full significance. They suggest that direct investment be regarded primarily as a movement of entrepreneurial talent and only incidentally as a capital flow, and stress that direct investment takes place when a firm can obtain a peculiar advantage from the multinational operations, such as access to new markets, raw-materials supplies, special technology, managerial experience, or a broader financial base.[2] Although this is much closer to truth than the orthodox notion which equates direct investments with multinational enterprise, it still falls far short of conveying the fact that multinational enterprise is much broader than the flow of managerial talent and funds; that, in addition, it extends to legal forms of organization, to ownership affiliations, to the physical location and design of the facilities, and to the entire functional spectrum ranging from distribution of products to fundamental research, to payrolls, to labor-union organizations, and to relations with foreign governments and people. In sum, multinational enterprise represents the totality of organizing and operating business establishments in an international context.

Evolution of the Multinational Enterprise

In its contemporary form the multinational corporation is a truly new phenomenon, a product of the twentieth century. However, its roots extend to antiquity. To explain better its varied and highly complex nature, this chapter reviews how it has emerged, what elements it embodies, how it differs from earlier schemes to operate international business, and why its forerunners have been transformed into the present multinational enterprise.

The Early Antecedents

Individual ventures

Nearly 5000 years ago, Mesopotamian merchants attempted to form trading companies for penetration into other lands. Their business was interkingdom, interregional, and intertribal traffic in wool, spices, silver, slaves,

[2] Cf. Kindleberger, *International Economics,* p. 411.

and art objects; their aims were profit and adventure; their main burden was to convey the goods from the point of origin to the marketplace despite extreme risks and costs. Permanent settlements were few, and connections among them even fewer. Overcrowding in the mother cities forced people to move to virgin areas or to settle in foreign lands and "colonies." Carthage and Syracuse are well-known examples of such colonies. As a result, colonies and trading cities arose, among which the earliest foreign-trade activity developed.

For three millennia, this intercity system of "world" trade continued with but minor change. With certain exceptions in the Roman era, foreign trade remained almost exclusively a matter of individual ventures, mostly for merchant-adventures, until the sixteenth century. The distinction between trading and robbery was often blurred by the practices of the early merchants. "Besides slave trading, the robber merchant also engaged in 'hijacking' the cargoes of others to stock his own ships, or fell upon defenseless, coastal towns, particularly in the Near East, where religious cloak could be given to any kind of rapine practice upon the Infidel."[3]

At the end of the Middle Ages, however, some regularized forms of commercial associations, known as *commenda,* began to develop. They consisted of capitalists, who stayed at home, and merchants, who traveled abroad and conducted the trade. The commenda were not permanent organizations, but task forces organized for a particular expedition and reorganized or disbanded after its completion.[4] However, here was the seed from which more elaborate commercial enterprise emerged.

Emergence of company ventures

With the invention of the magnetic compass and the subsequent discovery of the New World, trade expanded rapidly and its organization took new forms. The greater investment for long voyages, the size of the newly discovered riches, and the rising governmental ambitions in overseas area forced the merchants to band together in commercial companies to pool their resources and share the risks, and also to capitalize on the political opportunities which were opening up for strong organizations capable of governing colonial lands. Thus, the commenda gradually transformed into *commandite,* the initial form of permanent commercial enterprises. Their basic scheme provided for one active partner, who conducted the business and was personally responsible for it, and several inactive partners, who furnished the capital and shared in the results.

Parallel with the development of trade, the first institutional structure of international finance developed with its base in Italy. Three powerful groups of Italian financiers—the Medici, the Grimaldi, and the Peruzzi—established agencies in Rome, Lyons, Bruges, Paris, Antwerp, London, and

3 Miriam Beard, *A History of the Businessman* (New York: The Macmillan Company, 1938), p. 58.

4 Max Weber, *General Economic History* (New York: P. F. Collier, Inc., 1961), p. 159.

other centers throughout Europe. These agencies were not mere correspondents. They were comparable to branch banks in that they received deposits, granted loans, and engaged in other banking transactions. The structure of these financial groups, or *maggiori,* as they were called, consisted of a combination of separate partnerships controlled by the same groups of senior partners. They thus resembled modern holding companies. Many of their clientele were kings and lesser sovereigns who were in need of arms and military supplies. "Nothing is, in fact, more revelatory of the internationalism of business in Renaissance Europe than the manner in which the British equipped themselves with the arms, which they could not possibly have made themselves, for raising their military might above those who supplied them.... Armor was made in Nürnberg or Augsburg, sold perhaps in Venice or Milan and smuggled out of Antwerp, ostensibly on the Spanish side, with the aid of agents of Spain, and paid for by money raised from all regions."[5] However, despite their great power and international outlook, the participation of the maggiori in the affairs of the state and of the Church eventually led them to direct involvement in military campaigns which ultimately met with disaster.

Whether the maggiori should be ranked as the first manifestation of business internationalism or whether they should not because they predated the modern idea of national loyalty remains a moot point. Except in England, no sense of nationalism existed among the merchant class. But with the rise of national states the situation reversed itself.

Colonial enterprise

The nationalistic state did not tolerate political indifference. Commerce and finance were subordinated to the nationalistic aspirations of the state and were rewarded for support and cooperation with exclusive rights. This practice led to monopolistic enterprise. In the colonizing countries, giant commercial companies emerged which were granted by the government the exclusive right not only to trade with a particular colony but also to exercise the political powers of the state in the territory involved. The best-known commercial companies of that era were the British East India Company, the Levant Company, the Dutch East India Company, and the Hudson's Bay Company. The following quotation reflects the nature and scope of their activities: "The merchants of this company [the British East India Company] received the entire rights over all of India that they could bring under their sway.... As its director, Sir Josiah Child, once boasted, the India Company was 'a sovereign state in itself. It declared war on the Mogul Empire, it had a fleet, an army, and fortified settlements, it could coin money and make laws. Businessmen administered India in their own fashion, and a very lively fashion it was for a long time.... This business administration of India was not ended until Victoria's reign.' "[6] In accordance with the mercantilist doctrine, these commercial companies exploited the colonies to supply the mother country with

5 Beard, *A History of the Businessman,* p. 59.

6 P. T. Ellsworth, *The International Economy* (New York: The Macmillan Company, 1964), p. 33.

raw materials that could be converted into manufactures for export or be substituted for imports. Colonies were therefore considered an economic appendix to the home country and regulated to serve its interests. Trade was closely controlled through the commercial companies and through strict navigation laws which aimed to centralize all colonial trade upon the metropolitan home country and to prevent diversion to other areas. Economic development in the colonies was limited to products wanted in the metropolitan country for consumption or reexport; duplication of the metropolitan industries and development of competing products were suppressed.

Industrial Revolution

The advent of the Industrial Revolution marks the downturn of the influence of the colonial companies. Government functions were differentiated from business activities and gradually taken away from the companies. The specialization and the concentration of production which the new factory system encouraged forced the nations to abandon self-sufficiency and to depend more on foreign trade. As a consequence the mercantilist philosophy, which to that time had dominated international economic relations, was replaced by the concept of free trade expounded by Adam Smith and other classical economists. However, colonial trade still remained under the close control of the metropolitan country. This was especially true for primary producers, which were kept entirely dependent upon the metropolitan markets, such as England, France, and Holland.

The new methods of organization and production introduced by the Industrial Revolution required skills which were unavailable in the colonial areas. European administrators, technicians, and skilled workers had to be attracted to the colonies. Whereas in the earlier periods permanent settlement had been limited to the Americas and colonial capital was often kept in a floating form ready to be withdrawn on a short notice, investments in the nineteenth century were set up on a more permanent basis. They took the form of subsidiary operations of metropolitan trading or manufacturing companies in need of raw materials. More than any previous development, these colonial subsidiary arrangements of nineteenth-century metropolitan firms foreshadowed the modern multinational corporation.

The key resemblance between the two is the transfer of capital, knowhow, and people to permanent operations in overseas areas. But similarities are hard to find in objectives and methods. As already indicated, the central purpose of the colonial business establishment was the search for raw materials for the metropolitan company. Only incidental attention was paid to development of the economies of the colonies themselves. Instead of being integrated in the local economy as the modern multinational corporation is, the colonial subsidiary formed an economically as well as a socially insulated enclave which cohabitated with, rather than participated in, the native economy. The effects of its investments—expansion of income, markets, skills, techniques, and other external economies—took place not where the investment was physically located, but where it originated—in the metropolitan country. As H. W. Singer succinctly puts it, these extractive facilities "never became a part of the internal economic structure of those underdeveloped countries themselves, except in the purely geographical and physical sense."[7] One might say that they were domestic operations located abroad.

Another difference from multinational operations, which also stresses the domestic character of the colonial operations, was the virtual absence of risk and uncertainty in the colonial environment. The task of local officials was to protect the metropolitan interests, and the legal environment in which the colonial companies operated was more domestic than foreign. All negotiations, contacts, and communications were with the Europeans rather than with the indigenous populations.

A third difference is that the colonial investments were geared directly to specific natural resources, especially minerals and tropical plantation agriculture. In Africa, for instance, two-thirds of the total foreign capital invested between 1870 and 1936 went to the mineral districts[8] and much of the rest went into tropical fruits, nuts, and forest products. The colonial affiliates were almost exclusively in the extractive industries and conspicuously not in the manufacturing and service industries.

Finally, there is a fundamental contrast in marketing and finance. Since the principal goal of the colonial-enterprise complex was to supply materials for processing and sale at home, the parent company staffed the affiliates with production and physical-operations specialists. Marketing and financial questions were left to the metropolitan headquarters. In a multinational enterprise, the reverse is usually true; the overseas affiliate is first of all utilized for marketing purposes and often also plays an important financial role, especially in areas where currency restrictions and political uncertainties prevail, while the production function follows at a later stage. And, when it does, the production is oriented to serve first the indigenous market and second the natural export markets of the country rather than the interests of the headquarters country.

The Start of Multinational Enterprise

In the nineteenth century, the problem of industry was that of maximizing production. The demand arising from an extraordinary population increase and from industrial growth kept the European market in a chronic state of undersupply. Today the industrial world faces a different situation. The production plant is no longer dependent on heavy and bulky coal; mass production and automation have been mastered; and the capabilities for immense outputs have been achieved. The problem now is marketing—to develop

[7] "Foreign Investment in Underdeveloped Areas: The Distribution of Gains between Investing and Borrowing Countries," *American Economic Review,* XXXX, No. 2 (May 1950), 476.

[8] Richard D. Tobinson, *International Business Policy* (New York: Holt, Rinehart & Winston, Inc., 1964), p. 15.

the uses, users, and markets to match the production power. The consumer has become the prime mover. Even extractive industries must shift from the search for raw materials to that for markets, as is reflected in this quotation:

> At the end of one five-year period after World War II, the Standard Oil Company (N.J.) reported that, whereas the overseas market had formerly absorbed 35 per cent of its sales, it was now taking up 65 per cent. This company, first seeking wealth underground, found new riches on the surface: local consumers. Now, while it still competes for new fields and wells, it is strangely engaged in a battle for its share of foreign markets, for other oil companies have responded in like fashion to the new attraction of foreign buying power.[9]

Furthermore, the colonial empires have crumbled. The preferential treatment and political protection upon which the nineteenth-century enterprise system was founded have been submerged by the rise of new nations and the spread of nationalism throughout most of the world.

Canadian Ventures. Like the United States and Germany, Canada adopted a protective attitude and imposed high tariffs. This policy represented a departure from British free-trade views and was based on the "infant-industry" argument. However, unlike the German and U.S. objectives, the purpose of Canadian protectionism was to entice capital investments from foreign enterprises to accelerate its economic growth. To a considerable degree, the policy was effective, and foreign investment in Canadian plants and other productive facilities ensued. Among the first were duPont's purchase of two Canadian power mills in 1876 and the Edison Company's Canadian branch in 1883, which subsequently became the Canadian General Electric Company.[10] The significance of the Canadian ventures was that for the first time in history, foreign-owned companies were accorded substantially the same rights and privileges under formal charters of incorporation as were domestic firms. This was a large step toward multinational enterprise.

European Ventures. In Europe the first breakthrough was made by the Swedish inventor and industrialist Alfred Nobel, who founded the first foreign branch plant in Hamburg, Germany, in 1866. The prime motive for local manufacture in this case was a technical one—to avoid long-distance transporting of explosives, a task the carriers of the time were ill-prepared to do. The Hamburg plant was followed by others. However, Nobel did not set up any comprehensive international organization. The only connecting link among his various companies was his personal financial and managerial interest in them.

Another European innovator in international business was William Lever of Britain. He founded the Lever Brothers Company, which he later merged with a Dutch group of margarine companies called the "Margarine Unie" to form the now-global Unilever Company. But unlike Nobel, Lever was a true

9 Thomas Aitken, Jr., *A Foreign Policy for American Business* (New York: Harper & Row, Publishers, Inc., 1962), p. 25.

10 Howe Martyn, *International Business* (New York: Crowell Collier and Macmillan, 1964), p. 29.

pioneer of international business organization. Since protectionism prevailed in many countries and since margarine was perishable and was often damaged in storage and transit, Lever acquired facilities for local manufacture and distribution in foreign countries. In this he was eminently successful. A multinational corporate family emerged, bound together not only by Lever's personal participation but also by an organizational structure tailored to its needs. The international structure of this diversified complex of marketing and production enterprises was solidified under Lever's successor, Sir d'Arey Cooper, who decentralized operating control and delegated much policy-making authority to regional and functional specialists of the firm.[11] As a consequence, Unilever evolved into a truly multinational company which now operates in 60 countries.

Following the Lever example, a number of other European companies, including such contemporary giants as Nestlé, Imperial Chemical, Degussa, Philips, Ericson Telephone, and Royal Dutch-Shell, started organizing on a multinational basis. The search for new markets combined with the resurgence of protectionism in the interwar period provided a continuing impetus for this trend.

Early International Ventures of U.S. Business

Throughout its colonial era the United States had served England as an agricultural outland to supply the metropolitan motherland with cheap food and raw materials. The British imperial policy aimed to prevent industrial development in its colonies and to limit their trade to the imperium, centered on London, by severely taxing extraimperial trade through a punitive system of tariffs. Nevertheless, a considerable amount of industrial development did take place in the American colonies. When independence came the newborn nation had already achieved what at least in the terms of the late eighteenth century passed as a semiindustrial stage. The enormity of the new nation and its rapidly growing home markets fully absorbed all indigenous industrial energies for the first one hundred years of its existence. Export and import trade developed, but very little else. It was, therefore, only toward the end of the nineteenth century that American business made its debut on the international business scene.

Markets for Inventions

Unlike the European colonial companies, the early U.S. direct investors abroad were not seeking raw materials and foodstuffs but markets and profits. The frontier to the West was still open and untold natural treasures remained untapped. There was no shortage of natural resources. Technology and markets, however, were another matter. Interestingly enough, the search for technology

[11] Gilbert Burck, "Unilever—III: The Conversion," *Fortune,* XXXVIII, No. 2 (February 1948), 78.

led also to the discovery of new markets to technological inventions and ultimately to foreign manufacturing operations. The American companies that pioneered in multinational industrial operations in the late nineteenth century invariably received their initial impetus from some technical inventions or product which, on one hand, confronted it with the opportunity to acquire a legal monopoly on an almost global scale through patent rights, and on the other hand, impelled it to establish foreign-based production facilities to prevent local imitators from preempting these markets. In those days the main markets lay almost wholly in Europe.

Thus we find among the first U.S. direct foreign investors manufacturers of sewing machines, telephones, electric lamps, airbrakes, and cameras, all of which had sprung from American inventions or innovations. Singer obtained a patent on his sewing machine in 1851; fifteen years later his company broke ground with its first overseas factory in England. As the patent came under heavy competitive pressure in the continent, Singer affiliates in other European countries followed in a rapid succession. From this has emerged the company's present global network of affiliates and facilities.

The Western Union telegraph, Bell Telephone, and Edison's electric lamps, as well as his subsequent central station power generating equipment, and National Cash Register had almost identical early histories, though in their later development each moved along a different path. Each was based on an invention, acquired patents, and proceeded to establish its corporate presence in Europe to prevent competition from cashing in on the invention.

Not too different were the cases of Westinghouse and Kodak. George Westinghouse was first to perfect the airbrake, which was to revolutionize railroad transportation of his day. Since this occurred when railroad networks were introduced or significantly expanded in all civilized countries, his product had an immense ready-made market. In a few years the company's operations spanned the European continent from London, England, to St. Petersburg, Russia.

Kodak had built the first successful American camera. When he in the 1890's linked up with Eastman's photographic plate firm of England, a marriage was consummated from which the present world-wide Eastman Kodak company has evolved.

Among other late nineteenth-century American manufacturers who entered into international business were International Harvester agricultural machinery, Otis brothers' elevators, Babcock and Wilcox boilers, Remington typewriters, Burroughs calculators, Yale cylinder locks, and Colt guns. Again, they all were motivated by the particular technical advantages that derived from patentable inventions.

Oil Companies

Oil companies were catapulted to a global orbit by the perfection of the internal combustion engine which completely revolutionized transportation. Both the motive and the method for international expansion in this industry were quite different from what we have been discussing to this point. The initial push for oil companies to globalize was the search for oil; and although the search for markets has been added to it in the more recent past, the oil companies have remained, essentially, seekers and exploiters of petroleum resources in their main international ventures. In this they bear a close resemblance to the colonial companies whose shadow has never ceased to haunt them.

Legal Impetus

A new impetus to internationalize was provided by the Sherman Antitrust Act of 1890. This law prohibited collusion among business firms in restraint of trade. The rapid industrialization of the American economy in the second half of the last century had inflicted the society with clandestine monopolistic schemes to bleed the consumer and to threaten the economic as well as social health of the nation.

In an attempt to curtail the corporate malpractices, the Sherman Act prohibited cartels, trusts, and other collusion in restraint of trade among business firms that were potential competitors. Business responded to the law in two ways. First, since cooperation was outlawed but mergers were not, a wave of corporate mergers swept the land which in a short time brought into being a number of large firms in the U.S. These represented unprecedented concentrations of corporate power. Their expansionary force was soon felt abroad when the American "mammoths," as U.S. corporations are still often called abroad, embarked upon the practice of buying up foreign firms. Although temporarily interrupted during periods of political upheavals such as the two world wars, the policy of acquiring foreign-based affiliates has continued to date with an ever accelerating momentum.

Cartellistic Advantage

In the early days, the U.S. judicial authorities interpreted the Sherman Act as being limited in its scope to domestic business activities. Collusion, including formal cartel agreements between American firms or between American and foreign firms, was a matter of official indifference as long as such actions were taken abroad and did not directly affect the domestic market. Thus monopolistic collusion, outlawed in the United States by the Sherman Act, could be practiced with impunity in foreign markets by American firms. This provided a special stimulus for international expansion. It also broadened the base for such expansion. While the direct foreign investors to this point had been primarily manufacturers of patentable products, they were now followed by traders in nonpatentable goods and service industries in search of special marketing advantages. Their sudden appearance sharply underscores the lure that the relatively greater freedom to engage in market-sharing, price-fixing, and competitive retaliation seemed to have offered. Life insurance companies were the first to appear on the scene and rapidly enveloped all European empires during the 1880's and 1890's. Ocean shipping was not far behind. It started with J. P. Morgan's purchase of Leyland Shipping Lines in 1901 and was quickly followed by others.

In the biased interpretation of the antibusiness historian, these turn-of-the-century foreign ventures of American business were motivated by insatiable corporate appetites and fueled by illicit schemes and monopolistic manipulations. The opposite bias of company historians (always paid agents of the company involved) invariably ascribe the rise of the early American business ventures abroad to dynamic and brilliantly resourceful management, aggressive and imaginative marketing, and superior efficiency in production and service. While both biases harbor a grain of truth, each not only overstates its point but ignores the other side of the coin completely.

It has also been speculated that since Europe in those days was incomparably more advanced and sophisticated than the young, ex-colonial United States, business leaders as individuals received a deep sense of personal satisfaction from being able to score a success in the old world. This was to have made the major league. Any study of personal biographies of American business leaders of that era would confirm that a very large majority did, indeed, aspire for European connections and recognition and that most spent both wealth and effort in this pursuit. Yet, any direct connection between such personal aspirations and corporate goals has escaped documentation.

Foreign Operations Atypical to Early Industry. Although a number of American firms did move abroad in the early years, they were a small minority. The vast majority of firms were preoccupied with a growing domestic market. The principal exceptions were oil companies, mining companies, and some tropical agriculture plantations. At the end of 1940, U.S. direct investments amounted to $7 billion, most of it in petroleum properties. Very few U.S. firms had invested in overseas manufacturing ventures designed to supply the local markets. The immensity of the domestic market was still overwhelming, and isolationism mitigated against international business relations.

Recent Expansion

World War II changed many things, including the international business relations of the United States. The contacts, experiences, and necessities thrust upon both individuals and firms as part of the nation's war effort became the spawning grounds for new attitudes and approaches to international trade, investments, and corporate operations. U.S. business embarked upon internationalization as a continuous, long-range process.

Direct Foreign Investments. Direct foreign investments, which in 1943 stood at $7.9 billion, shot up to $11.8 billion by 1950. This 50-percent increase was attributed to postwar dislocations and other abnormalities, which had to be overcome to reconvert the world economy to civilian production. In part at least this must have been true. The Marshall Plan, Point Four, and other foreign-assistance programs played a role in the international investment activity of that period, as will be shown later. But this was only the beginning. By 1966 the figure stood at $55 billion, having nearly quintupled in the fifteen-year interval, and in 1969 the U.S. government reported $71 billion as the official amount and for 1972 the estimates ran between $75 and $77 billion. If anything close to these rates of increase continues, the volume of American direct foreign investments will pass the $100-billion mark in the mid-1970's. From the prewar base the growth is reflected in the following index numbers:

Year	*Index 1936 = 100*
1919	58.3
1929	112.5
1936	100.0
1950	176.2
1957	377.5
1964	662.7
1970	1060.5

In terms of activity, the greatest growth of U.S. involvements in foreign business has been in manufacturing, which now accounts for more than two-fifths of all U.S. direct investments. In the second place is the petroleum industry with about one-fifth, followed by mining and smelting as a distant third with less than 10 percent of the total. Public utilities, construction, and miscellaneous other industries—many related to infrastructure—make up the rest.

In terms of geography, Western Europe with 33 percent and Canada with 31 percent dominate the picture. Europe has gained significantly since the creation of the Common Market. The relative importance of Latin America has declined correspondingly; the area now has less than 20 percent of the total. Japan, whose importance is on a sharp increase, is likely to overtake Latin America in volume of U.S. direct investments in the next few years.

Economic theory postulates that the movement of productive factors is guided by their relative scarcities, which determine their marginal productivities at different localities. Since capital is very scarce relative to labor and land in developing countries, the theory-based prediction would visualize direct investments to flow primarily from the developed to the less-developed parts of the world. Actual data do not conform with the theoretical expectation. American direct investors have found the industrial countries of Western Europe, Canada, and Japan incomparably more attractive than the less-developed areas. Nearly four-fifths of U.S. direct foreign investments have gone to the industrial countries and only one-fifth to the developing nations—many official inducements not withstanding. A similar preference is reflected in the foreign investment statistics of other industrial countries. The tendency of capital to avoid and often even to escape from the poor countries is an old economic paradox to which we shall return in later chapters.

SALES. Since official reporting systems are yet to be designed for accurate statistics on international business activities other than export-import and payments transactions, even experts lack firm figures regarding the sales of U.S.-owned foreign businesses. This leaves the matter open for speculation and estimation. Dependent on assumptions made and methods used widely varying estimates have been produced. Close to the low end are the U.S. Department of Commerce estimates which cover manufacturing and mining affiliates only; for 1968 this figure was $51.8 billion. The government considers an affiliate to be American if 25 percent or more of its equity is owned by a U.S. parent. On the high end are some private studies which claim a much greater total. A reasonably good guess puts the current annual sales of U.S. business affiliates abroad in the range of $130 to $160 billion. This estimate drops the 25 percent equity requirement and includes not only manufacturing and mining establishments but also all other types of subsidiaries, branches, joint-venture enterprises, licensees, construction contracts, and contract management arrangements such as those used by hotel and other service industries.

GROSS PRODUCT. A popular method to measure the size of American industry abroad is to compute its annual output of goods and services as a ratio of its investments. The ratio applied varies from 2 : 1 to 2.5 : 1. On this basis the gross product of all U.S. business establishments abroad would fall between $142 and $177.5 billion for 1971. If portfolio investments, nearly $20 billion, are added the total value of American-financed foreign production would reach the range of $180 to $225 billion in 1971. Rough as such simplistic methods are, they nevertheless help us to form an order of magnitude in this vast new aspect of international reality.

The investment figures are but one indication of the internationalization process of U.S. business and, at that, a deceiving one, for as going concerns, most overseas affiliates' worth vastly exceeds their initial investment as well as their book value. Furthermore, the figures have a strong downward bias. Both tax and local charter restrictions encourage companies to use accounting concepts that minimize their assets. Nondisclosures, inadequacies of the reporting system, and the limiting definitions used by government statisticians also compress the investment figure.

PROFITS. Profits of foreign affiliates are another indicator of the international growth of U.S. business. For the war and early postwar years profit figures were highly erratic and are difficult to interpret because of the peculiar circumstances surrounding them. From 1950 to 1969 aggregate overseas earnings nearly quintupled by rising from $2 billion to over $9 billion.[12] For the decade of the 1960's, rate of return on all direct foreign investments averaged 13 percent per year as compared to 11.5 percent for domestic investments. Yields in less-developed countries were considerably higher, mostly due to petroleum.

[12] Computed from U.S. Department of Commerce data.

Since many affiliates represent very recent investments, their yields have not reached their full potential trend, and even higher yields can be expected in the 1970's. It is interesting to note also that the profits of foreign affiliates have been less subject to fluctuation than domestic profits.

The tendency of published records is to undervalue the actual earnings for tax and political reasons. Another limiting factor in the profit data is their dependence on internal decisions regarding transfer prices, costs, and accounting methods. It may be argued, however, that corporate judgments in such matters vary enough to cancel out any overall bias. This, one must admit, is not a very convincing argument, because matters such as currency-control legislation and general business conditions tend to produce a similar effect on all companies in a particular country and thus to prejudice their action in the same way.

Behind the aggregate profit data lie some spectacular achievements by companies which have pioneered in the international field. A study by Walter Stern shows that a group of 37 U.S. companies depends to the following extent on foreign operations:[13]

Foreign net income as percent of total net income:	49.3
Foreign net assets as percent of total net assets:	35.1
Foreign sales as percent of total sales:[14]	33.1

Shift in Emphasis. Another characteristic of postwar international expansion has been the escalation of direct investments from primary to secondary and even to tertiary levels of production. Investments in mining and smelting have increased in dollar volume but declined relative to aggregate investment. Petroleum investments, although bypassed by manufacturing investments, remain a major component. Both the mining and particularly the petroleum figures conceal the escalation effect since, in contrast to earlier periods, their foreign operations have been shifted more and more from serving the U.S. market with crude and semicrude products to meeting overseas requirements for finished goods both locally and on an export basis. For example, petroleum-industry affiliates have reduced their exports to the United States to below 1 percent of their total annual sales. The shift in marketing objectives has been accompanied by changes in product mix and an increase of emphasis on nonextractive aspects in vertically integrated companies. To what extent such intraindustry escalation will continue cannot be predicted. However, the phenomenon should be kept in mind in using and interpreting investment data.

Experience in Other Countries. Business firms in other industrial countries have also shown a growing tendency to internationalize. Even some semideveloped countries can now lay claim to being headquarters countries for one or more multinational companies. The value of direct foreign investments of non-American firms for 1972 was estimated to be about $74 billion.

[13] "U.S. Direct Investments Abroad," *Financial Analysts Journal,* XXI, No. 1 (January–February 1965), 96.

[14] Only 22 of the 37 companies disclosed foreign sales.

Added to the U.S. companies' foreign holdings, this gives us a world total for direct foreign investments of $150 billion that produces an annual output of $375 billion.

A large share of the non-American companies' foreign investments have gravitated to the United States. Though extending back for many years, the foreign business investments in this country have shown a specially rapid growth since the mid-1960's. In 1971 the estimated total was between $14 and $15 billion. That sum is still relatively small in comparison with the size of the nation's GNP and with its own overseas investments. Yet the names such as Bayer, Ciba, Dunlop, Electrolux, Massey Ferguson, Nestlé, Olivetti, Pechiney, Shell, SKF, VW, and Yamaha reflect the diversity of business activities carried out by non-American companies in the United States. It is not coincidental that the acquisition of Atlantic Richfield by British Petroleum ranked as the largest international investment transaction of the world in 1969. Several other very sizable foreign acquisition prospects have made headlines in American press in the recent past, including Brown Bovari of Switzerland, Mitsubishi of Japan, ICI of England, BASF of Germany and scores of other companies from many countries.

Continuation and probable acceleration of the inflow of foreign direct investments to the United States are pointed up by the fact that more and more foreign firms have been setting up sales and service subsidiaries in this country, a step which is frequently followed by processing, assembly or complete production facilities a few years later.

Foreign portfolio investments in the United States approximate $25 billion, varying in value with price fluctuations in the securities market. When the U.S. stock market recovers from its current (1971–72) depression, this total will increase substantially.

10

Causal Factors of International Business Expansion

In the discussion of economic incentives for international business the central concern was the national advantage and disadvantage patterns. It was a macroview. This chapter focuses on the individual motivation of enterprises. From macroanalysis management can normally gain a first approximation of profitable or nonprofitable international ventures. But, for choosing concrete objectives and formulating policies, it has to narrow down the broad national patterns to the specifics relevant to its own case. Each company is a different microcosm characterized by a particular combination of resources and capabilities. Although this combination is seldom easily defined and is sometimes misinterpreted by management itself, it nonetheless is the ultimate source of any true managerial power and, as such, governs a company's specific advantages and disadvantages as opposed to those of the country as a whole. Indeed, the micro- and the macropatterns can at times be not only different but even conflicting. Competition, anticipations, aspirations, previous commitments, and many other factors may cause a company to set its own course at a particular point in time.

Long-Term Advantages

The objective here is not to catalogue such subjective combinations, which obviously are innumerable, but to survey the major advantages sought and compulsions felt by business managements in setting their international objectives. In this chapter the factors of long-time historic relevance are surveyed. A detailed discussion of the reasons for the contemporary rapid rise of the multinational firm follows in the next chapter.

Raw Materials

To start with an area on which both economic and managerial analysis closely agree, we will scan the search for raw materials and markets. The differences in resource bases explained in Chapter 4 make certain industries and companies dependent on imported raw materials and create for others cost-reduction opportunities through procurement from foreign sources. In general, the intensity of the search for raw materials varies with the nature of the enterprise. Resource-oriented firms have the strongest motivation to respond to international differences in the availability and the cost of materials. Oil companies, steel mills, and chemical plants provide well-known illustrations of this category. As some resources near depletion and rise in cost while others are being discovered, advantages derived from foreign procurement are subject to constant change.

When one moves from the raw-material-processing industries to complex manufacturing and refining enterprises where the inputs come from a wide variety of sources, the importance of any particular raw material tends to decline, if not from a physical at least from an economic standpoint, since the price of any one input in a multiinput operation is but a fraction of the total raw-material cost. Accordingly, such firms are less responsive to international price differentials but tend to react vigorously if the physical availability of some critical material is in question.

Markets

The search for markets has been another prime motive for international business operations. Historically this search has been strongest among two types of companies: those facing stiff competition or market saturation at home, and those capable of economies at outputs greater than the domestic market can absorb. Mechanization and automation offer increasingly greater possibilities for lowering per-unit costs through increased output (greater utilization of capital equipment) and thereby intensify the search for export markets in all industries affected by them. This intensification is particularly apparent in smaller countries, and, as will be explained later, it has been a major force for international economic integration in both Europe and Latin America.

It would be misleading, however, to imply that only these two types of industries have sought international markets. Particularly in recent years the search has become almost universal. Management in general has become more world oriented and has learned that, unlike domestic trade, which consists largely of the interchange of goods between businesses and consumers with similar standards, international trade can flourish on differences in production and consumption standards and, in this way, can provide alternatives and additives to the domestic market.

Although in the past firms contemplated markets for their existing product mixes, more recently they have often expanded their objectives. Rising living standards and changing fashions have outmoded many products and made them economically obsolete in industrial countries, while the demand for them continues in less-developed areas of the world. As the products become outmoded, so does most of the specialized machinery and equipment designed for their production. To avoid massive write-offs and scrapping of such equipment, management has sought, often successfully, to replace the losses in domestic sales through aggressive export campaigns.

Increased emphasis on research and development by U.S. management has created still another reason for the search for foreign markets because of the increasing number of new product possibilities it has yielded. What to do with these possibilities is rapidly becoming a major unresolved problem of U.S. business, which we will not deal with here in its entirety. A partial solution for more and more firms, however, is the development of product lines primarily or exclusively for particular markets abroad.

Industry Position

Among the basic criteria for managerial success is a company's position in its industry. Its rank is usually based on the volume of sales, but it may also be in terms of total assets, number of employees, or profits. A similar measure is the "share of the market" figure, which relates company sales to industry total (the ratio of company sales to industry sales expressed as a percentage) and ranks the membership of the industry on this basis.

To demonstrate its effectiveness, management normally strives for improvement of the company's industry position; maintenance of the status quo, that is, growing at the same rate as the industry, is considered the practical minimum. However, since competitors are pursuing the same objective, the success of one company means the failure of another in this relative sense. To make up losses at home, a company may have to go abroad as a last resort to protect its industry position. Others find foreign markets less rigid or more responsive (than the domestic scene) and look for growth in the international realm while being content with maintaining their share of the domestic market. More often than not, the desperation overseas moves have opened new corporate vistas that have engendered autogenous processes for subsequent international growth.

Head Start

For certain industries and companies expansion into international business has been fundamentally due to the fact that they gained a head start in a particular product line. Whether this was the result of extraordinary foresight or pure accident makes no difference. During the lead period the firm can decisively influence consumer concepts of the value and the utility of the new product and create "in its own image" the qualities, preferences, and loyalties that will form the pattern of the emerging market. It can, in other words, capture the new market not only as a supplier in the physical sense but also as the architect of the value system that will govern and direct its growth.

In theoretical terms these tendencies can be expressed as successive shifts in the cost and demand curves in Figure 10-1. The cost curve shifts downward and to the right as the pioneering enterprise develops more effective production techniques and machine tools to increase productivity. This gives the company an advantage over any potential competitor, who, lacking access to the advances made by the head-start firm, must begin with the C_0 cost schedule.

FIGURE 10-1

Successive Shifts of Cost and Demand Curves for Head-Start Firm

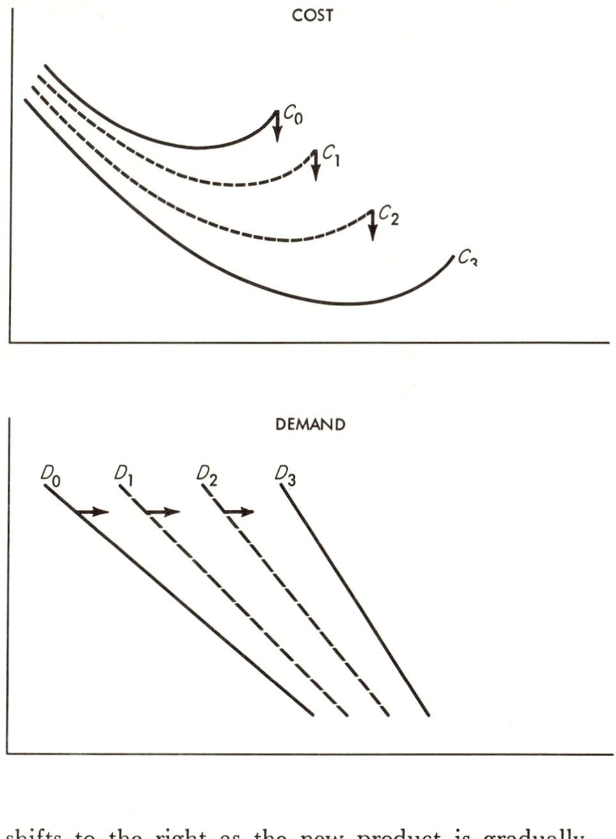

The demand curve shifts to the right as the new product is gradually adopted by the public as the standard for the industry. It also becomes more upright as the growing prestige of the product makes the demand for it less elastic. The more successful the firm is in building a dominant image, the more immune it will become to competitors' efforts to challenge its position. And, conversely, the more vulnerable will any prospective competitor be to the head-start firm's preemptive impact.

Numerous firms have been successful in building up such technical and marketing advantages, and they have maintained their leads over extended periods through constant technical improvements and vigorous marketing, including preventive promotion, which either thwarts competition in its infancy or requires from it massive effort and expense to make up the differences.

International expansion

Dominance in the domestic market compels international expansion. To preempt foreign markets before indigenous competition has emerged is an almost self-evident strategy, as is the tying up of key resources and of marketing channels. To prevent emerging foreign competition from becoming a menace, it must be challenged on its home ground; to fill foreign orders and to accept invitations to supply foreign requirements are natural reactions of any enterprise. Thus, the dominance gained by head-start firms has a built-in tendency to flow across international boundaries either because of the centrifugal force that the very dominance itself generates or because of the pull of the vacuum abroad.

Illustrations of such international business expansion are numerous. The most classic ones are these industries:

The *German optical industry* dominated world markets for several decades and has been seriously challenged only in the postwar period. Whether that challenge would have been possible without the wartime technical assistance of Germany to Japan and the early postwar control of German industry by foreigners is a moot point. The industry was completely divorced from any natural advantage in the sense of underlying resource endowments. Silica sand and ashes, the main ingredients of glass, are found in unmeasured quantities in all parts of the world; and the art itself ranks among the oldest of industrial skills. Yet, the German products were unmatched and their quality unduplicated. The key to this success, of course, was the head start that the German industry gained through a rather accidental incident—one man's strong avocation for optics.

The *British bone-china industry* has a similar history. It too is completely unrelated to any advantage in the physical resources of the country. Bones, linked with animal life, are distributed in all regions where life exists. Yet, only the British were able to produce and market bone china successfully, and to date they have remained the leaders in this field.

The *Swedish bearing industry* provides a somewhat different example. The SKF (Sovenska Kugellager Fabrikerna) bearings are still to be surpassed. It has been argued that Hitler did not occupy Sweden when he had control of the rest of Scandinavia mainly because he feared that the sources for bearing supplies, so important to his war machine, might be destroyed. Dependent on high-quality steel made from the exceptionally high-grade iron ore found in the deposits of the Dalarna region, this Swedish industry has a definite connection with the resource base. But, although not universal, high-grade ores do exist in a number of other countries. It must, therefore, not only be the ore but also, and perhaps more importantly, the specific techniques and the good reputation which have maintained the SKF legend.

The *French fashion industry* represents the ultimate in gaining and maintaining dominance in an industry on a world-wide scale. The nearest connection with the physical environment it has is its use of textiles. But to say that it depends on a specific fiber or fabric is totally fallacious. It is not the fabric that makes Paris fashion houses but the fashion houses which make or break the market for a fabric.

In spite of aggressive schemes to break its power, through imitation, substitution, and indifference, the French fashion industry continues to reign supreme. New York City, Rome, London, and Hollywood have emerged as open contenders to the throne, and a flock of other metropoles can claim a niche in the court of high fashion. Yet, there is no indication that the French lead has been cut at all. The other centers have merely gained from a general forward motion of the entire industry; all contestants have advanced, but their relative positions are unaffected.

The *Swiss watch industry* is another classic. All the metals that make up its material inputs must be imported. Skill in precision work has been the historian's explanation for the renown which the Swiss timepieces have the world over. Even if it were true in the past, this claim has no factual foundation in the lifetime of the present generation. Precision work of much greater complexity and finer tolerance than is required in watchmaking is now a precondition for manufacturing many modern products ranging from medical instruments to weapon systems. If the Swiss industry were to start today having available all the skill in precision work it now possesses but lacking the lead position and the production and marketing advantages, would it rise to the dominance that it now enjoys? No more than have the Swiss makers of computers, control instruments, or any other precision product. Indeed, prudent executives might view aspirations for such dominance as utterly eccentric.

The *complex-component industries,* such as automobiles, aircraft, television, weapons, and various modern production systems ranging from hospitals to oil refineries, can seldom produce all the components in their own facilities. At least some, and often the majority, of the components must be acquired through subcontracting and purchases. Many of the components are made by highly specialized branches of industry which require heavy capital investments and have relatively limited ways in which to employ their facilities. Their number is usually small even in large countries. Where can one find a multitude of manufacturers of automobile transmissions, TV picture tubes, or X-ray installations, not to mention jet engines, computers, or atomic reactors?

Because of the small number or the complete lack of component sources at home, manufacturers of complex-component products must turn to foreign suppliers. Such component procurement normally requires much closer cooperation with and involvement in the supplier's business than does importation of ordinary commodities because of the greater loss which would result if the component failed to function in the final product or if it were not delivered. The loss in such an event could far exceed the value of the component itself, as it would tie up the whole assembly process and possibly the entire production operation. A recent illustration is the near paralysis which a Swedish car maker suffered when Hardy-Spicer of Britain failed to come through with contracted deliveries of motors, for which it was the manufacturer's sole source. This company no longer depends on a single supplier or on a single country for its motors.

How many crises such as this have occurred and how many have been forestalled by managerial planning can only be surmised. But there is little doubt that the complex-component industries have all become internationally involved to a greater or lesser degree and that this involvement is being looked upon as normal rather than exceptional and as basic rather than supplementary to any domestic involvement. Even giants, such as Boeing, Radio Corporation of America, and Fiat, dare no longer depend on domestic self-sufficiency.

Product Life Cycle

Through deductive extrapolation the head-start phenomenon has recently been restated as the theory of the product life cycle. This theory postulates that at its introduction, the market for a given product is small and confined to high-income countries, because of the greater number of financially capable consuming units there than in the less-developed countries; that is, the primary markets for most new products are found in the most highly developed countries. And since the primary market and necessary subcontractors, capital, and technical imports also are in the developed countries, production will first remain limited to these countries. However, as overseas markets for the product grow, manufacturing locally becomes profitable. When this point is reached, the exporting company will be compelled to invest in overseas production facilities or either a local firm or some other foreign investor will preempt the opportunity.

Due to tariffs and transportation costs, the United States exporter would not be able to compete with the local producer and if not capitalizing on the investment opportunity itself would have to concede to others the earning capacity which they may later use to compete more effectively against the original producer of the product, even in its own home country. Thus, investment in multicountry production facilities becomes mandatory not only for retaining the market abroad but also for protecting the company's position in the headquarters country itself. While this concept is too narrowly based to be of value in explaining the motives to invest of all companies, it does provide a reasonable rationalization why market-oriented companies such as manufacturers of pharmaceuticals, foods, and so on, have shown an increasing tendency to replace export operations with multinational production facilities.

The expectations for changing production loci as a product goes through its life cycle are true basically on products in which there are substantial economies of scale in production. If there are not economies of scale, production is economically possible in many markets at early stages of the product life cycle. For example, products for which there are not large economies of scale in production would include some pharmaceuticals and certain processed foods.

Thus, the multinational firm is subject to two opposing pressures. First, there is a need for decentralization of engineering and product development in order to design or adapt products to each marketplace; and in opposition, there is the pressure for centralization regarding standardization of products. Along these lines different economies can be gained from quality and cost controls. It is possible, of course, that rather than the economics of the product cycle as postulated in this concept, it has been simply a function of corporate learning through export marketing to know the real overseas opportunities which have led the manufacturers to shift from exports to multinational production. Once the foreign market is known and the operational superiorities of the multinational firm understood, there remains not much need to rely on the product cycle concept, nor much to go through the export phase, before multinationalizing the production capacity of the firm.

Buy-National Requirements

Discrimination against foreign suppliers is a world-wide practice that may take many forms. Its most overt expressions are *buy-national* laws such as the Buy-American Act, Buy-Indian Act, and so on, which require government agencies including armed forces, postal service, and other public enterprises to limit their purchases to domestic sources unless specified (usually very substantial) price advantages can be gained. Less obvious are indirect regulations, for example patent laws that require that a patent be "worked" to maintain validity in a country, or industry regulations like the French railroad and German electric utility regulations, both of which make it exceedingly difficult to utilize any foreign suppliers. In its most covert form the official discrimination against nondomestic sources takes place in administrative practices and guidelines of which no accurate account exists.

Regardless of its form, the discrimination provides an inducement for potential foreign suppliers to establish indigenous operating affiliates to escape from the foreign classification. Westinghouse, for example, built its first factory in France to supply French railroads that lay beyond the reach of its facilities elsewhere. Similarly, Nobel built his explosive plants in several countries because domestic supply was officially insisted upon. Most any contemporary multinational firm can illustrate one or another incident of buy-national discrimination as the initial incentive for particular direct investments.

11

Causes of Ongoing Multinationalization

Expansion across international frontiers no longer characterizes exceptional corporate behavior but has since the 1950's become a generally pursued objective by business firms both in the United States and many other countries. Gone are the notions that investments abroad were to be justified in terms of something unusually compelling or exceptionally attractive. Also gone is the notion that export and import trades represent the only normal conduits to foreign markets. A new notion of normalcy which has literally crashed to the current business scene holds multinational operating structures as natural not only for resource-based industries and unique technical products but equally to all types of manufacturers and service industries from banks to consulting firms.

The change from the old to the new has been sudden—almost violent as such things go—and many of its incipient forces are yet to be unraveled. Such a fundamental change in the socioeconomic structure can seldom be fully explained contemporaneously; it requires distant view—a retrospect of time—for all factors to be identified, measured, and arranged. Nevertheless, a reasonably consistent pattern of causation has been emerging from a rapidly mounting volume of research on the multinational firm. The factors that have been instrumental in sparking and sustaining the new trends are in part environmental and in part managerial.

Environmental Reasons

Supporting the growth of factories, warehouses, and other affiliated establishments of U.S. companies are certain broad international developments which, although difficult to associate directly with any specific business action, have changed the overall context in which the opportunities and uncertainties of international business ventures are weighed by management.

Multilateralism

The most inclusive among the external changes has been the shift from bilateralism to multilateralism in international economic relations. Between the two world wars, business dealings among countries were handled bilaterally. A country negotiated separate, often exclusive, arrangements with each individual foreign nation, there being, at least in principle, as many different arrangements for such things as treaty provisions, trading rules, formal regulations, tax and entry privileges, measurement and valuation standards, and documentary requirements as there were other countries with which the nation maintained official economic relations. As a consequence an incredible maze of legislative and bureaucratic technicalities surrounded international transactions in most countries. These complexities acted not only as an invisible tariff, which reduced international business by raising its cost, but also as a deterrent to all but professional specialists to involvement in any kind of international business. The mere mechanics of international transactions were often insurmountable for the typical corporate executive. There were thus compelling operational reasons for channeling international trade transactions through export and import intermediaries and for depending upon the latter's leadership in the formulation of corporate policies in reference to overseas developments.

The deterring effects of bilateralism were not limited to the mechanics but went to the heart of international economic relations. For bilateralism provides a means for according different treatment to the products, investments, and enterprises of different countries; it is a vehicle for discrimination in international commerce. This discrimination manifested itself in many ways—in tariff and quota treatments for products from different countries; in foreign exchange regulations; in taxes and visas; and in many other aspects of international intercourse. As such, it interfered with the normal flow of goods, capital, and services, and created perverted patterns of international trade and investments. When this structure of invisible barriers was superimposed upon the highest visible trade barriers of any peacetime period, the total deterrent became a massive fortification against international trade.

Since the war, multilateralism has greatly reduced both visible and invisible barriers. The organizational vehicle for multilateralism has been the General Agreement for Tariffs and Trade, commonly referred to as GATT, to which nearly the entire noncommunist world now belongs. Its history and specific activities are treated in a subsequent chapter. But it is relevant to mention here that under the GATT format international trade matters are negotiated and settled in an open forum in Geneva, Switzerland, and any privileges granted by one country to another become automatically applicable to the entire membership.[1] This method prevents discrimination, at least in the formal schedules and rates or in whatever norms may be involved in the negotiations. By meeting together, the member countries have standardized many basic practices, procedures, performance standards, and to some degree even customs procedures. Thus, much of the invisible superstructure of trade barriers has been eliminated, and the execution of international transactions has been greatly simplified. This simplification explains the relative ease with which manufacturing concerns have been able to circumvent the foreign-trade middlemen and to absorb their functions in recent years. But, like bilateralism, multilateralism goes much deeper than the mechanics of international commerce. Its real meaning and value lie in minimizing the abnormalities and perversions and in enabling international business relations to develop according to the normal price and cost patterns rather than according to arbitrary restraints. Multilateralism has opened up new areas of profitable endeavor for business and industry and has paved the way for direct contact with and among operating facilities in foreign areas. Especially, it permits the different national affiliates of a multinational firm to specialize to trade among themselves, thus forming an integrated international system.

Foreign aid

Another factor which has facilitated the movement abroad of manufacturing concerns has been the massive U.S. aid which many foreign countries have received. Much of the aid dollar inevitably becomes a trade dollar when it is used for purchases by the recipient country. From the exports which the aid monies have generated have sprung many foreign factories, subsidiary companies, and joint-venture enterprises abroad.

Since helping other countries to industrialize has been one of the principal purposes of foreign aid, the U.S. government has often in the past enticed, and occasionally pressured, private enterprise to establish or operate productive facilities in some foreign country as its contribution to the aid program. Once abroad, a company has a tendency to stay, to grow, and to spread.

Communist threat

Still another external force giving impetus to the internationalization of business enterprise has been the imperialism of the two communist giants —the U.S.S.R. and China. The fear of this threat has compelled the free nations to tighten their military, political, and economic ties in order to find safety in collective action. Although not free from internal friction, the structure of joint defense against communist imperialism has been a formidable force not only for economic cooperation among governments but also for business participation in building the defense system. For, to have substance and strength, the free-world military alliances and geopolitical programs must

[1] The cornerstone of multilateralism is the most-favored-nation principle discussed in Part IV.

be reinforced by, if not based upon, close economic and business relations. Hence, the political and military *rapprochements* have engendered the same tendency in the business sphere.

Managerial Reasons

Reasons for initial direct investment

As part of a study of foreign-based affiliates a survey was conducted in 1959 of 104 international companies and their 533 affiliates.[2] The survey revealed that the motives which have impelled U.S. companies to initiate operations of permanent facilities abroad are often complex; instead of one single motive, several different factors may be responsible for a company's action. Since the motives did not lend themselves to meaningful classification, each company having its own peculiar combinations, the responses to the survey were tabulated in terms of the primary reason for establishing foreign-based affiliates. The results were as follows:

Primary Reasons	*Percent of Sample*
Legal restrictions (tariffs, quotas, etc.)	21
Lower cost of production (savings on labor, raw materials, or processing)	20
Inefficiency of native marketing institutions	14
Competition	12
Dissatisfaction with international middlemen	11
Long-range expansion policy	7
Invitation by foreign companies or governments	6
Tax advantages	4
Other reasons	5
Total	100

Thus the most important single reason for establishing company-controlled affiliate operations abroad has been governmental restrictions of trade. Among these, three are considered by business to be the most crucial: import restrictions, especially quantitative controls and licensing practices; monetary restrictions, including the availability of dollars for foreign imports and the artificial exchange rates; and priorities given to goods originating in soft-currency countries. To minimize these difficulties firms have decided to get behind the barriers by operating from within the respective markets. Invariably these companies have extended their foreign operations beyond marketing activities in order to identify their products with a soft-currency area and profitably to employ their inconvertible funds accumulated abroad.

The decrease in costs obtained through employment of local labor and raw materials has been the second inducement for international expansion. Companies which depend heavily on manual labor, which have internal econo-

2 See Endel J. Kolde, "Les fonctions des sociétés affiliées domiciliées à l'étranger dans la structure administrative d'une enterprise commerciale internationale," *Revue Economique et Sociale* (December 1962), pp. 154–84.

mies limited in size, which patronize foreign sources of supply, or which have any combination of these benefit from this opportunity. As may be expected, such companies have been eager to decentralize their production facilities, which normally set the pattern for their marketing organization also.

The third reason has been the inability of foreign marketing institutions to provide intensive coverage of the market and aggressively to promote the products of the U.S. exporter. In this respect the most common complaints are difficulties in synchronizing domestic and foreign programs when they are not centrally administered and particularly in inducing the foreign distributors to adopt modern marketing methods. As a result, the competitive position of a company has, as measured by its "market share," often been endangered. Competition appears to have increased sharply in most foreign areas since the mid-1950's because of local industrial development, the more aggressive export policies of Japan and the European countries, and direct investment enterprises. In certain instances, pressure has developed for on-the-spot processing and service facilities because of changes in market and in consumer expectations.

Dissatisfaction with international middlemen stems from similar problems, with the additional complaint that their efforts are often spread over several types of merchandise or over several countries or both, a situation which does not permit sufficient concentration on any particular manufacturer's line or market.

To be able to compete more effectively with local and international adversaries is another principal reason companies have established amalgamated operating units abroad. Although given as the principal reason by only 12 percent of the firms studied, it was listed among the top three reasons by 62 percent and as a contributing reason by another 16 percent. Depth interviewing revealed that more decisive than price rivalry in this regard are the nonprice aspects of competition, particularly credit terms, prompt delivery, ability to accept small orders, and customer services. All these, of course, require local representation and warehouse facilities to avoid unwarranted risks and excessive costs of operation. Also, continuous contact with the market is important for quick adjustments to changing market conditions and for counteracting competitors' promotional measures before they can cause shifts in customers' patronage.

These four sets of reasons—lower production costs, inefficiency of local market institutions, competition, and dissatisfaction with international middlemen—all are closely interrelated and have a common denominator in their ultimate objective, which is to increase operating efficiency. Together, these four factors had motivated the establishment of 57 percent of the foreign-based affiliates included in the sample studies.

By accepting legalistic restrictions as environmental conditions beyond the control of business enterprise, regardless of how arbitrary they may seem from an economic point of view, one must regard them too as impediments to operating efficiency and thus must combine them with the other four factors. When this is done, it is seen that 78 percent of the foreign-based affiliates emerged from the drivefor better and more economical cultivation of overseas markets, i.e., the drive for increased efficiency.

Reasons for expansion and growth

A follow-up survey in 1965 probed not so much the original reasons for entering foreign areas as the incentives for their continued growth and proliferation. Special attention was paid to the actual experiences as contrasted with the preconceived expectations that executives might have held before their company's international involvement.

Classified into four broad categories, the advantages gained through having operating affiliates in different foreign countries, as revealed by the survey, are as follows:

1. MARKETING INCENTIVES

1.1 No tariffs or quotas

1.2 Lower cost of transportation

1.3 Lower inventory requirements and savings on warehousing (economic distance between point of production and point of consumption shorter)

1.4 Easier to serve market—no long preplanning required

1.5 Easier to conduct market research

1.6 Easier to plan and execute advertising campaigns

1.7 Less sales resistance (This was applicable to about 50 percent of respondents. Ten percent had the opposite experience. Both product and country seem to affect this point.)

Strategic Flexibility

Having a resident affiliate in each country provides the multinational firm with the capability to adjust its marketing strategies within wide ranges whenever conditions demand. Unlike the uninational firm, it depends neither on international trade controls nor on domestic sourcing limitation. This is not to say that it is immune to changes in trade controls or in sourcing possibilities; only that the multinational firm possesses means for compensating for these changes which its uninational competitor lacks. If and when the conditions warrant, the multinational firm markets across international boundaries and consolidates several national markets; but under different conditions, it can move in the opposite direction and segmentize its marketing operations into sharply segregated national markets, for example when either trade barriers or other factors make this optimal. Between these two extremities lies a wide range of possible strategies which are available to the multinational firm. They may be varied in reference to degrees of national market segmentation as well as to different regions of the world.

Such a broad range of options for realizable strategies provides the multinational firm with a high degree of immunity against environmental adversities, be they internal business conditions of a country, restrictive governmental policies, or disturbances in international affairs.

This flexibility is not limited to marketing of already established products but extends also to new product introductions as well as to other marketing innovations. Thus it encompasses all the developmental aspects which constitute marketing dynamics in economics terminology. Take for example the introduction of a new product. The multinational firm can choose from among a wide variety of different countries the market in which to test the product. For a typical consumer product, the initial testing might be done in a small country such as Belgium, Denmark, or Finland where regional variances in demand characteristics are small and where the preexistence of highly refined statistical information provides an environment for completing the tests at relatively low cost. In contrast, the uninational company has hardly any alternative to its own home market to do the testing regardless how well- or ill-suited that may be in a given ease. The lack of own marketing capacity precludes other countries from serving as operationally acceptable test markets.

2. PRODUCTION INCENTIVES

2.1 Lower plant construction cost
2.2 Lower wage costs including fringe benefits
2.3 Better quality control
2.4 Availability of specialized skills (e.g., design, fashion, artistry)
2.5 Easier to meet engineering standards
2.6 Easier to adapt product to local consumption requirements
2.7 Procurement economies (cost of raw materials and parts lower)
2.8 Availability of special raw materials
2.9 Transportation economies (freight rates lower on raw materials than on finished goods)

Potentially the greatest operation superiority of the multinational firm over its uninational rival lies in its ability to combine marketing and production arrangements throughout the world in an optimal fashion, that is, it need not limit its choice to completely customized and globally standardized models, but can choose modular designs in which certain modules or subassemblies are standardized globally, others continentally, and still others to specific countries or even subsections of a country. This enables it to achieve any desired degree of customization to individual country consumption requirements without sacrificing the economies of mass producton and international specialization. The multinational company achieves economies of scale from mass-producing the global and continental modules at the same time it benefits from international specialization by having each module produced in the country possessing the most advantageous conditions for it.

For complex-component industries (automobiles, appliances, aircraft, computers, electronic systems, and so on) commonality is typically achievable in a significant share of components or subcomponents if production planning is focused on multinational maximization of their use. Business press reports that through the policies of emerging multinational firms in Europe "British, French, and Spanish companies are gradually being harmonized." Rootes announced that it will move toward a greater interchange of components, such as transmissions and engines, with Simca and Barreiros. This could lead to total commonality, which Ford has achieved with its Capri and Escort models produced in Britain and Germany.

"Commonality, which American companies . . . are building into their

European operations, permits them to shift production from one country to another as easily as production is juggled from one plant to another in the U.S. Ford already has been threatened with a slowdown by 150 British draftsmen who are protesting a transfer of some of their technical work to the Ford plant in Cologne." (*Business Week,* February 21, 1970, page 51.)

Only recently have multinational companies begun to understand the existence of this flexibility and to purposefully use the marketing superiorities flowing from this flexibility. In this new type of rivalry the uninational firm has found itself badly outmatched and outperformed. By combining sourcing and marketing motivities, the multinational company can greatly increase the number of options and alternatives over and above those available to a uninational form. This gives it superiority both in the efficiency of production and in the competitiveness of marketing.

3. FINANCIAL ADVANTAGES

3.1 Lower taxes and tax-deferral privileges (Tax savings can be used for reinvestment.)

3.2 Capital cost allowances for research and development

3.3 Greater depreciation allowances

3.4 Greater flexibility for moving earnings and assets from one country to another without incurring U.S. tax liability in the process (for example from a high-risk area to a more stable country)

3.5 Freedom in respect to timing the repatriation of earnings and to moving assets from one affiliate to another without prior clearance from the U.S. internal revenue officials

3.6 Higher rates of interest available for short-term holdings of company liquid assets

3.7 Access to local sources of capital—both equity and borrowed funds (emphasized only by smaller firms)

Cost of Capital

Both economic and regulatory determinants of the cost of capital vary internationally. Each country has its own structure of interest rates and, even more importantly, the changes within this structure seldom bear any direct correlation to interest rate patterns elsewhere. Divergencies in long-time trends are also often present. As a consequence, the cost of capital, be it short-, medium-, or long-term, can vary considerably from country to country at any particular point in time.

Besides interest rates, there are numerous regulatory and institutional factors that tend to further widen the range. Many countries have instituted programs to support or to subsidize certain types of investment programs; these may be limited to particular industries, to particular localities, to infrastructure projects, or whatever has been deemed important by the public authorities. The support itself may take the form of governmentally guaranteed low-interest loans, direct capital contributions (usually on a participation basis) of equity capital, reduction of taxes or complete tax holidays for a number of years, accelerated depreciation and write-off privileges, special allowances for research and development, foreign-exchange guarantees, and even governmental purchase contracts to assure a satisfactory return on the contemplated investment.

Thus, it is not only the cost of capital acquisition, but also its subsequent utilization and profitability which vary among countries. It is well to be reminded here that the real measure of cost is its ratio to return. If capital from different sources can produce the same return, then the obviously rational action is to carefully compare the acquisition costs for different sources of capital and to use the least-cost source. This is the typical textbook prescription which works quite well in a one-country context. In a multinational setting our calculus must go beyond the mere acquisition cost since the equal-return hypothesis no longer holds. That is to say, capital acquired in country A may be burdened with very different utilization costs because of different taxes, depreciation, restrictions, and so on, and be capable of earning quite different revenues due to governmental subsidies, support programs, purchase guarantees and the like than in countries B or C. In sum capital utilization is subject to international differences on three levels: the acquisition costs, the utilization costs, and the profitability expectations of capital, therefore, the financial possibilities available to the multinational firm can never be duplicated in any one-country context. The multinational firm, consequently, has a number of financial alternatives and options open to it which are unavailable to the uninational firm. These options must be looked upon as superior powers which a company derives from its multinational structure for otherwise they would not exist. They range through the whole spectrum of financial typologies, from short-term borrowing to equity investments on one side and from interest earnings on liquid holdings to payback periods and amortization rates on capital investments on the other side.

In financial literature the multinational firm is typically viewed as a foreign investor. In point of fact, an already established multinational firm is neither foreign nor necessarily a new entrant investor; rather, it holds a dual status being concurrently a resident enterprise and also a member of an international corporate family. Its investments normally have the purpose of expanding locally existing enterprises—its affiliates in the country—and do not cause new firms to enter the country from outside. The only exceptions are the investments made for expanding the territorial scope of the firm to new countries, which is the case primarily during the conversion from uninational to multinational structure. After that the push to enter any additional countries weakens rather abruptly and further outward expansion plays only a minor role in the firm's investment expenditures.

This is to say, the discriminatory regulations can retard a multinational company's activities only in its initial entry phase to a particular country. Thereafter, the restrictions act for its advantage by serving as a shield against other entrants and potential competitors. The rhetoric of discriminatory retardation of international investments must, therefore, be dismissed as inappropriate for explaining the financial motivities of the multinational firm. In the next section this point will be elaborated upon from another perspective.

Transferability of Funds

A uninational company is wholly dependent upon its home-country's constraints in reference to any international capital transfers, be they short- or long-term transactions. If there are no official restrictions this dependence becomes academic. If, however, restrictions do exist, as has been the case with the United States and many other countries, the uninational company's ability to respond to foreign opportunities or to participate in international ventures is accordingly curtailed. The tighter the regulations the greater is this constraining effect.

The multinational company, on the other hand, can develop a high degree of immunity to restrictive currency controls and need not lose its operational flexibility because of them. First, having separate juridic personalities in many countries—its different national affiliates—it has a wide range of choice as to which of these will act as the principal in any particular venture. If the U.S. exchange restrictions foreclose a particular undertaking, the Swiss or Swedish affiliate of the company may not be similarly constrained; and if no single national entity of the multinational firm can fully achieve the desired international objective, several of them may combine into a consortium to meet the need. Second, this juridic apparatus is reinforced by the multinational distribution of existing capital reserves as well as the potentialities to borrow. That is, the firm may, by an appropriate distribution of its capital reserves and borrowing, perform a wide variety of international investments, devestments, and transfers without violating the currency and exchange controls of any particular country, which may be wholly impossible for the uninational firm.

The superior flexibility is not limited to neutralizing the negative consequences of official restrictions. It applies equally in the case of official investment stimulation policies. Such programs as governmental investment guarantees, low-interest investment loans, tax holidays, special aid programs, and other official measures to stimulate economic growth have become commonplace in a multitude of countries. While varying widely in scope and continuity, the governmental support programs for growth have become an important source for corporate opportunities throughout the world. But only the companies who possess the flexibility for the inward transfers of the needed financial resources can capitalize upon them. Needless to add, the same is true for investment and growth opportunities unaffected by governmental measures.

4. GENERAL MANAGEMENT INCENTIVES

4.1 More promising growth alternatives for company than at home

4.2 Stabilization of earnings through diversification of markets and productive facilities

4.3 Outlet for technological slack (profitable reemployment of product ideas, techniques, facilities, and management skills threatened domestically by obsolescence)

4.4 Company image (*International* means "big league" business, hence, more significance than a national company has. Much of this effect seems to be simply the result of emulation.)

4.5 Better relations with suppliers, distributors, customers, and foreign government agencies

4.6 Access to foreign manpower

4.7 Access to technical innovations, research results, and product ideas of other countries (products licensed by parent for U.S. or third-country manufacturing)

4.8 "Localization" of administrative practices and procedures in terms of national custom

The survey also revealed that a strong new attraction for U.S. direct investments is the European economic integration movement. The prospects of having one or two mass markets with no internal trade barriers and a high standard of living seem to have exerted an immense pull on U.S. companies both big and small.

Impediments Versus Incentives

The plurality of the multinational business environment can, of course, also constrict managerial freedom and impose upon it new and different standards of behavior. Often the constrictive effects are illusory, in that they result from management's own attitude of not accepting the outside world in terms of its realities; attempts to suppress and change these realities to fit management's own culture-conditioned format create the difficulties. Once that rigidity is relaxed and greater understanding of the international environment is acquired, the constrictions tend to become new opportunities and incentives.

More tangible impediments to managerial freedom stem from legislation and from governmental regulations for business, which vary from country to country in countless ways. Tariffs and other import restrictions are among the most troublesome. But even here the inherent tendency of the multinational environment to create more alternatives often easily counterblances the rigidities and restraints. Tariffs, for example, are no longer visualized as insurmountable barriers to international business but as complications which may necessitate the entirely different approach of building foreign-based affiliates rather than pursuing exports.

The multinational environmental complex is not a static but a highly dynamic one. Its mutations defy description. Living standards zoom in some countries and stagnate in others, reshuffling market demand and variegating the opportunities for business expansion and new growth; indigenous industrial development takes hold and annihilates a previously lucrative export market but also opens new vistas for local manufacture as well as for exportation of the capital equipment needed in the industrial buildup. Population shifts, urbanization, resource discoveries, political changes, economic trends, and cultural developments all add to the volatility and rediversification of the multinational business scene.

Governmental Inducement

For various reasons governments at home and abroad have induced business enterprise to cooperate in public programs and to participate actively in carrying out certain government policies. Industrial development plans and programs for road building, power plants, and other projects to create a modern infrastructure require industrial know-how which the developing countries usually lack. To alleviate this problem their governments have invited American and European companies to cooperate in these efforts, either as principals or as partners, often on a guaranteed-return basis. Other countries have taken an indirect route by providing special advantages to foreign investors in their countries. They have initiated incentive programs to attract capital to boost their industrial growth. These programs affect corporate investment decisions in two ways. First, nearly always the program is given considerable publicity built around the natural advantages and business potentialities in the country concerned. Even though the assessments may be quite far from being perfect, publicity of the alleged advantages draws the attention of foreign enterprises, often leading to further studies and to expected or unexpected opportunities.

This is not to say that the official incentives themselves are ineffective. As a rule they are not. A survey of investment experience made by the National Industrial Conference Board revealed that the companies of 12 industrial nations whose operations were spread to 88 countries had frequently given significant weight to the special development incentives or privileges officially offered to foreign investors by the host governments. The most effective development incentives had been these:[3]

Duty waivers on imports of capital equipment
Duty waivers on imports of necessary parts and supplies
Tariff protection
Infant-industry benefits
Tax holidays
Tax concessions or deferrals or both
Liberal depreciation allowances
Low-cost government loans for factory construction
Other long-term subsidized loans
Government subsidies for industrial buildings
Preferential allocation of foreign exchange for materials and parts

[3] Cf. National Industrial Conference Board, *Obstacles and Incentives to Private Foreign Investments* (New York, 1966), pp. 34–42.

Guarantees of profit remittance and capital repatriation
Subsidy for training personnel
Free port or foreign trade zone
Government railroad subsidies
Favorable conditions for developing industrial site
Use of government port facilities

The U.S. government has enlisted business firms all through the postwar period in a variety of foreign economic-aid programs where their technical skills and organizational capabilities have been essential. Building and repairing agricultural machinery and implements and constructing steel mills, food-processing plants, sanitation systems, and transportation facilities illustrate foreign activities which received their initial impetus from an econonic-aid assignment.

More recently the U.S. government, confronted with a chronic balance of payments deficit, has sponsored an intensive campaign for export expansion. According to the U.S. Department of Commerce, a large number of firms have responded and have initiated programs for marketing abroad. Besides moral suasion, the government has offered several practical aids and incentives for foreign sales. Among them are listings of international trade leads, trade missions sent to different regions of the world, and active participation in international fairs.

Capital import impediments

The effects of the incentives have been minimized by the presence of obstacles. Quite often, the principal reason for the incentive program is the existence of a generally antagonistic atmosphere for business growth and especially international business activity. The impediments listed in 12 countries by managers of multinational ventures in the 88-country sample referred to above stressed among others the following obstacles:

Exchange restrictions and balance-of-payments deficits
Restrictions on foreign enterprises, investors, and executives
Import controls, including duties and exchanges
Inconsistent and unpredictable legal protection
Political uncertainty
Labor problems
Financial instability
Tax discrimination
Inadequate infrastructure

The survey made no effort to measure the significance of the different impediments. It therefore does not permit ranking them in any systematic way.

Capital export incentives and impediments

Official measures encouraging domestic enterprise to acquire foreign facilities have generally been much more limited. Most industrial countries, if they have any favorable treatment at all for capital-exporting enterprises, limit the incentives to projects in the underdeveloped countries. It would be generally true to say that the obstacles, both visible and invisible, which most countries place in the way of capital exports more than neutralize the export incentives.

Tactical Motives

Case studies show that changes in business conditions, both internal and external, may create tactical advantages that induce a company to enter international business. Some of these changes are discussed below.

UNUSUAL OR UNPREDICTABLE CHANGES IN FOREIGN BUSINESS CONDITIONS. These include an exceptionally prosperous economy in a particular foreign area; the start of a new industry which will create or substantially augment the demand for the firm; the failure or setback of a major international competitor (such as a head-start company) whose marketing advantages may be neutralized by the difficulty, thus creating a temporary opportunity for a firm to establish itself; the relaxation of quota and license restrictions on imports; and the elimination of discriminatory taxes and other governmental restrictions aimed against foreign branches and subsidiaries.

UNUSUAL OR UNPREDICTABLE CHANGES IN DOMESTIC CONDITIONS. A serious recession or depression may compel a company to seek safety abroad. Technical or organizational rationalization within the firm may free from their previous responsibilities a significant number of people who cannot be reabsorbed by the firm without international business. Overproduction or unexpected sales resistance may result in excessive inventories, which, if dumped into domestic channels, could destroy the established price structure and stability of the market. Exports are usually the way out of these dilemmas.

Cash and other liquid resources accumulated in excess of anticipated needs may be most productively used in a foreign area. Because rates of return on capital have been higher abroad than in the United States, several industries have greatly accelerated the international expansion of corporate facilities in recent years.

Minimax Strategy

This discussion would be incomplete if the internationalization of an undefinable but significant segment of American business were not accounted for. This segment consists of the followers rather than leaders; their goals are set by their competitors, their industries, or what is called the *mainstream of business*—current managerial fashions. Hence, when other companies have established international operations, they too take these steps. The formal logic for such behavior is the *minimax principle*—if one does what most others do, one cannot be more wrong than the majority. This idea is purely probabilistic and has no substantive relevance, but, with the increased dependence on computers and statistical decision making, many executives have accepted the minimax principle.

Self-Sustained Growth

Once a company has broken the international barrier, its foreign involvement multiplies and reorganizes itself for a self-generating expansion which may take a variety of forms. Since this expansion is an inextricable aspect of the foreign branches and subsidiaries of U.S. firms, elucidation of it will be postponed until the growth and organization of the multinational company are discussed in later chapters.

12

The Organization of Multinational Companies

Modern organization theory recognizes two fundamentally different aspects of business organizations—*formal organization* and *informal organization*. Formal organization refers to the structure for rational action: to the division of work; to the allocation of personnel, functions, and resources to produce the greatest efficiency. Formal organization also includes the communication systems and the chain of command required for the coordination and the control of the different parts as well as of the total system. The positions and relationships of the organization are conceived as institutionalized entities free from sentimental caprice and emotional uncertainty. The office rather than the officer is the criterion. Individuals are thus replaceable, and the structure is independent of variations in the personal qualities of the personnel. In its pure concept, formal organization is synonymous with rational action—scientific management.

The central thesis of informal organization is that besides the formal structure in every company there will develop more or less spontaneously a social structure of positions and relationships governed by a different value system and different dynamics than is the formal organization. The differences are presumed to arise because individuals respond to irrational impulses just as readily as to rational ones. Consequently, their personalities cannot be scaled to fit perfectly the particular molds that the formal structure attributes to them. Instead of confining themselves to these delineated roles, they remain whole people whose behavior is determined by a much more intricate network of interests, hopes, and fears than that which any functional assignment in an organization encompasses. Thus behavioristic aspects[1] become dominant in the informal organization.

Since these two concepts constitute the bedrock of modern organization theory, it would be wise to use them in the analysis of multinational enterprises. Yet, they are much less useful in this study than in the study of limited structures, such as factories or stores, where the atomistic elements of the organization—the individual employee and his functional task—can be made the pivotal points. Although not unessential, the atomistic elements do not present the most complex problems or the greatest challenges in the multinational business organization.

The emphasis here is primarily on the architecture and secondarily on the bricks and mortar, because the multinational enterprise is primarily a complex of companies rather than a combination of departments or individuals. Juridically, it is a compact among autonomous units of different national jurisdictions; socially, it is a multicultural aggregation of both formal and informal structures conditioned more by the environments of their respective countries than by the behavioral experience in any single national culture. The contrasts among its parts in economic, political, and social milieu; the differences in technology and resource bases; the obstacles to international mobility of manpower, assets, and ideas; and the divergent trends and uneven tempos of development all combine to create organizational problems peculiar to the multinational enterprise. These problems are in many ways of a different order and magnitude than those encountered in typical domestic situations. It is to these problems that the analysis in this chapter must be directed.

To avoid unnecessary confusion with the general literature on organization, the standard terminology of *formal* and *informal* organization is retained; but often *managerial* is substituted for formal and *social* for informal. The synonyms are used to minimize confusion from another source which to date has escaped the scrutiny of organization theorists—the legal, or juridic, form of organization as defined by the respective country's law and imposed upon a company by its official charter. Although influenced by it, the managerial (formal) organization seldom coincides with the juridic form. Usually they are significantly different from each other, as will be shown subsequently in this chapter. Both are in a sense formal organizations. However, the juridic form can lay a greater claim to the term than the managerial one can. What is worse, international relations people, as well as the legal profession, think of the juridic form of a company as its formal organization.

Thus, perfect terminological clarity is unattainable here. It is therefore better to refrain, where possible, from using *formal organization* in either sense and, as suggested above, to substitute *managerial* or *de facto* organization for it in the sense of organization theory, and *juridic* or *de jure* organization for it in the legal or official sense. The concept of informal or social organization need not be changed.

[1] A forerunner to this concept was the so-called *human relations school,* which was in vogue a decade ago.

The Structural Scheme of International-Trade Management

Multinational business organization has been changing rapidly. In the process new concepts have emerged which have greatly expanded the once rather standardized pattern. To capture the dynamics of this evolution it is necessary to start with an analytic reformulation of the international trade structure. As was shown in Chapter 29, the historic pattern consisted of three different business institutions: the domestic firms, including manufacturers, growers, and distributors in the country of origin; the international trade intermediaries, such as exporters, importers, and custom brokers; and the foreign firms which performed the distribution function in the country of consumption or served as sources of supply for imports.

Thus, the management of foreign trade was divided among the three institutional zones, the firms in each zone carrying out a certain part of the process and depending on firms in the other two for its completion. To visualize graphically this managerial specialization among the institutional zones, the total scope of management jobs might be viewed as a line connecting the point of production in the country of origin with the point of consumption in the country of destination as shown in Figure 12-1. The functions performed by each zone can then be sequestered as three successive segments in the total management process. Although interdependent, the institutions in the different zones were not integrated with those in the others through either ownership or control.

FIGURE 12-1

Managerial Phases of the Foreign-Trade Process under the Traditional Institutional Structure

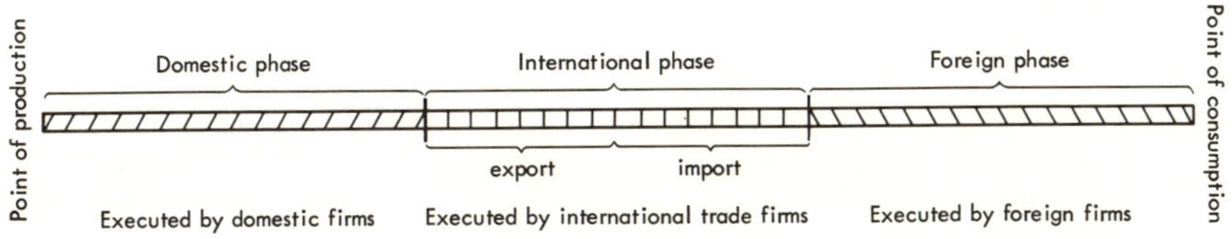

Requirements for executive capabilities varied from zone to zone. Those in the domestic zone needed, and typically only possessed, the most rudimentary acquaintance with any nondomestic aspect of the overall process. Since they functioned entirely within the jurisdiction—both legal and cultural—of the country of origin, they had minimal contact with the market overseas. For all practical purposes the domestic phase of foreign-trade management was not different from domestic business itself; the same laws, the same costs, the same courts, the same unions, the same banks, the same interest rates, and the same language applied. The transactions between the firms in the domestic zone and those in the international zone were, at least from the standpoint of managerial preparedness and competence, hardly different at all from like transactions consummated between two domestic companies. The only special capabilities required of export management on the manufacturing level were a thorough knowledge of the firms in the international zone and the ability to cultivate those relations with them which best served the foreign-trade objectives of the company.

The vitality and power in foreign-trade management lay in the international zone. The export and import intermediaries possessed the know-how and techniques for penetrating trade barriers, reconciling incongruities among different laws and customs, and handling the commercial and financial formalities required. The expertise of the intermediaries was rated as professional competence of such high order that many countries accorded to their foreign-trade practitioners special rights and privileges similar to those granted to doctors and lawyers.[2] The process analysis in the previous chapter further elaborates the competence region of the intermediary zone.

Conceptually the foreign phase in this scheme is the mirror image of the domestic one except that pragmatic differences in business conditions and practices between the countries distorted the two in most respects. This organizational pattern evolved during the middle third of the nineteenth century and became accepted as the "normal" structure of international trade. However, arrangements in recent years are forcing a massive expansion of the structure and challenging the lingering on of the "normal" structure. In quantitative terms, traditional foreign-trade business has shrunk to less than a fifth of the total international business of the United States, while the business carried on under the new arrangements has increased correspondingly. The discussion here will focus on these newer arrangements.

Early Structural Models of International Industrial Companies

Deviations from the three-zone structure can be traced to the colonial companies. However, outside the colonial realm such deviations remained rather exceptional until the period between the two world wars, when extreme protectionism severely limited opportunities for international trade. Since the tariff walls were too high to climb, the only way to reach foreign markets was by being established behind them. Consequently, acquisition of foreign-based production facilities became a growing factor in international business.

Yet, both the philosophy and the organizational ideas remained embedded in the traditional concept of foreign trade. Where the choice existed, a company was interested not so much in going new ways as in gaining control of the traditional route, not so much in developing foreign production bases, except in the extractive industries, as in circumventing the international intermediaries. Accordingly the main thrust of the industrial corporation was to

[2] This notion has been revived in some foreign-trade circles, especially in Philadelphia, in the last few years, and proposals for professional accreditation of export-import executives have received considerable attention and publicity. In the light of the very basic changes in international business it seems highly unlikely that such accreditation would make any real contribution to business management.

create its own foreign-trade organization in the image of the export and import firms it was to displace. In smaller firms the new trade organ was a foreign-trade or export department; in large ones, a foreign-trade division or *export-selling company.* The latter represented the ultimate under the foreign-trade concept. It was a wholly owned subsidiary located in the same country as the parent concern and prepared to perform all the functions previously left to the independent intermediaries. It represented a channel for direct trade and an instrument of centralized control over both the domestic and the international phases of the foreign-trade process.

When tariffs compelled direct investment in overseas facilities, the model arrangement was the so-called *allied export company*—a firm incorporated and situated abroad in which the U.S. parent held some stock but which it seldom owned outright. Although the allied export company was also engaged in manufacturing activities, its principal purpose remained export marketing, as indicated by its name. Frequently, the manufacturing operations were conceived by management as a wedge for prying market openings from within when import restrictions made markets impenetrable from without. The logic was that a company established within a country can mobilize public support and governmental interest to win special consideration and privileges in regard to foreign-trade restrictions. However, manufacturing was not purely a camouflage for the import strategy. Often the manufacturing activity outranked trade in its growth and generation of profits. But, since the top management of the parent firm was guided by an inward-looking, nationalistic perspective, exportation was generally preferred over plant and production abroad.

Both the export-selling company and the allied export company are rapidly approaching extinction. Those forms which have emerged in recent years have either absorbed them or displaced them. This process was particularly conspicuous in the 1950's.

An Overview of Alternative Organizational Arrangements

The main organizational arrangements which now exist are shown in Figure 12-2. The shaded areas show the international entities of the company. In a general sense, the alternatives also reflect the stages of growth from indirect exporting to a fully integrated international corporate structure. Lately, however, there has been an increasing tendency to skip the intermediate stages and to move directly from alternative *A* to *D, E,* or even *F.*

Structural Models of Multinational Companies

The most significant organizational change in the postwar period has been the replacement of foreign-trade departments or divisions with international-operations establishments. From this shift has evolved nearly all that

FIGURE 12-2

Types of Functional Relations between Parent Organizations and Their International Entities

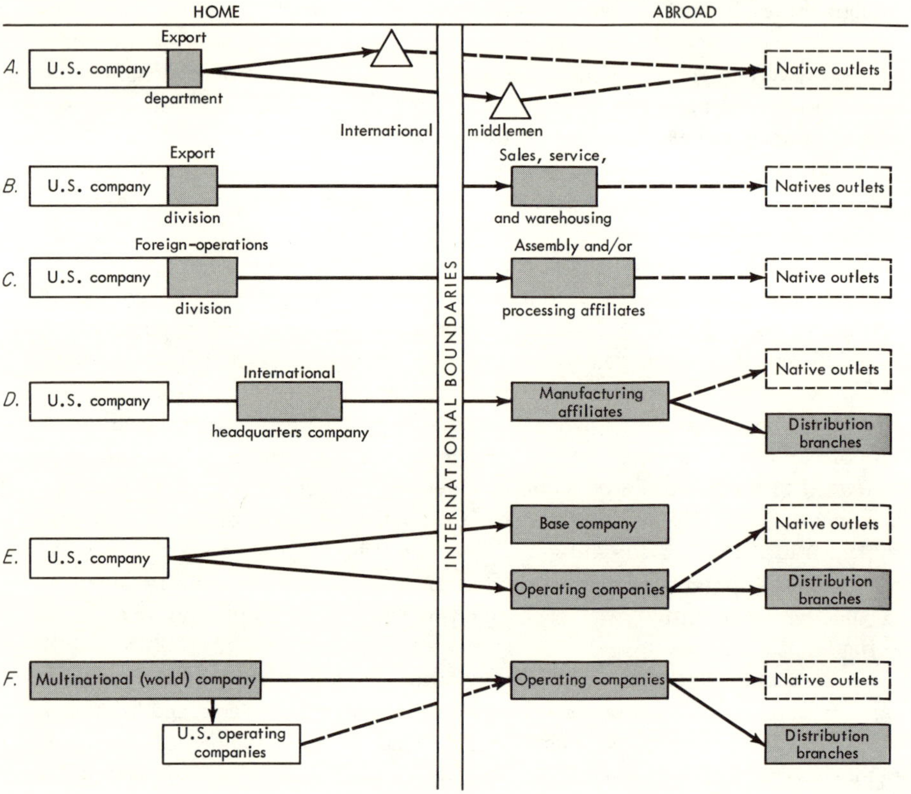

is peculiarly characteristic of the modern multinational corporation. From this shift, also, has come an entirely new and different structural framework for international economic relations. The organizational expression of this shift can be reduced to four prototypal models: the international-headquarters company, the foreign-base company, the world company, and the transnational company. The models are not exact reproductions of a particular firm but are the conceptual expressions underlying the design of the organization. In practice such models must always be suited to the particular circumstances of a specific company.

The International-Headquarters Company (IHC Model)

The emergence of the international-headquarters company marks an important turning point in the organization of international business. Although an outgrowth of the export-selling company in older firms (but not in others), it is structurally and functionally different. Unlike the older forms, it drops all pretense of being an offshoot of the sales organization (a subordinate outlet with narrowly defined objectives) and assumes the role of an operationally autonomous enterprise whose factories, warehouses, employees, and customers are not located in its country but are scattered in different foreign areas. Production and finance are thus organic to it, and export selling is expanded to international marketing, with aspirations and capabilities of a higher order. Any need to be organized in the image of the international middlemen firms is thus eliminated and a new structural model emerges. It is shown in Figure 12-3.

In this prototype the top echelons of the parent company remain unaffected except for the addition of a vice-president to serve as the contact officer between the parent and the subsidiary. The latter has its own policy-making organs: board of directors, president, and staff vice-presidents for each functional area. In the chart, these latter functionaries are indicated by the oval boxes, as are their counterparts in the parent firm. The line officers, on the other hand, are indicated by rectangular boxes. The IHC board is chaired either by the contact officer or the president of the parent.

The line organization of the international-headquarters company follows the territorial principle. Divisions or subsidiary companies, set up for all appropriate world regions, carry out the actual operations of the firm. These in turn control the foreign-based affiliates—wholly owned subsidiaries, joint-venture companies, or others.

From export management to international management

The underlying principle of the new model is not functional but geographic. The international-headquarters company is not limited to exporting or to any functionally dilineated responsibility as such, but undertakes all functions the company carries out abroad. Its managerial jurisdiction is defined not by the nature of the job but by the geographic scope or location of the job. Accordingly, the international-headquarters company may be compared to the State Department of the U.S. government or to any ministry of foreign affairs. Its functional dimension knows no limit, but its territorial dimension is sharply defined.

THE FUNCTIONAL SPECTRA. Based on this concept, the new model also creates new requirements for managerial preparedness, although the requisites for export management remain. Figure 12-4 shows how the spectrum of managerial functions is changed. Under the export scheme functions were limited to selling and shipping tasks; now they encompass not only a more complete multinational program but also, and more importantly, many nonmarketing responsibilities.

In fully developed international-headquarters companies the spectrum of management functions is actually wider than that of the parent corporation itself because the former encounters problems peculiar to multinational activities: international transfer pricing, dealings with foreign governments, negotiations with supranational bodies. In addition, it must be able, on the one hand,

FIGURE 12-3

Structural Model of the International-Headquarters Company

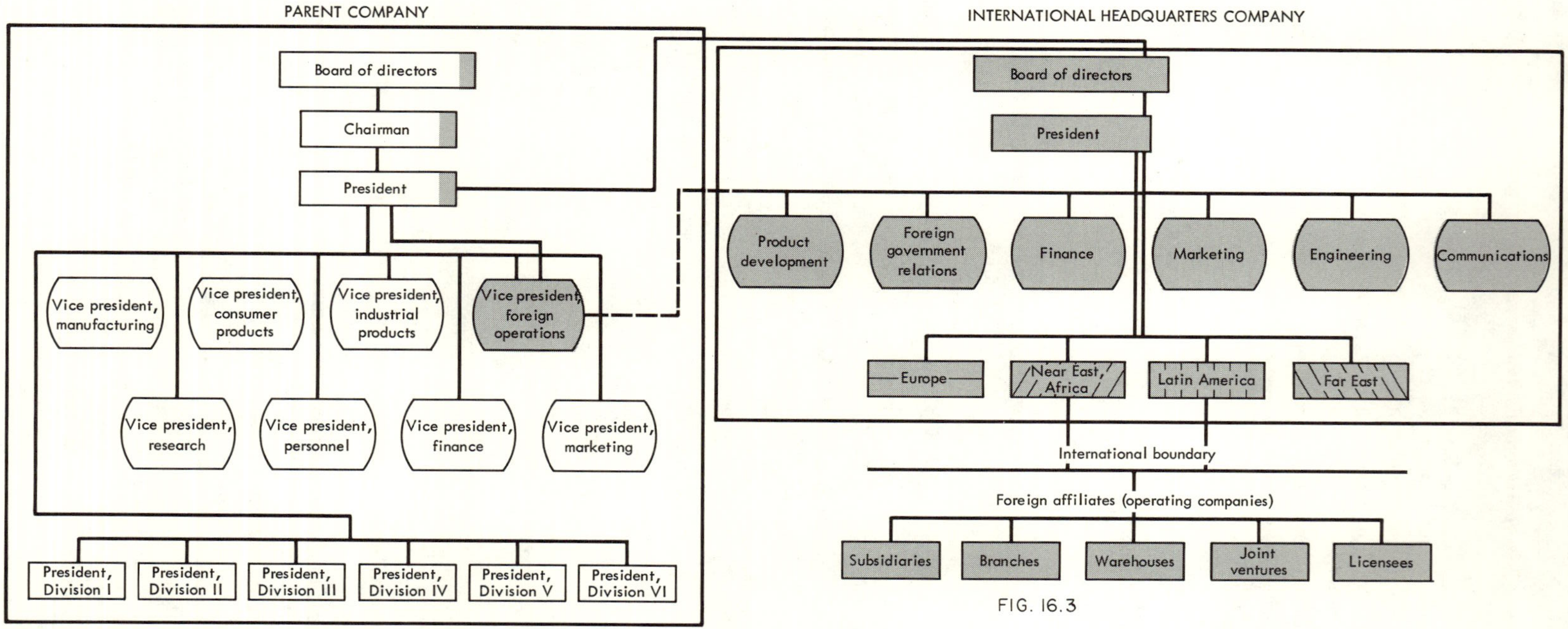

Note to Figure 12-3: Corporate entities with international responsibilities are shaded in the chart, and those with domestic responsibilities are not; the directors, chairman, and president of the parent have secondary responsibility in international management, as indicated by partial shading.
Source: Endel J. Kolde, "Business Enterprise in a Global Context," California Management Review, VIII, No. 4 (Summer 1966), 39.

FIGURE 12-4

Comparative Spectra of Functional Responsibilities: A Schematic Sketch

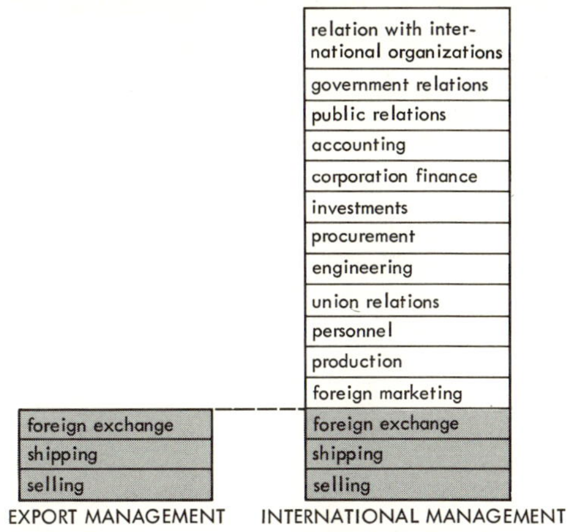

to adapt its objectives, policies, and methods to the social and cultural conditions of each country in its territory and, on the other hand, to create sufficient uniformity and continuity for effective coordination and control of the entire multinational structure. In complexity, the skills and capabilities which the management of a multinational enterprise must possess dwarf those of the traditional foreign-trade executive. Consequently, the new scheme marks the beginning of what now is called *international* or *multinational management* as distinct from *export* or *import management*. And, at the same time, it completely changes the concept of an international executive, together with the requirements for becoming one.

The changeover to the IHC plan reached its apex in the late 1950's, and by the early 1960's it had become the dominant organizational format for U.S. business, including both industrial and nonindustrial companies. Even service firms such as management consultants, market research agencies, and accounting firms adopted this plan.

The Base Company or Overseas Regional Headquarters

The base-company format had its beginning in the search for sanctuaries where foreign-source income could be accumulated with minimum tax depletion. Wide differences in corporate income taxes among countries induced the search. The low-tax countries—especially the Bahamas, Panama, Liechtenstein, Switzerland, and Hong Kong—became the preferred locations for the *tax-haven,* or *profit-sanctuary,* subsidiaries, as the initial base companies were commonly called. Many of these were paper corporations without physical facilities or administrative capabilities. Their value derived from the fact that the U.S. internal revenue laws did not cover foreign-source income as long as it remained abroad. But, although the tax savings were real, they were not the only advantages of the foreign holding company. Many firms found it both ethically and organizationally desirable to endow them with the authority of actual management by making them the headquarters for their foreign operations.

The 1962 Revenue Act wiped out the pure tax-haven companies by making foreign-source income of most U.S. firms taxable irrespective of where the funds were kept.[1] This helped to make the base company an international-headquarters company located abroad rather than in the same country with the parent firm. In its structure the base company duplicates the international-headquarters plan with the exception of its location. The advantages that it offers over the IHC model are (a) better integration of top management and operations, (b) greater autonomy and less likelihood of interference by the parent, (c) greater financial flexibility in transferring earnings and assets from one country to another, and (d) spreading political and financial risk of the enterprise as a whole. The negative aspects are (a) complications of management—domestic routines and practices which can be employed in the IHC must be reformed; (b) loss of U.S. treaty and diplomatic protection; and (c) closer scrutiny by U.S. tax and trade authorities.

The base-company concept has two main variations: a monocentric system with one base company functioning as the top management organ in international operations; and a polycentric system in which international management has been divided into geographic zones and a separate base company has been established for each. Figure 12-5 sketches each type. In addition to these variations, the base-company idea has recently been grafted onto the IHC plan by some multinational firms which retain the IHC as the central organ but establish one or more base companies as subordinate management centers. In such secondary base companies the responsibilities tend to be more operations oriented than policy oriented compared with those in the base company as such.

The World Company

The process of organizational development has not ended with the IHC. A new and still different structure has emerged. Its basic plan is shown in Figure 12-6. Although in the IHC model the dichotomy between domestic and international was emphasized as the fundamental criterion, the world-company model abandons this dichotomy and integrates the American and international operations by subordinating domestic to multinational affairs. The top echelons of the parent corporation, which under the IHC plan retain their inward-looking, domestic orientation, are thus reoriented to the global point of view, and the previous dualistic structure is eliminated from the policy-making organs. The entire headquarters staff becomes multinational in managerial responsibility and outlook.

The operating units are again organized on the territorial principle, each

1 See Chapter 17 for elaborations.

FIGURE 12-5

Geographic Patterns of the Base-Company Model

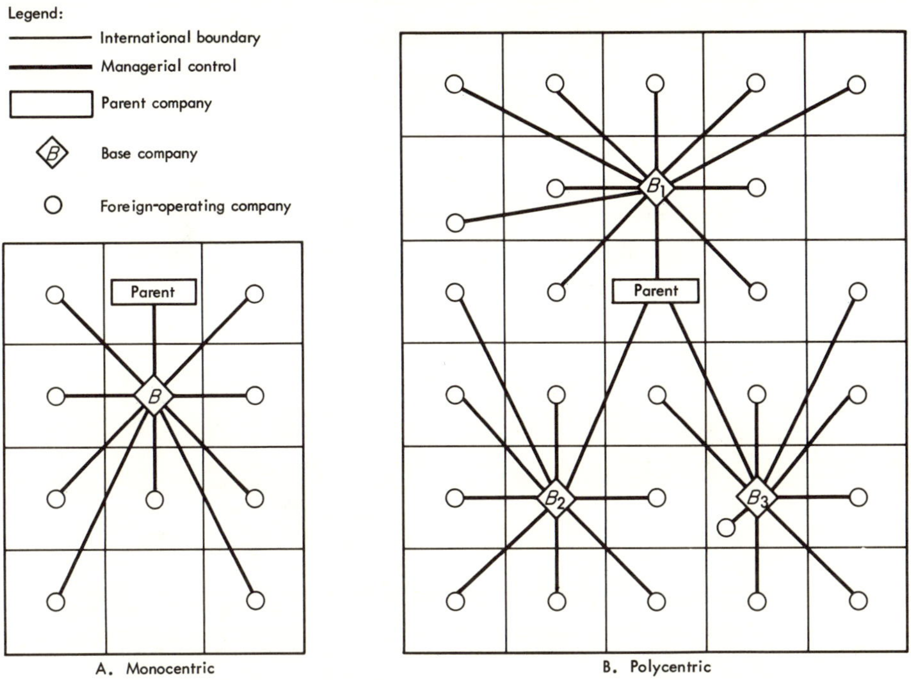

being defined in terms of a particular world region and thus adapted to the economic and cultural peculiarities of it. Needless to add, area expertise thus takes precedence over functional and product knowledge for general-management positions on the operational level. Some firms are now attempting to insert a product organization in the world-company framework; but, for the time being at least, no clear-cut conceptual solution has emerged. When it has been tried, the result has been a double structure utilizing both territorial and product principles.

Although the world-company plan is still in its infancy, having been first attempted in the mid-1950's, the conversion to it has been considerable, especially among companies whose product line has a relatively universal demand, such as petroleum, soft drinks, and drugs. It might be added that the model is being adopted not only by industrial giants but also by more and more smaller firms, many having skipped the IHC stage.

The Transnational Company

The transnational company originated in Europe. It differs from the world company in that both ownership and control of the corporate structure are international. Its management is polycentric; there is no parent company

FIGURE 12-6

Structural Model of the World Company

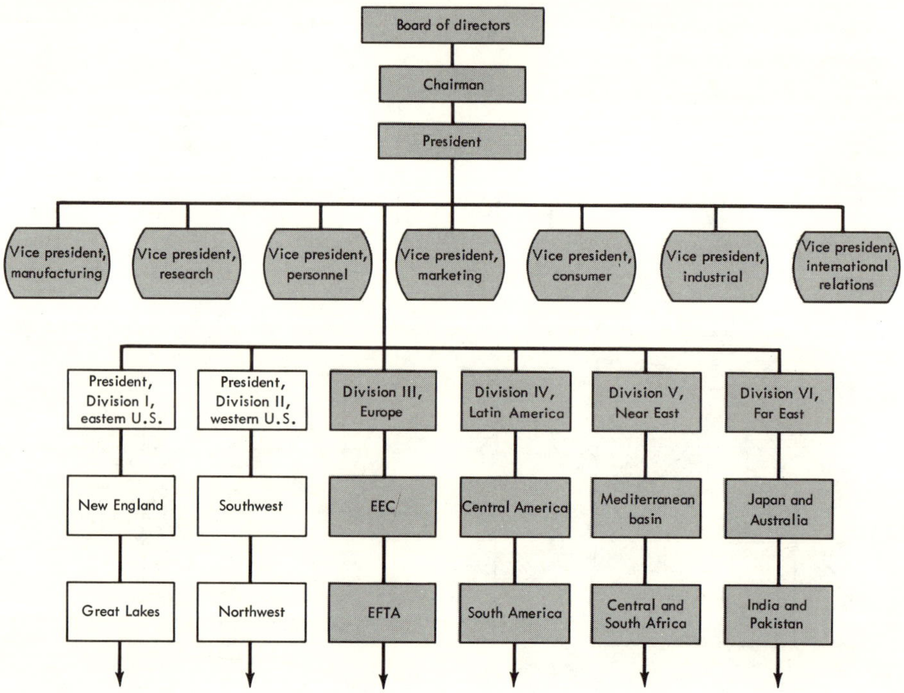

as such, no central source of power, no domestic market or principal domicile. Its capital is raised from whichever capital market provides the best source for a particular venture; and top management is divided among several headquarters, each in a different country, and functions as an international coalition rather than as a command hierarchy. In essence, then, the transnational company can be visualized as a group of management centers jointly administering a network of operating companies.

Although a few such polycentric multinational firms now exist (Unilever, Royal Dutch-Shell), the attitude of international executives toward this plan remains reserved. Whether it will ever reach a status comparable to that of the other plans seems doubtful at this time. However, the development of foreign-base companies with strong subsidiaries of their own resembles the transnational concept.

Contrast between the New Models and the Traditional Scheme

How basic a change these new models represent is demonstrated in the structural model of the typical industrial corporation of the foreign-trade era in Figure 12-7. As in the previous charts, the international organs are indicated by shading. Here the international aspects of management are limited in terms of both function and position. The operation is not well organized as a hierarchy. The chief international executive—the export manager—is subordinate to a functional department head rather than being part of general management. No top executive has his primary responsibility in the international field.

FIGURE 12-7

Export (International) Department in Traditional Corporate Structure

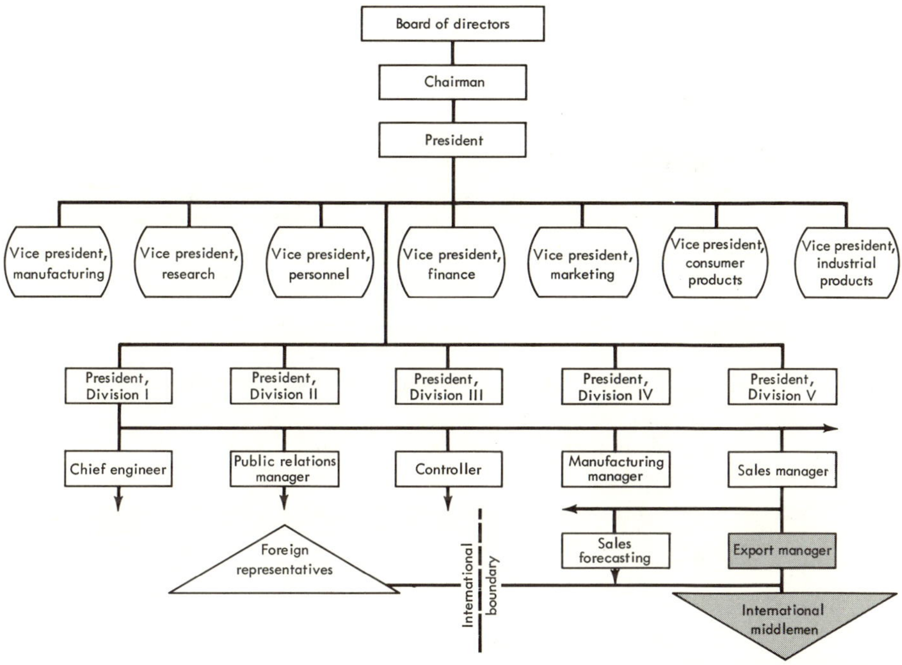

Foreign-Based Affiliates

How the foreign entities of a company are organized is basically a matter of law. To gain entry in a particular country a company must comply with all the legal provisions applicable to it. Since the laws of no two countries are identical, the legal aspects of establishment must always be handled as special cases.

Generally speaking, visas for corporate entry into a country are subject to more restrictions than are those which apply to people, goods, or capital.

To meet the requirements a company has four alternative approaches: qualify for a branch license; form a subsidiary company under the laws of the host country; create a joint venture with one or more indigenous companies; or enter into a licensing agreement with an existing firm. The last two alternatives are discussed in separate chapters; the first two are the subject of the remainder of this chapter.

Foreign Branches

From a legal standpoint a branch is not a separate juridic entity but only a physical offshoot of the parent firm. As long as both the branch and the parent are in the same country they are subject to the same national jurisdiction. The legal status of the branch is of small concern, as the parent company remains responsible for any legal action taken either by or against the branch. If, however, a branch were located in a different country, a legally intolerable situation would arise. The branch with its physical and economic powers would function as a legal nonentity over which the host country's government had no control since its juridic embodiment, the parent firm, would be outside the country's jurisdiction and thus beyond the reach of the juridical organs of the government. No government can permit such immunity to law in its territory. For this reason licenses are issued for branch operations to nonresident companies only if the branch is *domesticated* by having a responsible national of the host country serve as the legal custodian of the establishment. The custodianship must be based on a formally executed power of attorney, in which the company conveys to the foreign citizen or firm involved complete jurisdiction over the branch. Since such an arrangement creates subtle problems and additional uncertainties, branches are relatively uncommon in multinational companies except as subunits of a national or regional subsidiary limited to one single country.

The foreign branch has other weaknesses also. Business licenses may be of short duration, and frequent renewals involve considerable expense; regulations and governmental surveillance may be tighter;[3] the taxable base may be so defined that the branch becomes taxable not on the basis of its own earnings or assets, but on the basis of the total profits or capitalization of the multinational corporation as a whole.

Foreign Subsidiaries

To avoid such discriminatory treatment most companies prefer to organize their affiliates as indigenous enterprises under the laws of the host country. Although the legal forms of enterprise (partnership, corporation, etc.) have over the years become relatively similar, significant differences still exist. The most significant among them is the existence of organizational forms other than the corporation which have juridic personalities separate

[3] For example, the branch may be required to patronize local suppliers, not compete with local industry, or refrain from employing nonnationals.

from their owners and in which the owners' liability is limited to their investments in the enterprise. For example, German law provides for a limited-liability company (G.m.b.H.) which resembles the U.S. corporation in all features essential to management yet enjoys much greater freedom of action under law than does the German equivalent of the corporation (A/G). Thus the American term *to incorporate* is often as misleading as is the popular notion that the various national affiliates of a multinational company are corporations in form. Many are not. And many others should not be. With the growth of the multinational company, U.S. management has become more aware of the legal differences, and more sophisticated use is now being made of the various organizational opportunities which the laws of different countries provide.

To qualify for establishment in most countries, the law requires that a certain number of directorships or other key positions in the firm be occupied by local nationals. Compliance with this requirement produces a *statutory* or *de jure administration* which many companies find unsuitable for the actual management of the affiliate, so they limit the functions of these statutory executives to those prescribed by the charter: holding an annual meeting, signing necessary forms and reports, sanctioning legal contracts, etc. To safeguard itself, the parent company must fill these positions with people of unquestionable integrity, or, more commonly, counterbalance their official powers with contractual constraints such as leasing the assets to the *de jure* administration with the proviso that the officers "delegate" the operational responsibilities to individuals appointed by the lessor.

Another typical requirement for incorporation is that a specified portion, sometimes more than half, of the capital invested in the affiliate be controlled by local citizens. In countries where such restrictions exist, the U.S. parent company usually enters joint-venture or partial-ownership arrangements. It either buys part ownership in an existing foreign concern or induces a foreign firm to coinvest with it in a new venture. This latter practice has become popular in recent years, especially among manufacturers and distributors of technical products, for whom local facilities and technical personnel are essential for making installations and servicing their customers. To enable the foreign company to contribute the legally necessary capital, it may be permitted by the parent to turn over some existing assets such as its building, equipment, sites, production processes, and even goodwill. Monetary values can be assigned to all of them by mutual agreement, and thus the need for a cash contribution by the local concern is minimized. How far a company is willing to go in this respect depends, of course, on the alternatives available to it and the profit potential of the particular market.

Dual management

Although to some extent conditioned by official charters, the *de facto* management of the foreign-based affiliates is often different from the *de jure* administration and is invariably subordinated to the parent company's international headquarters whatever its form. No clear-cut interrelationship between the *de facto* and *de jure* managements exists. In some companies they are completely divorced. In others they are quite closely interwoven, with most titular officers serving as operating executives also. But in the great majority of cases the actual management is in the hands of people other than the law-prescribed directors and officers.[4]

The complete separation of *de facto* and *de jure* administrations is illustrated by the organizational structure of a large West Coast company which operates affiliates in a number of Latin American countries. Each of these affiliates is incorporated under the laws of the respective country, but none of them functions as a separate administrative unit; instead, they "buy" their management from a U. S. subsidiary of the parent company, organized for that purpose exclusively. This so-called *management services corporation,* reporting to the international-headquarters company, is responsible for and actually performs all the activities of the company in the Latin American area. Its internal organization parallels that of any other operating company in the same industry, with the usual departmentalization and executive hierarchy.

It is not clear whether the cleavage between the *de jure* and *de facto* structures of the foreign-based affiliates is likely to widen or lessen. Until the mid 1950's the trend was toward an alienation of the two through new organizational and legal devices invented for that purpose. But in the last decade multinational companies have initiated training and executive development programs for local nationals and have begun to emphasize the use of local talent to a much greater extent than previously. Where such programs have been in existence for some time, the results are most encouraging.[5]

Managerial Functions and Autonomy

Most of the foreign-based affiliates function, from an administrative standpoint, as operating auxiliaries to the international-headquarters organization. They are relatively autonomous in making many operational decisions but are usually subordinate in making decisions on business policy. Although the degree to which administrative authority is delegated to a foreign affiliate in any particular case depends on special circumstances, in general it varies with the size of the affiliate and with the organizational pattern of the parent company. Both of these factors deserve additional comment.

As an affiliate grows in size, its administrative responsibilities increase in magnitude and in diversity. The case of an instrument manufacturer illustrates this point. The company started a sales office in Italy in the late 1940's to service the orders placed by Italian importers and to enable the company to consolidate shipments to that country and thus reduce transportation costs. As sales increased, the company found it desirable to expand the

[4] Cf. E. J. Kolde, "The Administrative Structure of International Business with Special Reference to Foreign-Based Affiliates," *University of Washington Business Review,* XXII, No. 3 (February 1963), 38–50.

[5] Kolde, "The Administrative Structure of International Business," pp. 38–50.

office until in 1960 the original staff of two executives and three secretaries had swelled to 800 permanent employees and workers. Along with the additions to personnel, the office had successively assumed such additional responsibilities as prospecting, calling on customers, advertising, operating a service and repair department, carrying inventories in leased facilities, acquiring a company-owned warehouse, and, finally, expanding the service department to a plant capable of assembling and manufacturing certain products. To finance this expansion, the investment in the affiliate increased from $44,000 to nearly $1.7 million in the 12-year interval. Many affiliates have grown in a similar fashion.

The increase of sales volume and its corollaries—increase in investment, personnel, and administrative responsibilities—places greater demands on the executive of the affiliate and elevates his stature within the administrative hierarchy of the parent company. Thus, irrespective of the basic organizational setup of the company, the growth of the affiliate increases its influence on top management decisions. Incidentally, this explains the difference in policy autonomy between production and marketing affiliates. Since, on the average, the former are considerably larger and perform a greater variety of functions than the latter, they are given correspondingly greater freedom for independent action.

It appears that an affiliate's autonomy is affected more by its relative size than by its absolute size. The European affiliates of two American chemical companies, for example, have had substantially equal shares of the European market since 1949. One of them represents about 4 to 5 percent of the parent company's total sales and is subject to close operational control by the latter; the other represents 13 to 15 percent of its parent's total volume and is accorded the status of an autonomous subsidiary.

Compared with their domestic counterparts, the foreign-based affiliates have considerably more independence. This difference is due to some extent to distance and to the problems of remote control, but primarily to differences in operating environments. In the words of one executive, "We consider our Mexican branch as a distinct entity because it must deal with a whole range of problems that our domestic divisions never need to bother about—problems peculiar to Mexico. On the other hand, there are matters which are of vital concern to the domestic divisions but of no consequence as far as the Mexican branch is concerned."[6]

A survey made by this author showed that only 16 percent of parent companies regarded their foreign affiliates as being synonymous with their domestic branches.[7] Most of these were companies which were distributing a standardized line of staples or which had been active in foreign markets for only a short period. Regardless of size, the older foreign-based affiliates differ more often and in a greater number of ways from their domestic coun-

6 Quoted in Kolde, "The Administrative Structure of International Business," p. 44.

7 Endel J. Kolde, "The Functions of Foreign-Based Affiliates in the Administrative Structure of International Business Enterprise," *Revue Economique et Sociale* (December 1962), 155–83.

terparts than the newer establishments do. It was not definitely established whether a company relaxes control over its foreign affiliates as they get older because the management learns to appreciate better the environmental and operational peculiarities or simply because they tend to grow in size. It is plausible to presume that the degree of autonomy granted to affiliates is, to some degree, correlated with both of these factors.

Composite Structure

The actual power structure of a multinational enterprise is a composite of managerial requirements, formal juridic organizations, and ownership ties among its national components. The popular notion that power is primarily a function of ownership is more often false than true, except, possibly, in wholly owned affiliates. Usually, the key criterion here is managerial efficiency. To achieve its objectives, top management must be able to exert its will upon the various national entities of the complex. Accordingly, a managerial hierarchy, however simple or complex, must be constructed to satisfy this fundamental requirement. If there were no legal restrictions, the managerial hierarchy, primarily because of performance criteria, would also constitute the formal organization. However, this is seldom the case. The laws of each country provide not only for different business charters but also for different qualifications for company officers, different numbers of stockholders, and different ownership distributions.

Most of these provisions are based upon nonmanagerial criteria and, thus, have a generally restraining effect upon business efficiency. The restraining effect is multiplied by the differences, contradictions, and incongruities in the multinational realm. Yet the legal requirements must be met regardless of how well or ill suited they are for a firm's functional objectives. And accordingly, a *de jure* structure, based on national laws and regulations, is erected to give the enterprise its legal existence. More often than not, this *de jure* structure fails to satisfy the requirements for managerial performance or competitive efficiency and, as indicated above, a *de facto* command exercises actual management control. To minimize the complications which the existence of the *de jure* and the *de facto* functionaries might raise, many firms prefer undivided ownership of their international ventures.

13

Joint Ventures

> More U.S. corporations are changing their tactics in foreign companies. Increasingly they are sharing ownership and pooling investment capital with businessmen, shareholders, and even government in other countries.[1]

In the past, the wholly foreign-owned subsidiary was the most common approach to overseas investment. Complete control and ownership were seen as the most logical policies for an international firm. The success of a worldwide strategy by the parent company depended upon complete control over all foreign units. However, more and more host countries, especially the underdeveloped ones, have concluded that the wholly foreign-owned enterprise does not contribute to the country's economic interests as do joint ventures. And as a consequence, a relative shift from the wholly owned subsidiary to the joint venture has occurred in international business organization. As the joint ventures increase in number and importance, they deserve critical study and evaluation. Some analysts already rank them as the typical vehicle of American participation in foreign industry.[2]

1 *The Wall Street Journal* (New York), March 30, 1965, p. 1.

2 *The Wall Street Journal* (New York), March 30, 1965, p. 1. See also: Robert B. Shaw, "Joint Ventures by American and Foreign Companies," *The Magazine of Wall Street,* CIV, No. 11 (August 15, 1958), 592–95; "Overseas Investments: What's Really Involved—Who Makes the Decisions?" *International Trade Review,* XXXVIII, No. 11 (November 1964), 26–28.

Definition of Joint Ventures

A joint venture is sometimes defined as an overseas enterprise which is not completely owned by the parent company.[3] This definition would embrace not only foreign-based enterprises owned by two or more different firms but also those whose stock is partially held by the general public. From a purely legal point of view a case can be made for classifying the latter enterprises as joint ventures. But from economic and administrative points of view such an extension of the joint-venture concept undermines its central idea—partnership. There can be no partnership in the pure sense of the word between a foreign corporate owner and the local or, for that matter, the international stockholders of an enterprise. Although the stockholders are entitled to exercise control over the company's activities, they do not legally share in practice in the management and direction of the firm.

Here, a joint venture is a business enterprise in which two or more economic entities from different countries participate on a permanent basis. The participation is not limited to equity capital but normally extends to control of the undertaking through manufacturing processes, patents, trademarks, managerial know-how, or other operationally essential factors. When the partners' rights stem from their equity participation, the enterprise is classified as an equity joint venture; when one or more of the partners have made no equity contribution, the enterprise is a nonequity joint venture. From a legal standpoint, the equity joint venture is a creature of company or corporation law, while the nonequity joint venture is based on contract law.

Quantitative Data

There are relatively few statistical data on the percentage of equity ownership in U.S. direct investments. The latest figures were published by the U.S. Department of Commerce for 1957. At that time, the great majority took the form of wholly owned subsidiaries. "Nearly three-quarters of the U.S. direct investment is in enterprises in which the U.S. share of equity is at least 95 percent, including foreign branches of U.S. companies. About one-fifth of the total is in enterprises where the proportion of U.S. ownership ranges from 50 to 95 percent; and about 5 percent is in enterprises where the U.S. participant has a minority interest but where the aggregate U.S. equity is at least 25 percent." The report noted, however, "a continuous though moderate shift toward lower proportions of U.S. equity participation in the newer enterprises."[4]

These figures compare closely with those provided by a study conducted by Professor R. F. Mikesell, of the University of Oregon, on 115 companies which accounted for about two-thirds of the value of U.S. direct foreign invest-

[3] W. G. Friedmann and G. Kalmanoff, *Joint International Business Ventures* (New York: Columbia University Press, 1961), p. 94.

[4] Office of Business Economics, U.S. Dept. of Commerce, *U.S. Business Investments in Foreign Countries* (Washington, D.C.: Government Printing Office, 1960), p. 6.

ment. The Mikesell study showed that the companies predominantly held subsidiaries abroad—over 87 percent of the affiliates were owned 50 percent or more by the U.S. company. On the other hand, 46 of the 115 companies held a minority interest in their overseas ventures. However, 13 of them, all in the extractive field, had no partnerships with host capital. And, of the remaining 33 companies, relatively few expressed the desire for an association with foreign partners. Thus, Mikesell concluded, "Though joint ventures are accepted by 40 percent of U.S. companies, they are as yet popular with only a few of them."[5]

The highest proportion of equity joint ventures exists in public utilities and in mining operations. However, it is very likely that most of these are not with local partners but with associates from other countries. Very high figures for agriculture and trade reflect a definite preference for the branch form in these industries. The Mikesell study showed that over 42 percent of all selling companies were branches, compared with less than 7 percent in manufacturing. In agriculture, the proportion was 50 percent, according to Department of Commerce Statistics.[6]

As a rule, the number of joint ventures is higher in developed than in underdeveloped countries. About 83 percent of U.S. direct investments in economically backward countries represented wholly owned subsidiaries, compared with only 76 percent in Europe and 62 percent in Canada. In aggregate, joint ventures represent 31 percent of the investment in industrialized countries and 17 percent in underdeveloped areas. The rather high percentage of joint ventures in Africa reflects the importance of old colonial relationships.

Reasons for Joint Ventures

The host country's attitudes

The most decisive factor in the expansion of joint-venture enterprises is government attitudes toward foreign ownership of business. In general, this attitude has shifted in favor of joint ventures and against wholly owned subsidiaries. This shift is most pronounced in underdeveloped countries which are closing their borders to U.S. companies unless they are willing to take on local partners. This attitude is defended on several grounds. First, a joint venture permits local capital to participate more fully in profitable and productive undertakings. This belief rests on the assumption that foreign industries are likely to concentrate on the most rewarding opportunities and that the market for these industries is too small to permit more than one plant of efficient scale. Hence, through coflotation local capital is directed into the most productive fields. Second, a joint venture transmits techniques and

5 *U.S. Private and Government Investment Abroad* (Eugene, Oregon: University of Oregon Books, 1962), p. 85.

6 Office of Business Economics, U.S. Dept. of Commerce, *U.S. Business Investments in Foreign Countries,* p. 97.

managerial know-how more effectively and rapidly than wholly foreign-owned enterprises. Third, a joint venture eliminates the danger of undue domination of industry or of improper political influence on the part of the foreign investor. Valid or not, such distrust of foreign investment is encountered throughout most of the underdeveloped world, and the creation of wholly owned subsidiaries is restricted as a consequence. Fourth, some countries prefer joint ventures as a means of strengthening their balance-of-payments position through minimizing dividend transfers and repatriation of foreign capital.

For these reasons, some governments require native participation in any foreign venture. In India, for instance, the late Prime Minister Nehru declared in a policy statement in 1949, "The major interest in ownership and effective control of an industrial undertaking should, as a rule, be in Indian hands."[7] However, most of the time, the enforcement of such policies is quite flexible. In some sectors local capital may be unavailable or insufficient, and in others the need too pressing to wait for it to become available. Nevertheless, the screening of foreign-investment projects has become increasingly rigid and restrictive.

In other cases, the foreign investor may be prohibited by law from investing in certain industries except on a joint-venture basis. In Burma, for instance, the law requires 60 percent Burmese control in any corporation which exploits timber, minerals, forests, fisheries, coal, petroleum, or other natural resources. Similarly, Mexico has a constitutional provision which limits a foreigner's control to a maximum of 40 percent in corporations engaged in agriculture, radio or television broadcasting, motion pictures, publishing, advertising, fishing, transportation, and a number of other activities.[8]

The new business class

A second factor that may explain the recent expansion of joint ventures is the growing sophistication of foreign businessmen. Increasingly an international managerial class is emerging. Not only are administrative techniques and organizational know-how transmitted from country to country, but also the attitudes and points of view characteristic of modern industrial executives have spread throughout the world, even to the Soviet realm. This does not mean that no more important differences and conflicts of interest exist between partners in joint ventures. They do exist, but the trend is clearly toward greater homogeneity; and the fundamental divergences between businessmen in different countries are no longer so great as they were in the 1930's and 1940's.

Labor shortage in Europe

Because of its rapid economic growth, continental Europe suffered a general labor shortage since 1958. Incoming investors thus found that the

[7] Quoted in Friedmann and Kalmanoff, *Joint International Business Ventures,* p. 194.
[8] Friedmann and Kalmanoff, *Joint International Business Ventures,* p. 199.

easiest way to gain entry into the market was to acquire interest in a concern that already had a labor force. Many American firms, therefore, entered joint-venture agreements under which they provided technology, patents, and merchandising know-how while the European company furnished the plant, the facilities, and the labor force.

The influence of the U.S. government

The desire of American firms to have majority ownership has declined to some extent since the passage of the 1962 Revenue Act. Under this law, a parent company which owns over 50 percent of a foreign firm must pay U.S. income taxes on its current overseas profits regardless of whether they are repatriated or not. But companies whose holdings are less than 50 percent of their foreign affiliates are not subject to this requirement. As a result, the interest of U.S. firms in joint venturing abroad has increased—especially in the former tax-haven countries.

Finally, the trend toward joint ventures has been encouraged by the recent efforts of the U.S. government to curb the outflow of gold. Restrictions on direct foreign investments have compelled more companies to raise money from overseas sources, a task easier to accomplish in partnership with a local firm than alone.

Types of Joint-Venture Enterprises

A joint venture may take several forms depending upon (a) the identity of the partners and (b) the extent of the ownership by each partner. (See Figure 13-1.) Regarding partners, a firm has basically three choices: local companies (private enterprises), government agencies, or parties from a third country. Regarding ownership, the key decision is whether to acquire a majority or to accept a minority position; subsidiary issues involve the degree of flexibility and adaptability that the particular proposition warrants.

The Identity of the Partners

Association of foreign private interests

Veteran international operators, such as most of the oil companies, have long favored joint ventures abroad. The early joint ventures were often associations among partners all of whom were alien to the country where the enterprise was located. For example, a U.S. company combined with a British firm for oil exploration in Arabia, or a French and a Swiss company joined efforts to mine phosphate in South America. In most cases, the advantage of common enterprise arose from pooling the different resources and capabilities of the partners. One may have had the capital but lacked the experience or the

FIGURE 13-1

Types of Joint-Venture Partners (All Names Fictitious)

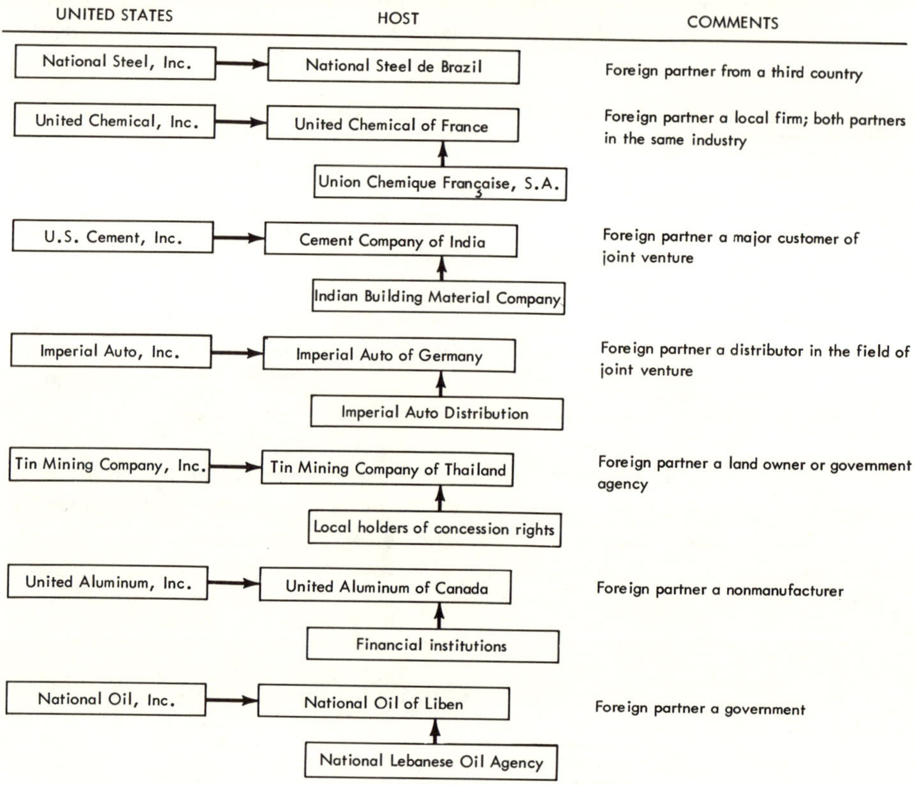

political entrée to the country; and the other firm may have possessed the latter. In highly speculative investments spreading the risk was also an advantage. Such multiple ownership is not uncommon among the joint ventures formed before World War II. This practice aggravates what usually is considered the inherent disadvantage of joint ventures, namely, the differences in managerial philosophy, organizational structures, and operating policy which the partners must overcome to have consistency and intrinsic cohesion in management. For this reason, only one or two partners are assigned primary managerial responsibility. The others participate mainly through the contribution of capital, technology, or material and through representation on the board of directors.

When no party to a venture is a local national—that is, all partners are from different foreign countries—the enterprise is comparable to a wholly foreign-owned subsidiary and, as such, is faced with the problem of gaining public acceptance and identification with local interests. In part, the fact that all parties are subject to the same antiforeign laws and policies and to essentially the same nationalistic and cultural prejudices, although the latter may vary, may be considered an advantage to the firm; it helps to avoid interpartner differences and to solidify the venture's managerial objectives and policies. However, this is not enough to make up for the disadvantages of not having a local partner.

Association with local private interests

Normally, the native partner in a joint venture is a company of some significance. As such it can contribute existing production facilities, markets, distribution outlets, labor, and management to the new enterprise. The need for starting from scratch is thus eliminated; the typical initial losses are minimized; the developmental period is shortened; and both the investment and the uncertainty for the foreign partner are reduced.

A joint venture may also be formed with a local partner operating in some related field. In India, for instance, the Tata Engineering and Locomotive Company (locomotives and heavy engineering products) organized an automobile division with Daimler-Benz of West Germany; and, in the Philippines, the Intercontinental Hotels Corporation has formed a joint venture with a Philippine real-estate firm.[9] And there are others. This kind of association is usually initiated by the foreign firm, which seeks out a local company for some specific reason; the more common reasons are these:

To gain entry into the country

To keep the dollar portion of the new investment under a desired limit

To achieve vertical integration of operations where either supplier-consumer or supplier-distributor relationships are involved[10]

To gain access to natural resources, patents, or other valuable inputs which a native company may control

In some cases, joint ventures are formed by partners who have no industry connection or functional relationship. For instance, Monsanto Chemical holds 40 percent of the stock of an Italian company, Sicedison S.p.A., a diversified manufacturer of organic and inorganic chemicals, for which the native partner and majority owner is Societe Edison, a large Italian hydroelectric company.

Other less common local partners in joint international business ventures consist of small financial groups prominent in the local business community, of financial institutions such as commercial banks, of life insurance companies, and of others.

Association with public agencies or governments

Joint ventures are not confined to private capital. Public enterprise and, of greater interest although relatively new to the field, governments appear to

[9] Friedmann and Kalmanoff, *Joint International Business Ventures,* p. 88.

[10] For example: (a) In Bristol de Mexico, an aircraft overhaul and repair firm, the native partners are the largest airline companies in that country: Cia Mexicana de Aviación and Aeronaves de Mexico. (b) American Cyanamid Company formed Cyanamid Italia by purchasing a part interest in its former licensee, Aziends Laboratori Farmaceutici (Alfar).

be taking more interest in this type of international organization. Direct participation by official agencies in equity joint ventures is already quite widespread, especially in the underdeveloped countries. Governments have come to emphasize public participation in business enterprise primarily because of the growing concern with economic growth. This is clearly reflected in the names of the governmental agencies commissioned to enter joint ventures with foreign capital. They bear such titles as Corporación de Fomento de la Producción (Chile), Nacional Financiera (Mexico), Industrial Development Corporation (Pakistan) or their titles include some other phrase about industrial development or economic progress.

The main activities of such public corporations are investments in heavy industry and other sectors considered basic to a particular country's economy. They also boost lagging industries for a better overall economic balance. As pointed out by one author, the main functions of such a development corporation are "to assist in the promotion, financing, and organization of new industries; to broaden the opportunities for private investors; and to move on to new investments with the rotation of its funds from earlier investments."[11] The implication here is that participation by the public corporation is essentially a temporary booster operation which will continue long enough for an enterprise to achieve a desired maturity. At that point the public corporation will withdraw from the venture and will be succeeded by private investors. Sensible as it is, this plan is only a future possibility. It is perhaps more correct to conceive government participation in joint international ventures not as a temporary phenomenon but as a long-range trend toward a "mixed" enterprise system.

In an increasing number of countries certain sectors of the economy are blocked out for governmental control and development. This is true not only in the newer nations such as India, the United Arab Republic, and Algeria but also in Italy, Great Britain, Sweden, and France.

Doctrinaire Opposition. Private investors in the capital-exporting countries, especially in the United States, often vigorously oppose partnership with branches of foreign governments. The main reason is generally a rigid, doctrinaire adherence to the classical free-enterprise concept. In his study of 172 American firms with foreign interests abroad, Richard D. Robinson notes some interesting comments by executives from different U.S. companies about entering into partnership with foreign governments: "We'd say the hell with it, that is not our idea of free enterprise"; or "We are a business, not a government agency."[12] Their common supposition is that mixed companies are retarded by government participation and therefore less efficient than wholly private operations. They also believe the government corporation will resort to political pressure rather than to administrative efficiency to guide the mixed venture. It is too early to know if there is any general validity in these assumptions. Friedmann thinks there is none: "Joint ventures with local

[11] Friedmann and Kalmanoff, *Joint International Business Ventures,* p. 175.

[12] "Management Attitudes Toward Joint and Mixed Ventures Abroad," *Western Business Review,* VI, No. 1 (February 1962), 14.

government have generally proven to be no less successful than entirely private joint ventures."[13] And, regarding the alleged political pressure, such pressure is seldom unknown and is often a strategic constraint in wholly owned subsidiaries. Indeed, one cannot resist the question of whether private enterprise could not strengthen its position in some countries by interlocking its organization and institutions with those of the public domain.

There is some evidence that the purely ideological barrier to entering a mixed-ownership joint venture is being broken down by private enterprise and that a more flexible point of view is gaining currency. This is especially true in the petroleum industry. In many countries mineral resources belong to the state. Hence, oil production is directly dependent upon state participation in one form or another. Also, the oil-surplus countries have often capitalized on this one resource as the source of revenue for the government. The resulting profit sharing between the operating companies and the government has brought about a variety of different organizational arrangements, many peculiar to the petroleum industry. One of these is the joint venture in which both partners are governmental bodies. For example, Societe Irano-Italiene des Petroles (SIRIP) is a venture formed jointly by the Italian government-owned ENI (Ente Nazionale Idrocarbuni) and the National Iranian Oil Company, an agency of the Irani government. An interesting feature of this particular partnership is its profit-sharing formula. It provides in accordance with Irani law for a 50–50 division between the government and the company. But, since the production company is half Irani and half Italian, the company's share is further divided on a 50–50 basis. The net result is that the Irani government receives 75 and the Italian government 25 percent of the total.

The Ownership Policy

Management attitudes toward equity participation vary greatly from one company to another. Some firms adopt an inflexible policy of retaining complete ownership; others insist on taking only a minority equity in all their foreign ventures; and still others are willing to vary their equity participation either within a certain range or all the way from complete ownership to a minority position, depending upon conditions in the host country. The extent of equity ownership depends primarily on these factors: the nature of the product; the financial and managerial strength of the company; the economic, social, and political environment in the host country; and the views held by top management.

Product

The complexity of the company's product induces some firms to retain full or majority control over foreign operations. Also, there is less pressure on them from host governments for local participation than there is in the case of simpler and more familiar activities. The IBM World Trade Corporation,

[13] Friedmann and Kalmanoff, *Joint International Business Ventures,* pp. 174–75.

for instance, has no joint ventures despite its far-flung, global structure. Its executives are convinced that the highly specialized nature of IBM products sets their company outside the general policies and regulations which many countries apply to foreign enterprises. On the other extreme, utility companies and producers of staples and other goods of simple design lend themselves to standardized operations. Public participation here is widespread, partly because of governmental pressure and partly because of the desire to obviate any such pressure by accepting a minority position. Pan American World Airways has been reduced to a minority position in most of its foreign ventures for these reasons.

Business environment

The economic, social, and political situation of the host country may also have an important bearing on the equity ratio between the native and the foreign partners. In underdeveloped and unstable economies, the number of joint ventures is likely to increase relatively faster than the number in industrialized countries both because of the more nationalistic attitude of host governments toward foreign investments and because of the necessity for the foreign partner to protect itself by spreading the risk.

Capital and management resources

A small firm with limited capital and management resources is more likely to seek strong foreign partners than is a large company operating a network of production facilities in numerous countries. The larger firm wishes to ease its productivity and selling capability by buying or taking over a firm and is often less concerned with the efficiency of the overseas company than it is with the activities of the company and its contacts with the market, the government, and the raw-materials supplier. These are the factors which determine whether the potential venture can or cannot be well integrated into the parent concern's world-wide organization. Such a large company seeks majority control in order to install its own methods of management, production, and marketing rather than having to depend upon the local methods. On the other hand, the smaller company does not have the financial resources to acquire foreign units or the managerial strength to run them on a centralized basis. Lacking size and power, it emphasizes flexibility, adaptation to local situations, and decentralization of management authority. Also, instead of ownership control, small companies may seek nonownership control over the venture through a technical or a management contract, and in this they often do succeed. As Theobald points out, "An equalitarian grouping of firms of limited size in a number of countries might be able to achieve far better results than the conventional. . . joint-venture approach, in which the U.S. company characteristically becomes the dominant member."[14] The same author

[14] Robert Theobald, *Business Potential in the European Common Market,* American Management Association Study No. 62 (New York, 1963), p. 36.

mentions also the approach followed by Ansul Chemical Company, a medium-sized firm: "One of the things we found out in our investigations has been the advantage of what we could call partnerships in the various countries. Because of our size, we think carefully about invading a market alone. We try to get a partner in a particular area and develop a 50–50 relationship with him so that he has his interest and we have ours. This idea seems to be growing in acceptance because neither one side nor the other dominates and dictates. In other words, you don't have to come into a foreign country and start your own operation and employ people (nationals) there. In a partnership you share in the economy and the culture. Then, in case of expropriation or any of the other problems which might arise, you have a local partner who is vitally interested and in position to act. From a small company's standpoint, it seems to me that foreign partners offer a real advantage. . . ."[15]

Top management attitudes

All of the above factors may be important in explaining the ownership policies of U.S. companies, but such objective criteria are not the only bases for the policies. In his study of 172 American firms, R. D. Robinson found, "Fixed attitudes in respect to such undertakings [joint ventures] are compounded largely of prejudices, as demonstrated in the author's inquiry by the fact that opinion among executives on the merit of 100 percent U.S. industry-owned subsidiaries, joint and mixed ventures, seemed to be divided, and could not be correlated with any objective business factors."[16] So, "statements by executives in support of majority. . .ownership of foreign enterprises revealed the highly personal or nonbusiness nature of many decisions."[17] Wolfgang Friedmann reaches the same conclusion when he analyzes the motivations for joint ventures: "In such matters, unconscious attitudes are understandably present, for example, attitudes toward familial patterns, social and cultural difference, and hierarchical and impersonal relationships versus human relationships based on equality and face-to-face dealings."[18] These findings caution against reliance upon purely economic analysis and interpretation of the arguments in favor of or against joint-venture enterprise. Most U.S. companies prefer a controlling equity participation in joint ventures, but for how long this will be true remains to be seen. The pendulum is swinging slowly but surely from the majority-ownership policy toward a minority position.

That business at the present time is searching for a new formula for its overseas equity position is abundantly clear. An increasing number of large companies have declared their willingness to accept minority participation under certain circumstances; others have adopted a policy of deliberately seeking minority equity in their foreign ventures, even if other alternatives are open; and still others have in fact proceeded to make such a policy a reality.

15 Theobald, *Business Potential in the European Common Market,* p. 41.
16 "Management Attitudes Toward Joint and Mixed Ventures Abroad," p. 15.
17 "Management Attitudes Toward Joint and Mixed Ventures Abroad," p. 15.
18 Friedmann and Kalmanoff, *Joint International Business Ventures,* p. 125.

Robinson mentions the case of two large hotel companies searching for foreign opportunities on a minority basis though accompanied by management controls. Their managements refused to consider projects requiring any substantial investment by the companies themselves.[19]

Multiple objectives

Most companies pursue multiple objectives in their ownership policies. They are prepared to vary their position from case to case and may be involved in a wholly owned subsidiary in one country, a majority-controlled venture in another, and a licensee arrangement in a third, depending upon the circumstances of the particular country or the venture in question. In Robinson's study, a large chemical company had equity interest in its foreign affiliates ranging from 2 percent to 100 percent. Such a policy provides the company much wider latitude than the single-criterion policies of some companies. A flexible policy permits the company to synchronize its structure and strategies with national objectives and local peculiarities so as to benefit from rather than to be penalized by them.

Multipartite Ventures

Most joint ventures are bipartite. Their traditional model calls for a foreign majority partner and a local minority partner, the former providing the management and the latter serving to anchor the venture in the indigenous economy. The insistence on majority ownership and undivided managerial authority limited multipartite venture formation, since local partners regarded fractional shares of minority ownership too small for any real influence.

Increasing political objections and legal restrictions against foreign domination of joint ventures, especially in the developing countries, have fostered growing corporate acceptance of minority positions in joint venture creation. Experience has shown that majority position does not exclude local interference—it sometimes causes or compounds it—nor is minority position necessarily synonymous with lack of influence and managerial control over the venture.

> As long as the foreign investor is needed because of his capital investment, his managerial expertise, and his technological know-how, he is not likely to suffer from the position of a minority stockholder, and he is not subject to the accusation of dominating the enterprise. . . . A foreign minority participation will usually classify the joint enterprise as "national" and thus save it from general legislative or administrative measures directed at foreign enterprises.[20]

Relaxation of the majority policy has opened for multinational firms and other direct foreign investors opportunities to participate in projects which

[19] "Management Attitudes Toward Joint and Mixed Ventures Abroad," p. 10.

[20] Wolfgang G. Friedmann and Jean-Pierre Beguin, *Joint International Business Ventures in Developing Countries* (New York: Columbia University Press, 1971), p. 12.

the host governments guard jealously against overt foreign control. Power, railroads, port facilities, hospitals, public service facilities, and other aspects of the infrastructure constitute the hard core of this category. Basic resource-oriented industries such as mining, tropical agriculture, and lumber, where majority positions or complete foreign ownership used to be common, are now required by host countries to relinquish majority control to local nationals, often a government corporation, and to limit its interest to 49 percent or less. Refusal of several old-line companies to comply with this requirement has led to complete expropriation of the ventures. Their fate has had a sobering effect on others.

The acceptance of minority position and willingness to enter into partnership with state enterprises have removed two corporate taboos which since colonial times have blocked the formation of multipartite joint ventures. Now the way is open. Although the tradition-bound older firms, as well as the many overly-centralized ones, still reject the new flexible approach, several younger industries are already enmeshed in multipartite ventures. Since they require from management greater cross-cultural sophistication and more adaptive decision-making processes than the old bipartite arrangements, the multipartite venture is likely to grow only to the extent to which the quality of international management advances to equal this new option.

Motivation

The value of international joint-venture enterprise is complex to assess. Each joint-venture investment is in some respect different from others and as such requires separate analysis and evaluation. No a priori criteria can therefore serve as the basis for a completely rational joint-venture policy. The companies which follow some pre-established rule are running the risks of limiting their international opportunities and of entering into less profitable associations while more profitable ones are rejected. However, a theoretically satisfactory analysis is not always possible in practice. Limitations in time, manpower, and particularly skill in analyzing and projecting international business problems encourage reliance on some a priori rules. The following systematic exposé of the positive and negative reasons for joint-venture enterprise can serve as a framework for a rational analysis of any particular case and provide a broader basis for a priori criteria where they are necessary.

The Case for Joint Ventures

The merits of joint ventures may be classified into three broad categories: economic, political, and social. Each deserves separate discussion.

Economic advantages

If a principle of joint-venture economics exists, it must be to optimize the returns to two or more enterprises, each of which controls different resource inputs required for a new company. This procedure is more than pooling. To be sure, capital outlays of the partners are reduced through the pooling, permitting larger-scale and lower-cost operation than the partners could individually support. But the crux of the matter often lies not so much in the amount but in the form or forms of the investment inputs necessary. People may be reluctant to sell out a traditional family business or permit foreigners to acquire land. Also, placing an appraisal on the value of land to be used for an entirely new purpose may present some very difficult questions, ones that bear directly upon the size of the capital contribution of each partner to a venture.

Preexisting marketing network and supplier relations, intangible though they are, are especially crucial for the success of new ventures since they require time, sometimes extended periods, to develop. At least in the early years then, an enterprise has no other opportunity to acquire these marketing and supply capabilities than through a native partner.

Acquiring an experienced labor force presents a similar problem. Many countries' business systems suffer from chronic shortages of skilled labor and competent technicians. In others, full employment or overemployment, as has existed in continental Europe for several years, seriously retards any new investor's ability to secure adequate manpower resources. The difficulties for foreign investors are usually compounded by discriminatory regulations and attitudes. A native partner can surmount such difficulties by supplying the initial work force and by utilizing its established channels for recruiting the balance. Key technicians, foremen, department heads, district representatives, and other strategic cadres proficient in the local language and business practices can similarly be obtained.

Less often found in practice, but no less valid in theory, is a product which is inaccessible without a joint-venture agreement. Patented, trademarked, or otherwise protected products of great potential belong to this category as do products requiring point-of-sale or point-of-consumption service and face-to-face contact which only a native staff under local supervision can effectively supply.

Finally, there is the tax advantage for U.S. companies which own less than 50 percent of the joint venture. As indicated earlier, the Revenue Act of 1962 imposes U.S. income tax on all foreign affiliates of American firms in which the parent has majority interest; in the case of insurance companies the tax liability starts at 25 percent equity. This means that such affiliates must pay U.S. taxes on their current earnings annually regardless of whether the profits stay abroad or are transferred to this county. For affiliates in which the U.S. partner's investment constitutes less than 50 percent, or in the case of insurance companies less than 25 percent, no U.S. tax liability accrues until the profits are repatriated. Since income-tax rates in most other countries are substantially lower than those in the United States, the savings that result from not being compelled to pay the U.S. tax are normally a major source of funds for the venture. A significant percentage of the growth of foreign affiliates of U.S. firms is attributable to such tax savings.

Political advantages

Discrimination against foreign enterprise is universal. No country accords all the rights and privileges enjoyed by native firms to foreign companies. Such discrimination is inherent in the concept of the sovereign nation, which, in terms of its logic, must promote and defend the interests of its citizens vis-à-vis the rest of the world. Whether a politically independent nation can have any substance at all after the economic differences between domestic and foreign interests are removed will be better understood once the European economic integration under the Treaty of Rome has been completed. For the present, there is no prospect that the differences will disappear. Even if the European Common Market becomes a reality, it will only substitute a larger realm for the six smaller ones. An improvement—yes; an elimination—no.

The relevant question, then, is not whether there is discriminatory treatment of foreign affiliates but what form it may take and how great it is. Answers to both questions depend on the country and the industry involved. Most countries do not have separate laws for foreign enterprise. Instead, the discriminatory provisions are scattered among different codes and regulations such as immigration laws, investment controls, and corporation law. Superimposed on the statutory regulations are administrative decrees, policy declarations, and bureaucratic practices, which in most countries form a greater barrier than the laws themselves.

To overcome those barriers can be a compelling reason for an investor company to seek association with a native enterprise rather than to attempt a wholly owned venture. Furthermore, the local party in a joint venture may not only provide protection against discriminatory governmental actions but also place the enterprise in a position where relief from burdensome domestic regulations can be sought and generally favorable governmental treatment expected. Governmental attitude is crucial for a new international enterprise in most countries but especially in those where central planning, socialization, and public regulation of the economy are present. Import licenses, foreign exchange quotas, transfer permits, and work and residence visas to engineers and executives are examples of "routine" controls by which local or national officials can quickly undermine a firm's operations. On the positive side are tariff protection, tax exemption, low-interest loans, and other special privileges used in an increasing number of countries as incentives for industrial development. The friendliness of local officialdom is therefore an essential precondition for the success of new international ventures. The best way to cultivate it is to integrate the firm in the national business system through joint ownership and management.

Social advantages

The political and social aspects of joint ventures are not easily separated. The general fields of public relations, in the broad sense of a company's social image, and labor relations, including trade unions and employee-morale problems, qualify more as social than as political problems, although elements of the latter are undeniably present.

In public relations, joint-venture operations are of great importance, as people in all countries identify a joint venture with their own society and regard it with greater affection and tolerance than they do foreign enterprises. Public regard is especially important for the consumer-goods industries, since it directly affects the acceptance of their products. The same could be said about service firms, such as banks, insurance companies, hotels, and common carriers.[21]

In labor relations, the joint venture enjoys three important advantages: It can bargain with unions without being vulnerable to anti-American attacks or other foreign-relations vicissitudes which often beleaguer the wholly owned affiliate; it is not pressured to issue comparative, and often embarrassing, wage statistics for all the operating facilities in its multinational structure; and studies in industrial psychology show that employee morale has a tendency to rise after local capital enters a previously all-foreign enterprise—no less among the white-collar staff than among the blue-collar laborers. In the emerging countries, where leadership is supersensitive to its national identity and people are subjected to intensive indoctrination in nationalist ideology, the gains in morale are potentially more significant than the gains in the other two areas.

The Case against Joint Ventures

Joint venturing is still a novelty and, as such, is distrusted in the more conservative sectors of American business. Friedmann observed that objections to joint ventures were most prevalent among companies which had never tried them, and that this distrust and the arguments against joint ventures which are based on it stem from a general lack of confidence in the ability and integrity of businessmen of other lands. Whether it is engendered by misconceptions, chauvinism, or naive egotism, such an attitude is dangerous in international business. In the discussion which follows, no effort is made to probe the psychological aspects of the subject except where the factual record itself has such connotations. The objectively negative arguments regarding joint ventures center around managerial dissension and profits.

Managerial dissension

Wherever individuals from different national, economic, ethnic, and cultural environments join in a common effort, there is a high probability of conflicting views and value judgments and of different ways of looking at problems in general. The history of allied military campaigns, church organizations, and political movements offers centuries of testimony to this effect. Interpersonal friction in the multinational management group of a joint-

21 Firms catering to the international tourist or foreign trade are unlikely to be affected.

venture enterprise must, therefore, be regarded as a basic but normal problem of management. Like similar problems elsewhere, it requires methods and policies specifically designed to deal with it. The fact that the problem lacks an exact duplicate in mononational management does not place it in the unpredictable class; it only means that a different perspective is required to identify and prognosticate the problem correctly and to have the staff and experience to meet it effectively.

The potential causes for dissension are many. First, there are different influences. The foreign partner operates in an international environment, and the native partner in the more limited sphere of its own country. For example, the foreign partner is subject to taxation in both countries, while the local partner is affected by the tax provision of its own government only. Or, the foreign partner is eager to coordinate the venture's policies and products with those of its other international affiliates, while the local partner may be influenced by a "separatist" course more in accord with its concept of domestic opportunity.

Second, there are the general difficulties of nonunified management. Each partner is faced with the problem of explaining and justifying to the other or others, as the case may be, its respective home office's decisions and actions in respect to the operations of the joint venture. Hence, administration is made more difficult and psychologically demanding. Related to this are conflicting objectives and implicit differences in ethical standards. For example, the family-controlled companies, typical in many foreign countries, confront their nonfamily-owned U.S. corporate partner with demands to make top executive appointments from among the family membership, to pay frequent and high dividends, and to divert company resources to the family's other consumptive needs.

However, serious as such problems are, the general outlook is encouraging. Business education and professionalism in management are spreading and displacing many traditional differences with relative harmony in basic philosophy and attitudes of management. Indeed, the growth of joint ventures may prove to be an important testing ground for multinational management practices and theory.

Profit limitations

The profit-limitations argument is that, by sharing the ownership, the party to a joint venture denies to itself the future opportunity for full profits, thereby limiting its potential earning power. In a sense, it is the reverse side of the investment-advantage argument, i.e., joint venturing reduces investment input. But unlike the latter, the profit-reduction argument lacks merit. The reverse could be argued with an equal or an even greater degree of persuasiveness.

A more serious charge relates to the disposition of profits, especially to reinvestment and expansion of the base. Opponents of joint ventures believe that local partners are against liberal reinvestment policies and thus are a deterrent to company growth. In individual instances this has been true, but in the majority of joint ventures the fear has been exaggerated. Friedmann notes, "On this point, there is considerable evidence that serious conflicts have not arisen and that joint ventures have followed a policy of liberal reinvestment for growth. Enterprises in the more advanced countries do not ignore altogether the interests of their stockholders in dividend distributions and the effect of dividend payments on the value of their securities on the public exchanges. Cases are not totally absent in which the relative attitudes of the foreign and local partners toward reinvestment policy are the reverse of what is expected. In a situation of sharp exchange depreciation, the foreign partner may wish to remit dividends rather than reinvest profits, while the local partner may prefer to reinvest profits for working capital rather than to borrow locally."[22] To this we might add that any unacceptable attitude regarding the treatment of profits would be uncovered during the negotiations preceding the joint-venture association, and, if the attitudes were unalterable, the association simply would not materialize.

Another negative aspect of joint ventures was explained to the author by a businessman: "The danger is that after a while one partner is contributing more than its share, and the other party is receiving disproportionate benefits. Some intangible elements brought by one of the partners, such as certain affiliations, know-how, patents, or processes, may not have been adequately capitalized in the beginning. The partners gradually lose sight of their relative inputs as the joint venture expands into new fields, and, after some time, the contribution of one may be disproportionately large while the other gains a return incommensurate with its contribution." The businessman was not clear on how an alert management could permit a situation where it is not receiving its legitimate share of the profits to arise. But there must be some rationale to the argument, for it has more than negligible following among businessmen as evidenced by its recurrence in different studies.

22 Friedmann and Kalmanoff, *Joint International Business Ventures,* p. 172.

14

Foreign Licensing

Licensing makes available to a foreign firm some intangible industrial property such as a patent, a manufacturing process, or a trademark for the purpose of cultivating the foreign licensee's market. This obviates the licensor company's need for entering the foreign market through export trade or capital investment. In return for the property rights transferred to it, the foreign firm pays royalties normally based on its output or sales of the licensed product.

The Licensing Agreement

A licensing arrangement is always formalized in a written agreement which stipulates which property rights are being transferred; the royalties or other considerations paid; where and how the rights are to be utilized; under which circumstances the rights are to revert to the licensor; and the degree of participation the licensor is to have in the licensed operations of the licensee or in the marketing of the licensed products. The contract may further cover the period of time; the size of the territory covered by the arrangement; the methods of control and payment; the applicable law in case of conflict; and the method of arbitration, if appropriate.

Besides providing an alternative to export-import trade and direct investment, licensing agreements also provide an inexpensive means for exploring and testing a company's growth potential in a particular foreign area before any irretrievable investment is made. From a risk standpoint, licensing agreements entail greater risk than normal export operations but considerably less risk than direct investments. For this reason, licensing is frequently used as a transitional phase between export and foreign manufacture in a company's international expansion process and is succeeded by a more extensive commitment. So-called *royalty and stock participation agreements* are specifically designed for gradual conversion from licensing to equity operation. They provide for a low or a declining royalty plus a stock-purchase commitment in a new or existing establishment to succeed the licensing arrangement. The licensee acquires a partial ownership interest in the successor company through the stock purchases. In cases where local equity capital is not available in sufficiently large blocks to establish a joint-venture facility, the facility may initially be financed by the U.S. licensor and gradually converted into a joint enterprise under a royalty and stock-purchase agreement. Thus, such arrangements permit equity financing from the proceeds of the very product for which the equity was intended.

Licensing has sometimes been defined as exporting of know-how. However, it is also a continuous cooperative relationship between the parties for their mutual benefit. It is correct to classify licensing as a nonequity joint venture where pooling of resources among the partners is the overriding characteristic. It is not to be equated with direct investment; the industrial property rights are not sold outright but leased or loaned for a definite period, and the proceeds are royalties—not dividends or profits.

Geographic distribution

Licensing agreements are more dominant in the developed countries. In a survey, the National Industrial Conference Board found that 65 percent of the 500 licensing arrangements identified were located in the industrial countries of Europe, in Canada, and in Australia.[1] The percentage of franchises in Canada was relatively small, reflecting the fact that most U.S. companies conceive the Canadian market as part of their domestic structure. To develop this market local branches, subsidiaries, or equity joint ventures are used instead of licensing agreements.

In Latin America and Asia, the licensing agreement is a relatively new but growing method of international business. Generally, the agreements in less-developed areas require more assistance with plant facilities, machinery, technical know-how, and marketing than potential licensors are prepared to offer. Also, fewer potential licensees limit the opportunities. For these reasons licensing arrangements in Latin America are concentrated in Mexico (4.8 percent), Argentina (2.9 percent), Brazil (2.7 percent), and Venezuela (1.0 percent). In Africa they are concentrated in the Republic of South Africa—3.3 percent out of the 4.6 percent total according to the same survey.

Industry distribution

Generally, licensing is used for the same products that are exported and directly invested in abroad, i.e., machine tools, electrical and industrial equip-

[1] National Industrial Conference Board, *Foreign Licensing* (New York, 1958), p. 13.

ment, automotive products, household appliances, rubber products, chemicals, drugs, and pharmaceuticals. For products which do not lend themselves to export—because they are too heavy or bulky or because foreign production is more economical—licensing is used as a preliminary step to establishing equity operations in the particular foreign market. In the last ten years increasingly more consumer-goods manufacturers have discovered the advantages of licensing their know-how and trademarks; and the practice is spreading rapidly.

Types of Licensing Arrangements

Licensing is a flexible and variable working arrangement which can serve the international needs of a great variety of different partners. The simple licensing agreement is limited to a patent or trademark. A complex licensing agreement may involve not only scores of patents and brands but also comprehensive manufacturing and distributing systems, active participation of the licensor in the management of the franchised enterprise, and possible ownership affiliation. Between the two exists an infinite variety of legal arrangements which transfer property rights, industrial know-how, and business services to organizations abroad.

The common element of all licensing agreements is the permission given by the licensor to the licensee to use an industrial property right for a royalty. Beyond that, licensing agreements may differ in three important respects: the licensee, the licensor, and the limitations placed on the use of the licensed rights.

Identity of the Licensee

The most typical licensee is a well-established national firm engaged in the same industry as the licensor. It should have sufficient financial strength and productive capacity to carry out the objectives of the arrangement. In some cases, the licensee has a monopoly position, partly or wholly protected by the government, and no effective alternative except licensing is open to the licensor in that country.[2]

Where large firms do not exist or where they will not or cannot enter licensing arrangements, such arrangements are sometimes made with a small native company. In such situations the licensor retains much more control over manufacturing and marketing operations than it does under regular licensing agreements. Occasionally, the licensee may be a small financial group or even a private individual with no existing plant or equipment. The intention of such arrangements is to start a new business with active local participation, usually as a prelude to a subsequent joint-venture investment.

2 Charles H. Lee, "How to Reach the Overseas Market by Licensing," *Harvard Business Review,* XXXVI, No. 1 (January–February 1958), 78.

Intracompany licensing

Ordinarily, the foreign licensing agreement is concluded between companies which have no ownership ties. However, in recent years formal licensing agreements have become increasingly popular between the parent company and its foreign affiliates. Branches, wholly owned subsidiaries, and joint-venture companies have been authorized like any other licensee to use the parent's property rights or services for regular royalty payments. Similar arrangements are also increasing in multinational corporate structures. Among the latter, the usual royalty arrangement is often replaced by a cross-licensing clause under which one property right (trademark *X*) is exchanged for another (trademark *Y*), and both parties are simultaneously licensors and licensees.

Whether intracompany arrangements should be included among licensing agreements is debatable. Some writers argue that they are essentially something else, but close examination leaves the author less than certain that this is so. In many instances the intracompany agreement not only is legally as valid as intercompany franchises, but also requires from the partners considerations as significant as any others. A possible criterion for accepting and rejecting intracompany arrangements as bona fide licensing agreements is the existence of a royalty payment or an equivalent consideration such as cross-licensing. Royalty-free arrangements would thus be excluded.

Triangular arrangements

A special case is presented by the triangular relations among a licensor, its foreign licensee, and a foreign joint-venture company owned by the two. As indicated in the beginning of this chapter, a rather common arrangement in such situations is the royalty and stock participation agreement, from which the licensor can derive several important advantages: (a) greater total return by combining royalties and dividends than through straight royalties; (b) greater continuity of return, as the dividends would not cease if the agreement were terminated; and (c) greater control over the licensee through the joint venture. More complex arrangements involving several major and minor partners in combined licensing and joint-venture relationships exist. These are, however, newcomers to the international business scene, and there is insufficient experience with them to justify any generalization.

The Licensor

Any division, department, or subsidiary of a company located at home or abroad may be the licensor. It may license directly—i.e., its own products, know-how, or rights—or indirectly, by being authorized to license the property of another entity in a multiunit international firm. In the latter case, it acts as a licensing representative for that other entity, and its licensing functions extend only to the territory covered by its normal operations. It has been common practice for foreign-base companies to act as licensing representatives for the parent corporations and their domestic subsidiaries.

Licensing pools

A unique roll in foreign licensing is played by patent and licensing pools organized for this specific purpose or joined together with a combination export management firm or a manufacturer's export agent. The latter type "acts as licensing as well as export representative for a number of manufacturing companies. It solicits and receives permission to negotiate licensing agreements, subject to the approval of company management. It recommends licensing policy, conducts the exploratory research and actual negotiations, and undertakes the supervision and servicing of the completed arrangements."[3]

Normally there are no direct financial ties between the licensees and the licensing pool. However, a middleman-operated pool such as the one described in the above quotation acts in a *del credere* capacity guaranteeing payment of royalties to the original licensor, i.e., to its domestic client company. In return for its services, the pool operator receives a certain percentage of the royalty and, in recent years, has often acquired a stock interest in some licensee concerns.

Limitations on Licensed Rights

Exclusivity is an important principle of foreign licensing arrangements. Virtually all franchise agreements contain certain exclusive features, but the number, the kind, and the extent of these features vary widely from case to case. Some manufacturers grant exclusive production rights to only one firm in any foreign country; others follow regional or continental schemes. Some grant exclusive manufacturing rights but follow a nonexclusive distribution policy; others may do the reverse. What can be done is more often a function of the circumstances than of any strict policy. For example, a thin market may induce a licensee to accept an agreement only if complete exclusivity is guaranteed. In a large urban market, where competition is less decisive, the licensor has more alternatives and consequently greater flexibility.

One of the most common licensing restrictions is the *mutual restraint*—licensors and licensees contract to stay out of each other's markets. The licensor grants an exclusive production and distribution right, and the licensee promises to remain within his designated territory.

Limitations depend also on the applicable laws of the host country, especially those which regulate competitive business practices, trademarks, patents, and foreign relations. In some instances the licensor's domestic legislation, too, may be relevant. For example, if the contract restricts the market territory of the licensee, it may be objectionable to the U.S. antitrust authorities. However, the laws affect the language and phraseology of the licensing agreement more than its intent. Even in the absence of explicit limitations in the contract, there will normally be at least a tacit understanding between the licensor and licensee that the rights and know-how will be used only in

3 National Industrial Conference Board, *Obstacles and Incentives to Private Foreign Investment* (New York, 1965), p. 32.

designated areas or for designated purposes and the licensee will refrain from interfering with the licensor's arrangements in other areas.

Possible conflict

But exclusivity has its negative side. It commits a company to the arrangement and may become a serious block if changes later become desirable. The principal drawback is the licensee's potential power to prevent direct manufacture or other alternative methods for serving the market. From the licensee's standpoint, also, there may arise a need for greater flexibility than an exclusive commitment permits.

In practice, exclusive protection seems to be accorded quite readily for manufacturing, but not so readily for sales. The reason for this is that "the reservation of the right of the licensor to sell in competition with its licensee may be a safeguard against potential antitrust action as well as a persuasive factor in making the licensee develop his market."[4]

Reasons for and against Licensing

According to some authors, licensing is a sign of weakness or lack of interest in establishing facilities.[5] And indeed, many cases can be found where the licensor was unable to expand directly in foreign markets and was forced to find a local firm to produce and to sell its products overseas. However, other motivations and other elements also explain the importance of licensing, for even the strongest and the biggest companies use this method.

Reasons for licensing

The advantages inherent in any cooperative international ventures, such as the saving of capital and management resources and the favorable attitude of local government, apply also to licensing arrangements. In addition, there are at least five other areas of motivation for foreign licensing; these are discussed below.

ADDED REVENUE FROM INDUSTRIAL PROPERTY RIGHTS. Licensing of industrial property rights is a source of income which has little relation to the licensor's previous manufacturing and marketing operations. This is particularly true for markets which are not covered and for unused patents and processes. Some companies use licensing only for such purposes. The added income obtained from licensing may cover research costs or maximize returns from research and know-how. For instance, some of the big oil companies regularly license European producers to use patented processes which they have developed for their own use in the United States. In these cases, the oil company is not interested in the foreign market as such but primarily in the royalties it receives; these partially offset the costs of discovering and perfecting the new

[4] Carol McCormick Crosswell, *International Business Techniques* (Dobbs Ferry, New York: Oceana Publications, Inc., 1963), p. 115.

[5] Andrew W. Brainerd, "License or Equity," *International Trade Review,* XXXVI, No. 9 (September 1962), 18.

processes, i.e., they finance the research and development effort the company wishes to sustain.

Licensing as a Marketing Tool. Licensing has often helped a company build goodwill and popular acceptance for its products abroad. This has been true even when only one of several products is licensed. As the local people become familiar with the company's brand through the licensed product, other products exported to the country share in this acceptance.

For high-tariff countries, licensing provides more effective access to the market than exportation does. The same argument applies to countries with other import restrictions. For technical products which require service in connection with sales, the licensing offers the only viable alternative to equity investments.

Protection of Patents and Trademarks. In a number of foreign countries, the only way to protect a patent or a trademark is to "work" it. A licensing arrangement will not only prevent the piracy of products, trademarks, or patents by a local concern but also yield a royalty to the firm.

Reciprocal Benefits from Foreign Know-how. Reciprocal rights to new technology and new products developed abroad by the licensed concern are sometimes included in the licensing contract or handled as another, parallel link between the two partners. Some companies report that such reciprocal rights are of greater value than the royalty payments received under the licensing arrangement, since the foreign research talent is obtained at a comparatively low cost.

Other Advantages. Licensing agreements can be used also for accumulation of capital for direct investment, for testing the potential of a market, and for meeting the needs of parent-owned foreign manufacturing plants which depend on American equipment.

Reasons for not licensing

If the licensing arrangements have been carefully drawn up with clearly defined objectives, they are often useful. However, this method of foreign operations is a limited one and can often constrict the long-term development of the business by putting the incentive in the wrong place. Generally such arrangements encourage the licensee to make the maximum effort in his own interest, simply using the licensed product to that end. They seldom result in the development of a product or service to its fullest possible extent. This is especially true for distribution rights. Therefore, when a competitive sales and advertising job is needed for a product, licensing is not often the most successful arrangement, primarily because the licensor is divorced from the consumer.

Another danger of licensing arises when the licensor assists a foreign company to develop and to expand to the point where the licensee no longer requires the services of the licensor. Thus, the licensor will have been instrumental in building up a local competitor. If, at some future date, the licensor thinks it advisable to engage in direct manufacturing, his position will be much more difficult than if he had undertaken direct manufacturing from the start.

Other reasons advanced for not licensing include: the inability of the licensor to insure quality control; the limited profit potentialities of a licensing operation, especially in expanding markets; the difficulty in changing a royalty to be commensurate with the value of the licensed development; the uncertainty about the application of antitrust laws to licensing activity; the high taxes levied on royalty income by some countries; and the exchange difficulties.

Organization of Licensing Activities

So far, no typical licensing organization has emerged. Very few companies have made permanent staff appointments in which the primary responsibility is licensing. Most firms operate on an *ad hoc* basis. In large firms where specialized units are set up to handle licensing, they consist of representatives of the engineering, financial, legal, and marketing departments. If the company has a separate international headquarters, it is the president of that organization who typically heads the licensing group and under whose personal supervision the foreign arrangements are made. Where there is no international division or headquarters company, licensing and exporting are parceled out on a functional basis to the various domestic divisions.

Within the international division, licensing operations are often subdivided along the same product, regional, or functional lines as are the export marketing or the overseas manufacturing operations of the division or both. For example, if the international operations are organized along product lines, licensing is handled by the heads of the product divisions; if the operations are organized on the territorial principle, each regional manager has charge of licensing in the countries within his territory. Where the export marketing and the overseas manufacturing operations have separate organizations or follow different principles, the licensing arrangements are typically delegated to manufacturing management.

A few companies have made overseas subsidiaries responsible for licensing. In those cases, assistance and advice are frequently sought from the legal, research, and production divisions of the parent company. Moreover, in most instances licensing responsibility extends only to the region in which the subsidiary is located.

Other Nonequity Affiliations

Technical service agreements

In a number of countries, especially the less-developed ones, U.S. companies have entered agreements with local firms or government agencies for performing some technical or operational function in exchange for predetermined royalties or other payments. Typically the services rendered involve developmental activities such as exploring for minerals, planning and constructing specialized industrial or agricultural facilities, or modernizing an existing plant. These are more than ordinary construction projects, for their main emphasis lies on the developmental and operational aspects and their duration normally exceeds the time required for building construction. In fact, some require only incidental or no construction.

A well-publicized case of technical service arrangements is the Indian government steel projects being constructed by German and British companies and by the Russian governmental enterprise. The plants are entirely owned by the Indian government; there is no equity participation at all by any of the foreign partners. The agreements call for no particular structures but for operational plants with agreed technical and economic capabilities. A different illustration is provided by the Mexican petroleum monopoly—a nationalized industry—which has long commissioned American and European oil companies to do much of its prospecting and exploratory drilling. The foreign firms are not paid for the cost of the exploration, but for a 25-year period share in the returns of any discoveries they make.

Management contracts

In the newest type of joint venture, operating facilities are owned by one partner but managed by another. This has become the pattern in the hotel industry. Western International Hotels and the Hilton group, for example, run large hostelry plants around the world which are either completely or primarily owned by non-American capital. The typical management contract continues in effect for an indefinite period and entitles the management corporation to a fixed minimum annuity plus a share of the profits.

Another type of management contract is used for foreign packing and assembly operations.[6] The product is exported in bulk to a foreign firm which processes, assembles, packages, and markets it for the U.S. company under a management contract. This arrangement, too, provides for profit sharing by the partners.

Industrial lease agreements

Related to management contracts are industrial rental agreements, under which a foreign government leases a complete facility to a U.S. company. The rent consists normally of a fixed annual sum plus a scale of payments based on the output of the plant. As a rule such lease arrangements are limited to relatively complicated operations in which technical or managerial know-how is decisive.

6 George D. Bryson, *Profits from Abroad: A Reveille for American Business* (New York: McGraw-Hill Book Company, 1964), p. 148.

15

Normative Aspects of International Management

Theories of management are really subtheories. Each provides some insight into certain structures or processes of management, but none provides a complete framework for the subject as a whole. Some postulate that a business enterprise is a social system and that management's job is to make the system function effectively; others argue that management's task is to fuse an organization with its individual members; and still others maintain that management must initiate, organize, plan, direct, and control. All agree that management manages by making decisions which determine the scope and character of an enterprise.

Research shows that management involves all of these functions. Learned, Ulrich, and Booz, after studying U.S. corporations, concluded that executives primarily concentrate on keeping the business alive, meeting competition, and making a profit. They are constantly concerned with their relations with the community, government, and labor. They must solve financial problems and whittle down projects which exceed resources. "Explicit understanding of human factors, which is soundly based in experience, does make executive action more consistently and systematically effective."[1] The management job, then, is extremely broad, involving many external and internal relationships. But, since all aspects of it are not of equal importance and since some remain virtually unchanged while others involve radically different complications when placed in an international context, the discussion in this chapter will

[1] Edmund P. Learned, David N. Ulrich, and Donald R. Booz, *Executive Action* (Boston: Harvard Business School, 1951), p. 15.

center on the aspects which are the most essential for a multinational enterprise.

Management's primary job is acquiring and organizing inputs—material resources and manpower—and processing them efficiently and effectively into outputs—goods and services—demanded by the society, a customer, or a client. One author described the job succinctly when he said that management's first function is economic performance.[2] Through the processes of dividing the work, directing, coordinating, and planning, management obtains economic performance. Affecting this performance and being affected by it are the subgroups in the organization, both formal and informal, and the personality of the organization itself. Throughout these processes and in the midst of these interrelationships, the members of management are continually making decisions. Information from the input, processing, and output areas, as well as from areas external to the organization, must be communicated to them to provide the basis for decisions to be made and implemented. Change is the only constant in the management process.

Encompassing the organization and the external elements with which management must deal is the cultural environment. Whereas the behavior of the external and internal elements of the organization affect management and the behavior of management affects these elements, the cultural environment largely determines the parameters of behavior.

Management, to perform its primary economic or service function, has working relationships with many people, groups, and institutions and goes through many processes. As was expounded in previous chapters, all these relationships are influenced by the cultural environment within which they exist. To operate effectively within this network of interrelationships, management consists of "men in motion." Professor Sune Carlsson time-studied 12 top industrialists of Sweden over a period of several months; not one worked over 20 minutes uninterrupted.[3] Burns found that 80 percent of the time of middle managers was spent in contact with people inside and outside the organization.[4] This apparent need for frequent face-to-face or phone contact by top management leads to those particular requirements which will be discussed at the end of the chapter.

It has been pointed out before that the primary distinction between international and domestic business lies in the environmental framework and the organizational and the behavioral responses that flow from it. The entire managerial process is affected. Although the executive functions remain in theory what they are in domestic management, their application may be radically changed; although people interact and form groups of various kinds, the nature of both the interactions and especially the dynamics of intracorporate groups is changed. In addition, the multinational scope of the

2 Peter Drucker, *The Practice of Management* (New York: Harper & Row, Publishers, Inc., 1956), p. 7.

3 Quoted in Drucker, *The Practice of Management,* p. 103.

4 Tom Burns, "The Direction of Activity and Communication in a Departmental Executive Group," *Human Relations,* VII (1954), 73–97.

enterprise creates some new areas of managerial responsibility derived primarily from the interrelationships among the different national subentities of the corporate family and also from certain supranational functions which a multinational company must perform. This significance will become evident in the discussion of coordination below.

To paraphrase, the cultural and institutional plurality of the international environment confronts management with a quite complex and variegated reality, which is the source and justification for international management as distinguished from management per se. International, or multinational, management, then, is the source of direction for an enterprise in a plurality of cultural environments and national institutional structures. Whether an enterprise's becoming multinational will or will not affect the basic theories of management must remain debatable until the enterprises have matured and become better established. However, it does affect the conceptual structure of management as it is currently understood. Whatever one's theory of management may be, its application in terms of methods, techniques, performance standards, and both internal and external relationships is certain to be quite different and more demanding in an international administrative situation than in a national one.

Among the key concepts of management theory are delegation, coordination, and communication. They will be the basis for constructing a theoretical model for multinational management in the ensuing discussion here. The main thesis of the author is stated in terms of four basic propositions, each followed by a brief exposé of its rationale. The reader will find further documentation throughout this book.

Delegation and Decentralization

In this area there are two propositions which appear basic to international, or multinational, management. One is outward looking, the other inward looking; one focuses upon the contacts between the company and the outside world, the other on the contacts between the company and its internal elements.

External Factors

PROPOSITION I: *The plurality and diversity of external factors make it necessary for any national or continental suborganizations of a multinational company to possess the power to solve problems and issues which are peculiar to its domicile. Decentralization, therefore, is fundamental.*

Both evidence and reason support this proposition. Studies in this country and abroad show that management must continuously interact with people inside and outside the organization, and that its members—the executives—must constantly be ready to interject themselves at the interfaces when something threatens to disrupt the equilibrium of the organization. Many such threats and problems require immediate face-to-face contact. A decision maker who is stationed in a different country is seldom in the position for direct personal action.

Besides the obvious restraints of distance, time, and travel cost (which are decreasing in importance because of faster transportation), there are the more serious barriers of language, points of view, attitudes, beliefs, and values, which tend to restrain international personal contacts, complicate communications, and protract the discussions and negotiations necessary. Furthermore, a central decision maker is at a great disadvantage as far as being informed about all the relevant peculiarities of each country. Here are some illustrations of national peculiarities.

Laws and public policies governing corporate behavior and defining the limits of entrepreneurial freedom and action differ in countless respects. There are no two countries whose laws and policies are the same. An action which is perfectly legitimate in one country may constitute a criminal or civil offense in another; or again, an action regarded in the best interest of one community or public may be construed as antisocial in another. In the United States, the variation in laws among states, cities, and districts causes enough problems. Yet, the Constitution, federal legislation, and courts provide a common system of laws and principles which serve as basic ground rules for managerial action and executive behavior. A multinational corporation has no common constitutional structure, no federal laws, and no other common juridic framework. The laws and public policies encountered are often based on different premises and vary in countless respects; and, what is worse, they frequently are incongruous and irreconcilable in specific provisions. For example, the incorporation laws in one country may be loose; in another the requirements may be strict. In some countries, like Spain and Mexico, a specified percentage of stock must be held by local nationals. Such a restriction may necessitate the use of dummy stockholders. In other countries, like Ethiopia, the permission to enter business may be obtained only after repeated visits and long negotiating with officials simply because such a procedure is customary. Because of the political situation, a major dairy firm shared ownership of its Lima subsidiary with a Peruvian family. One member of the family belonged to one political party and another member to the other party. The presidency of the company alternated between the two, depending on which party was in power, because business prosperity there depended greatly on good relations with the government.

Each country has a different set of tax laws, which change constantly. The collection system varies. In some countries, income and property taxes are paid not only on the basis of financial statements but after negotiation with the tax authorities.

Import and exchange restrictions may be changed frequently. The treasurer of a Brazilian subsidiary spends most of his time on foreign exchange problems. He may even be required to "loan" the government foreign exchange credit which is repaid at times favorable to the government.[5]

Industrial relations also require national treatment. Few unions cross international boundaries. Each country has its own labor organizations and policies regarding wages, working conditions, and settlement of disputes. For example, in Brazil the government establishes wage scales, working hours, and vacations and imposes strict limitations on management's freedom to discharge. The unions are primarily concerned with political matters and exercise little control over shop practices. There are no shop stewards and, consequently, few industrial relations managers. In the former British colonies in Africa, grievances which cannot be settled on the spot are referred by law to a joint consultative committee. Often the first body intervening in a labor dispute will be the government inspector to whom the worker presents his grievance. If it is not settled to his satisfaction, he may appeal ultimately to a government labor court. Strikes are forbidden while the prescribed procedure is being followed. These examples illustrate the diversity of union problems which require local solution.

Public relations is another function which often requires decisions handled more effectively locally than from corporate headquarters. The behavior of the executives on the spot is an important determinant of favorable or unfavorable public opinion. Although most large firms have a separate public relations director, who lobbies, donates to charity, and makes speeches, most good public relations are created by a product or service which satisfies the public, by advertisement of that product, and by management's behavior in what the public believes to be a reasonable and proper manner. But reasonable and proper is a variable standard. What is reasonable and proper in the Congo is unreasonable and improper in Japan. The climate in the United States is generally favorable for private enterprise and the capitalist system. But in many other countries, especially in Asia and Africa, *capitalism* connotes plutocratic exploitation, social irresponsibility, and the subjugation of spiritual values to materialistic greed.

However unfounded, such antibusiness prejudices are widely held. Thus, the public relations director abroad may have to fight an unfavorable image before his company even has a product or service ready to distribute, or he may find his firm a pawn in a political contest. For example, "Yankee Go Home" signs may appear on factory walls; foreign plants may be burned; students may riot in front of the office building; or other anticompany actions may occur.

A recent survey of Brazilians' opinions of the United States showed that half of the respondents believed that American companies were trying to take over Brazil's industry and commerce to exploit the Brazilian people. The idea was strong among students who thought of capitalists as "robber

[5] Claude McMillan, Jr., Richard E. Gonzales, and others, *International Enterprise in a Developing Economy* (East Lansing, Michigan: Michigan State University, 1964), p. 97.

barons." The people were especially sensitive to the remission of profits and interest.[6] Even Canada is sensitive about the amount of U.S. investment, and Europe has become so in recent years.

The programs needed to build good public relations vary from country to country; these needs must be identified by national management, and the activities must be carried out by national management. The program must also be sensitive to the public relations effects of its everyday operations. But no nation-oriented public relations program should undermine the company's image or objectives in some other country. Therefore the development of the program requires cooperation between national management and corporate headquarters. The basic image must be decided at the multinational level, and the primary effort of the national public relations programs should be adopting and cultivating this image in the respective national settings.

In some foreign countries, the gaining of a favorable image may be a task beyond the resources of any one firm. In Venezuela, for example, several foreign oil companies have worked together to establish a multimillion-dollar fund to finance community health, recreation, and educational improvements in an effort to develop more favorable public opinion.

Economic and market conditions, too, require diverse approaches of management. That people of different countries have different tastes, different levels and patterns of income, and different consumption habits is obvious. From these differences come varied criteria for product characteristics, advertising appeals, distribution channels, and marketing policies.

Procurement policies and vendor relations present similar problems. A purchasing agent of a U.S. corporation would not think of using a cottage industry; in fact, he probably could not find any. But in Japan, cottage industry is integrated with large enterprises. To illustrate, one manufacturer for the bicycle industry had four simple machines in the front room of his home. With his daughter and four employees he manufactured nuts which he sold to the factory from which he obtained the raw material. Next door another householder finished hub castings.[7]

In Saudi Arabia, Aramco has spent a great deal of money training Arabs to become contractors for many of the supplies and services the company needs. In France, when a local supermarket chain started business on a self-service, low-price basis, it found many of its supplies through the regular distribution channels cut off. The small shopkeepers had put pressure on the distributors. The chain then had to develop direct sources from the manufacturers.

Although there are different purchasing problems abroad, with today's computerized information networks it is possible for a subsidiary's purchasing agent to forward quickly to the director of purchases at corporate headquarters the necessary data for issuing the purchase order. An automated procedure like

6 McMillan, Gonzales, and others, *International Enterprise in a Developing Economy,* p. 21.

7 Henry G. Aubrey, "Small Industry in Economic Development," *Studies in Economic Development* (New York: Holt, Rinehart & Winston, Inc., 1962).

this enables the headquarters to screen all purchases without losing the important face-to-face contact provided by the national purchasing agent abroad. Such contact is particularly important in a buyer-seller relationship where personal negotiations are often decisive for obtaining low prices, where goodwill depends on prompt service, where only conversation can bring out the latest trade information and news about innovations, and where speed is essential for taking advantage of a good offer.

In summary, to deal effectively with the plurality and diversity of external factors, the different national and continental operating units of a multinational enterprise must possess the power for meeting the problems peculiar to their respective domiciles. That power is gained through the delegation or the lowering of decision-making authority to the various national suborganizations of the multinational structure.

Effect of Environmental Plurality on Internal Factors

To this point we have focused on external factors. Turning now to internal factors we come to the second basic proposition.

PROPOSITION II: *The environmental plurality of a multinational firm tends to induce an analogous plurality in its internal structure.*

In support of this proposition are offered the following observations: Organizational and leadership patterns depend greatly on the environment. To use an oversimplified dichotomy as an illustration, the executive hierarchy in the United States is characterized by a greater height and larger number of levels than are typical abroad. Authority is delegated and responsibilities decentralized to a much greater degree. But decisions are often made in committees or other groups and not by individuals. Or, the decisions are interlocking in the sense that an executive will act only if he is certain of some other executive's attitude or reactions to his decision. There is widespread use of staff personnel and sharing of information with subordinates and superiors. This spreading and "collectivizing" of management responsibility results in very little social distances between the levels of management. It improves interaction and understanding between senior and junior executives and induces upward mobility, which makes progression from one level to another a normal process.

Outside the United States these norms are often conceived as abnormalities. Differences in decision-making behavior are greater than is generally appreciated. Even the European executives, although culturally they are the closest to American managers, complain, "Americans in Europe cannot make decisions on their own, are always on the phone to New York or Chicago, and insist on doing things by the book."[8]

According to Harbison and Myers' study, the idea of centralization permeates French society; the French top manager relies very little on his

8 "Those American Managers Don't Impress Europe," *Fortune,* LXX, No. 6 (December 1964), 138.

middle managers. The foreman is not even included in management. Entry into top management is by birth, by marriage, by attendance at one of *les grandes écoles,* or by transfer from a high civil service post. It has been rare, although it is becoming less so, that a man works his way up. The top executives form a small, class-conscious elite separated from the lower echelons by a social gulf.[9]

The traditional role of the Italian employer is that of *padrone*—the boss who is like a father to his workers and who treats them like sons whom he can boss around with relatively unlimited authority but whom he takes care of when the worker's family is sick or needs help. Loyalty to the employer is expected, although the workers generally do not like the capitalists.

The top executive in Germany, the *unternehmer,* believes that he has a moral right to authority and obedience. He belongs to the professional elite and does not mix with subordinates, who belong to a lower level.

This writer's research in the European countries suggests that the European industrialist belongs to the highest social class. The hired manager may or may not be accepted in this class depending on his family and educational background. He does, however, hold a high rank within his organization, and the deference shown by his subordinates is generally greater than that shown in the United States.

Perhaps in no industrial nation is there such a feeling of mutual obligation as there is in Japan. A strong, lifelong bond of solidarity and loyalty binds the individual and the organization: One expects a lifetime job; the other, lifetime service. This applies from the top to the bottom of the organization's structure.

In the new, excolonial countries, executive expectations and decision-making behavior present a bewildering maze of different patterns, most of them not sufficiently studied to permit any substantive generalizations. To a certain degree the management methods of the previous colonizing power are usually evident; in Burma things are done more as in Britain than as in France or the United States; in Indonesia the model is Dutch; and in Algeria it is French. But this is not saying much. In all these countries the colonial heritage is submerged under indigenous forces which engender new and distinct administrative systems, most of them highly autocratic, often even militaristic, in character.

Many American management theorists, especially those with a sociological bent, condemn the authoritarian and paternalistic leadership patterns, but it is difficult to see how a multinational firm could follow their advice. Indeed, it is difficult to find fault in terms of results with these patterns in countries like Germany, Italy, or Japan. It would be doctrinaire foolishness for a multinational corporation to attempt to impose upon its various national entities any Americanized organization structure or leadership system particularly when the subunits are manned by local nationals. At best such attempts

[9] Eugene W. Burgess, "Management in France," in *Management in the Industrial World,* Frederick Harbison and Charles A. Myers (New York: McGraw-Hill Book Company, 1959), p. 217.

would alienate the local nationals from corporate goals, and more likely they would place the company in the neocolonialist category and thwart its opportunities.

An analogous situation exists in reference to recruitment and training. Multinational headquarters cannot effectively prescribe common recruitment and training procedures for national personnel. In many countries manual work is done by the lower class, and there is a stigma attached to it. Education is the vehicle for climbing the socioeconomic ladder. As a consequence, the educated people in most underdeveloped countries do not want to be associated with manual labor. In Venezuela, even a person with a sixth-grade education refuses to do manual work; that kind of labor is for fourth graders. College graduates resist association with field activities.[10] It is even difficult to select salesmen in South America. Lower-born men who actually do start at the bottom are not readily accepted by their new colleagues as they rise in rank. In a country like India, the caste system institutionalizes social stratification and makes vertical mobility extremely difficult or impossible. In fact, promoting a lower-caste man over a higher-caste man may wreck havoc in the Indian organization. Although not so acute elsewhere, the problem is encountered even in countries like Britain and Sweden. Again, the diverse problems of recruitment suggest that, for lower-level personnel, staffing be left to local management.

If decentralization is valid for multinational firms, and the foregoing discussion suggests that it is, then the national management is responsible for the performance of the enterprise in its respective domicile. Decentralization can be very useful in supplying powerful motivation to the indigenous managers. When decision-making power is delegated to them, their initiative and creative energies are released, and the total power of the corporate complex is increased. In other words, delegation not only distributes the power the multinational headquarters possesses but also generates new power throughout the system. Both domestic and international studies prove this point. Herzberg, Mauser, and Snyderman[11] found in 1959 that delegation in a domestic setting was a positive incentive for higher productivity. Haire, Ghiselli, and Porter[12] report, in their study of executives in the international realm, that managers in all countries surveyed put self-actualization and autonomy at the top of the scale of aspirations. My own work suggests that increased autonomy improves these executives' performance at least to a point. Once they understand the overall objectives and goals of the multinational firm, their capacity to set the subordinate national goals, to make plans to achieve them, and to exercise leadership is increased if not straight-jacketed by centralized interference from the top.

[10] B. F. Hoelitz, "The Recruitment of the White Collar Workers in Underdeveloped Countries," in *Underdeveloped Areas* (New York: Harper & Row, Publishers, Inc., 1957), p. 181.

[11] Frederick Herzberg, Bernard Mauser, and Barbara Block Snyderman, *The Motivation to Work* (New York: John Wiley & Sons, Inc., 1959), pp. 107–19.

[12] Maison Haire, Edwin Ghiselli, and Lyman Porter, "Cultural Problems in the Role of Manager," *Industrial Relations,* II, No. 2 (February 1963), 95–117.

To summarize the argument for decentralization: To deal effectively with the plurality of external factors in a multiplicity of dynamic environments the management of a multinational firm must possess the internal plurality and flexibility which only a decentralized structure of organization and administration can provide.

Coordination

PROPOSITION III: *To function effectively as an organic whole in its pluralistic international environment, the multinational corporation must coordinate all decisions which transcend in application or consequence any national subentity of the company.*

Coordination presumes that there is a central purpose and a power to pursue this purpose, i.e., that there is centralization. That the overall objectives and strategies must be decided on the multinational level needs hardly to be emphasized. But equally important, and usually much more difficult, is the coordination of specific functional aspects of the multinational structure. Here, the arguments for decentralization and centralization are on a collision course, and only diligent and discriminating analysis can show how both principles are best employed in any particular situation. There are, however, certain areas which stand out.

In marketing, centralization becomes a necessity when several national entities participate in serving the same customers.

In production, the costs of component fabrication, raw materials, and assembly operations vary from country to country because of different labor rates, prices, and trade regulations. This presents the headquarters management with alternative choices and opportunity costs which the national submanagements can neither have nor be expected to use in an impartial way.

In finance, the differences in interest rates, taxes, and currency stability and the availability of foreign exchange necessitate central planning and close coordination on the multinational level. Decisions to make substantial investments, to undertake major expansions, or to cease important operations require centralized handling, and normally top management retains the power for such decisions. Because many governments have restrictions on exchange of currencies and because the income-tax rate and base vary from country to country, central control over cash and the disposition of earnings is advantageous to the firm. Socony-Mobil headquarters management, for example, buys foreign exchange at lower cost than some of its affiliated companies can. The company pools and clears sales and purchases of foreign exchange itself rather than paying to have the funds transferred. To eliminate interest charges headquarters management negotiates a line of credit for several countries with a bank which has branches abroad. Local management can draw on these funds. Central management also keeps local management informed on the money markets.

In transfer pricing, too, centralization is imperative. The prices which the various national subsidiaries charge one another in intracompany trade determine the international distribution of the company's revenues and taxes and the currency composition of its profits. These concerns are vital to the welfare of the organization as a whole; yet, the self-interests of the national and the multinational management on these matters often conflict. To prevent this conflict, the decision on transfer pricing must be made on the multinational level.

Management training and executive development in personnel matters deserve central guidance. Indigenous managers must be taught the objectives, policies, and expectations of the company. Many societies do not have the necessary attitudes toward efficiency and productivity; and many societies do not have the same attitudes toward them as U.S. society does. Many able foreigners have developed neither scientific attitudes nor a sense of teamwork. A study of Latin American managers showed that they rarely used the scientific method, that they relied heavily on intuition, and that to them action was more important than results.[13] Such executives must be reoriented and remotivated before their full potential can be harnessed by the company.

Studies of authority patterns indicate that the European, Latin American, or Asian chief executive is accustomed to making most of the important decisions himself. Therefore, for him to operate as a team member with his peers or with corporate-level staff men requires reorientation. "Until 1960, International Telephone and Telegraph Corporation's executives in Europe frequently competed against each other for the same export sales. They even refused to disclose prices and other information to each other."[14]

Many an American looks at business as a way of life. The higher his position the more he is committed to his firm—the more it becomes the center of his world. The French businessman does not usually believe in business as a way of life.[15] The managing director may be totally committed to the success of his enterprise (the subordinates much less committed), but he usually retains a family or social life or other commitments beyond those of his business associates and connections. To the Italian businessman, business is a means to an end—family survival, prosperity, and position.[16] The Chinese and Indians also have clan obligations which take precedence over business commitments. This attitude toward business led to the situation in which a key European executive of a U.S. corporation whose vacation was due at the height of a crisis in its advertising campaign and its manufacturing operations at the same time insisted on taking it anyway. He found nothing abnormal about leaving, but his American superiors were shocked.[17]

[13] Eugene C. McCann, "An Aspect of Management Philosophy in the United States and Latin America," *Academy of Management Journal,* VII, No. 2 (June 1964), 150–52.

[14] McCann, "An Aspect of Management Philosophy in the United States and Latin America," p. 149.

[15] Roy Lewis and Rosemary Steward, *The Managers* (New York: New American Library, Inc., 1961), p. 184.

[16] Franco Ferrarotti, "Management in Italy," in *Management in the Industrial World,* Harbison and Myers, p. 247.

[17] *Wall Street Journal* (New York), March 30, 1965, p. 1.

In most cases like those cited, the native manager needs training in the parent company's philosophy and mode of operation. Use of the scientific method; the search for facts, goals, and quotas; and a certain amount of team effort have been found productive. They do not run contrary to a deep philosophy of life, although they may not conform to attitudes currently prevailing among the managers. Whenever people of a different nationality than that of the headquarters personnel are employed in a managerial capacity, additional training and orientation are indicated.

To develop their foreign managers, some firms bring them here to work in the U.S. headquarters or branches for one to two years. The foreigners are expected to learn the practice of management in their particular firm and its objectives, and to gain an understanding of how the American environment affects the behavior of American managers. Other foreign managers go to business schools or special management seminars, either abroad or in the United States, which present effective management techniques for various situations. Still other overseas managers are trained when they are promoted into a new job in a new environment. Perhaps the most effective and widely used training device is the centrally coached but nationally run training program of the multinational organization itself.

Central management may also insist on a policy of training replacements for its national managers abroad because of the lone-wolf attitude already cited and because of the scarcity of good men. Local nationals capable of running a large operation and adjusting to American ways of doing business have long been scarce in many foreign countries. But this problem has become especially critical in recent years as U.S. companies have sharply stepped up their overseas activities.

The plurality of attitudes toward management which prevails because of the plurality of cultural environments requires that central managements of multinational corporations train their top managers abroad so they can operate effectively in the corporate organization structure.

Similar arguments can be advanced for central coordination in respect to the transnational functions and activities of the multinational company. The discussion to this point can be summed up by saying that a multinational management should be conceived as consisting of two vertical spheres: *a nationally and culturally decentralized base structure designed to deal with pluralistic conditions through strong, autonomous subentities on the national and local levels; and a centralized superstructure to guide and coordinate the organization as a whole on the international and multinational levels.*

Communication

PROPOSITION IV: *Multinational management control is predicated upon effective international communication.*

This is perhaps the most crucial area of international management. Even in a domestic context communication was ranked by Chester Barnard as one of the three most important elements of management.[18] In the international context its role is crucial. The multitude of languages, ideologies, and cultures in a multinational organization makes communication both difficult and hazardous. An obvious preliminary is that managers of the multilingual organization learn a common language. The American executive in this respect is in a preferred position as English has, so far at least, been accepted as the common language. (This acceptance has its drawbacks, too.) But language alone does not suffice for communication. The process has many nonlinguistic expressions, gestures, and acts which Hall and Whyte point out in their study of intercultural communications.[19] International executives must not only acquire linguistic skills but also become sensitive to how their acts and behavior are interpreted by people from different cultural backgrounds. The friendly slap on the shoulder by an American may insult an Indonesian; getting down to business right away with an Argentine may offend him deeply; pressing an Arab for a deadline may cost a friendship. People who work together must learn both to be sensitive to what their behavior actually communicates and to be tolerant of what is unintentionally communicated. On their capacity to anticipate and to avoid mistranslations and misinterpretations and on their tolerance for the uncustomary phrase and the peculiar accent depends the functioning of the international channels of communication.

A second requirement for international managerial communication is comparability of standards. If the different national subsidiaries are to be compared, standard formats must be employed. This is more easily said than done. Local laws and custom often frustrate efforts to install unified reporting standards in multinational settings. In their stead, specially designed conversion methods and formulas must be devised.

The third requirement in any organization is that the areas of responsibility be defined sufficiently so that various members know to whom to direct a particular message. Since in a multinational firm the *de jure* (legal) organization very often differs from the *de facto* (managerial) structure, this requirement is particularly crucial.

The fourth requirement of international managerial communications is rapid and uninterrupted feedback. Since, as explained before, the basic structure of the organization must, by necessity, be decentralized, close supervision by the multinational headquarters is not possible. Therefore, prompt feedback becomes decisive for coordination and control.

A fifth requirement for international managerial communication is multiple management. Frequent face-to-face contacts between the multinational and national spheres avoid misunderstandings and correct misperceptions. This is generally recognized. But if frequent face-to-face contacts are

[18] Chester I. Barnard, *The Functions of the Executive* (Cambridge, Massachusetts: Harvard University Press, 1954), pp. 82, 89–91.

[19] Edward T. Hall and William F. Whyte, "Intercultural Communications: A Guide to Men of Action," *Human Organization,* XIX, No. 1 (Spring 1960), 5–12.

important, then more than one decision maker is required for most problem areas on the multinational level because face-to-face contact presumes that the multinational executive spends much time in different countries cultivating contacts. The very plurality of the corporate structure and its environment, too, require multiple management. To work simultaneously with subunits in many countries is often impossible for any one person. There is a tendency, therefore, to overlap the decision-making authority for most top-management functions in deliberate violation of the undivided-authority dictum. In a few companies the division or overlapping of authority has been carried all the way to the chief administrators' level. Nestlé, for example, has two managing directors; General Motors retains the traditional titles of chairman and president but gives both equal powers; Royal Dutch-Shell has in effect two sets of executives; and Unilever—the most decentralized of the worldwide enterprises—relies on multiple headquarters operating as equals in an international corporate coalition.

Integrated Planning

To take advantage of the benefits of decentralization and to focus on common objectives, international management must employ integrated planning. A plan provides a scheme of action or a programmed decision process. The people affected have a program which directs their activities and the activities of others around them so there is less duplication of effort and unnecessary competition. The plan contains also a goal or series of goals or standards against which performance is measured. It provides the constraints within which decentralized decision making may occur.

Headquarters management cannot unilaterally impose a plan upon its overseas affiliates because of the plurality of factors discussed above. A multinational plan must be developed from the bottom up. The operating units of Unilever, for example, each make an operating plan which is sent to the superordinate management group. This group, in turn, consolidates the plan with its own and sends it for approval to a three-man special committee, which reports to the Board of Directors. Upon approval it becomes the operating program for the period.[20] During the planning process and the implementation, the national or regional headquarters are in continual consultation among themselves in what might be called triangular planning. (See Figure 15-1.)

Evaluation of managers in a decentralized multinational organization should utilize the technique of *management by objectives.* The phrase means that the managers of different operating affiliates make their own plans and

20 Rykens, "Local Autonomy and Central Control," in *Business Leadership in a Changing World,* Robert Baker (New York: McGraw-Hill Book Company), p. 386ff.

FIGURE 15-1

Triangular Planning

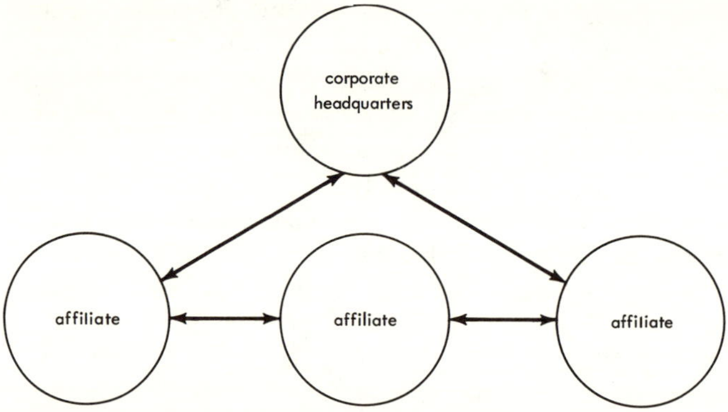

set their own goals or targets in cooperation with their multinational superiors and are held responsible for reaching the goals.

Management appraisal is a very important element of good international management and an essential part of integrated planning. McKinsey and Company investigators made a survey of executive-performance appraisal in Latin America and in Europe. They discovered that salary and bonus decisions were only rarely influenced by individual performance. They concluded that ineffective and inadequate appraisals of executive performance were the cause of one of the greatest economic wastes that management incurs.[21]

In a plurality of external factors and cultural environments, it is erroneous to rate a man as some executives are rated in the United States on the basis of aggressiveness, tact, cooperativeness, leadership, people consciousness, etc. These are inadequate bases for judging performance in a domestic firm; they are even more inadequate when the rater and the person being rated have different cultural backgrounds and environments.

Where possible, the goals—profit increase, sales increase, improved market standing, quality improvement, cost reduction, or successful innovation—ought to be quantified. Quantified goals are much easier to measure than subjective goals. In some cases, however, innovation, good labor relations, public relations, or government relations may be of greater importance, and they cannot be quantified.

Even the achievement of quantified goals may not reflect actual performance. In one instance, raises were given to a British management group because the total business of the British factory had risen markedly. Upon further examination the parent firm found that the increased output had been exported to a market developed by another group and that the local

21 Bruce McLagan and John D. Woodthorpe, "Measuring Executive Performance in a World Enterprise," *International Business Management* (Belmont, California: Wadsworth Publishing Co., Inc., 1964).

British sales had actually declined. A few months after the managers had received raises, they were fired.[22]

Global Viewpoint

A global viewpoint is a necessity for top managers of a multinational corporation. They must look at all the free world as their market and at all its peoples and resources as their potential of production. Economic performance is their objective, and prejudice against nations and customs has no place in their code. On the contrary, awareness of different customs and values and a sensitivity to the effect of their own behavior are essential characteristics. They need to have the ability to pick good men, the courage to delegate to them, and the wisdom to weld all of them together into a unified whole.

22 McLagan and Woodthorpe, "Measuring Executive Performance in a World Enterprise," p. 61.

16

Intracompany International Transfer Pricing

Decentralization of operations and the use of multiple profit centers require a system of transfer pricing for intracompany trade. In the United States domestic transfer pricing became a major concern in the early 1950's. Definitions which came into being at that time are applicable throughout this book.

Transfers mean movements of products among operating units within the largest policy-making unit, regardless of corporate entities; for example, transfers within the family of companies represented by Cities Service Oil Company or among the divisions of E. I. duPont de Nemours and Company.

Product is broadly interpreted to include raw materials, components, and intermediate products and services as well as finished products in the ordinary sense of the word.

Transfer price refers to the net value per unit; it is used for recording transactions on operating statements.[1]

Transfer pricing for a multinational firm is concerned with the value per unit of a product which is transferred across the borders of at least two countries from one affiliate of the firm to another. Such transfers are subject to a number of restrictions and barriers which the crossing of international boundaries presents. Transfer prices can be of two types: the established price that does not have an effect on the final sales price of the product regardless

[1] Joel Dean, "Decentralization and Intracompany Pricing," *Harvard Business Review*, XXXIII (July–August 1955), 75.

of the significance of the transfer price in relation to the sales price; and the transfer price that has an effect on the final sales price—for example, when a higher transfer price results in a higher sales price.

The primary purposes of international transfer pricing are (a) to secure an economic allocation of resources among the company's affiliates in different countries—that is, to maximize aggregate profits on a long-run basis, and (b) to provide criteria for measuring the profit performances of the affiliates. Secondary objectives may also be attained through transfer pricing. They include increasing the size of the market, strengthening the ability of the firm to compete, attaining economies of scale, reducing the effect of domestic and foreign restrictions, and others. In a broader sense, however, all the various secondary objectives are auxiliaries to the primary objectives—profit maximization and measurement of profitability.

The Systems Approach

The use of the systems approach in calculating transfer prices is desirable since the rational philosophy is to achieve a synergistic result. The systems concept as applied to transfer pricing involves combining all the different facets of marketing, distribution, and production in order to create a meaningful price for the product(s) in question. If each separate subsidiary or branch looks at pricing in this fashion, an efficient outlook will be obtained for the world company. The systems concept implicitly states that the organizational structure and the decision-making authority will be allocated along the lines which make for the greatest efficiency. Hence the company structure will be geographically oriented, and the delegation of decision making will be along profit-center lines, although transfer pricing will still be a central function. In other words, where economies of scale reaped in one country with greater efficacy than in another, then a transfer of goods between these two countries will take place at the expense of the excess capacity that may exist in a third country. Therefore the aim of each individual unit or division will be suboptimization of price-output combinations; each unit will contribute to the maximum long-run profit of the world company rather than to the maximum profit of the foreign unit. The underlying logic of this reasoning has been aptly translated into an action guide for the maximization of international profit by Seymour L. Linfield:

(1) Invest wherever the investment can get the best return.

(2) Purchase raw materials or partially manufactured components wherever they are cheapest.

(3) Manufacture either finished or component parts wherever it can be done productively.

(4) Market the goods wherever the firm reaps the greatest profit.[2]

2 "Overseas Corporations," *Harvard Business Review,* XXXVIII, No. 5 (September–October 1960), 45.

Conceptual Model of Multinational Transfer Pricing

Multinational pricing is complicated because each country is in some respects unique and because certain differences among them are irreconcilable. How can such different and conflicting conditions be reconciled under any overall pricing policy?

Although it is agreed that decentralization of decision-making functions, including pricing, would resolve many of these serious conflicts, still there is no simple solution to the problem of intracompany transfer pricing. The "idiosyncrasies" exhibited by each country have to be looked at from a world point of view, and, in fact, they may necessitate decisions which do not seem logical from the local point of view.

Any model of multinational transfer pricing has to take into account not only the tangible, real barriers to a freely competitive system, but also the intangible barriers erected by the uncertainties and risks inherent in each foreign country. And recognition of the tangible barriers does not necessarily obviate the intangible barriers. In any business transaction a certain amount of risk is attached to all activities. These risks take on greater meaning in international business and are somewhat commensurate with the real barriers existing to the free flow of goods and services. These greater risks are usually reflected in intracompany transfer prices. Thus risk differences among various countries, though intangible, are barriers to the free flow of trade and have to be taken into account as idiosyncrasies peculiar to particular countries.

It is quite true that a subsidiary may obtain a cheaper source for certain raw materials and manufactured components than that which another foreign division of the multinational company can obtain. However, within the systems approach of centralized responsibility for strategic planning and control, it may become necessary for that subsidiary to suboptimize its profit maximization for the sake of overall profit maximization.

In many cases the transfer price for a component part will be agreed upon by a formal contract between the parent company and its divisions, with a written reservation that prices do not exceed the level on the world market. For example, CIBA, Ltd., in Switzerland, made arrangements in a joint venture with ATUL, in India:

> Price to be charged to CIBA is to be full cost of production and an amount equal to 15 percent of the prime cost, providing this price is not in excess of delivered world prices, in which latter event CIBA reserves the right to buy elsewhere.[3]

Although other factors restrict the free flow of goods and hence prices, it should be noted here that on an economic basis realistic pricing tends to give balanced growth to intracorporate trade. Joel Dean points out that

[3] Quoted in Wolfgang G. Friedmann and George Kalmanoff, *Joint International Business Ventures* (New York: Columbia University Press, 1961), p. 383.

"intracompany pricing must preserve the profit-making *autonomy* of the division manager so that his self interests will be identical with the interests of the company as a whole."[4] Thus it is vital for multinational companies not only to apply the philosophy of the systems approach but also to remain sensitive to external competition. Any firm that blindly attempts to force all the international trade strictly on an intradivisional basis will only grease the sliprails for a collective descent into the abyss of inefficiency and stagnation.

The interesting question now is: How does a firm know when its transfer prices are no longer externally competitive? Within its framework of centralized planning and control it is important for the company to be thoroughly familiar with world markets and prices. The Ford Motor Company, for instance, has its Mexican subsidiary export assembly features to 14 Ford plants around the world. It is doing so at prices equal to or lower than those offered by non-Ford vendors. Adherence to the systems concept with a suboptimization philosophy for subsidiaries comes either from causes uneconomic in their incipiency or from the existence of nationalistic or political barriers to the free flow of currency and trade.

Economic objectives, indirectly tied to long-run profit maximization, can be attained through the use of transfer prices. Objectives such as increasing the market share, increasing the competitiveness of the firm, and overcoming domestic and foreign restrictions all involve the forsaking of immediate profits so that the firm can realize a greater long-run profit in that particular country. There is a three-way relationship among the economic allocation of resources, the measurement of profit performances, and the incentives for divisional company managers. Management can both effect and obtain certain efficiencies in these areas through the price-transfer system.

Although a domestic yardstick can be used for divisional profits, it is not easy to project such a comparison to subsidiaries in different foreign countries. In the international environment, the use of statutory devices to protect and enhance profits often distorts the significance of such operating results as net profit and return on investment, and the logistics pattern determined by headquarters executives may in fact restrict the return available to certain operating affiliates. Although many such problems restrict the applicability of our three-way relationship, the primary concern should be on the development of a correct price and on the decentralization of decision-making responsibility. An index for determining the disparity of real profits due to different techniques of measurement or general currency stability can be constructed. However, such an index should be used with care, since the headquarters company should avoid becoming involved in operational decisions of the affiliates, as was earlier argued.

Problems also arise in regard to the actual production cost imputed in the transfer prices for partially manufactured components. An accountant would treat the acquisition price as a variable cost, "even though the transfer-

[4] Dean, "Decentralization and Intracompany Pricing," p. 66.

ring division has been credited with an amount that covers some fixed factory cost, burden changes, or profit."[5] If the recipient company used marginal-cost pricing to effect a flexible marketing policy, it would seem that problems would arise on the downward side of any pricing decision. The inclusion of overhead profit from the transferring affiliate would contract the decision maker's ability to use a completely flexible pricing policy. This is especially true when the amount of overhead and profit is a considerable proportion of the transferred price.

Example

Suppose that the transferred price for a component part is $2 and that this amount can be broken up into overhead $0.50, profit $0.50, and variable cost of manufacture $1. The value to be added by the firm (transferee) in the country of destination is $1 and the burden and profit is $0.50. Therefore the expected resale price of the product is $3.50. Hence the flexibility of retail price policy here involves a movement from $3 to $3.50. But the true range of price flexibility should be from $2 to $3.50. A clear separation of the variable and fixed components of each transfer price would overcome this problem.

Problems and Barriers to Free Trade and Their Effects on the Transfer-Pricing System

Because a perfectly free market seldom exists, transfer prices are based on a number of factors that often bear little relationship to investment in the integrated segments of business. From the tangible factors it will be seen that obvious barriers are usually reflected in transfer prices. Economic stability, political uncertainties, regulations, foreign exchange problems, tariff and quota restrictions, repatriation rules, and incentives all involve a restraint on or an enhancement of the transfer price.

Tariffs

We saw before that a tariff raises the landed cost of a product or component part. Usually the duty to be paid for nonassembled products will be lower than that for assembled items. The duty may be a fixed amount to be added, or it may be ad valorem. These rates vary depending on the treaties in force among the countries. The type of good—i.e., whether it is a necessity or a luxury item—also may cause a difference in the duty exacted.

A tariff impinges directly on the profitability of a firm, and hence it is common sense for a firm facing high tariff barriers in one country to use the

[5] Paul W. Cook, Jr., "New Techniques for Intro-Company Pricing," *Harvard Business Review,* XXXV, No. 4 (July–August 1957), 74.

lowest transfer price possible when dispatching parts, subassemblies, or finished goods to its affiliates in that country. A tariff can affect the competitiveness of a firm by increasing costs, reducing profit margins, and generally forcing the firm out of the market. This, of course, may be the aim of the foreign government in order to bolster local competition.

In instances such as in the European Free Trade Area, where the percentage of value added to products originally imported from outside and then transferred among members is used as a basis for applying tariffs, a low transfer price can be of value to the firm. For example, if less than 50 percent of the value of the product is added in the Free Trade Area, a duty will be applied. If over 50 percent is added, a duty will not be applied. A low transfer price may increase the chances of having over 50 percent added in the member nation and therefore reduce the amount of tariff applied. For example, if $50 of value is added in the Free Trade Area, a transfer price of $60 means that less than 50 percent was added in the Free Trade Area, and tariffs will be applied. However, setting a transfer price of $40 means that more than 50 percent was added. This use of transfer pricing is beneficial to the company only if the final sales price is not affected.

Exchange control

Many countries, especially underdeveloped ones, suffer from an acute shortage of hard currencies. In order to overcome the inability to earn such foreign exchange, restrictions are placed on the use of local currency to buy it. These restrictions can be counteracted by lowering transfer prices. Thus a greater amount can be imported, and a smaller amount of foreign exchange is needed. Where restrictions on the amount of foreign exchange available exist, then the lower the transfer price, the greater the number of products that can enter intracompany international trade.

Nontariff import and export restrictions

Nontariff restrictions limit the amount of exports and imports entering a country through quotas, laws such as the Buy American Act, subsidies, and so on. The restrictions may vary in intensity with less effect upon component parts and more stringent effect on completed products.

The use of these restrictions is detrimental to the firm's objectives such as profit maximization, maintenance of and increase in the size of the market, and overcoming import and export restrictions. The direct effects of the nontariff restrictions can include a loss of economies of scale, a loss of competitive position, a loss of market, and an inability to meet the demand. If imports are restricted, a high transfer price based on costs may be required because of a loss of economies of scale. Or, viewed from the other side, import restrictions may make it imperative to use a low transfer price if imports are restricted to a certain value.

The same argument is applicable to export restrictions, only it must be viewed from the exporting country's side. Because of export restrictions, economies of scale may not be attained, requiring a higher transfer price if cost is used as a basis for transfer pricing. Exports limited to a certain dollar value require low transfer prices to export as much as possible. But attempts to export an increased amount because of lowered transfer prices might be foiled by customs authorities. Even under close scrutiny, however, the company should try to determine the lowest price allowed by the customs authorities in order to attain the highest profit possible.

Different types of ownership of affiliates in other countries

The proportion of ownership in an affiliate and the type of affiliate in a foreign country can affect the determination of a transfer price. In some countries the governments have established a maximum percentage of ownership which can be held by people other than nationals. Governments also favor subsidiaries as opposed to branches because the subsidiary may require the use of more nationals and of more products of that country. In addition, more local control can be imposed on a subsidiary. Favoring subsidiaries may bring about a lower tax rate for them and also other benefits.

If a certain percentage of ownership is required, it can affect the transfer price, as a "fair" amount of earnings should be accumulated in that country to maintain good relations with the foreign owners. If the country is a low-tax area, transferring the earnings to that country gives excessive earnings to the foreign owners. In the reverse situation of high taxes, it may be advisable to remove earnings from that country upsetting the relations with the foreign owners. Setting the price at a "fair" amount may result in a loss of profits because taxes cannot be minimized. Similarly, nonmaximization of profits also results if a branch is in an area where subsidiaries are taxed at a lower rate or favored in other ways.

The alternatives to transfer pricing are limited, since there should be an attempt to maintain good relations with foreign owners. The use of a "fair" price is the desired solution. In those instances where taxes are heavier on branches, a high transfer price to the country involved reduces the tax effect.

Taxation

The main problem that arises here is that a company's profits may suffer double taxation, i.e., taxation may be applied on the earnings of the company in the foreign division as well as on those of the parent company. Also, many countries have different rules and regulations regarding the accounting of profit and the actual tax rates to be employed. These two problems can be overcome by transferring those profits to the low-tax areas and hence maximizing world profits.

For example, if country *A* has a tax rate of 50 percent on earnings while country *B* has only a 25 percent rate on earnings, it would be to the company's advantage to transfer the products from *A* to *B* and lower the amount of profits in country *A*. The transfer price should be as low as possible to enhance the profits in country *B*. (See Figure 16-1.) If country *C* supplies

FIGURE 16-1

Transfer Pricing

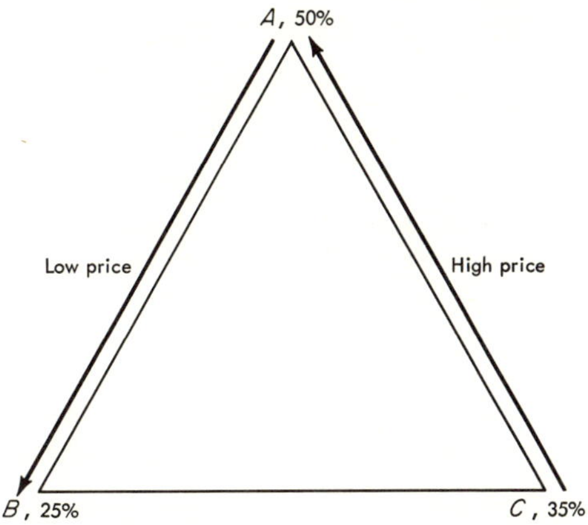

country *A* with a component part, *C* should charge *A* the highest price possible. This course of action may be advisable even though economies of production are reaped in country *B* since the enhanced profits due to the lower tax could be greater than the profit from reduced costs. Unfortunately the U.S. government frowns on artificially rigged pricing in trade with a subsidiary so that more income than is proper is generated in a nation with more favorable tax laws. The U.S. tax laws stipulate that a fair market price must be charged to a foreign subsidiary. This seems to indicate that the diversion of profits is illegal. However, since the "fair price" has not been specifically defined, there are the problems of deciding or determining what price is a fair price and of deciding how an established price can be justified by the company in case of federal inquiry.

The problem is first to determine what profit an affiliate should receive and then to establish the transfer price. Should the price be cost plus a reasonable markup even though manufacturers sometimes sell at cost or without profit in arm's-length transactions to develop foreign markets for their goods? In ascertaining the fair price, does the firm take into account the risks and uncertainty of foreign operations? In addition, should the price take into account only marginal costs incurred by increased production resulting from foreign sales, or should it include a proportionate amount of the fixed costs? The main difficulty in the taxation problem is to establish a price which will not be so low as to cause the government to reapportion the profits and which will minimize the taxes of the firm.

Profit maximization can be accomplished by using a low transfer price for products transferred to a low-tax area if the following assumptions hold: the selling price remains the same regardless of the transfer price, and the transfer product represents in cost a major portion of the final product. The low transfer price reduces the profits in the high-tax area and increases the profits in the low-tax area. In a similar manner, a high transfer price is used for products transferred to a high-tax area.

Competition of government-owned and subsidized firms

Any government assistance to a competitor or to the ownership of a competitor may present a large barrier for the multinational firm to overcome. The barrier is especially large if it allows the competition to sell at a lower price. The forms of government assistance besides direct ownership can include direct subsidies, transportation benefits, tax benefits, freer capital movements, and special contracts.

The firm can be affected by a loss of the market resulting in a loss of profits, by a loss of economies of scale, and by an inability to compete if the transfer price which affects the sales price is too high. Sales will probably decrease if the only difference in products being sold is the lower price of the government product. The loss of sales may decrease production below the most economical scale, and profits will decrease to an even greater extent.

A transfer-pricing alternative may not be available to the multinational firm, depending upon the objectives of the government. If the government wishes to force the multinational firm out, the government can subsidize the competitor to the point of making the market unattractive from an economic standpoint. If the government does not go to this extent, a low transfer price may allow the multinational firm to compete and perhaps even uproot the competition. This situation can occur only if the transfer price affects the final sales price of the completed product. Otherwise lowering the transfer price will have no effect.

Repatriation controls

The repatriation of profits in the way of dividends is controlled by levies imposed by a foreign government on outgoing earnings. These restrictions attempt to keep funds in the country as retained earnings for further investment. The use of withholding taxes in the overseas country and also in the country of the parent company, especially if the base rate overseas is less than that in the parent country, is commonly found. The fact that nationalists in underdeveloped countries criticize the foreign control of firms in their countries and hence attempt to repress the remittance of profits outwardly manifests itself in government sanctions and pressures.

These taxes on dividends transferred reduce the profit realized by the world company and can be lost permanently where inflation is prevalent. The use of a high transfer price to the restricting country is an effective means of transferring out these profits. The taxation of dividends repatriated in the parent country can also be overcome by inclusion of a certain amount of profits in the transfer price. But this technique is not without its difficulties. It penalizes affiliates which are forced to pay more than necessary for their parts and supplies and thus makes cost comparisons and profit performance measurements complicated.

Restrictions associated with the permanency of affiliation

Restrictions are also based upon whether the affiliation with the foreign corporation is long run or short run in nature. The objectives of the firm determine the permanency of affiliation, and the permanency influences the transfer price to be used. These restrictions affect the profit-maximization objective.

If an affiliation is temporary or short run, minimum profits should be transferred to that affiliate, resulting in high transfer prices. To flip to the other side of the coin, with a long-run affiliation, the setting of the transfer price depends mainly upon all the other factors discussed in this section. High profits may be required by part owners of the affiliate, who might, if not receiving high enough profits, break their affiliation and affiliate with a competitor. Other business goals of an affiliate may also dictate a specific transfer price.

Restrictions resulting from the laws of various countries

Restrictions on transfer pricing are present in fair-pricing laws and antitrust laws. These restrictions may be in the form of minimum limits on transfer prices when the transfer prices have an effect on the final sales price and prove detrimental to competition. Maximum limits may also be placed on the transfer prices; these limits affect the final sales price as well as the achievable objectives of transfer pricing.

The alternatives to the use of transfer pricing to overcome restrictions are limited. In fact, transfer pricing may be useless unless the company can determine the minimum to maximum range of allowable transfer prices. Once the range is determined, the company can operate to lessen the other restrictions and problems discussed in this section.

Instability in political relations

To maintain its operational structure intact, a multinational firm must have great flexibility in coping with disturbances in international relations. For instance, if the United States fell into disfavor with India, it would be wise for a multinational company to divert its United States–Indian trade to United Kingdom–Indian trade. The cost of manufacturing the component parts might be higher in the United Kingdom, but in order to keep the selling price competitive in India, the parts would be shipped at an appropriately adjusted transfer price from the United Kingdom affiliate. (See Figure 16-2.)

The general political health of a country is highly geared to the extent of industrial development. Where unemployment, inflation, corruption, or an increasing trend toward nationalization is prevalent, the transfer price will be greatly affected by these trends. Inflation itself is a most dangerous variable and it eats away at a company's profits. A multinational company should use a high transfer price with some of the profits accounted for rather than wait for the remittance of dividends which after a while may be worth only half the original amount in foreign exchange.

Although a multinational company is in a business for the profit, any stabilizing influence it has on employment, on the increase of infant industries, and on direct investment will in the long run help it in that market. Current business thinking in developed countries maintains that a social and benevolent outlook by an international firm will in the long run be to its own benefit. Hence the transfer-price system can develop a market and help stabilize the economy. A low transfer price can help to stimulate employment and create a greater distribution for the product, while a high transfer price only skims the cream of the market without generating any further activity.

FIGURE 16-2

Adjusted Transfer Price

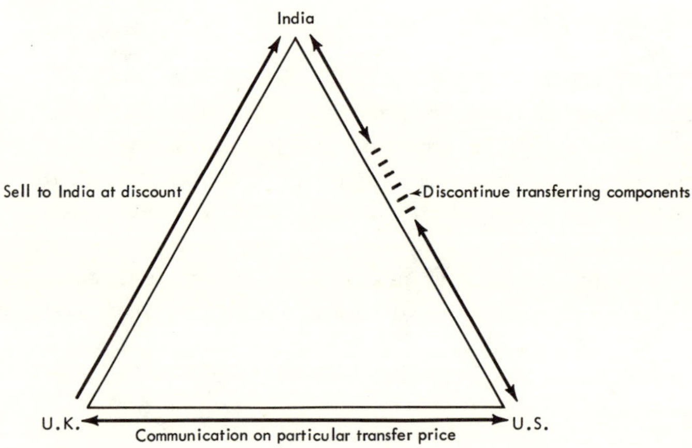

Toward a Deterministic Model for Intracompany Transfer Pricing

By making a distinction between the tangible barriers which now exist and the intangible barriers (future risks), we can make the logic behind transfer pricing a valuable tool for corporate planning and policy formulation. The probability of inflation, nationalization, repatriation controls, and corporate tax increases can account for the deviation of transfer prices from a purely economic model. By applying these latent barriers as constraints in imputing variables and by using probability estimates on the likelihood of their occurrence, one can form a workable model for decision-making purposes. A computer can be programmed to account for both tangible and risk barriers; however, it might be advisable to separate the subjective estimates from those which are either objective in nature or exist at the moment.

EXAMPLE I. For example, one could estimate the probability of various degrees of inflation over the next five years.

For Country A

Percent Increase in Inflation	*Probability of Inflation*
2	0.45
5	0.25
8	0.15
11	0.10
14	0.05
	1.00

EXAMPLE II. A cumulative estimate of the probabilities of nationalization over the next ten years would be helpful in explaining latent factors in the transfer price.

Years	*Cumulative Probability of Nationalization*
0– 1	0.10
1– 2	0.15
2– 3	0.25
3– 4	0.35
4– 5	0.40
5– 6	0.60
6– 7	0.80
7– 8	0.90
8– 9	1.00
9–10	1.00

These estimates may be either subjective or based on the experience of other foreign interests in the country in question and extrapolated into the future or both.

EXAMPLE III. The probability of a tax increase over a one-, two-, or five-year period could be estimated for the country in question.

Tax Increase over Next (2) *Years*	*Probability of Tax Increase*
5 percent	0.55
10 percent	0.30
15 percent	0.10
20 percent	0.05
	1.00

With this information on probabilities collected and computed for a meaningful time period, one can begin to see a valid relationship between the transfer price and the underlying causes. The time period for forecasting estimates has to be consistent with the time period used for budget and control forecasting and has to be correlated with a desired return on investment.

The use of expected value criteria based on these rough estimates may also be helpful in formulating a decision-making model. If the desired return on investment were to be locked into the transfer price, an increase of the local corporate tax would decrease the profit per unit of the transfer price. For example, if the probability of a 10 percent tax increase is 0.70 for the next year, then for every \$1 of original profit (net of taxes) transferred, the multinational company would have an expected value of \$0.93, i.e.,

$$\text{expected tax increase} = 0.70 \times 10 \text{ percent} \times \$1 = 0.07$$

Again, the use of Bayesian statistics, with the revision of subjective probabilities given an event takes place, can be an ongoing process for the calculation of transfer prices. Thus whether the expected value of the future \$1 to be transferred increases or decreases, it will still affect the actual transfer price contemplated for the ensuing period.

In sum, the aim of any model formulation is to couch its philosophy in such a manner that it will be workable and deterministic. Theoretical analysis based on the aggregation of supply and demand on an international basis would lead the decision maker into the vagaries of marginal cost and marginal revenue, which in a multimarket, multiproduct context present difficulties both to the practitioner and to the theoretician.

The systems approach applied to transfer pricing involves a suboptimization criterion on the part of the various affiliates in order to optimize aggregate world profits. This fact is even more evident when we arrange the barriers to the free flow of goods on a tangible and intangible basis. The tangible barriers (tariffs, repatriation controls, exchange controls, taxation, and political and economic stability) can be measured in meaningful terms. The problem arises in the measurement of the risk factors, i.e., the probability of the tangible factors either increasing or decreasing in the near or distant future. Careful study and experience with different methods, coupled with continual observation and periodic revision of the estimates, are likely to make transfer pricing an effective means of multinational management.

17

Taxation of the Multinational Firm

The multinational firm faces varying tax rates from one nation to another. Argentina taxes foreign companies 33 percent on income and an extra 12 percent on remitted profits; Bermuda has no income tax. Cambodia has 25 percent income tax; Burma has 98 percent income tax on all income in excess of 100,000 kyats.

The multinational firm also faces varying tax rates over time within countries, i.e., the tax rates in many countries fluctuate more than does the United States tax rate. For example, in contrast to an increase from 26 to 28 as a percent of GNP in the United States between 1960 and 1970, the tax rate in Sweden skyrocketed from 30 to 41 percent.

The multinational firm because of its many locations is particularly vulnerable to the number of fluctuations it will encounter. Yet, at the same time it is less vulnerable than a uninational company because it does not have all its eggs in one basket. Its tax risk is spread around.

The international tax problem has many other dimensions than rate differentials. The types of taxes, collection methods, and fiscal policies compound the problem. Some countries rely mostly on direct taxation such as the income tax, others emphasize indirect taxes, and most combine different forms of taxation into a mix which cannot readily be compared with any others. Although progress is being made toward greater comparability among countries through international conferences of fiscal specialists and officials, through tax treaties, and through international integration (common-market agreements), the tax environment for the multinational company continues to present a legally perplexing and financially intriguing aspect of international management.

Theory of International Taxation

"In a world of separate taxing authorities, problems arise from the fact that the entity taxed may not exist under the same taxing jurisdiction as does the base on which it is taxed, or one or both may in some sense belong to more than one taxing authority."[1] An individual or business may have his or its residence in one country, do business in another country, and be a citizen of or have headquarters in still another country. How is this individual or business taxed, and what should the criteria be? The controversy centers around two basic points: the right of the individual to equal taxation or freedom from excessive taxation; and the right of the different authorities to tax revenue. In other words, concern is for individual and international equity—equitable tax burdens imposed on the taxpayer and equitable division of tax revenues among the authorities. In addition to these legal and political problems, the taxation of foreign income also raises economic questions. Differential tax burdens, like tariffs, may induce an inefficient allocation of resources, or differing tax policies may be used to direct capital resources throughout the world. Thus a third important aspect is introduced—that of economic efficiency.

Economic Principles of Taxation

Three criteria have been suggested as the bases of developing a policy for taxation of the corporation with foreign source income.

Efficiency Principle. Economic efficiency is the first principle. "An economically efficient system of business income taxation would be one in which investment and other *business decisions were unaffected* by internation differences in tax rates or types of tax treatment."[2] Under this concept a tax policy would result that would make the investor neutral as to his location of investment. Thus capital would be invested where the real rate of return was highest. The use of tax incentive systems and subsidies would be nonexistent. A system of this nature would be almost impossible to achieve in practice, especially with a multitude of tax structures and rates; however, it serves as the theoretical model against which the soundness of any tax structure must be tested.

Equal-Treatment Principle. The second principle pertains to the equal tax treatment of investors. It implies that, within a taxing authority's jurisdic-

[1] Peggy Richman, *Taxation of Foreign Investment Income* (Baltimore: Johns Hopkins Press, 1963), p. 5.

[2] Richman, *Taxation of Foreign Investment Income*, p. 9

tion, recipients of income should be treated equally; a dollar of foreign earnings should be treated the same as a dollar of domestic earnings.

The problem that arises in this connection is how to treat the taxes paid by the affiliate to the government of its domicile. The national taxing authority of the United States has proposed three possible solutions. First, to ignore foreign taxes and to tax the gross income of the affiliate at the U.S. rate. Second, to consider the foreign tax a cost of doing business (allowing the corporation to deduct this from its income) and tax the remainder at the U.S. rate. Third, to allow the foreign tax as a credit against U.S. tax liability and to assess only the difference between the two.

THE EQUITY PRINCIPLE. This refers to the distribution of the tax base between the capital exporting and capital importing countries. It contends that the tax revenue of the foreign source of income (foreign investment) should be equally divided between the two countries. In her study, Miss Richman suggests four elements which should be considered in determining intercountry equity in this respect:[3]

(a) A country should be able to claim some return for benefits provided —benefits from the host country (importer) versus those from the exporter.

(b) The changes brought about by capital movement in the national income and tax base of the countries involved should be the basis for taxation.

(c) A country should be entitled to some allowance for national costs and external diseconomies caused by corporate activities; these would be recouped by means of proportionate tax claims.

(d) A country should have the right to some tax claim on moral and legal grounds.

The last point alludes to rights of jurisdiction and to the notion of national property rights.

Of the four elements, the one that suggests that a country is entitled to some return based on loss of income and reduction of the tax base is the most realistic and easiest to qualify. The claim that some return is due the home nation because of the benefits provided is probably the most controversial. The U.S. taxing authority argues that, no matter where income is earned, the corporation is benefiting from the fact that it is associated with the United States. To the corporation accrue such benefits as recourse to advice from American consulates in a foreign nation, protection of the corporation's assets from repatriation by a foreign government, and the psychological advantages which come as a carryover of the U.S. image. Those people who argue against this reasoning do so on two grounds. First, although the benefits suggested above may accrue to a person, they do not apply to a corporation. Second, since these benefits do not exist, the taxing authority is overstepping its jurisdiction when it crosses national boundaries to tax affiliated companies located in foreign territory.

[3] Richman, *Taxation of Foreign Investment Income,* p. 102.

Legal Principles of Taxation

There is wide agreement that a country has a right to tax the income and wealth of its residents or citizens because their rights to the protection and the services provided by the state are matched by their duties to the state, among which is the duty to pay taxes.[4] In general a nation might claim the right to tax on legal grounds similar to the following:

(1) property within its territory owned by foreigners
(2) property originating within its territory but located and producing income abroad, whether owned by nationals or foreigners
(3) property located abroad but owned by its nationals

The concept of fiscal responsibility of residents and citizens of a state would allow a country the right to tax income of its nationals whether the income were derived from assets at home or abroad. Less clearly delineated is the right to tax foreigners owning property within a nation. However, since the foreigner receives certain rights and benefits, he has the duty to pay taxes and this is the *rationale* behind the tax. In general, when considering the legal philosophy behind taxation of foreign-source income, taxation by domicile is more realistic. When one considers the distributional effects of national income, taxation by source is more desirable.[5] For an equitable policy of foreign-income taxation, a combination of both is justifiable, the exact mixture being a subjective question.

Thus, it is clear that no single policy with respect to the taxation of foreign-source income will meet the desirable objectives of both neutrality and equity. It appears that a policy emphasizing the tax-credit approach is superior, because it is neutral as to capital location and equitable as to tax burden.

Development of Current U.S. Tax Policy

From the inception of the corporate income tax, the United States has asserted jurisdiction to tax on the basis of two factors: citizenship and source of income. Thus a taxpayer is taxed on his worldwide income. But, until recently, a jurisdictional rule insulated foreign-based affiliates of U.S. companies from taxation. Under this rule, the income earned by the affiliate remained immune to U.S. taxation until it was remitted to the U.S. parent company in the form of dividends. Since the deferral of dividends was equivalent to an interest-free loan from a financial standpoint, it did not induce profit repatriation and greatly stimulated reinvestment of the affiliate's earnings abroad. Also, it gave rise to the "tax-haven" concept—the location of

[4] E. R. Barlow and I. T. Wender, *Foreign Investment and Taxation* (Cambridge, Massachusetts: The Law School of Harvard University, 1959), p. 173.
[5] Richman, *Taxation of Foreign Investment Income,* p. 102.

subsidiary operations in countries which had minimal or no corporate income tax (Panama, Switzerland, the Bahamas, Liechtenstein, Venezuela, and, recently, Canada). These tax-haven subsidiary corporations acted as investment clearinghouses for all foreign operations of their parent companies—accumulating income and taking profits from operations in one country and investing them in another without any tax liability to the United States.

Thus, compared to domestic income, the earnings of foreign-based affiliates enjoyed a distinct tax advantage not only in the right of deferral as such but also in making it possible for management to avoid affiliate dividends at times when domestic profits were high and to declare them when domestic earnings were at a minimum. This action caused a lower total tax liability in the long run than equivalent domestic earnings would have caused. A further reduction of the tax was possible by liquidating the foreign-based affiliate and transferring its earnings to the United States as capital gains rather than as profits. As a consequence, the objective of the U.S. tax policy for equal treatment of domestic and foreign income frustrated rapid growth of multinational operations, and increased sophistication in international taxation widened the gap between the objective and reality to the point where an adjustment became imperative.

The 1962 Revenue Act

The overriding purpose of the 1962 revision was the tax neutrality of investments in a foreign country (especially developed nations) and those in the United States. This purpose necessitated dropping the jurisdictional rule and eliminating the deferral privilege of foreign-based income.

But the singlemindedness necessary for so sharp a turn in tax policy was not present in Congress and a compromise measure incorporating what really are contradictory concepts was passed as the 1962 Revenue Act. It is inconsistent in principle and confusingly complicated in application. The law retains the old rule that the place of incorporation determines taxing authority. By this rule profits earned by foreign-based subsidiaries and other affiliates who are created under host-country law as separate entities are not subject to U.S. taxation unless and until distributed to the parent company or to other U.S. shareholders.[6] But a qualification was added in so-called Subpart F which for most practical purposes renders the general rule inoperative.

Subpart F obligates the headquarters company to add to its taxable income certain earnings of its foreign affiliates even though the earnings have been neither repatriated or distributed to the parent. This obligation applies to three types of affiliate income:

1. *Foreign holding company income* which includes dividends, interest, royalties, rents and any other distributions received from the ownership of stock or securities in other foreign companies, for example, in subsidiaries of the affiliate.

[6] Foreign branches of U.S. firms lacking juridic identification with host-country law are subject to U.S. tax as before.

2. *Foreign base company sales income* which is the name given in the tax law to income derived from purchase and sales transactions between related parties (affiliated companies) where goods traded are both produced and sold (or bought) outside the legal domicile of the affiliate. For example, if an Italian affiliate of a U.S. company bought goods from a Spanish affiliate and sold them to an Austrian buyer, the Italian affiliate would be termed to be the recipient of base company income.

3. *Foreign base company service income* which relates to income from services rendered outside the host country for an affiliated company or related person. It parallels the base-company sales income.

This puts all foreign-based affiliates which trade with one another under U.S. tax obligation irrespective of in which country their profits may be. Only manufacturing affiliates who sell direct to third parties can claim immunity against U.S. tax authority until the earnings remain in the host country. But since such isolation defeats the inherent advantages of the multinational firm, the strictly localized manufacturing subsidiary is a rare exception rather than the rule.

The American headquarters company must comply with the Subpart F requirement irrespective of whether the affiliate earnings have been transferred to the United State or not. Clearly, this qualification contradicts the main rule itself: the place of incorporation can no longer be the controlling criterion if firms incorporated in other countries are subjected to U.S. taxation. The law shields this substantive contradiction in its provisions behind a formality. Namely, if the affiliate profits are retained in the host country and, thus, remain outside the U.S. tax jurisdiction under the main rule, the Subpart F income is "deemed to be a dividend" to the parent firm and as such taxable in the U.S. The amount of the "deemed dividends" is based upon the so-called "minimum distribution requirements" which decree that a specified share of affiliate profits should be distributed annually to the U.S. parent. That any requirements in themselves violate the place of incorporation rule hardly needs to be pointed out.

Meaning of Affiliate

To tax the income of foreign-based affiliates, it was necessary to define and clearly distinguish between American and non-American enterprises abroad. In the 1962 Revenue Act this distinction is made on the basis of ownership: if 50 percent or more of the equity capital of a foreign-based affiliate is owned by the U.S. parent company or other American stockholders, each of whom owns at least 10 percent of the total equity, the firm is considered to be American and its income subject to U.S. taxation regardless of whether it is transferred to the stockholders or kept abroad; if less than 50 percent of the equity is owned by U.S. stockholders or if their holdings are fragmentized into units of less than 10 percent each,[7] the firm is considered

[7] Stock of shareholders who own less than 10 percent is never counted toward the 50 percent.

foreign and its income is beyond the tax jurisdiction of the United States. For insurance companies the ownership ratio is 25 percent.

Attribution rule

In determining the U.S. citizen's ownership percentage of a foreign firm, both direct and indirect ownership is considered. For example, if a U.S. firm owns only 5 percent of a French company's stock but at the same time owns a Swiss-based company which holds a majority interest in the French company, the U.S. company is *attributed* with a controlling (more than 50 percent) interest in the French company, and the latter company's income becomes taxable in the United States. Regardless of how roundabout the ownership relationship is and how many different foreign corporations are involved, the attribution rule still applies. Thus organizational gimmicks cannot be used to circumvent the intent of the new law.

Incentives for Investment in Underdeveloped Countries

Special tax concessions to private investors in underdeveloped countries are believed in U.S. official circles to be justifiable as incentives for redistributing world investment flows so as to bring about a more balanced development and to reap the large external economies which most underdeveloped countries offer. A further argument for concessions is the need to demonstrate the fallacy of the so-called *risk illusion,* which is caused by investors' ignorance and unfamiliarity with the actual conditions in the backward countries.

Opponents of the concessions are unconvinced by either of the official arguments. They fear that tax concessions are ineffective as incentives for new investment and only provide windfall profits to existing affiliates. Instead, they prefer government-sponsored investment programs or investment guarantees to deal with the question of risk and uncertainty. To date, the opposition has been unsuccessful in making any noticeable impression on the actual tax policy which is being implemented. And it appears that as concessions were made in the early postwar years to facilitate European rehabilitation, so will they be made in many years to come to accelerate capital formation in the underdeveloped countries. The prime vehicles for formalizing and conveying the concessions are tax treaties negotiated and ratified by the countries for whose benefit the concessions are intended.

Tax Treaties

International tax agreements first reached a degree of importance in the latter part of the 19th century. The rising tax rate caused by World War I is considered the principal reason for these agreements, which have recently become prominent. The impact of taxes of two countries on the same income aroused serious concern and led to a cooperative effort to eliminate the burden of double taxation.

The tax treaties were negotiated to minimize the burdens which double taxation entails. Their typical provisions are concerned with three main topics:

(1) the problem of payment of taxes to two jurisdictions
(2) the problem of dealing with double taxation and record keeping under two different tax systems
(3) problems resulting from inconsistent tax requirements.

Indirectly, tax treaties can be utilized for improving tax equity and administration by authorizing the tax authorities of the signatory countries to exchange information and to seek administrative consensus on matters about which there can be reasonable differences of opinion. In other words, the treaties make it possible for the tax authorities of one country to have continuous liaison with those of another, permitting them to deal more effectively and equitably with current problems.

A tax treaty with a developed country involves tax reductions or equal concessions by both parties. This type of treaty is advantageous to both countries because both have foreign traders and investors operating in their markets; loss of foreign tax revenue is replaced by an increase in domestic tax revenue. Since underdeveloped countries have few people involved in foreign investment, this type of treaty would involve a loss of revenue to them that in most cases would more than offset the gain in revenue from new investment. The tax treaties now being negotiated attempt to stabilize the taxation policy of the underdeveloped countries for the duration of the treaty. The purpose is not to reduce significantly the tax paid by an American corporation, because they already enjoy the foreign-tax credit, but to attempt to equalize foreign-income taxation, to eliminate sliding rates, and to provide stability and certainty as to the future tax burden. Tax treaties with underdeveloped countries provide incentives for U.S. investment in these countries and, at the same time, provide for scaling back the revenue sacrifice which the standard tax treaty demands of the source country.

Finally, other incentives that differ from previous policy have been offered by the government to stimulate investment in underveloped countries. A tax deferral is offered when an American firm gives patents or technical information for stock in a foreign corporation[8] for example.

Taxation Policies of the United States That Differ from Those of Other Developed Countries

The United States is most unusual among developed nations in making the place of incorporation or legal organization a determinant of income-tax

[8] Stanley Surrey, "The United States Tax System and International Relationships—Perspective in 1964," Treasury Department Bulletin (Washington, D.C.: September 21, 1964), p. 27.

jurisdiction. As contrary examples, let us take some members of the Common Market plus Great Britain. Generally speaking, these countries ignore the place of incorporation. The underlying concept of the British statute is that business income has its source wherever the "control and management" of the enterprise are located.[9] Practically speaking, this is a test of corporate or fiscal domicile as distinguished from legal domicile. The accepted European principle, to which the United States does not subscribe, is that the business income of a corporate branch or permanent establishment is subject to tax only in the country (source country) where the establishment or branch is located.

Regarding capital gains, too, most developed nations have a different philosophy than the United States does. Canada and some countries in the European Common Market do not tax capital gains as the United States does. Another difference is the method of assessment of taxes. In the United States the filing and assessment of income tax are left to the individual corporation. In contrast, the European countries use what may be called a *forced tax system,* under which the determination of the tax owed to the government (or its computation) is conducted or overseen by a governmental agency.

There are innumerable minor differences between the U.S. income-tax policy and that of other countries. The difference that causes the most concern and the one that seems to stand above all the rest is the U.S. policy of making the place of incorporation rather than the place where control and management are located the controlling test of income-tax jurisdiction.

The result is that the United States does not treat foreign subsidiaries the same way foreign governments treat their corporations. In international taxation policy, the United States has placed domestic neutrality ahead of foreign neutrality as the desired objective.

Value Added Tax (TVA)

The Tax on Value Added is a recent French innovation. It was developed in response to dissatisfaction with the "very pyramided" turnover tax previously used by most European countries. The turnover tax was a consumer's tax applied at each level of a product's life. It began with a tax at the raw materials purchase level, was applied again at the wholesale level, again at the retail level, and finally at the consumer level. Each time it was applied the tax compounded itself, "pyramiding" as it passed from one stage to the next such that no one really knew how much he was taxed on previous taxes or the value of the good.

The TVA gets away from pyramiding by taxing only the value added at each stage of the production process. The value added is the difference between what the firm takes in as sales revenue and what it pays out to other firms for materials and services used. For instance a company that produces a product

[9] Palmer Baker, "European Taxation of Foreign Source Income," *Taxes and International Business, a Symposium* (New York: National Association of Manufacturers, November 19, 1964), p. 12.

that sells for $500 before taxes and pays $360 for materials, transportation, and brokerage fees is taxed on (500 − 360) × tax rate, say 15 percent, giving a tax of $21 per unit. The cost to the buyer then would be $521.

Since the tax is calculated on value added and clearly invoiced as a separate item (not hidden in the sales price) there is no pyramiding and the tax is easily identifiable for rebating to companies that export. In this way the TVA does not fall on foreign consumers and serves to make European Common Market exports more competitive with exports from countries whose tax system is not adaptable for rebates.

There are several other advantages of the TVA which, because of French success, has become the tax to be used by not only all Common Market countries but throughout Western Europe.

1. Adaptability. The French use three basic rates ranging from 20 to 6 percent depending on the type of commodity. Luxuries are levied the higher rates and necessities the lower rates. Flexibility is increased by altering the tax base. For example, general construction and housing industries are stimulated by lowering their tax base. General construction is taxed at 60 percent of the normal base and housing at 50 percent of the normal. In this way the TVA can be adjusted to the prevailing economic problems and priorities.

2. Elimination of the pressure for firms to integrate vertically in order to reduce payments under the turnover tax, or ordinary sales tax.

3. Efficiency. TVA speeds up the replacement of manual methods with mechanized and automated processes since it lays a heavier tax burden on high cost manufacturers than low cost manufacturers. This is believed to be particularly important in encouraging technologically backward companies to modernize and to give all firms a greater incentive to stress research and development. Although the TVA falls on both labor and capital and the ratio of labor outlay to capital returns is high for low-profit enterprises and relatively low for high-profit companies, low-income labor-intensive companies will be taxed proportionately more.

4. Profitability. "Value-added taxes are likely to tax high-profit companies relatively less—not more—than low-profit firms." In this fashion it again rewards success and penalizes inefficiency. Take for example two companies with identical sales but different profits as shown in the illustration below:

		Low-Cost Company		*High-Cost Company*
Sales revenue		$600		$600
Purchases:				
raw materials	$ 80		80	
parts and subassemblies	40		40	
services	30		30	
TOTAL		$150		$150
Value added:				
wages	200		260	
overhead	130		130	
gross profits	120		60	
TOTAL		$450		$450
TVA (10 percent)		$ 45		$ 45

Expressing the taxes as percent of profits, the low-cost (high-profit) company pays 37.5 percent while the high-cost company pays 75 percent; under an income-tax system their respective obligations would be the opposite. Notice particularly that smaller labor costs reduce the tax burden on the company. Under the U.S. system of income taxation the reduction of labor costs would increase taxes unless passed on to the consumer in the form of lower prices.

The TVA makes no distinction between types of firms: cooperatives, unincorporated, and even government enterprises are treated in the same way.

The Influence of Foreign Taxes on the Multinational Firm

The net effect of the TVA on the multinational firm is difficult to precisely determine at this point because the TVA has two faces. One face frowns on the multinational firm and the other face favors it. Today the multinational firm is vigorously fighting the TVA for a very important reason: U.S. tax credit for taxes paid on profits earned in a foreign country and repatriated to the U.S. applies only to income taxes paid. The TVA is not an income tax in spite of the fact that it does in part tax profits. In American frame of reference the TVA is a sales tax. The consequence is double taxation of European affiliates.

The TVA also eliminated one of the historical advantages of some multinational firms: the large-scale vertical integration that permitted some multinational firms to avoid turnover taxes by producing all subparts, while their competitors had to buy components and therefore pay taxes on their purchases.

Transfer pricing—an important tool of the multinational firm in its global tax minimization scheme—is reduced in effectiveness by the TVA. Where emphasis shifts from income tax to value-added tax, the determination of cost of goods sold to find profit becomes less important and the use of transfer pricing for tax purposes, though not for other purposes, becomes of less value.

To the extent that the TVA stimulates greater efficiency in domestic industries it works against the multinational firm. Rewarding high profits and encouraging capital intensiveness will aid multinational firms and domestic firms alike to be sure, but to the extent that European companies which were stuck in tradition and now are forced to adopt more dynamic and progressive methods, the edge of the multinational firm over domestic firms is diminished.

The other face of the TVA favors the multinational firm. For those multinational firms already established within the Common Market the TVA opens new opportunities by taxing old hang-on enterprises more heavily and limiting their ability to survive.

Also, the equal treatment given to state corporations, private corporations, and cooperatives under the TVA system places the multinational firm in a more equitable tax position than it was under the traditional methods of taxation. Finally the tax rebate given for exports from the European countries must be attractive to the multinational firm with subsidiaries elsewhere. It more than any other type of organization is equipped to enter Europe for production with its eye set on sales elsewhere...in order to pick up the tax rebate.

Taxation of Foreign-Owned Companies in the United States

Until 1966, foreign-owned companies and aliens on a nonresident status (not having a permanent immigration visa) were subject to discriminatory taxation by the United States. This discrimination was eliminated by the Foreign Investors Tax Act of 1966, which represents the first major revision of these tax provisions in the postwar period. The central principle of the new law is to treat the U.S.-based foreign entities in the same way as a domestic firm or individual would be treated under like circumstances. However, since the foreign company often has special relationships with its overseas establishment, a series of special rules and formulas are provided for dealing with such specifics.

Tax-Shelter Corporations

To stimulate international trade, especially the exports of American goods, Congress has authorized the formation of certain tax-shelter corporations which enjoy specific tax savings not available to other firms. They seldom exist as separate operating entities but are set up as paper organizations, staffed by accountants and lawyers, to minimize the tax burden of the parent company. Their characteristics are explained in Chapter 29 along with other export institutions.

18

Interaction of the Multinational Firm with Host Societies

The presence of the multinational firm is a profoundly significant aspect of contemporary reality in much of the world. Most countries have wooed it through official incentives for inward foreign investments, tax holidays, tariff protection, foreign-exchange privileges and by many other means. The multinational firms have not always been happy to comply. Many prominent personalities and nongovernmental groups, anxious to push back the tyranny of material wants, low productivity, and aversion to change in their respective countries, have joined in the crusades and broadened the appeal to the multinational firm through private initiative.

On the international level, liberalization of transboundary business activities and closer economic cooperation among nations have become familiar themes to which all countries attest as common ideals. Even the Soviet Union and other communist countries have started to seek ways to entice companies from abroad to cross their previously ironclad borders. Thus, the evidence favoring the propagation and growth of the multinational firm is almost overwhelming.

Yet the issue is bitterly contested. Increasingly, the presence of the multinational firm has become a source of concern and, at times, acute resentment in many countries. Canada, France, Guinea, Iran, and Peru are publicized sites for recent dramatic clashes between the host governments and the multinational firm. Similar conflicts have surfaced elsewhere throughout the world.

Visionary illusions to one side, the frictions between the host societies and the multinational firm defy explanation by patent clichés. It is not the diabolical designs of avaricious plutocrats and insatiate imperialists but the inherent complexities of the mutually adaptive interactions between the uninational society and the multinational firm which harbor the real causes for conflict and tensions. Identification of the potential conflict situations in this multidimensional process is a necessary prerequisite for any rational interpretation, let alone the prevention and resolution of the conflicts. An understanding of these conflict areas is, therefore, critical for the leaders of both business and society.

Host Nations' Perceptions of Peril

Fear of Corporate Centralism

Governments and private groups in host countries have started to show the fear that as multinational companies expand, more and more business decisions affecting their economies will be made at parent-company headquarters abroad. In the light of the tendency of many multinational companies to centralize and integrate their various affiliates in ways which benefit the total enterprise, the possibility of divergent interests between the firm and its host societies cannot be ignored. The multinational firm's allegiances are inward-looking. With due regard to the limits set by the host government and belief in conveying the "good citizen" image, its overall objectives are growth and profits, which generally require increasing market penetration. The primary means of achieving these objectives is efficiency in the functional areas of management: production, marketing, finance, and so on, which the top management often feels can best be achieved by having undivided control over all aspects of the firm's affairs.

Empirical evidence indicates that a multinational firm tends to be more centralized the greater the interlocking of affiliates in production and marketing; the more intensive the development of rapid communication, frequent visits, and computerized data-gathering; and the more substantial the capital outlay required. But centralization also results from inflexibility of parent-company policies regarding product, manufacturing processes, and organization. Thus decisions are centralized regarding product mix for each affiliate, extent of interaffiliate sales of semifinished and finished products, pricing of products, exports and intracompany sales, input procurement, packaging, long-range planning, research and development, and particularly financial management. The tendency to centralize by the multinational firm signifies to the host governments an erosion of their own powers and controls. As the authority over these vital business decisons is shifted away from their jurisdictions they can hardly be expected to remain indifferent. Clearly, centralization is exacting a price from the multinational firm. This price the firms are yet to learn to calculate. However, when things are sorted out the price may well turn out to be far greater for many firms than the operational simplifications gained by centralization. And the trend is up.

Governments, particularly in the lesser-developed countries, are assuming more responsibilities for the achievement of economic growth and social goals than formerly. To be successful they need a fairly high degree of certainty in the business sector. The presence of affiliates of multinational firms is perceived to introduce uncertainties and uncontrollables into the economy which make it increasingly difficult for the government to plan and police its policies. With substantial segments of industry owned and directed from abroad and with headquarters-country governments, such as the U.S. government, bent on interfering in the affairs of the affiliates, the host governments see a serious challenge to their ability to effect the desired economic and social programs. The more responsibility for economic growth and stability the government accepts, the greater its direct involvement in business regulation and direction, and the greater the possibility that the multinational firm will be perceived as a potential agitator of the national plans. For example, the French minister of industry recently charged that foreign-owned affiliates in France were both unconcerned with objectives of the national plan and had means of avoiding its guidelines. Host governments see their planned goal achievement frustrated to the extent that the multinational firms take their cues from the headquarters country and tend to pursue policies that deviate from the indigenous national goals.

Fear of Industrial Dominance

The fear of industrial dominance derives to a large extent from the size of the U.S. enterprises and their affiliates, from their concentration in a few key industrial sectors, and from their aggressive behavior. In permitting foreign investors to control key industries, nations are in the precarious position of gradually losing control over strategic sectors to the seemingly omnipotent multinational enterprise. In Canada, for example, the concentration in a few major industrial areas is accompanied by a high percentage of control over the key industrial sectors and by a concentration of that control in the hands of a few foreign affiliates. United States companies' ownership of Canadian industry is so concentrated that several sectors are clearly dominated by these firms. In 1968, American firms owned 54 percent of the production of petroleum and natural gas, with 62 percent under their control, while American companies owned 54 percent of mining and smelting activities and controlled 52 percent.[1] Examining the European market, we find U.S. firms owned about 25 percent of the German production of automobiles during 1963–65. Belgian automobile production was wholly American-owned and in France about 20 percent was American-owned. In total, as of 1966, 1500 U.S. companies held or had interest in over 3900 European companies, nearly 20 percent of which were in chemicals, 15 percent in electrical manufacturing and 16 percent in

1 Computed from OECD statistics.

mechanical manufacturing (includes automobile manufacturing).[2] Hence the fear of industrial domination is no chauvinistic fiction but in many instances an obvious truth.

Fear of Unfair Competition

The multinational firm with its abundance of skills (financial, managerial, production, and so on) is often at an obvious competitive advantage when compared to the domestic firm. Local enterprises accuse foreign-owned enterprises of exercising this competitive advantage to the point of being "unfair" and against the nation's best interests. Oftentimes when multinational firms enter the host country they possess already a strong market position built on prior imports. This makes it so much more formidable in the eyes of local competitors, who may see in it overwhelming odds against their own aspirations. Some multinational firms place their direct investments in the host country in acquisitions of preexisting indigenous firms. To the nationals of the country this may look like a gradual takeover by foreigners of entire sectors of their economy. In smaller or less-industrialized countries the point is quickly reached when no nationally owned companies may be left in a particular industry. Thus, the appearance if not the reality of a foreign monopoly condition is created. A number of nations have, therefore, started to restrict acquisitions to prevent the elimination of local competitors and to try to channel inward foreign investments into the establishment of new firms which make a larger real contribution to the host economy and restrict the disturbance in the market which major acquisitions typically cause.

The affiliates of the multinational firm are also thought to have a distinct "unfair" advantage in financing. In support for this fear are cited the financial power of the headquarters company, high earnings of affiliates, ability to transfer assets among different affiliates and/or to the headquarters, and the easier access to external money and capital markets. The affiliates are also said to have a competitive advantage in being able to tap local banks more readily and at lower costs than domestic businesses due to its credit standing enhanced by the collateral value of the headquarters-company's assets.

Affiliates have been accused of price-cutting to simultaneously reduce the number of competitors and to obtain a larger share of the market. The affiliate could very well reply that due to its efficient production methods, costs are reduced and passed on to the consumer in the form of lower prices. French industries have, for example, complained that the American affiliates in France are responsible for price wars and unrest in the French labor force, in addition to being ignorant of social responsibility of business, using unfair promotional practices and disrupting established commercial patterns.

Still another charge against the multinational firm is that it reduces competition by creating overcapacity within an industry which forces the indigenous firms, whose financial reserves are limited, into cutthroat competi-

2 *Ibid.*

tion and ultimate suicide. For example, a French company, Moulinex, producing household appliances, lost a "safe" competitive position to French affiliates of Singer, Hoover, and Scoville; the last also is asserted to have rid Moulinex of its staff.

On examination of the methods utilized by the multinational firm to establish foreign subsidiaries, it is apparent that they invariably have a competitive advantage. Without it they would have hardly any rational reason to enter a country. The existence of an advantage is inherent in all direct investments and business ventures. There is nothing illegitimate or unfair about competitive advantages as such; in fact, they are the means for greater efficiency and productivity. But if the advantages are obtained through illegitimate or unfair means they do become socially destructive and politically indefensible. The fears of competitive superiorities of the multinational firm often blur this very important distinction.

Fear of Technological Dependence

The ability of the headquarters company to determine whether, when, and how the newest techniques are employed by affiliates has aroused fears in host nations of an increasing dependence on the multinational firm for its technological progress. It has been argued that this dependence is attributable to a technology gap between the U.S. and other countries. A lesser commitment of European and other non-U.S. industries to research and development is given as the cause for the gap. Researchers who have attempted to go beyond the expenditure figures discredit the technology gap theory by showing that technological inventions and innovations have come no less frequently from Europe than from the U.S. Furthermore the European inventions have tended to fall in the major breakthrough category. Thus the issue is by no means clear as far as Europe is concerned. However, there is no room for argument in reference to the developing areas.

The fear of the necessity of relying on U.S. technology, in turn, leads to the fear of foreign control and ownership of industry. As a given industry sector is taken over by multinational companies, the host country becomes dependent on the technological in-transfers of the foreign-headquarters firm for its growth and product development. Once achieved, the dominant position of the multinational firm is believed to be self-perpetuating. Dominance itself provides the affiliate with resources to help perpetuate its role as the major innovator. National policies aimed at greater independence in technology are a mixture of the desire for local research and development facilities and their ownership as well as the desire for technically advanced items produced locally. However, it appears that in a large number of countries no alternative will exist but to rely on foreign technology in order to avoid a stagnated economy until indigenous conditions have changed, especially in reference to managerial flexibility, increased investment in education, business attitudes towards research and development, and government subsidies for it.

Fear of Loss of National Sovereignty and National Identity

Loss of national sovereignty appears to be the all-pervasive fear resulting from the expansion of the multinational firm into all spheres. This loss may be the consequence of the dependence on foreign technology, foreign industrial dominance and the multinational firm's general ability to effect its own desired results. Losing its sovereignty, the nation loses its power, and without power the existence of nationhood, even its identity, becomes problematic.

Lack of managerial diplomacy in headquarters companies helps to feed such fears. For example, there was a strong French reaction to the closure of a French plant by Remington Rand. This reaction was not focused on *what* action had been taken, but rather on *where* and *how* the decision had been made. In this case, the decision was cabled from the American parent, allegedly without prior consultation with either the management of the affiliate or with the officials of the host government. This is by no means an isolated incident. Much resentment is caused in the host countries by the multinational firm's failure to communicate its intentions and motives to the host government and other local bodies whose interests may be affected. With the tendency of the firms to centralize, such problems are increasing.

Differences in relationships among societies must be recognized by the multinational enterprise if the fear of loss of national sovereignty and identity is to be allayed. These differences may be economic—income structure, compensation structure, capital-labor relationships—or personal. Diversity of institutional settings is evident.

By increasing the international factors, the multinational firm reduces choices open to the host government regarding the most appropriate means of guiding the domestic economy. How its policies and activities affect the balance of payments, economic planning, competitive policy, and the development of technologies of the host nation, resulting in increased pressure for greater cooperation and consultation among governments—a definite threat to national sovereignty intensified by sensitized nationalistic sentiments will be surveyed in the next section. As the reader will notice, they do in many ways reinforce the perception of peril to the national society which host-country people have started to lament. So long as the multinational firm insists on centralization of control over its affiliates, the host-country fears are certain to push the political climate against the multinational firm and threaten punitive governmental actions such as we have seen recently in several host countries.

Conflict-Causing Corporate Policies

Although the multinational firm has no power over the host government, it may have considerable power under that government. By being able to influence certain critical factors, the firm has the opportunity to help or harm national economies; in this sense, it may be said to have even power *against* host governments.

The critical factors subject to the influence of the multinational enterprise may be categorized: (a) financial policy, (b) export-import policy, (c) accounting methods, (d) transfer of currencies, (e) pricing policy, (f) research and development, and (g) employment policy.

Financial Policy

As a matter of financial policy the multinational enterprise can choose to invest its profits either in the host country or elsewhere. The host-country's government would naturally like domestic investment, but the power lies with the headquarters company to determine where the profits will be allocated.

The multinational enterprise may help relieve a deficit in the host country's balance of payments and many examples exist to illustrate this fact. Of course, no conflict arises from this situation. But the firm may also contribute to the worsening of the host country's balance of payments. For example, an investment by a U.S. parent may produce a larger demand for U.S. capital equipment thereby increasing the deficit in the host country. The multinational enterprise has been indicted for causing capital flows to fluctuate and even reverse. In addition, increased investment in the host economy could very likely increase the market share held by the affiliate, which could be in conflict with host country interests. This makes the allocation of profits a very sensitive area. If the parent decides to invest or declare dividends outside the borders of the host, the latter gains no benefits from the investment potential of the firm. Also, the return of earnings to the parent company fluctuates from year to year, disturbing the payments position of some countries.

The source of borrowed funds can also create conflict. The MNF has a very broad base from which to choose as its source of borrowed funds; it can borrow from local sources (the host economy), U.S. sources, third-country sources, or multinational sources. This makes the multinational firm a much greater threat to import large sums than a uninational company which poses a further threat to the balance of payments position of the host country.

Also, host-government's domestic monetary policy may be easily undermined by the countering efforts of the multinational enterprise. A typical example involves the multinational firm's extension of credit to a foreign subsidiary at times when the host nation is attempting to dampen domestic purchasing power through import restrictions and exchange controls. Thus the foreign-owned affiliate has the power, cash, and credit and it can readily avoid efforts by the state to constrain credit and investment. Hence certainty in the effectiveness of governmental restrictive controls to achieve national objectives is unattainable and uncertainty the result.

Even though the magnitudes involved are not large in comparison to major elements in the balance of payments, and many countries have substantial earnings from overseas investments, these points are overlooked when attitudes are formed toward foreign investment within the host country. And the exact impact of an inward foreign investment on a country's balance of payments is usually too complex to be easily explained.

One aspect of the multinational enterprise's operations complicates the picture in ways not discernible in aggregate data. This aspect is the shift of funds among the entities of the enterprise through intracompany (inter-affiliate) sales (discussed later under pricing policy), royalties, technical-assistant fees, and allocation of headquarters expenses. The potential significance of these flows to the balance of payments is indicated by the report that remittances by Canadian companies to U.S. parents apart from intercompany sales and dividends were four times the inflow of loan funds from the parents in the mid-1960's.

Export-Import Policy

The export-import activities of the multinational firm can also have an effect on the host-country balance of payments. Exports from affiliates are subject to the desires of the parent company and probably fit into an international marketing scheme of the international enterprise. This means the affiliate's exports could go to the parent or other affiliates instead of to customers desired by the host economy or government.

Another charge against the multinational enterprise is that it may allocate export territories among its affiliates, thereby preventing them from exporting as they might otherwise and damaging the prospects for expansion of exports of the host economy.

Importing policies are also dictated by the headquarters company. Affiliates may be directed to import from the parent itself or from other affiliates instead of using resources from the host country, thus further contributing to a trade deficit on the part of the host.

However much the multinational enterprise may contribute to the objectives of economic growth and stability in the host country, the fact that the parent has the ability to alter the activities of the affiliates increases the uncertainty facing the host government. The further fact that the decision center is outside the jurisdiction of the host government compounds the uncertainty. Informal means of control, such as persuasion and inducements, are not as effective across national boundaries. Consequently, the ability of the host government to carry out its economic plans and policies is circumscribed by the spread of the multinational enterprise, which itself is pressed by several influences to adopt sometimes conflicting policies relating to financing, transfer of funds, exporting and importing, that jeopardize the balance-of-payments position of the host government.

Pricing Policy

The controversial aspects of multinational company pricing relate in part to intracompany pricing or transfer pricing and, in part, to pricing policies concerning customers outside the company itself.

When trading goods and services among affiliates or between the parent and affiliate, the transfer prices can be so calculated as to serve various other objectives besides the trade transactions as such. If the host countries employ foreign-exchange restrictions, the transfer price may be designed to circumvent the restrictions; if a particular host country has high-profits taxes, the transfer price may be used to reallocate the profits to a low-tax country; and when economic or political instability plagues some host countries, transfer prices can be used to keep to a minimum the company's cash reserves in that country. Transfer prices can also be used to strengthen the competitive position of a company, or to neutralize the competitive advantage of others. In these or similar applications the transfer price can become an obviously objectionable device which is detested by both the indigenous uninational companies and the host governments.

In outside pricing, local industry fears the ability of the affiliate to cut prices to any level necessary to achieve not only a foothold but to increase its market share. As put by a European journalist: "It is possible for General Motors to give away every Opel sold in Germany and not reduce its total profits by more than 50 percent." Although nobody in Europe takes this statement literally, it conveys the point that the multinational firm does possess far-reaching powers in this respect and that there is reason for the local people to be fearful about it.

Some enterprises have established a global single-price policy, that is, the same price applies all over the world. By doing so the company denies itself the ability to respond to the demands of individual country markets or to utilize to its maximum advantage the oligopolistic market structure of most host countries. The problem becomes further complicated when the company can point to trade barriers that give it reason to charge different prices as well as government pressures on prices through controls of purchases of some goods.

Affiliates of U.S. multinational enterprises have, at times, entered into price-restraining agreements. But normally they are not permitted by their parents to establish cartellistic relations because of U.S. antitrust laws. In countries where cartels are commonplace the affiliates' refusal to participate creates a gnawing doubt among local industrialists as to whether the American affiliates will behave by the agreed-upon rules. At the Crotonville Conference in 1965, this conflict was seen by U.S. and European businessmen as one of the most difficult in trying to work out good relationships.

Research and Development

In more than one aspect, the area of research and development can cause a conflict in interests between the parent company and the host country. The first of these aspects is the placement of the research-and-development facilities. Most of the host countries have urged multinational enterprises to establish local research-and-development facilities. Having creative work going on in their economies is expected to accelerate efforts in other areas of scientific research and innovation. However, there is a strong tendency for the multinational firm to concentrate research efforts normally in the parent organization or at least directly under its control. Whatever the scope of the affiliates' research and development program, growth of such a department is dependent on the parent. And, whatever the pattern of relationships concerning research within the firm, it is not one that eliminates the dependence of the host economy on the parent-company's decisions.

Even if research is done by the affiliate in the host country the issue of the ownership rights over the findings can cause conflicts. Should the company decide to use the results of the research in some other country, the host government may feel that no benefit accrues to the local economy, since the utilization of the results is beyond the control of the host country, and parent-company decisions assume both significance and suspiciousness from the nationalistic perspective.

In sum, the multinational enterprise usually helps the host country reach a higher level of technology. But it also demands a claim on national resources for research. And it leaves a major problem of who controls the results of the research. So long as domestic ownership and control over key sectors and key technology have not been achieved, national governments appear to feel threatened. The conflict of ownership will become increasingly important even though the research base is expanded by the activities abroad, the absence of domestic ownership and control is likely to become an even more serious source of tension.

Management Personnel

In the early stages of its international growth, a firm usually tends to keep the management responsibility over its foreign-based operations in the hands of headquarters-country nationals, most of whom are transferred abroad and some exercising their power through "remote control." The advantages here are twofold: first, simplicity of selection, appointment, and promotion, all of which can be done in a unilateralist frame of reference without disturbing the established headquarters practices and routines; and second, the relative uniformity of backgrounds of all managerial cadres throughout the multinational structure—everybody is the product of the same national and corporate cultures and has reached his position by playing by the same rules. American-headquartered multinational firms seem to be among the most committed to the dependence on the expatriate transferee in their foreign-based affiliate management.

Another source of executive manpower is the third-country expatriate, who may be defined as a manager who is a citizen of country *A*, works in country *B* for a company headquartered in country *C*. Most of them are multilingual Europeans, many being refugees from communist countries. Third-country nationals are reported to be more adept in integrating themselves into new situations and making friends in a foreign environment than are American expatriates. A number of U.S. companies have expressed definite preference for third-country nationals in overseas management positions. Burroughs Company, for example, had only three Americans operating abroad;

the rest of its overseas divisions were run by third-country nationals. The versatility of third-country executives may indicate high mobility toward top management positions. For example, an established world business, Nestlé, has opened up top corporate posts for nonheadquarters nationals. Of the top eleven members of Nestlé's present board of directors, six are non-Swiss. All expatriates are a potential source of difficulty since the local people resent their presence, not always so much as individuals but as decision makers and holders of superior positions.

Racial or religious biases often compound these problems. Foreigners may be welcome as long as they are 'not white,' 'not Hindu,' or 'not Asiatic,' while the same race or religion may be perfectly welcome or acceptable in the neighboring country. In the Congo in 1965, it was so dangerous to be a white foreigner that any multinational firm operations involving whites were out of the question. The multinational firm must try to sense and be guided by the strength of these nationalistic and xenophobic feelings. Host reactions will range from slowing of permits and documents in government offices, to expropriation or overt acts of violence and destruction by the population.

The host society generally has mixed reaction to the expatriate executive. The upper class may resist him because he is a relatively affluent outsider who threatens the local power and prestige structures. At the same time, they realize that advantages will most likely accrue to their country and themselves from the new technologies and behavior patterns which the expatriate brings with him.

A third source of executive personnel is host-country nations. In companies which have been established internationally for a longer time, there has been a clear trend toward the employment of an increasing percentage of local nationals in management positions. The reasons for this trend have been both economic and cultural, the need for knowledge and understanding of the local environment, the rapid growth of overseas operations requiring speedy expansion of the management group, the increased ability to utilize individuals with different national backgrounds successfully in the corporate structure, and direct or subtle pressures by host-country authorities for replacing expatriate managers with indigenous employees. While all host governments appear to strongly favor their people in executive assignments, they nonetheless can violently object to the salary policy of the multinational firm. In this area the company can be damned if it holds fast to local salary standards (as underpaying local nationals in comparison with headquarters executives) and damned if it exceeds the local standards (as undermining local firms and pirating their best people). This is a real dilemma.

Work Force

In the area of employment policies, there are several potential conflicts. The most important of these is the attempt to impose the home country's methods, mannerisms, and behavior patterns on the host society through the operations of the affiliate. Behrman cites the case of an Italian affiliate which attempted to increase productivity by changing the working hours and days of work to approximate those of the U.S. parent. The company was working a half day on Saturday and allowing two hours for lunch. Due to the expense involved in operating the half-day shift, a change was instituted dropping the Saturday shift and shortening the lunch time to forty-five minutes. This attempt met such strong resistance from the Italian workers that it had to be abandoned.

The hiring and firing policy of most U.S.-based multinational firms parallels that of the parent company, that is, the firm shifts its management personnel, removes redundant employees, regroups and retrains labor to meet new tasks. These dynamic and sometimes harsh policies are contrary to the social values of many foreign countries, where both managers and labor generally receive more stable treatment by the firm and are tied to the firm for extended periods of time.

The multinational firm is especially open to labor relations difficulties due to its "foreignness." It is usually easier for union leaders to incite local citizens against it because of the resentment of foreigners.

In the area of worker recruitment and training the multinational firm finds several problem areas. The most obvious problem in recruiting abroad (especially in less-developed areas) is the scarcity of skilled people. Shortages of skilled workers, managerial personnel, research and development scientists, and technicians, create a potential area of conflict. If the firm imports the needed skills, the host country loses both the training and the jobs for its own nationals, and for the multinational firm to undertake the required training programs locally is often financially prohibitive.

In certain host countries manual work cannot be included in any training programs for supervisory personnel because a strong social stigma is attached to it. The same may be true about sales. There is difficulty for the multinational firm to interest educated nationals to take sales positions in certain countries because, in their value scale, sales work rates as undesirable.

Conflicts may arise also from the promotion policies of a multinational firm. Some countries have rigid social stratification in which on-the-job achievement and economic performance are not recognized. Merit-based promotion of the most competent or deserving personnel to management or supervisory positions, thus, flies in the face of expectations and notions of social propriety. Perhaps the best example of this problem would be the promotion of a lower-caste member to a position of supervision above a member of a relatively higher caste in India. While less obvious, the same conflict is encountered in many other, particularly developing, countries in a more subtle context.

Host-Country Regulation of the Multinational Firm

To preserve the nation's control in its own sphere of influence, host governments have applied restrictions which are felt to be in the national interests of maintaining internal control with a minimum amount of external interference. The areas in which such disturbance may occur are those in which the host governments look for positive contributions: growth targets in key industries, price and wage stability, balanced regional development, financial stability, and an improved balance-of-payments position. To achieve these objectives, governments have sought means of reducing or persuading foreign businesses to alter investment levels, change employment practices, expand exports, or substitute for imports. To facilitate the attainment of these objectives, nations have instituted particular requirements that must be met if foreign investment is to transpire.

The affiliate's repatriation of dividends, royalties, and so on, to the parent may be kept at a minimum to prevent the outflow of exchange reserves which may jeopardize their perhaps already delicate balance-of-payment positions. Import restrictions may be levied on raw materials, machines, and spare parts to induce foreign industry to purchase more of its supplies within the host country and thereby create markets for local industry and decrease the degree of importation. Some countries have gone so far as to require foreign investors to use a specified minimum of locally produced raw materials and components.

The continuing foreign-exchange shortages have also necessitated many host nations to institute obligatory export requirements by the multinational firm.

Tax controls have also been established resulting in a squeeze on profits, especially as the business prospers; oil companies have found this a frequent problem. There have been cases where the initial agreement called for specific tax rates only to have them increased considerably after some degree of success was attained by the venture. Related to the profit squeeze is the exercise of price control by governments.

Some host nations are requiring installation of research and development facilities in the host nation so as to stimulate interest in science in the universities, increase employment opportunities locally, and thereby reduce the brain drain and payment for technology.

Exclusion from certain industries can be discovered in virtually all nations, though to be sure, the degree of such exclusion varies from country to country. Natural resource development by foreigners is often restricted; ownership of public utilities, airlines, shipping lines, banks, and communications is reserved for nationals in a majority of countries; agriculture is almost entirely closed to private foreign entry in a number of countries; and many other areas of activity can be found in the sector reserved for local investment.

In many countries, labor unions have strong government support enabling the unions to effectively use such support in obtaining special concessions from business. Layoffs may be forbidden, profits may have to be shared and an extraordinary number of services may have to be provided. In addition, there might be requirement of employment of local personnel, personnel whom the multinational firm may feel are insufficiently educated and oriented toward parental policies and whose loyalties may be bent away from the interests of the firm. To superimpose this requirement of engaging local nationals in the multinational firm's operations, restrictions against employment of expatriate personnel (i.e., managers, technicians) are being imposed in a variety of ways by the host nation.

Requirement of certain officers of a corporation or a percentage of the board of directors to be nationals has been demanded in a number of countries. In Trinidad and Tobago, for example, some firms are reportedly faced with a regulation requiring the general manager to be a local national. Countries like Norway require at least half of the foreign subsidiaries' board of directors to be Norwegian residents. Nations such as Japan, Mexico, and India maintain the requirement of local majority ownership in many industries. This compels multinational firms which have an aversion to any type of joint venture to reconsider their ownership policies.

Finally, the possibility of expropriation and nationalization of production facilities exists. Expropriation stems from the belief that a country's national goals and self-interest can best be served by government ownership rather than by a foreign parent. Nationalization is usually justified on the grounds that the industry is critical to national defense, national sovereignty, national wealth and/or national economic growth. Most nationalizations have been further officially rationalized by the charge that foreign businesses have typically exploited the national wealth of the host country, taking everything from the country without giving anything in return. Nationalization has been most prevalent in the extractive industries such as oil and mining except for socialist countries where private ownership of business in general may be restricted or completely outlawed.

Corporate Adaptation to Host-Country Cultures

Although the conflicts between the multinational firm and its host societies usually take the form of a concrete economic or administrative controversy, their true substance is often hidden in the more fundamental and elusive forces of national culture. Economists, engineers, and the traditional business executives who took their intellectual cues primarily from these disciplines abhor the thought of having to grapple with anything as ill-defined and alien to their frames of reference as is the all-pervasive notion of culture. In self-defense some have rushed to lament and ridicule the whole idea. Yet the realities cannot be escaped. Cross-cultural conflict cannot be avoided by either economic or engineering manipulations—though both may help—nor can the multinational firm survive in the long run if it is incapable of adjusting to and being integrated with its host-country societies.

The traditional methods of dealing with the cross-cultural conflict in international business have been to try to ignore it, to pretend it does not exist, or to suppress it by financial power or political influence. Neither offers a viable solution in the contemporary world. This lesson is grudgingly being learned and positive approaches to constructively deal with the cultural conflict are now under serious study. This is a great leap forward, though ethnocentric inertia can be counted upon to restrain any hopes for massive results in a short time.

The most promising positive concept envisages the multinational firm not as a cultural extension of the headquarters country nor of one or another of the host countries but as a semiautonomous region of an international superculture which bridges the many underlying national cultures.

By exchange of experience and information, through meetings and seminars of executives and managers of multinational firms, a sifting and refining of experiences is taking place with the objective to find optimum solutions to culture-caused business problems and generally acceptable operating principles which all multinational firms could jointly adopt and serve as a frame of reference to the international businessman. This set of values and principles does not exist today, but through purposeful and continued search of this type, a *cosmopolitan corporate culture* is slowly emerging.

The great advantages of a common cosmopolitan culture for the entire multinational business sector in a global context would not only help the decision maker and provide consistence of dealing with cultural conflict but also redirect the focus of any particular clash of values from the individual firm or its home government to this broader system of values which the cosmopolitan culture will represent.[3] Then the negative confrontation between the host society and the individual multinational firm would be avoided and a creative process of cross-cultural adaptation take its place. Consequently, the stakes are very high for multinational business to push forward with vigor in forging a cosmopolitan corporate culture, a buffer culture both to absorb the impacts and to furnish the leadership in cross-cultural conflict situations.

3 For further elaboration of cosmopolitan corporate culture see E. J. Kolde, *Organization and Management of the Multinational Firm* (New York: Harper & Row, Publishers, 1973), Chapter 5.

IV

Financial Structures and Processes of International Business

We often buy money very much too dear.

W. M. Thackeray

19

Conceptual Systems of International Monetary Relations

Every nation has its own monetary unit, which serves as the common measure of value and the legal medium of exchange in its territory. All economic relationships, business transactions, and accounts of assets and liabilities are based on this unit. In the contemporary world, the issuance of currency is a governmental monopoly. Only it can mint the bills and coins which are recognized as official money, which can be tendered and which must be accepted as the normal means for settlement of financial claims.

In the international realm no legal tender exists. Values must be measured, accounts kept, and payments made by conversion of one currency into another. This conversion process is known as *foreign exchange*; the value or price of foreign currency in terms of domestic money is the *rate of exchange*. Sometimes the term *foreign exchange* denotes the holdings of foreign-currency assets, which more properly should be called *exchange reserves*.

The foreign exchange process is the central problem of international finance, and it is a highly complex one. Despite centuries of serious effort, no satisfactory solution exists, and the search for one must continue. Since the exchange process utilizes the links that tie one national currency to another, the search must center first of all on the nature and the behavior of these links.

International Currency Systems

From a theoretical standpoint international monetary affairs can be arranged on three different principles: a generally accepted medium of exchange—a universal currency; separate national monies but unhampered conversion from one to another on a free and open exchange market—integrated national currencies; and separate national monies segregated by official controls—disintegrated national currencies, or national exchange monopolies. Since the actual system in use today is a peculiar blend of all three principles plus a number of political and administrative compromises, it is helpful to review separately each of the theoretical systems before attempting to unravel the composite reality.

Universal Currency—The Gold Standard

Although other universal currencies are conceivable, the only one which has in fact been used is the gold standard. Extensive literature and much research are a rich fund from which its operations can be learned. It therefore provides a more concrete explanation of the workings of a universal-currency system than any fictitious units could.

In its pure form the gold standard relates all national currencies to gold. Although the unit denominations, the numerical scales, and the actual circulation media may differ from country to country and although each currency may have a different gold cover, all are convertible into gold at their respective mint parities to gold. Gold thus serves as the common denominator of all national currencies or, more correctly, as the universal money upon which the values of national currencies rest. Schematically this system may be visualized as in Figure 19-1.

If paper notes or nonauric coinage is circulated, as was typical under the gold standard, the relationship between such circulation media and gold is maintained through the freedom of any bearer or holder of the nonauric media to demand redemption in gold at the official mint parity. This right

FIGURE 19-1

The International Gold Standard

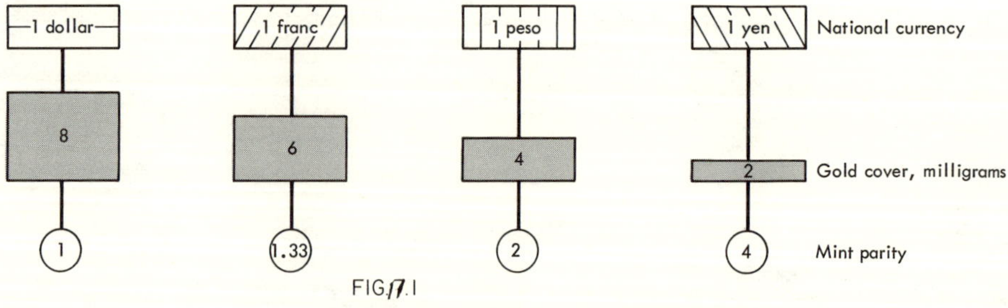

of redemption compels the monetary authorities of the nation to keep the money supply in the parity-prescribed relationship to its gold reserves at all times. Any change in the gold reserve will cause a corresponding change in the money supply and thus tend to adjust the country's price level either up or down depending upon whether the gold is flowing in and augmenting the money supply or flowing out and contracting it. This process is carried out through the banking system in the following manner. If, for example, a payment in gold is demanded from an importer by his foreign source, the importer buys it from a bank paying by check on his account. The commercial bank obtains the gold from the central bank by surrendering the equivalent amount of its reserve assets, i.e., gold certificates or cash. And, the result is that the bank's liabilities to its depositors as well as its reserves are reduced.

To reiterate, since under the gold standard all currencies bear some specific parity to gold, they can be interchanged at any time on the basis of these parities. What matters is not how many dollars, francs, or rupees one has but how much pure gold the particular currency represents. Consequently, the gold standard serves as the basis not only for national monetary systems but also for the international monetary system. However, day-to-day exchange transactions are executed in legal tender rather than in gold for two reasons: the instruments of exchange must be made out in a particular legal tender; and importers, exporters, and other parties to international transactions need sooner or later to convert their proceeds into their own domestic money. Therefore, the short-run exchange rate is subject to the current supply-demand relationship on the exchange market and may shift away from the mint-parity rate at which gold-standard currencies should theoretically exchange. But such shifts cannot exceed the cost of redeeming a currency in gold, for at that point gold will be demanded by the party against whose interests the rate is shifting. The redemption cost consists mostly of transportation, insurance, and handling costs for the gold shipments plus possibly some loss of interest. The extent and the limits of exchange-rate fluctuations are illustrated graphically in Figure 19-2A. If the demand for Swiss francs in New York exceeds the mint-parity rate of \$0.20 as shown by lines S_1 and D_1, the exchange rate will move above the mint parity to R_1 (about 20.4 cents per franc); if on the other hand the supply outstrips the demand, as is the case under the S_2-D_2 relationship, the rate will drop below the mint parity (in this instance to about 19.1 cents per franc).

However, if the demand for the franc (supply of the dollar) still exceeds the supply of the franc (demand for the dollar) when the exchange rate reaches the gold export point, dollars will be converted into francs to satisfy the excess demand, as illustrated by the R_3-D_3 section in Figure 19-2B. Such a situation may arise because of a sudden increase in Swiss imports to the United States or a decrease in American exports to Switzerland. In this case, only q_1 francs are earned through U.S. exports, and the q_1-q_2 amount is paid from the gold reserve. Conversely, if the demand for the franc (supply of the dollar) is insufficient to absorb the supply of the franc (demand for the dollar), as under D_4-S_4 conditions, the exchange rate will drop to the gold import point;

FIGURE 19-2

Exchange Rate Determination under the Gold Standard

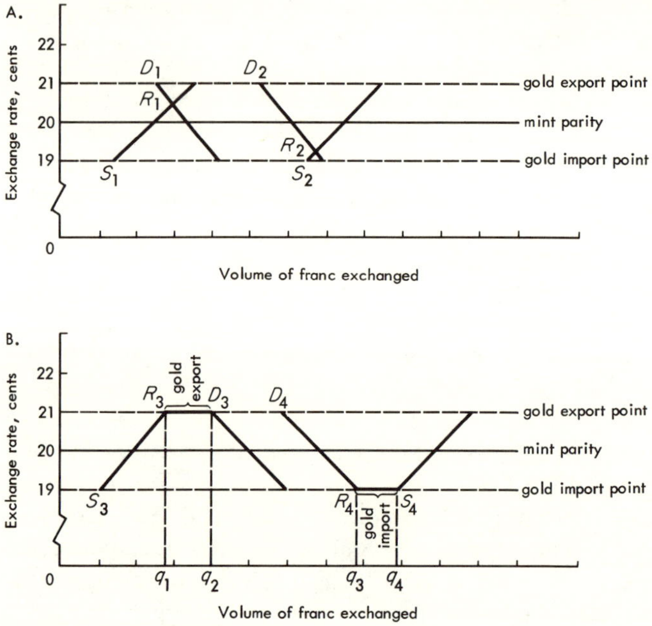

and, since there still are not enough buyers of the franc in the New York market to enable all holders of franc assets to settle their dollar obligations, i.e., not enough dollars to clear the franc supply, gold will be imported to make up the difference. A sudden rise of American exports to Switzerland or a decline of Swiss imports to the United States or both may cause such a disbalance in the franc-dollar exchange.

In reference to Part B of Figure 19-2, the deficit of Swiss receipts compared with its remittances, or from the other direction, the surplus of U.S. receipts over its payments, means that the Swiss are able to pay through their own exports of goods and services q_3 francs for their imports from the United States, and must pay for the rest, the q_3-q_4 portion, in gold. As a result, Swiss gold reserves and, with them, its domestic money supply shrink, and the U.S. gold reserves and money supply expand. The deflationary trend in Switzerland will tend to reduce Swiss prices relative to U.S. prices, and simultaneously the inflationary trend in the United States will further raise the U.S. internal prices relative to Swiss internal prices, with the consequence that Swiss goods and services become less expensive for American consumers than before and American goods more expensive for Swiss consumers than before. The relative price changes which the movement of gold triggers will sooner or later reverse the export-import relationships both in the United States and in Switzerland and thereby restore balance between the supply of and the demand for franc exchange.

Criticism of the gold standard

The most common argument against the gold standard is the direct interrelationship of domestic and foreign prices as described above: this system integrates a country's economy with those of other countries and permits foreign business trends to influence the internal economy freely. Employment and credit conditions thus revolve around the relatively immovable exchange rates, and the scope of countercyclical and other government policies aimed at economic stabilization and monetary management is extremely narrow.

Another criticism, on theoretical grounds, is the dependence on the availability and distribution of gold. Like any other product, gold is subject to supply-demand fluctuations, which affect its own value relative to other commodities. The supply comes from new production and the demand from the growth of business activities to be financed. If the two are growing at the same rate, the established price structure can be maintained. But, if the output of new gold fails to keep pace with economic growth, a deflationary trend starts, which normally discourages further business expansion and thus stifles economic progress. If, on the other hand, the production of new gold runs ahead of new monetary requirements, the resulting inflationary trend undermines the stability of legal tender and causes a redistribution of wealth and income in the society. In history, the price of gold has shown extraordinary stability. Until World War I a London-centered gold market and since then a New York-London axis have maintained world gold prices for extended periods.

The gold standard along with many other economic concepts was overcome by the devastating avalanche of the Great Depression and thus became identified with its suffering and misery in the minds of many. However, recent difficulties with international liquidity and disequilibria have helped to wear off the emotional daze, and a serious dialogue between the proponents and opponents of the gold standard not only has gained momentum but also has escalated to a widespread belief that some universal monetary system will have to be the long-range objective of our shrinking world.

Market-Integrated National Currencies

Unlike the gold standard, the concept of market-integrated national currencies involves no universal money. Instead, each country's currency represents a different monetary system linked to the others through the foreign exchange market. The market is *completely free* from government intervention, and the currencies are readily convertible; payments can be made in any amount, at any time, for any purpose, in any currency, at any place without interference from any source. The exchange rates are determined by the unhampered interplay of supply and demand very much as commodity prices are determined; and, like commodity prices, the rates respond to variations in the supply-demand relationship—hence the phrase *freely fluctuating exchange rates.* There are no gold export or import points to delimit the amplitude of the fluctuations or any common denominators in terms of which the value of any particular currency can be expressed except the rates at which it can be openly traded on the foreign exchange market. Since the trading takes place primarily in commercial paper bills, drafts, and acceptances, this monetary system is often labeled the *paper standard.* Strictly speaking, the paper standard is a somewhat different, although not conflicting, concept which denotes the lack of metallic cover for a currency with or without a free exchange market.

Under this system international adjustments are brought about by exchange-rate movements which equilibrate the supply and demand for a currency at the point where the market can be cleared. This means that international remittances and receipts are balanced by making the domestic currency either more or less expensive for foreigners. This balancing alters the relationships between domestic and foreign prices of goods and services. If the rate moves up, i.e., more U.S. dollars or cents per unit of foreign currency, merchandise imports become more costly; it takes more dollars than before to buy a unit of imports as prices in terms of the respective local currencies remain unchanged both at home and abroad. For the reverse reason U.S. exports become cheaper to foreigners and therefore can be expected to enjoy an increased demand; correspondingly, the export business in the United States becomes more profitable. If, on the other hand, the rate declines, it will take fewer dollars than before to acquire a unit of imports, and simultaneously a unit of exports will bring fewer dollars in revenue; hence, the rate of exchange will tend to increase the imports and decrease the exports of the United States.

The amplitude of exchange-rate fluctuations depends to a considerable degree on the lag between the initial change in the rate and the reaction of the import and export sectors of the economy. If the reaction is instantaneous, the fluctuation will be negligible; if it is slow, the rate fluctuation may assume violent proportions. In the absence of government interference the lag appears to be determined by the "normal" order period, i.e., the time between signing the purchase contract and making the payment on the shipment. However, short-term capital from both trade and nontrade sources can greatly increase this sensitivity of the exchange market to the initial change and can shorten the lag between the rate change and adjustments in import-export volumes.

Regardless of the amplitude or frequency of rate fluctuations, a country's foreign exchange dealings cannot drain its domestic monetary reserves under the market-integrated currency system. The country's money supply and internal price level are shielded against any disturbances in international financial relations. However, the appreciation and depreciation of its currency as the result of changes in the exchange rate cause shifts in the ratio of domestic to foreign prices and costs; and these shifts integrate the economy of the country with that of the world.

Purchasing-power parity

The theoretical foundation for exchange rates under the market-integrated currency system is the purchasing-power-parity doctrine advanced by the Swedish economist Gustav Cassel. This theory holds that the rate of exchange on a free market will seek the level at which the internal purchasing powers of the two currencies are equal. It recognizes that disturbances in the exchange market may cause the short-run rate to divide from the purchasing-power parity, just as they cause similar deviations from the mint parity under the gold standard. But such deviations are postulated to be short lived and the market to have the tendency to correct itself and to restore the equilibrium or parity rate. In other words, the short-term market rates revolve around the parity rate, which in the long run equalizes the real values of the domestic and foreign currencies in terms of purchasing power. Should inflationary or deflationary tendencies change the real purchasing-power relationship of two currencies, the exchange rates would move accordingly. For example, if the parity or equilibrium rate in the base year were \$0.20 per franc but in the subsequent period the price index in the United States climbed from 100 to 120 while in Switzerland it declined from 100 to 80, the new parity rate would be

$$\$0.20 \times \frac{120}{80} = \$0.30$$

Attempts to work out mathematical formulas for purchasing-power parities have been unsuccessful because (a) international payments other than those for exports and imports also affect the supply and demand of exchange; (b) the product mix of one country is never identical to that of another—certain goods are unique to certain countries and others vary in grade and quality; and (c) price indexes are misleading in that they conceal the actual price structures—that is, the relative value of one product in terms of another[1]—and create a numerical comparison which is fictitious. The third point has caused much confusion for statisticians and economists who have tried to work on the basis of the comparative "price levels" as defined by index numbers. Such attempts are predestined to failure. To equate the price levels of two countries one must first make sure that the product mixes of the countries contain the same products in the same proportions and that their price structures are identical. If, contrary to all probability, a pair of countries satisfied these conditions, it is obvious from the theory of international trade that neither would possess any comparative advantages for trading with the other and that, therefore, no trade could take place between them. Consequently, most of the statistical criticism of the purchasing-power-parity theory that one encounters in the older and even in some of the contemporary economic literature is really naiveté. Cassel, who was a mathematician before becoming an economist, must have been well aware of this statistical problem.

But how relevant is this? The importance and value of this or any other theory do not depend on its susceptibility to statistical implementation but on

[1] A typewriter in country *A* may be equal in price to ten pairs of shoes or two woolen suits or 2 pounds of liverwurst; in country *B* the same typewriter may be worth 15 pairs of shoes or one woolen suit or 80 pounds of liverwurst.

its premises and logic. On the latter grounds purchasing-power parity cannot be questioned and, in fact, is the only rational explanation so far advanced for exchange-rate determination in the absence of a universal currency. But even the statistical difficulties are becoming smaller than they once were. New insights into the complexities of international financial relations have revealed more and more variables which can help to make more meaningful comparisons between two currencies: capital movements; income distribution; consumption habits; changes in taste, techniques, and expenditure patterns. Still others may be discovered in the future. During the same time the electronic computer has immensely increased our ability to correlate and otherwise process these variables with the basic price data themselves. As a consequence, calculations of purchasing-power parity cannot only serve as the first approximations of what the equilibrium rate or exchange should be but also reflect quite accurately the composite behavior of the forces which underlie the long-term supply and demand for exchange.

Pegged exchange rates

In a variation of the theoretical market-integrated currency model, a governmental authority fixes an official par for exchange on the basis of purchasing-power parity and endeavors to enforce it through pegging operations. The central bank utilizes an exchange-stabilization fund to maintain the exchange rate close to the official par. When the market rate falls, the central bank enters the market on the demand side and buys all surplus exchange instruments at or close to the official par; when the rate rises, the fund or the bank enters on the supply side and offers to sell exchange at or near the official par to meet the otherwise unsatisfied demand. Thus fluctuations of the rate are minimized, and the exchange market is stabilized.

Pegging operations can succeed only if the official par is at or very near to the purchasing-power parity. When the par overvalues the currency, the central bank must constantly supply exchange at the lower official rate to business firms and to individuals who have foreign payments to make; sooner or later the exchange reserves of the stabilization fund will be exhausted, and, if the pegging operation is to be continued, the government will have to replenish the stabilization reserve at the free-market rate, which, since it tends to approximate the purchasing-power parity, will be higher than the overvalued official par. Obviously, the loss which results from such pegging operation cannot be absorbed over an extended period, and the authorities will be compelled either to devalue the currency by raising the exchange rate or to resort to exchange rationing through licensing, quotas, and similar devices.

When, on the other hand, the currency is undervalued and the rate is pegged, the government will continually have to buy large quantities of exchange, as the demand will otherwise fail to clear the supply and will cause the rate to fall. Such operations again become untenable in the long run, because the accumulation of exchange by the government cannot go on forever without straining the country's monetary and fiscal resources. Any attempt to dispose of the exchange will bring financial loss, since, as long as the currency remains undervalued, its free-market rate will always be lower than the pegged rate; and, what is worse, any sales of exchange by the government under these circumstances will increase the supply and further aggravate the pressure on the official par. Fortunately, undervaluation seldom occurs, and this problem is not so likely under pegged rates as is the opposite problem.

Disintegrated Currencies—National Exchange Monopoly

Perhaps a better name for the concept of disintegrated currencies is *segregated currencies,* but since *segregation* has become an emotion-laden word for reasons quite remote from international finance, it is better left alone. The central idea in this third theoretical approach to international payments is the establishment of a governmental monopoly over foreign exchange. The government can direct all receipts of exchange into a national pool in order to subject it to rigorous inspection and control. More specifically, the exchange-control authority fixes the exchange rate by an official decree, requires all recipients to surrender their foreign exchange assets to the central bank or to some other agency at the official buying rate, and rations the exchange through quotas, licenses, and exchange permits.

The country's currency is thus rendered inconvertible, and its exchange rate is rigidified. Supply and demand in the exchange market can affect neither money supply nor prices. The domestic economy is entirely shielded against foreign influences, and the government experiences no international restraint or compulsion regarding domestic business affairs. In such apparent freedom from the discipline of the world market lie what have proven to be the irresistible appeal and also the serious dangers of this system.

Only in rare exceptions have governments been able to resist the temptation of using this freedom. Political pressures for monetary expansion are nearly always present to increase employment, to ease credit conditions, to maintain or accelerate economic growth, or to raise the standard of living. In the absence of external standards, internal monetary discipline and restraint are extremely difficult, and overvaluation of currency is unavoidable. Consequently, internal prices rise, not as a result of international financial disturbances but because of the easy-money policies followed at home. The demand for imports increases as foreign products become underpriced at the fixed, overvalued exchange rate, and at the same time domestic prices rise; exports become overpriced abroad, and the demand for them declines. The emerging disbalance between the country's foreign payments and receipts necessitates tighter rationing of foreign exchange and sooner or later leads to the imposition of direct controls over imports. These controls, in turn, accelerate the inflationary trend—import competition declines; supply is curtailed and thus the selling prices of imports rise; and domestic prices go up still further. Overvaluation of the currency becomes a self-generating process which can be stopped only by deflationary measures internally and by limitation of imports externally.

DISCRIMINATION. All exchange controls are *ipso facto* discriminatory. They encourage importation of goods which the regulatory agency favors and retard the importation of others; hardest hit are products which are considered luxury or nonessential. The controls discriminate not only against goods but also against currencies. The importer's decision on merchandise is not based on cost considerations but on the question of which country's currency is most easily obtained from the control authority.[2] The controls invariably also cause a redistribution of profitability in the import sector. The relatively greater scarcity of the restricted imports leads to higher reselling prices, which increase profits to the import firms with exchange permits while denying other importers their normal opportunities. At the same time, the control restrictions protect certain domestic products against import competition despite the fact that this was not an original objective of the control. As a consequence, a redistribution of productive resources may follow in the long run, and the protected sectors of the economy may grow at the expense of the others. Since the most rigid restriction is usually applied against the nonessential luxuries, the irony of exchange control is that domestic production tends to shift toward luxuries and away from the essentials, which have greater export demand and exchange-earning capacity. Again, the restrictions generate increased restriction.

BLACK MARKET. Another corruptive corollary of restriction is the emergence of illegal exchange dealings, which occur in direct proportion to the degree of overvaluation. Although no official statistics exist on black-market operations, it is believed that in some soft-currency countries as much as two-thirds of total exchange is sold outside legitimate channels. When the black-market rate is far above the official rate, exporters find it profitable to participate in the illicit operation by double-invoicing their shipments—underbilling the cargo on the document submitted to the exchange-control authorities, but sending to the foreign importer another invoice with instructions to deposit the difference in a foreign bank. Importers, conversely, arrange with their foreign suppliers for overbilling of their purchase. The excess exchange which they obtain at the low official rate can then be sold at the high black-market rate or an easy windfall or can be deposited in a foreign country. Hence, capital can escape the country despite exchange control. And, when this occurs, more stringent controls are necessary to suppress the flight. In general, exchange control deals with symptoms and fails to come to grips with basic causes. Suppressing the capital flight or the black-market operations through stricter policing and greater penalties does not cure the underlying political or economic malady.

2 In practice the dispensation of exchange permits and licenses is based on a variety of methods ranging from first-come-first-served to complex tie-in arrangements requiring importers to match their foreign purchases with an equal, or some other, quantity of domestic goods. Also, requirements as to the currency in which payment is to be made or received have sometimes been prescribed by the control authority.

Remedial uses of exchange restrictions

Under certain abnormal conditions exchange restrictions can serve a positive purpose. A serious difficulty in recent years has been the flight of capital from certain countries either because of higher interest rates abroad or because of business and political uncertainty at home. Where the interest-rate differential is the cause, the best remedy clearly is to raise the rates at home. But this solution may take time, during which the flight could assume dangerous proportions and seriously imperil the country's international financial position. Checking the flow by using exchange restrictions allows a basic corrective to be worked out and implemented without undue haste. If the cause for the flight is business and political uncertainty, no rational remedy may be available, and the control of exchange becomes chronic, as in certain Latin American countries.

Exchange restriction is also justified when a country is faced with a sudden shift in the relationship between its international receipts and its remittances, especially when there is an abrupt reduction on the receipt side or a sharp increase on the remittance side. A sudden disbalance of this kind may cause undesirable and unnecessary instability in exchange rates, gold flows, import and export trade, and employment. Exchange restriction can be used to absorb the shock of the shift and to enable the country to ride out the storm if the disturbance seems temporary or to make the necessary adjustments to restore the balance if the condition seems permanent.

Still another situation in which exchange restriction can play a useful role is when there is a widespread scarcity of goods, such as in early postwar years. To permit the exchange rates to climb in response to extreme and abnormal supply-demand conditions would bring undue hardship to some and unearned profits to others. Exchange control can facilitate, and in fact has facilitated, more normal trade relations and orderly payments than would otherwise be possible.

Theoretically, exchange controls are justified also when the demand for imports and the supply for exports is inelastic. Such inelasticities make the volume of commodity trade relatively immune to changes in exchange rate and prevent the market mechanism from performing its adjustment functions. However, there is no reliable evidence that this situation can arise in reality, except in the case of individual commodities or industries.

20

The Foreign Exchange Market

Conceptually the foreign exchange market consists of three components: sellers, buyers, and the banking system which converts one currency into another. The sellers are individuals or organizations which have acquired foreign currencies or financial claims and wish to convert them into domestic money, and the buyers are those which have incurred financial obligations to foreigners. The buyers and sellers of exchange represent the opposite sides of transboundary remittances, which derive from a variety of international and multinational activities. The principal types of payments are these:

—trade payments: remittances for export-import shipments

—direct foreign investments: acquisition of production facilities such as plant and equipment abroad

—portfolio investments: purchases of foreign securities (stocks and bonds) as corporate or personal investments

—loans: drawing on the loanable-funds supply of another country

—interest: payment on borrowings from another country

—repatriation transactions: (a) repayments on principal of foreign loans or investments, and (b) return to parent organization of profits earned by a foreign affiliate

—taxes: payment on nonexempt income earned abroad

—tourist spending: expenditures of individuals traveling abroad

—governmental spending: payments for goods and services acquired abroad by governmental agencies

—foreign aid: assistance by one country to another

—miscellaneous: professional gifts, philanthropic grants, penalties, and so on.

All international trade and payment transactions are recorded in the balance of international payments, which serves both as a common depository for all transactions which give rise to international financial obligations and as a measure of a country's remittances to others and its receipts from them.

Exchange Instruments

It is not shipments of dollars, francs, or rupees from country to country but the transfer of bank deposits and credit instruments that serves as the means of international payment. In multinational business, especially in trade transactions, the international payment process depends mainly on the use of credit instruments, which as the following discussion will show are designed for carrying out almost any conceivable payment obligation.

The system of instruments of international payment and credit which now exists is based on the realization that a certain risk is inherent in all international transactions. Although the risk can be shifted from one party to the other, it cannot be eliminated. This concept is illustrated in the diagram below, where the line *r* represents the inherent risk which must be taken by either the exporter *E* or the importer *I*.

$$(E)\ \vdash\!\!\overset{r}{\text{—————————}}\!\!\dashv\ (I)$$

The size of the risk, the length of *r*, depends on the country; the customer or the party with which the transaction is undertaken, and the terms, including the method of payment. If the country and the customer are given, the question of who bears the risk will turn on the terms specified for the transaction and finally on the credit instrument chosen to implement the terms. Each instrument represents different rights, privileges, and conditions for both parties. The instruments fall into two categories: drafts and letters of credit.

Drafts, or Bills of Exchange

The draft, or bill of exchange, is the basic instrument of international payment. It was reportedly first introduced by Lombardian merchants of the seventh century to avoid the shipment of large quantities of gold and silver in payment for their foreign purchases. The draft is a formal order from the exporter or any other possessor of a foreign financial claim to the respective importer or debtor to pay a specified sum of money to a third person, normally a bank, at a certain time. It thus establishes a triangular relationship in which the three parties are formally identified as the drawer (the exporter or maker of the draft), the drawee (the importer, debtor, or his bank), and the payee (the designated recipient of the payment, normally the exporter's bank). Being a negotiable instrument, a draft can be easily transferred, sold, discounted, or otherwise traded.

The time dimension of a draft is composed of two elements: the time (number of days) it takes to deliver the draft to the drawee and the usance, i.e., the time allowed to make the payment. Since the delivery may require the participation of three or more banking institutions, it can rarely be precisely determined. The usance, however, is always fixed. From the usance standpoint, two general categories of drafts are distinguished: *sight drafts,* which are payable immediately upon presentation to the drawee ("Pay at sight to the order of. . . ."), and *time drafts,* which permit the lapse of a specified number of days before falling due ("Pay 30 days after sight to the order of. . . ."). Confusingly, the time drafts are sometimes referred to as 30-day sight drafts or 90-day sight drafts, depending on their usance.

A variation of the time draft is the *date draft.* Its usance commences on the date of issue rather than on the date of sight, which effectively eliminates the time variable. However, the length of the overall credit period still remains a variable because financing must start with the signing of the export contract rather than with the date of issuance. All time drafts are presented to the payee for acceptance as soon as they can be delivered. When presented, the payee stamps or writes the word *Accepted* across the face of the draft followed by his signature and the date. For the regular time draft this date will denote the beginning of the specified usance. Figure 20-1 illustrates the different types of drafts and their time sequences.

FIGURE 20-1

Time Relationships under Draft Financing

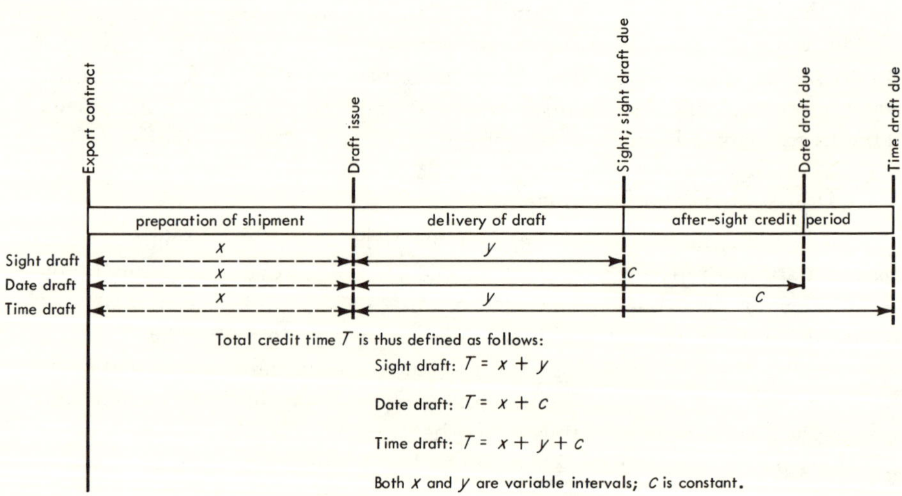

Control of delivery

In trade transactions drafts are normally accompanied by all the required documents; hence the term *documentary draft.* The key document for control purposes is a negotiable copy of the bill of lading, the document of title to the cargo. Since the import company cannot claim the cargo from the carrier without surrendering an endorsed copy of the bill of lading, the exporter can compel the importer to comply with the financial terms of the transaction by instructing the bank not to release the documents unless he does; sight drafts specify D/P, meaning documents against payment, and time drafts D/A, documents against acceptance. Although in the latter case, the import firm gains access to the cargo without making the actual payment, the acceptance of the draft formally commits it to a bank in its own locality and, should it subsequently fail to honor this commitment, a serious deterioration of its credit standing would result. But no promise, however sincere, can be equated to an actual payment; factors beyond the control of the import concern may intervene even with its most sincere intentions. Therefore, the control mechanism of the documentary time draft must be rated substantially below that of the documentary sight draft.

Drafts without documents attached, known as *clean drafts,* lack any control capacity and are, therefore, used in export-import business only if that aspect is unimportant or if other arrangements for preventing delivery in case of nonpayment have been made—for example, if the bill of lading has been made out to the order of the shipper himself or to the bank instead of to the import concern. Except in trade transactions such as these, the clean draft serves primarily as the medium of international payment where no physical cargo is involved—e.g., settlement among banks, remuneration for services, or repayment of loans.

Letters of Credit

A letter of credit is a formal instrument for substituting bank credit for the importer's or distributor's own credit. It is a formal document issued by a bank on behalf of an importer guaranteeing payment of the exporter's drafts drawn according to the stipulations in his agreement with the importer. The stipulations regarding the amount, the timing, and the shipment must be restated in the letter of credit itself to be legally binding; mere reference to an export sales contract will not suffice. In effect, the letter of credit establishes a conditional account for the exporter in a bank in his own country on which he can draw as soon as he has complied with the condition—namely, delivered the goods as ordered by the import concern. Figure 20-2 illustrates the relationships in a letter-of-credit transaction.

The letter of credit performs four unique functions:

(1) It shifts assessment of the importer's credit worthiness upon a bank-

ing institution in his own country and community which normally is in a better position to do this than the export company itself.

(2) It protects the exporter by substituting bank credit for the importer's own credit.

(3) It protects the importer by enabling him formally to communicate to the paying bank the exact stipulations which must be met by the beneficiary before his drafts are honored; thus, payment will be prevented in case of nonperformance or deviation from the specifications of the transaction.

(4) It eliminates or minimizes the risk that foreign exchange restrictions or other government trade regulations might interfere with completing the payment after the exporter has already committed himself—for example, after he has procured the cargo for the transaction.

FIGURE 20-2

Letter-of-Credit Transaction

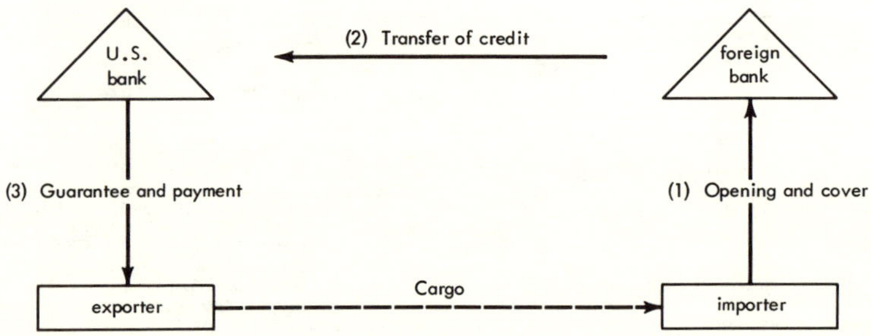

(a) To open a letter of credit the importer must satisfy his bank's credit standards and agree to supply the bank the funds to honor the beneficiary's (exporter's) drafts when they are drawn against the l/c; and to pay the customary commission to the bank for its services. Title to the shipment will pass to the bank if the importer should fail to provide the necessary funds; no additional cover or collateral is normally necessary.

(b) The importer's bank either issues the formal letter of credit itself or asks its correspondent bank to prepare and issue the letter for it and to transfer the credit to a bank in the exporter's locality. The channel of transmittal may contain several different banks, but the opening bank always remains responsible for the ultimate payment unless some other bank expressly agrees to share in this responsibility by confirming the letter of credit.

(c) The local bank advises the exporter about the arrival of the letter of credit and usually also honors his drafts on behalf of the opening bank when he presents documentary evidence that he has carried out his commitment, i.e., presents all shipping documents. At times the advising and paying functions are divided among different banks: *advising bank,* located in the exporter's community, notifies exporter about the arrival of the letter of credit and presents it for his examination and approval; *paying bank* is the one on which the drafts must be drawn and which accepts or pays them subject to reimbursement by the opening bank; *negotiating bank* is any financial institution not named in the letter of credit which voluntarily accepts or pays the drafts by the beneficiary (exporter); for this service it charges a fee or it discounts the draft.

In the interwar period it was customary for certain traders, especially British and continental traders in colonial commodities, to use what is known as the *revocable letter of credit.* Under this instrument the importer retains the right to unilaterally cancel the credit any time before the exporter's drafts against it have been honored by the accepting or paying bank. Since it leaves the exporter vulnerable for cancellation, revocable credit has been increasingly confined to transactions where the risk element from the exporter's standpoint is relatively low, or where the importer is in a relatively strong bargaining position. From the exporter's standpoint, the benefit of having a revocable letter of credit is that it permits the drafts to be drawn on a bank instead of on the importer, which makes them cashable at a lower rate of discount on the foreign exchange market than bills drawn on commercial firms.[1] Also, the exporter gains in that the formal participation of the banks in the letter-of-credit transaction adds an important element of judicature to the process, which serves to discourage misbehavior on the importer's part. From the importer's standpoint, the revocable letter of credit is desirable when there is a need for protection against *mala fides* (bad faith) on the part of the seller.

The normal practice now is to issue only *irrevocable letters of credit,* which, once approved by the exporter, cannot be changed in any way without the mutual consent of both parties. If the exporter considers the irrevocable credit of a foreign bank an insufficient guarantee for his risks, he may require that the credit be *confirmed* by another bank, usually the paying bank in his own country. By confirming the letter of credit, the domestic bank assumes the liability of paying the exporter should the foreign bank fail to do so. Hence, a confirmed letter of credit carries with it the guarantees of both the opening and the confirming banks and is thus as nearly risk free as any arrangement can be short of prepayment. Naturally, the confirming bank will charge for its participation an appropriate fee, which contributes to the overall cost of the transaction. The need for confirmation may arise because of political risks—governmental instability, revolution, war, etc.—or because the financial strength of the opening bank is deemed insufficient to provide adequate protection against the beneficiary's risks. This is usually the case if the foreign bank is a small institution with a weak asset-liability ratio or if unusually large sums of money are involved in the transaction.

From a strictly legal standpoint, confirmation relieves the exporter also from a contingent liability to refund the payments made by the paying bank against his drafts drawn under the letter of credit—a liability which he otherwise must bear until the opening bank has, in fact, reimbursed the paying bank

1 See the discussion of bank acceptances later in this chapter for further explanation.

and others for the drafts drawn against the credit. In other words, if, for any reason within or outside its control, the opening bank fails to make the reimbursement, the paying bank would have recourse to the exporter. Such a situation cannot arise under a confirmed letter of credit unless the confirming bank also fails to discharge its commitment.

The letter of credit is a very flexible instrument which can be adapted to a great variety of international credit and payment requirements. Some typical uses as reflected in the different types of letters of credit are described below.

—*Periodic letters of credit* provide that the transaction can be repeated after a specified time interval has lapsed (i.e., a new draft can be drawn against the credit to the same amount as the original one); such credits can stay in effect for an extended period.

—*Revolving letters of credit* permit repetition of the transaction as soon as the first or previous draft is paid by the opening bank.

—*Cumulative letters of credit* permit drafts on partial shipments and/or application of unused portions of the credit to another transaction between the same parties.

—*Back-to-back letters of credit* are issued by the paying or the notifying bank in favor of a party other than the original beneficiary—for example, to make payments to the exporter's supplier; they are based on the original letters of credit and can never exceed them in amount or tenor.

—*Circular letters of credit* are issued without designating any bank; the beneficiary may either send the drafts directly to the issuing bank or, as occurs more frequently, present them to any other bank for negotiation, i.e., for discount or collection or both.

—*Standby letters of credit* are issued by American banks for the account of U.S. companies (such as contractors) doing work abroad. This provides them with the needed credit facilities in the particular foreign country. The credit is issued in favor of a foreign bank with provisions that the foreign bank may draw drafts on the issuing bank at any time the American firm fails to meet the terms of his credit.

—*Performance letters of credit* are used to guarantee the completion of a contract undertaken abroad; they represent a type of an international performance bond.

—*Deferred payment letters of credit* provide for:

(1) Presentation of required documents by the beneficiary within a specified time, or on a specified date, and

(2) Payment to be made to the beneficiary at a specified date after presentation of the documents, or after date of shipment, or any other specified date.

—*Traveler's letters of credit* are issued by a bank for the benefit of a traveler authorizing him to draw drafts against the bank's correspondent institutions abroad; they are circular instruments carried by the traveler himself and issued on the basis of his personal credit standing or an appropriate collateral or prepayment. If the credit is not fully exhausted, the letters can be revoked and the balance is refunded to the traveler.

Authority to purchase

Under an authority to purchase, a bank is authorized by the importer to negotiate drafts drawn by the exporter; i.e., the bank accepts or pays the drafts subject to reimbursement by the importer. The bank and its correspondent act only as the importer's agents and assume no financial responsibility for the final payment. If the importer refuses to honor a draft drawn under the authority to purchase, the bank has full recourse to the exporter and is entitled to recover the funds advanced to him. As such, the authority to purchase is not, as is sometimes mistakenly believed, synonymous with a letter of credit.

Supplementary Financial Arrangements

Trust receipts

If a firm lacks the necessary funds to meet the financial requirements of an import transaction, it may obtain them from a bank by signing a trust receipt on the contemplated cargo. Authorized in the United States under the Uniform Commercial Code of 1966, this arrangement gives the bank a lien on the property to be imported in return for accepting or paying the exporter's drafts on the importer's behalf. This in no way interferes with the importer's right to take possession of and to sell or otherwise dispose of the cargo in his regular course of business. However, any proceeds from the imported goods have to be credited to the bank until the obligation is fully settled.

Through this method it is possible for importers to finance transactions from their own sales returns with a minimum of working capital. Also, trust-receipt financing may help an importer's bargaining position, since the bank's acceptance of the credit liability will greatly reduce the risk for the exporter. To be valid under U.S. law, a trust-receipt agreement (the formal document establishing trust financing) must satisfy these three points:

—Goods or other movable property must be transferred to the trustee (the importer) by the entruster (the bank) or by a third party (the exporter).

—A party other than the seller must take a trust receipt entitling him to a lien on the property in question; this third party is usually the bank.

—The trustee (importer) acquires a monetary commitment to the entruster (bank), such as the obligation to reimburse the bank for drafts honored.

If the cargo is already in the importer's country when the need for financing arises, the trust receipt is not available under U.S. law, and regular domestic credit instruments such as mortgages or warehouse receipts have to be substituted for it.

Bank acceptances

If a bank accepts an exporter's or importer's time draft, it makes the instrument easily salable and thus provides a source of ready cash to the drawer of the draft. The bank itself does not have to purchase the acceptance;

it may do so if its portfolio of commercial paper is lower than desired, but this is irrelevant for the cash value of the draft. What matters is that the bank has accepted the obligation to honor the document at its maturity, and anybody who buys it can count on this commitment.

The most typical use of bank acceptances is by importers faced with D/P terms who wish to extend the financing until the proceeds from the cargo can be utilized to pay for the purchase. In such a situation the importer will draw a time draft on his bank in an amount sufficient to meet his obligation to the foreign exporter and, after securing the bank's acceptance, sell it for cash with which to pay for the exporter's sight bill. The usance of the acceptance is chosen to enable the importer to sell the cargo and to be able to pay for it from the sales revenue the cargo itself produces, just as under the trust-receipt arrangement. Here, too, the bank acquires ownership interest in the cargo when the acceptance agreement is signed and has a preferred claim on the revenue materializing from its sale until the full amount of the acceptance has been recovered.

Trading in international credit instruments

If drafts are drawn in foreign currency, they are bought and sold at the going exchange rate for the particular type of instrument. As explained elsewhere, the rates on any given day vary with the usance of the bill, and for each usance there is a differential between selling and buying rates. If the bills are drawn in the domestic currency there is no exchange problem, and the only variable is the discount rate, i.e., the interest that should be deducted from the face amount to induce buyers to purchase the instrument. If the drawer of the draft wants to utilize only partially the cash value of the draft, he may obtain a percentage advance against it from a bank which will handle the collection of the draft.

If a draft is not honored, that is, the drawee refuses to pay or to accept the terms, an official protest may be launched. It consists of a formal demand prepared by a notary public to the drawee to honor the draft. If he still refuses, a certificate of protest is prepared and all interested parties notified. In most civil or Roman law countries, the protest empowers the plaintiff to attach the property of the drawee for the period of litigation and to get quick court action, sometimes within three days. In the United States and in British common law countries, the effect of the protest is limited to the adverse publicity which the drawee receives through the protest notifications and the unavoidable damage to his credit status. Banks protest all drafts which they have bought or discounted in order to establish the official basis for their recourse action against the drawer. Business firms should follow the same practice.

Standard Terms of Export Transactions

Credit terms for export shipments are normally chosen from the seven alternatives in Table 20-1. Up to the late 1950's U.S. companies insisted on either prepayment at the time of delivery to the international carrier or a prearranged irrevocable letter of credit. In the last few years, however, competitive pressures from exporters in Europe and Japan have brought about more liberal credit policies, and alternatives (3), (4), and even (5) in Table 20-1 have become relatively commonplace. For example, over 70 percent of all American exports were letter-of-credit transactions in 1955, but only 40 percent were in 1965. A contributing factor to this shift has been the establishment of export credit insurance, which eliminates most of the political risks and some of the commercial risks attached to a transaction. Installment sale, or hire purchase, as it is known in international circles, is employed primarily in the field of industrial installations and heavy equipment. Consignment transactions are seldom used in contemporary foreign trade. Under the consignment transaction the exporter ships the goods unsold to a foreign firm whose only commitment is to offer them for sale in his country of domicile on behalf of the exporter, and, if he sells them, to remit the proceeds after

TABLE 20-1

Term-Instrument Relationship

Terms	*Instrument*
(1) Prepayment: a. cash with order b. cash against certificate of manufacture	 Banker's draft or acceptance Banker's draft or acceptance
(2) Payment on delivery of goods to port of exportation (to the carrier)	Irrevocable letter of credit plus sight draft
(3) Payment on delivery of goods to port of destination	Documentary sight draft (D/P) or banker's draft
(4) Payment after delivery of goods to importer	Documentary time draft (D/A) or documentary date draft (D/A)
(5) Open book credit	Clean draft
(6) Hire-purchase (installment sale)	Clean draft
(7) Consignment transaction	Subject to agreement, usually banker's draft or acceptance

deduction of his commission to the exporter. The exporter bears not only all credit risks but also all ownership risks in such a situation until the goods are finally sold by the consignee. For these reasons, the consignment transaction is used only as a last resort in situations where the exporter is convinced that the demand exists for his goods abroad but fails to acquire any purchase orders to make an outright sale. Manufacturers of some novel items and small companies with relatively unknown brands may find themselves in such a predicament.

Organizational Structure of the Exchange Market

The foreign exchange market has no formalized structure comparable to the stock and commodity exchanges. It embraces the entire banking industry which participates in the financing of commercial enterprise plus exchange brokers and dealers who specialize in certain aspects of the exchange process. The institutional structure of the market is determined by three basic functional relationships: dealings with the buying and selling public, dealings among banking institutions, and dealings among domestic and foreign exchange institutions. These may be called, respectively, the retail, wholesale, and foreign sectors of the exchange market.

Retail sector

On the customer level, there are the various commercial banks which serve their local communities' exchange needs and provide the auxiliary banking services necessary for efficient handling of international payments. For this purpose the banks maintain foreign exchange departments, which may be independent or may be a subsection in the international banking operations division, a new development in bank organization.

Most inland banks, especially the smaller ones, work through large metropolitan banks in New York City or in some other major foreign trade center. Others, including the major metropolitan banks themselves but also many inland banks, maintain their own working balances in the form of deposits in correspondent banks abroad. These overseas balances are replenished by the purchases of exchange assets from business firms and individuals and from sales of domestic currency to foreign exchange institutions.

Inland banks which do not have their own exchange deposits abroad maintain correspondent relationships with large metropolitan banks in New York City or San Francisco, under which they can utilize the latter's exchange resources either in this country or abroad. Normally the inland correspondent is authorized to draw drafts directly against the foreign balances of the metropolitan bank and to accept deposits of them at specified rates and in predetermined amounts.

Along with banks, foreign exchange dealers are active in some areas in buying and selling exchange to the general public. In the United States, the exchange dealers tend to operate in the marginal, high-risk markets, and their importance varies with the international financial climate. In the early postwar years, when most foreign currencies were inconvertible and settlement of international accounts ran into innumerable obstacles, the exchange dealer played an important role by providing what often was the only means for exchange transactions. Since the dealers are not subjected by law to the same governmental supervision as banks, they can engage in more venturous, higher-risk operations and thus can undertake transactions beyond the legitimate capabilities of a bank. In the late 1940's and early 1950's it was not uncommon for some large exchange dealers to receive and ship foreign currencies in carload lots. With the return to convertibility of major currencies, the dealer's opportunities and importance have become limited to the soft currencies of the underdeveloped and iron curtain countries.

Wholesale sector

In the course of its retail trading activity, each bank can use purchases to offset sales and thus can finance much of the local demand from the local supply. In large cities with diversified international activity, the opportunities for such internal clearinghouse operations are good. In less diversified centers imbalances between demand and supply may cause large surpluses or deficits in a bank's foreign exchange accounts. To even out any imbalances banks must turn to the interbank or wholesale exchange market.

In the United States the interbank exchange market has no uniform pattern. Some seek to clear their daily balances first on the local and regional basis; others deal directly with the New York market, which is the principal foreign exchange center of the country. Most of the larger banks refrain from direct trading with one another but depend upon the foreign exchange brokers for their interbank transactions. The brokerage firm's main function is to bring together the buying and selling banks and to arrange the necessary supply or placement of exchange that a particular bank may need. Like other brokerage houses, it does this through continual contact with the market and an intimate knowledge of the supply-and-demand condition at any particular moment. The typical brokerage firm maintains direct telephone lines to the foreign exchange trading rooms of all the leading commercial banks and keeps in continual contact with the bank traders. The latter can thus concentrate upon their customers' needs, while the bids and offers are matched up by the brokers. For his services the broker is paid a commission by the selling bank.

The U.S. exchange market is also affected by such supranational financial institutions as the World Bank and the Export-Import Bank, which transact most of their business through New York. Although these institutions cannot be regarded as regular components of the market (their activities being limited to certain specialized functions and objectives), they have a significant influence on the New York exchange market not only through the industries which may participate in their far-flung economic programs but also through various indirect means which affect supply and demand. The influence of these supranational institutions on other exchange markets is seldom more than marginal.

In the London, Lisbon, and Paris markets governmental agencies specialize in investments and other monetary transactions among the respective metropolitan country and its associated areas overseas, as explained in a later section of this chapter.

Foreign sector

The need for exchange trading between U.S. and foreign banks arises in part from the imbalance which may arise in the wholesale sector and in part from the foreign supply-and-demand conditions, which vary in response to international business activity. To meet their own requirements the foreign banks participate continuously in the U.S. exchange market. This participation is not limited to the buying or selling of dollars in the interest of commercial enterprises but extends to profiting from differentials in the rates of exchange or of interest that may arise. The U.S. banks, of course, behave in a similar manner. The activities of foreign central banks, which may enter the market either as buyers or sellers, are usually designed to prevent excessive swings in the exchange rate and are, therefore, often the most decisive factor of the market as a whole.

The Structure of Rates

The theoretical analysis of exchange-rate determination in Chapter 7 emphasized the fundamental supply-and-demand forces which determine what may be called the *basic equilibrium rate.* This basic rate is an analytical abstraction and is never received or paid by traders and investors in practice. Besides being influenced by supply-and-demand forces, the actual rate-making on the exchange market is influenced by factors which refer either to the manner and speed of the exchange or transfer process, or to the credit and financial services which the banks may render in connection with the exchange process of a particular type of transaction or exchange instrument or both. As a result, the market has not one but a multitude of exchange rates at any particular time. It is significant to note, however, that it is the invisible equilibrium rate which underlies the visible rate structure and determines its long-term level and behavior.

All exchange rates are quoted in pairs of selling rates and buying rates, the former being the price which a bank will charge and the latter the price it is prepared to pay for a particular exchange instrument or arrangement. The difference covers the bank's expenses and earnings. Since this duality is universal, a single exchange rate makes no more practical sense than a trouser or a scissor.

The buying and selling rates in turn vary with the exchange instrument and the method of payment involved. The basic exchange methods are discussed below.

Cable transfer

A cable transfer is a telegraphic order by a domestic bank to its foreign correspondent bank to pay a certain sum in the foreign country's currency either to the buyer of exchange or to the party designated by the buyer. When a Seattle bank sells a cable transfer to an importer of French fashions, it cables to its correspondent in Paris to transfer the necessary amount from its own account to that of the fashion house and collects from the Seattle importer the dollar equivalent of the transfer. The chief advantage of this method lies in the speed with which it can be effected. A decade ago, cable transfers required three days for completion; currently it is two—i.e., the release of funds is made the day following the purchase of the transfer—and same-day transfers are coming into increasingly greater use as a result of new communications techniques.

The exchange rate on cable transfers takes into account the cost of the telegram, the prevailing interest rate in the country of payment, and the time differential between cable and mail transfers (or sight drafts) as the basis for the "loss" of interest income to the bank. Where the mailing time is short or the interest yield on foreign deposits low, exchange rates of cable transfers exceed those of other sight and demand instruments only by the cost of the cable.

Mail transfer

Under mail transfer all elements are identical to cable transfer except the speed and cost of communication. However, with the almost universal switch from surface to airmail transfers and the use of transcontinental jet planes, the time differential has been greatly reduced. For many cities the difference has dwindled to the point where the cable can offer no significant advantage and its higher cost becomes unjustifiable. As a consequence, the great bulk of international transfers are currently made by airmail. But for cable or mail transfers, the rate for any transaction of consequence to the bank, such as a substantial import or export shipment, is often tailor made by the bank's trading department, which tries to anticipate the movement of the market and at the same time straighten out its own exchange position. Companies engaged in international business shop around by telephone among the banks and exchange dealers for the best price before making a commitment.

Drafts

As to the exchange rate, drafts present a varied picture. In general, the rate for a draft varies first with its usance—sight drafts command higher rates than time drafts, and the longer the usance the lower the rate. This difference is due to the fact that when a bank buys a time draft it must either wait until maturity to cash it or sell it at a discount equivalent to the anticipated interest income on the face amount plus compensation for any possible credit risk attached to the draft. It is relevant also that, if the draft is drawn by a foreign party, the rate at which it is discounted is determined by the interest rate prevailing in that foreign country. Second, the rate on a draft is higher if it is issued or accepted by a bank than if not; in the latter case, the rates may vary further with the credit standings of the parties to the draft. Finally, the rate for any particular type of draft, but especially for trade drafts, depends on the supply-and-demand conditions at the time it enters the market. Like the buyers and sellers of cable and mail transfers, the parties to bills of exchange, particularly if large sums are involved, seek the most favorable rate quotation by contacting several banks before making an actual sale or purchase.

Forward exchange

The rates discussed to this point are *spot rates,* as they involve an immediate transfer of the exchange either through bank balances or through drafts and acceptances. If a business firm anticipates an exchange obligation or receipt at a future time and does not wish to speculate on the rate fluctuations, it may buy *forward exchange.* An exchange contract is executed between the company and its bank calling for delivery at a future date of a given sum of foreign currency and a simultaneous dollar payment based upon the exchange rate fixed in the contract. When the contract matures, it will be settled on the basis of the predetermined rate, regardless of whether the spot rate has moved up or down during its life. Forward contracts are normally made over the telephone and subsequently confirmed in writing.

The standard forward quotations call for 30-, 60-, 90-, or 180-day delivery. They are often expressed as a schedule of discounts and premiums applicable to the respective spot rate. Since business needs for exchange can seldom be adapted to these delivery dates, most transactions require a separate negotiated rate for which the standard rates serve as a basic guide.

Demand for long-term forward exchange has been increasing because of increasing direct investments in foreign subsidiaries and in joint-venture companies as well as because of the emergence of export-import transactions involving major structures and installations, such as steel mills, chemical plants, and electric-power stations, which require a long time for both negotiation and completion. Two- and three-year forward exchange contracts have thus become a regular, although not dominant, feature of the exchange market.

To illustrate, suppose a U.S. contractor wishes to submit a bid to build a flour mill in Mexico. The dollar cost is calculated at $4,000,000 and delivery is 18 months after contract date. If the current peso rate is $0.10, the bid should be made at 40,000,000 pesos. But, if the rate should rise during the construction period to $0.11, the dollar return of the contractor's bid would drop to $3,636,364. If the rate should drop to $0.09, the contractor would collect $444,444 and thus make a windfall. But, since on the basis of recent monetary experience the probability is greater that the rate will rise and since, normally, manufacturers and contractors are primarily interested in earning and safeguarding their functional rather than their speculative profits, the firm will settle the matter by taking an option on an exchange contract for the bid period and, if successful in getting the business, convert the option into a firm forward exchange contract guaranteeing the calculated $4,000,000 return.

Hedging

The use of forward exchange by business firms shifts the risk of rate fluctuations upon the banking system. But banks, like manufacturing and trading firms, seek to minimize the risk and to protect their normal earnings against speculative loss. They do this by covering forward sales with forward purchases and, if a balance is left, by hedging against any speculative loss by entering the spot exchange market on the opposite side of the balance. Such hedging is based on the theory that the movements in forward and spot rates will parallel each other and that, whatever the direction of the rate movements, the bank will gain on the spot as much as it will lose on the forward or vice versa, thus eliminating the exchange risk.

Determination of forward rates

Forward exchange rates depend on the composite effect of six different variables: interest rates, the time interval, the exchange risk, the demand, the supply, and market imperfections. In terms of economic theory, the forward rate for one currency in terms of another depends on the differential between the prevailing interest rates of the two countries concerned. If the interest rate is higher in Italy than in Japan, lira exchange at a discount from the lira-yen spot rate because funds held in lira yield a higher return over the forward period than those in yen; and, yen exchange at a corresponding premium over the yen-lira spot rate since funds kept in yen yield relatively less in interest than those in lira. Theoretically, then, the size of the discount will be determined by the rate differential and the length of the forward period, as follows:

$$(r_I - r_J) \times t = \text{forward rate}$$

where r_I denotes the interest rate per annum in Italy, r_J the interest rate per annum in Japan, and t the forward period in years.

When the actual discount or premium equals the interest rate differential, the forward exchange rate between the two countries is at its theoretical equilibrium, which is referred to as the *interest rate parity.* If, for example, $r_I = 10$ percent, $r_J = 6$ percent, and $t = 6$ months, then.

$$\text{the parity forward rate} = (10-6) \times 0.5 = 2 \text{ percent}$$

In practice the other five factors listed above often cause the actual market rates of forward exchange to deviate from the interest rate parity. As for the exchange risk, the forward rate is particularly responsive to speculative influences, which are more violent in times of international monetary and political uncertainty than in periods of stability. When, for example, a particular currency such as the yen is in a weak position and its depreciation is anticipated, foreign earners of yen not only will liquidate their current holdings of yen but also will try to sell their prospective yen receipts as forward exchange. Consequently, the speculative expectation of yen devaluation will swell the supply of yen in Italy, and for that matter other countries, and will generate downward pressure on the forward rate of yen. At the same time Japanese earners of lira will delay converting their exchange to yen in hopes of making a windfall on the devaluation. As a result, the demand for yen exchange will be curtailed and the downward pressure on its forward rate compounded. An opposite deviation will occur when an appreciation of yen or depreciation of lira becomes a reasonable anticipation.

At the present time fluctuations of forward rates are also affected by the numerous exchange controls and monetary restrictions in different countries and by internal economic conditions, especially the overall liquidity of the economy, which determines the amount of short-term capital available for interest arbitrage. When the liquidity preference at home is low—that is, there are idle liquid funds—a small incentive may be sufficient to bring the idle funds into the exchange market. However, if the liquidity preference is high, only large differentials in interest rates and exchange rates can cause any significant flow of capital for arbitrage purposes.

Cross rates

When currencies are truly convertible, any differences between exchange centers such as New York and London are quickly ironed out by arbitrage operations—buying the exchange where the rate is lower and selling it where the rate is higher. When, however, currencies are made inconvertible and rates are fixed by control authorities, arbitrage becomes impossible. Direct differences, such as in the dollar rate in New York and in London, will, as a rule, be avoided by the control authorities. But cross rates—for example, the dollar rate in terms of francs in London or in terms of pounds in Paris—may become disparate and inconsistent with the bilateral direct rates. To illustrate, suppose the dollar-pound rate is $2.80 in both New York and London, the dollar-franc rate is $0.20 in both New York and Paris, and the franc-pound rate is Fr. 13 in both Paris and London. Thus, direct arbitrage is neither possible nor necessary. But the rates are inconsistent. Suppose a U.S. bank is authorized to spend $140,000 to buy foreign exchange and that it needs pound sterling. If it buys direct, the sterling it would acquire at the $2.80 rate would be 50,000 pounds. But if the bank buys French francs first, as it certainly would under the conditions, it would obtain Fr. 700,000 for the $140,000. Converting the franc acquisition into pounds it would receive 53,846 pounds total or 3,846 pounds more than through direct purchase. This type of maneuver, sometimes misleadingly called three-point arbitrage, will not, however, correct the disparity of the cross rates under exchange control. Indeed, broken cross rates have proved to be unavoidable byproducts of inconvertibility. They distort and corrupt international financial relations.

Market Zones

The world exchange market is characterized by a variety of arrangements for international cooperation which have a greater or lesser degree of influence on both the organization and the functioning of the market. The most important of the cooperative exchange arrangements are those outlined below.

THE STERLING AREA. It includes all members of the British Commonwealth and certain countries which previously belonged to it. This is the current list: Australia, Burma, Ceylon, Cyprus, India, Kuwait, Libya, Malaysia, Nigeria, Western Samoa, New Zealand, South-West Africa, Rhodesia, Malawi, Sierra Leone, Singapore, Iceland, Ireland, Jordan, Republic of South Africa, plus the various British colonies and protectorates.

The main reserve currency for this vast area is the pound sterling and the main exchange center the London market, which has specialized agencies to handle the investment and monetary problems of the members of the sterling area. Based on intergovernmental agreements, the sterling-area monetary arrangements encourage a relatively greater degree of freedom and uniformity in financial transactions among its members than in those with the outside world. For example, exchange controls may apply on extra-area transfers of sterling while intra-area transfers are unregulated; if regulations are imposed on intra-area transfers, they are likely to be standardized for all members and implemented simultaneously.

THE FRANC ZONE. This is another multinational group which acts in close cooperation in matters of international finance. Membership in the franc zone includes, in addition to metropolitan France and its appendices (Corsica, Oasis, Sauora), the following countries: Algeria, Guadeloupe, Martinique, Guiana, Réunion, Comoro Islands, Saint Pierre and Miquelon, New Caledonia, French Polynesia, Cameroun, Chad, Central African Republic, Dahomey, Gabon, Republic of Guinea, Ivory Coast, Malagasy, Mali, Mauritania, Monaco, Morocco, Niger, Senegal, Togo, Tunisia, and Upper Volta.

In the zone the new French franc serves as the principal reserve currency, and Paris is the exchange center. Since most of the zone members are subindustrial areas with relatively weak currencies, franc-zone members depend much more directly upon the exchange reserves and financial aid of France than do sterling-area members on Britain. Indeed, in much of the postwar period, the London market depended heavily upon the inflow of reserves from the member countries of the sterling area, while Paris provided much of the liquidity for the franc zone. As for exchange controls and monetary policies, the franc zone, too, and perhaps to a higher degree, provides standardization and stability to the exchange market in its sphere.

THE ESCUDO ZONE. This exchange area embraces the Portuguese sphere of influence. In addition to Portugal itself, the members are the Azores, Angola, Madeira, the Cape Verde Islands, Portuguese Guinea, Sao João, Baptista de Ajuda, the Islands of São Tomé and Principe, Macao and Timor, and Mozambique. The escudo serves as the international exchange medium of the zone and Lisbon as its central market. Smaller in size and in impact than the pound sterling or franc, the escudo nevertheless plays a highly significant role by making regular trade and payments transactions possible for its members, many of which would otherwise be beyond the reach of normal financial intercourse. An intrazone reserve fund was organized in 1963 to serve as the central source of exchange for the area.

European monetary agreement

In the early postwar years a special monetary bloc, *the European Payments Union* (EPU), was organized. Since it was designed to cope with the catastrophic consequences of the war, its relevance to the current financial situation is only historic. Its principal purpose, however, was to restore convertibility among European and other major currencies. This objective was achieved by 1958, when the EPU was liquidated and the European Monetary Agreement (EMA) was put into effect. Under the EMA each signatory country agrees to maintain its exchange rate in a specified relationship to gold or the U.S. dollar or both and to limit its fluctuations to a prescribed range. Special bilateral payments agreements as well as other discriminatory tactics are discouraged by the requirement that settlements under any such arrangement be effected through the facilities of the EMA. Although other international balances may be settled through the EMA, the penalty for doing so stems from a provision which prescribes that this can be done only at an exchange rate less favorable than the prevailing free-market rate. Also, the central bank balances, if they are to be cleared via the EMA, are calculated on the basis of the least favorable selling rate of the particular currency on the exchange market. Through these and related provisions the EMA places a premium on free and open methods of international payments and helps to enforce the monetary discipline of the exchange market.

The Eurodollar Market

In the mid-1950's some European banks started the practice of accepting dollar-denominated deposits and making dollar-denominated loans, providing a non-American alternative to owners of dollars for banking their holdings, and enabling borrowers of dollars to satisfy their requirements through European sources. This Eurodollar market originated with a few banks in Paris and London but rapidly spread to other financial centers and is now worldwide in scope.

The initial reasons for its emergence were (1) the desire of the communist-bloc banks to have their dollar working balances in Europe rather than the United States, and (2) the need of countries whose own currencies were inconvertible—and nearly all were until 1958—to use dollars as the unit of account and means of payment in international transactions. Widespread convertibility after 1958 did not destroy the Eurodollar but accelerated its use, the main reason being the regulations which prohibit the banks in the United States to pay any interest at all on demand deposits and strictly limit the rates on time deposits. Thus the American banks were unable to pay to international depositors the interest that on the world money market was offered by foreign banks. Direct and indirect exchange controls imposed by the United

States for "balance of payments" purposes have been another stimulant to the Eurodollar market. These include the interest-equalization tax, the "voluntary" controls on foreign investment and lending, and the compulsory controls which President Johnson established.

In amount, the Eurodollar transactions range from modest sums to very large, with an average in the five to eight million range. In tenor they extend from overnight deposits to several-year term facilities; 60-, 90-, and 180-day loans seem to be the most typical.

Since the U.S. banking regulations do not apply abroad, major American banks have tapped the Eurodollar market by establishing branches in Europe, Hong Kong, and other world financial centers. To their initial purpose of pumping it—the U.S. banks' indebtedness to the Eurodollar market at this writing exceeds $9 billion—these banks have more recently found that many of their major domestic customers have switched from New York to the Eurodollar market to maximize interest earnings on their cash resources. This has further broadened the depositor base of the Eurodollar market including the foreign branches of U.S. banks. While a large part of the foreign branch deposits are transferred back to the head office, an increasingly large share has in recent years been utilized for providing working capital to the local affiliates of multinational firms, to indigenous companies, and at times even for governmental purposes. Thus, the U.S. banks have, in fact, become active participants in the Eurodollar market.

Much of the original supply of Eurodollars came from the U.S. balance of payments deficits which left many foreign banks with large holdings of dollar claims, most in the form of deposits in American banks. However, with its present volume of $35 to $40 billion the Eurodollar market has far outgrown this initial source. Now, the Eurodollar supply, just like our domestic money supply, derives in most part from *fractional reserve banking*. Eurodollar deposits like domestic dollar deposits can exceed multifold a bank's actual dollar reserves because only a negligible fraction will be demanded in the form of actual currency. The rest of the bank's obligations are typically discharged by providing a credit or deposit at another bank. Only for the small fraction who demand currency does the Eurodollar bank have to hold actual dollar currency reserves on hand. In any period, owing to the fact that the bank not only pays but also receives dollars, it can redeem much of its cash obligations from day to day as a matter of course. The same principle applies to deposits at American and other banks. Like currency, deposits at other banks need be only a small fraction of assets since the bank is in a continuous process of remitting to and receiving from other banks which to a very large degree balance the bank's positions. Reserves are needed only to provide for temporary discrepancies between its remittances and receipts.

In the United States a minimum level of bank reserves is established by legal regulations; these are considerably higher than would normally be needed for purely financial operations of a bank. The Eurodollar banks including the foreign branches of U.S. banks are not subject to the American reserve regulations. Each country has its banking laws. In many countries they are more liberal than in the United States. A typical Eurodollar bank, therefore, can cascade its reserves in dollar currency plus its initial dollar holdings in other banks into a volume of loans and deposits which is several times greater. Some writers have claimed that the amount of Eurodollar business done at any time is limited to the volume of dollar transfers from U.S. banks; this is pure nonsense. Once a foreign bank has launched its Eurodollar operations its initial dollar holdings have little further significance. From here on, the only limitations on the bank's ability to expand its Eurodollar business are (a) its total assets, (b) the need to have at least a certain, though yet undeterminate, share of the bank's business in the local currency, and (c) the banking regulations regarding reserve requirements of the particular nation. The bulk of Eurodollar business volume is neither dollars nor in Europe. It consists mainly of dollar-denominated credit instruments from short-term drafts to multiyear term certificates and Eurobonds which the banks abroad create, carry, and trade. Their holdings at U.S. banks are helpful but not essential to this business.

The Eurodollar system of accepting nonresident-denominated deposits has in the last few years been expanded to include a number of other currencies: Swiss franc, West German deutsche mark, Dutch florin, French franc, Italian lira, Japanese yen, and some others. Strictly speaking, therefore, we should rename the Eurodollar market *Eurocurrency market,* but here as in many other practices the original term will probably continue to be used despite the new developments.

The Eurocurrency system stimulates cross-convertibility of currencies, facilitates the flow of funds from surplus to deficit countries, and provides means for financing international business operations and other major transactions. Its other effects are not fully understood. The editors of *Business Week* have this to say about it:

> —It is a big, open market, seemingly capable of almost limitless growth, able to funnel huge amounts of dollars to anyone willing to pay the price. . . .
> —It is a valuable market, because it has enabled world economies and world trade to keep growing despite pinched world liquidity and a spreading web of controls over the movement of national currencies. It has allowed U.S. corporations to keep growing in overseas markets, even though rules tightly limit the export of dollars. . . .
> . . . more and more institutions the world over—banks, corporations, governmental agencies, even the growing band of international mutual funds—have come to use the Eurodollar market as borrowers or investors. "We need the Eurodollar market," declares Fritz Leutweiler, director-general of Switzerland's central bank. "If we didn't have one, we should have to get one."[1]

[1] *Business Week,* No. 2162, Feb. 6, 1971, p. 31.

Appendix to Chapter 20

The Risk and Insurance Aspects in International Trade Payments

In international trade transactions the risk elements attached to credit and payments often have a decisive influence on the position which the management of a firm will take. While the sources of these risks are numerous, they can be grouped into two distinct categories—those associated with the country involved and those associated with the particular customer involved—and must be analyzed accordingly.

Country Analysis

Unless an exporter is in a position to prescribe his own currency as the means of payment, the first critical decision in an international payments transaction is which currency to be used: exporter's, importer's, or that of some third country. Rapid inflation and lack of monetary discipline in many, and apparently a growing number of countries, have pushed the currency problem into the forefront of payments considerations in recent years. It remains true, however, that the majority of trade transactions are payable in either the exporter's or the importer's currency. This probably remains so not because of its financial soundness but because of the national and patriotic price which even a faltering and inflated currency can command. The country analysis, therefore, is mostly limited to the economic and particularly the monetary situation in the other party's country. It must answer three different kinds of questions. First, what governmental restrictions and controls are employed which may interfere with international payments: exchange quotas, licenses, multiple exchange rates, special guarantees, etc.? Second, how closely does the official exchange rate—the price of the foreign currency in terms of domestic money—reflect its true purchasing power? And third, how stable can the currency be expected to remain? Only if each of these questions is answered in such a manner that the element of uncertainty can be assessed and compared with those of alternative currencies is the management in a position to render a rational decision. To arrive at such judgments it is often necessary to undertake a comprehensive study of the country's economic and political conditions. Since many firms cannot justify the cost of such a study on the basis of their export expectations, they are compelled either to rely on the advice of financial intermediaries (the banks) and mercantile credit agencies or to try to shift as much of the risk as possible upon the other party. As shown below, the selections of international credit instruments depends primarily on the degree to which the exporter can induce the importer to share in bearing the risk burden.

Customer Analysis

Whereas the country analysis attempts to ascertain the influences external to the payor which might influence an exporter's risk, the customer analysis centers on the payor, i.e., the importer himself. As in domestic credit work, the objective here is to determine the integrity, the liquidity, and the solvency aspects of the importing company.

The *integrity criterion* is best ascertained on the basis of past record; banks, other suppliers, and mercantile credit agencies are the standard sources for information on a firm's characteristic behavior regarding punctuality, sincerity, and honesty of fulfilling its financial commitments. As contrasted with domestic credit analysis, the mercantile credit agencies play a much smaller role in international finance, because their sources and staffs are seldom adequate for a reliable analysis of foreign customers.

The *liquidity criterion* is used to establish the firm's capacity to generate liquid assets, primarily cash, during the contemplated credit period and thus to establish both the amount and duration of any credit to be granted to it. The ideal indicator of the liquidity status is the firm's cash budget, which unfortunately is seldom available from non-American firms. In its stead the would-be creditor must depend primarily on profit-and-loss statements supplemented with whatever other financial data may be obtainable either from the foreign import firm itself or through banks or other interested third parties to establish as closely as possible its current assets–current liabilities ratio. An often neglected source of financial information is the Commercial Registry in countries which use the civil law (Roman law) system. At the Registry, which normally is attached to the patent office, audited balance sheets and profit-and-loss statements of private firms are kept on file and are available for inspection without charge. The firms are required by law to file these statements annually with the Registry. Since in the United States this source of information does not exist, and since American credit practice seems to have been patterned after the domestic format, the Registry records have remained an untapped source of financial information on foreign firms.

The *solvency criterion* is designed to be the ultimate line of defense against credit loss. Whereas the liquidity test was made to determine credit terms which would fall into the range of the importer's capabilities, the solvency analysis attempts to ascertain the overall asset-liability relationship of the foreign firm and whether it is likely to change during the credit period considered. The basic question here is not if the company can pay on schedule but if it can pay at all if the liquidity assumptions do not materialize. The main sources of information for this analysis are the balance sheets and other records describing the character of the assets and liabilities of the import company. Some conservative export firms base their solvency studies on the bankruptcy assumption; i.e., they devalue the prospective debtor's assets to what might be expected to be their value in the case of involuntary liquidation. Such procedure is difficult to justify, particularly when the assets of the importing firm contain a high percentage of capital equipment, structures, or other special-purpose facilities which, although costly to acquire and very valuable as productive resources of a going concern, may have little more than scrap value if disposed of individually on the open market. This is true because, in a going concern, i.e., in a productive combination, these assets possess the capacity to produce finished goods which give them value. If the productive process is discontinued, as in liquidation of the firm, the capacity to produce is destroyed and, with it, the derived value. All that remains is the market value of the machine or structure as a separate article. Hence, the bankruptcy assumption will grossly undervalue the assets of industrial firms and imply an unnecessarily restrictive credit position to the exporter. On the other hand, firms whose assets consist mainly of inventories of finished consumer goods would hardly be affected at all by this procedure, because the value of such products is quite independent of the question of whether the seller is a going concern.

There is no simple rule concerning how the solvency test can best be conducted. It must be stressed, however, that whatever the formula, the structure of the assets as well as liabilities of the firm must be established and projected against the background of the overall profitability of the concern before any definite conclusions can be reached. Credit analysis of foreign prospects is in its relative infancy, and much remains to be learned and uncovered. Until the early 1960's, U.S. exporters rarely sold any unsecured account and thus had no serious need for a reliable analysis of the prospect's credit worthiness. The pressure of international competition, especially that of the European Common Market and of Japan, has forced American businesses to shift toward a more liberal credit position in the last few years, and this trend can be expected to continue; from it, no doubt, will emerge the experience, techniques, and institutional arrangements to meet this new managerial challenge.

International Credit Insurance

The extension of credit to foreign customers is subject not only to the regular commercial risks (illiquidity, insolvency, and impropriety) but also to risks arising from political instability and governmental manipulations of foreign monetary exchange and trade controls. Although instruments such as confirmed letters of credit are available to minimize these risks, their use implies a restrictive credit policy which, on one hand, compels the company to reject certain customers and, on the other, makes its terms of sale unacceptable to some others. Such a policy, while eliminating credit losses, would at the same time restrict exports. In recent years the responsiveness to credit terms has reached high elasticity in most world markets because of increased competition. This has made credit terms a crucial factor in export success for both companies and countries.

Some credit losses will always occur. An ideal credit policy is not one that eliminates all credit losses, because such a policy could only be implemented through cash transactions. Thus, along with credit losses the policy would eliminate credit sales and all the potential profits derived from them. Instead, an ideal credit policy is one which would maximize the gross income of the firm. Since the income is a product of sales volume times gross margin (price less cost per unit), increasing the volume through credit sales represents an addition to company profits as long as credit losses remain smaller than the income from these sales. When the credit losses have risen to the point where they add as much to the cost side as additional credit customers would add to the revenue side, the maximum policy has been achieved. The theoretically ideal credit policy would equate the marginal revenue from credit sales to the marginal credit losses.

In countries where capital is scarce and interest rates are high, liberal credit terms provide a potent means for increasing sales. But, typically, the same countries present highly variegated and unpredictable credit risks. Thus, extensive credit exports may expose any firm's position to serious peril.

Efforts to Reduce the Risks of Foreign Credit

Since it is in the national interest of each country to encourage exports, various programs and institutions have been set up in almost all industrial countries to provide exporters with a credit insurance system covering the regular commercial rates and the political risks as well. The form of this insurance varies from country to country, but, as will be seen, essentially similar institutions have been developed to insure both short-term and medium-term export credit. In the past, the main emphasis was on medium-term credit, up to five years. More recently, however, there has been a trend to increase the availability of both short-term (up to six months) and long-term (five to twenty years) credit insurance. As will also be pointed out, attempts have been made to separate commercial and political risk coverage, thereby reducing the cost of insurance to the exporter. American and several European exporters may now insure for political risks only.

As to ownership of the underwriting institutions, the systems differ greatly; some are completely governmental undertakings, and others are privately owned or mixed systems. Some standardization of methods and practices is fostered by the International Credit Association headquarters in Zurich, Switzerland. A common feature to all international credit insurance schemes is the requirement that the insured must retain an interest in the credit transaction; that is, complete coverage is never granted to avoid exporters' carelessness and misuse of the insurance protection.

Export Credit Insurance in the United States

The United States has been a relatively late entry into international credit insurance. The Export-Import Bank began in 1954 to assist exporters of capital goods by lending them up to two-thirds of invoice amount "without recourse" on long- and medium-term projects. In 1960 the Bank adopted a policy of covering political risks only but extended the coverage to short-term credits also with the proviso that all the insured's shipments had to be covered. The insurance was issued in a form of guarantee to private insurance companies or banks who actually granted the export credits.

The foreign credit insurance association (FCIA)

Since the Export-Import Bank's program was limited to heavy industrial goods, it left a vacuum for lighter industrial goods and the entire consumer goods sector. To fill this vacuum the FCIA was created in 1962. It is composed of 57 private insurance companies and the Export-Import Bank. Its program consists of two types of policies: a comprehensive commercial and political coverage of U. S. exports sold to friendly nations, and political-risks-only coverage. The commercial risks are defined as "insolvency and protracted default," that is, outstanding export accounts more than six months overdue. The political risks covered include (a) expropriation, confiscation, inconvertibility, war, and civil commotion, and (b) restrictions or cancellation of a valid import or export license after shipment of the cargo. Commercial risks are insurable up to 85 percent and political risks up to 95 percent under the comprehensive policy. If insured separately, political risk coverage is lowered to 85 percent.

U.S. commercial banks

Backed by the FCIA, certain commercial banks in the United States have recently adopted the Swiss practice of *without-recourse* financing, which shifts both commercial and political risks from the exporter to the bank. Without recourse means that once the bank has bought an exporter's paper (international credit instrument), it assumes the entire risk for the credit. Should the instrument, for whatever reason, subsequently turn out to be uncollectable, the liability will not revert back to the exporter as it would under regular acceptance procedure but will have to be borne by the bank itself. The banks, on short-term credit, cover 100 percent of the risk in many of the principal trading nations and 85 percent in remaining countries, all without recourse to the exporter.

From the exporter's standpoint, without-recourse financing is preferable to credit insurance in that there is no continuing involvement after the paper has been liquidated (sold to the bank) and that the rather complicated procedures of securing export credit insurance are avoided.

21
The Balance of Payments

International Social Accounting

The balance of payments is a system of accounts designed to show how a nation finances its international activities and what role it plays in the world economy. Its focal point is the nation's external liquidity—the relationship of current assets to current liabilities—which measures its ability to meet claims from the outside world and to acquire the goods and services it needs to import. The accounts are set up to summarize all economic transactions between the residents of the nation and the residents of other nations during a given period of time, normally a year, a quarter, or a month. As such the balance of payments registers the changes in the nation's financial claims and obligations vis-à-vis the rest of the world. It is a national accounting tabulation comparable more to a firm's profit-and-loss statement, which shows what has happened during a year, than to its balance sheet, which presents the total assets and liabilities at a particular point in time. Hence the balance of payments does not measure the total foreign assets or liabilities which a country's citizens may possess at any particular moment, but it does show what changes are taking place in them and how these changes affect the external liquidity and other financial relations of the nation.

Although the primary purpose of the balance of payments is to answer questions pertaining to the country as a member in the world community of nations, i.e., to its international financial position, it also serves as the central framework for analysis and interpretation of a wide range of problems dealing with specific aspects of the country's economic and business life. For example: What effect would currency depreciation or appreciation have on the nation's business and on its gross national product or on the export opportunities of a particular industry or company? What impact would tariffs have on another country's market for American goods? How would employment conditions in a particular area or industry respond to a specific foreign development such as closing a mine or building a factory? What are the results to the consuming public of direct foreign investments by the U.S. oil companies? What is the real purchasing power of a particular currency? How great is the import potential of Argentina? Questions such as these have come increasingly to the attention of management because of the growth and the expansion of multinational operations as shown in Chapter 9. Thus, the balance of payments has become a critical tool for analysis, prediction, and policy formulation in business administration as well as in national administration.

Definitions

TRANSACTIONS. For balance-of-payments purposes economic transactions include all transfers of property which can be valued in monetary terms from a resident of one country to that of another. This rule is employed without qualification. Transactions in kind and in credit are accountable just the same as cash transactions; and, transactions for which no payments are received or expected, such as shipments of equipment to a foreign branch plant by the parent firm, or, conversely, of component parts from the branch to the parent, are included along with sales and purchase transactions. Indeed, the question of *quid pro quo* is irrelevant in balance-of-payments accounting, as unilateral transfers of value, such as personal gifts, government grants, and philanthropic donations, are also recorded. From a strict accounting standpoint the balance of payments is not a record of international payments but of international transactions.[1] However, its meaning and usefulness derive not from the accounting manipulations of the transactions but from the external-liquidity changes which the accounts reflect.

RESIDENTS. The term *resident* is defined by the International Monetary Fund as all persons and institutions identified with the country concerned. Resident institutions include all business enterprises, government agencies, and nonprofit organizations. International agencies are regarded as a special case and are not treated as resident institutions of the countries in which they are located. Government officials and members of armed forces stationed abroad are treated as residents of the country of citizenship. Foreign branches and subsidiaries of business firms are treated as residents of the countries in which they are located, whereas transactions with agents are regarded as transactions

[1] The International Monetary Fund definition of balance of payments is, "A systematic record of all *transactions* during the period between residents of the reporting country and residents of other countries."

with the principal for whom they are acting. A further distinction is made between *branch* and *agency,* depending on the operation of the local office in question. If the local office acts as a principal for its own account, it is regarded as a resident of the country in which it is located; if it acts for principals abroad, it is treated as a resident of the principals' countries. Travelers, commuters, temporary residents, and other individuals with dual or multiple residency are classified by the so-called *center-of-interest* rule, which assigns them to the country of their principal interest. The residency concept in general refers to normal location rather than to nationality, except for government and military personnel.

CREDITS AND DEBITS. According to the double-entry principle transactions are recorded in the balance of payments either as *credits,* if they give rise to receipts from or claims against foreigners, such as export of merchandise, sale of securities overseas, and rendering services to foreign consumers; or as *debits,* if they cause such payments or indebtedness to foreigners as importation of goods, tourist expenditures abroad, and purchase of foreign bonds. Each business transaction must give rise to a claim of resources by one country and a counterclaim for payment by the other. Thus an export of goods creates a claim for payment in the country of origin and a counter-claim for goods in the country of destination: a purchase of French securities by a Canadian capitalist creates a claim for ownership by the Canadian and a claim for payment by the French concern. There is a duality in all international transactions except unilateral transfers. This duality problem is solved in balance-of-payments accounting by making opposite double entries in the accounts of the two countries involved, in the same way that they are made in the books of two business firms. A further explanation of this process follows the discussion of the structure and contents of the different accounts.

The System of Accounts

For greater utility in analysis and for statistical convenience the international transactions entered into the balance of payments are grouped into a hierarchy of accounts based upon the degree of homogeneity among the different transactions. On the data-collection level, transactions of identical purpose or character or both, such as railway charges, port fees, and exports, are each recorded in a separate account; on subsequent levels the more homogeneous transactions are combined into composite accounts according to the headings in Table 21-1. The rationale of this system is that the transactions in the homogeneous accounts differ from those in the other accounts in both their behavior pattern and their effect upon the nation's financial position.

1. CURRENT ACCOUNT

1.1 Merchandise Trade (Visibles)

For most countries, exports and imports of merchandise are the largest single component of total international payments, often accounting for two-thirds or more of their overall international transactions. As we have already

TABLE 21-1

Balance of Payments Conceptual Scheme

Classification	*Entry*	
	Debit	*Credit*
1. Current account		
1.1 Merchandise trade (visibles)		
Balance of trade		
1.2 International services (invisibles)		
Current account balance		
2. Transfers (donations, unilateral transfers)		
2.1 Private		
2.2 Governmental		
Total donations		
3. Capital account		
3.1 Long-term capital		
3.11 Private		
3.12 Governmental		
3.2 Short-term capital		
3.21 Private		
3.22 Governmental		
Total capital account		
4. Monetary-reserve account		
4.1 Gold movements		
4.2 Convertible currencies		
4.3 Other convertible reserves		
5. Errors and omissions		
5.1 Incomplete information		
5.2 Inaccurate valuations		
5.3 Estimates versus accounts		
5.4 Differences in timing		

observed, exports of goods from a country give it a claim upon foreigners for payment, and the value of the goods is therefore listed as a credit entry. On the other hand, imports represent a payment obligation and are therefore entered as debit entries in the account. The net result of the merchandise account is the country's *balance of trade*, a concept often confused by the layman with the balance of payments itself. Merchandise transactions are referred to as *visible trade,* as distinguished from *invisible trade* or, more correctly, *invisible transactions,* i.e., international business dealings which do not involve physical products.

1.2 International Services

(A) Foreign Travel. This account includes all tourist expenditures: fares, lodging, food, entertainment, and articles bought while abroad. Such expenditures are comparable to imports. Conversely, foreign visitors' consumption and purchases while in the country concerned are similar to exports. For many countries, such as Switzerland, Denmark, Italy, and Spain, receipts from foreign tourists constitute a major source of foreign exchange. For the United States it has been a debit item, as much more is spent by Americans abroad than by people of other nations in the United States. The expenditures of the foreign service and of other governmental representatives are not included in this account but in the governmental services account.

(B) INVESTMENT INCOME. This account comprises transfers of dividends, interests, and repatriated profits of foreign branches and subsidiaries of transnational firms. Dividends are entered when officially declared, interests when credited or paid by the bank, and profits when paid or due. Income from portfolio investments is treated the same way as dividends from direct investments. All these data are entered at their book value.

(C) PRIVATE SERVICES. Under this heading come payments to various private parties: royalties; rents; consulting and engineering fees; reinsurance commissions; charges for international cable, radio, and telephone operations; motion-picture rentals; and all other international charges for services rendered and received by nongovernment institutions and personnel. Since the available data for some of the service subaccounts are quite incomplete, such as those for purely personal services, copyrights, and travelers' expenditures, this account represents the least accurate component of the balance of payments and contributes to the errors-and-omissions part.

(D) GOVERNMENT SERVICES. The principal transactions recorded in this subaccount are the regular international transactions of a country's government: diplomatic and military representation; administrative and operating expenses; salaries and wages to foreign employees of embassies, consulates, etc.; purchases of foreign products; payments for land and buildings; membership fees in international organizations; and similar expenditures. In the case of the United States, the transactions of government-operated business enterprises such as the post office and the Panama Canal are also recorded in this account. Goods shipped and services rendered under U.S. military-aid programs are not in this account, for they do not affect external liquidity.

2. TRANSFERS (DONATIONS) ACCOUNT

2.1 Private

Included here are international noncommercial transactions by private citizens and institutions. Personal gifts of all kinds, philanthropic activities, cultural donations, and relief-organization shipments are the main categories. Although such transactions flow in both directions, the U.S. net has been heavily outward for many years.

2.2 Government

This account consists of transfers by government agencies of money, goods, and services as aid to other nations, i.e., where nothing is received in return. Under U.S. practice, it includes grants made under economic-aid and defense-support programs but excludes direct military aid. As such, this account has been a large and controversial debit post in the U.S. balance of payments ever since World War II. For aid to dependent countries, it is a significant credit; for most of the others it is inconsequential. Where the foreign-aid grant takes the form of goods and services, the debit entry is offset by crediting either the exports or the services accounts, and there is no immediate effect on the country's liquidity; where the aid is given in the form of cash transfers, it represents a corresponding reduction of the country's liquid reserves. It is aid of this latter type that causes serious deficit problems unless neutralized by surpluses from other accounts.

3. CAPITAL ACCOUNT

3.1 Long-Term Capital

This account shows the inflow and outflow of capital commitments which have a maturity longer than a year. The account is divided into subsections for private and for public or governmental capital transactions. Private long-term capital items range from the extension of commercial credit to the acquisition of physical properties such as mines, mills, and factories abroad. Stocks, bonds, new issues of securities, redemptions, long-term bank claims, and miscellaneous other interests in property constitute the majority of its entries.

Governmental long-term capital includes loans to and from other governments, financial support in economic-development projects abroad, and, particularly significant for the United States, loans by the Export-Import Bank, subscriptions to the Inter-American Development Bank, and participation in the financing of other foreign projects either directly or through international institutions.

3.2 Short-Term Capital

Short-term capital movements are generally confined to commitments whose duration is under one year. Frequently the maturity date is only 30, 60, or 90 days. Movements in short-term foreign-capital accounts commonly include additions to or subtractions from foreign bank balances; purchases or sales of marketable foreign government bonds (of relatively short maturity); and acquisitions of bank deposits, other foreign-currency holdings, foreign exchange instruments (commercial paper), and other liquid or near-liquid assets. They are normally used to finance international trade, to pay for international services, and to settle other accounts. The short-term capital account also is divided into private and governmental subaccounts. The basis for the division is the same as that for long-term capital accounts. For balance-of-payments analysis, particularly for forecasting financial conditions, this division is a significant one, since the two groups react quite differently to certain changes in the economy.

4. MONETARY-RESERVE ACCOUNT

4.1 Gold Movements

Since gold may serve as universal money for the settlement of international accounts or as an ordinary industrial material, its accounting in the balance of payments presents a peculiar problem—namely, which transactions to include in the monetary gold account and which in the merchandise account. The League of Nations developed a formula now used by the International Monetary Fund and most of its member nations, including the United States. The formula allocates the difference between commercial (nonmonetary) gold consumption and the annual production of gold to the merchandise account as a credit if positive and a debit if negative; any changes in the country's monetary gold reserves are recorded in the gold account and are offset by an opposite entry in the short-term capital account. The phrase *monetary-gold movements,* although in general use, is a misleading one. A large number of international transactions in gold involve no physical movement but are handled through "earmarking" operations, by which the title to the gold is transferred from one nation to another while the bullion remains in Fort Knox, Bern, Paris, or London. Such passing of ownership is a sufficient basis for the appropriate balance-of-payments entry.

4.2 Convertible Currencies

Official holdings of other countries' currencies which are freely convertible on the international money market are kept by countries for the same reason they keep monetary gold. Since the most widely held reserve currencies are the U.S. dollar and the British pound, most other countries have significant movements in these two currencies. Since the early 1960's several other hard currencies, particularly the West German deutsche mark, the Swiss franc, and, to a lesser extent, the French franc, the Dutch gulden, and the Swedish krona, have taken on an increasingly important role in international money reserves. The United States, which refrained from using other currencies as reserve-account assets, now has an official policy to emphasize their use by both this country and others in order to relieve the strain which its extended international position has placed upon the U.S. dollar. It should be added that only purchases and sales by official monetary authorities, such as the U.S. Treasury and Federal Reserve Board, the Bank of England, or the Swedish Riksbanken, are entered in this account.

4.3 "Paper Gold"

The International Monetary Fund provides credits in the form of regular and special drawing rights (SDRs), gold tranche, and loans which have become increasingly important reserve assets to its member countries.

5. ERRORS AND OMISSIONS

Although in theory the balance of payments should always balance, because all debits are offset by credits and vice versa, in reality it never does balance because data are incomplete and they lend themselves to different interpretations by different people and agencies. The specific reasons for deviations depend on the particular country's data-collection and data-processing systems and as such defy generalization. The following are the main causes for the internal disbalances in the U.S. balance-of-payments statement.

5.1 Incomplete Information

(a) Records of commissions, fees, royalties, and rental income received by local residents from foreign sources are inadequate.

(b) Purchases and sales of real property between local residents and foreign residents are not recorded by customs or other agencies from whom balance-of-payments data are derived.

(c) Transactions of securities made by local residents directly through foreign brokers are not known to the balance-of-payments authorities.

(d) Illegal transactions to evade customs or monetary control, such as smugglings or briberies, are unavoidable.

5.2 Inaccurate Valuations

(a) Inconsistent valuation of merchandise in different countries creates statistical difficulty.

(b) Transfers of funds in the absence of international transactions—funds transferred to foreign residents (capital flight)—which are recorded as a reduction in liabilities will appear to be a capital outflow (or debit) when in effect no international transaction of any kind has taken place.

(c) The existence of exchange control or of tariffs based on the value of the merchandise may also give shippers in foreign trade an incentive to report some value other than the true one.

5.3 Estimates Versus Accounts

(a) Tourist expenditures are estimated from sample surveys based on questionnaires and are subject to considerable error.

(b) Interest and dividends are estimated from income-tax returns of corporations and individuals supplemented by questionnaires for the largest corporations operating in the foreign field and are also subject to substantial error.

(c) Arbitrary valuations of intercompany transactions in raw materials or semifinished goods are often used.

(d) Nonmarketable gifts such as those sent by parcel post and household effects of migrants do not lend themselves readily to valuation procedures.

5.4 Differences in Timing

The transactions and the payments of international accounts may be set up so that payments will be due after the compilation of balance-of-payments data.

The errors-and-omissions post is not an account, and no transactions are ever recorded in it. It represents the arithmetic difference between the total debit and total credit entries (exclusive of the balancing transactions of the monetary-reserve account), which should be equal by definition. The possible influence of this post on the country's liquidity position will be discussed later.

Balance-of-Payments Techniques

The tabulation of international transactions in the balance of payments is based on double-entry accounting. Every entry must have a counterentry—for every debit there must be a corresponding credit and for every credit a counterbalancing debit. As indicated earlier, the distinction between debit and credit transactions may be made on the basis of the receipts and payments criteria: If a transaction causes a payment it is a debit, and if it results in a receipt it is a credit. Because of its relative simplicity the receipts-payments or claims-payments approach is widely used in nontechnical discussions of the subject.

Another way to distinguish between debits and credits in the balance-of-payments account is to use the asset-liability criterion, as is done in corporate accounting. This approach is normally employed in official balance-of-payments statistics. Any transaction which increases a country's assets is a debit entry (just as an addition of goods to the inventory of a business firm is), and one which decreases the country's assets is a credit entry (just as a withdrawal of goods from a firm's warehouse is). On the liability side any transaction which decreases the country's liabilities is a debit, and one which increases its indebtedness is a credit.

Accordingly, a merchandise import to the United States is a debit entry, for it adds to the material wealth of this nation, but the payment for it is a credit because the draft drawn upon the importer adds to American liabilities to foreigners; if the purchase term calls for cash or a sight draft, the payment still is a credit, for it is subtracted from the overseas assets of the U.S. bank which converts the currency or honors the draft. How this principle can be employed throughout the entire balance-of-payments system is demonstrated in the next section. The counterbalancing requirement of double-entry accounting must always be met by simultaneous entries in one of these combinations:

(a) debit (increase) of assets ....credit (increase) of liabilities
(b) debit (increase) of assets ....credit (decrease) of assets
(c) credit (decrease) of assets ....debit (decrease) of liabilities
(d) credit (decrease) of assets ....debit (increase) of assets
(e) credit (increase) of liabilities ......debit (increase) of assets
(f) credit (increase) of liabilities ......debit (decrease) of liabilities
(g) debit (decrease) of liabilities ......credit (decrease) of assets
(h) debit (decrease) of liabilities ......credit (increase) of liabilities

The only exceptions to the counterbalancing entries are the donations or unilateral transfers which create no payments claim by the country of origin. They are treated in different ways depending upon the nature of the donation. A shipment of goods as a gift (food packages, school books, Red Cross shipments, etc.) is a visible export and, therefore, a credit in the merchandise account, which is counterbalanced by a dummy debit entry in the donations account. Grants and gifts of money in the form of checks, drafts, bills, and international postal money orders are credited to short-term capital, since they must be paid by some resident in the donor country when due; the balancing entry again is a debit in the donations or unilateral transfers account, which is used for all grants and gifts.

Posting of Entries

Table 21-2 illustrates how international economic transactions are recorded in a country's balance of payments. For simplicity, the country is designated *A* and the rest of the world *B*. It is assumed that all entries are recorded correctly and there are no omissions; hence, the balance of payments as a whole must always remain balanced because of the offsetting of debits and credits either within a particular account or among the different accounts. The latter process—interaccount balancing—is the object of this illustration. The accounts involved are indicated by parenthetical references to the two symmetrical postings in Table 21-2. The transactions are these:

1. Country *A* exports merchandise worth $10,000 and draws a sight draft upon the importer in *B*. The importer pays by an acceptance of his local bank, which holds deposits in *A*.

Entries: The export is a credit because it creates a claim by *A* against *B* and reduces its merchandise assets (A1). The payment is a debit because it entails a movement of short-term capital from *B* to *A* and thereby increases *A*'s bank balances abroad, or alternatively could reduce *B*'s bank balances in *A*, which decreases a liability (or could increase an asset). (F1)

2. Country *A* imports $8000 worth of goods and agrees to pay by means of a draft drawn by its exporter on his domestic bank's correspondent in *B*.

Entries: The import is a debit entry in the merchandise account (B2), and the payment is a credit entry (F2). Explanation is the reverse of that for transaction 1.

3. A resident of *A* consumes $2000 for food, entertainment, and transportation services while vacationing in *B* and pays for them by travelers' checks issued by a bank in *A*.

Entries: The consumption is debited, as it adds to the assets of *A* (by conserving them) and gives *B* a claim against *A* (C3). The payment is a credit because, when the travelers' checks are tendered, they decrease *A*'s assets in *B* (bank balances) or increase its liabilities (F3).

4. A firm in *A* receives from its foreign-based subsidiary $5000 of

TABLE 21-2

Balance-of-Payments Accounting: A Summarized Statement Based on Some Hypothetical Transactions

Items		*Debit* (−)	*Credit* (+)
A. Exports (1)			$ 10,000
B. Imports (2)		$ 8000	
Balance of trade (*A* − *B*)		—	2000
C. Services			
Tourist expenditures (3)		2000	
Income on investments (4)			5000
Balance on current account (*A* − *B* − *C**)		5000	
Private donations (5)		5000	
Government grants (6)		10,000	
D. Unilateral transfers			
E. Capital account			
Long-term private direct investment (7)		200,000	
Government portfolio investment (8)		100,000	
Net current transfers and capital Balance (*A* − *B*, *C** − *D** − *E**)		310,000	—
F. Monetary-reserve account			
Increase (+) of *B* bank balances in *A*			
	(2)		8000
	(3)		2000
	(5)		5000
	(6)		10,000
	(7)		200,000
	(8)		100,000
Net Increase (+)			325,000
Increase (−) of *A* bank balance in *B*			
	(1)	10,000	
	(4)	5000	
Net decrease (−)		15,000	
Balance in monetary-reserve account		—	310,000

* Indicates net changes.

dividends, which is remitted in the form of a draft from the subsidiary's bank in *B* on its correspondent in *A*.

Entries: Declarations of the dividends increases *A*'s assets and is a debit (C4), and when the draft is cashed it decreases *A*'s foreign assets or respectively increases its claims and is therefore a credit (F4).

5. A foundation in *A* donates $5000 as a research grant to a scholar in *B* and transfers it by a check on a foreign branch of its local bank.

Entries: The scholarship grant is a credit (D5), and the check, when cashed, is a debit (F5); the reasoning is analogous to that in the previous transactions.

6. *A*'s government makes a $10,000 grant to a village in *B* for irrigation

construction and pays for it by drawing a check on its local bank's correspondent in *B*.

Entries: The government grant from *A* increases *B*'s assets, for it gives *B* a claim against *A*, and thus it is a debit (D6). When the check is cashed by *B*, it decreases *A*'s assets in *B* (bank balance) or increases *A*'s liabilities to *B*, and thus it is a credit (F6).

7. A citizen of *A* invests $200,000 in a business in *B*. Payment is made by a bank in *A* drawing a foreign-currency bank draft on its balances in a bank in *B*.

Entries: The investment made by the citizen in *A* constitutes a claim against *A* by *B*, thus it is a debit (E7). The payment increases *A*'s liabilities to *B* or decreases its assets, and thus it is a credit (F7).

8. *A*'s government buys stocks and bonds worth $100,000 from *B*'s government and citizens and pays for them by drawing checks on its local bank's foreign correspondent in *B*.

Entries: The purchase of stocks and bonds creates claims for *B*'s government and citizens, for it reduces *A*'s assets, and thus it is a debit (E8). The checks add to *B*'s assets (bank balances) in *A* or increase *A*'s liabilities and are a credit (F8).

International Differences

International efforts to standardize and unify balance-of-payments principles and techniques have a long history. Especially good progress was made under the League of Nations in the interwar period and more recently within the framework of the International Monetary Fund. Despite the great strides toward uniformity, the many remaining differences and inconsistencies make it difficult and often hazardous to combine, contrast, or compare the balance-of-payments data of different countries. Lack of comparability is perhaps the greatest handicap for the international organizations, including the multinational business concerns, which often need international comparisons for making rational decisions regarding their policies and programs.

Format

Since there is no acceptable way to catalogue the specific differences and since, as indicated, they are declining, it is more useful and economical to focus our attention here on the points of convergence rather than divergence. The basic format is the International Monetary Fund standard schedule in Table 21-3. This format has been accepted, at least in principle, as the goal toward which the world's financial community should strive in its efforts to harmonize the various national balance-of-payments systems. And in the interim the standard schedule serves if not as the common denominator at least as a fixed point of reference, since each member country is required to provide the necessary retabulations if its own balance-of-payments system does not conform to the standard. In this way, it helps make more revealing juxtapositions among them. However, retabulation to meet a form requirement is not necessarily an acceptable substitute for an original accounting system designed to produce the prescribed data.

Statistical systems

In the method of data collection, balance-of-payments systems vary considerably. Since in the free countries the people's contacts with the outside world include all conceivable transactions, legitimate and illegitimate, the collection and recording of the primary balance-of-payments data are formidable tasks. Indeed, no country has yet been able to achieve anything approaching completeness in this respect. The difficulty stems not only from the fact that the transactions may vary in number and character over the widest imaginable range for one country, but even more from the fact that each country differs to some degree from all others regarding institutional structure, legal requirements, public behavior, and business practices, making it extremely difficult to adopt standard methods and practices. Even if they were adopted, the results still might remain quite diversified and differentiated. This belief has been so strongly shared by all international financial organizations, including the IMF, that no international agreement or even recommendation regarding the reporting system and the sources for balance-of-payments data exists. Instead, the matter is left for each individual nation to decide for itself.

Reporting systems

In principle there are two different reporting systems for balance-of-payments data. One, the *American system,* is used by the United States, and the other, the *French system,* by the European countries (and is best described in French literature).

The American system is perhaps best characterized by the absence of a system in the strict sense of the term; it has no central source of information, and debit and credit entries of the same transaction or account are not made simultaneously or even based on the same data. For example, the import of merchandise is debited in the U.S. balance of payments on the basis of customs records, while data for the corresponding credit entry—payments for the imports—customs records are ignored, and the books of financial intermediaries such as banks and exchange brokers are substituted for them; the credit is thus entered quite independently from the debit and can differ from it not only in timing but also in amount.

The rationale for this method lies in the flexibility which it permits in utilizing a great variety of different sources for data, and thus it purportedly maximizes the coverage and completeness of the balance-of-payments statement. To put it differently, the American asymmetrical method does not strictly adhere to the simultaneous offsetting entries required by the double-entry principle. Both the magnitude and the timing of the two theoretically simultaneous entries may differ greatly in practice. Thus, this method is open

TABLE 21-3

International Monetary Fund Standard Balance-of-Payments Schedule

Reporting Country ______________________ *Period Covered* ______________________
Currency ____________ *Unit* ____________ *Exchange Rate: U.S.$* ______ *Per* ________

A. Current Transactions

Item	*Credit (Receipts)*	*Debit (Payments)*	*Net Credit (+) or Net Debit (−)*
1. Merchandise (1.1 plus 1.2)			
1.1 Exports and imports (both f.o.b.)			
1.2 Other			
2. Nonmonetary gold movement (net)			
3. Foreign travel			
4. Transportation (4.1 plus 4.2)			
4.1 Gross freight			
4.2 Other			
5. Insurance			
6. Investment income (6.1 through 6.3)			
6.1 Direct investment			
6.2 Other interest			
6.3 Other equity			
7. Government, not included elsewhere (7.1 plus 7.2)			
7.1 Military expenditures and surplus property			
7.2 Other			
8. Miscellaneous			
Total goods and services (1 through 8)			
9. Donations (9.1 through 9.4)			
9.1 Personal and institutional remittances			
9.2 Other private transfers			
9.3 Reparations			
9.4 Official grants			
10. Total current transactions (1 through 9)			
Errors and omissions (16 minus 10)			

B. Movement of Capital and Monetary Gold

Item	*Net Movement Increasing (+) or Decreasing (−)*		
	Assets	*Liabilities*	*Net Assets*
Private (excluding banking institutions)			
11. Long-term capital (11.1 through 11.6)			
11.1 Direct investment			
11.2 Portfolio securities: bonds			
11.3 Portfolio securities: shares			
11.4 Amortization			
11.5 Other contractual repayments			
11.6 Other			

TABLE 21-3 (Cont.)

12. Short-term capital (12.1 plus 12.2)
    - 12.1 Currency, deposits, government obligations
    - 12.2 Other

Official and banking institutions

13. Long-term capital (13.1 through 13.6)
    - 13.1 Official loans
    - 13.2 Bank loans
    - 13.3 Portfolio securities
    - 13.4 Amortization
    - 13.5 Other contractual repayments
    - 13.6 Other
14. Short-term capital (14.1 through 14.4)
    - 14.1 Payments and clearing agreements
    - 14.2 Liabilities to IMF and IBRD
    - 14.3 Other liabilities to official and banking institutions
    - 14.4 Other
15. Monetary gold
16. Total movement of capital and monetary gold (11 through 15)

for what might be called *internal disbalances* resulting from the differences in the data on which any particular pair of debit and credit entries are based. This weakness, it is argued, can be tolerated because scrutiny of many sources will maximize the balance-of-payments coverage and the internal disbalance, the errors-and-omissions post, is not an unreasonable price to pay for this.

The French system requires consistent adherence to the double-entry principle. It utilizes the same or closely related sources for any pair of balance-of-payments entries with the consequences that (a) any two posts are in fact identical sums or very nearly so, (b) the internal balance remains undisturbed, (c) time lags between entries are eliminated, and (d) the errors-and-omissions post in the balance of payments is minimized. The nerve center of this symmetrical system lies in the government's foreign exchange control authority usually together with the central bank of the country, which draws its basic data primarily from the financial records of governmental and semigovernmental agencies.

The system works best in countries which employ foreign exchange controls for which written applications have to be filed and exchange permits issued. These records provide an easy and near-perfect source for data on international transactions. One might argue, as some critics of the symmetrical system have, that the documents do not always reflect the true uses of the exchange, as the applicants may, at times, either deliberately or due to sudden changes in circumstances, divert the funds to an international transaction other than the one stated in the application form or the permit. Some of this no doubt does happen. But the deviations tend to stay within the limits of the same use category—the same subaccount—so that the balance-of-payments entries are hardly affected by them. Since most countries use some exchange control, the symmetrical French system is in much wider use than is generally realized.

An objection to the dependence upon foreign exchange records arises when a country has direct foreign investments and other international dealings where settlement may be effected by means other than foreign exchange. Obviously these transactions would not be reflected in the exchange control records, and compilation of supplementary data becomes necessary. A more serious difficulty arises when a country relaxes exchange controls or abandons them completely. The consistency and convenience of the control records are thereby lost, and dependence on multiple sources becomes unavoidable. It should be understood that neither of these difficulties derives from the system as such; they refer only to the sources of data. Although multiple sources are substituted for a single one, the principle of symmetrical entries can still be applied by basing both the debit and the credit entries for any particular transaction or account on the same source, although for another account a different source may be utilized.

22

The Balance-of-Payments Equilibrium

Equilibrium, as used here, refers to the relationship between a nation's international receipts and remittances during a given period. If the aggregate value of receipt-producing transactions coincides with the aggregate value of remittance-producing transactions, the two flows neutralize each other and the nation's financial position vis-à-vis other nations remains unchanged. This is the equilibrium position; all foreign purchases (goods, services, and securities) can be financed from the proceeds of foreign sales, and no excess of international receipts or remittances is created. Since the only mechanism necessary to carry out international payments is an efficient implementation of the clearinghouse principle, there will be no delays or other constraints retarding the receipt-remittance neutralization process. In theory, then, a country which is in the equilibrium position needs no gold or other international monetary reserves to finance its economic relations with the rest of the world; the relations are both self-generating and self-liquidating.

In practice, the receipt-remittance neutralization is not instantaneous, primarily because both flows comprise countless autonomous transactions which follow their individual and independent paths, and secondarily because the international clearing process takes time to work itself out, as the banking channels through which it flows are not entirely free from rigidities and restraints. Thus, no nation can in reality finance its international relations without monetary-exchange reserves. But in the equilibrium position its reserve requirements are limited to what is necessary to bridge leads and lags in the receipt and remittance patterns. The equilibrium reserves represent the country's "working-capital" requirements, which depend on its volume of international business and on the oscillations characteristic of that business.

If, however, the aggregate value of receipt-producing transactions differs from the aggregate value of remittance-producing transactions, the neutralization of one by the other can only be partial and there is a residue of either receipts or remittances. If the residue is in the receipts column, it is termed a *surplus* and constitutes a net addition to the nation's monetary-exchange reserve. If the residue is in the remittance column, it is called a *deficit,* which causes an equivalent net reduction of the monetary-exchange reserves of the country. In either case the nation's international equilibrium has been disturbed. The surplus signals a positive disequilibrium in that the nation's exchange reserves are growing, and the deficit signals a negative disequilibrium in that the exchange reserves are diminishing.

The surplus will be reflected first in the nation's foreign bank balances and holdings of liquid assets abroad, which will increase, or alternatively in the foreigner's balances in its own banks, which will decrease, and later in an inflow of gold, SDRs, or other accepted reserve assets to balance the surplus. Conversely, the deficit is first manifested in the decline of the nation's bank balances and liquid assets abroad or in the rise of foreign holdings in its own financial institutions, which will ultimately lead to the outflow of reserve assets to pay for the deficit.

Both surplus and deficit disequilibria in the balance of payments endanger the nation's international relations and may have a profound effect upon its domestic economy. Their arrest and adjustment pose highly complex problems to which no completely satisfactory solution has yet been discovered. The search for it will, no doubt, engender serious study and disagreement in the future, as it has in the past.

Measurement of Disequilibria

To compute the deficit or surplus in the balance of payments, *autonomous transactions*—those which take place for reasons of their own, such as exports, imports, investments, travel expenditures, etc.—must be distinguished from *induced transactions*—those which are carried out by the government for the purpose of correcting disequilibria or coping with the country's international financial position. The induced or settlement transactions consist mostly of sales and purchases of reserve assets (gold, foreign exchange, drawing rights, and so on).

In theory, then, the disequilibria are measured by the difference between the autonomous receipts and autonomous payments: the amount by which autonomous payments exceed autonomous receipts shows the size of the deficit, and in the reverse situation, the excess of autonomous receipts over autonomous payments shows the surplus. In practice the problem is not that simple. While the principle remains the same, neither the power nor the will exists always for a complete and correct separation of the autonomous transactions from the induced transactions. While there is little difficulty with such things as merchandise exports and imports, transfers of capital often defy any easy classification since the balance-of-payments authorities have no way of telling what their purposes were. Consequently, their classification cannot be based on factual record but must be left to "accepted accounting practices" and "professional judgement."[1]

Therefore, there is no absolutely correct or precise measure of a deficit or surplus. The actually reported figure is always affected to some degree by the judgment used in classifying capital transfers. And since such judgment is required the monetary authorities can deliberately increase or decrease the reported figure by juggling the questionable capital transfers to suit their political purposes. However, their latitude to do so is limited.

Liquidity balance

Traditionally the United States balance-of-payment accountants have used a method called the *liquidity balance*. Computed by this method a deficit includes a loss of official gold and foreign exchange reserves plus any rise of foreign holdings of short-term claims in the United States: bank deposits, treasury bills, marketable or convertible U.S. government obligations (even long-term bonds because of their ready marketability), bank acceptances, and similar short-term exchange instruments. All long-term capital transactions are excluded from the computation and viewed as settlement transactions. A surplus is measured by reversing the signs in the above formula.

A peculiar feature of the liquidity method is the treatment of short-term private capital transactions asymmetrically: changes in the U.S. liquid liabilities to private holders abroad are counted as part of the imbalance while the changes in private U.S. claims on foreigners are counted as reserve account transactions or settlement items. If, for example, an American company acquires one million Swiss francs in a European bank and in the same period incurs an indebtedness of $230,000 (equals one million francs) to another European bank, the first transaction is treated as an autonomous capital outflow increasing our deficit, but the second transaction is counted as an indirect or settlement transfer and is not included in the computation. Proponents of the method argue that this asymmetry is justified by the fact that all foreign holders of dollar assets, public and private, have a potential claim on the U.S. gold stock since the private holdings could be transferred to foreign central banks or other financial authorities to whom the U.S. is obligated to sell gold on demand. And for reverse reason, namely that private U.S. claims on foreigners are not readily available for U.S. government as reserve assets and cannot be used as such, they must be counted as part of the disequilibrium.

Because of its asymmetry, the liquidity method results in overstatement of the reported U.S. deficit, exaggeration of the threat to U.S. gold stock and other reserves, and understatement of its surpluses. It is an overly cautious

[1] For the United States the problem is further complicated by the fact that most foreign countries keep a certain amount of their monetary reserves in the dollar. When they make settlements these reserve dollars are shifted in and out of the country, showing up as international capital transfers on the United States balance of payment. Were they autonomous or induced transactions? Neither, so far as the United States is concerned.

method. Many foreign countries use the U.S. money market for holding working balances for financing their international business and diplomatic operations. Though varying in size, these balances are always needed and their becoming a claim against American reserve assets is less than likely.

Official reserve balance

Adopted first in the late 1960's, this new method of computing the balance-of-payments disequilibrium differs from the liquidity balance in that it treats private foreign claims, either long-term or short-term, as autonomous transactions, changes in which are included in the computations, and regards all transactions of monetary authorities as reserve account or adjustment entries. By treating American and foreign short-term capital alike it eliminates the asymmetry of the liquidity method and avoids its distorting effects. It should be noted however, that to make the distinction between official and private holdings of dollar instruments is not always easy. Central banks can and do influence the foreign exchange methods and holdings of private banks and business firms in such a way that the official balance is affected. The liquidity balance is immune to such policy-induced shifts.

A number of other techniques of computing the disequilibria have been proposed, but they have not been adopted by the monetary authorities. The United States now publishes both the liquidity balance and the official transactions balance figures regularly. Figure 22-1 shows how the two compare.

FIGURE 22-1

U.S. Balance of Payments Comparisons

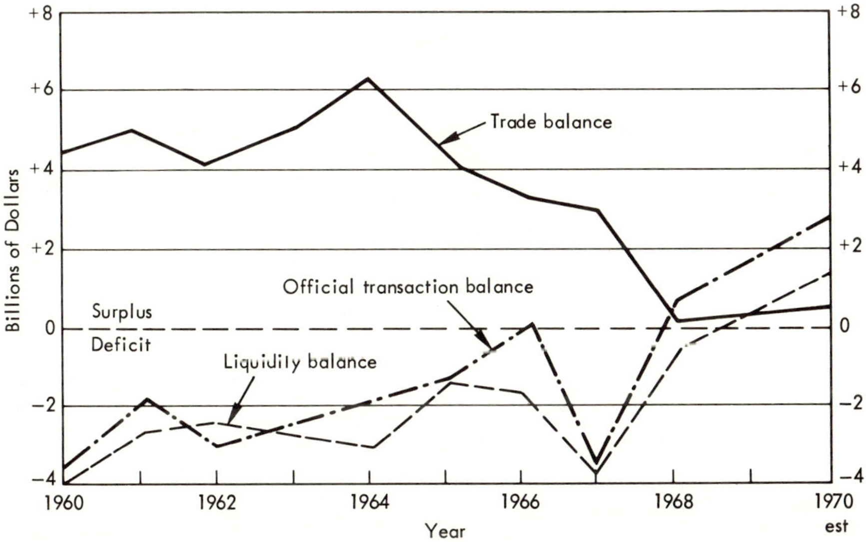

Source: U.S. Dept. of Commerce data

Equilibrium in Unmixed Systems

The basic approach to the equilibration problem depends on the international monetary system under which it is to be solved. As explained before, there are three basic schemes for international monetary relations: universal money (gold standard), the free-exchange market (paper standard), and exchange monopoly (regulated or disintegrated currencies). To cope with the mixed system that, in fact, exists in the contemporary world, it is necessary to understand fully how the adjustments are made under each of the conceptual schemes and then to untangle their combined effects under the mixed system.

Equilibrium under Universal Currency

The gold standard is the only universal currency which has been in actual use. In its pure form, the gold standard means that the value of national currencies is firmly anchored in gold through their respective mint parities and that exchange rates can move only between the gold export and gold import points. If the demand for a nation's currency exceeds the supply at the gold import point, gold will flow into the country, expanding the money supply, and, conversely, if the demand is insufficient to absorb the supply at the export point, gold will flow out of the country, contracting its money supply. How the adjustments of disequilibria will then take place is demonstrated in the following example.

Suppose that the following data apply to two countries, Alpha and Omega:

	Alpha	*Omega*
Currency unit	dollar	franc
Mint parity	600 milligrams	120 milligrams
Cost of transport	5 percent	5 percent
Parity rate of exchange	0.20	5.00
Comparative cost advantages	pens	stemware
Domestic prices:		
Pens	$2	Fr. 10
Stemware	$1	Fr. 5

Suppose further that the elasticities of supply and demand of both products are greater than one—a condition which always holds in practice for the aggregate exports and imports of a country but which may not hold for a single commodity—and that although both Alpha and Omega trade with third countries in a diversity of goods and services, trade relations with each other are confined to pens and stemware.

Negative disequilibrium

Assume now that a negative disequilibrium, a deficit, develops in Alpha's balance of payments because of insufficient exports to cover imports or because of the withdrawal of foreign investments from the country. What will be the consequences of the balance-of-payments deficit on the nation's economy under the gold standard?

PHASE I: 1. The exchange rate in Alpha will rise to the gold export point of 21 cents per franc (fewer francs per dollar) but no higher.

2. If the deficit still persists, importers in Alpha will start buying gold from their own government and deliver it in payment for their purchases in Omega. This will cost them 21 cents per franc (120 milligrams plus 5 percent shipping). The effective exchange rate thus cannot rise above 21 cents per franc.

3. The outflow of gold from Alpha will cause its money supply to contract, as its monetary authorities must maintain the parity relationship to the country's gold reserve at all times; the central bank rediscount rate will be raised, interest rates will go up, and credit conditions will tighten.

4. As the money supply shrinks while the factories and farms continue to produce at their normal rate, the relationship between the quantity of money and the output of goods and services must change; there are fewer dollars for the same volume of products. This means that the purchasing power of the dollar goes up in the domestic market and the prices of products go down. In brief, the deficit leads to deflation, but the process does not end with the downward adjustment of the price level.

PHASE II: Suppose the deficit-induced deflation hits particularly hard the two products being exchanged by Alpha and Omega and that the prices decline by 20 percent—pens from $2.00 to $1.60 and stemware from $1.00 to $0.80. What will this do to the balance of payments?

5. For pen exports, the price in Alpha is $1.60 and the price in Omega is Fr. 10 as before; exchanged at parity the foreign price produces a per-unit revenue of $2.00 and thus an excess profit of $0.40 less transportation costs. Hence pen exports will zoom.

6. But what about stemware imports? Since prices in Omega have not changed, the purchase cost for Alpha is still the same as it was in the original equilibrium position—20 percent below the domestic retail price of Fr. 5 per unit or Fr. 4 net. In dollar equivalents the cost of imports would thus be $0.80 per unit, which is identical with the average selling price in Alpha and leaves no room for transportation costs and other import expenses. The result is that imports of stemware decline sharply and continue only where nonprice factors, such as some consumers' strong preference for the imported product, provide grounds for price differentiation or for some business houses to absorb the loss as a matter of institutional prestige.

7. The cutback of imports then will cause a corresponding decline in the country's international remittances, i.e., outflow of gold, at the same time the

boom in pen exports (see point 5 above) is building up franc receipts and inducing an inflow of gold from abroad. Consequently, the balance-of-payments deficit has produced its own antidote by adjusting the domestic price level downward. This adjustment makes the country's products cheaper for foreigners to buy and thereby strengthens its international competitive position and, simultaneously, makes foreign products more expensive to domestic consumers, thus decreasing imports. This process continues until the outflow of gold is reversed and the international equilibrium restored.

Positive disequilibrium

If a surplus develops in the balance of payments the price-specie-flow mechanism will reverse the processes described in the deficit adjustment. Referring again to the Alpha and Omega data, this is what would happen.

PHASE I: 1. The exchange rate will go down to the gold export point of $0.19 per franc but no lower.

2. Gold will start flowing in from abroad.

3. The money supply will expand, the central bank will lower discount rates, and the interest rate on credit will go down.

4. The purchasing power of the dollar will decrease as price inflation sets in.

PHASE II: Suppose the surplus-induced inflation leads to a price hike of 20 percent. What will this mean in terms of the international receipt-remittance relationship?

5. Pen exports will drop or cease entirely, as the domestic price is now $2.40 and that in Omega the equivalent of only $2.00. The cutback of exports will be mirrored in the earnings of the franc.

6. Stemware imports will skyrocket because they not only bring in more profit per unit than before but also command a higher price than that in Omega's domestic market. Alpha's domestic payments increase in proportion to its imports from Omega; gold starts flowing out, and a contraction of the money supply follows.

7. Again, the disequilibrium has provided its own remedy. The upward adjustment of the domestic price level has arrested the excess inflow of gold by making Alpha's exports more expensive abroad and expanding its import markets, thus draining off the surplus and establishing a new equilibrium.

Criticism

The gold standard has been criticized by some economists on the grounds that the price-specie-flow mechanism failed to bring about the needed adjustments in the 1920's and that this failure led to the abandonment of the gold standard when the Great Depression paralyzed the world economy. This criticism confuses historical facts with theoretical causation and as such has never been satisfactorily substantiated. The disequilibria that existed in the 1920's were attributable to the colossal dislocations and shifts of power which

World War I had produced in the world economy. The maps of three major continents—Europe, Asia, and Africa—had been completely redrawn; the industrial capacity of continental Europe had suffered severely and that of the United States had enlarged immensely; Russia, with its gigantic Eurasian land mass, had been isolated from the rest of the world through the Bolshevik Revolution; the Austro-Hungarian empire had collapsed; and numerous other changes had taken place, each of which alone was capable of seriously threatening the international equilibrium. In combination their force was devastating. Moreover, during the war years, trade relations had been disrupted and the gold standard had been put into "storage" to await the return of normalcy. That day never came. When an attempt was made to reinstitute the gold standard in the 1920's, the basic dislocations and disintegration of international trade relations had eroded the structure of the world monetary system, and it was facing inevitable collapse.

Adjustment under Market-Integrated Currencies (Floating Rates)

With marked integrated currencies, the exchange rates depend entirely upon the supply-demand relationships on the foreign exchange market. Currencies are freely convertible, and the market is free from governmental intervention. Since there is no common denominator, such as gold, for the different currencies, disturbances in a nation's balance of payments cannot affect its domestic monetary reserves or bring about any changes in the internal money supply. However, the appreciation and depreciation of its currency on the exchange market alter the relative relationships between domestic and foreign prices and costs, and it is these relationships which integrate the country's economy with that of the rest of the world.

How are disequilibria in the balance of payments adjusted under such a system? Consider two countries Alpha and Omega again, but assume that both have converted to the paper standard and are operating without artificial exchange controls. Assume further that the prevailing cost and price situation is the same as described earlier, i.e., the exchange rate is $0.20 per franc, Alpha is exporting pens at a price of $2 or Fr. 10 per unit, and Omega is paying for them by exporting stemware at Fr. 5 or $1 per unit; the two countries' balances of payments are in equilibrium. Also, the higher-than-one elasticity assumption is retained.

Suppose now that Alpha's payments position deteriorates and a deficit develops in its balance of payments. The supply of dollars in the form of drafts, bills, etc., exceeds the demand for them on the international money market, and the franc-dollar rate of exchange rises to $0.30 as the currency depreciates. What will the consequences be?

1. Exports of pens will become more profitable as the Fr. 10 price at the new exchange rates will convert into $3, yielding an excess profit per unit of $1 over the equilibrium profits (which were included in the domestic $2 price); as a consequence, pen exports will increase.

2. Imports of stemware will decline because the Omegan price is still

Fr. 5, which at the new rate requires a $1.50 outlay per unit, i.e., $0.50 more than before. Only where the demand for Omegan glasses is inelastic in Alpha can imports continue at all.

3. Supply of franc exchange goes up, since the increasing exports produce increasingly more franc holdings to residents of Alpha. This puts pressure on the existing exchange rate, because some holders of franc claims, not finding ready markets for them, will start settling for a lower rate, i.e., accept less than $0.30 per franc.

4. Demand for franc exchange declines in response to the drop in stemware imports. This intensifies the pressure on the exchange rate, as fewer buyers are willing to pay $0.30 per franc.

5. The exchange rate will start moving down again due to the pressures of both supply and demand. This will continue until the deficit in the balance of payments is eliminated and a new equilibrium position is reached.

If a surplus develops in the balance of payments, the reverse consequences result; as Alpha's currency appreciates, its exports become more expensive for foreigners and its imports become cheaper for its own residents, hence:

1. Exports decrease—fewer Omegans can afford Alphan pens.
2. Imports rise—stemware is less expensive for Alphans.
3. The supply of franc exchange goes down.
4. The demand for franc exchange goes up.
5. The exchange rate rises, since fewer francs can be bought for a dollar on the exchange market. This continues until the disequilibrium disappears from the balance of payments.

As these illustrations show, a free international exchange market can automatically adjust balance-of-payments disequilibria under convertible paper-standard currencies; the equilibration is a self-generating process. However, emphasis here is on the word *free.* If the exchange rates are not permitted to float in response to disequilibria, the adjustment process will not be initiated or completed and the system will fail. In practice, the exchange rates have never been permitted to perform their equilibration function on a multilateral basis without governmental interference. In all attempts to use this system, government interference in various forms has counteracted the corrective adjustments. The objections to free rates originate from the fears (a) that the supply and demand of exchange in the short run will not balance because of various lags, such as seasonal ones, which will make the rates fluctuate more than is desirable; (b) that under conditions of uncertainty exchange speculation may appear and further exaggerate the fluctuations, destabilizing international financial relations; (c) that incessant variations in rates would complicate cost calculations and profit planning for export and import concerns and tend to disrupt or depress international trade; and (d) that depreciation of the currency would affect domestic prices and spark an inflation. All these are possible dangers, but they are not different from similar dangers from other sources; since the system of a free-exchange market with unregulated rates has never been given a fair test by the major trading nations of the world, the criticisms must be tempered with the observation that exaggeration of the dangers may well be greater than the standard textbooks admit.

Equilibration under Exchange Monopoly

The central idea in the third alternative—exchange monopoly—for dealing with balance-of-payments disequilibria is to replace the free-exchange market with a complete government monopoly, which as the reader will recall will fix the exchange rate, pool all international receipts, and ration the use of exchange. The currencies are rendered inconvertible, and the country's internal business affairs insulated against any foreign influence.

Under this system any negative disequilibrium in the balance of payments, even a large deficit, can be suppressed by restricting the volume of exchange made available by the government for import purchases, direct investments, and other foreign expenditures. A surplus, if one should occur, is easily eliminated simply by relaxing the exchange restrictions and permitting greater expenditures abroad. In practice, a balance-of-payments surplus is almost a self-contradiction under exchange control in a noncommunist country, because the basic reason for the implementation of the control is to protect the exchange rate against market influences which would force it up, that is, to protect the currency from depreciating and to restrict what is considered by authorities to be excessive or unnecessary imports. By so doing, exports, too, are restricted to the extent to which the exchange rate is overvalued and the purchasing-power parity is distorted.

Consequently, the exchange monopoly tends to equilibrate international payments primarily by restriction—curtailing imports and foreign investments by direct action and holding down exports indirectly through an artificially low exchange rate. That the total trade and investments of the country under such conditions must be smaller than in the absence of the monopoly is obvious. And, although the restriction balances "the books" of the nation, it does not remove the underlying disbalance between domestic and foreign prices and costs. If anything, the disbalance between internal and external prices tends to increase rather than decrease under prolonged restriction.

Income Effects

Changes in national income tend to induce variations in the volume of imports, exports, and to some degree also in foreign investments. When income rises at home, imports increase since people have more money to spend for them; when incomes rise abroad exports (imports to foreigners) are stimulated. Consequently, a balance-of-payments deficit can be reduced or sometimes even eliminated by either an increase of foreign income or a decrease of domestic income or by a combination of the two, as prices, exchange rates, and exchange controls remain unchanged. Similarly, a surplus can be adjusted as a result of an increase in domestic income or decrease of foreign income.

Under stable economic conditions income effects are small and do not seriously interfere with the adjustment processes discussed before. However, when income either at home or abroad is subject to rapid changes, its effects either reinforce or counteract the normal adjustment processes, and as such, play an important role in international monetary policy.

How great the income effect on the balance of payments is in any particular country depends on the *propensity to import* which is defined as the ratio of imports to the national income and can be expressed in terms of average or marginal propensities. A slightly different measure of the effect is the *income elasticity of demand for imports* which is computed by dividing the percent change in imports by the percent change in income.

While changes in national income affect the balance of payments, changes in the balance of payments affect the national income. It is a mutual dependency. National income is conceived in real terms as the aggregate production of goods and services by the national economy, or in money terms as the aggregate expenditure on this production. For our purposes the national money income is the more useful one.

Where do exports and imports belong in reference to national income? Exports are part of national income since they represent goods and services produced by the national economy; but imports are not, for they have been produced elsewhere. Demand for exports originates abroad and is, therefore, independent from domestic income; demand for imports originates at home and is related to domestic income (propensity to import). Since exports add nothing to domestic consumption expenditure, their effect is to increase the stream of income from the sales of goods and services very much like the effect of domestic investments. Imports, on the other hand, represent a leakage from the domestic income-expenditure flow, similar to that of savings, as moneys spent on imports do not reenter the national income stream.

These relationships cause all three factors, national income, exports, and imports, to move in the same direction, though not at equal rates. A change in one can trigger corresponding changes in the others. Theoreticians used to perceive exports to be the primary variable. Their reasoning went like this: if exports increase, national income will increase also as more goods and services must be produced to supply the increase in exports; the resultant increase in national income will cause imports also to rise due to income elasticity of imports. Conversely, a decrease in exports would result in a cutback in the aggregate domestic production or national income, and the decrease in income will transpose a shrinkage on imports.

Empirical evidence does not support the theoreticians' belief that changes in exports have primacy over the changes in the other two variables. It is more realistic to say that, at least in large countries such as the United States, the variations in the national income are the important or least responsive of the three factors. This is so because the size and growth of the national income is subject to many other influences besides the balance-of-payments position of the nation. Due to other influences, the national income may remain irresponsive or underresponsive to changes in exports and imports for extended periods. Therefore, the balance-of-payments adjustment through income changes, though potentially powerful, is unreliable and rarely complete. The income swings may be too small to fully counteract a deficit or surplus or it may be large and persistent, causing a disbalance in the opposite side. The income swings represent, so to speak, a shifting of the coordinates for the other payments-adjustment mechanisms which must be taken into account but they are not a solution to payments disequilibria as such.

Adjustments by exchange-rate manipulation

Devaluation and Revaluation. In order to overcome the economic disbalance which the imposed balancing of accounts cannot remedy, the exchange monopoly may devalue the currency by raising the exchange rate. This stimulates exports as the external prices of the nation's goods and services are reduced correspondingly; a unit of foreign currency will exchange for a greater amount of domestic currency and thus buy a larger quantity of goods for export, and imports will be retarded for the reverse reason. How strong these effects will be depends on the degree of devaluation, especially on whether the reduced rate eliminates completely the disparity in purchasing power which existed before, and also on the elasticities of supply and demand for foreign exchange.

In theory, the country could depreciate its currency drastically and generate the degree of export stimulus which it desires. In practice, any significant underevaluation of currency can be undertaken only in a grave crisis, or other countries are likely to retaliate by devaluating their own currencies, neutralizing the export-stimulation and import-retardation effects for all or setting off a rate war from which no country would benefit. If devaluation were adopted as a policy of the monetary authority and periodic adjustments in the exchange rate were made, speculation in anticipation of these devaluations would become a serious destabilizer in the international financial market. Any devaluation, even a relatively small percentage, abruptly changes relationships of internal and external prices and creates windfall profits for exporters and other holders of foreign exchange assets and penalizes importers, investors, and other debtors who have foreign currency obligations outstanding at the time of the devaluation. Politically, too, devaluation may bring undesirable repercussions, as the general public is likely to interpret it as a sign of serious trouble which the government may find difficult to explain.

Revaluation is the downward adjustment of the exchange rate to appreciate an undervalued currency. Its effects are the opposite of those of devaluation. In practice, revaluation is rare. A balance-of-payments surplus, which it implies, is unlikely to occur under a controlled currency, as explained before, and, if it should occur, the strong reserve position is consistent with the usual governmental objective to achieve a favorable balance of trade regardless of theoretical considerations; consequently, there is no serious internal pressure to revalue the currency. Only the 1971 monetary cataclysm can be credited with a number of sizable revaluations. Before that there had been but three token revaluations undertaken to pacify foreign critics, particularly the United States and the United Kingdom, which were suffering serious balance-of-payments deficits at a time when Germany and the Netherlands were accumulating surpluses.

MULTIPLE EXCHANGE RATES. An exchange monopoly must, by definition, be discriminatory by market standards, as it allocates the exchanges by methods other than free choice made by the public under competition. The discrimination affects both products and currencies, as described in Chapter 19.

The discriminatory powers of the exchange monopoly can be magnified by the use of multiple exchange rates—fixing different rates for different purposes. For example, a low selling rate (less domestic money per foreign unit) is set for imports of goods and services classified as necessities. A medium rate is set for essentials, and a high rate for luxuries. Analogously, a high purchase rate (more domestic money per foreign unit) for exchange instruments is earned by exporters of commodities the authorities want exported, and progressively descending rates are earned for other commodities. Consequently, certain imports and exports are subsidized while others are taxed, and still others are unaffected by the multiple-exchange-rate structure. From an equilibration standpoint, the adoption of a multiple-exchange-rate system or the expansion of the range between the lowest and the highest rates in an existing system is tantamount to a partial devaluation; the export-stimulating effect of the devaluation action is felt only by those whose products are given preferential classification, and the import-retarding effect is concentrated only on products which are classified as less essential or which originate from countries whose currencies are discriminated against.

The principal justification for multiple rates is that they allow a deficit country to conserve exchange for essential imports and to limit other foreign expenditures on a selective basis without the large bureaucratic apparatus which direct quantitative controls of imports and exports would require. At times, they have been employed not for balance-of-payments purposes but to open up new export markets, to exert competitive pressure on a particular foreign industry, or to avoid taking the necessary but politically unpopular economic measures, such as checking domestic inflation, which undermine the purchasing power of the currency and cause its overvaluation at a fixed exchange rate.

The most serious criticisms of the multiple rates are (a) that by restricting imports they conceal the basic disbalance in the country's international financial position; (b) that by reducing export profits through unrealistic rates, the major motive for export expansion is eliminated for large segments of the economy; and (c) that by helping to balance the nation's international accounts through such restrictive measures they contribute to chronic disequilibrium.[1]

[1] Indirect adjustments in the balance of payments may be induced by changes in national income which tend to affect flows of exports and imports.

Equilibrium under the Contemporary Mixed System

None of the three theoretical concepts singly can explain the processes by which balance-of-payments disequilibria can be adjusted under the contemporary international monetary system, since, being a mixture, the IMF system does not fit any of the theoretical models.[2] The mixture incorporates certain features from all three and combines them with diverse philosophical views as to what objectives an international monetary arrangement should have and what is correct conduct for its individual members. From an economic standpoint the essential characteristics of the mixture are these:

(1) The system rests on a modified gold standard but discourages the use of gold for settling international accounts except as a last resort.

(2) Superimposed on the gold standard is the key-currency concept which makes the U.S. dollar the primary international medium of exchange. Reserve-account assets may be held in the dollar and IMF drawing rights in lieu of gold. More recently, the key-currency idea has been broadened to include several secondary key currencies, any of which can serve as a general means of exchange, thus increasing the legal base for international liquidity. The German mark, the Japanese yen, the British pound, the French franc, the Swiss franc, and, in its own zone, the Portuguese escudo, have acquired some secondary key-currency stature. But it has been difficult to use them because international banking practices have been geared to the dollar.

(3) Exchange rates are fixed by administrative action, and all countries are bound to employ exchange-control methods to maintain rates within the official IMF band around the central parity.

(4) International payments as well as the settlement of national balances are made through the mechanisms and processes of the foreign exchange market, in spite of the fact that rates can move in restricted bands.

(5) The IMF provides clearing facilities for countries with inconvertible, i.e., chronically overvalued, currencies.

(6) The IMF has resources to augment temporarily a country's exchange reserves and to help it out of a deficit position under specified conditions.

Hence, from a theoretical standpoint the system is a peculiar composite. It is based on gold but relies primarily on key currencies and drawing rights and tries to minimize gold movements; it fixes rates administratively but tries to utilize the free-exchange market as the primary balancing mechanism; and it tolerates both convertible and inconvertible currencies at the same time. Like so many other international compromises, the IMF system, which was supposed to become a horse, turned out a three-humped camel. Yet, many believe that with all its imperfections and inconsistencies it has provided a better monetary arrangement than any of the theoretical models; as indicated in Chapter 23, opinions on this are no less mixed than the system itself.

[2] A complete description of the IMF system appears in chapter 23.

Analytically, such a system defies treatment as a whole; it requires piecemeal analysis tailored to any particular set of facts. The respective roles of various component parts borrowed from the different models must first be identified and isolated and then their interactions must be studied in a given situation, for the fruitful techniques will sometimes follow and sometimes contravene a given principle. As the situation changes, the relative roles and with them the appropriate techniques may change too, and the process has to be started again. No formula, therefore, can be derived for the adjustments process in this mixture of different principles, compromises among conflicting opinions and interests, empirical precedents, and *ad hoc* arrangements. Instead, one must choose from all possible combinations of the three analytical formulations the appropriate remedies for a particular disequilibrium. That this is not an easy job is amply evidenced by the fact that a number of balance-of-payments deficits, including those of the United States, Great Britain, and many subindustrial countries, have belied the advice of scores of economists and countermanded governmental promises and proclamations year after year to the dismay of both experts and politicians.

As a practical matter, the difficulties arise in two different stages: the diagnosis and the prognosis. In the diagnosis, disagreement rages over the specific causes of a particular deficit. This disagreement gains scope and vigor the larger the size and industrial diversity of a country. In the prognosis stage, the search for correctives can succeed only if the real causes are known and understood. Uncertainty and misinterpretations provide no basis for rational remedial action. But even when the causes are well understood, the choice of correctives may, and often does, remain a difficult decision. Predictability under any mixed system is quite low, and in the current monetary system it is further lowered by the fact that any projections are subject to subsequent administrative influences from many sources.

Thus there are no clear-cut solutions and no proven formulas for correcting balance-of-payments disequilibria under the contemporary mixed system, although many people believe that they have the alchemical secret which will cure the problem with a simple prescription. The fact is that the various national business systems have become managed economies to a much higher degree than most people realize or wish to admit. Administrative action and political expediency often play a role equal to, if not greater than, that of the market mechanism. And, if the external monetary discipline imposed through the competitive processes of the market—objective and impartial as it is—should counteract domestic economic aspirations, the latter will prevail; or so it seems from recent experience. It remains to be seen whether the arbitrary subordination of international financial soundness to domestic policy constraints can stand the pressures which chronic disbalances will amass in the long run.

The Critical Variables

Capital Flows. The world's capacity to save and to generate liquid assets —money and near money—has increased immensely in recent years. The population explosion; economic growth; and the drive to convert backward areas from their destitute agrarian existence, where barter and local self-sufficiency dominate, to industrial societies with money-based business systems have been the main contributors to the world's money supply. To be sure, the rate of increase has not been uniform. Some countries remain on the threshold of industrial civilization; others have entered it to different degrees. However, the reliance on money and credit and, with it, the internal money flows have increased without exception throughout the world.

Monetary assets are the most volatile and the most sensitive to differentials in comparative advantage. They are especially responsive to differentials in interest rates and in the safety of the principal.[3] Since both interest rates and the safety factor vary constantly from country to country, they produce international movements of capital which are not connected with trade or long-term investment transactions but which seek to maximize the short-run interest return or to escape a domestic disturbance which might endanger the safety or purchasing power of the internal currency. Often, one cannot tell from the international transfer transactions whether the capital is to stay in the country of destination for a short or a long time. Indeed, in many cases the owners themselves cannot predict with any degree of accuracy what their next moves will be; these depend on future events which may change their comparative-advantage position.

In balance-of-payments accounting, all transactions without fixed maturities in excess of one year are lumped into the short-term capital account. Hence, it is this account which has become the most unpredictable and unmanageable. Theoretical economics assumes that most short-term capital movements or for that matter any capital movements are induced by import and export transactions, which in turn may be subject to income or price effects but which for purposes of the theory are the pivotal activities in international financial relations. As stated before, this assumption does not correspond with the present reality. Thus, the theoretical concepts cannot help us deal with problems such as capital flows in search of higher interest or of security.

Some economists label the short-term capital flows speculative and convey the impression that they are somehow illicit or immoral. This is absurd, for it is the central edict of economics that the factors of production seek to maximize their returns. It is up to the economics profession to forge ahead and to develop new and more adequate theoretical concepts rather than to cry default where events outrun the traditional notions of international economy. Speculation is responsible for a part of international capital movements, as it is for part of internal capital movements and for part of any other business activity. This is only normal and unavoidable. But the great bulk of the transfers are made not by Arabian oil sheiks or other scheming tycoons, but by multinational companies who seek to place their liquid holdings in currencies which yield the best interest or avoid unacceptable risks of devaluation.

[3] Auxiliary reasons for autonomous capital flows include these: more easily obtained bank credit in the United States, expectations that the dollar will be devalued or some other currency revalued, and extension of credit to foreign affiliates by multinational companies.

Another factor influencing capital movements is the liquidity preference of different countries. For relatively obscure psychological reasons, the public's valuation of liquid holdings vis-à-vis other assets varies greatly from country to country and also from time to time in the same country. Where or when the liquidity preference is high, it builds up the nation's liquid holdings and thus adds to the pool from which international capital flows. A low liquidity preference, on the other hand, acts as a stabilizer of the short-term capital account.

INVESTMENT FLOWS. Although much that goes into the short-term capital account may actually be an investment, the two are distinguishable in that liquid assets move in response to interest differentials while investment capital moves in response to profit differentials. There is also a difference in timing; liquid assets respond to present interest returns and investments to anticipated profit possibilities.

Investment flows, too, have become a critical factor in the contemporary balance-of-payments analysis. The reasons for this are associated with those for the short-term capital flows. The most important among them has been the drive for industrialization and general economic growth throughout the world. These factors have multiplied investment needs and opportunities on technological, industrial, and international planes. The rise of the multinational company, international economic integration, and generally greater knowledge of foreign areas—due mostly to improvements in communication—all have contributed to more rational and broader approaches to international business enterprise than the traditional export-import doctrine could have accommodated.

The global alternatives for investments, coupled with a rapid rise in entrepreneurial knowledge, evaluating, and cultivation of the best of these alternatives, contrast sharply with the traditional notion of regional and national spheres of investment alternatives. As a result, international investments have multiplied in number and in volume. This trend, again, is in complete accord with the return-and-productivity-maximization edict of economic theory. Yet, like the short-term capital movements, the international investment flows have incited traditionalists to devote their energies to schemes to stop the investments through punitive taxation and outright prohibition. How such attempts could succeed is difficult to conceive. It is like trying to stop a river; if one bed is blocked, it will make itself another and keep flowing. Even the restoration of exchange rationing could at best halt the investment trend temporarily; nothing is likely to stop it, not to mention reversing it, as long as the rights of capital and enterprise to seek more efficient and remunerating employment are recognized.

The continuing swell of international investments has raised serious questions about the adequacy of international economic theory and underscored the desperate need for a broader and more flexible frame of reference. Regrettably, there are no indications that any breakthrough on the theory front is in the making. All recent work has focused mainly on technical detail and has been almost completely backward looking as far as conceptual approaches to international problems have been concerned. It would seem that nothing less than a major breakthrough could bridge the presently widening gap between theory and contemporary international reality.

Until the now-confining frontiers of the theory are thrust outward, business administration will have to provide an increasing share of the diagnostic tools and the prognostic criteria for the equilibration and management of international financial relations. As in other areas of administration, greater reliance will have to be placed on the relatively young but rapidly growing family of administrative sciences, including simulation, operations research, mathematical models, and other quantitative techniques.

Foreign Aid. A third disbalancing factor peculiar to the contemporary international monetary system is the large-scale flow of donations, primarily foreign aid, for which no payment is received or contemplated. Many long-term, intergovernmental, low-interest-rate loans, which are loans in name only, also belong to this category from a financial standpoint. Based almost entirely upon political rather than business or economic motivation, unilateral aid transfers cause both disbalance and instability. They also distort the normal trade and payments patterns by artificially increasing trade flows to areas receiving aid, financing industries making those products on which the aid funds are spent, and simultaneously placing the non-aid-receiving countries in a relatively weaker position. The corruption and inefficiency which the aid operations have engendered are now public knowledge, and it is reasonable to hope that in the future aid transactions will shift closer to normal business transactions and their administration will be placed on a long-term basis. Both these changes would help to minimize the negative effects of aid on the balance-of-payments equilibria.

U.S. payments deficit

Increasing dissatisfaction has been voiced over the prolonged deficit in the U.S. balance of payments and its effect on world financial relations. The critics' arguments are elaborated in chapter 23.

The easy-money policy, they argue, more than compensates for its international defects by boosting new investment, industrial expansion, and employment within the country. If internal growth withered, which might happen if monetary policies were tightened, the resultant recession might cause a much greater international disturbance because of the relative size of the U.S. economy than the excess liquidity does now.

Both the critics and the respondents have their points, and the dialogue is certain to continue. Hopefully, it will be centered more on facts, logic, and reason than prejudice and chauvinistic pride, which so far have tinted the debate with unconstructive emotionalism and rigidities of views.

23

The Contemporary International Monetary System

For nearly three decades international financial relations have been based on a compromise arrangement worked out in the early 1940's in a series of meetings and consultations by governmental experts of different countries. The plan was completed at a conference in Bretton Woods, New Hampshire, in July 1944, to which 44 nations had been invited. By the end of the next year, 30 nations had formally signed and ratified the Bretton Woods Agreement, and it became the controlling instrument of international financial relations.

The agreement created two institutional entities, both supranational in character: the International Monetary Fund (IMF) and the International Bank for Reconstruction and Development, usually called the World Bank. The IMF regulates and coordinates overall international financial relations; the World Bank serves specific credit needs relating to postwar reconstruction and to economic development of financially weak areas. For the purposes of this chapter, the bank has no direct relevance; it will be discussed later in connection with developing countries and foreign investments.

The Nixon administration's startling decision to suspend gold payments against the dollar in August 1971 signified that a turning point had been reached and that a general revision of the world monetary system is in the offing, however, events to this writing indicate that any forthcoming changes will be limited to a greater or lesser reform of the Bretton Woods plan but not any new system altogether.

Original Design of the IMF System

The basic characteristics of the Fund may be divided into two broad groups: the legal aspects, including its organizational structure and constitutionally defined powers, and the functional aspects, embracing its objectives, policies, and operations. Since an understanding of the legal aspects is imperative for a realistic interpretation of the functional aspects, they are presented first.

Legal Aspects

QUOTAS. Membership in the Fund is open to all nations. The member countries number 118. To qualify, an applicant nation must pay a subscription quota based on its national income, monetary reserves (gold and foreign exchange holdings), foreign trade and payments patterns, and general economic conditions. At least 25 percent of the quota or 10 percent of the country's net holdings of gold and U.S. dollars, whichever is less, must be paid before the membership becomes effective; the payment must be in gold.[1] The balance of the subscription is payable in the member's own currency under a schedule agreed upon by the Fund and the member. Every five years the quotas and unpaid balances on subscriptions are reviewed and may be adjusted if conditions warrant. Several upward revisions have been made. Table 22-1 lists the quotas as of April 1971 for the entire membership.

VOTING. The voting power of a member country is related to its subscription. At the time of entry, each member acquires 250 votes plus one additional vote for each $100,000 in its quota; e.g., a quota of $45 million gives 450 additional votes or a total voting strength of 600.[2] As in many other organizations, the matters and issues to be voted upon are ranked and different requirements for passage apply, ranging from a simple plurality to a four-fifths majority and, for some matters, unanimity.

ORGANS. The voting powers are exercised through the Board of Governors, to which each member nation appoints one of its officials and an alternate. Besides the Board, the IMF organizational structure includes 18 executive directors, of whom five are appointed by the largest subscribers—the United States, the United Kingdom, West Germany, France, and India—and the others are elected by the governors. Their function is to oversee the general operations of the Fund on a continuous basis and to select the managing director, who serves as the chief operating executive responsible for the implementation of the policies and decisions of the organization and for the selection,

[1] In a few instances involving newly created nations without any appreciable financial means, this requirement has been waived temporarily.

[2] The voting power decreases when the country draws support from the IMF financial reserves.

development, and supervision of its professional and clerical staff. All transactions and official contacts of the IMF are limited to those with governmental authorities, primarily ministries of finance, central banks, stabilization funds, and other national agencies.

TABLE 23-1

IMF Subscription Quotas in Effect 1972
(million U.S. dollars)

Afghanistan	37	Guatemala	36	Niger	13
Algeria	130	Guinea	24	Nigeria	135
Argentina	440	Guyana	20	Norway	240
Australia	665	Haiti	19	Pakistan	235
Austria	175	Honduras	25	Panama	36
Barbados	13	Iceland	23	Paraguay	19
Belgium	650	India	940	Peru	123
Bolivia	37	Indonesia	260	Philippines	155
Botswana	5	Iran	192	Portugal	75
Brazil	440	Iraq	109	Rwanda	19
Burma	60	Ireland	121	Saudi Arabia	90
Burundi	19	Israel	130	Senegal	34
Cambodia	25	Italy	1000	Sierra Leone	25
Cameroon	35	Ivory Coast	52	Singapore	30
Canada	1100	Jamaica	53	Somalia	19
Central African Rep.	13	Japan	1200	South Africa	200
Ceylon	98	Jordan	23	Southern Yemen	29
Chad	13	Kenya	48	Spain	395
Chile	158	Korea	50	Sudan	72
China	550	Kuwait	65	Swaziland	8
Colombia	157	Laos	13	Sweden	325
Congo (Brazzaville)	13	Lebanon	9	Syrian Arab Rep.	50
Congo, Dem. Rep. of	113	Lesotho	5	Tanzania	42
Costa Rica	32	Liberia	29	Thailand	134
Cyprus	26	Libyan Arab Rep.	24	Togo	15
Dahomey	13	Luxembourg	19	Trinidad and Tobago	63
Denmark	260	Malagasy Republic	26	Tunisia	35
Dominican Rep.	43	Malawi	15	Turkey	151
Ecuador	33	Malaysia	186	Uganda	40
El Salvador	35	Mali	22	United Arab Rep.	188
Ethiopia	27	Malta	16	United Kingdom	2800
Equatorial Guinea	8	Mauritania	13	United States	6700
Finland	190	Mauritius	22	Upper Volta	13
France	1500	Mexico	370	Uruguay	69
Gabon	15	Morocco	113	Venezuela	330
Gambia, The	7	Nepal	10	Vietnam	62
Germany, Fed. Rep. of	1600	Netherlands	700	Yemen Arab Rep.	10
Ghana	87	New Zealand	202	Yugoslavia	207
Greece	138	Nicaragua	27	Zambia	76

Functional Aspects

OBJECTIVES. The principal purposes of the IMF, as defined in the Bretton Woods Agreement which created it, are these:

—promotion of exchange-rate stability
—maintenance of orderly exchange arrangements
—avoidance of competitive currency depreciation
—establishment of a multilateral system of payments and the elimination of exchange restrictions
—creation of a stand-by source of exchange reserves available to individual countries in case of maladjustments in international payments

The emphasis upon stability, orderliness, and multilateralism reflects the two basic concerns at the time of the Bretton Woods Conference: the general financial instability, disorder, and discriminatory bilateral payments relations which had prevailed in the immediate prewar years; and the major economic depression accompanied by chaotic international relations that was anticipated soon after the war. In retrospect, both of these appear to have been given exaggerated weight in the Articles of Agreement, with the result that rigidity rather than flexibility later became the weakness of the system.

EXCHANGE RATES. The IMF uses a mixed exchange standard which incorporates certain features of all three theoretical systems: the gold standard, the paper standard, and the exchange monopoly. At the time of admission, a country's currency is assigned a par value based on its rate of exchange in U.S. dollars at that time. The dollar par is in turn converted into a gold par on the ratio of $35 per ounce of pure gold ($38 per ounce after 1971 dollar devaluation) and is expressed in the metric system. Thus, regardless of whether a particular currency has any legal gold cover internally, it is given a gold parity by the IMF. And, as pointed out before, either dollars or gold must be used to pay a portion of the country's subscription quota. Table 22-2 presents the monetary units of selected countries, showing both their gold and dollar parities in the original system.

Like the gold standard, the IMF plan is predicated upon exchange-rate stability. In place of the gold points, the rules of the agreement prescribe that exchange rate fluctuations be kept between fixed limits. The original band was one percent above or below the official parity. After the 1971 reform the band was widened 2.25 percent each side or 4.5 percent total. Each member must pursue policies which help to keep its own rates within this range. The parity requirement applies also to gold; all official purchases and sales of gold by the members must be made at parity rates. And the membership is refrained from engaging in any practices which might jeopardize the rate structure without prior approval from the Fund.

TABLE 23-2

Selected Monetary Units and Parities, before 1971 Dollar Devaluation

Country	Monetary Unit	Subunit	Gold Parity (Milligrams)	Dollar Parity	
				Units Per US Dollar	US Cents Per Unit
Afghanistan	Afghani	100 puls	19.748	45.00	2.222
Argentina	Peso	100 centavos	** nm	83.00	
Austria	Schilling	100 groschen	34.180	26.00	3.846
Belgium	Franc	100 centimes	17.773	50.00	2.
Burma	Kyat	100 pyas	186.621	4.76	21.
Canada	Dollar	100 cents	822.021	1.08	92.5
Ceylon	Rupee	100 cents	149.297	5.95	16.8
China (Mainland)	Yuan	100 chiao	36.125 nm	2.46	nm
China (Taiwan)	New Taiwan dollar	100 cents	22.217	40.00	2.5
Costa Rica	Colon	100 centimos	134.139	6.63	15.094
Denmark	Krone	100 öre	118.489	7.50	13.333
Ecuador	Sucre	100 centavos	35.547	25.00	4.
Ethiopia	Dollar	100 cents	355.468	2.50	40.
France	Franc	100 centimes	160.00	5.55	18.004
Germany (fed. Rep. of)	Deutsche mark	100 pfennigs	242.806	3.66	27.322
Guatemala	Quetzal	100 centavos	888.671	1.00	100.
India	Rupee	100 naye paise	118.489	7.50	13.333
Indonesia	Rupiah	100 sen	* nm	315.00	
Iran	Rial	100 dinars	11.732	75.75	1.320
Israel	Pound	100 agorot	253.906	3.50	28.571
Italy	Lira	100 centesimi	1.422	625.00	0.16
Japan	Yen	100 sen	2.469	360.00	0.278
Jordan	Dinar	1000 fils	2488.280	0.36	280.
Lebanon	Pound	100 piasters	405.512	2.19	45.631
Liberia	Dollar	100 cents	888.671	1.00	100.
Malaysia	Dollar	100 cents	290.299	3.06	32.667
Mexico	Peso	100 centavos	71.094	12.50	8.
Morocco	Dirham	100 francs	175.610	5.06	19.761
Netherlands	Gulden	100 cents	245.489	3.62	27.624
Nigeria	Pound	20 shillings 240 pence	2488.280	0.36	280.
Norway	Krone	100 öre	124.414	7.14	14.
Philippines	Peso	100 centavos	227.864	3.90	25.641
Poland	Zloty	100 groszy	222.168 nm	4.00	
Portugal	Escudo	100 centavos	30.910	28.75	3.478
South Africa	Rand	100 cents	1244.141	0.71	140.
Spain	Peseta	100 centimos	12.695	70.00	1.429
Sweden	Krona	100 öre	171.783	5.17	19.330
Thailand	Baht	100 satangs	42.725	20.80	4.808
Turkey	Lira		59.245	15.00	6.667
United Arab Republic	Pound	100 piasters 1000 milliemes	2551.870	0.35	287.156

TABLE 23-2 (Cont.)

United States	Dollar	100 cents	888.671	1.00	100.
U.S.S.R.	Ruble	100 kopecks	987.412 nm	0.90	
Uruguay	Peso	100 centesimos	120.091	7.40	13.514
Yugoslavia	Dinar	100 paras	71.094	12.50	8.

* Par value not established.
** Restrictive controls in effect; dollar parities computed by the International Monetary Fund.
nm: nonmember
Source: *International Monetary Fund's official records.*

Adjustment of par values

To permit adjustment of the parity system to changing business realities, the par values can be changed under the following conditions.

—Any member is free to change its parity rate by 10 percent from its initial par value at its own discretion but in consultation with the Fund.

—Any change exceeding 10 percent must receive prior approval from the Fund; such approval is accorded if the change is designed to correct a fundamental disparity or economic maladjustment.

—The Fund itself is empowered to initiate a simultaneous change of all parity rates (i.e., change the official gold price) of the system; such initiative is subject to veto from any member (currently only the United States and the United Kingdom) whose quota exceeds 10 percent of the Fund's total subscription.

If a change of parity involves reduction of the gold cover for a currency, the country's subscription will be revalued on the basis of the new rate and the member will be required to pay to the Fund the difference in its own currency. Should the parity be adjusted upward, the member is entitled to withdraw from the Fund its currency in an amount equal to the difference.

Exchange regulation

The Fund rules permit no restriction on payments which arise from international trade and service transactions, including imports, exports, short-term credit, interest and dividend payments, reasonable amortization of loans, depreciation allowances, and remittances of living expenses. All such transactions are left to the foreign exchange market to regulate except in unusual circumstances. However, this requirement to abolish exchange restrictions has been bypassed by the great majority of IMF members under Article XIV, which allows a country to retain the exchange restrictions in effect when that country entered the Fund. The decision of when to abandon the exchange restriction was left to the member, and, what now seems a serious oversight, no time limit was set for such action. Only 25 members have abolished all restrictions on current payments: the remaining 87 continue to use them.

All discriminatory payments practices, such as bilateral payments agreements and other exclusive arrangements, are prohibited regardless of whether they concern trade or investments.

The IMF charter recognizes two legitimate uses of exchange restrictions: to arrest a balance-of-payments disturbance and to restrain capital flight. In neither case should the restriction endanger multilateral trade and payments. But because of Article XIV these basic premises have been circumvented. Regulation of capital movements including foreign investments are exempted from this provision, and the members may regulate them at their own discretion. Heavy outflow of capital and balance-of-payments deficits are the usual causes for members' turning to the IMF for aid.

Drawing rights

A member country is entitled to an annual purchase with its own money of any other member's currency up to a maximum of 25 percent of its quota. These drawings may be repeated before repayment, but the accumulative total cannot exceed 200 percent of the buyer's quota. The first 25 percent drawn is termed the *gold tranche,* which theoretically is the normal limit for the Fund's contributions. The connotation of the gold-tranche criterion is twofold: as long as the accumulative drawings remain within the tranche they are covered by the member's own contribution to the gold reserves of the Fund; and the drawings up to the tranche limit will not increase the Fund's holdings of the member's currency above its total quota. To draw in excess of the gold tranche, a country must apply for a waiver of the gold-cover requirement, which will be granted if deemed desirable from the standpoint of the Fund's objectives.

Special Drawing Rights. Creation of the Special Drawing Rights (SDRs) in 1969 significantly increased the reserve potential of the IMF system. The SDRs denominated in *units of account* equal to 888.671 milligrams of gold, i.e., equivalent to the U.S. dollar at its pre-devaluation par value and consist of book entries in a Special Drawings Rights Account set up separate from the General Fund Account. This paper gold serves as an unconditional reserve asset created to enlarge the total pool of reserves available to the IMF members. The first allocation of SARs, based on regular subscription quotas, was made in 1970 and totaled 3.4 billion units. All member countries elected to participate in the SDR program except Ethiopia, Iraq, Kuwait, Lebanon, Libya, Nepal, Portugal, Saudi Arabia, Singapore, and Thailand.

The SDRs may be used any time when the country has a need for additional reserves. All participating member countries are obligated to accept SDRs on IMF's request to the point where the particular country's total SDR holdings reach three times its original allocation. When a participating country wants to trade its SDRs against currency, the IMF will designate which member's currency is to be used with the proviso that the currency be "convertible in fact." Normally the IMF designates the currencies of countries who have strong balance of payments positions or who must acquire SDRs to meet outstanding obligations of their own. SDRs may also be transferred between member countries without IMF designation. A country acquiring convertible currency by trading off some of its SDRs can use it for settlement transactions or in the foreign-exchange market transactions at its own discretion.

Signs of Weakness

For its first decade the IMF system ran smoothly. Its key currency—the U.S. dollar—was strong and accepted around the world. Any fears about its soundness were assayed by a massive U.S. gold stock (peaked at $24.6 billion) that assured ready convertibility of the dollar into gold. From the enchantment of this initial success sprang grandiose illusions of a perpetual dollar hegemony which, though gratifying to American nationalistic ego, overlooked the inherent weaknesses of the IMF system and ignored the fact that in the early postwar years international economic relations were far from normal.

The original IMF model, based on a key currency, is open for serious criticism from both economic and political standpoints. It ties the international monetary system inextricably to the domestic conditions and policies of the key currency nation, i.e., the United States. Economic and monetary programs designed for American domestic purposes become automatically global in effect; any internal monetary disturbances involve the entire world monetary system. And, conversely, actions of other countries cause undesirable and unintentional effects upon the United States, especially regarding money supply, liquidity, and balance of payments. When the other countries' needs for foreign exchange increase (for example to finance increasing trade between themselves or for reserve assets), they draw dollars out of the United States; the increase of their dollar assets means a corresponding decrease of the money supply in the United States, necessitating certain countermeasures in this country. When the foreign requirements for the dollar decrease, the excess liquidity tends to gravitate back to the United States, who is committed to accept its own legal tender and all the disturbances that such an influx of liquidity could cause.

The real dilemma of the key-currency concept lies in its functional dualism: the key currency must simultaneously serve as domestic money, and also as the medium of international exchange and the reserve asset of other countries, i.e., the universal currency on which the values of all other currencies depend. The key-currency country cannot escape financial crises precipitated by actions and interactions among other countries unless it resorts to restrictions and constraints on the transnational flows of its currency. If this is done, the key-currency system has destroyed its own objectives.

Escalation of Crisis

When in the 1950's the world economy recovered from its early postwar ills, the IMF system began to show signs of serious strain. In 1950 the U.S. balance of payments swung into deficit and has shown a deficit every year except 1957 and 1968 until the 1971 crisis; by that time the cumulative deficit from 1950 was some $50 billion.

As the deficits persisted, confidence in the dollar waned. The key currency no longer was "as good as gold" and the demand for the bullion increased as foreign holders started seeking to convert their dollar assets into gold. The first open crisis occurred in 1960 when a run on gold in the London market pushed prices to $40 per ounce. Only concerted intervention by the major central banks could bring the price under control. The U.S. tried to discourage conversion of dollars to gold and to bolster the sagging dollar with frequent official declarations of its invincibility. When the French government under de Gaulle started turning in dollars for gold in 1962, it became the demon for the key-currency protagonists, the right to convert guaranteed in the IMF charter notwithstanding.

The drain on U.S. gold stock forced the government to resort to arbitrary restrictions on the international movement of the dollar. Interest-equalization tax on foreign borrowing in the U.S. was imposed in 1963; "voluntary controls" directed at foreign investments and other dollar transfers by American firms were introduced in 1965; then controls were made mandatory and requirements for repatriation of profits and dividends by U.S. firms were added in 1968. While the purpose of the restrictions was to protect the United States' financial position, the inevitable outcome was to cripple the dollar in its international role as the key currency of the IMF system.

A second run on gold in London, Zurich, and Paris markets rocked the system in 1968. A two-tier gold price system—one price for official monetary purposes and another for the free gold market—was devised to help slow the efflux of U.S. gold. The two prices, given the reserve currency status of the dollar, were equivalent to two exchange rates, one fixed and the other floating. The dollar, thus, became officially semi-inconvertible, something it had unofficially been for some time as a result of pledges from most major countries' central banks to refrain from converting their dollars into gold.

Revaluation of the German mark provided temporary relief. In 1970 the Special Drawing Rights were authorized but even this new device failed to reverse the trend. The world dollar glut continued to worsen and soon reached catastrophic proportions. Faced with an irresistible onslaught, President Nixon suspended convertibility of dollars into gold for foreign treasuries and central banks in August, 1971. This unilateral action cut the dollar completely loose from gold and cast it afloat in the money markets of the world. No change was made in the official price of gold, however. Thus, the

IMF system had come to a standstill and only through a major reform could it ever be revived.

Controversies about Causes

Much disagreement has raged over the strength and weaknesses of the IMF system. The main arguments revolve around international liquidity, inflation, and exchange rate parity.

International Liquidity

Perhaps the most fundamental criticism of the Fund relates to the use of gold as the ultimate basis for the system. It is argued that world gold production, which has increased an average of about 1.5 percent per year, cannot keep pace with the growth of world business, which has been increasing at 5 to 6 percent per year. If those rates continue, sooner or later gold will not provide the liquidity necessary to finance international economic relations. In this view the one breakdown of the system was caused by the inadequate flow of gold into the monetary system—inadequate in the sense that the demand for gold by the world's monetary authorities could not be met without drawing down U.S. reserves; it was simply a matter of too little gold and too many dollars.

Although quite convincing on the surface, the validity of this argument has not been easy to document. First, international liquidity under the IMF system is by no means synonymous with the gold supply. Gold has been used only as the last resort; the U.S. dollar has served as the principal liquid medium, and other convertible currencies can serve the same function. The supply of international liquid media is not gold alone but the sum of all the available convertible currencies plus gold. Second, the supply of convertible currencies is not limited by the supply of gold as long as the exchange rates reflect the underlying purchasing-power parities. Only when a currency deviates from the purchasing-power parity and becomes unacceptable to other nations (inconvertible) must the nation draw upon gold resources. Naturally, the more members whose currencies are overvalued, the greater the requirements for gold reserves in the system as a whole, including those of the IMF itself. Most decisive is the convertibility of the key-currency. To the degree it becomes overvalued, its convertibility is impaired and gold must take its place. Thus, the demand for more gold arises primarily from financial malpractices and maladjustments and only secondarily from the volume of business activity.

In the IMF parity system the quantity of gold is, as a matter of principle, quite irrelevant to the rate structure; instead of the quantities indicated by the present parities, the gold cover could be only one-half or for that matter one-tenth of the present par values without affecting the exchange rate structure in any way. What such changes *would* affect is the capacity of the system to sustain abnormalities and deviations. An increase of that capacity can open the way to a relaxation of the financial rigidity which the original parities imposed.

An influencial segment of the world's financial community, especially outside the United States, considers *the increase of the price of gold* as the only correct means of strengthening the monetary system. While they consent to the relaxation of the rigid discipline that gold imposes, they refuse to completely eliminate it. In this conception, domestic, economic, and monetary policies of all countries should be subjected to international financial discipline through the use of gold. This is not only to prevent "adventurous domestic policies," but also to preserve a reserve asset that has intrinsic value, as distinguished from drawing right, and that can be used on any country's sole initiative and thereby maximize financial sovereignty.

This view is diametrically opposed by those who look upon gold as a barbaric relic devoid of any intrinsic value. Their prescription for a better international monetary system is *floating exchange rates,* i.e., market integrated currencies, or substitution of special international credit instruments for gold. American official position has shifted increasingly in this direction in recent years. Questions of national prestige and international equity have contributed to the shift. Devaluation is never a politically prestigious or internationally glorious act. In the case of the key-currency country the devaluation against gold has also direct effect on existing financial relations because:

(1) Countries with large gold holdings would gain large additional exchange reserves.

(2) Countries with small gold holdings would not gain much.

(3) The communist-bloc countries would make a windfall, as their gold reserves would double in value in reference to prices in the free countries.

(4) All gold-producing countries would benefit from the higher price of new gold mined; there would be no corresponding gain for the nonproducing countries.

(5) Since the poor countries, which are in need of financial assistance, have the smallest gold holdings relative to others, they would be worse off than before.

Consequently, any raising of the gold price would favor the rich and penalize the poor. Thus, how to eliminate from the IMF system pressures for maintaining the status quo remains an unanswered question.

American Inflation

As long as the U.S. dollar is the key currency of the IMF system, it serves both as the principal medium of exchange in international financial transactions and as the primary reserve asset in all countries. Except for short-term transactions, the stability of the dollar is, therefore, very important to the entire monetary system. Persistent inflation in the United States has afflicted the dollar with chronic deterioration of value (see Figure 23-1) which undermines its integrity as a key currency, especially as an international reserve asset.

Though not unrelated, the domestic and international effects of American inflation are quite different. In the domestic economy the decline in the purchasing power of the dollar affects primarily those whose incomes are fixed by preexisting contracts, especially pensioners and holders of long-term bonds. In the rest of the domestic economy the value of a dollar bill as such is not as important as are the offsetting flows of incomes and costs—both of which show nominal increases more or less paralleling the rate of inflation. This means that individual dollar bills buy less but since there are more of them streaming in and out the real purchasing power of the individual or firm need not decrease at all. In other words, for most people and businesses it is not the value of the dollar bill but the relationship between the reserve stream and the cost stream that determines their real purchasing power. If there are leads and lags in the individual's revenue and cost streams, there will be corresponding gains or losses for him caused by inflation. The point here is not to argue that inflation is inconsequential—that would clearly contradict Chapter 24—but to stress the fact that in the domestic context the inflationary process creates its own counterbalance in a very substantial degree by inflating both the incomes and expenditures of people and businesses.

FIGURE 23-1

Purchasing Power of the Dollar

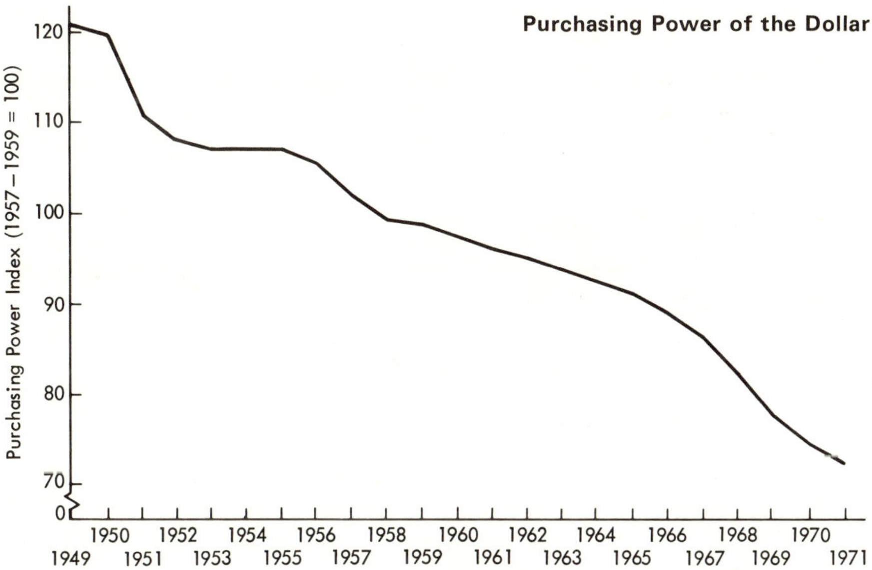

Source: U.S. Bureau of the Census, *Statistical Abstract of the United States,* 1970 (91st edition), Washington, D.C., 1970., p. 338. United States Government Printing Office.

In the international context this is not so. When the dollar is held as a reserve asset by a foreign central bank there is no revenue—cost-stream relationship, but only the value of the dollar bill counts.[3] The foreign government acquires the dollar for its own currency and thereafter depends upon the value of these dollar bills just as the pensioner or other fixed contract holder in the U.S. If that foreign country experiences a slower rate of inflation than the U.S., the value of its dollar-denominated reserve assets deteriorates not only in real terms but also relative to the country's own currency. Since the dollar is the key currency and the standard of the IMF system, the onus of adjusting the exchange rate falls upon the other countries. To realign their own currency with the constantly depreciating dollar, they must periodically revalue their currencies.

Experience shows the revaluation to be politically an even tougher move for a government to make than its opposite, the devaluation. The reasons for this are not entirely clear. One major source of resistance to revaluation is the fear that the country's international trade position as well as its balance of payments will suffer. Apparently, they would rather accept distorted currency values than accept the reasons associated with revaluation. Since no country has so far undertaken periodic revaluations to neutralize the effect of the American inflation upon international monetary relations, the problems of purchasing-power disparity and key-currency instability have emerged as critical dysfunctions of the IMF system.

Under the key-currency system with fixed-dollar parities, rapid inflation in the United States is tantamount to a de facto devaluation of other nations' currencies whenever their own inflation rates are lower. Their exports are stimulated and their imports impeded by the process. To the United States itself the inflation puts a break on exports and accelerates imports. That pushes more dollars into the coffers of apprehensive foreign authorities.

As a consequence of this process a number of other currencies have kept gaining in strength compared to the dollar. As their IMF parities were not adjusted to offset the gain (except minor revaluations of the German mark and Dutch gulden), their purchasing power parities suffered serious distortion. Thus, besides the general undervaluation of gold, the dollar became overvalued vis-à-vis many other currencies—though in different degrees. The IMF system's lack of flexibility to harmonize purchasing power and exchange rate parities became painfully evident as prolonged international maladjustment endured under its regime.

Conflicting National Attitudes

The IMF's inflexibility was compounded by certain official attitudes of the key-currency nation. The U.S. viewed its chronic payments deficit with "benign neglect." This posture rested on the mistaken notion that since the U.S. economy was big and strong and its foreign trade balance typically

[3] Interest in U.S. government bonds may increase to very slightly counteract the loss in dollar value.

positive, the payment deficits were largely a matter of passing interest. The only permanent factor, in this view, was direct foreign investment which was to be held in check by restrictive government controls. Neither the rise to dominance of the multinational firm nor its significance and power were understood. Instead of disappearing, the pressures for foreign investment continued to grow.

Similar indifference characterized the U.S. official attitude toward the massive accumulation of dollars abroad. It was variably argued that these accumulations, far from being dangerous, were actually useful as a means of providing badly needed liquidity for growth of world economy; or that if some country considered its dollar receipts excessive, it could revalue its currency.

Other countries disagreed. They not only refused to unilaterally accept the onus of adjustment, arguing that this burden should be shared, but feared that they would be stuck with a dollar standard forever if they revalued. Such a fear was whetted by both inward-looking economic policies and vigorous advocacy of dollar-based monetary reform schemes. The polarization of official attitudes between the key-currency nation and its major trading partners made an ultimate breakdown of the system inevitable. This came when the U.S. President pulled the linchpin of the system by terminating the convertibility of the dollar in August 1971.

Toward a New IMF System

The U.S. President's dramatic action prompted a frantic search for a new monetary order. The first urgent objective was realignment of currency values. This was attempted in December 1971. The agreed-upon formula was for the United States to devalue the dollar and for the other countries to revalue their currencies, largely by allowing them to float against the dollar.

The official price of gold was raised by 8.57 percent from \$35 to \$38 per fine troy ounce. That devalued the dollar by 7.8 percent.[4] The new parities that resulted were termed "central rates" and considered "temporary working values" subject to change when a final accord is reached on a complete reform of the IMF system. That underscored the general understanding that the repositioning of currencies was only the beginning and that settling all the basic disagreements was a long term project.

The overall effective devaluation of the dollar against other currencies —our devaluation plus their revaluation against gold—was estimated by U.S. authorities in January 1972 to have amounted to 12 percent, against specific currencies it varied from plus 16.9 for Japan to minus 43.9 for Ghana.

Contrary to official predictions, the 1971 dollar devaluation failed to restore purchasing power parities and stability in world exchange markets. The flight

[4] The 1934 devaluation raised the price of gold from \$20.67 to \$35, equivalent to a 41 percent devaluation.

from the dollar continued. Central banks of hard currency countries, notably of West Germany and Japan, bought massive amounts of dollars in a concerted effort to help to maintain the new exchange rates but with no avail except to prolong the agony. When, due to dwindling resources, they slackened their purchases the pressure against the dollar quickly reached crisis proportions making a second devaluation inevitable; it came in February 1973. Thus, the 1971 devaluation had ended in a fiasco. The new rates had not only failed summarily the test of the market but had in the process also inflicted punitive losses upon the countries that in a bona fide effort to support the dollar found the value of their huge dollar holdings overnight reduced by the second devaluation.

The 1973 devaluation reduced the value of the dollar by 10 percent in terms of gold and SDR's. That raised the official U. S. price of gold to $42.22. Other countries responded in four groupings: those holding their gold parities, in effect revaluing their currencies upward by 11.1 percent against the dollar; those following the dollar down with a 10 percent devaluation; those devaluing by less than 10 percent; and those floating their currencies.

The world exchange markets again refused to confirm official predictions. Confidence in the dollar was not restored and the pressures to convert dollar assets to gold and hard currencies continued to undermine monetary relations. Causes of this double failure remain a matter of intense dispute. The main battle line runs along the gold vs. credit (paper) standard arguments. Despite the two devaluations, the disparity between the official American price and the world market price of gold has not decreased but increased from roughly 1:2 in 1971 to 1:3 in 1973 ($42 against $125). How to eliminate this crippling disparity will be the primary challenge in any further efforts to reform the contemporary international monetary system.

The Revised Blueprint

Although setting a new official price for gold, the U.S. postponed indefinitely the resumption of gold payments for the dollar, ostensibly to push for a rapid completion of the reform, but more correctly to prevent itself exposure to foreign gold demands, which, based on their official dollar assets, were five times greater than its remaining gold reserves. So long as the world money markets had not fully adjusted to the repositioned values and confirmed their equilibrium, the risk of reopening the U.S. gold window was very great.

The postponement of convertibility left the other countries only two choices of response to American deficit: to accept more dollars; or to eliminate their own surpluses by appreciating their currencies, inflating, or imposing restrictions on capital inflows. It was hoped that this postponement would accelerate completion of the reform, thereby satisfying their desire to escape from this predicament.

As of June 1973, the previously divergent positions among major world capitals are converging to a point of global consensus on these five strategic objectives of the reform:

1. To end rigid exchange rates and to depoliticize the adjustment process by providing equal incentives to adjust for surplus and deficit countries. This would mean smaller scale and more frequent exchange rate changes and international rules to minimize political interference with the process. The widening of the official band for rate movements from 2 to 4.5 percent around the parities that were part of the 1971 realignment can hardly be enough. The IMF needs powers to induce changes in the parities themselves when unbalances are pending to prevent their actual occurrence.

2. To phase out the dollar from its key currency role. There is a near unanimous opposition abroad to the dollar's hegemony. Any recurrence of the situation where a country can pay its foreign debts by simply printing more of its own money is unthinkable in the contemporary world. The United States, too, wants to divest the dollar from its reserve currency functions to escape from the international political problems that beset the domestic monetary initiatives of the key currency country, and to avoid the externally induced exports and imports of its currency.

3. To expand the use of Special Drawing Rights to replace the dollar as reserve asset. (The dollar will in all likelihood remain the dominant medium to finance private international transactions.) Through the increased dependence of credit based reserve assets like the SDRs or some completely new unit the IMF system can acquire a greater ability to rationally match the growth of international liquidity to world needs.

4. To retain gold as the ultimate reserve asset, but in a decreasing ratio to the SDRs. Gold has been fundamental to the IMF system. First as the unit of account in which all currencies are measured—even the SDRs bear specific relation to gold—second as the basis for convertibility of the dollar. Foreign critics point out that gold losses provided the only effective discipline in the United States until its suspension of convertibility. When the dollar was cut loose to float, gold even more than before, became the only peg and anchor of the IMF system. Furthermore, gold is the only medium which in peace and in war has been accepted everywhere by private buyers and governments in unlimited amounts. This has an inevitable public appeal. The value of any purely credit-based reserve asset will rest on international cooperation. A breakdown of that cooperation may destroy the asset. For this reason, even the radical protagonists of "paper gold" advocate "war chests" of real gold against such a contingency.

5. To liberalize trade. Dismantling of non-tariff trade distortions is considered particularly important for avoidance of future monetary crises and the growth of world trade. Further reduction of tariffs is also on most countries' lists.

Conspicuously absent from the reform agenda despite their tremendous importance is the multinational corporation with all its transboundary inter-ties. It may require a quantum leap to move from the GATT style trade negotiations to encompass transfers of technology, intracompany international trade, cooperation on trade adjustment programs, and environmental control standards in addition. But there is hardly any alternative. A revision of the GATT agreement to accommodate multilateral cooperation on all these increasingly critical areas will have to be part of the monetary reform. The reformation process, therefore, has only begun.

24

Method Analysis of International Investment Decisions

Investments in foreign environments confront corporate management with a variety of risks and uncertainties which differ materially from those involved in domestic investment decisions. Political context, monetary environment, costs, and revenues all present different combinations of factors which bear directly or indirectly upon the potential profitability of an investment. How to analyze and evaluate international investment opportunities, how to deal with uncertainties, and which tools to use in the decision-making process are the subjects of this chapter.

Political Uncertainties

For direct foreign investment the attitudes of the people and of the government officials in that country have to be carefully considered. This analysis should include a thorough study of the country's laws and of their enforcement. In some countries such as Burma there are official statutes which favor direct foreign investment. These include liberal tax exemptions, guarantees against expropriation, and immunity to certain exchange controls. But the statutes have never been implemented, and the government generally disregards them. At best these laws can be construed as indications of governmental power rather than as rights of business enterprise. And since the Burmese government has been socialistic in outlook, it has effectively blocked private enterprise from benefiting from the statutes. In such a climate the political risk to direct foreign investment is high, irrespective of formal assurances to the contrary. In addition, experience has shown that a business investing in Burma may face considerable price competition from nationalized enterprises and from Communist sources which aim at eradicating private enterprise. There are other situations where takeover by a hostile government in the future is a distinct possibility or where the political climate is so unstable or unpredictable that no long-range projections can be made short of intuitive guesses. Although quantitative techniques, which will be described later, can be useful in decision making under such conditions, nonquantitative factors based on judgment and experience must provide the basic assumptions and financial criteria for the numerical analysis. Yet, the presence of political uncertainty is not synonymous with a void for investment incentive.

The primary criterion for business investment is anticipated return. Secondary criteria include economic growth, employment, and other aspects of public welfare in the country concerned. Political instability is particularly characteristic of underdeveloped countries, where the need for new industry, employment, and economic development is extremely intense but where capital and entrepreneurship are generally scarce; thus, the return on investment is high. The main criterion for international management is not the presence or absence of political uncertainty but the balance between the uncertainty and the potential profits. High risks can be neutralized by high profits, which enable the investor to recoup its principal in a proportionally shorter period and to realize a net gain at an early stage in the physical life of the facilities involved. Consequently, the feasibility of a foreign investment depends upon the relative magnitude of the uncertainty, including political risk, compared with the profit potential that the particular country may offer. The crucial variable is time rather than the risk as such—how fast the capital of a contemplated investment could be recovered and how much longer it would take to earn an acceptable net return on it.

Revenue and Cost

Preliminary Analysis

A logical investment analysis should start with a survey of the alternative opportunities for the company concerned. The more complete the initial survey, the better the chances that the best alternatives will ultimately be chosen. Although many companies still treat international investments apart from domestic ones, this practice is to be discouraged, as it lacks economic rationale. The only justification for separating the two is management's ability to understand and judge the domestic opportunities and uncertainties compared with its relative unfamiliarity with international conditions. Where this is a fact it must, of course, be recognized. But as a matter of principle and as an objective, each company should strive to acquire the managerial capabilities which would permit it to analyze investment opportunities in an international rather than in a national context and to make the investment decisions on the basis of such analytical comparisons rather than on arbitrary assumptions regarding the foreign areas.

Capital Budgeting

From the data compiled during the preliminary analysis a more formal and systematic schedule of different investment opportunities can be derived. The preparation of such schedules is commonly called *capital budgeting.* Its objective is to provide a numerical basis for investment decisions by presenting comparable profit estimates on all alternative investment opportunities known to the firm. An international capital budget, therefore, would show the estimated size of the investment in each country or world region, the cost of the capital required, the anticipated revenues, and the risks peculiar to each country and project. To arrive at these data capital budgeting requires the following information:

(1) An assessment of political uncertainties
(2) An economic forecast including the possibilities of inflation
(3) An analysis of the differences in financial costs and risks with particular reference to
- (a) currency controls
- (b) exchange risks
- (c) character of money and capital markets of each country involved

(4) A projection of the impact which any particular investment will cause on the cash flows of the firm
(5) A measurement of capital availability under different alternatives
(6) Methods to compute the cost of capital on the basis of the capital-availability estimates
(7) A method for reducing the items in different currencies to a common denominator reflective of the real values involved

In all stages in the capital-budgeting process time must be taken into account. Since money has a time value and since investment decisions involve costs and revenues at various future dates, the budgeted figures must be converted to their present value to make them meaningful and comparable. This conversion employs the *discount principle,* which is based on the fundamental proposition that a dollar today is worth more than a dollar in the future. For the quantitative techniques and procedures of capital budgeting, the reader should consult specialized literature on this subject.

Qualitative ranking

Capital-budgeting techniques are being adopted by an increasing number of multinational companies. However, small firms, and also many large ones, still rely on qualitative evaluation and ranking of their investment opportunities abroad. Such rankings emphasize the uncertainties in various countries, the urgency of different projects, and the past experience of the company and the industry to which it belongs. But instead of mathematical techniques, they utilize quasi-intuitive judgments. Supporters of the qualitative method believe that experienced executives can determine with relatively little effort—primarily through their personal judgment and hunches—which investments are profitable and which are not. No doubt this approach will always have many supporters simply because the capital budgeting of an international investment usually represents a substantial cost—it is, in fact, itself an investment—which often seems unjustifiable in comparison with the results which can be obtained by a much less costly qualitative decision—that is, the reduction in uncertainty may be less than the expense of the quantitative budgeting. This judgment is more valid for small than for large investments. But almost all investments involve aspects and factors which defy meaningful quantification, such as the actions and reactions of competitors and other external forces, style changes, innovations, and political conditions.

The weakness of the qualitative method is the lack of objective standards for reviewing and testing investment decisions. Possibly, if a decision were analytically dissected, the hunches and judgments used would be modified or completely discarded. The purely qualitative decision is no better or no worse than the insights and the judgments of the executives who make the decision. Superior people are likely to make superior decisions on investment projects of which they are well informed. But the reverse is equally true. In addition, superior people are likely to make bad decisions on projects which they do not fully understand—a situation quite normal in the international context.

The Cost of Capital

To this point the discussion has emphasized the revenue aspects of international investment analysis. Although the same principles and approaches apply also to the cost aspects, certain additional observations are in order. To start with, the true cost is opportunity cost. Unfortunately only crude measurements can be made of opportunity costs in an international context. To the extent to which this is possible they should be utilized. Normally the opportunity-cost concept is employed, explicitly or implicitly, in the preliminary rankings of different projects as well as in the final comparisons. The international investment analysis, however, must depend primarily upon the supply cost of capital.

The supply cost depends on the volume, as is typical of all supply schedules under normal conditions—the greater the amount, the higher the cost per unit of capital. Thus, theoretically, a company could draw up a cost schedule by varying the size of its projected investments and move from the lowest obtainable cost toward the point where the marginal cost of capital equals the anticipated revenue. But since the size of the different projects is typically determined by engineering efficiency, by market demand, and by such local constraints as building codes, public utilities, and labor supply, management has relatively limited opportunity to vary the size of the investment in response to the variations in the cost of capital.

What makes this problem much more difficult than it may appear is the fact that the cost of capital is a composite of different debts and equities: retained earnings, proceeds from the flotation of new common or preferred stock, bonds, regular bank credit, Eximbank and World Bank loans, and credits from respective national governments—just to mention a few. Each has its own cost, which may depend upon the total mix of the capital inputs or on the projected capital structure of the investment project. If all sources were readily open to the firm, the solution to the problem would be purely mathematical: namely, to design a capital structure which would minimize the cost of the capital needed for a given project. In reality the capital structure is subject to a great many noncost constraints: legal requirements for local participation, political factors, the policies and criteria of lending agencies, tax considerations, the accumulated reserves of the company, and the financial philosophy of its management.

The types of securities as well as loans and lending agencies are products of national legislation. As such they vary significantly from country to country. Despite the unifying effect of past colonial empires, the international scene represents a bewildering plurality of capital structures as well as financial practices when compared with the United States or any other nation. To an undetermined degree the foreign norms can be disregarded if they interfere with rational action. But it is seldom possible to transplant into a foreign situation one's domestic (such as American) financial methods without modification. Even where it is possible legally, such a course can be questioned from a public-relations standpoint.

Like revenue, the relevant costs in an investment decision are those which affect or are affected by the future, not by the past. Investments, once made, become sunk cost and cannot be recovered in any other way than through productive utilization of the facilities in which the investments were made. Only the sales revenues generated by the facilities can repay the investors. Investment decisions represent irrevocable commitments which can rarely be changed through subsequent managerial action. The past cost of capital, therefore, cannot be used as the basis for new investments. The two are conceptually distinct.

Separated or Integrated Financing

From the standpoint of financial theory an international corporation may be conceived as a multidenominational pool of funds in which the different national currencies are but different legal forms of the underlying purchasing power and, as such, interchange freely in response to the total needs and resources for liquidity of the firm. All the national affiliates are then subject to the same financial criteria, and the headquarters is the logical control center for the financial pool; it borrows in the country where terms are most favorable and transfers the funds to the country where they can be employed most profitably.

In practice the pool-of-funds concept, although valuable as a general guide, can rarely serve as a basis for financial policy in a multinational corporation. First, there are exchange controls, which interfere with the transfer of funds from one country to another, the degree of interference depending on the restrictiveness of the controls. Each restricted currency represents to a greater or lesser degree a separate or autonomous system in which both the costs of capital as well as the profits are neither comparable nor exchangeable with those in other countries in any direct way. Second, some sources of funds are available only for particular purposes: for example, government development loans, matching funds, special amortization privileges, and mortgage loans. Third, differences in interest rates may be offset by the indirect or noninterest costs of borrowing or by differences in debt limits set by the various national governments. The opportunity to borrow a greater proportion of an affiliate's capital requirements increases the leverage on the equity part of the investment. A high debt ratio in one country may, if consolidated with the ratio of the parent company, push the combined or pooled figure beyond the legal limits of the headquarters country. Fourth, if the affiliate is a joint venture or a partly owned subsidiary, the determination of comparative costs of capital becomes particularly involved. Also, as explained in Chapter 14, foreign-licensing agreements often involve standing commitments for particular dispositions of returns such as earmarking for or reinvestment in a new venture.

Because of such deterrents, unified financial management of all member institutions in a multinational corporate family is seldom possible. But this does not mean that the pool-of-funds concept should be abandoned. The company must understand the peculiar rigidities of each national jurisdiction and design its financial policies and controls accordingly. Only in light of the actual barriers to international transfers of corporate funds and to their acquisition is it possible to determine when centralized action is indicated and when a decision must be made locally.

Some Analytical Techniques

Pro Forma Statement. This is a numerical expression of management's best judgment as to what the financial condition of the company would look like at some future date if a particular investment were made. The statement is broken down into as much detail as possible. Estimates are made of cash, accounts receivable, inventories, plant and equipment, liabilities, equity, revenue, expenses, taxes, and net profit. A *pro forma* statement is a guidepost for estimating the total dividends that could be paid, based on earnings; working from that figure management can estimate the total amount that might be repatriated, in view of the exchange restrictions.

If a *pro forma* statement indicates a possible lack of liquidity, the problem then is finding a source of funds. With no currency restrictions, the headquarters management could transfer funds from other countries or from the corporate treasury to the new affiliate. Dollar loans also could be arranged. With currency restrictions, management might be reluctant to invest more dollars but could explore the possibility of obtaining loans in local currency.

Such funds would neither enter nor leave the country. Earnings made abroad could be spent abroad, and a growth situation could develop despite foreign exchange restrictions. This growth could be either in anticipation of the time when funds would be freely repatriated or for permanent expansion of the corporate organization.

Management might also consider the possibility of foreign partners, who could provide part of the capital for direct investment and so reduce the risk to the company itself. Foreign partners might not particularly favor large repatriation of earnings by the company, and from their point of view currency restrictions might not necessarily be undesirable. Yet American management would have a good talking point sometime in the future if restrictions were to be lifted. The U.S. management could simply point out that their return on investment had been severely limited for many years and that they were now entitled to increased dividends.

Rate of Return. There are three basic ways of measuring the rate of return: to divide the net income figure by net sales; to divide net income by equity; or to divide net income by total assets. It is, of course, possible to design a combined method based on all three. The rate of return is also linked to asset turnover. The return on total assets involves not only the rate of return on sales but also the number of times the capital invested in the assets turns over in a year. Therefore, rate of return on total assets is equal to rate of return on sales times the asset turnover.

Trading on the Equity. Under partial or full currency exchange restrictions, management might use the technique of trading on the equity. Since U.S. owners would want to avoid further dollar investment, a loan might be arranged in local currency from a local bank. For example, if the cost of this loan were 10 percent and if the firm could earn 15 percent or more with the borrowed funds, then the loan would make a 5 percent contribution to the earnings of the firm. Growth might thus be quick, providing the maximum possible repatriation allowed by law and at the same time strengthening the company's position in the country concerned.

Trading on the equity, also called *financial leverage,* is normally expressed in the United States in an amount equal to the percentage increase in earnings per share after taxes and interest divided by the percentage increase in earnings before taxes and interest. In international investments this definition is inconvenient and at times impossible to employ. It is more useful to drop the "per share" criterion and to measure the leverage either in terms of the total borrowing or in units specifically designed for this purpose.

Annuity Method of Depreciation. Exchange restrictions represent a risk. To deal with them, management must apply the best possible techniques for the greatest accuracy. Also, if a U.S. company is party to a joint venture with a foreign firm, each side is most probably going to use the methods of accounting that best support its own position. During a period of currency restrictions, American management might desire to show the lowest possible return on sales or assets and to use this return as a bargaining point later on, especially since full dividends could not be paid for the time being. If there is reason to believe the situation will improve, then the evidence of past low returns on assets would provide a valid bargaining point for U.S. management to secure a higher payout later to compensate for the previous years.

Straight-line depreciation increases the return on assets. The book value of the asset base declines steadily, assuming no new purchases, but the annual depreciation expense stays the same. A declining asset base divided into a constant net income means a higher rate of return each year, as is shown in the following hypothetical illustration:

$$\frac{\text{1960 income } \$\ 10{,}000}{\text{1960 assets } \$100{,}000} = \text{10 percent return on assets}$$

$$\frac{\text{1965 income } \$\ 10{,}000}{\text{1965 assets } \$\ 50{,}000} = \text{20 percent return on assets}$$

The annuity method of depreciation amortizes the asset cost as well as the theoretical interest that could have been earned if the asset had been used differently. Currency restrictions on dividends and interest taken out of a country are a matter of concern. The theoretical interest that could have been earned on an alternative investment is included in the depreciation expense and is also shown as earned interest. Fixed assets are reduced in value by the difference between the total depreciation charge and the theoretical or imputed interest earned. For example, assume an investment of $500,000, a going rate of interest of 8 percent, and an estimated depreciation life of plant of seven years. The following calculations would be made:

$$\frac{\$500{,}000}{5206^{(1)}} = \$96{,}045 \text{ depreciation expense}$$

Eight percent of $500,000 = $40,000, interest earned. At the end of the first year the books would show:

Depreciation expense	$96,045	
Imputed interest		$40,000
Accumulated depreciation		56,045

The plant-investment account would then show the reduced value $543,955. At the end of the second year, interest earned on plant assets would be calculated as 8 percent of $543,955, the reduced asset base. Net income is not affected by including the imputed interest, since depreciation is increased to the extent of the interest in subsequent years, thus neutralizing the interest over the life of the investment. Since the annuity method smoothes out the rate of return and presents an accurate picture of costs and profits, it is well suited for international investments, where yearly fluctuations are normally

1 Present value of $1 annuity for seven years at 8 percent.

greater than in domestic business because of uncertainties and governmental interferences.

Rate of Return on Total Assets. A firm may capitalize on exchange restrictions by deploying its resources for the expansion of its sales in the country, even if this lowers the current profits to some degree. Since dividends would be limited anyway by the exchange restrictions, management might find it less desirable to bank the funds (not to mention keeping them idle) than to reinvest them to increase its share of the market. If this reinvestment were made, higher profits might result in the long term, and perhaps by then repatriation of funds would be allowed. In order to judge to what extent expenses could be allowed to gain and profits to be reduced, a rate of return on total asset calculation could be used. This calculation is made by multiplying the rate of return on sales by the asset turnover.

For example, Company *A* may depend on its higher profit margin with lower sales to get a 15 percent return on assets. Company *B* may depend on a higher volume of sales with a smaller profit margin to get its 15 percent rate of return. Under restrictions on dividends a firm could operate similarly to Company *B,* establishing itself in a wide market. When restrictions on dividends were lifted, the firm might increase its net profit margin, which would increase correspondingly its rate of return on total assets.

Institutions Which Specialize in International Investment Loans

There are a large number of agencies, both private and government owned, designed specifically to assist and stimulate direct international investment. These agencies make direct loans, invest in equity, and make available various guarantees. They are growing in size and number, and their significance to multinational business is increasing accordingly.

International Bank for Reconstruction and Development—The World Bank. This bank was created by the Bretton Woods Conference in July 1944 as a companion organization to the International Monetary Fund for two basic reasons: to provide immediate and emergency assistance in countries devastated by World War II, and to stimulate international investment and economic growth after rehabilitation. Most of the free-world countries at the Bretton Woods Conference joined the bank, and by 1966 its total membership exceeded 80 countries.

Each member subscribes to capital stock and in return has voting rights. By 1966 the bank's total capital actually subscribed was $21,000,000. The bank makes both loans and guarantees of loans to governments and private firms. However, it is not supposed to compete with private commercial banks, and the loans and guarantees are made in situations in which the borrower would otherwise be unable to secure a loan. If the bank makes a loan to a private firm, the country in which the firm is located must guarantee the repayment and servicing of the loan, and the loan must be made for a particular reason, such as for industrial or agricultural development purposes. As a second safeguard the bank must attempt to lend only to borrowers who will be in a position to repay the debt. It is not a gift. Third, the proceeds of the loan must go specifically for the purpose given. No general-purpose loans can be made. Fourth, the loans made usually consist of the furnishing of the foreign exchange specifically needed for the project. Any local expenditures necessary must come from private sources.

International Finance Corporation (IFC). An affiliate of the World Bank, the International Finance Corporation was set up in 1956 to serve private investment needs, especially in reference to industrial projects. Its basic policy is to lend only to private investors and not to firms that are owned or operated by a government to any sizable extent. The loans are limited to 50 percent of the total investment of any one borrower. Besides the usual direct loans which bear interest, the IFC is authorized to make equity investments, but it will not assume managerial responsibilities under normal conditions. It attempts to keep equity investments from becoming frozen by selling them as soon as it is feasible. The purpose of the originators was not to create a large institution but rather to create one which would have a multiplier effect on foreign investment—in other words, not to dominate but to stimulate foreign investment.

Loan maturities are from 5 to 15 years; loans are usually repaid in dollars, but at times local currency may be used. Loans may be used to buy equipment or to pay for local costs such as land and building and even for working-capital purposes in general, but it may not be used to refund. The interest rate is negotiated.

Edge Act Corporations. In 1919 Congress enacted the Edge Corporation Act, which authorized U.S. banks to form subsidiaries for foreign banking purposes. These subsidiaries were created to stimulate direct foreign investment. The Chase National Bank of New York City was the first bank to set up such a corporation. Now there are 34 Edge Act corporations and five additional corporations operating in agreement with the Board of Governors of the Federal Reserve Banks.

Edge Act corporations may purchase equity up to $200,000 or 25 percent of foreign bank stock without permission of the Federal Reserve Board. They may invest in business in the form of equity and may underwrite stock issues. They may make direct loans for working-capital and refunding purposes. Terms are medium length, and interest charges range from 7 to 10 percent. The authority to have equity interest in client firms is coupled with the right to share in the client company's profits, receive additional new issues of stock, and buy warrants. Most loans by Edge Act corporations are made to well-established businesses in developed countries.

Private U.S. Investment Firms. In addition to Edge Act corporations, other private companies such as private investment banks or firms make loans abroad. Examples include the American Express Company, the Deltec Corporation of Panama, and the American International Investment Corporation of San Francisco. Loans are basically medium- or short-term.

AGENCY FOR INTERNATIONAL DEVELOPMENT (AID). This federal government agency, started after World War II as part of our overall foreign aid program, deals to a large extent with foreign governments; it makes what are known as *soft* or *semisoft* loans—long-term loans which extend to 40 years with interest terms as low as $\frac{3}{4}$ of 1 percent. At times they are payable in dollars, but often foreign currency is acceptable. Under certain circumstances AID lends to private business, but these loans are made at or near commercial rates of interest and are repayable in dollars. Loans are limited to 50 percent of equity and are made primarily for developmental purposes, such as purchase of plant and equipment and land acquisition. AID will also underwrite the cost to private business of conducting investment surveys by sharing the cost up to 50 percent. If the investor uses the information and makes an investment, the funds advanced by AID are to be repaid. If the survey is not used and no investment is made, the survey is turned over to the U.S. government, and the funds advanced by AID are written off without repayment. The agency does not lend to borrowers in industrial countries, its emphasis being on underdeveloped areas.

AID further encourages direct foreign investment by offering a program of investment guarantees to private business. New investments are offered guarantees against three risks: convertibility-of-currency problems, expropriation, and war. Guarantees against convertibility problems are available in 57 countries, against expropriation in 56, and against war in 36.

DEPARTMENT OF AGRICULTURE AND COMMODITY CREDIT CORPORATION. Under a 1962 amendment to Public Law 480, the Dept. of Agriculture and the Commodity Credit Corporation can make certain funds available to banks, corporations, and other private businesses. These loans are made for 20 years at low interest rates for the purchase of commodities on the U.S. surplus list. The interest rate is 4 percent, and the loans are repayable in dollars.

EXPORT-IMPORT BANK (EXIMBANK). The Export-Import Bank was created in 1934, with an initial capital of $1 million and $10 million borrowed from the Reconstruction Finance Corporation, to assist in financing and facilitating exports and imports and the exchange of commodities between the United States and other countries or the agencies and nationals thereof. Since that time it has grown into an institution with $1 billion capital stock—all owned by the U.S. Treasury—and Congressional authority to borrow $7 billion.

Originally managed by a Board of Trustees representing various agencies of the government, its affairs are now the responsibility of a full-time bipartisan board of five directors appointed by the President with the advice and consent of the Senate.

An amendment to the Bank's charter now provides for an Advisory Committee of nine members representative of finance, commerce, industry, agriculture, and labor. The Committee is appointed by the Board of Directors on the recommendation of the president of the Bank and meets with it in

Washington three times a year to discuss all questions of policy governing the operations of the Bank. The individual members of the Advisory Committee are used as consultants throughout the year.

The Bank operates primarily to help finance exports and imports of the United States by (a) extending credit to private enterprise and government agencies for buying U.S. capital equipment (project credits) and (b) helping foreign countries maintain their imports from the United States under adverse dollar shortages (emerging-foreign-trade credits). Its clientele includes numerous foreign credit institutions, state enterprises, and private firms. All its loans are restricted to purchase of American goods and services and cannot be used for local costs.

INTERNATIONAL DEVELOPMENT ASSOCIATION (IDA). This agency, established in 1960, promotes economic development by making loans to governments and firms that do not meet the banking standards of low risk and stable yield. The loans are established to mature in up to 50 years with a grace period of ten years before repayment starts. IDA may charge interest or may make interest-free loans as it wishes. But the credits granted must be invested "in a normal, businesslike way," and the projected finances must have high enough prices to recover the investment. Its credits are available to foreign firms, joint ventures, and governmental bodies.

INTER-AMERICAN DEVELOPMENT BANK. This bank was set up to encourage direct foreign investment in Latin America. The terms of loans are six to 20 years with interest at 5.7 percent. Loans are usually made in dollars, but local currency loans are made at times. Both private and public entities of any member country (the United States is a member) can qualify for its loans.

FOREIGN INSTITUTIONS. There are a variety of agencies abroad, such as development corporations or development banks, that give assistance for international investment. These may be privately owned, government owned, or both. Some grant intermediate-term credit, and others are engaged mainly in economic planning. Still others operate stock exchanges or act as fiscal agents. Some specialize in building projects for governments. Among the well-known examples are the European Investment Bank, the International Bank for Resettlements, the Pakistan Industrial Credit and Investment Corporation, and the Industrial Credit and Investment Corporation of India. In all there are about 125 such firms. In addition, European commercial banks are active in lending for direct investment purposes.

25

Management under International Inflation

The pressure for prices to rise has been universal throughout the postwar period. No country has been completely successful in suppressing it, and all currencies, therefore, have declined in real value. Figure 23-1 shows the depreciation of the U.S. dollar.[1] Since under the IMF system the values of all other currencies are measured in dollar parities, the decline of the dollar is synonymous with the deescalation of the entire international monetary structure. Within this structure, each national currency has had its own history with regard to rates and patterns of purchasing power decline, and, as a consequence, the real, as distinguished from the official, values of currencies have been shifting in countless ways. For international enterprise, this has meant a constant mutation in the financial environment, in comparative costs, and in other financial factors.

Causes of Inflation

Inflation is a basic, yet poorly understood, problem of the contemporary world. The lack of understanding comes from the great complexity of the

[1] It has been argued that part of the increase in the postwar price indices is compensated for by increases in product quality. Since it is impossible to empirically evaluate this argument, it has been confined to academic speculation.

problem. Since the answers are hard to find and often inconclusive, both the causes and the consequences of inflation provide room for controversy.

To cope with the managerial implications of inflation, both financial and political, an international executive must possess not only the statistics on a particular country but also a conceptual framework within which the facts can be evaluated and interpreted. There are three theoretical explanations of the inflationary process: demand-pull, cost-push, and structural inflation.

Demand-Pull Inflation

The central thesis of the demand-pull theory is that inflation is caused by increases in the money supply which are not neutralized by matching increases in the supply of goods and services. It assumes that the level of prices depends directly and proportionately on the money supply of the country.

Figure 25-1 shows a graphic model of such inflation. For simplicity it is based on the assumption that the country has full employment and no further employment of resources or manpower is possible. Aggregate income at full employment is at Y_0. Now, if the supply of money should increase either because of new bank loans to business or because of a new issue of currency, demand for goods and services would increase accordingly. But, since at full employment all resources and manpower are already utilized, the supply is completely inelastic at the Y_0 level, and any increase in demand will cause prices to rise from the original equilibrium point P_0 to some higher level such as P_1 or P_2. In case of a shrinkage in the money supply the opposite effect would occur.

Keynesian modifications of inflation theory shift the emphasis from the

FIGURE 25-1

The Model of Pure-Demand Inflation

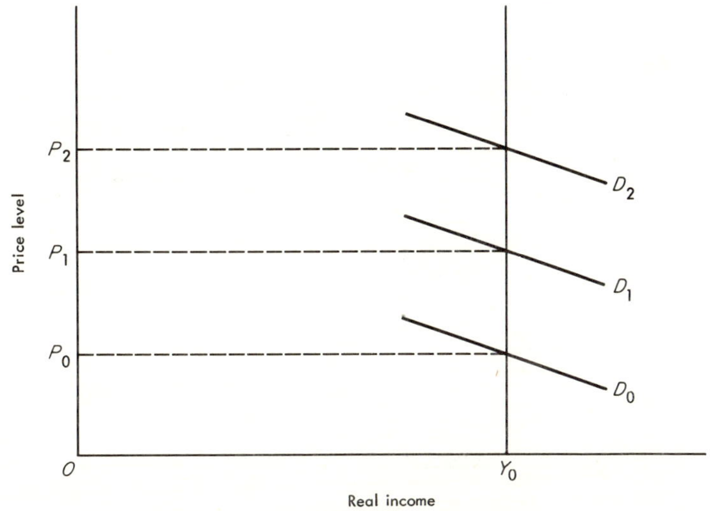

stock of money to income and expenditure flows which are determined by the "liquidity preferences" of different segments of the society. In Keynesian analysis inflation may occur even in the absence of any expansion in the money supply. For example, a deficit in the government budget could be financed by inducing some people to hold government securities instead of cash (thus releasing cash for other purposes and thereby increasing the velocity of circulation).

The Keynesian demand-pull inflation analysis is usually expressed in the concept of an "inflationary gap," shown in Figure 25-2. Real income and real expenditure must lie on the 45° line labeled $Y = C + I + G$ (income = consumption plus investment plus government spending). Full employment is assumed to occur at the aggregate real income level OF. Consequently, real income cannot exceed OF and real expenditure cannot exceed OX. If aggregate demand is at the level $(C + I + G)$, the system is in equilibrium and no inflation is experienced.

If for some reason total demand rises to the new level $(C + I + G)'$, an upward pressure on prices will be exerted since the equilibrium income level OF' is unattainable because of the full-employment constraint. Monetary expenditures will be OX', and prices will rise as money chases goods and services. The differential AB constitutes the inflationary gap. The upward pressure on prices will continue unless the aggregate expenditures can be reduced through curtailing government expenditures, increasing taxes, decreasing the money supply to $(C + I + G)$, or expanding productive capacity to OF'. The speed and stability of the inflationary process depend upon the length of

FIGURE 25-2

Keynesian Inflationary Gap Analysis

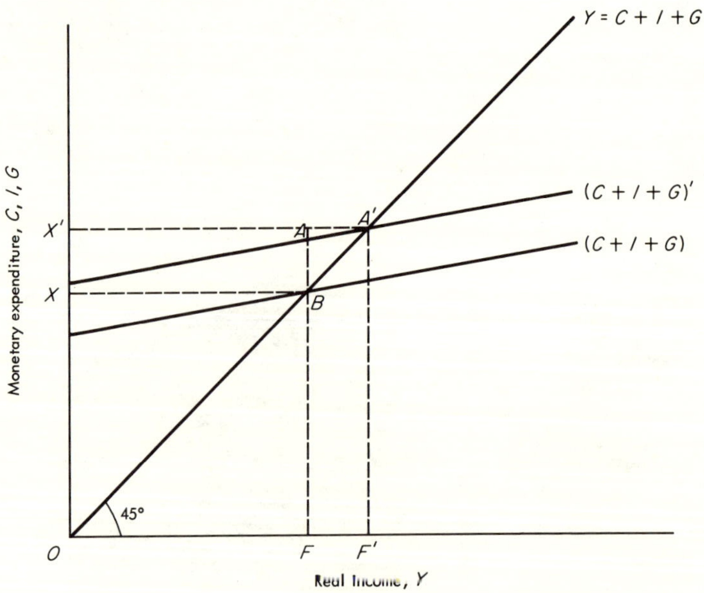

the lag between the sales of goods and services at the higher prices and the corresponding rises in monetary income.

Cost-Push Inflation

The critics of the demand-pull theory argue that since the labor market is imperfect in the sense that factors (unions, labor legislation, etc.) other than supply and demand affect wages, it is unrealistic to presume that demand-pull can explain inflation. Instead, they believe the explanation lies in wage increases which outstrip productivity trends and thus raise the cost of production. The higher cost results in higher prices of goods.

The wage demands may stem either from increasing profits, which on one hand incite labor leaders and on the other hand enable employers to yield to union demands for wage increases, or from labor shortages, which induce employers to lure workers from other industries by higher wages. Regardless of their cause, wage increases cannot normally be absorbed by business unless productivity can be increased simultaneously at the same rate. If productivity remains constant, management has to raise prices or reduce employment to keep its total cost at its previous level.

In its pure form the cost-push theory can be reduced to the model in Figure 25-3. The vertical axis represents the price level, and the horizontal axis indicates the real income level. The aggregate supply curve S moves upward because of the pressure of autonomous organizations. Assume that at full employment the real income level is at Y_0. When aggregate supply increases from S_0 to S_2, the price level must go up from P_0 to P_2 as the income level is at its maximum. Simultaneously demand must rise from D_0 to D_2. If aggregate demand is held at D_0, under rising supply, real income falls progressively to

FIGURE 25-3

Pure Cost-Push Inflation

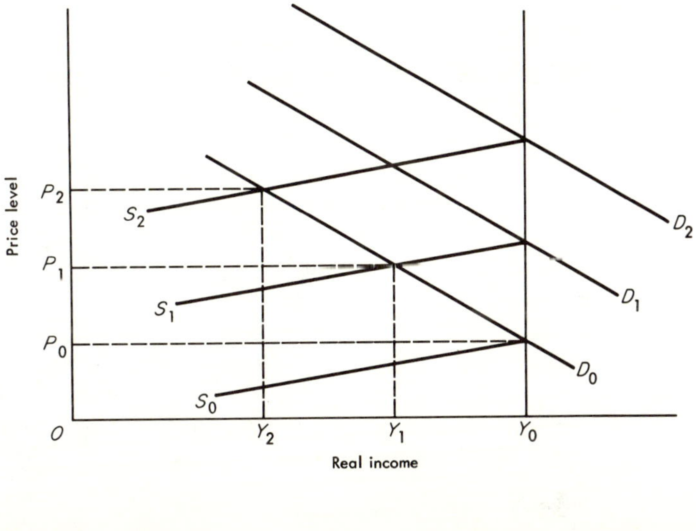

Y_1 and Y_2, even when the price level rises from P_0 to P_2. Therefore, unemployment results from holding prices closer to the level P_0 or to any previously achieved level.

Structural Inflation

The structural theory of inflation holds that, even though the aggregate demand is not excessive, the demand in specific industries of the country may be excessive while in others it may be insufficient. In the industries with the excess demand, prices will rise. But this rise will not be balanced by corresponding price declines in industries with insufficient demand because both prices and wages in the contemporary world are flexible upward, but rigid downward. To the contrary, therefore, the excess demand will raise the price and wage standards of the entire economy.

Empirical evidence shows us that raw-material prices react to both positive and negative shifts in demand and supply. Prices of partially processed goods and materials are also flexible upward but tend to be rigid downward. This effect occurs because semifinished products have fewer substitutes than do raw materials and are, consequently, less susceptible to competitive pressure to lower prices. If demand for a finished good increases, demand for materials used in this good will also increase and their prices will rise. If these same materials are used in products which are experiencing declining demand, firms which produce these products will be faced with a problem of increasing variable costs in addition to their problem of declining sales volume.

In general, prices of materials which are consumed by inflation-aided industries rise since excess demand for the final goods usually implies excess demand for specialized materials. However, materials used mainly in industries with deficient demand do not fall in price unless the demand deficiency is large. Thus, excess demand in particular industries leads to a general rise in the prices of intermediate goods, semimanufactures, supplies, and components; and industries which are not experiencing excess demands find themselves confronted with rising material costs.

Wages also are bid up in excess-demand industries, and wages in other industries then follow. Even though demand for labor is not excessive, firms cannot allow the wage differential between themselves and other firms to get too large because they do not wish to experience the inefficiencies and lowered productivity which result from dissatisfaction over widening differentials.

Producers of finished goods find themselves confronted with a general rise in the level of costs, even when the demand for their products and their own demands for materials and labor are not excessive. Therefore, the more cost determined the prices of the industries involved, the greater the degree of inflation. In competitive industries rising costs are at least partially absorbed.

In summary, structural inflation may arise initially from a rapid growth of a particular industry, a concentration of population in a particular region, a social policy, or any other change which causes excess demand in some sector of the nation's business system. But it leads to a general inflation because wages and prices tend to be cost determined and their flexibility, for institutional and social reasons, is relatively immune to downward pressures but sensitive to upward trends. Thus, neither the upward push of costs nor the aggregate demand can fully explain inflation.

Empirical Reasons for Inflation

Although there is rarely a sole reason for a country's inflation, the main sources of it are reasonably clear. In the industrial countries post-World War II inflation has been primarily of the cost-push type, as wages have tended to increase faster than productivity. The reasons for the discrepancy vary from area to area: In the United States it has been the strength and aggressiveness of labor unions reinforced by prolabor legislation and public policies and, more recently, also the Vietnam War; in the European Economic Community it has been overemployment, which has widened the gap between the supply and the demand of labor; in others there has been a sharp increase in social insurance, unemployment protection, paid vacations, and other social costs. Although industry has striven to counteract the rising labor cost by emphasizing mechanization and automation, they have achieved but partial success. Also, the increased interdependence of national business systems has made inflation internationally contagious. The result is imported inflation, to which the smaller countries have been particularly susceptible.

In the less industrialized countries the overriding cause for inflation has been demand-pull generated by the "revolution of rising expectations" and excessive deficits in governmental budgets. The former generates a massive upgrading of the public's conception of consumer needs, and the latter is spurred by national ambitions for industrial growth. A contributing factor has been the increasing costs of imports; this increase has upset the balance of trade and forced a structural shift in expenditures from domestic to foreign recipients.

Measures of Inflation

Since inflation affects different segments of the society at different times and to different degrees, there is no generally accepted measure of it. The cost-of-living index, usually synonymous with the retail-price index, is the most widely used indicator. In the underdeveloped countries it is the only national measure of prices available; in others it is preferred to wholesale-price and industrial-production indices by businessmen because it is more comprehensive than the other two. However, the wholesale-price index may in fact produce more accurate results for management purposes since it is less affected by government price-control and taxation policies. Also, the wholesale-price index is usually less weighted by food and clothing than the cost-of-living index.

A more sophisticated measure of inflation than any ordinary price index is provided by the so-called *implicit price deflator,* which is the difference between a country's gross national product computed at current prices and that computed at constant prices. As such it is an all-inclusive index encompassing all sectors, private as well as public, and all price levels from raw materials to consumer goods. For many countries this measure is difficult to attain, as no price-deflator computations are published by the authorities. Private companies often lack the capabilities for developing such data by themselves.

Reasonably satisfactory results can be obtained for most managerial purposes by using a number of available measures and averaging out the result in a manner which seems appropriate in a particular instance. Depending upon the country, the more readily available measures may include: cost-of-living index, retail-price index, index of agricultural prices, index of manufacturing prices, index of housing costs, and indices of export and import prices. The free-market rate of exchange used as a supplementary measure can show the change in the external value of a country's currency—a particularly valuable measure in countries where the speed of inflation is faster than elsewhere. In Latin American countries it has become standard practice for business firms to depend on the free-market rate of their national currency rather than on the U.S. dollar as the main indicator of comparative international values.

Social Effects of Inflation

Inflation affects the entire society. It is most malicious for people living on fixed incomes, especially for the passive-income claimants such as the aged and pensioners who lack the means and opportunities for hedging against rising prices. On the other hand, inflation benefits those groups whose earnings rise at an equal or a higher rate than the prices. In some Latin American countries, for example, industrial wages have kept pace with inflation while the earnings of the rural population have not, resulting in a redistribution of purchasing power. Such redistribution affects nearly all segments of the society, since certain types of income and assets rise less rapidly in value than others.

The resultant income disparities cause social stress and political instability. This is particularly pronounced in underdeveloped countries where the redistribution of income has been primarily in favor of the very few highly developed industries and secondarily in favor of industrial labor as such. As a consequence, there is an influx of people to urban centers; this population increase in turn puts unbearable strains on the cities' abilities to provide housing, sewerage, water, and other public services. Vast suburban slums—shantytowns—then form around these industrial cities of the developing world, accentuating their unemployment problems and creating social conditions laden with political explosives.

Inflation also weakens the general confidence in money. By reducing purchasing power, inflation makes currency as well as other monetary assets unsuitable for protecting one's real income. People therefore attempt to convert these assets into price-flexible and quick-yielding tangible properties. Thus inflation discourages investment in price-rigid infrastructural sectors, which are a prerequisite for industrial development and economic growth. Also, when confidence in monetary assets is undermined, the public's will to save is weakened, thrift is discouraged, and spending habits are changed in favor of consumption expenditures. The savings which do accumulate often escape the country and seek safety in a hard currency abroad. In most developing countries the problem is further aggravated by the nonexistence of a security market through which savings could be channeled to productive investments.

Effects of Inflation on Business Conditions

The decline in savings and the tendency of capital to flee the country dry up the supply of capital available for business purposes. At the same time the demand on the capital market increases because of the failure of business firms to raise their depreciation charges to offset the price escalation. If the inflated profits are distributed as dividends, business will be consuming its capital stock and sapping its internal strength for growth even further.

Since inflation discourages saving at the expense of consumption, its general effect is to stimulate the demand for goods and services. But the degree of the stimulus varies in a broad range. On the positive extreme are the groups whose incomes in real terms are increasing the most and on the negative end are those whose purchasing power is decreasing the most. Since the consumption patterns of the gainers and the losers are likely to differ and to become even more different as inflation progresses, the redistribution of income is followed by a redistribution of market demand among different goods and services. Suppliers of the inflation-benefited segments of the market gain, while the suppliers of the other market segments lose. If the demand of the two segments is composed of different product mixes, as is normally the case, its redistribution will be reflected not only in changing market shares but also in the relative profitabilities of different industries and companies. Thus the redistributive effects of inflation are transposed from the consumer level down to the production level. Here windfall profits attract new investment into the inflation-benefited sectors, while the others decay.

Inflation also shifts the demands for exports and imports. For trading nations this is crucial. Inflated costs weaken the competitive position of the country's industries in export markets, and simultaneously the inflated prices stimulate imports. This situation in turn puts pressure on the exchange rate and undermines the country's balance-of-payments position—both potential sources of restrictive governmental action and curtailment of business opportunity.

For the decision maker the redistribution of costs, prices, and purchasing power poses serious complications. The criteria on which decisions are normally based become warped, and executive judgment is distorted by attempts to anticipate and offset the impact of inflation. Long-range planning becomes more complicated and is a questionable alternative to short-run policies and speculative behavior. Why, for example, risk one's investment in a project which after five or six years may have become unprofitable because of unpredictable inflation if profits can be made by speculative manipulation of the assets and the properties on hand?

Price-Level Accounting

How does a foreign company, for example, an American one, report on and measure the impact of inflation? How can it tell whether its operations are keeping pace when, even within the short space of a year, inflation can heavily affect the value of its cash and receivables? This problem can be solved—at least to some extent—by the use of price-level accounting, which attempts to adjust the financial statements to take the effects of inflation into account. In doing so, it pushes aside the traditional accounting assumption that fluctuations in the purchasing power of local currency may be ignored in preparing financial statements. Instead, historical cost figures of transactions and ending balances are converted to the current value of money, as measured by a wholesale- or retail-price index or by a specially constructed composite inflation measure of the type discussed previously in this chapter.

To illustrate the conversion procedure assume the following index numbers:

1962	100
1965	120
1966	168
1967	180

If the analysis concerns the year 1967, all assets, current liabilities, and capital stock items, except inventory and plant assets, would be in terms of that year's currency; so no adjustment would be made, except for the two items: inventory and plant assets. To adjust the preceding year's statement it would be necessary to divide the 1967 index number, 180, by the 1966 index number, 168. Each item in the financial statement for 1966 would then be multiplied by the resulting quotient, which would convert the statement to 1967 dollars. The same procedure would be followed for 1965: Divide 180 by 120 and multiply each item in the 1965 statement by the new quotient.

Inventory, plant assets, and accumulated depreciation are composed of both current dollars and past year's dollars, depending upon the date of acquisition. In respect to the 1967 statement a portion of these three items would be in current dollars. However, that portion representing 1966 acquisitions would have to be adjusted by that year's index, as described above, and so would the portions acquired in 1965 and in each of the previous years. When all the items were adjusted, the three annual statements would conform with purchasing power and, as such, directly compare with one another.

Each noncash item on the financial statements would be expressed in a common denominator: the purchasing power of the currency at the balance-sheet date.

Table 25-1, the summary statement of the Trans-Liberian Mining Company, illustrates this method.

According to the customary financial statements (in historic dollars) the Trans-Liberian Mining Company shows a healthy growth between 1965 and 1967; total assets are up by more than 30 percent, sales have increased by nearly the same rate, and profits show an increase of 29 percent. But, when the 1965 figures are converted to the same purchasing-power base as the 1967 data (constant dollars), an entirely different picture emerges; instead of the 30 percent growth there has actually been a 13 percent decline of company assets, sales have not increased in real terms but decreased by 13.4 percent, and profits have declined (14 percent) rather than increased. Furthermore, it should be noted that in the historical statement the capital-stock base remained the same, assuming no stock was issued or retired. However, the constant or uniform currency statement shows a decline in the capital-stock base; this situation reflects a decline in the value of constant currency units.

Such distortion of real values is dangerous to the company on two counts. One, the capital-stock base is a protection to creditors in the sense that at least that much of the assets must be left in the firm; during inflation this protection is declining, but the relative proportion of retained earnings to capital stock is shown by the historical-cost statements to be growing. Two, if a foreign government were inclined to believe that the profits which a firm is making are excessive, the presence of a high ratio of retained earnings to capital stock could be interpreted as proof of the government's contention and could invite restrictive regulation of the company.

Inventory Policy

A rapid inflation such as has occurred in Brazil and Chile requires a company to have a careful inventory reevaluation procedure because the cost of the inventory is often a major factor in income determination. For example, consider this simplified illustration: The cost of goods is \$2 per unit and the price is \$3; the firm sells 10,000 units and realizes \$30,000. Disregarding operating expense, we see that the profit is \$10,000, which conceivably can all be distributed as dividends to the owners. But if during the sales period the price of inventory purchases rises to \$2.50 per unit, the company will be able to replace only 800 units with the remaining \$20,000. Or, to put it another way, the company will be short \$5000 to maintain the inventory requirements.

The LIFO method of inventory pricing is suggested for firms involved in inflation. It assumes that the merchandise which is purchased last is the first to be used up or sold. The time interval between the purchase and sales dates is thus substantially reduced and the inventory is valued at close to the current cost of acquisition. By contrast the FIFO method of inventory valuation assumes that the merchandise which is first acquired is first to be used,

TABLE 25-1

Trans-Liberian Mining Company
Condensed Financial Statements in Historical Dollars
(thousands of Liberian dollars)

Assets	*1967*	*1966*	*1965*
Current assets			
Cash and other liquid assets	2283.2	2107.2	1299.2
Accounts receivable	1622.4	1422.4	1203.2
Inventory	3864.0	3313.6	2937.6
Total current assets	7769.6	6843.2	5440.0
Plant assets			
Plant and equipment	6128.0	5200.0	4480.0
Less accumulated depreciation	3678.4	2822.4	2080.0
Total net plant assets	2449.6	2377.6	2400.0
Total assets	10,219.2	9220.8	7840.0
Equities			
Current liabilities			
Accounts payable	1512.0	1356.8	977.6
Wages payable	369.6	345.6	292.8
Estimated taxes payable	571.2	492.8	468.8
Other current amounts payable	113.6	97.6	84.8
Total current liabilities	2566.4	2292.8	1824.0
Long-term notes payable	800.0	960.0	880.0
Owners' equity			
Capital stock	640.0	640.0	640.0
Retained earnings	6212.8	5328.0	4496.0
Total equities	10,219.2	9220.8	7840.0
Income Statements			0.4
Net sales	12,947.2	11,131.2	9968.0
*Cost of sales and operating expenses	11,788.8	10,152.0	9070.6
Net income	1158.4	979.2	897.6
*Depreciation included	440.0	384.0	358.4
Assets	*1967*	*1966*	*1965*
Current assets			
Cash and temporary investments	2283.2	2256.8	1948.8
Accounts receivable	1622.4	1523.4	1804.8
Inventory	3864.0	3548.9	4406.4
Total current assets	7769.6	7329.1	8160.0
Plant assets			
Plant and equipment	6128.0	5569.2	6720.0
Less accumulated depreciation	3678.4	3022.8	3120.0
Total net plant assets	2449.6	2546.4	3600.0
Total assets	10,219.2	9875.5	11,760.0

TABLE 25-1 (Cont.)

Condensed Financial Statements in Constant (1967) Dollars (thousands of Liberian dollars)

Equities			
Current liabilities			
Accounts payable	1512.0	1453.1	1466.4
Wages payable	369.6	370.1	439.2
Estimated taxes payable	571.2	527.8	703.2
Other current amounts payable	113.6	104.5	127.2
Total current liabilities	2566.4	2455.6	2736.0
Long-term notes payable	800.0	1028.2	1320.0
Owners' equity			
Capital stock	640.0	685.4	960.0
Retained earnings	6212.8	5706.3	6744.0
Total equities	10,219.2	9875.5	11,760.0
Income Statements			
Net sales	12,947.2	11,921.5	14,952.0
*Cost of sales and operating expenses	11,788.8	10,872.8	13,605.6
Net income	1158.4	1048.7	1346.4
*Depreciation included	440.0	411.3	537.6

at least for accounting purposes. Cost of goods sold is computed on the basis of the earliest prices. In this case old costs are matched with current revenues. Under inflation the FIFO method gives a larger profit figure than the LIFO, since it fails to correct the data for the depreciation in currency value. FIFO, therefore, gives management a false sense of gain and also an excessive tax liability.

The smaller profit produced by LIFO is more representative of the true earnings of a firm under inflation. But even here a correction is necessary. Since LIFO charges current, higher costs against current revenues, the units unsold are valued at older, lower costs. Thus an inventory using LIFO will be valued lower on a balance sheet than its actual replacement cost. The longer the items have been on the books, the greater the discrepancy between LIFO and the real values.

To compensate for this defect the current-cost method can be used. Under this inventory-evaluation system the current market price of each item in the inventory is determined, and the composite of these values is the inventory figure:

$$I = \sum_{i=1}^{n} P_i Q_i$$

where I = inventory

P_i = current market price of 1 unit of the ith item in stock

Q_i = quantity of the ith item in stock.

The resulting sum replaces the traditional LIFO or FIFO figures on the balance sheet, and the retained earnings section is correspondingly adjusted to make the sheet balance. The income statement, of course, will show a greater cost of goods sold and a correspondingly smaller profit.

Despite its compelling logic the current-cost method is still used by only a minority of U.S. companies. Rigidities of tradition in the accounting profession, coupled with some peculiar tax provisions, have helped to perpetuate the FIFO and LIFO conventions. Multinational companies, however, increasingly supplement the traditional systems with the current-cost system, especially for purposes of pricing and planning and for other strategic decisions.

Depreciation Policy

Inflationary trends require the use of accelerated depreciation methods so as not to present inflated profits. Under straight-line depreciation the historical cost of an asset is written off at a fixed, unchanging amount each year, depending on the estimated life of the equipment. An assset costing $20,000 may have an estimated useful life of ten years. One-tenth of $20,000, or $2000, is depreciated for each year in the ten-year period. If at the end of that time a replacement asset could be bought for $20,000, the depreciation charge, which allows cash to accumulate to that extent since no money is spent for depreciation, would theoretically provide the funds for replacement. However, if the price of the asset increases during its life from $20,000 to $40,000, the depreciation accumulation is clearly entirely insufficient to pay for its replacement. Hence, from a financial standpoint an accelerated depreciation must be substituted for the traditional straight-line method to prevent erosion of company assets under inflation. From the legal standpoint, however, the matter is subject to specific restrictions which vary widely from country to country. Most foreign countries have more liberal depreciation laws than the United States, implying that multinational companies should decentralize their depreciation policies to take full advantage of the local laws.

In Great Britain, for example, the 1960 law specifies basic depreciation rates on machinery of 9⅜ percent, 12½ percent, 15⅝ percent, and 25 percent when calculated on a declining balance. In addition, in the year of acquisition there is a special investment allowance of 20 percent and an additional initial allowance of 10 percent. In the first year (using 12½ percent as the basic rate) the total permissible depreciation is 42½ percent.[2]

Until 1956 Sweden gave businesses full freedom to set their own depreciation rates. In 1956 two alternatives were specified: depreciation by plan, which means assuming a basic life for five years and then writing off 20 percent

[2] R. W. Lindholm, "Taxation Considerations" (mimeographed paper, University of Oregon, School of Business Administration, n.d.), p. 13.

each year; and the bookkeeping basis, which allows the business to write off 30 percent of the book value at the start of the year plus the cost of acquisition and less any realizations during the year.[3]

In the United States all depreciation schemes have an upper limit set by the historical cost of the asset. European and Latin American countries usually allow depreciation accumulation up to the actual replacement cost. The rationale of the latter provision is to conceive of depreciation not as a means of paying back the money which was originally spent on an asset but as a means of maintaining the productive power or real value that the asset represents.

Dividend Policy

A foreign-based firm may have dividend problems not only because of exchange controls but also because of inflation. If old costs are matched with current revenues, the resulting net profit is higher than if current costs are matched with revenues. For instance, with an apparent large profit, management may pay out 60 percent of the reported income in the form of dividends, believing that this represents a distribution of only a portion of current earnings. Before this, however, the profit and loss statement should be adjusted for uniform dollars, which may reduce the apparent profit more than 60 percent, indicating that the profit contained a large element of inflated prices and a small portion of real income. In this case the payment of a dividend may take all the "real" profit in terms of purchasing power and may even take part of the equity. If pursued for some time, such a policy will eventually drain the company of its cash, causing slow payment of trade debts or making it impossible to replace inventory or plant as needed.

Liquidity

In a period of rising prices firms suffer losses in the purchasing power of their cash and in the value of assets that are claims against cash, such as accounts receivable. In countries where inflation is a problem, a firm should keep cash at the minimum amount necessary for safe operation. Any surplus cash should be invested in assets which tend to increase in price along with the inflationary trend. Such assets include securities, gold, hard currencies, extractive rights to natural resources, and real estate. Multinational companies often adjust their intracompany transfer prices so that the excess cash will be shifted through intracompany trade to some country with stable currency. (See Chapter 16.) Investment in larger inventories is perhaps the most common device employed by business under inflation. Direct foreign investments in the form of plant and equipment are also common.

Regarding trade credit, inflation requires both a strict and a restrictive policy. To keep the accounts receivable from deteriorating in real value during

3 Lindholm, "Taxation Considerations."

the credit period, it has become customary in many countries to mark up the current selling price by an amount equal to estimated depreciation of the currency during the given credit period. Since inflation may drain a company's cash resources, it is imperative that tight control be exercised over collections and receivables in general.

Inflation will benefit firms that make use of fixed monetary obligations to finance their asset purchases. When monetary assets (cash and accounts and notes receivable) are held while prices rise, the purchasing power of these items can decrease drastically. However, in the case of monetary liabilities (accounts and notes payable) the results are reversed; the continued existence of a fixed-money debt will result in a "gain" for the firm since less of substance is owed. Businesses will, therefore, tend to increase their monetary liabilities if the price level is expected to rise, i.e., go deeper into debt to benefit from inflation. If firms are able to carry large amounts of fixed debt, they will also be able to make a substantial purchasing-power gain from holding monetary liabilities. This strategy is an inflationary hedge against losses which would be incurred from holding monetary assets during the same period.

V

Marketing in Multinational Context

Every land has its pleasures, its style of wit,
and its own ways.

26

Multinational Market and Product Strategies

Strategy is the grand design of policies and programs to carry out a mission or to achieve an established objective—military, political, or economic. As a design for action, strategy can be conceived only in terms of the realities under which it is to be implemented. In business, realities consist on one hand of the present and future opportunities and constraints of the firm and, on the other hand, of the resources and capabilities, both actual and potential, of the firm itself. The development of strategy, therefore, presupposes a realistic assessment of both the opportunities and the capabilities of the firm.

From another viewpoint, strategy is a creature of the objectives and goals which a company has set for itself. Apart from an objective no strategy can be designed. However, this relationship is not unilateral, for apart from strategy the objectives may never be achieved. The interdependence of objectives and strategies is an organic one, and the planning of both must in practice be carried out if not concurrently then at least closely together. This broader process embracing decisions on both the goals and the strategies is often labeled *strategic planning*.

In this chapter we are concerned with the strategic planning of marketing operations in the international or multinational sphere of business enterprise. Since space does not permit us to treat the subject in its entirety, our attention will be focused on the critical aspects, i.e., the decisions which commit a company to one type of international structure or another.

Market Strategy

Selection of foreign markets has often been by accident rather than through planning. Business history abounds with examples of an international venture sprouting from a company official's hunting trip to the Andes, a social or family contact with residents of another country, military or missionary assignments, an unexpected order from a foreign firm, or some other unintentional international contact. Contrary to what one might expect, this method of selection has played a role even in the post-World War II period, as indicated by studies of both the foreign trade and the investments of the United States. However, it appears that recent developments, especially the rise of the multinational corporation in the last several years, have greatly reduced, if not eliminated, those opportunities for successes through accidental discoveries. Although coincidence will always remain an element in international business, as in other spheres of life, we can discard it from further consideration without risking any perversion of contemporary reality.

In a conscious search for international markets, business has been guided by four strategic criteria:

(1) preferential treatment
(2) the "safety-valve" principle
(3) similitude
(4) market research

Preferential Treatment

If we look back to the colonial era, especially to the interwar periods, we see that the world was divided among the major powers into spheres of influence. This division not only included the colonial empires, but also included the noncolonial independents, which were mostly small nations. This political division was inseparable from economic and business relations. The ideas of privileged treatment and discrimination among nations were extended to trade, payments, and international economic policy, and the global market was divided into bundles according to influence and to special relationships. These divisions determined both the opportunities and the constraints for international enterprise and defined the strategic considerations for marketing policy. The bundles were often held with loose and tangled string. And, aside from colonial control, they were wrapped in patriotic slogans and diplomatic decorum. But their effects were unmistakable—namely, bilateralism and protectionism.

Through extreme tariff walls, quota restrictions, multiple exchange rates, and a multitude of other restrictive devices—both visible and invisible—business relations among nations were constrained to the extreme. One's opportunities to do business abroad depended more on his ability to penetrate the barriers than on any other factor. Accordingly, management's primary objectives and its strategic efforts were focused on this point.

The principal ways to pry openings through the barriers were by intergovernmental treaties and trade agreements which accorded special treatment to products or investments or both coming from the other contracting country on a reciprocal basis.

A secondary method of penetrating the barriers was direct negotiations between a company and a foreign government; if successful, they resulted in special concessions granted to the firm under a contractual arrangement or a special charter. Needless to say, this latter opportunity arose only under unusual circumstances; business, in general, was dependent on intergovernmental treaties and agreements. But, whichever the case, access to foreign markets was a special privilege rather than a normal aspect of business operations. And, accordingly, management's first preoccupation in the international field was developing the access routes to foreign markets rather than the markets themselves.

Although bilateralism and protectionism have been swept aside by the multilateral system of trade which has emerged since 1948 through GATT (General Agreement on Tariffs and Trade), the philosophy and concepts of that era are still very much in evidence. Privileged treatment, such as tax exemption, special tariff protection, and exclusive production or importation rights, continues to dominate the international strategies of certain firms and industries. And, one must add, preferential treatment is not a ghost of a previous age. Governments of some nations, ill advised to be sure, have hoped to boost their retarded economies by giving exclusive preferential treatment to certain firms or industries to the detriment of all others. Nearly all the new countries seem to be in a desperate hurry to reach higher levels of industrialization, and no device, including privilege peddling, may safely be written off. However, the forces of international economic integration and multilateral trade hopefully will continue to erode such discriminatory policies and practices. As a result, the strategy of special privileges and political protection will hold increasingly less promise for business success. Indeed, as a strategy it is approaching obsolescence. It persists in companies with roots in the colonial era—primarily companies in the extractive industries. For them a change is overdue.

The Safety-Valve Principle

Another strategy is to use foreign markets as a safety valve for disposing of surplus production or for utilizing excess capacity in periods of slack demand in the home country and, thus, to achieve a stable output at minimum cost. In such cases, international operations are clearly subordinate to domestic activity. To achieve this objective two conditions must be fulfilled: foreign markets must be found where demand for the product exists, and the demand must either remain untapped or be readily reconvertible to the company when it commences its intermittent operations after a temporary absence.

In the sellers' market of the first post-World War II decade the safety-valve strategy was successfully employed by a great many U.S. firms, despite its disruptive effect upon foreign distributors and consumers. Since these firms were not interested in penetrating deeply into the export markets and since their business abroad was based on price appeal (a policy of flexible low prices), they were not concerned with accurate measurements and projections of the market potentialities. It sufficed to establish contact with interested parties in other countries through international trade journal references or through the U.S. Dept. of Commerce trade lists and to achieve limited turnover (sales) objectives abroad.

But as competitive conditions were restored in world markets, the safety-valve strategy became increasingly precarious to follow. The companies which still adhere to it have been forced to steadily increase their foreign contacts and either to shift from area to area or to engage in skimming operations similar to those of a speculative trader. Besides its operational limitations, this method is denounced by government authorities and in editorials as being detrimental to the image of a country's business abroad, and its role is likely to decline even further.

Similitude

With the liberalization of international economic relations the critical decisions have shifted from the political and legal instrumentalities discussed above to market analysis. For this shift business was, and in many ways still is, ill prepared. Statistical data and other information for assessing the different world markets are scarce and difficult to obtain. Methods and techniques of market research, developed primarily in the United States and Canada, are difficult to employ in the international realm because of linguistic, social, and cultural differences. The paucity of commercial research organizations in the vast majority of countries leaves the company with the alternatives of (1) engaging an American team to conduct the studies at very high costs, or (2) reaching its decisions without the relevant facts. Neither solution is satisfactory.

Efforts have been made to meet this need by several marketing and management-consulting firms which in the last few years have established overseas offices and developed native cadres to do the research. Large manufacturing concerns, too, have tackled the problem, and several have built quite significant research units specializing in international markets.

The results have varied from company to company. In general a substantial amount of progress has been made. But in reference to the standards of the United States and Canada, and also to the requirements of realistic planning, a gigantic job remains before adequate information becomes accessible at a reasonable cost.

What complicates international fact finding is the discouraging discovery that neither the design nor many of the methods of market research are transplantable from one country to another. Cultural settings, social attitudes, and economic structures make most countries sufficiently unique to cause serious complications for many multinational research projects and to completely void some others. Many standard research techniques such as mail questionnaires, telephone surveys, and personal interviews still lie largely beyond reach of a researcher in vast areas of the world because of taboos and technological conditions. The result is that very often market research programs must be tailored to each foreign country. Although the few big ones may have the potential demand to support a separate research program, the many small countries almost never do.

When facts do not suffice, theory must do. As reliable data on foreign markets have been scarce and expensive, the principle of *similitude* has become the strategic guide for international action. What does it mean? In essence, the principle of similitude states that the best foreign market for a company is the country which is the most like or the least unlike the markets now served by the firm. Likeness is judged in terms of the general standard of living, cultural background, and social behavior. The theory behind this proposition is that the greater the similarity between the two countries in these broad terms, the easier it is to transfer products, services, and practices from one to the other. Proponents of the principle cite as proof of its validity pairs of countries such as the United States and Canada, Sweden and Denmark, Germany and the Netherlands, and France and Belgium, and insist that, unlike the preferential treatment idea, the similitude principle rests upon the empirical fact that trade between two industrial countries is greater than between an industrial and a subindustrial country under the same general circumstances. If followed to its ultimate conclusion, the principle of similitude would direct a firm to start its foreign operations in a country most similar to its home market and expand in succession to less similar areas.

The critics of the principle of similitude point out first that while it may apply in a large context, its use is not always justified in the smaller economic setting of a particular firm; individual opportunities in the final analysis are determined by the specifics rather than the national aggregates. Second, they argue that in the consumer-goods sector similarity may have its validity, but in the capital-goods field such general notions as the standard of living and cultural setting are of little value. To this might be added that this principle would present a most discouraging prospect to a firm located in a less developed country. Yet, any study of international market strategies confirms that most U.S. firms are in fact following the similitude theory in the great majority of cases where governmental guarantees or other nonbusiness influences are not a factor.

International Market Research

Before any scientific measurement of a market can be attempted, it is necessary to clearly define its dimensions. Although the word *market* is loosely used with several different meanings, in research its usage must be strictly limited to the product of three variables: population, purchasing power, and propensity to buy. Designating the three factors as P_1, P_2, and P_3, we can express the basic dimensions of market as

$$M = P_1 \times P_2 \times P_3$$

The underlying rationale of the formula is self-evident. Without a population no market can exist. The population may, of course, consist of either individuals or institutional consumers; in either case the size of the population, its geographic distribution, its consumer types, and its behavior over time are primary determinants of what and how much it will demand. All market research, therefore, must start with the delineation and measurement of the relevant population—schoolgirls, family units, drugstores, oil refineries, missile sites, etc. But population alone does not make a market. The population must have the financial ability to transform its latent needs to effective demand; this it can do only to the extent to which it has purchasing power that can be allocated for the acquisition of a particular product. Therefore, measurements of population take on marketing significance only after coupled with corresponding measurements of purchasing power.

Both P_1 and P_2 lend themselves to numerical counting and any desired quantitative treatment. The same cannot be said about P_3, propensity to consume. Clearly, no amount of information on population and purchasing power can make a market unless the population is willing to spend the purchasing power on the product or service for which the measurements were made. Thus, although intangible and unmeasurable in a direct sense, the propensity to consume is also fundamental to the basic notion of a market.

Literature on domestic market research often fails to emphasize the significance of this triangular relationship. It does this presumably under the dual assumption that (a) the variance in the population regarding P_2 and P_3 is relatively small as far as any particular product is concerned, and (b) pre-existing information can supply the P_2 and P_3 necessary to complement any particular set of population data. Therefore, domestic market research is often preoccupied with population measurements, and pays relatively little attention to P_2 and P_3.

Such an approach to international market research would be disastrous, for the level of income and its distribution vary sharply from country to country, as do consumer requirements and motivation. Any analogy of a Swiss or Swedish consumer's financial ability and propensity to consume to the same characteristics of a Congolese, Bolivian, or Indian consumer, for example, would result in a misconstruction lacking any real relationship to the factual market. This, of course, does not prevent unscrupulous commercial research agencies from selling such market information to unsophisticated clients.

Sources of Information

Any objectively accurate evaluation of markets must be based on the analysis of pertinent factual information. The collection of such information represents a most important and formidable task in international marketing, not because factual data are more important in international marketing than in national or local marketing but because the collection of authentic and sufficiently detailed market data is vastly more complicated and costly internationally than in the United States. Although there are inherent reasons for this complexity and cost, as the ensuing discussion will show, the effect is artificially magnified by a relatively low level of knowledge about foreign and international sources of data; this lack of knowledge leads to misappropriation of the data and misinterpretation of the factual situation.

The most common source of confusion is the differences in statistical reporting systems. American analysts and executives are accustomed to the U.S. government's official reports, particularly the U.S. Bureau of the Census publications (censuses of population, of business, of manufacturers, of housing, etc.), which contain nearly any kind of basic economic and social facts about the country. In addition to the complete censuses published periodically, the government publishes a variety of current reports based on sample surveys or official estimates to update the basic information. This official reporting system is so much a part of marketing activity that it has, to a very great extent, become the frame of reference used in factual market analysis.

No other country has an identical system. Each has its own, and each is unique in some or most respects. The locating of relevant information on foreign markets, therefore, presupposes a thorough understanding of the particular countries' statistical practices. Differences in data-collecting and data-reporting methods do not necessarily affect the type or the reliability of the data, as is often erroneously assumed. What they do affect are the form and the contents of the publications in which they are released. Many countries put out outstanding compilations of socioeconomic information. Other reports are superior in one aspect or another. Most industrial countries publish a great many statistics which are generally reliable and available at a nominal cost. The same cannot be said about the underdeveloped countries, except for two or three; if they exist at all, their data are usually inadequate and inaccurate—often based on nothing more than "official opinion." Governmental sources in dictatorial countries, especially those of the communist bloc, are unsatisfactory because of deliberate biases and falsifications introduced to serve propaganda purposes rather than objective truth.

U.S. Government Sources

Since the mid-1950's the U.S. government has come to recognize the need for better information on markets beyond its own boundaries, and several programs have been initiated or improved to deal with the so-called *export-information gap*; they include the following services:

Overseas Business Reports. This information service consists of four different series or parts: Part I—*Economics* presents economic surveys on individual countries, emphasizing aspects particularly relevant to exporters, shippers, and creditors; part II—*Operations Reports* deal with property rights, trademark protection, patents, foreign-trade regulations, shipping practices, and related information; part III—*Statistical Reports* provide monthly data on U.S. exports and imports by country and on foreign trade among other nations; part IV—*Utilities Abroad* is a compendium of transportation and electric-power industries abroad.

World Trade Directory Reports. This is a service rendered by the U.S. commercial attachés and consuls at foreign posts upon request of U.S. companies. A directory report outlines the characteristics of a particular foreign firm, listing its supplies, export markets, and other pertinent facts.

Trade Lists. Compiled by foreign-service officers on an individual-country basis, these lists, classified by product category, contain the names and addresses of foreign companies which either have expressed or are expected to have interest in American goods or services.

Other. Among the many other attempts of the U.S. government to provide information on the world market, the *Marketing Handbook* series provides comprehensive reports on the market for U.S. products in different countries. Regrettably only a half dozen countries have been covered to date.

The *Survey of Current Business* and the *Federal Reserve Bulletin* are useful sources of income, foreign exchange, and balance-of-payments information. Finally, the *Statistical Abstract of the United States* presents annual summary data on all basic aspects of U.S. foreign trade.

International and Foreign Sources

The United Nations is rapidly becoming the most important source of socioeconomic data on an international scale. Its statistical reports present data on 250 countries (the number has been increasing). Two other important sources of international data on a wide range of subjects are the Organization of Economic Cooperation and Development (OECD) in Paris and the European Economic Community in Brussels and Luxembourg. The Pan American Union, too, might be added to this group.

On more specialized topics the International Monetary Fund (IMF), the International Labor Organization (ILO), and the General Agreement on Tariffs and Trade (GATT) office serve in their respective fields as major information sources.

In reference to published information from a particular country itself, no general source can be listed for reasons explained earlier. However, there are at least two and often three well-established channels through which the sources can be not only uncovered but also reached. First is the U.S. commercial representation in the country involved. The lists of U.S. embassies and consulates are available from all Dept. of Commerce and Dept. of State field offices in all large cities. Also, requests can be transmitted to the commercial foreign-service offices abroad through the field-office staff. A parallel channel is provided by foreign governments' commercial representatives in the United States. Besides the consuls, commercial attachés, and counselors, some countries use foreign-trade secretaries or special trade representatives to encourage closer contact between their official trade-promotion organ and the business community abroad. A third channel may exist in the form of a special industry export association which, for purposes of goodwill and reciprocity, catalyzes the information flow between its own and other markets.

Banks and Business Organizations

For current business and credit conditions foreign departments of major commercial banks can be of significant help. Although they seldom undertake formal market studies, they do keep abreast of daily trade situations in a number of foreign countries and are usually ready to share their information with companies concerned with the particular area.

A number of trade associations, chambers of commerce, port authorities, and various service firms offer auxiliary sources on various aspects of world markets. The quality of their data varies widely, and much of it consists of an assortment of uncritically assembled data. Like the consulates and trade representatives, these organizations can be useful not for data but for information on the sources of data.

Field Research

Data gathering through field work must fill the gaps left by the insufficiency and inconsistency of available published information. Desk or library research, which is based on existing data, and field work to generate new data represent different phases of market research. The latter requires research skills and capital expenditures of an entirely different order. Even in the United States field research is vastly more complicated and costly than desk research. In the international markets, these complexities and costs are greatly magnified. Experience and expertise, therefore, can pay very high dividends in international market research.

Foreign Market Surveys

The central idea in the survey method is to substitute sampling for a complete account and to estimate from the sample data the actual size and characteristics of the statistical universe which was sampled. This substitution is necessary because a complete census is normally beyond the financial capabilities of any one firm and because absolute accuracy is unnecessary for most business decisions. To be valid the sampling must be based on the mathematical laws of probability so that the data collected reflect a true cross section of the particular universe. The techniques and practices of sampling are well covered in numerous books on this subject. The concern here is not with the sampling as such but with the peculiar problems encountered in international market research.

LANGUAGE. The need to use one or more foreign languages greatly complicates questionnaire design and personal interviewing, as well as the analysis and interpretation of results. Market researchers are no different from the rest of the U.S. business community, and their linguistic abilities can rarely be practically used in their professional fields. In both interviewing and questionnaire design, precise and sophisticated use of language is often decisive for the clarity and the nonambiguity of the answers and also for the controls and double checks which may be necessary to protect the integrity of the data against any biases held by the informants. Literal translations of words and phrases are of little value in this type of communication.[1]

CULTURAL OBSTACLES. Willingness to provide information in response to requests from strangers is less than complete in all countries. However, the degree of reluctance is often much greater abroad than in the United States. Cultural attitudes and social customs account for the differences. Information on personal preferences is often considered private, and all attempts to probe their nature are suspect. In some cultures, certain topics are acceptable for discussion only among men, others only among women. Also, class structure may preclude communication of certain types between members of different strata. The social level and the sex of the interviewer are major considerations. The practice of purdah, restricted mingling of the sexes, persists in many parts of the world. No self-respecting housewife in such a society is prepared to give a man interviewer access to her home, much less her kitchen. On the other hand, many foreign men find it beneath their dignity to discuss their personal preferences and habits with a female interviewer. In some countries he may refuse to answer questions put to him by a man of inferior social standing. Workers in lower economic and social classes may be just as reluctant to talk with an interviewer from a higher stratum of society.

Another difficulty encountered in international business research is the suspicious attitude aroused by inquiries pertaining to money or business matters. In some foreign countries such matters are regarded as strictly private affairs. Concern about tax payments or about the possibility of giving away business secrets or of tarnishing the existing image of one's family or firm act as strong suppressants. Business firms as well as individuals are reluctant to give out facts that relate to economic status or purchasing power for these reasons. Promises of anonymity and offers of the use of the final results have

[1] If English-language questionnaires are distributed in a non-English-speaking market, it is essential to enclose a glossary of at least the most significant words and phrases used in the survey.

almost no appeal to the average foreign businessman, who sees little or no personal gain in this latter proposition.

In less-developed countries field work may suffer from inadequate literacy levels and inability to conceive and articulate the desired information. This drawback is very valid for products and services uncommon in the country or otherwise new to the respondent. For example, it is difficult for a person to express an attitude toward an electric stove or gas heater if he has never seen or used them and cannot recognize the value or usefulness of these products.

Experience with multinational questionnaires shows that the same questions tend to elicit varying answers in different countries. This is frequently true even in studies where the informants are statisticians, economists, or other professionals. International market research staffs must, therefore, carefully study the cultural and social structure to anticipate and to compensate for any special circumstances in each country which might bias or invalidate the responses.

Particularly sensitive are questions which may be construed as reflecting the nation's international status or the informant's patriotism. Especially in the newer nations, but often also in older ones, national fame and glory often take precedence over objectivity, and answers bearing on these attitudes easily become exaggerated or distorted. The need for thorough planning and "cultural conditioning" of any survey program—be it mail questionnaire or personal interviews—is further underscored by the fact that the research staff normally has no independent evidence or other standards against which the reliability of the survey results could be tested.

Selection of respondents

In the United States listings of individuals, business firms, and social institutions which are actual or potential consumers of various goods and services are readily available. The basic sources are the membership rosters of innumerable formal organizations that embrance the great majority of the population. Specialist firms on market research and public-opinion polling not only have refined the rosters into information systems from which almost any desired consumer group can quickly be identified together with all the necessary details for mailing and canvassing but also have complemented the organizational materials with specific prospects.

In most other countries neither of these conditions exists. Very few people belong to any formal organization, and specialist survey firms are seldom found except in the Western European industrial countries. Thus neither the raw materials nor the listing expertise is at hand. Although progress is being made in this field through the efforts of some private research organizations and advertising agencies, the international market researcher remains largely dependent upon his own ingenuity and skill in locating the respondent population in most foreign markets.

Cost of International Marketing Research

Research is a highly technical job. Besides formally trained and experienced professionals, it requires specialized organizations in order to function effectively. In the United States and Western Europe most business research is bought from various market and other commercial research firms rather than carried out by companies themselves. The research firms design research projects to best serve their client companies' needs, and carry them out through their own personnel and intelligence organization. Research is thus functionally specialized both in terms of personnel and of institutions and, as such, is seldom a responsibility to be discharged by operating managements.

Outside the Western industrial area marketing research is still in its infancy. Indigenous researchers, not to mention research agencies, are rarities, and the opportunity seldom presents itself for delegating the research function to independent specialists as in the industrial countries. Consequently, the burden of research falls on the operating company itself. This is a doubly difficult proposition. First, as already indicated, the operating companies are not normally equipped with market research capabilities, and, second, the task of researching foreign markets presents many problems and complications not encountered in domestic market research. In many companies for which these problems have been great, the use of formal research has been abandoned in favor of similitude or pure judgment. Others have sought help from U.S. or European research firms. Although some research firms have been making rapid progress toward acquiring research capabilities outside their home country, the typical research firm is still unequal to the international task. Indeed, the vast majority of U.S. commercial research agencies make no claim to international capability and do not hide the fact that they would have to use a substantially higher schedule of fees in international than in purely domestic research. There is, of course, no guarantee that despite the higher fees the results are not merely foreign data set into a basically American structure of values and ideas and, as such, are dangerously misleading.

But even a fully qualified research organization frequently cannot do marketing research abroad at a cost comparable to that for the same research in the United States simply because many of the elements of research cost are unaffected by the size of the country which is studied. Project design, organization, adaptation of methods, training of the field force, and most other planning and preparatory activities belong in this fixed-cost category. But, although unaffected by the size of a country, these costs are affected by the environmental peculiarities of a country and may, therefore, vary from one foreign market to another in no relation to their size. Costs in the data-processing and the analysis phases of a project are also relatively independent of the size of the country or region. It is only in the field-work phase that costs tend to vary in direct proportion to the size of the territory studied. As a consequence, the overall cost of international market research bears little relationship to the size of the potential foreign market. Usually, it is considerably costlier to carry out any particular project abroad than in the United States or Canada. This difference becomes particularly pronounced if the research costs are expressed on a per-unit basis; i.e., the costs are distributed over the potential sales that may result from the project.

Because of the high cost and the low yields of business research abroad, the planning of international objectives and strategies has been hampered by a paucity of reliable and relevant factual information. Despite gradual improvement, this condition remains a major bottleneck for the individual firm, especially for the smaller companies.

Methods and Control

Despite being the functional field which has the longest history of international application, marketing can lay no greater claim on maturity or methodological sophistication than other aspects of international management. For long, international marketing programs have been built on one of two basic assumptions.

One, known as the extension approach, assumes that "domestic products, marketing experience, and marketing programs would be as successful in foreign markets as in the United States."[2] From this naively ethnocentric perspective U.S. solutions are universal solutions, and there is no need for international marketing know-how of any kind. Its proponents, diminishing in numbers, have pointed to unqualified successes of certain companies who have transplanted their American marketing programs abroad without any change. Close examination shows, however, that these companies have enjoyed a strongly monopolistic position due either to the uniqueness of their product or the lack of indigenous competition. Thus, they have succeeded not because of but in spite of their exported marketing methods.

The second approach has been to assume as a fact that each country is so entirely different from all others that it needs to be treated as a separate and distinct marketing unit. That has meant complete decentralization with consequent proliferation of parallel organs and programs throughout the world. While more defensible on analytic grounds and with a better track record, this approach shares the basic weakness with the extension method that there is no overall strategic planning of the global marketing activity.

For a fully rational and effective multinational marketing program the firm must recognize both the critical differences and essential similarities among different national markets. This task requires an overall view and a high degree of cross-cultural sophistication which no single affiliate of the firm can be expected to possess. It is, therefore, a headquarters task, an important aspect of multinational strategic planning and policy formulation.

2 Warren J. Keegan, "Multinational Marketing: The Headquarters Role," *Columbia Journal of World Business,* Vol. VI, No. 1 (Jan.-Feb. 1971) 85.

Product Strategy

Product strategies can be developed only in the context of specific market information. To be exportable, products must be acceptable to consumers abroad. In competitive markets they must not only be acceptable but also be preferable to other similar products. Something received willingly by consumers in the United States or Canada (or whatever the country of origin) is not necessarily suitable for another market; differences in taste, economic status, technical standards, or legal codes may make changes and adaptations necessary before the product can meet foreign consumer requirements. The following examples illustrate some of the most common differences:

Electrical Current. Voltage and cycles vary from country to country. In most areas of the world the voltage is substantially higher than the 110-volt standard in the United States and Canada, making all electrical goods unusable unless adapted to the voltage requirements of the export markets.

Radio Networks. U.S. radios are too weak to be useful in many export markets of the world because American network broadcasting systems obviate the need to own powerful receivers. This technological condition is not present in most overseas markets. Hence, the product is largely unsuitable for export.

Weights and Measurements. With a few exceptions, including Canada and the United States, nations have adopted the metric system. As a result, North American products designed and packaged in nonmetric units are subjects to resistance on three counts:

(1) They may not fit into the scheme of things—for example, automobiles, desks, files, accessories, tools, containers, prefabricated houses.

(2) They may involve costly alteration and waste; examples are lumber and building materials which have to be recut and possibly refinished by the foreign consumer to meet metric standards. Both labor and the import material itself have to be expended to do this.

(3) Surveys in European countries show that housewives abroad are reluctant to buy consumer goods packaged in containers the dimensions or weight of which they cannot comprehend and which may not fit the storage shelves, recipes, or other standards of their homes.

Tariff Laws and Regulations. Import duties are levied on many products. The bases for these levies vary widely from country to country, not only in terms of rates but also in terms of the classifications that underlie the rates. Minor alterations such as removing metallic ornamentation from a drum or a piece of braid from a garment can move the product from one classification to another and change the duty very substantially. The limited studies of this author point to immense possibilities for savings through designing products with the duty requirements of the export market in mind. It may be true that a greater return would accrue if some of the funds now spent on income-tax accounting were converted to duty analysis by international firms.

Other fixed product criteria

Food and drug laws, building codes, safety regulations, and engineering standards provide similar examples. Most important are the intangible, often hidden, elements of buyer preference; these come under the purview of motivation research. What little we know of the basic motivations strongly suggests that our motivational mechanism, whatever its makeup, is more a creature of the culture to which we belong than of the instincts and drives of the species.

A comparative analysis of market requirements, based upon factual studies, is but the beginning phase of planning international product strategy. Specific product characteristics based on this information must be determined. A practical way of distinguishing these characteristics is by identifying each market factor and rating its relative impact like this:

Environmental Factor	*Rating* 1 2 3 4 5 6 7 8 9 10	*Adaptation*
(1) Labor cost	__________	Automation or manualization of production
(2) Literacy	__________	Re-marking and simplification of product
(3) Income	__________	Quality and price change
(4) Interest rates	__________	Quality and price change
(5) Maintenance	__________	Changes in tolerance
(6) Climate	__________	Product adaptation
(7) Isolation (heavy repair)	__________	Product simplification, reliability improvement
(8) Standards	__________	Recalibration of product
(9) Availability of other products	__________	Greater or lesser product integration
(10) Power availability	__________	Resizing of product
(11) Special conditions	__________	Product redesign or invention

The continuum-weighting factors (1–10) are only a suggestion for establishing the relative importance of each environmental factor.

The Cost of Product Adaptation

From specific ratings such as those above conclusions can be drawn as to the nature and amount of product change necessary to meet the consumption requirements of the export market concerned.

But almost any change will affect the cost of the product. What the effect will be depends not only on the change itself but also on the production methods and organization of the firm. For example, even a minor adjustment may be very costly in a highly mechanized and automated plant; on the other hand, a job-order factory may easily accommodate even major changes with no significant effect on costs. In some exceptional instances the product change can result in a reduction of production costs and thereby make the product change doubly desirable, i.e., from the standpoint of the market as well as of the cost. More often, however, a product change results in an increase in production cost. Unless the demand is highly inelastic, such an increase in cost will inversely affect the sales volume and thus tend to defeat the purpose of the adaptive change in the product.

Where the need for changing the product arises from technical or legal conditions in the foreign market, the decision will hinge on the incremental effects which the product change will have on the cost and the volume of the firm. Where, however, the need for the product change arises from nontechnical resistances to sales, such as tastes or consumer habits, a further variable must be considered—namely, promotion. If the resistances are such that they can be overcome by information, persuasion, and education of the consumer, the costs of these efforts must be compared with those of the product change to make a rational choice between them. Such comparison is possible only if the company has reliable data on its advertising effectiveness as well as on the behavior of its production costs. It might be added that the relationship between the costs of product change and the costs of advertising to achieve the same sales target without product change is not a linear one but varies with the degree of change involved. Typical behavior of the two cost components is illustrated in Figure 26-1.

Export selling costs decline rapidly when the most critical adjustments of the product to foreign-market requirements are made. To this category belong such changes as adaptation of packaging, relabeling, introduction of metric measurements, different styling emphasis, and conversion of electric current. After the critical changes have been incorporated, further reduction of export selling costs, primarily advertising costs, is possible only by more substantial changes in the product.

The cost of production has an opposite tendency. The initial changes cause a high incremental cost because the established processes or routines have to be broken and new ones introduced. But once a sufficiently large number of workers and machines have been converted, the incremental costs of further changes in the product decline as illustrated by the flattening off of the curve in the chart. This decline continues until changes in the original product concept end. From this point, the cost of adaptation will turn sharply upward, and no further adaptation is feasible. If, at this point, the product is still not salable in the export market, introduction of an entirely new product is the answer.

The opposite tendencies of the export selling costs and the product adaptation costs place the decisions of adaptation among the most controversial and tension-ridden ones in a firm. Production people want no part of product change; marketing people never have enough of it. The intracompany battle lines are especially sharp when production and marketing divisions are organized as separate profit centers within the firm. To assure that due con-

FIGURE 26-1

Typical Effects of Product Adaptation on Costs of Production and Export Promotion (Selling)

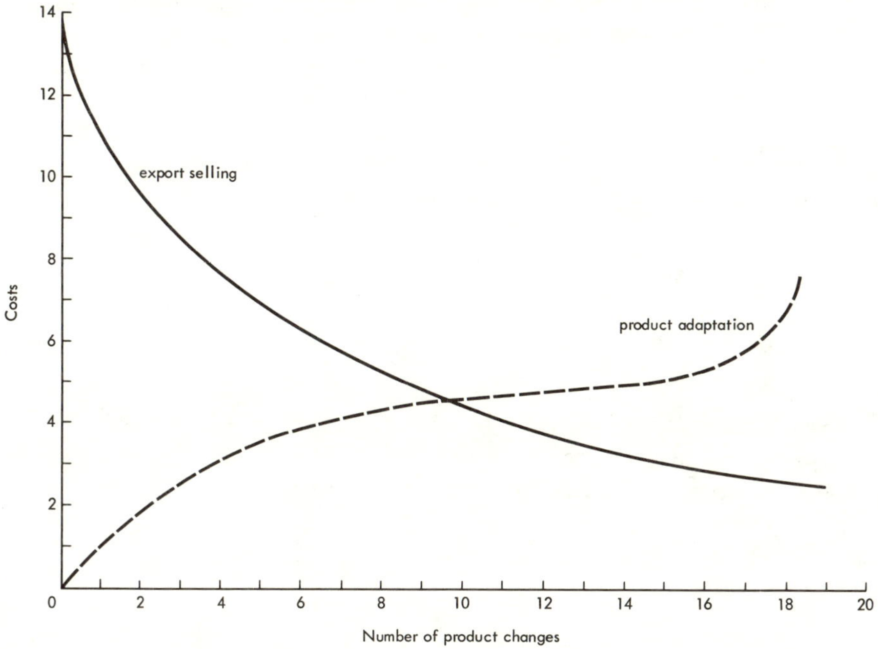

sideration is given both tendencies and that their combined effect on the firm's profitability is used as the basis, the final decisions on these matters should not be delegated to the functional executives but should be reserved by top management for itself.

Adaptation of Trademark

One of the knottiest problems in connection with product adaptation is branding and trademark policy; i.e., should a company continue to use one trademark or brand, or should it establish a different identity for the product in each national or regional foreign market? Having the same brand but different quality characteristics would violate the orthodox theory of branding, which postulates that in order to be effective a brand must become synonymous with a particular quality standard. Hence any adaptive changes in a product should be reflected in its brand.

On the other hand, the critics point out that any attempts to localize branding prevent the company from building up that multinational image which, they maintain, has an important impact on the separate markets which it serves. The risk of confusing the consumer by quality differences is believed to be more than outweighed by the international carryover which a uniform international brand would provide. Although neither school has won the argument, the weight seems to be shifting toward the one-brand proponents. But more study and research must be done before we really know.

Methods and techniques of planning international product strategies are only beginning to emerge. But progress is being made, and the traditional notion that "a good product at home is a good product abroad" is being replaced by an awareness that a company's international potentialities can often be increased through systematic efforts to tailor its products to the foreign demand. The successes of some European and Japanese firms are to a high degree attributable to their pioneering efforts in international product strategy.

Appendix to Chapter 26

Survey Materials Collected in the Developing Countries: Sampling, Measurement, and Interviewing Obstacles to Intra- and International Comparisons[3]

Robert Edward Mitchell

Scholars, government officials, and commercial interests in the developing countries are increasingly recognizing that survey research methods provide the only means by which systematic information can be collected and analyzed for a wide range of purposes of both scholarly research and policy making. . . .

The present paper attempts to outline and catalogue some of the major issues involved in the conduct of survey research in the developing countries. A concern with the use of existing materials for purposes of secondary analysis, especially for international comparative purposes, initiated this review. . . .

The analysis of available materials is under three headings or types of bias: sampling, measurement, and interviewer bias.

Sampling Errors

Poor workmanship

In many countries it is only an analytical fiction which permits one to discuss sampling and nonsampling errors separately, for the same staffs and procedures used in interviewing respondents are also used in preparing the samples. This is the situation in particular with regard to preparing samples of certain specialized populations for which no locator or parameter informa-

3 Reprinted from the *International Social Science Journal,* XVII, No. 4 (1965).

tion is available. In these instances, the interviewing staffs frequently prepare the information which is used in drawing the sample.

Relatively few countries have adequate sampling information even for their major metropolitan centers, and, as a consequence, various incomplete, outdated maps are used, or, in the absence of alternative registers (for example, voting or housing registers), agencies will prelist their sampling areas. Some studies in nonurban areas employ random-walk procedures...without the benefit of prelisting and, therefore, the interviewer is at the same time a sampler. Interviewers also often select the respondent within the household, although it appears to be an increasingly common practice to have the interviewer first list the members of the household and then use a table of random numbers to select the actual person to be interviewed. Interviewers, of course, play a crucial sampling role in studies based on quota samples.

Unfortunately, there is abundant reason to question both the competence and honesty of interviewing-sampling field staffs in many countries, and, consequently, to question the adequacy of the samples which are drawn.

Coverage and comparability of sampling frames

Given the lack of sampling resources available in developing countries, and given the sampling obstacles created by poor and often mobile populations, it is probably inevitable that sampling frames often fail to include large segments of the population within a single country and that samples used for international comparative purposes are typically based on non-comparable sampling frames. . . .

These problems of the comparability of frames between countries are no less serious within single nations. For example, one might question the comparability of Rio de Janeiro samples with samples of São Paulo. Since survey studies in most developing countries tend to be conducted within the major city or in the city where the major research agencies are located, the sampling resources are differently distributed throughout the nation. Therefore, a so-called *national urban sample* based on a number of cities will utilize sampling frames which differ considerably in their completeness. . . .

Social and cultural accessibility (noncompletion rates)

Even if a researcher is satisfied with the sampling frames and procedures prepared for his study, he will still have to overcome obstacles created for him by nonrespondents, an especially acute problem in comparative studies. Nonrespondents are typically not distributed randomly throughout the sample but differ according to variations in the cultural and social accessibility of distinct population segments. . . . A number of studies and research experiences in Asia indicate that women are culturally and socially inaccessible to interviewers,[4] whereas the experience elsewhere indicates that men are rela-

[4] However, in one Southeast Asian country, two commercial agencies differed in their estimations of whether men or women had the higher refusal rate.

tively inaccessible, and, as the Almond-Verba study suggests, there are national differences in the availability of different types of respondents even within the Western world.

These same problems arise for samples within a single country, since groups may differ in their degree of accessibility to interviewers in different parts of a nation. In Latin America, some of the major intranational differences in response rates seem to occur for members of the upper class, since they are difficult to interview in urban areas.

Intranational as well as international differences in response rates have implications for the way the data can be interpreted. As will be indicated again later, there is good reason to believe that respondents and nonrespondents differ in their ability to provide equally good and complete information; therefore, certain comparisons—such as rural-urban or center-periphery—will typically introduce biases. For example, the absence of membrs of the urban upper class may lead to an understatement of rural-urban differences. . . .

Measurement Errors

Sophistication and meaningless evidence

Until recently, social science research in the developing countries was conducted almost exclusively by anthropologists, as it is today in a great many areas. Anthropologists have made a number of cogent criticisms of survey research, especially opinion studies. Two criticisms are especially relevant: doubt as to the existence of any such thing as private or public opinion, the mechanisms for decision making and opinion formation being thought to be absent in lower-class roles, especially in tradition-directed societies. Second, the critics imply that even if the native does harbor personal opinions, it is not possible to measure these opinions by means of standard interviewing techniques.

While it might be argued that the proponents of these views tend to generalize experiences gained from observation of primitive societies to the kinds of problems which are likely to be encountered in modernizing areas, and although these critics sometimes ignore the fact that survey research methods are used for gaining factual as well as attitudinal information, still there is considerable general support for their criticisms. For example, almost any study which includes consistency checks within the research instrument will discover a very high proportion of inconsistent responses. . . .

The second criticism raised by anthropologists also has apparent support, for there is little doubt that asking questions, as in a personal interview, is alien to many societies. Keesing, among others, has argued that to answer a question is to make a decision, which only certain individuals in a society have a right to do. . . . Other studies. . . have amplified this issue by noting that lower-class respondents typically are unable to answer questions which require that they take the role of others. These difficulties have encouraged some researchers to sample only known opinion holders (the elite), whereas other researchers, less concerned with general public opinion than with specific behavior and basic values, have interviewed unsophisticated respondents with considerable success. . . . Many studies, of course, are not concerned with general opinions but, rather, with factual information and basic values. One might expect that there would be relatively minor difficulties involved in obtaining factual information on household expenditures and income, media exposure and voting behavior, and family control techniques and family size. Many of the obstacles to obtaining factual information have been observed by others; for example, demographic surveys have difficulty in obtaining correct information in societies which do not have the Western concept of time; and economic surveys in largely nonmonetary markets and in rural areas have discovered that employment, income, debt, and consumption vary in size over the farming year, thereby making it impossible to generalize about the economy on the basis of the limited information that respondents are able to recall at only one time period. . . .

Many of the criticisms against survey research focus specifically on precoded questions, since they obviously provide the answers which respondents mights not otherwise be capable of formulating for themselves. To avoid the dangers involved in these questions, as well as similar problems which might arise in open-ended questions, Converse suggests that the respondent be encouraged to volunteer that he has no opinion on a particular topic. . . . There is no reason why such an invitation or filtering technique could not precede precoded questions, although the general approach could possibly be overtly effective in societies where respondents are eager to give the answer they think you want from them. They would volunteer "no opinion" when in fact they had one. . . .

Culturally sensitive topics raise special problems for the comparative researcher, since what is sensitive in one country may not be in another. For example, it is said to be extremely difficult to obtain religious information in Moslem Pakistan, but relatively easy to do this in Hindu India. In some African areas, as well as in other parts of the world, there is a reluctance to talk about dead children and the number of people in a household—obstacles to demographic researchers. In the Middle East there is a reluctance to discuss ordinary household events. . . , and Chinese businessmen in any country are reported to be especially secretive about any and all facets of their work and personal lives. In many countries, respondents are reticent about political topics in general and party preference in particular. On the other hand, it is by no means clear that family planning is nearly as sensitive an issue in the developing countries as might be expected.

Questions raised with regard to both meaningless opinions and opinions on culturally sensitive topics suggest the need for new measuring devices, especially devices to measure basic values. To this end, some studies have experimented with projective tests, role-playing, and various sentence-completion techniques, but, unfortunately, the relative merits of these approaches were not reported....

It will be some time before we can be assured that various segments of a population are offering responses which are comparable in terms of amount and quality. For even though respondents are willing to answer questions asked of them, there remain cultural differences regarding respondents' abilities to express themselves. For example, if one examines marginals from studies conducted in Malaysia, one will notice that the Chinese, when compared with the Indians, have a much higher proportion of "no answers" to precoded questions and fewer answers to open-ended questions. One of the reasons for this is that the Chinese are quite reticent, whereas the Indians are loquacious. This creates problems in comparing the two groups; and, of course, if the Chinese, Indians, and Malaysians are treated as a single national sample, the Chinese will be underweighted and the Indians overweighted....

Mention might be made of some additional means by which these various obstacles can be overcome, or at least means by which measurement errors of these kinds can be statistically controlled in the analysis of survey materials. For example, if respondents have a short span of attention, then interviewing might be conducted in several sessions, although this might be too expensive a procedure for most project budgets. At least the consequences of a short span of attention could possibly be measured by charting the proportion of "poorly answered questions" at different phases of the interview session. The proportion should increase toward the end of the session. Another obvious approach is to spend much more time and resources on the pretesting of the research instrument, even if this requires that a smaller sample is interviewed in the final study. Researchers might also establish beforehand the amount of error they will tolerate in their materials, and then, on the basis of a small follow-up survey, decide whether the materials fall within the stated error limits. If not, then the materials and the research project might be abandoned entirely. Another procedure is to include numerous measures of verbosity, sophistication, credulity, conformity, extremism in responses, inability to differentiate, filter questions, information questions, items to measure the strength with which opinions are held, and various reliability or consistency checks. These measures can be used to differentiate population groups whose answers are biased and who need separate consideration.

Conceptual and linguistic equivalence

Problems of conceptual equivalence are especially troublesome to the comparative researcher, since he will often find that the concept he is working with is not found in the local culture. Researchers have discovered this difficulty with regard to concepts of time, of the future, of distance or height with regard to visual scaling devices, and of a number of concepts which have clear evaluative overtones, such as "table manners." In one recent study, the English word "aggressive" was used to describe various groups. This created problems in at least one country, since it was later discovered that "aggressive" had to be expressed either with a negative term or a positive one (one which implied pioneer). The positive one was used, which created some confusion on the part of the client.

Considerable knowledge of the local culture and language is needed in order to gain conceptual equivalence, or, as some call it, *functional equivalence.* Agencies in the field which are aware of this are becoming increasingly opposed to what some of them refer to as "canned questionnaires sent from the United States." They feel that a client's attempt to preserve the exact form of his questions, especially precoded ones, can only lead to major errors. One agency now insists that clients attach a paragraph of explanation or a *rationale* to each question submitted. Once the agency discovers the intention behind a question—that is, the kind of answer which is desired and how the question will be used—it formulates its own version.

This approach deserves further exploration, for it attempts to gain functional equivalence with regard to the information which the researcher wants to elicit rather than with regard to the form of the questions used to elicit this information. (For the latter approach see Almond and Verba's five-nation study.) To attempt to gain functional equivalence in answers may require four questions in one country but only one question in another. While these four questions certainly would add to the value of the information from that single country, obvious difficulties are created for the researcher who wishes to make international comparisons. Not only are different procedures used in gaining the same kind of information, but also, the key terms in the questions are often different. This would occur in studies asking questions about decision making and authority structures, since the relevant issues and reference groups would be different in different areas. . . .

There is general agreement on how the actual translation of the questions should be made. First, the original instrument is translated into the local language, and then another translator independently translates this translated version back into the original. The original and retranslated versions are compared and the discrepancies are clarified. . . .

Unfortunately, relatively few research agencies have these linguistic resources. The implications of this are suggested by a recent study using a number of languages: The client decided to check the language versions which the contractor had prepared and discovered that approximately one-fourth of the translations made for any one language would have led to major biases.

In some areas, no attempt is even made to prepare a translation into the local language. Rather, this is left to bilingual interviewers. This seems to be a fairly common practice in Africa, where many of the languages do not have alphabets. So far as I have been able to discover, some of these African projects do not even decide on common terms for key concepts. Apparently, if the respondent speaks the Western language in which the questions are written, this is the language used in the interview. In other multilingual areas, research agencies interview in the language which the respondent speaks in his home.

Needless to say, the language used in an interview may have important implications for the information elicited, for languages may differ considerably in their richness and expressive quality. These problems arise even in a single-language culture, as shown in the class differences in language behavior in the United States. . . . Since those who prepare and translate questionnaires are typically from the middle and upper classes, the instruments they produce are likely to be somewhat inappropriate for large segments of the population.

Interviewer Bias

Clinical witnesses

It seems that the personal interview—that is, where an interviewer interviews a person in private—is relatively rare in a great many countries. For example, it has been estimated by some of my informants that at least 50 percent of the European interviews are conducted in the presence of third parties, whereas in many areas of the developing countries—for example, in nonurban Pakistan—almost all interviews are conducted in the presence of other people. Some researchers have referred to these other people as *clinical witnesses.*

The implications of these third parties for the data which are obtained seem to depend on a number of factors, including the content of the question, the status characteristics of the third parties, and the general cultural rules defining interpersonal relations. Reports by people working in the field suggest that the "third-party" effect is considerable in societies characterized by sharp status and authority cleavages. In part, this is because the most important people are often interviewed first. Field workers report that after each answer given by the first interviewed, the assembled crowd nods its approval, saying that the answer also represents the views of others. Not only does this create or help crystallize consensus, it also often produces resistance to being interviewed on the part of others.

As with many other topics previously mentioned, third parties sometimes have a mixed effect. For example, in studies seeking information rather than attitudes, third parties may help keep the respondent honest and also help him to remember the requested information. In other instances, especially with women and younger people, respondents may refuse to be interviewed unless a third person is present. It is common practice in many areas at least to obtain the permission of a third party—the local headman— before commencing field work. . . .

Several procedures have been developed to avoid the assumed consequences of third parties. For example, for some questions the respondent is asked to cast a ballot rather than to give an oral reply. This procedure could possibly reduce biases in politically oriented studies. . . . A second and administratively popular approach is to use teams of interviewers. The team saturates a village so that the field work is completed in a very short time. . . . The third approach, which is a more recent development, is to use resident interviewers. These interviewers, like the traditional ethnographer, live in the local community for a fairly long period of time. Some researchers, especially those who have worked in Southeast Asia, claim that this is the only technique which can assure complete and unbiased information. The resident interviewer acquires knowledge and contacts to permit him to check on the information he receives; he recognizes errors and inconsistencies which can then be quickly clarified; he may be able to eliminate the recall problem; and by being a member of the community, he is able to overcome the natives' resistance to giving truthful information to outsiders. On the other hand, the use of resident interviewers and field-work procedures which assign a very large area to only one or two interviewers limits the number of sampling points which can be used and may, therefore, decrease the representativeness of the sample. Since interviewing assignments cannot be randomized, the entire information for a single sampling point is the product of one man's biases; also, spending long periods of time in one area may involve the field worker in community problems and provide him with so much "inside" information and so many personal contacts that his respondents refuse to provide him with information because they fear it will not be kept confidential. . . .

Courtesy bias

The second type of interviewer bias has been referred to as *courtesy* or *hospitality bias,* a bias which seems to be especially common in Asia, everywhere from Japan to Turkey. . . . Courtesy bias means that the respondent provides information which he feels will please the interviewer. He behaves this way because the norms governing interpersonal relations in general and relations with upper-class strangers in specific call for him to do so. . . .

There is some indication that the direction of the courtesy bias is different in different countries. For example, the humility of the Japanese is said to lead them to underevaluate their own achievements, class positions, and the like. On the other hand, some researchers in the Middle East claim that respondents there tend to exaggerate their achievements, class position, knowledge of the world, and extent to which they are modern rather than traditional. In practical terms, this means that the type of question-wording appropriate to Western countries would be inappropriate to Japan, and what is appropriate in Japan and the West would be inappropriate in Turkey or Iran.

Some of the effects of the courtesy bias can be reduced by concealing the sponsorship of the study, by more effective training of interviewers, and by more careful wording of questions. With regard to wording, it is advisable to avoid the use of "moral" words which require either the respondent or the interviewer to pass judgment on the other. Above all, it is important to maximize the ease of giving a socially unacceptable answer, such as might be done through the standard practice of opening the question with, "Lots of people feel this way...and lots of people feel the other way. Which direction do you lean toward in...?" Leading questions also might be appropriate here.

Perhaps courtesy bias is easier to control than its opposite, which might be called the *sucker bias.* Sucker bias is found in areas where...all outsiders are considered fair game for deception....

Interviewer-respondent status congruency

The third type of bias arises from communication obstacles created by the relative status characteristics of interviewers and their respondents....

In some countries, for example, interviewers are often considered as government employees, and since the local population does not readily differentiate policemen from tax collectors from political party workers, the interviewer has considerable difficulty in socializing the respondent into a new type of questioner-answerer relationship. In these situations, respondents are reported to be very reluctant to provide interviewers with accurate information. This may be one (but only a minor) reason why economic surveys often find that respondents exaggerate expenditures and under-report income, wealth, and savings. To overcome these suspicions, noncommercial research groups often seek an academic affiliation or sponsorship, denying any direct government connection with their activities. Unfortunately, owing to the lack of local personnel, the field-work staff are often required to rely on government employees—not only on teachers but, as in some Asian countries, also on "moonlighting" secret police.

Research agencies in many countries recruit their interviewers from among college students, which means that they come from middle- and upper-class backgrounds, and are themselves educated people. This type of interviewer creates a communication problem, since there are certain traditional ways in which members of different classes interact. For example, custom demands that lower-class persons use polite forms of address, be humble, and not express themselves freely to members of the upper classes. Recognizing this, some researchers have questioned whether the equalitarian-oriented interviewing techniques used in the West are appropriate in societies which have sharp status and authority cleavages. Respondents also might be confused if a nonnative associated with the former colonial ruling group were not demanding in his questioning....

27

International Marketing Communication

Effective communication between the company and its consumers is a basic prerequisite for successful marketing. Such communication not only conveys important factual data such as product characteristics, prices, and terms of sales but also creates images of the company as an institution—its personality, economic importance, and social status. Communication may take many forms. Executives, sales representatives, delivery trucks, packages, brand names, services, and the products themselves all contribute to the impressions and ideas which determine the public's attitudes toward the firm.

To be effective these communications must reach all the people who have a bearing on the firm's well-being. Besides consumers, who themselves may represent several distinct categories, there are stockholders, creditors, government agencies, competitors, and various social groupings who provide funds, issue directives, or react to the firm's actions depending upon their understanding and interpretation of the facts and the images communicated to them.

A systematic communication program, designed to enhance the company's objectives, is a basic managerial responsibility. In international marketing the role of communications is often crucial. A nonresident firm, a foreign product, and an alien salesman are strangers and, as such, are generally more suspect than their indigenous counterparts. Whenever this negative effect is encountered, it requires additional "communicating" to have it neutralized. Often, too, the consumers in international markets are unaware of the uses to which a product can be put or how its value can best be utilized. A basic education through the communications program, then, must precede any physical distribution effort.

International Advertising

Advertising is the most important form of marketing communication. It is defined by the American Marketing Association as "any paid form of nonpersonal presentation or promotion of ideas, goods, or services, by an identified sponsor." To be effective, the advertising process must be completed not only in the sense that the intended message be transmitted from the sender to the receiver but also in the sense that it become *internalized*—that is, that it enter into the receiver's future decision making either explicitly or implicitly. How full and effective the transmission is depends upon the advertising media used; how complete and effective the internalization is depends on the impact which the transmitted message has on the target consumer. Although both the media selection and the message production are basic to any advertising, they assume new dimensions when the advertising process transcends international boundaries.

Decision Areas

An advertising campaign, properly conducted, represents the following system of sequentially related decisions:

(1) Defining objectives to be accomplished
(2) Determining to whom the communication should be directed to accomplish the objectives, i.e., defining the target consumers
(3) Choosing the message with the right appeal, i.e., the maximum internationalization potential for the target consumers
(4) Selecting the media which can best reach the target consumers
(5) Producing the actual advertisement
—illustration }
—slogan } layout
—copy }
(6) Planning and managing the campaign
—budget
—timing
—coordination

Except point (2), which is a matter of market research, a subject discussed previously, each of these areas deserves further elaboration.

Objectives

Like other areas of management any systematic advertising program can be defined only in terms of its objectives. Without definite objectives, the entire campaign lacks a foundation, and there can be no rational criteria for the media or message strategies, not to mention the measurement of the results. In determining objectives management must make two basic decisions: What reaction does it wish the advertising to create in the market? And what role is advertising to play in the overall exporting effort? From answers to these general questions management can proceed to determine the specific objectives of the campaign. Typical objectives of international advertising include the following:

—introducing an existing product to a new market (country, region, or city)
—introducing a new product to existing markets of the firm
—expanding existing markets
—informing consumers about new developments (product change, new application, company plans)
—eliminating sales resistances
—providing sales representation in the absence of salesmen
—preparing the way for salesmen (raising the level of awareness and interest)

The objectives of the campaign determine who the target consumers are and thereby define all other elements of the program.

Media

In reference to territorial reach, it is useful to divide advertising media into three groups: transnational, intranational, and local.

THE TRANSNATIONAL MEDIA. This group consists almost exclusively of printed periodicals and radios. In Central Europe and a few other regions television can also be included to some degree. The transnational periodicals are directed either to the educated general public—*National Geographic, Der Spiegel, Paris Match, Reader's Digest,* etc.—or to technical or business professions—engineering, pharmaceutical, machine-tool, automotive, and similar journals. The foreign circulation of popular magazines usually is limited to the upper strata, who possess the means, the linguistic facility, and the interest to patronize foreign journals. For the most part, these are people from the top of the income structure. As such, they represent a scattered minority whose tastes as well as consumption standards are more cosmopolitan than national. Being often more consumption oriented than people of equivalent income in the United States, the foreign cosmopolites are prime consumer prospects for deluxe quality goods, which, therefore, can bring real benefits from promotion in these periodicals. Except for some emulation effect, the possibility of any international popular magazine reaching the middle and lower income mass markets is relatively negligible.

Technical and professional journals have a well-defined circulation. But, not unlike the popular journals, they reach the elite in their respective fields of specialization and are seldom read by the majority of the profession or by businessmen abroad.

Thus the foreign coverage of both types of transnational periodicals is generally thin. They may reach many countries but seldom penetrate far below the surface layer of their markets; hence, they are called *umbrella media.*

Regarding radio the possibilities are different. The introduction of the transistor has made the income level almost entirely inconsequential for radio ownership. Receivers are now as commonplace, if not more so, in primitive bush country as in metropolitan Europe. But, although the technical ability to communicate through radio to mass consumers has taken a giant leap forward, the economics of transnational radio communication lags far behind. Only a few countries, and the United States is not one of them, have broadcasting transmitters powerful enough to send out signals which can be received by regular transistor radios abroad. In European countries this problem has been solved by building large and powerful receivers to compensate for the weakness in signals. But the cost of European receivers puts them into the deluxe category, and thus they miss the mass market. It seems reasonable to expect that this problem will soon be solved in response to the massive demand for better radio service in the vast majority of countries.

Intranational Media. Intranational media are by far the most significant for international marketing communications, for most people patronize their own periodicals, radio, and television much more than they do foreign media. Compared to the U.S. experience, media selection in other countries presents a more difficult problem because information on the circulation of periodicals and listener audits is often very crude or completely lacking. Independent agencies which prepare unbiased data on media coverage do not exist in many countries. The only sources for circulation figures are the media themselves, which for competitive reasons grossly overstate their circulations. Experienced advertisers are known to discount the media claims by 30 to 70 percent in some countries. Another rather general problem is that of finding the right mix of media. One medium is rarely enough to reach the majority of the potential buyers. Although the same can be said about the situation in the United States, the difference lies in the size. In a large country all media can reach a sufficiently large market to justify the cost of an advertising campaign; in a small country the potential demand may be too small to justify such an expenditure.

Local Media. A penetrating coverage requires the use of local media—newspapers, radio, television, cinema, posters, billboards, and point-of-sale displays. When and how any of these should be used depend not only on the objectives of the advertising campaign but also on the legal and ethical constraints placed upon their use.

The most regulated are the broadcast media. In a number of countries commercials on radio and TV are completely prohibited. In others, including much of continental Europe, commercials are permitted but must be segregated from the rest of the broadcast and programmed as a separate item for a specified time, much as news is in U.S. broadcasts. This item in the program usually goes under a heading such as "Announcements and Advertising." That such a requirement removes the cutting edge from an American commercial should be self-evident. In addition, a variety of specific restrictions is encountered in many countries. In Mexico and Italy spot TV commercials cannot exceed 20 seconds and must be visual only; in Venezuela sound tracks are permitted but only if the announcer is a native of that country; some Latin countries require that wedding rings be worn by actors depicting married couples; and Australia bars all commercials produced on foreign film. These few illustrations point out the great diversity of restrictions that prevail in different countries.

Conceptual scheme

The basic approach to media selection may be visually summarized as in Figure 27-1. The horizontal dimensions stand for geographic coverage; the vertical, for penetration power.

The strategic questions in message preparation are (a) to what motive of the target customer should the message be addressed—his personal desires, professional needs, or business requirements; and (b) what specific appeals would offer the best guarantee that the message will be accepted.

Answers to these questions must be sought in the inner sanctums of motivation research and the psychology of advertising. Since neither of these yet has the status of science and since both are subject to continuous molesting by the less scrupulous elements of the advertising industry, the appeal selection remains the least systematic and most precarious aspect of marketing communication. In U.S. domestic advertising the inability to analytically develop precise criteria for effective appeals is, at least to a degree, compensated for by customary appeals which have evolved from many years of advertising experience.

But the appeals which work well in the United States are not necessarily effective abroad. Experience has shown that the so-called *pseudo-scientific appeals* are especially treacherous in international use. These appeals simulate

FIGURE 27-1

Coverage and Penetration of Advertising Media: A Conceptual Scheme

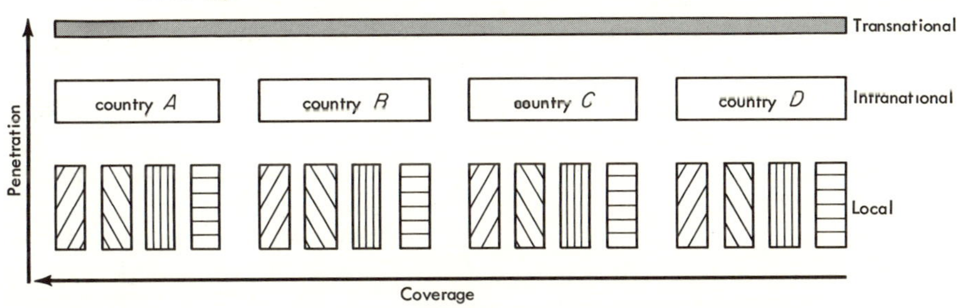

FIG. 21.1

doctors, scientists, and all kinds of technical apparatus to create an aura of objectivity and accuracy for their sales pitch which, to make the entire message consistent, itself is phrased in scientific vernacular complete with technical "precision" ("the nasograph shows," "44.72 percent better," "the liquid in the left tube turned yellow," etc.). What makes people in some countries rebel against pseudoscientific jargon defies simple explanation. The negative reaction, to be sure, may derive from entirely different sources in different cultures.

Hard-sell commands such as, "Hasten to Masen's; buy it today; don't miss this once-in-a-lifetime chance," illustrate another category which often runs into trouble abroad. In some areas such appeals evoke people's resentment against the autocratic bossism under which they live; in others, where trading and bargaining are second nature to lower class people (the Arabs, for example), such commands downgrade advertising to the practices of the common tradesmen, whose popular image is not always distinguishable from that of impostors and thieves.

The *raw appeals to sex,* which have more recently become prominent in U.S. advertising, represent a third category which is ill-suited for international adaptation. The reference here is to advertisements such as the one which depicts a well-dressed young man standing next to a partially disrobed young woman who lies on a couch in a most suggestive pose; and, as if the illustration were not erotic enough, the headline urges: "Come on strong, go all the way with [name of product]." The U.S. preoccupation with sex cannot be attributed to the influence of Freud; people in other countries are no more immune to Freudian ideas, and some have indeed formally declared for them. Rather, the sex paradox is a historic relic. If the American frontiersman had not for generations been deprived of normal sexual relations because men greatly outnumbered women and, if this maldistribution had not driven him to sexual criminality, neither the excessive preoccupation with sex as a psychological force nor the world's most antisex statutes and city ordinances could have developed. The latter have helped to perpetuate the obsession.

Humor is apparently the most universal appeal. A latecomer to the U.S. advertising scene—its power was released only by the advent of the television cartoon—humor has long been the backbone of effective advertising in many countries including one as closely tied to the United States as Great Britain. But to say that humor has a universal appeal does not mean that a humorous advertisement is internationally transplantable. What is funny to a Moroccan may be silly or even insulting to a Finn. For the British, American humor is often flat and banal; for Americans, British humor is frequently too sarcastic and cruel. The French like to sport the piquant; and the Japanese with many other orientals delight in the adumbrative and benign.

Rather than to attempt to give any cookbook rules on appeals—an effort doomed to failure—it is important to reemphasize the fallacy of such cliches as "human nature is the same" or "people everywhere want what we want." Whatever validity they may have as abstract philosophical notions is lost when specific and concrete matters, such as different people's motivations to buy particular products, come into question. Cultural and social values often conflict in the international markets, as do ideas of beauty and ugliness, honesty and treachery, courage and cowardice, comedy and tragedy, necessity and luxury, plus the innumerable other axes that delineate a particular people's pursuit of happiness and define their ideals, hopes, and aspirations. Only an understanding of the sources of these values can bring about an intelligent adaptation of marketing communications to national cultures and customs. American and other Western advertising has failed notoriously in certain Far Eastern countries, not because the advertisers ignored the details of the local situation or did not follow the accepted procedures, but because they tried, subconsciously, of course, to superimpose their Western logic on the facts and attitudes pertaining to a non-Western culture. The result was astonishment for both the companies and the local nationals. What they could have done was dig to the bedrock of the particular area's structure of thought. For example, in a considerable region of the Orient the basic values and social relationships are based on the Confucian legacy, which conflicts with Judeo-Christian principles in more ways than can be discussed here. Yet the Confucian picture has an inner logic as strong and consistent as the Western view of man and his place in society. This logic may explain the most "irrational" behavior traits of the individual Oriental.

When an American holds a door for a woman, he does not think consciously of the customs of medieval chivalry or the 2000 years of Christian reverence for the Virgin Mary and, through her, for all women. In the same way, a Far Eastern gentleman, unless he happens to be thoroughly Westernized, would never think of holding a door for a woman because such an act and attitude are quite alien to Confucian thinking. But the idea of sending his aged father or mother to a poorhouse or even to an expensive home for old people would strike him as something positively obscene—a crime against humanity.

When attitudes as different and as powerful as these become mixed in marketing communications, they can cause all kinds of troubles unless they are seen, recognized, and understood. To carry the point a little further, Western thinking holds that the unit of society is the individual and that society is the sum of such individuals. To a Confucian, society is based on a set of relationships in which the person who is inferior must show respect and deference to the person who is superior. Thus children must respect parents, the young must respect the old, the wife must respect the husband, the subject must respect the ruler, and the living must respect the dead. Of all these relationships, that of the family is the most important. Society is thus not a sum of individuals but a web or fabric of interlocking relationships. In Confucian society, every individual has his proper place—and has significance only in his proper place.

Thus, even a moderate knowledge of Confucian principles could clarify many of the puzzling consumer attitudes, reactions, and motivations in those countries. Needless to add, other regions have similar legacies that serve as the bedrock for their philosophical system. For international communications to succeed—in the form of advertising, diplomacy, or cultural relations—it is imperative that the practitioners not only are technical experts but also have the necessary grasp of the philosophical framework of the cultures concerned.

Transferability of Advertising

A recent survey shows that advertising research has hardly scratched the surface of the cross-cultural adaptation problem and that most marketing executives are poorly prepared to realistically cope with this problem. Of 73 international marketing executives interviewed only 23 were conscious of the need for "cultural or psychological adaptation of their advertising."[1] Even this proportion probably overestimated the true stress laid on such factors. Many of the executives believed cultural concepts were too vague for actual use, although they readily admitted that they were important. One concept that marketing executives watched carefully, though, was whether there were any cultural taboos which might influence sales.[2] Economic market criteria were, however, studied much more carefully, and the advertising was quite frequently adjusted in one or more respects to the findings, as shown in Table 27-1.

TABLE 27-1

Extent to Which U.S. Advertisements Are Used Abroad

Type of Advertiser	*Translated and Used As in U.S.*	*Copy and Head Rewritten*	*Copy and Illustrations Changed*	*All Changed Except Theme*	*No Particular Similarity*
Cosmetics, soaps, and drugs	4	1	1	2	4
Food	—	—	—	2	6
Beverages	—	—	—	2	—
Automobiles	—	—	—	—	3
Miscellaneous	1	1	—	2	1
Total	5	2	1	8	14

Source: S. Watson Dunn, "The Case Study Approach in Cross-Cultural Research," *Journal of Marketing Research* (American Marketing Association), III, No. 1 (February 1966), 28.

According to the same survey the transferability and adjustment decisions were based on a rather uneven admixture of criteria. They are reproduced in Table 27-2.

1 S. Watson Dunn, "The Case Study Approach in Cross-Cultural Research," *Journal of Marketing Research,* III, No. 1 (February 1966), 26ff.

2 Dunn, "The Case Study Approach in Cross-Cultural Research," p. 29.

TABLE 27-2

Criteria Used in Appraising the Transferability of U.S. Advertisements

Type of Criterion	*Number of Respondents Who Mentioned*
Market or economic criteria:	
Competition	10
Education and literacy	4
Standard of living (discretionary income)	3
Distribution	3
State of economic development	3
Age distribution of the population	2
Homogeneity of the population	1
Relative importance of imports from United States	1
Similarity of product's use to that in United States	1
Urbanization of the population	1
Mobility of the population	1
Cultural or psychological criteria:	
Cultural or psychological barriers to acceptance of the product	5
Friendliness of people toward United States	3
Price consciousness of the population	3
Extent to which people accept advertising or other persuasive communications	3
Importance of religion in the culture	3
Acceptance of authority	2
Sophistication	1
Class consciousness	1
Attitude of people toward the human body	1
Political stability	1
Subjectivity of the concepts used in the advertisements	1
Attitude toward participating in voting	1
Media criteria:	
Availability of same media used in the United States	7

Source: Same as Table 27-1.

Production Problems

The main production problems of international advertising fall into three groups: technical, legal, and linguistic. The technical problems arise in part from the local peculiarities of the communication media, especially their physical capabilities to produce the desired quality of illustrations, size or clarity of copy, etc., and in part from the general lack of and dissimilarities among advertising agencies in different countries. Frequently the agency activities are limited to simple space brokerage for different media, and no production services are available. This shifts the entire production operation of international advertising upon the firm itself.

The weaknesses in local production capabilities are gradually being compensated for by large U.S. agencies which have been establishing international offices and training internationally experienced communications experts. Twenty percent of the 2600 U.S. agencies are reported to have some international connections, by having their own foreign departments, by working in partnership with some foreign agencies, or by owning their own overseas offices. Thus, the local-agency picture is being diversified and the range of advertising services broadened, especially in response to the demand from the multinational firms.

Legal Aspects

Although the psychological reactions of the target consumer are the basic considerations, advertising is also subject to legal constraints. Many U.S. practices are barred in various foreign countries—brand-X comparisons, any comparisons of one make of product with another, two-for-the-price-of-one offers, one-cent sales, box-top gimmicks, free tie-in offers, and claims to be the best or better than others in the industry. The legal codes on communication not only ban but also sometimes place positive requirements upon the advertiser by demanding that a certain condition be fulfilled or a standard met before a message can legally be communicated. The wearing of the wedding ring in some Latin countries, mentioned above, illustrates the point. As a rule, both the negative and the positive requirements which are expressly stated in the law are not excessively numerous, and they can be relatively easily indexed. The important thing here is for management to be aware of the problem and to do the checking before heavy outlays have been committed to a particular international campaign.

A much more subtle problem than that above is to evaluate the legality of appeals and claims which are not expressly banned by the law. Some U.S. agencies have proceeded on the theory that if something is not expressly prohibited it is legal. This theory may or may not work, depending on whether the country has a common law or a Roman law system. In the former the basic legal doctrine is *caveat emptor* (buyer beware), which means that the seller is legally entitled to praise his wares and the buyer is not entitled to legal redress if he allows himself to be misled or trapped by the seller's claims. The law restricts no claims except unmistakable falsification of verifiable facts. Allusions, implications, symbolic assurances, and suggestive promises are all legitimate methods of trade bluff. *It is on this legal doctrine that U.S. advertising experience rests.* It places the seller in a more favorable position than the buyer and sanctions in advance any messages that avoid express statements of falsehood.

In the Roman law countries the basic doctrine is *caveat venditor* (seller beware), which emphasizes the buyer's need for protection and restricts the seller to claims which he can actually verify or support. This restriction applies to both expressed and implied statements.

To illustrate the difference between the two doctrines, take an innocent claim like "Richfield is years ahead." In a common law country this is a perfectly legitimate claim since there is no verifiable fact involved; indeed the express portion of the statement lacks any meaning whatsoever since to be ahead requires some reference point which is not given. The real meaning of the claim lies in the implication or inference that the reader or listener makes mentally, namely, that Richfield is years ahead of the other gasolines. In a Roman law country this claim would be banned, not because of the expressed statement but because of the implied meaning. Even the simplest understanding of the *caveat venditor* doctrine could save much embarrassment and bewilderment for U.S. advertising people who repeatedly run afoul in the Roman law countries. Their approach has been trial and error with no conceptual base from which to draw the cues for the legality of their programs. The principles of the *caveat venditor* doctrine provide the necessary conceptual base.

Linguistics

The effectiveness of written and oral communications depends not only on what is actually said but also, and in advertising more often than not, on what is implied and what the total image or impression is that the communication conveys. The choice of words and phrases, therefore, is just as important as the choice of themes and appeals.

Advertising thrives on catchwords, inventive phrases, slogans, and other forms of word imagery which often lose their communicative impact when translated from one language to another. Sometimes they are entirely nontranslatable. To convert the message from one language to another it must be interpreted rather than translated, the objective being to convert the idea or imagery rather than the meaning of the words as such. A German advertising executive is reported to have offered anyone to name his own price for a German equivalent of "the pause that refreshes." Although the literal translation of this phrase could be accomplished by a relative beginner, the total impact of it defies both translation and interpretation.

Formal research on the linguistic convertibility of marketing communication is unknown to this writer. All the information that this writer has been able to uncover is based on the subjective observations of different individuals including the writer himself. Thus it appears that the best approach to interlingual conversion of advertising messages is to transwrite the copy, i.e., to start with the concept rather than the language and, once the desired message has been clearly defined in an unambiguous literal statement in the foreign language, to recast it into the most effective advertising vernacular of that country. Needless to add, the original English copy and the foreign copy thus constructed may have no literal correspondence whatsoever. This point deserves underscoring because the traditional notion of translating is among the most serious barriers to effective international business communication. The problem is not one of language but of linguistics.

Product Communication

The oldest form of advertising is by the product itself. In modern times the communicative aspects of the product must be purposefully cultivated through packaging, labeling, and branding.

Packaging

The term *packaging* covers two functionally different concepts. One refers to the wrapping of a product for physical protection and logistic convenience; boxing, crating, bundling, and baling serve this purpose. The other concept of packaging focuses on selling; its aim is to make the product more desirable to the stores and the consumers. To do this the package must match the consumer's requirements in size, shape, material, and artistic properties. If it does not, it defeats its own purpose. What a consumer's requirements are depends on his consumption parameters, both technical and psychological. The variance from country to country poses difficult demands on the managements of international operations.

An incident will illustrate the point. A few years ago a West Coast manufacturer started exporting baking powder to the Philippines. Prior to entering the market the company had conducted laboratory tests of competing brands sold in the Philippines and was completely satisfied that its product was technically better than those. Yet, its efforts to export the product met with very little success in the consumer market; in the institutional market it did much better. When the cause for this paradox was investigated, it was discovered that the Philippine housewife found the skyblue color of the company's cans repulsive and that she preferred cans which would be usable in certain ways after the powder had been consumed. She did not plan to discard the can but visualized secondary uses for it. The upshot was that the manufacturer had to change both the color (from sky blue to red) and the design of its can, a major expenditure. But this was not all. To buy the cans at an economical price, the can manufacturer needed a minimum production run far in excess of what previous export experience indicated could be used. Thus, the company had to choose between discarding the Philippine market or risking a substantial sum on a warehouse full of red cans of a unique design. It did the latter.

Labeling

A label contributes to consumer acceptance of the product by communicating to the consumer its essential qualities, technical characteristics, and sometimes also its various applications. To perform any one of these functions the label must be intelligible to the consumer first linguistically and second conceptually. An English-language label cannot make French or Japanese consumers any wiser about the product unless they learn English. But, as with advertising copy, translation alone is seldom enough. The value of a label as a selling tool depends on its close identity with the needs and the conditions that motivate the consumer. Unless this is the case, label, too, can become a liability instead of an asset. An American recipe on a food product is hardly appreciated by a Turkish or Polish housewife.

Branding

The internationally sensitive aspects of branding are symbolism, spelling, and phonetics. If a brand is to be a generator of demand, it must identify the product with the desired standards of quality and value. But expressions of quality and value, hard as they are to define in a domestic setting, take on cultural connotations in an international context. Even such a universally accepted welfare agency as the Red Cross must replace its emblem with a crescent in the Islamic world. Emblems, designs, and colors often have symbolic meanings which tend to be particularly intense in less developed countries but which can never be discounted even in the most advanced ones. Therefore, transplanting any trademark or brand design from one country to another is a potential source of trouble which only careful research and market testing can avoid.

In international brand names the twofold problem of spelling and phonetics arises from the fact that the same combination of letters frequently spells a different word in different languages. The conflicting meanings that such coincidences in spelling may have are reflected in the few random examples below.

American Word	*Meaning of Same Word Abroad*	*Language*
arc	face	Hungarian
acre	sour, tart	Spanish
ban	forest	Nepali
boom	tree	Dutch
brand	fire	Dutch
fond	bottom	French
home	mildew	Finnish
make	husband	Swedish
sale	dirty	French
tot	dead	German
vale	lie	Estonian

Thus a brand name that in English, or whatever the original language, has a positive connotation in that it associates the product with something elevating and harmonious may quickly turn into a word which is completely dis-associated with the product when a linguistic boundary is crossed. And what is worse, either the disassociation or the foreign meaning of the word may cast a negative reflection on the product. Export firms report instances where a highly successful brand name at home became an unutterable obscenity abroad, and, conversely, importers have had to reject technically superior articles because of the repulsive connotation of their brand. The latter problem is particularly frequent in small countries whose languages are generally less well understood in the exporting countries.

Phonetics can be equally treacherous. To be usable at all a brand name must be easily pronounced; to be effective it must be easy to remember and to repeat. Most foreign-language words are none of these, regardless of the native language. Words of nonphonetic languages, such as English and French, in which spelling is different from that in phonetic languages, are especially vulnerable on this account. The great majority of their words are either mispronounced in a variety of ways or not pronounceable at all for people who only know a phonetic language. For example, the brand name "Allright" in Estonian, a perfectly phonetic language (every letter represents a definite sound which almost never varies), becomes grotesquely distorted in speech and completely devoid of value.

The root of the phonetic difficulty goes deeper than the relationship between spelling and enunciation. Most occidental languages, with the exception of English and French, are more or less phonetic. Yet it is not uncommon that problems of pronunciation arise when a word is transplanted from Spanish to Estonian, for example, because the same alphabet serves different phonetic needs of different languages. The letters are the same, and, although they are pronounced consistently in one phonetic language, they may represent a slightly or considerably different sound with equal consistency in another phonetic language. Thus, even the internal consistency of phonetic languages does not avoid the inconsistency in pronouncing an international brand name. From this inconsistency come the accents that interfere with oral communication. The most troublesome letters are *j, g,* and what might be called the *sh*-group (*sh, sch, ch, z, zh*). The pronunciations of *r* and *u* also vary more than those of other letters. Brand names containing these letters deserve particular scrutiny when international use is intended.

Often the individual letters in the brand name are less decisive than the particular order in which they come. A classic example of this problem was provided in the late 1950's by the attempt to replace the brand name Esso, which, because of a U.S. antitrust ruling, could not be used in the Midwest and West Coast states, with a new brand name which could be promoted in the worldwide markets of the Standard Oil Company of New Jersey. There was strong support in the upper echelons to change the name to Jersey. Fortunately, before this selection was made final, the opinions of outside experts, including this writer, were sought, and they strongly advised against the proposed selection because Jersey would become in practically each foreign language something other than it is in English. Yarsei, Yersiu, Herrsi, Zerrsai, and Gersei are some of the multilations the word would suffer. In contrast, the word Exxon, which the company ultimately selected, is almost immune to mispronunciation in most languages. Also, it is as nearly perfect from other standpoints as one can wish.

Lavidge and Steiner Model[3]

The basic premise of the Lavidge and Steiner model is that consumers normally do not switch from being disinterested or indifferent individuals to being convinced purchasers in one instantaneous step. Rather, they approach the ultimate purchase through a process, or series of steps, which may be analytically distinguished and in which the actual purchase is but the final act.

The steps suggested are seven, not necessarily equidistant, and, in a sense, beginning at the point of "indifference."

(1) Potential purchaser is completely unaware of the product or service.

(2) Potential purchaser is aware of the existence of the product or service (though perhaps still on the point of indifference).

(3) Potential purchaser knows what the product has to offer.

(4) Potential purchaser has favorable attitudes toward the product.

(5) Potential purchaser has a preference for this product over all other possibilities.

(6) Potential purchaser has a desire to buy and a conviction that the purchase would be wise.

(7) Potential purchaser becomes an actual purchaser.

The six steps beginning at step 2 indicate three major functions of all "demand-stimulation" activity:

(a) The first two, awareness and knowledge, relate to information or ideas.

(b) The next two have to do with favorable attitudes or feelings.

(c) The last two, conviction and purchase, produce action.

This classification of functions can be directly related to a classical psychological model which divides behavior into three components or dimensions:

(1) the cognitive component—intellectual, mental, or "rational" states

(2) the effective component—"emotional" or "feeling" states

(3) the conative or motivational component—"striving" states, relating to the tendency to treat objects as positive or negative goals

In domestic business the promotional process can often be short-circuited because the target consumer has become preconditioned by having "coexisted" with the product concerned for a considerable time as the particular business has grown, and he has thus acquired a certain level of awareness about it, or, perhaps even a preference for it. The entry of a product into a new country almost always means sudden exposure to a product or brand of which the indigenous consumer rarely has any prior awareness. There has been no preconditioning of his attitude toward the product. To be effective under these

3 T. J. Lavidge and G. A. Steiner, "A Model for Predictive Measurements of Advertising Effectiveness," *Journal of Marketing,* XXV, No. 4 (October 1961), 59–62.

conditions any promotional campaign must be designed to embrace all the seven stages from indifferent unawareness to the buying action. Because this is difficult, if not impossible, to accomplish in one single promotional effort (e.g., an advertisement), a continuing campaign or sequence is required to move potential purchasers along the steps to the point of actual purchase. At least, such would be the case for the promotion of new or unfamiliar products. In countries to which exporting has been frequent the promotional job must be based on a careful analysis of the particular step which the relevant target market has reached so that the correct balance among the psychological components may be achieved.

28

The Export-Import Process

International trade is sales and purchase transactions which cross international boundaries. Depending on the direction of the transboundary movement of the products traded, the transactions are divided into import and export trades. Since the trade transactions give rise to international financial obligations, the trade movements are paralleled by payments transactions, which flow in the opposite direction. The macroview of the international trade process visualizes it as a continuum of imports, exports, and payments, which connect the different business systems of independent nations.

Transactions

A trade transaction is a commitment on the part of two or more parties to perform certain functions or to cause certain results, usually centering around delivery of a specified quantity and grade of a product in return for monetary or other material considerations. The product may be either tangible or intangible. Many different types of functional performance and individual acts are required to complete a typical trade transaction. Their nature and scope are presented in a later section of this chapter. Management must mobilize the necessary resources and skills to produce these specific performances and to coordinate and control them so as to complete the transaction at a minimum cost. To do this management must be thoroughly familiar with all possible alternatives and be able to compare and contrast them on a rational basis.

Trade transactions vary in complexity. For analytical purposes it is useful to distinguish between *simple transactions,* in which only one functional objective, such as filling an unsolicited order at the point of sale, is to be achieved, and *composite transactions,* which necessitate negotiating and carrying out subsidiary commitments—subtransactions. Simple transactions are the atomistic particles of the trade process which can be effected independently of the other elements. Analogously, composite transactions are the molecular constituents of trade relations. Except in rare instances, all export and import transactions fall into the composite category and have complex hierarchies of interdependent processes, as will be shown later.

Analyzing and understanding the links among the transactions and subtransactions are fundamental for rational and efficient administration of foreign-trade operations. By identifying and defining the elements and their relationships within a particular trade transaction, one may design a systematic program for optimum cost and efficiency. With rapidly advancing computer technology, operational research and process analysis have passed the point where customary practices can be accepted as a reliable guide for management action.

Transactions may be classified also in terms of the judicial system within which the particular commitment is undertaken and through which compliance can be enforced. This might be called *jurisdictional classification.* It consists of two different groupings of transactions:

Directional	*Nondirectional*
Domestic	Uninational
International	Binational
Foreign	Multinational

A transaction is domestic if all parties to it reside within the country in which the observer or analyst is located; it is international if the parties to it are domiciled in different countries; and it is foreign if neither of the parties is located within the jurisdictional boundaries of the analyst's country Thus, the point of reference is the analyst's nationality, and the same transaction may be classified differently by different analysts, depending upon which country they reside in. A domestic transaction for a U.S. observer is a foreign transaction for a Frenchman, and vice versa. The nondirectional breakdown is unaffected by the observer's nationality. A transaction is uninational if all its parts are performed within the same jurisdictional environment; it is binational if two countries are involved; and it is trimultinational if it is to be carried out in more than two foreign countries. That the two classifications can be combined in many ways for analytical purposes should be self-evident.

From a company standpoint any of the classifications can be further categorized as either intracompany or extracompany transactions. If a business firm runs a multiunit operation with establishments in several different countries, its units can, and normally do, engage in intracompany transactions which may cover the entire spectrum from uninational domestic to multinational foreign. Hence the classifications are applicable not only to the analyses of extracompany trade (transactions between independent firms) but also increasingly to internal analysis as the number and scope of multinational companies increase. Although fundamental to academic inquiry, the functional and jurisdictional analyses of international trade offer important new avenues for rationalization of managerial practices by helping to uncover the critical processes, to program the activity, and to allocate both load factors and benefits to the different structural elements of the trading system on a factual basis.

The State of the Art

This section delineates the scope and character of executive responsibilities in an international trade transaction. It is thus primarily a job description. But also, in following the path from the initial decision to seek foreign-trade opportunities to the final distribution of exported products, it portrays the entire export-import process and explains the functions of its multipronged components in their chronological sequence. This explanation should serve not only as a reference but also as a basis for realistic analyses of other aspects of international enterprise. The technique used here is a variant of the so-called *critical-path analysis,* which graphically identifies the critical elements of a business process together with the relative order and interdependence among them. In this way it exposes the key parts of the process and the skills required for carrying them out.

The critical path of the export-import process is depicted in Figure 28-1, which shows the process in its entirety regardless of who is to perform it. A specific company may or may not assume responsibility for the entire process. Often it divides the job with other firms, as is explained more fully later. The institutional framework for the diagram consists of the functional participants found in most international transactions. The two functionaries in this framework are the principals to the transaction—the exporter and the importer—and the so-called *facilitating agencies,* which perform the subfunctions. The latter include the supplier, the international carrier, the banks, the underwriter, and the governmental bodies of both principals. In any specific situation the institutional elements may be subdivided into several parallel entities, operating jointly in a particular functional phase. Although this complicates the mechanics, the basic functional relationships remain the same. The additional complications can easily be accommodated by extending the respective parts of the diagram. It might be added also that, although the institutions shown are those of a free-enterprise country, the basic framework is not materially different in a communist country, since the latter have patterned

FIGURE 28-1

Critical Path of Export-Import Processes

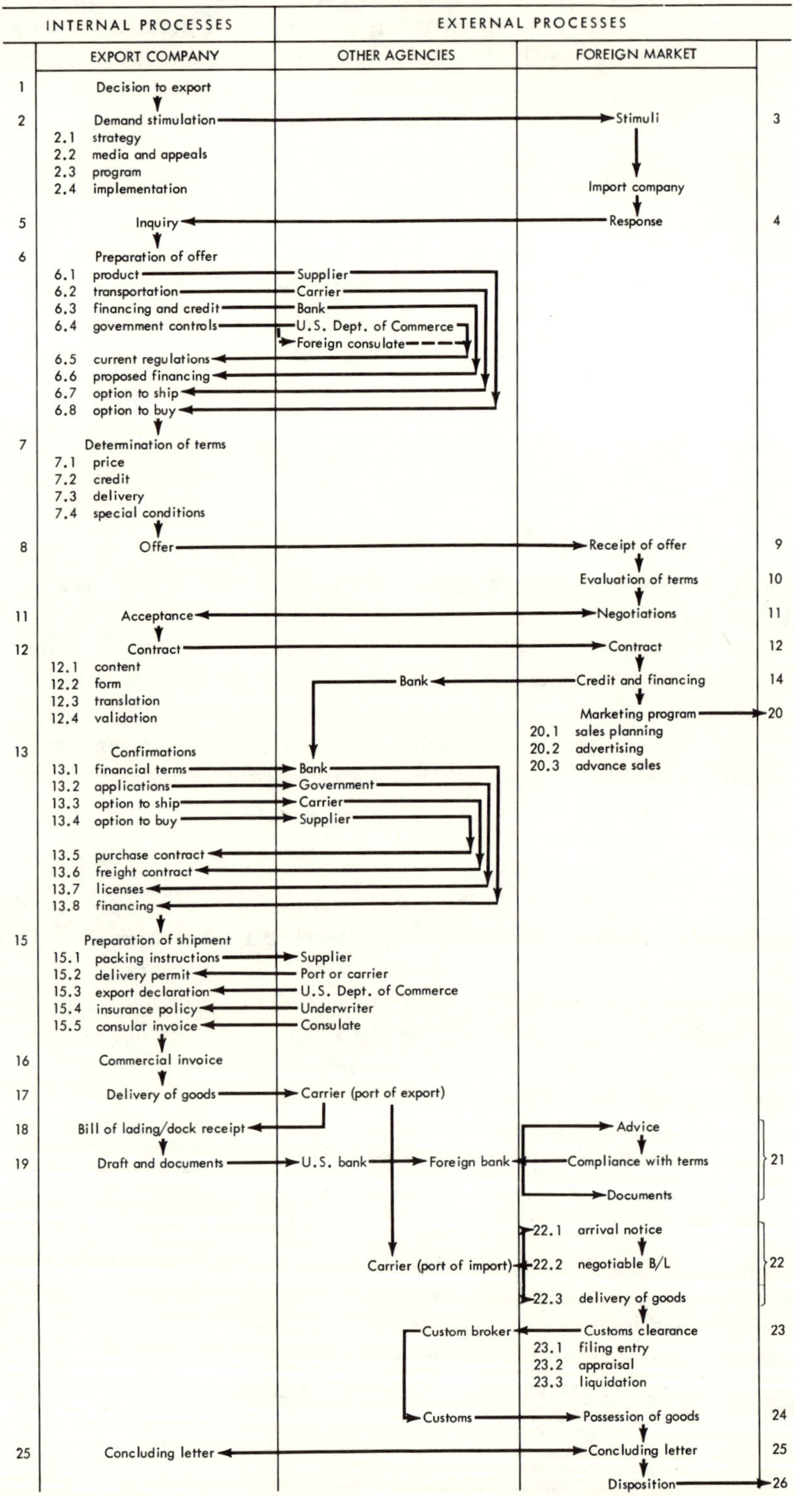

their international-trade agencies after those of the capitalist world. This is not to say, however, that either the control or the motivation of these agencies is synonymous with those of their capitalist counterparts.

Although a practitioner may benefit from this analysis, it is not intended to be a work guide so much as a graphic design of the interrelated activities in the continuum of transboundary trade. It thus lays bare the bedrock of operational functions; in it can be anchored the analysis of objectives, strategies, and policies. It also helps to evaluate and interpret the theoretical concepts of foreign trade and international economics from a managerial point of view. The importance of such links with operational realities cannot be overstressed, as they are generally absent in economics literature on international trade.

A view of the entire process should also help show what could and should be done with or about it. To show what should be done without grasping the actual possibilities may produce neater concepts and more amiable models, but these gains in form and method are often dearly paid for by losses in substance and usefulness.

Process Analysis

Although not a trigonometric graph, the diagram in Figure 28-1 may be thought of as having three dimensions; the exporter-importer axes, which control the cardinal commitments; the time axis, which reflects the ordinal sequence from the initial decision to export to the instant the products exported enter the distribution system of the country of destination; and the lateral spurs from the main axes to the service agencies. To synchronize the narrative with the chart, the numbers in the chart index the commentary which follows.

1. THE DECISION TO EXPORT

The incentives for an enterprise to consider overseas opportunities are many: knowledge of existing prospects, hopes for higher profits, lack of demand at home, governmental edicts, prestige, or the lure of adventure in uncharted markets. Irrespective of the specific incentive or the combination of factors which caused the decision to export, the subsequent processes must follow the same course except perhaps in minor details.

2. DEMAND STIMULATION

The first task is locating and stimulating demand in target export markets for the product line involved. Clearly, no trade can start before foreign demand has been built to the point where importers can expect sufficient consumer interest. Building demand usually requires tapping latent unsatisfied needs or shifting consumer preferences from competitive products, either local or international in origin. The promotional phase represents a complex galaxy of operations in which four processes control the results:

2.1 Strategy

The strategy—the overall promotional scheme which defines the objectives and indicates the methods and means to be employed in their pursuit—must be based on one hand on the nature and characteristics of the market and on the other on the resources and capabilities of the company. On the market side it involves decisions as to where the promotional efforts are to be directed, in which way each target country can best be approached, and how intensive the penetration must be. These decisions require study and knowledge of a great many factors: population, incomes, competition, consumption patterns, industrial development, and the spatial and temporal influences which affect the demand for a specific product in a particular market. On the resource side the strategy is based upon the money, the manpower, and the skills which the company can allocate for promotion. The plan should maximize goodwill for the products and minimize the number of different products in order to stay within the budget. This is possible only if the objectives, the methods, and the means are all planned simultaneously.

2.2 Media and Appeals

The selection of the medium through which the market can be reached effectively and economically and the choice of stimuli to elicit the necessary reaction in the market represent perhaps the most critical factors in the demand-creation process. The four basic approaches to export promotion include 16 categories of media:

(A) ADVERTISING. Periodicals, posters, radio and television, and direct mail

(B) DISPLAY. International fairs and exhibitions, industry and product fairs, trade centers, and public terminals (airports, squares, etc.)

(C) INDIVIDUAL CONTACT. Sample products, catalogues, correspondence, and visits

(D) PUBLICITY. News releases, conferences and meetings, editorials, and governmental representation

From them management must forge the best combination for its specific products and markets. The tools and techniques by which this can be accomplished are discussed in a subsequent chapter.

2.3 Program

The promotional program translates into action the objectives, strategies, and policies previously chosen. It is a precise plan with firm allowance of funds and specific definitions of the tasks, media, and locational element involved. A basic requirement in modern promotional practice, such a plan has two main functions: to minimize uncertainty by forcing management to consider all details before it commits itself to a particular campaign, and to provide a blueprint to be followed by the geographically scattered entities which are to carry out the campaign. Although less dramatic, this phase is no less crucial than the other three. Indeed, it is here that the irrevocable decisions have to be made.

2.4 Implementation

No promotional program, however well conceived and designed, can serve its purpose unless put into practice. The size and complexity of this task depend on various factors—media, appeals, frequency and intensity, participants, and budget. In multinational campaigns the implementation phase often hinges on efficient communication between the prospective exporter and his field force—the agencies or individuals or both who put the program into effect abroad.

3 and 4. STIMULI AND RESPONSE

As the promotional campaign unfolds, it generates stimuli which focus directly or indirectly upon the firms and individuals possessing the capacity to undertake the importation of the product promoted. If effective, the intensity of the campaign will rise until one or more of the prospective importers actively respond to it. Normally the response takes the form of an inquiry about prices, terms, and other specifics about the line or a request for a firm offer from the aspiring exporter. By taking this step, the importer does not have any legal or moral obligation; nevertheless this is a critical point in the process, as it opens the direct negotiations without which even the most routine transactions can seldom be consummated.

5. THE INQUIRY

For the export firm the receipt of the importer's response signals the beginning of direct negotiations. To negotiate effectively the export organization needs concrete information on all facts and conditions relevant to the transactions. It also needs to settle variable elements to protect itself against external change. These needs are met through a multipronged process of communication in which the following actions and relations are involved.

6. PREPARATION OF OFFER

6.1 and 6.8 Product

In order to make a legally binding offer without unpredictable risk the export company has first to confirm the supply in terms of cost, quantity, and quality (6.1). An export firm with no inventories of its own does this by obtaining an *option to buy* from its supplier. The option is an agreement guaranteeing the exporter the desired supply under terms which will remain fixed during the negotiations (6.8). Such an option provides the facts on which the exporter can base his calculation.

An industrial concern with its own export organization and inventories acts in very much the same way. Instead of an option, it places a hold on the required inventories with the manufacturing division or other appropriate department of the company. But, as industrial concerns have grown in size and complexity, multiple corporate entities and subcontractors have become essential elements in many branches of industry, especially the highly technical ones. In these situations the intracompany buying and selling procedures are often patterned after those used between independent firms. The export department may find it necessary to obtain an option to buy regardless of the fact that the supplier belongs to the same corporate entity. In some such instances the export organization may need not one but several options, as components of the final product, such as aircraft, may come from a pyramid of subcontracting concerns.

6.2 and 6.7 Transportation

The second absolute for the exporter is to have the transport capacity to deliver the shipment and to be able to do so competitively (6.2). Waterborne freight movements, which account for the bulk of international transportation, are comparatively irregular and infrequent in all but a few major ports of the world. Compared with U.S. land transportation, ocean shipping is characterized by greater distances, fewer carriers, and slower speeds, which place strict limitations on the regularity and frequency of contacts between the different countries and regions of the world. Furthermore, a large segment of merchant-marine carriers operates as tramp vessels, i.e., without any fixed sailing schedules or ports of call. Even the liner freighters, which do maintain prescribed routes and sailing dates, are subject to the perils of the sea and the vicissitudes of commerce and thus are allowed considerable latitude both in time and in choice of ports.

As a result, there is no certainty that delivery to a foreign port can be effected at a specific time unless a booking on a definite voyage is assured in advance. The exporter secures such assurance by seeking the most suitable carrier, either with or without the help of a freight broker or international freight forwarder, and obtaining a *shipping option,* which specifies the tonnage, the time, the destination, and the freight rate of the expected transaction (6.7). This option, like the purchase option, is left open for the short period, usually two or three days, needed to complete the negotiations between the export organization and its foreign prospect.

6.3 and 6.6 Financing and Credit

The cost of financing an international trade transaction varies with the credit risk, the currency, the instruments of payment, and the mechanism through which the financial aspects are processed (6.3). It is of critical importance for the export concern, therefore, to determine factually the relevant financial factors before establishing the offer (6.6). Although certain aspects of the financing, as of the product and the transport, may be adjusted in the negotiation, the export firm must reach rather concrete judgments before the outset of the negotiations regarding the limits. And, since financial arrangements affect the total cost of the transaction, it is often difficult to determine an acceptable price basis until the financial cost is either asserted or confirmed within a narrow range. In the United States this is normally done with the help of the international facilities of the commercial banking system; in many foreign countries specialized banking institutions exist for foreign-trade financing.

6.4 and 6.5 Government Controls

Simultaneously with the other preparations, the governmental controls applicable to the contemplated transaction must be ascertained for both countries (6.4). If quotas or some other severe restrictions are in effect, this matter takes precedence over all other preparatory measures, as it is a factor over which neither of the principals has any control.

The main government trade controls fall into two categories: U.S. export controls and foreign import controls (6.5). The U.S. export controls vary not only from product to product but also according to the country's international relations at any particular time. As a consequence the system of controls is a complicated one including quotas, many different licenses, destination controls, and, at times, complete embargoes.

The official source of information on U.S. export controls is the Department of Commerce, which operates field offices in all states and in most of the principal cities. In a compendium, "Comprehensive Export Schedule," specific definitions of licenses and regulations applicable to export shipments are published. It is essential that the nature of the applicable restrictions be determined and fully understood before any commitment to export is undertaken by an individual or a firm.

Foreign import restrictions vary from country to country. Although quota restrictions are outlawed under GATT, they are still widespread and can be expected to continue indefinitely. This is particularly true concerning agricultural commodities on an almost global basis and industrial goods in the economically backward countries. The recent tendencies toward managed economies as distinguished from market economies make the outlook for complete elimination of quantitative import quotas rather bleak.

The inevitable accompaniment of quotas is a rigid system of import licenses. But import licenses are generally used even if no quotas are in effect. The license requirements present particularly troublesome problems in dictatorships, where they are often used in an unpredictable manner. Tariffs, duties, and import taxes are essential cost elements in the overall export-import process. Who pays for them depends on the agreement between the export and import companies, but they must be entered into the calculation from the beginning to assess the feasibility of the transaction as such. Special regulations—health laws, engineering codes, certifications of origin, etc.—must also be checked and their criteria evaluated in the light of the pending proposition.

Information regarding import regulations can be obtained in most instances from the consulate of the respective country or from the U.S. commercial attaché stationed in that country. In practice the two principals often agree to divide this task so that each secures the information applicable to his respective country. But, unless there is complete mutual confidence, the exporter should verify the facts regarding all applicable controls.

7. DETERMINATION OF TERMS

The information accumulated in the previous stages is now combined with company data on operating costs, packing, inland freight, markup, and profit rates, to provide the raw material from which management must forge the precise terms that it can offer to the specific prospect abroad. As shown in Figure 12-1, judgments on at least three conditions are required price (7.1), credit (7.2), and delivery (7.3). Often there are special conditions—technical, legal, or commercial—which too require evaluation and definition (7.4). All the terms must be sufficiently accurate for the company to accept them as firm commitments. Whatever padding is put in for tactical purposes should be fully recognized as such to avoid errors and misjudgments in the negotiations.

8. THE OFFER

The offer itself is a legal act. It consists of drafting a brief statement of the terms in definite, unambiguous language and transmitting it to the prospect by airmail, cable, or Telex.

9 and 10. RECEIPT OF OFFER AND EVALUATION

Upon receipt of the offer the import firm can evaluate the prospective relationship with the exporter much more concretely than before. By studying the terms and juxtaposing them with other alternatives as well as with the requirements of its market, the importer can judge the prospects for a profitable transaction.

11. NEGOTIATION AND ACCEPTANCE

Depending upon this judgment, the offer is either accepted, rejected, or countered with proposals to change the terms more in the importer's favor. Such proposals may in turn be recountered by the export firm which attempts to maintain the original offer as nearly intact as practicable. The dialogue between the negotiating parties may be short or long; it ends in either an unconditional acceptance or rejection by one party. In the negative event, the process ends at this point, and no trade transaction will materialize. In the positive event, a legal agreement has in fact been consummated, although not always in form.

12. CONTRACT

The instrument for formalizing and validating the substantive agreement is the written export contract (12.1). Although theoretically it is immaterial which party drafts the contract, it is customary to place this responsibility upon the exporting concern (12.2). The contract is not just a formality; it double checks the specifics of the understanding, clarifies possible ambiguities, and expands points that may have been overlooked or inadequately explained during the bargaining phase. Or, to paraphrase, it defines all the rights and privileges of both parties in such a way as to make them amenable for appraisal and adjudication by impartial third parties if any dispute should later arise. The export contract must be complete in all details, written in simple and clear language, and drafted in strict compliance with the provisions of both nations. Clarity of expression and good syntax are particularly critical if bilingual copies of the document have to be made (12.3).

In many civil law (Roman law) countries contracts must be validated by a notary or by the consul of the country (12.4). This process consists of payments of stamp fees and certification of the contract as a bona fide legal instrument. In most such countries the original of the contract is retained by the validating official and serves in case of dispute as the prime evidence of the agreement. That such a practice protects either party against forgery is self-evident.

13. CONFIRMATIONS

Signing and validating the contract commit both parties irrevocably to the terms of the transaction; both must fulfill these terms. For the exporter, the potential to fulfill them was acquired during the preparatory phase (see point 6). It is now incumbent upon management to convert the potential into the actual by settling optional arrangements.

It confirms the purchase option or hold on goods and places a firm order for the quantities and the quality desired (13.4 and 13.5). The shipping option is replaced by a freight contract (13.3 and 13.6), under which the carrier legally obligates itself to take the cargo to the port of destination under the terms stipulated by the export contract; and the exporter is committed to provide the cargo and to pay the freight rates as agreed. Thus, both the exporter and the carrier make a firm legal obligation and subject themselves to damage claims if their performance deviates from the agreement. The necessary applications for licenses and other documents are now filed (13.2 and 13.7), and the arrangements for financing completed with the bank (13.1 and 13.8).

14. CREDIT AND FINANCING

If the contract calls for a letter of credit, prepayment, or the posting of credit guarantees, the importer's participation in completing the financial arrangements becomes necessary at this point. The desired measures typically are worked out through banking channels with the exporter's and importer's own banks as the main instruments. Financial cooperation may be started as early as the initial contract between the principals and may continue throughout the negotiating phase until the actual financing is decided upon.

15. PREPARATION OF THE SHIPMENT

At this point, the documentary mechanics of the shipment have to be performed. First, the supplier is provided specific packing instructions for proper protection of the goods during the voyage (15.1). Boxes, crates, and other containers, which are standard in domestic shipping, are seldom adequate for ocean cargo. Both design and materials deserve attention because marine rates are charged on gross weight or volume, whichever produces greater revenue to the carrier, and because in some countries either all or part of the containers is considered dutiable cargo. Hence, lighter, though costlier, packing materials of equal strength may profitably be substituted for standard containers. Depending on the rules, it may be more economical to run a calculated risk of breakage and loss than to seek complete protection.

Second, transportation to the dock must be provided. Since only authorized cargo is admitted to loading piers, it is necessary to obtain a *delivery permit* from the carrier, its agent, or the port authority in charge of the pier or quay from which the vessel will sail (15.2).

Third, all exports leaving the United States must be declared on an official form. The *export declaration* serves no purpose for the export firm but is of great significance to the government as the basic source of trade information and as a practical means of implementing export-control regulations. The forms are obtained from the U.S. Dept. of Commerce (15.3).

Fourth, marine insurance for the cargo is needed to protect it against the perils of the sea and other risks for which the ocean carrier is not legally responsible. Evidence of such coverage is provided in the form of either a marine-insurance policy or a marine-insurance certificate, depending upon whether the exporter takes out separate insurance for the particular shipment or holds a so-called *floating* (*open-end*) *policy* to cover all his shipments (15.4).

Fifth, depending on the country of destination, an official invoice prepared on forms provided by the government involved and certified by its consular representative may be required. As a rule a fee is connected with the consular invoice (15.5). Most major trading nations have eliminated this requirement.

16. COMMERCIAL INVOICE

The basic document in an international trade transaction is the *commercial invoice,* which incorporates all the essential facts about the shipment and serves managerial rather than legal or formal purposes. If properly prepared, it shows the following information:

(1) Name and address of seller and of buyer
(2) Quantity and description of merchandise
(3) Price, per unit and total
(4) Number and type of packing containers
(5) Port marks and numbers
(6) Other documents involved (insurance, consular, etc.)
(7) Name of carrier
(8) Ports of export and import
(9) Ocean or air freight charges
(10) Terminal charges (handling, wharfage, etc.)
(11) Special fees and costs, if any
(12) Any other factual information pertaining to the shipment

Which cost items need to be declared in the invoice depends upon the specific price terms under which the export shipment is made. It is in the interest of the exporter to make the document as complete as possible. Omissions, inadequate information, and errors in commercial invoices are by far the major reasons for misunderstandings, delays, and penalty charges in connection with processing international cargoes through customs. It behooves management to avoid such difficulties by making sure that the commercial invoicing is properly executed. As a rule, much of the difficulty can be avoided by designing an invoice form for export purposes different from those used in domestic marketing.

17. DELIVERY OF GOODS TO PORT

At this point the physical movement of the international shipment starts. The first leg of the journey is from the source of supply to the port of export—usually a seaport but, for more and more cargo, an international airport. Besides inland freight charges, delivery to the port of exit may involve switching charges, lighterage, and wharfage—all of which represent costs of exportation and have to be considered in the calculation under point 6 above.

18. DOCK RECEIPT AND BILL OF LADING

At the port the condition of the cargo is examined and any irregularities —observable damage to containers or contents, inaccuracies in quantities and numbers—are recorded on the *dock receipt* or *bill of lading* issued as documentary evidence of the physical transfer from the shipper to the carrier. When the goods are subsequently loaded on board the vessel, the dock receipt is replaced by the bill of lading unless the process was short-circuited at the time of delivery and the bill of lading was issued immediately.

The bill of lading serves both as a receipt and as a contract of carriage. In the latter capacity it replaces the freight contract, and its issuance terminates both the dock receipt and the freight contract. If desired, the bill of lading can be issued in a negotiable form, in which case it will also serve as a document of title to the cargo and greatly facilitate both control and resale activities.

19. DRAFT AND DOCUMENTS

With the bill of lading the exporter has all the normal documents of an export shipment.[1] The documents are now compiled and presented to the exporter's bank together with a draft for the price of the shipments. This for all practical purposes completes the transactions as far as the exporter is concerned.

20. OVERSEAS MARKETING PROGRAM

The time between contract commitment and the arrival of the cargo is normally considerable, in many cases between three and six months. This delay is caused by the preparation of the shipment, the ocean voyage, and the customs clearance involved. In that period the import company must not only develop the plans for distributing the cargo but also start both promotional and actual selling activities to maximize the turnover and the profitability of the transaction (20.1–20.3). How extensive these preparatory activities are depends in part on the market, the product, and the aptitude of the management of the import organization.

21. COMPLIANCE WITH TERMS

As shown in Figure 12-1, the process splits into two parallel channels when the export company delivers the goods to the carrier and the documents to the bank. The former will move via the shipping network, the latter via the banking system. As a rule the documents are the first to reach their destination. They are processed through the importer's bank in accordance with the instructions supplied by the exporter and his bank. Typically, the instructions prescribe that the import firm either pay or accept the exporter's draft before the documents are released to it.

22. DELIVERY BY CARRIER

At the port of destination the carrier releases the cargo as required by the contract of carriage—the bill of lading (22.1). If the lading is a non-

[1] If the export contract provides for special documents in addition to these, the exporter is obliged to obtain them.

negotiable instrument (straight bill of lading) calling for delivery to a specified consignee, the cargo can theoretically be released without the presentation of the documents. In practice this is seldom done. The typical lading provides for delivery "to the order of" the consignee and is thus a negotiable instrument by which title to the cargo can be transferred through proper endorsements (22.2). As such the order bill of lading must be surrendered to the carrier when it releases the cargo. Through this mechanism the financial and the transportation channels of the process are again joined, since the documents are required in order to take delivery (22.3).

23. CUSTOMS CLEARANCE

Delivery by the carrier is only a titular transaction, for, physically, the cargo remains in the custody of customs authorities until it has been cleared according to regulations. The clearance process consists of the following activities: filing an official entry form provided by the customs service and accompanying it with a full set of documents on the shipment; appraising the merchandise, i.e., determining the classification and the import duties applicable; and liquidating the entry by paying the assessed duties and taxes and complying with other requirements the authorities may impose. Since clearance through customs requires highly specialized knowledge and experience, it is rarely done by the import firm itself but is entrusted to customhouse brokers, who specialize in this service.

24. POSSESSION

Liquidation of the entry releases the shipment from customs and permits the import firm to proceed with its plans for physical distribution. If the liquidation is delayed because disputes, litigations, or consultations arise concerning interpretation or application of some relevant regulation, the cargo may be released under special procedures requiring that the importer post a bond in an amount sufficient to cover any duties the final decision may impose.

25 and 26. ACKNOWLEDGMENTS AND DISPOSITION OF CARGO

As a matter of etiquette the two companies exchange letters acknowledging the fact that the other has fulfilled its commitments and exploring opportunities for a continuation of the relationship. With this the international process dissipates into the marketing system of the import country, whose indigenous institutions and processes control the final disposition of the cargo (26).

Conclusion

The export-import process is not a matter of mechanics, as erroneously described in some books. Neither the exporter nor the importer can execute the process routinely even if it operates its own foreign-based subsidiaries.

The usual export-import transaction is a composite in which many parties other than the buyer and the seller have a role and an influence. Only through negotiations, adaptations, and technical know-how are import-export transactions made efficiently and effectively.

29

The Institutional Structure of International Trade

The structure of international trade—the functional and spatial framework for the global system of exchange—is composed of the various productive entities which participate in trading operations. Although the process of trade was earlier described as a continuum of export, import, and payments transactions, the structure could be visualized as a galaxy of institutions, organizations, and establishments which actively constitute the trade process or have the capacity to influence its character and course. They provide not only the channels through which world trade flows but also its content and locomotion. All trade transactions and processes are either actions of or interactions among the institutional components of the system.

Trade institutions have evolved as creatures of the economic and cultural realities of the respective peoples. Their size, character, and behavior vary in uncountable ways from country to country, and the intricate system of interconnections with which they circle the globe is not even textured but quite rough hewn. However, the effect of national and regional environments upon international trade institutions is often more apparent than real; their manifestations are more in the form and the configuration of the trading firms than in their economic purpose and social substance. Despite differences in organizational and operational detail, the underlying functional and juridical members of the trading system constitute a relatively consistent core. This apparently is true more of the international trade institutions per se than of manufacturers, processors, distributors, and other business establishments not directly engaged in international trade. The *raison d'être* of trade institutions is to bring about economic interactions between two or more countries—not only to initiate the interactions but also to produce the actual transboundary transactions. To this cardinal objective are subordinated all other activities of the institutions. The individual firm may not aspire to this basic objective as such; it may be designed to fulfill only a fractional part of it. Yet the specific objectives of any enterprise in the international trade structure, however specialized or diversified it may be, must contribute directly or indirectly to the flow of commerce across international borders or either it is malfunctioning and heading to its ruin or it simply is not part of the structure.

In a broad schematic sketch the international-trade institutions might be visualized as organic appendages of a country's internal institutional structure; these appendages supply the cohesive subsystem and the channels for that country's trade with the rest of the world. International trade institutions extend beyond the periphery of a country's business system and function largely in an international area in that both their cardinal objectives and their crucial problems center largely on phenomena which are external to the country's business system itself and as such are of no direct relevance to the other institutional components of the system. Thus, by necessity, international-trade organizations differ from other business institutions in that they must be outward looking and, if not imbued with pluralistic cultural and social attitudes, then at least immune to cultural intolerance and political isolationism. As creatures of international dealings they can succeed and prosper only when these dealings serve the needs of the respective countries better than some alternative activity.

Prototypal Analysis

Analyses of the component institutions in international trade are hampered by the cultural environments that have shaped and conditioned the institutions in different countries. Since, as indicated above, these environmental forces manifest themselves particularly in the form and not so much in the substance of the organization, a meaningful analysis becomes feasible if the focus is shifted from the specific detail to the basic patterns of objectives, operations, and behavior. In this way one can obviate cataloguing the bewildering diversity that the international business scene reflects and also diminish the danger of exaggeration of trivial differences—a process which could overshadow the fundamental harmony of the basic structure.

In what follows, the structure of international trade is described in terms of its prototypal rather than its exact institutional components. Thus it is possible that the format and the functions have not always been visualized in their truest perspectives and that at times some of the essence is discarded along with the trappings and at other times too many trappings have been preserved. But in spite of these shortcomings prototypal analysis is preferable to the nearly impossible exact analysis of specific firms throughout the world.

The essence of prototypal analysis is the substitution of model institutions for actual ones. This is not a new technique. It has been used by institutionalists in many disciplines to construct the systematic relationships without which scientific inquiry cannot succeed. Here the prototypal models are constructed not on theoretical but on empirical evidence. Consequently, they are not hypothetical but natural, not devoid of reality but the very creatures of it. More precisely, they represent the typical functional combinations found in international trade institutions; each prototype is a structural unit capable of participation in international trade. The capabilities of these "molecular" units can be combined with those of the others to construct any desired potential for a diversified firm.

To simplify the presentation further the international business community itself is reduced to two models: an export country and an import country. This does no violence to reality as long as each model reflects the basic structural apparatus. And, by using only two models, an absolute minimum for any international analysis, retraction and repetition are eliminated.

The Classical Model

On the prototypal level the components of the international-trade structure fall into three distinct zones: the business system of the export country, the international intermediaries, and the business system of the import country. As shown in Figure 29-1, the two outer zones serve primarily as the supply and demand hinterlands which are little, if at all, affected by each other's organization. Their components, therefore, are of only secondary importance in the classical model, which recognizes no circumvention of the intermediaries; i.e., all international-trade activities are presumed to be channeled through the institutional apparatus of the middle zone. Consequently, all that which is in any way essential to and characteristic of international-trade relations in the structural sphere is to be sought in the intermediary zone.

The institutions belonging to this zone are shown in Figure 29-1. They form two different columns: one for the firms domiciled in the country of production; the other for those in the country of consumption. At first glance one might classify each as a separate zone rather than as parts of a whole. In certain respects this would be an advantage, but, as later discussions will reveal, the two columns are better conceived as belonging to the same basic zone, for they are by and large capable of affecting each other's functions, and whenever opportunity costs favor such substitution it does, in fact, occur. Nevertheless the two distinct columns in the chart strongly suggest that complete synonymity does not accurately describe their essential nature. If nothing else, each belongs to a separate national jurisdiction. But more importantly, each has, in the prototypal model in any case, a different objective and orientation, at least from a relative standpoint—the export column represents supply, the import column demand. Lest this latter point be misconstrued, this is true only in a secondary or derived sense, and for managerial analysis the supply-demand concepts, even if carried to basic relationships, are of no great moment. Perhaps the best way to identify the two columns would be to call them, respectively, the export and import subzones of the structure.

FIGURE 29-1

Institutional Structure of International Trade

DOMESTIC ZONE--BUSINESS SYSTEM OF COUNTRY OF PRODUCTION	INTERNATIONAL ZONE--INTERMEDIARIES			FOREIGN ZONE--BUSINESS SYSTEM OF COUNTRY OF CONSUMPTION
	Export subzone		Import subzone	
Producers	Export merchants export houses export trading companies	BOUNDARY	Import merchants import houses import trading companies	Service firms custom house brokers freight forwarders
Distributors	Export agents selling agents manufacturers' agents		Import representatives commission houses resident representatives	Carriers
Carriers	combination export managers international brokers		of foreign exporters	Banks Distributors
Banks	Export buyers commission houses (also		Consumer-owned import establishments	Dealers
Service firms freight brokers international freight forwarders marine-insurance agencies consultants	known as indent houses or confirming houses) resident buyers Producer-owned export establishments export branches or subsidiaries		manufacturers retailers cooperative buying groups	Consumers
	Legal-advantage organizations			
	Webb-Pomerane associates			
	Western hemisphere trade corporations			
	Export trade corporations			
MULTINATIONAL ENTERPRISES				

The Export Structure

The export subzone consists of four categories of participant institutions: merchants, agents, foreign resident buyers, and service agencies. The lines between these categories are sometimes blurred in practice because certain firms encompass the activities of more than one group and others specialize in borderline functions which are difficult to classify. But on the whole the picture is quite unmistakable.

Export Merchants

To this category belong the institutions which undertake export operations at their own risk, that is, which buy the products from domestic companies in the country of origin with the intention of reselling them abroad. The legal definition of a merchant rests on the ownership of the goods to be exported; if the export firm becomes the legal owner—takes title to the goods—it is a merchant enterprise, and if it does not, it is an agent or representative.

Since with the ownership go most of the basic risks of commercial activity, the role and behavior of the merchant enterprise are fundamentally different from those of the agents. Among the risks of taking title to the inventories traded are these: price decline, obsolescence, fashion change, physical damage, and loss. As a consequence administrative responsibility in the merchant institutions focuses upon turnover: the minimization of ownership risks and the maximization of the return on capital investment in the inventories of the firm. However, since the nature of the inventories as well as the *modi operandi* vary among the different firms, three prototypes of export merchants can be discerned: the full-function export house, the limited-function trading company, and the pure trader. Each of these deserves separate description.

The export house

The distinctive characteristics of the full-function export house include: permanent sales outlets in one or more major regions (continents) of the world, permanent suppliers and inventories for its principal lines of goods, complete capabilities for all export processes, a large departmentalized organization, its own sales force in the major markets, and a wide assortment of product lines traded. In addition, the firm either operates branch offices overseas or utilizes foreign firms to obtain continual representation throughout its marketing territory. Its strength lies in its central position between the producers of its own country and the consumers abroad. To the former the export house can offer an extensive, established network of export outlets without the heavy investment in organization and development that it entails. Furthermore, the fact that this network is already operational and possesses the managerial, technical, and financial resources necessary for far-flung international marketing operations permits it quickly to sense the receptivity to a manufacturer's products in different foreign markets and to achieve results. The lure to the manufacturers of the export house is thus multiplied: wide coverage of foreign markets, absorption of export risks, minimizing initial investment in the export program, and avoiding managerial complications. To its overseas customers the export house appeals primarily because of its capacity to provide a reliable, diversified supply and because of the relatively stable and nondiscriminatory pricing and operating policies of such companies as compared with those of other types of export institutions.

In the last decade export houses in the United States have radically declined both in number and in significance. In many port cities the export house as a distinct business has become completely extinct. The ones that remain are concentrated primarily in a few large centers, such as New York City, San Francisco, Los Angeles, and Chicago. The causes for this decline have been direct trading and especially the emergence of multinational corporate structures, which will be discussed in subsequent chapters. In foreign countries the decline has been generally much less pronounced, and the export house typically continues to occupy its historically central position.

The trading company

To the trading-company category belong a great number and variety of export merchants who deal in one or a few related products. The line may be lumber, canned goods, wheat and flour, citrus fruits, wood pulp, or any similar commodity. The typical merchant firm concentrates on staples or bulk commodities of standardized grade or quality.

Unlike the export house, which performs all marketing functions, the trading company is a limited-function establishment. Typically it is a small firm, often family operated, with modest resources and rudimentary organization aside from clerical tasks. The line authority remains centralized in the owner-president, possibly together with one or two close associates or partners.

The *modus operandi* in these firms calls for purchases only. Although the firm buys the product outright from its supplier, it does so only after having received an order for it or having been otherwise assured of immediate resale. The company rarely carries any inventory besides the goods in transit. The model firm in this category has no permanent field force overseas but depends entirely on foreign agents and more or less periodic travels of its top executives. Its market coverage is regional—the Far East, Europe, or South America—and its promotional activities restricted to immediate opportunities.

The pure trader

The term *pure trader* is used here to identify business firms, usually small, one-man operations, which specialize in a very small number, often one, of basic commodities and carry out arbitrage transactions in it internationally. Their particular skill lies in the ability to uncover local shortages and surpluses in widely separated parts of the world and to arrange offsetting transactions of purchase and sale in a very short time. Through their far-flung intelligence network they follow the world market in their respective commodities and are able to determine quickly when local deviations from the normal supply-and-demand relationship are about to develop. By buying at the depressed price in the surplus country and selling at the inflated price in the deficit country, the trader not only earns a quick profit but also helps to stabilize international commodity markets.

A pure-trading firm has no operating organization besides the intelligence and buying-selling mechanisms; it handles no physical distribution and never takes delivery of the goods it buys. All movements and operational problems are either left for the seller or the buyer to handle or are passed on to some other intermediary such as a limited-function merchant or a commission house.

A variant of the pure trader is the *international desk jobber*. Instead of engaging in rapid-fire transactions, the desk jobber serves a relatively well-defined international clientele, such as flour mills, furniture manufacturers, or any other homogeneous group, on a continual basis. He is franchised to sell the product of several producers to the particular industry, for example the coal of several coal-mining companies.

The international desk jobber differs from his domestic counterpart only in that his operations embrace a wider geographic area and entail many legal, linguistic, and financial complications which do not confront the domestic firm. Because of these complications, the international desk jobbers in the United States seldom go beyond Canada. In Europe and Latin America, where the language problem is a smaller hurdle (because of multilingual schooling) and the need for this type of operation has persisted for a longer period, jobbers with multinational operations are found in many commodities.

Still another variant of the pure trader is the *speculative trader,* whose basic objective is to capitalize on the possible price differences rather than on existing ones. In other words, he buys in anticipation of price increases and sells in anticipation of price decreases in very much the same manner as speculators in domestic commodity markets.

Agents

The (export) selling agent

Selling agents are large companies which distribute mostly semimanufactured or staple goods produced by small- to medium-sized manufacturers, such as unfinished cloth, plywood, and some building materials. The selling firm acts as the joint marketing agency for a number of factories or mills producing a fungible product. By being their complete and exclusive marketing arm, the selling agency will pool the sales volume of all its client producers and thus obtain much greater competitive strength than any of the producers could without it. Although some selling agents confine their activities to the domestic market (this is probably more true in the United States than in any other free enterprise country), most operate in a number of countries. For his services the selling agent deducts a commission from the sales proceeds before remitting the balance to the supplier. Although legally the manufacturers make all final decisions, in practice the selling agent controls the marketing policy *in toto.* The number of selling-agent enterprises has always been small because many manufacturers are frightened by the imparity in size and bargaining power between their own and the agent's organization.

The manufacturers' export agent

The concept of the manufacturers' export agent has unquestionably been the most abused institutional concept in foreign trade for a long time. It has been confused by some with the combination export management firm, by others with selling agents, and by still others with the commission houses. The reasons for this confusion are obscure. In reality the manufacturers' export agent is a prototypal trade concept which has remained unchanged since the dawn of industrialization. Such an agent builds a large volume of sales in a particular market by combining the products of several manufacturers or producers with a minimum of competition among them. To realize this objective the agent develops an assortment of complementary goods—products that satisfy related needs but cannot displace one another and that can be distributed through the same wholesale and retail outlets. With such a mix the agent maximizes the volume of orders received from any outlet or market served by him and provides representation for his producer-suppliers in countries and regions where the demand otherwise would not justify the cost of sales representation.

The requirement of avoiding competitive items has restricted the entry of manufacturers' export agents into trades of standardized, large-volume commodities and compelled them to concentrate on differentiated goods, i.e., branded products. As a result the manufacturers' export agency tends to be relatively small and limited in coverage to a few countries or a particular continental region. Furthermore, the manufacturers' export agent is seldom granted exclusive export rights on a global basis but only for the countries of his principal strength. Unlike the selling agent, the manufacturers' export agent may recommend but never decides export policies and specific terms of the individual manufacturer's sales. He, too, is paid a commission for his services.

The combination export manager

The awkward title of combination export manager describes the most original of the export-agent institutions. The combination manager firm contracts to serve as the exclusive export outlet for its client and functions as if it were the manufacturer's own export department. This eliminates the need for the manufacturers to have any export personnel of their own and provides them specialized and experienced export-management service. Since the combination firm pools the export potentials of many manufacturers of closely related products, it can maintain a specially trained headquarters staff reinforced by a locally based marketing organization in foreign countries, both of which would be beyond the capabilities of the individual manufacturers because of their much smaller export income.

In essence, the combination export firm combines in the export sphere the principle of complete and exclusive distribution rights, which is a characteristic of the selling agent, with the principle of a complementary or noncompetitive product line, which is characteristic of the manufacturers' export agent. This enables the combination firm to achieve greater volume, a more complete marketing programming, and greater competitive strength than the manufacturers' agent and wider choice of product suppliers than the selling agent.

A unique operating characteristic of the combination manager firms is that they camouflage their legal and factual independence from the client manufacturers. They normally use the manufacturer's letterhead, invoices, and other corporate identifications and behave in all matters as an organic part of the manufacturer's organization. It is argued by some that a favorable image of size, diversity, and international competence is thus created for the manufacturing concern and its export position is strengthened. The merits of this argument are debatable.

NEW VERSION. The combination export manager firm has been changing in the last decade in one essential respect. The traditional firm defined its mission as that of providing continual long-term exporting capability to manufacturing companies not able to acquire or interested in acquiring such capability themselves; the earnings of the firm came from a steady flow of commissions on export sales, many of which were repeat business and routine orders. New ventures and changes requiring special managerial effort were minimized, as in all other intermediary marketing organizations.

The new version of the combination export manager firm has shifted its objective from the long-term continuation of relatively routine trade to the creation of new export opportunities and capabilities for its client manufacturers. To paraphrase, it sees its principal mission as introducing a client's products to foreign markets; building an effective demand for them; establishing the appropriate marketing channels; and simultaneously developing the personnel, skills, organizational structure, and operating systems necessary for the manufacturer to acquire export capabilities of its own. And when this point is reached, the combination firm's mission has been accomplished and it withdraws.

This is in sharp contrast to the traditional concept, and it requires sophisticated problem-solving capabilities of consultant caliber from the firm to be successful. The new firm represents and utilizes a different and more potent mix of managerial resources and know-how and thus can undertake assignments beyond the reach of its traditional competitor. Since much of its contribution is made during the initial stage of the export program, the new combination manager firm must depend to a high degree on fees rather than on commissions for its income. The typical plan provides a minimum fixed fee per month and a commission rate applicable to actual export orders obtained. In the beginning months of a manufacturer's program, when there are no sales, the full fee will be charged; as the orders start coming in, the accumulated commissions are deducted from the fee, and the fee disappears entirely when the commissions equal or exceed the total fee amount.

Export brokers

The activities of an export broker closely parallel those of the pure trader except that the broker does not actually buy or sell but only mediates the transaction. He, too, keeps a close watch on the market of the particular product in which he specializes, but, unlike the trader, who bought or sold on his own account, the broker tries to locate firms or individuals who will in fact consummate an export transaction with his assistance. For his services he is paid a brokerage fee, usually a small percentage of the value of the transaction.

Export brokers are dominant in the areas of food, raw materials, and semiprocessed commodities. A particular variant of the broker specializes in what might be labeled *distress transactions,* i.e., filling unusual needs or disposing of abnormal surpluses.

Export buyers

Export Commission House. Often known as the *indent house* in the ex-British areas of the world, this is a resident buying organization for foreign firms. In routine purchases it serves as a simple order-processing and followup organization to which the foreign principal transmits its intentions; the requirements are satisfied by designated sources. This is particularly true for repeat business and standard commodities. In new orders and other nonroutine purchases, the commission house locates the most advantageous source of supply through inquiries or, as in cases of large transactions or technically complex products, by inviting firm bids on a competitive basis. In all transactions the principal objective of the commission house is to serve the needs of its overseas principals, which pay for its services in the form of a commission.

Because of its primary affiliation with the foreign buyers, the relationship between the commission house and the supplier remains stable only if the latter continues to be the low bidder for the particular business. Hence, from the manufacturers' standpoint, the commission house can seldom be anything else than a supplementary outlet for their export business. However, small firms in many countries are known to rely solely on this export channel.

Since the commission house operates in the border area between the merchants and the agent exporters, it has acquired certain characteristics of both and is, thus, a hybrid. It is an agent in the sense that it does not buy for its own account and that it derives its income from commissions rather than profits; but it is a merchant in the sense that it frequently places the purchase orders in its own name and not only guarantees but also actually processes the payment to the supplier of the goods.

The relative importance of the commission house has declined sharply in the United States and in Western Europe since World War II. In countries where trade institutions are less specialized and manufacturing establishments smaller, the need for the broad range of export services of the commission house appears to have kept it in a relatively strong position.

Buying Offices. Some governments and industries maintain offices in other countries to procure supplies which must be imported in substantial quantities. Such resident buying agencies form a minor segment of the export structure except in some smaller countries which trade heavily with the communist bloc. The organizational nature and operating characteristics of the buying offices vary widely with the purpose and the controlling interest and defy any prototypal synopsis.

Channels for Direct Exporting

The shift from indirect exporting toward direct dealings with foreign customers and financial participation in overseas production operations has produced a complex institutional structure which contains entities of greatly different functional and organizational makeup and capabilities. As in the previous section, the intent here is not to reproduce a photocopy of this great diversity but to portray the prototypal members of the structure.

Built-in export department

The built-in export department is an arrangement by which export activities are carried out within the jurisdiction of the regular (domestic) sales organization of the firm under the operational direction of an export manager, who reports to the head of the sales department or division. The department has no specialized staff besides the export manager himself and possibly his secretary; its work is done intermittently with domestic marketing activities by the personnel of the sales department.

Because of the relative ease of establishing it and its suitability to the initial stage of an export business, the built-in organization has been the historic forerunner of most other producer-controlled export organizations, both conceptually and chronologically. Its main functional characteristics may be summarized as follows:

Advantages	*Disadvantages*
(1) Nominal initial investment	(1) Inadequate capacity for original planning of export program
(2) Low overhead (export manager and his office space)	(2) Lack of specialized skills for effective handling of nonroutine work
(3) Work done by regular staff at slack periods	(3) Close supervision by export manager required to avoid errors and to help personnel
(4) Both domestic and foreign sales activities under same executive; better coordination	(4) Export work dependent on domestic load
(5) Minimum loss in case of failure to develop export business	(5) Export policy formulated by people from other phases of company operation
	(6) Export function relegated to subordinate status

Because of its characteristics, the built-in organization serves well if the export operations of a company meet one or more of these criteria: (a) the firm is still in an experimental stage with its export operations; (b) the product mix to be exported consists of a small number of simple, standardized goods which are ordered in large quantities; (c) the company's export capacity is small; or (d) its activities are confined to a limited foreign market. Conversely, the built-in department is organizationally ill suited for (a) exportation of complex products or diverse assortments or both, (b) operations in multiple foreign markets, and (c) large-scale export operations. But it should be added that much of the efficiency of the department depends upon the caliber of the personnel of the sales organization of which it is a part. Well-educated, well-trained employees with a constructive and cooperative attitude can overcome many of the organizational drawbacks. Needless to add, the built-in department is quite adequate for most companies utilizing export intermediaries for carrying out the actual export process.

Separate export organization

The built-in department is followed either by an export department divorced from the domestic sales organization or, in larger companies, by an export division with executive personnel, facilities, and influence approximating those of other major divisions of the enterprise. The difference between these two is more in degree than in character. The separation from domestic marketing removes the organizational limitations of the built-in department, but it also requires a substantially greater investment and overhead cost which, in turn, require proportionally greater export revenue.

It appears from case studies that the much greater latitude, in both policy and operational areas, which the organization gains through separation tends to be compounded, on the one hand by the pressure to justify the investment and overhead costs, and on the other by the incentive to excel, which tends to produce a rise in export efficiency and profitability. Only when the operations are too small or when the staff lacks proficiency in international trade is the built-in organization more satisfactory. Yet, in U.S. business, the separate export department as such has fallen into near oblivion, while the built-in department continues to play a recognizable role, especially in small business. The explanation of this apparent contradiction lies in the fact that the independent export organization has been escalated into an international division or subsidiary corporation with much more extensive ambitions than are conceivable within the traditional export concept. These developments are discussed in subsequent chapters.

Export selling company

In the interwar period, and in some instances even before that, the ultimate form of export organization was a subsidiary corporation created exclusively for this purpose. Although the ownership rested with the parent firm, which exercised overall control, the latter nevertheless was a relatively autonomous entity with a legal status and corporate officers of its own. Its management had complete freedom in all operational matters and a very strong voice in even the basic objectives and policies of the concern. Typically, it was effectively insulated against domestic influences which might have interfered with or otherwise been detrimental to export activity.

The rise of the multinational company in the postwar era has brought the export selling company to the verge of extinction. Although it still continues in name in some corporations, in functional substance it has assumed new dimensions which will be treated under multinational corporate structures. The same fate has befallen the *allied export selling company,* a forerunner to contemporary joint-venture operations. It, too, may still be encountered, but only as a remnant of the past in companies which have remained relatively static in their international programs for the last quarter of a century—rare exceptions indeed.

Legal-Advantage Organizations

International business has been subject to special legislation in all countries. These laws frequently provide for special types of business organizations to be employed under certain circumstances. It would be impossible to present a global survey of such organizations here. Suffice it to say that in nearly all instances they are designed either to promote export trade or to enhance the strength of the country's enterprise vis-à-vis international competitors, as illustrated in U.S. legislation.

The Webb-Pomerane association

The Export Trade Act of 1918, sometimes called the Webb Act or the Webb-Pomerane Act, permits cooperative export activities among U.S. companies. The law grants conditional exemption from certain parts of the Sherman Anti-Trust Act of 1914 and also from Section 7 of the Clayton Act to associations of business firms organized for the exclusive purpose of export trade. The exemption is granted only if the agreement made among the members and all the activities of the association comply with these three conditions:

(a) They do not restrain the export trade of any other company.
(b) They do not raise or lower prices in the U.S. market.
(c) They are not in restraint of trade within the United States in any other way.

An association formed under this law is required to file its organization papers, including the articles of association, with the Federal Trade Commission (ETC), and it remains under a close surveillance by federal authorities at all times. Its freedom to act is limited not only by the provisions of the Act, but also, and often more so, by the uncertainty which clouds the boundaries of these provisions in actual business practice.

Such requirements are not conducive to aggressive and imaginative export marketing. Their dampening and restraining effect on business is particularly apparent in those product lines which require a great deal of flexibility and creativity for satisfactory sales results. As a rule, the complexity of the export-marketing task increases with the complexity of the product itself. Highly standardized or otherwise uniform and simple products, such as staples, semiprocessed materials, and raw commodities, are sold primarily on the basis of price; the marketing techniques and procedures and to a considerable degree even the relationships which are involved in exporting these products are relatively simple to define, and they can be submitted to the supervisory authorities for approval in advance of an actual business transaction. The sale of complex and unique products, such as electrical apparatus, cosmetics, and fashion apparel, on the other hand, depends heavily upon imaginative nonprice strategies and tactics of marketing which are difficult to standardize and which usually do not lend themselves to advance approval by the supervising authorities.

Thus the danger of running afoul of the FTC and the antitrust authorities is very real for manufacturers of the latter products, and they find the Webb-Pomerane Act little help in their struggle for export markets. The fact is that the law was never intended for such companies. It was initiated and promoted by the staples and raw materials interests and it was thus tailored to their own problems; to expect it to benefit the more sophisticated industries would be not to know the history of this legislation. What makes the situation more critical today than in the past is the fact that during the half century the Webb-Pomerane Act has been in force the patterns of both production and export trade have shifted more and more toward manufactured products which are ill suited for exportation through the Webb Act associations. One must also observe that the law predates the birth of many marketing concepts, institutions, and procedures characteristic of the contemporary business scene. It is, therefore, not surprising that the Act cannot deal effectively with present export marketing problems.

What is surprising is the fact that even in the staples category the number and importance of the associations formed have been relatively small. A clue as to why this is so may be found in the following statement:

> Although the reasons for the Webb Act were peculiarly persuasive in the case of *small business* [my italics] the Act was drafted in terms of all export business, big as well as small. But, having made the Act general in its availability to exporters, Congress proceeded to have hedged its provisions in order to prevent exempt associations from being used to restrain the domestic competition or to put independent export competitors at a disadvantage. As a further safeguard ...it was later determined by the Supreme Court that the activities of the Webb Act Associations alleged to violate the Sherman Act were within the jurisdiction of the Department of Justice as well as the Commission, i.e., FTC.[1]

If the Act were designed to help small business and would not be applicable to big corporations, neither Congress nor the courts would have reason to worry about the potential misuse of the law as a means of creating undesirable concentration of economic power or monopoly, as now is the case. With the monopoly problem eliminated, an act of this type could lead to relaxed control of export associations without danger to the public interest.

The Western Hemisphere trade corporation

The Federal Revenue Act of 1942 established legal criteria under which an American corporation could be exempted from both excess-profit taxes and surtaxes and also qualify for certain reductions of its regular income-tax

[1] Kingman Brewster, Jr., *Anti-Trust and American Business Abroad* (New York: McGraw-Hill Book Company, 1958), p. 24.

burden. The specifics of this formula defy nontechnical explanation, but the criteria for a company to become a Western Hemisphere trade corporation can be summarized as follows:

(a) The company must be incorporated and domiciled in the United States.
(b) A minimum of 95 percent of its total business must consist of exports to Western hemisphere countries.
(c) A minimum of 90 percent of its gross revenue must be derived from the active conduct of trade rather than from investments or other nontrade activities.

The interpretation of the law and the determination of its applicability are made by the Internal Revenue Service. Since the law was written from a narrow tax standpoint, it has no regard for the organic unity and managerial efficiency of a corporation; as such, its influence is likely to continue to be strictly limited to the formalistic surface of the U.S. export structure and not to extend to the operating organization.

Export trade corporation

Prompted by the balance-of-payments crisis which has plagued this nation for several years, Congress in 1962 extended the availability of tax exemption to a new form of enterprise—the export trade corporation—in order to induce business to increase exports and to help reduce the payments deficit. The new form of enterprise is available to any company which has obtained 90 percent of its income in the three years prior to filing the application from foreign sources and the principal activity of which is the sale of products produced in the United States for consumption abroad by persons unrelated to the applicant. Sales to subsidiaries are not included. An export trade corporation is entitled to exemption from taxes on its foreign income in an amount equivalent to the smallest of these three measures:

(1) 150 percent of export promotion expenditures outside the United States.
(2) 10 percent of gross revenue from export trade.
(3) increase in export assets—working capital, inventory and handling facilities—during the tax year.

The income from foreign sources need not all come from the sale of physical products but may under certain circumstances include royalties, commissions, and fees charged for the use of patents, trademarks, secret processes, and related property rights belonging to a U.S. producer.

DISCs (Domestic International Sales Corporations)

In the fall of 1971 Congress authorized U.S. companies to set up special DISC subsidiaries to handle their foreign sales of American-made goods. The aim was export stimulation through tax incentive. The DISC subsidiary derives its export stimulus from the provision that shelters 50 percent of its profits from U.S. taxation indefinitely if they are retained by the subsidiary. These tax-deferred funds can be made available to the parent company as loans. To qualify for DISC classification a subsidiary must have at least 95 percent of its gross receipts from export sales. At this writing scores of corporations are intensively investigating the possibilities of this newest legal-advantage organization.

Criticism of legal-advantage organizations

From both economic and managerial standpoints legal-advantage entities are justified only to the extent to which they contribute to the elimination of arbitrary obstacles to efficiency and equality of opportunity in international business relations. Provisions along the lines suggested in the discussion of the Webb-Pomerane Act would then be healthy and desirable despite their possible conflict on some points with American philosophical dogma. At least they would compel the doctrinaire positions to be rationally analyzed in the light of the contemporary international business requirements.

But measures such as the establishment of the revenue-act corporations are harmful to overall business interests; they create artificial advantages for some and artificial disadvantages for others. (In competition an advantage for one is a disadvantage for the other.) Hence, they are discriminatory devices which contribute to inefficiency and inequality in the international system.

Import Structure

The institutional framework of import activity, although not a mirror image, is quite similar to that of export activity. This is only natural, for the import and export structures must form a functional whole if their joint objective—the flow of international trade—is to materialize. We are not concerned here with whom these institutions belong to or whose specific interests they serve, but we are concerned with how the apparatus for the trade is constructed. The import structure embraces three main categories of business institutions: import merchants, import representatives, and consumer-owned import establishments.

Import Merchants

The full-function import houses with a general line of merchandise, which dominated the U.S. wholesale trade in its early days and continued to play a significant role in the distribution structure of the country up to World War I, have all but disappeared from the scene. Extreme protectionism with its ultrahigh tariffs and other harsh restrictions plus the unemployment and the generally depressed conditions of the 1930's severely weakened the competitive position of the general import house, already under heavy strain from revolutionary changes in American marketing, especially from large-scale retailing organizations such as chain stores, ownership groups, and cooperative ventures. When World War II started, all these adversities were further aggravated, and the general import house, an international wholesaler, apparently ceased to exist. In some other countries this type of institution still may be encountered, but everywhere the trend has been toward the limited-function import establishments.

The limited-function import company is the dominant import intermediary today. It tends to specialize both in terms of the distributive functions which it undertakes and in terms of the products it will import. Typically it concentrates on a narrow range of products, either one line or a combined assortment geared either to the demand pattern of a specific group of consumers—textiles for suit manufacturers, engineering supplies for the machine-tool industry, specialty foods for delicatessens, antiques and art objects for decorators—or to the requirements of a particular domestic distribution channel—supermarket, gift, millinery, haberdashery, leather, and other specialty retailers.

In the consumer-goods sector the import merchant normally carries continuous inventories and is often the sole source of supply. His distribution organization is relatively limited—mostly a few salesmen and some clerical staff.

In the industrial sector, the inventory function is limited to replacement parts, display and demonstration models for manufactured products, and test samples for chemicals and raw materials. Only a few large firms, sometimes called raw-materials merchants, who specialize in one or two commodities in continuous demand, maintain inventories for immediate delivery as a common practice.

Import Representatives

As indicated earlier, the broker who is active in the export business is often also engaged in import activity. Contrary to customary terminology, most of them should be classified as international brokers. However, although some brokers do limit their activity exclusively to export transactions, this author has no knowledge of import brokers as such. In general the role that brokers play in import activity is a relatively negligible one, except under unusual conditions.

The Import Commission House

Unlike the export commission house, the import commission house in its pure form is strictly an agent institution which buys abroad on behalf of a U.S. consumer, makes all arrangements in the name of its principal, and acts in all respects in strict compliance with the authority granted to it by the principal (the U.S. consumer). It assumes no financial responsibility for either the foreign supplier or the domestic consumer and is remunerated by the latter by the purchase of the article procured at the agreed price.

In practice, the functions of the import commission house are sometimes combined in the same company with those of an import merchant or those of the export commission house. To avoid confusion and unnecessary complications it is highly important that such "mixed" firms clearly distinguish among the different transactions. In well-arranged companies, separate divisions handle the different institutional functions.

Resident Representatives of Foreign Exporters

To avoid direct investments in overseas sales offices or distribution branches, exporters of all types have long utilized resident representatives in different foreign markets to handle the export selling function, i.e., to generate import orders from the agent's country to the exporter. The representative may be either an agent or a merchant institution. The former concentrates on order-obtaining activities and serves as an information link between the import market and the exporter abroad. The latter in addition assumes the risks of ownership and carries out the physical distribution of the product involved.

Historically, the resident representatives have enjoyed exclusive rights to importing the particular manufacturer's products into their respective native markets. These exclusive rights were granted to them originally to minimize the number of establishments from any particular foreign area with which the exporter had to deal. Since knowledge about other countries' markets was limited and difficult to obtain and since information of a current nature was difficult to transmit—not only because of linguistic difficulties but also because of primitive communication methods—the exporter was strongly motivated to turn over to a native firm all the marketing functions in the particular export market. From this transfer the exclusive agency concept emerged; it now has gained widespread acceptance in all phases of business relations, both international and intranational.

Although cultural differences among national markets remain, knowledge about them has increased immensely and becomes available with much greater ease. Thus, the necessity for having an exclusive representative has been reduced, and it is now but one among several alternatives for obtaining representation. Too often, perhaps, agency arrangements persist not because of economic reasons but because of inertia or convenience. New methods of international marketing have also worked against the representative system as such, including the exclusive-agency arrangements. With planned objectives, targets, and research-based strategies, international marketing operations have assumed functions which the traditional agency firm has found difficult to adopt. As this process continues, it is likely that the traditional agent representatives will be relegated, as they already are to a high degree, to carrying out the routine business of smaller export firms and that the business which is not absorbed by company-controlled foreign outlets will be shifted to much larger and financially and managerially stronger companies which can keep pace with new advances in marketing and management technology.

Consumer-Owned Import Establishments

In importing, as in exporting, the shift has been toward direct control over the process and over establishments carrying it out. Manufacturing firms which use foreign materials or components have come to rely on their own import unit if this is the only foreign activity of the company or have transferred the procurement function to an international division if a variety of multinational operations is involved. The import department, where it still exists, resembles in many respects the export department but invariably has a product-based organizational plan instead of the territorial scheme which tended to dominate export departments.

Large retail stores—department stores, chains, and supermarkets, too—have set up their own import units, which deal directly with foreign sources or export intermediaries. The smaller retailers (such as independent department stores and local chains) have created import-buying groups, which usually function as a suborganization to their cooperative buying organization. Both these retail import entities have shown vigorous initiative in having their own resident buyers in the source countries and in seeking direct contact with potential merchandise resources for new products and product ideas.

30

International Pricing

Pricing is one of the most difficult tasks of international management. Differentiation of products, plurality of costs, contrasts and contradictions in markets, and international complications in logistics—all in the final analysis must somehow be incorporated into the pricing equation. To be sure, price is but one of the variables of the marketing mix, to be considered in conjunction with such factors as the nature of the product, the type and the amount of promotional activity, and the characteristics of the customers; however, price is the one factor upon which all other factors depend because the process is circuitous. The price of the output determines the revenue gained from sales and used to pay the costs of production, distribution, promotion, product research, and capital. If the firm's pricing process is improper or haphazard, it runs the risk of selling too little at too high a price or too much at too low a price. In either instance, all the firm's other activities will suffer because of lack of funds which could have been made available from sales revenue if proper pricing were employed.

Policy vs. Routine Pricing Decisions

Because of its crucial importance, pricing policy is always a primary responsibility of top management. Only in the case of very large, decentralized firms, such as multinational companies, is there any delegation of the authority to formulate pricing policies and strategies to subordinates and even then the pricing authority usually falls no further than to the national managements of the various overseas affiliates of the firm. In contrast to the formulation of pricing policies and strategies, the implementation of the policies—that is, the day-to-day operational price making or routine pricing—is rarely a direct concern of top management but is widely diffused throughout the organizational structure. This diffusion is often misinterpreted by textbook writers as evidence that pricing is handled as a matter of routine by minor executives and that the theoretical concepts and techniques of pricing are completely ignored. Close analysis will reveal that the pricing decisions which the minor executives make are nothing more than results of directions top management has issued to lower echelons. Through its pricing policies, top management coordinates the day-to-day decisions of managers in widely dispersed markets. Thus, consistency with the overall objectives of the firm is attained, and the operational aspects of pricing are simplified for increased efficiency. The policy directives can usually be adjusted to account for varying conditions in different countries.

In many instances these directives which translate policy into procedure take the form of markup formulas. The markup formulas may be adjusted in countless ways to reflect conditions in the particular markets in which they are used. But in approach the formulas are limited to two basic types. The first uses cost as a base of the markup (100 percent) to which a specified percentage is added. In its simplest form the cost-based markup is

$$\text{cost} + \frac{(\text{cost} \times \text{markup, percent})}{100} = \text{price}$$

The second basic type of markup formula is based on the selling price. Its basic formula is

$$\frac{\text{cost} \times 100}{100 - \text{desired markup (percent)}} = \text{price}$$

The two markup procedures are in reality two ways of saying the same thing. The markup on selling price is more popular for reasons of convenience, as it permits the invoice figures to be used as the basis for many kinds of statistical reporting without any adjustment. It is roughly equal to the gross margin.

The markup concept of pricing has been the object of a great deal of criticism in recent years. It has been said that markup pricing ignores the influence of demand upon price and may fail to account for all the costs of doing business. It is certainly true that many firms, particularly smaller companies, improperly use markup pricing policy and fail to consider many facets of policy formulation such as demand and opportunity costs. The only correct use of the markup technique is implementation and not formulation of policy. Firms can and do, however, make proper use of markup pricing by first employing economic analysis to formulate pricing policy and then translating the results of their analysis into appropriate markup formulas. In fact, the sheer size of many national and multinational firms makes formula pricing imperative at the level of the individual market.

The pricing formulas can be tailored for individual markets by adjusting the markup percentages, by including discounts and markdowns, and by applying different definitions of cost to various markets. The adjustment of the relative markup is an operational method of considering demand in price. Large markups can be assigned to markets with high demand and small markups to markets with low demand. The concept of cost can also be altered to include transportation charges, import duties, and fixed costs associated with foreign operations such as special taxes and licenses.

Theoretical Framework for Pricing Policy

Pricing policies may be designed to serve different objectives. Modern microeconomic theory has been built on the assumption that the sole objective of the firm is to maximize its profits (or to minimize its losses). Utilizing the marginal-cost and marginal-revenue concepts, this theory provides the basic models for formal price analysis. But, although invaluable as an analytical tool, the marginalist theory is insufficient for coping with pricing realities. Its limitation lies in the single-objective hypothesis. Factual evidence shows that management may emphasize other objectives such as market share, recovery of historic or accounting costs (as distinguished from economic costs), or, particularly significant in international pricing, avoidance of antagonistic political reaction in its various world markets. The prevalence of these other objectives has given rise to the so-called *behavioristic theory* of the firm, which postulates that instead of trying to maximize profits, management seeks to *satisfice* its various objectives as it defines and rates them at a particular time and place. The slogan, "The objective of businesses is to render a service to the public, and profits are a prerequisite for doing this," is a popular version of the behavioristic notion. It should be added that, although a firm's management may pursue multiple objectives, it does not abandon the principles of profit maximization; it only reduces the maximum by sacrificing some resources or revenues for the other objectives. However, the behavioristically oriented management views the pricing problem more often as earning an "acceptable" return over cost rather than as maximizing profits. This approach is further elaborated in the full-cost pricing section below.

Marginal, or Incremental, Cost Pricing

Marginal cost pricing uses economic theory as its conceptual framework. The decisive variables in the theoretical pricing model are marginal cost and marginal revenue, that is, the per-unit changes in total cost and total revenue which a pricing decision may cause. In practical application the term *incremental* is used instead of *marginal* to indicate that the firm is not concerned with minute differences such as variation of sales by a single unit but renders decisions on problems of greater scope, say 100 or 1000 units of volume. In this discussion marginal and incremental are used interchangeably.

Under the incremental approach, management tries to weigh the rewards and penalties of its pricing decisions; it juxtaposes the effects on sales with the effects on costs of any change in price or in output to find the position where the positive effects on one equal the negative effects on the other. That is, both cost and demand behaviors are given full consideration in pricing policy. To do this, the firm must critically analyze all its cost elements and have a clear conception of their relationship (variability) to output and sales. The relevant costs for incremental purposes are only those expenditures which will be affected by a particular decision, i.e., which will either increase or decrease because of the decision. All fixed costs are irrelevant in marginal-cost pricing, as they represent irrevocable consequences of past decisions and will continue regardless of new decisions. Since pricing decisions are always future directed, they should concern only the variable elements of cost which determine the marginal or incremental costs of the decision. The popular notion that incremental costs are almost impossible to determine in practice is one of the greatest economic fallacies. In fact the determination of incremental costs can be accomplished quite accurately in the vast majority of pricing situations. The real obstacle in incremental-cost analysis has not been the inherent complexity of the job but the lack of understanding of the marginal approach by executives and the naïveté of economics instruction and text materials. These weaknesses are now being remedied by increased economic sophistication, both in business management and business schools.

On the revenue side the problem becomes more complicated, for the determination of the demand schedule from which the incremental revenue can be derived is subject to market forces over which the firm has no control like that which it has over the cost. Also, information on the market forces is more elusive. But through modern methods of market research and forecasting reasonably accurate prognostications can be produced. The determination of demand is assigned either to the firm's market research staff or to outside consultants. In a multinational context separate surveys may be employed in the firm's different markets to establish the relative significance as well as the peculiarities so that both policy decisions and markup formulae can be adjusted for differences in demand.

The multinational firm often finds its pricing problems further complicated because of various forms of market instability and because of difficulties in communicating with its customers. Businesses in the United States and in the highly developed foreign countries operate in a relatively stable political environment which is not present in the less developed nations. Incidents of severe policy changes in these underdeveloped areas are numerous and have on occasion taken the form of serious civil disturbances, economic fluctuations, high taxation, or even nationalization of foreign operations. Firms contemplating operation in such regions should consider the possibility of drastic governmental policy changes and should adjust their expectations accordingly. Firms operating in such an unstable political environment often tend to use short-run pricing methods and exploit demand because of the fear that the market may be closed before the long-run profit expectations can be realized. However, it may be just such exploitative pricing which induces antagonistic action against the firm in its foreign markets. These actions and the probabilities of their occurrence should be given much consideration in international pricing decisions.

When the marginal-cost and marginal-revenue schedules have been determined for each product or group of products and when relative demands between markets have been ascertained, the firm has a good idea of what its price policy should be. However, the firm must not only take account of the present situation but also look to the future. Pricing policy should include provision for changes in demand over time and for "long-run" costs. Therefore, marketing life cycles of products, replacement costs associated with fixed assets, and anticipated changes in economic conditions must be incorporated into the policy. The nature of competition and its effect on the firm must also be determined before the pricing policy can be considered operational.

The amount of control the management of a firm can exercise over its price depends upon the industry it is in. No company has complete freedom in its pricing decisions, as complete monopoly is never encountered in multinational business. Every time a company expands its market by crossing international boundaries, it is likely to face a new set of competitors. Therefore, even those companies which enjoy a relatively highly degree of monopolistic control at home become more and more subject to competitive influences when they enter multinational markets. By theoretical standards multinational firms fall into either oligopolistic or monopolistic groups. Thus, they emphasize price stability, for price changes initiated by any one firm are quickly recognized and followed by the others. If all firms react to the price change, the company which initiated the change may have gained nothing and may have jeopardized its market position.

Price leadership

Because of this phenomenon, price leadership is not uncommon among multinational companies. One company is recognized as the price leader and initiates all price changes, either upward or downward, which the other firms then follow. In the U.S. antitrust legislation, price leadership is the form closest to domestic consort which the government will tolerate. In many other countries the government is more tolerant of the interactions among firms, and cartels are numerous. The firms in a cartel make joint decisions on pricing, output, and marketing areas; all firms are bound by these decisions. Consequently, a cartel is really a monopoly in which the productive factors are owned by separate parties. Multinational firms should be aware of the viewpoints of the governments of their different markets with respect to intercompany cooperation so that they may make the best use of cartels and other forms of industry cooperation when the opportunity arises.

Full-Cost Pricing

In full-cost pricing a company endeavors to set its price at a level which covers all costs, both variable and fixed, plus a predetermined net return on the investment. The notion that all costs are covered by the price has a widespread appeal because, by definition, it assures profitable business. Managers who lack the economic sophistication to employ the incremental approach or who cannot determine the position or shape of their demand schedules find the full-cost method a convenient shortcut to reaching pricing decisions. Other managers may prefer the full-cost method because it gives them what might be called a greater *political right* in pricing than does the incremental method. This belief stems from the fact that there is no concrete or generally accepted way of defining full cost; hence a definition can be devised by which all markets are charged the same price as a matter of "fairness and justice" regardless of the differing risks and costs among them; or, alternatively, each market may be assigned a quite different price because of the differences in the direct costs or for some entirely noneconomic reason. In other words, full-cost prices can be computed either as

$$\frac{\text{total cost}}{\text{total sales}} \text{ or } \frac{\text{cost of market } A}{\text{sales market } A} + \frac{\text{cost of market } B}{\text{sales market } B} \cdots + \frac{\text{cost of market } N}{\text{sales market } N}$$

The leverage in the definition of full cost is the overhead; the greater the proportion of total cost which is overhead, the greater the opportunity for devising diverse definitions of full cost and, consequently, the more different prices which can be "supported." It is not too great an exaggeration to say that the full-cost concept of pricing presumes no other constraints to pricing than those which management legislates for its own guidance.

Thus, in contrast to marginal-cost pricing, the full-cost method lacks not only theoretical consistency but also any inherent standard by which the economic soundness of a pricing policy could be determined; it places pricing in the realm of subjective judgment and the political influence of the price makers. Marginal pricing requires a careful study of, and adjustment to, the demand in each market; full-cost pricing is incapable of adjustment to demand. Marginal pricing adjusts the company's operations to the structure of the market and to the competitive conditions that flow from it; full-cost pricing does not. Marginal pricing utilizes incremental costs as the relevant determinants of profitability; full-cost pricing relies on average costs instead. Furthermore, in the full-cost method the costs are the accountant's costs, i.e., the historic or original costs and arbitrary allocations of overhead, both of which are quite often unrepresentative of the current values, not to mention opportunity cost. The fact that profitable operations can be maintained under full-cost pricing is of little consequence; the real question is not whether the result is a profit or loss—both of which are themselves debatable terms as they are used in accounting—but how effectively the resources at management's disposal are being used. A profit in one country or subsidiary may represent a more severe indictment of management than a loss in another when actual opportunities offered by the respective markets are compared.

Market Segmentation

As mentioned previously, it is quite common for multinational firms to face different demand schedules in each of their countries. The proper course of action for such firms is to set different prices with respect to the different demands in order to satisfy each demand and gain the maximum profit. The same situation can occur within one country; however, governments usually are concerned about firms which set different prices for different markets in the same country unless such price differences can be justified by differences in transportation or selling cost.

Figure 30-1 shows the proper pricing strategy under conditions of market

FIGURE 30-1

Pricing for a Two-Country Market

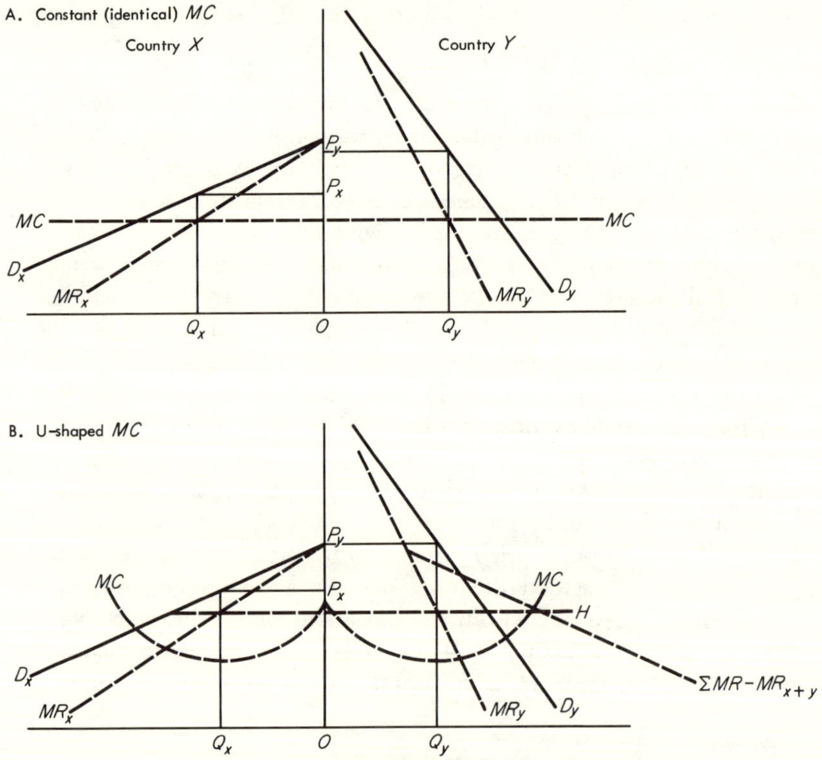

segmentation. A two-country, single-goods situation is described; however, the analysis can be adapted for more countries and more goods. Profit maximization requires that marginal revenue equal marginal cost and that marginal revenue in both markets be equal; therefore MR_x and MR_y must be added by using a horizontal summation of the quantities in each market at each level of marginal revenue. This summation gives an aggregate marginal revenue schedule Σ MR. The point of intersection of the MC and Σ MR schedules (point H) determines the total output which should be marketed in order to meet the basic condition for optimization, which requires that $MC = MR_x = MR_y$. The intersection of the horizontal line drawn through point H with the individual marginal revenue schedules (MR_x and MR_y) determines the correct prices as at the levels of P_x and P_y and allocates the sales between them as measured by Q_x and Q_y.

If the two countries are not adjacent to each other, price adaptation to their individual demand conditions is all that is needed. If, however, the two countries have a common boundary or if for other reasons commercial interactions between them are likely, the price adaptation needs to be reinforced by product differentiation to prevent leakage from the lower price country X to the higher price country Y.

Export-Import Costs

To arrive at a proper cost schedule for international pricing, all the expenses associated with export-import transactions must be taken into consideration in addition to other costs. These expenses stem primarily from the need to move goods over long distances, to use multiple carriers, and to cross international trade barriers.

In many instances, the cheapest form of transportation is not the most efficient. Frequently transportation problems involve a trade off between cost and time. If the product is perishable, it may need to be shipped by a fast, relatively expensive carrier such as air freight. In other instances, fast carriers may be used if demand is unsteady because it may be cheaper to use air freight for some items than to maintain a large inventory of them in a market which is quite distant from the production plant.

Since transportation, duties, and other export-import costs usually represent a very significant share of the total value of international cargo, they can render any price figure meaningless unless it is qualified by clear stipulation as to the amount of these costs included in the price. From generations of negotiations on this issue between importers and exporters, standard definitions of international price quotations have emerged; they are now in global use. In minor detail the price definitions vary from one country to another, but in basic structure and in disposition of the normal export-import costs they all are very much alike. The most generally used definitions on a worldwide basis are "Incoterms," published by the International Chamber of Commerce, in

Paris, France. Also in wide use are the "Revised American Foreign Trade Definitions" of 1941. The typical price definitions and the export-import costs that are associated with each definition are shown below. The U.S., British, and French names of the definitions are given.

	U.S.	*British*	*French*
(1)	Ex point of origin (ex factory, ex mill, ex warehouse, etc.)	Ex works	A l'usine (ex usine) (à la mine, ex magasine, en magasine, etc.)

1.1 Domestic selling price at warehouse, factory, etc., *plus*
1.2 Export packing and marking costs
1.3 Costs of checking quality (weighing, counting, or measuring), if any, *minus*
1.4 Export discounts, if any

	U.S.	*British*	*French*
(2)	F.O.B. inland carrier (named point of departure)	F.O.R. (free on rail) F.O.T. (free on truck)	Franco wagon Franco sur wagōn (point de départ convenu)

2.1 Costs 1.1–1.4 inclusive, *plus* the costs of
2.2 Cartage to freight station
2.3 Loading on rail carrier
2.4 All risks until carrier has taken custody of cargo

	U.S.	*British*	*French*
(3)	F.A.S. vessel (named port)	F.A.S. (free alongside ship)	F.A.S. (franco le long du navire)

3.1 Costs 1.1–2.4 inclusive, *plus* the costs of
3.2 Rail switching
3.3 Unloading
3.4 Handling and trucking (payments to longshoremen for moving and positioning the cargo on dock so as to put it in reach of ship's tackle)
3.5 Lighterage (the charges for the use of lighters or barges in loading large ships)
3.6 Wharfagĕ (fees charged for the use of a wharf)
3.7 Transit duties
3.8 Forwarder's commission
3.9 Clear dock receipt
3.0 All risks until goods are in custody of carrier or operator of wharf

	U.S.	*British*	*French*
(4)	F.O.B. vessel	F.O.B.	F.O.B. navire (port d'embarquement convenu)

4.1 Costs 1.1–3.0 inclusive, *plus* the costs of
4.2 Booking cargo space
4.3 Loading on board ship
4.4 Heavy lift (extra charge made for loading units over a limit, such as 6,000 lb, specified by local port authority)
4.5 Clean on-board bill of lading or ship's receipt (depending on country)
4.6 All risks until goods have passed ship's rail

	U.S.	*British*	*French*
(5)	C. & F. (cost and freight to named port of destination)	C. & F.	C. & F. (coût et fret, port de destination)

U.S.	British	French
5.1 Costs 1.1–4.6 inclusive, *plus* the costs and fees of 5.2 Export licenses 5.3 Export duties and taxes 5.4 Ocean freight to port of destination 5.5 All risks until goods have passed ship's rail		
(6) C.I.F. (cost, insurance, and freight to port of destination)	C.I.F.	C.A.F. (coût, assurance, fret; port de destination)
6.1 Costs 1.1–5.5 inclusive, *plus* 6.2 Marine insurance 6.3 Consular invoice, certificate of origin, inspection certificate, or any other document required under the terms of the transaction. 6.4 All risks until goods have passed ship's rail at port of shipment		
(7) Ex ship (named port of destination)	Ex ship	Ex ship (point de destination convenu)
7.1 Costs 1.1–6.4, *minus* fees for 7.2 Consular invoice and certificate of origin, *plus* 7.3 All risks until ship has docked at port of unloading		
(8) Ex dock (named port)	Ex quay (named port)	Ex quai (port convenu)
8.1 Costs 1.1–6.4, inclusive, cost 7.3, *plus* 8.2 Lighterage if the vessel cannot be wharfed 8.3 Unloading if not included in ocean freight 8.4 Import licenses 8.5 Customs duties and import taxes 8.6 Custom brokerage (customhouse broker's fee for clearing cargo through customs) 8.7 Trucking and handing 8.8 All risks until delivery to importer on dock or port of destination		
(9) Free delivered*	Free delivered	Franco rendu
9.1 Costs 1.1–6.4 and 7.3–8.8 inclusive, *plus* 9.2 Transport and insurance to inland point 9.3 All risks until cargo is delivered to specified point		

* There is less international agreement on this term than on the others, partly because its original definition excluded import tariffs but included export and transit tariffs. In this form it is more useful for deliveries by land carriers which must cross the territory of third countries.

Companies that use full-cost pricing follow the practice of simply adding on to the domestic selling price the charges which the exporter must bear under the price quotation he uses. This practice will often escalate the price of the exported product to two to four times its domestic price. If the markups of the foreign importers, jobbers, distributors, and retailers are also added, the escalation may be even greater. In absolute amount these markups in the foreign-distribution channel are substantially higher than their domestic counterparts. This is true for two reasons. First, as a general rule the import business uses the *landed cost,* which is the same as ex dock value, as the base figure on which their markup structure is erected. Second, in countries where firms are small and turnover slow, it is customary to charge higher markups than in the United States. The practice of stacking on the export-import costs to domestic price became widespread during the decade after World War II, when production capacity lagged far behind consumption requirements in much of the world. Thus, U.S. exporters had little reason to concern themselves with competition or the demand side in general in their export pricing. Since the late 1950's, however, the picture has changed. The supply has caught up with the demand, and keen competition has arisen in most export markets.

This competition has made export operations directly dependent on management's ability to convert from rigid full-cost pricing to a flexible policy designed to approach the problem from the demand side—to use the market conditions as its base—and to utilize the concepts of variable and incremental costs to test when and where to compete. The export-import costs, then, cannot be stacked on top of the domestic price but, instead, must be subtracted from the contemplated market price. If the residual is less than the domestic price, other variable costs will have to be subtracted to determine whether some part will be left for contribution toward overhead and profit.

The conversion from rigid full-cost export pricing to demand-based pricing has been generally much slower than can be justified in the light of prevailing market conditions. Too many executives are righteously resisting any changes in their unilateral "right" to prescribe the price for all their markets. This slavery to the past helps to explain many of the recent setbacks which U.S. industries have experienced because of their noncompetitive prices in various world markets. They have, literally, priced themselves out of the market, not because the market price was too low, but because their pricing policies and strategies were based on the wrong premise.

VI

Environmental Dynamics: International Integration

Multinational enterprise must function in a world of contrasts: old and new, primitive and modern, pious and agnostic, unutterably beautiful and sickeningly squalid, educated and ignorant, progressive and stagnant, sophisticated and naive—all in constant agitation. To interpret this volatile diversity, to make sense of this apparent chaos, we must try to identify the underlying forces—the prime movers—which produce the global dynamics. This is the objective of the chapters which follow.

Prologue to Part VI

Transformation from national to supranational is the essence of international integration. The *nation-state system* which superseded the autocracies of feudalist tyrants—principalities, kingdoms, and empires—has provided the basic blueprint for the organization of the world. This has been the most remarkable epoch in man's economic and social achievements. In much of modern thought and action the nation-state is not only taken for granted but also idealized as the epitome of self-determination and self-actualization of different peoples. National sovereignty, national policy, national economy, national culture, national honor, and national interest are but a few illustrations of the depth to which modern conceptualizations have been cast to the mold of the nation-state system. It is only in this organizational framework that industrial and postindustrial societies have emerged; and without them modernity as a comprehensive notion would yet remain to be invented. Thus, by all indications the nation-state has outperformed, outranked, and overpowered all earlier political formats.

Ironically, it is the massive weight of its successes that is now overloading the bearings and conduits of the nation-state system. Receding horizons in technology, science, and human expectations have pushed to the limits of this system and beyond. Wider and more flexible structure is the categorical imperative for a new epoch. The merging of separate nations into integrated *supranational systems* on a regional basis seems to be the format to meet this demand. Though of very recent origin, the international integration movement has already reached global dimensions. No continent, ideology, or nationality has escaped its effect. And this is only the beginning.

All organizations are inherently conservative especially when it comes to structural change. The nation-state is no exception. As the most autonomous and complete of any organization so far devised, it does not readily succumb to pressures for reorganization.

It would, therefore, be gross oversimplification to leave the impression that international integration is running its global course with smoothness and ease; on the contrary; its path is uneven and full of perils. In addition to internal political intrigue, East-West rivalries and the backwash of decolonization in the underdeveloped world obscure and retard its progress. But it cannot be stopped. As science and automation push back technological frontiers, possibilities for better and richer life are created—but only for those who can amass the investments and absorb the quantities required by the expanding scale of the *optimal plant.* Neither small companies nor small countries can, therefore, qualify. Can any nation deliberately deny itself that which its large neighbors and integrated supranational communities can enjoy? Not for long. More than anything the rising expectations of the consuming public everywhere are pushing to break the barriers that constrain the realization of its welfare aspirations.

If international integration will lead to an ultimate dissolution of the nation-state is for the future to show. More likely, it will transform the nation-state into a state in a united states—an entity for limited local rule in a larger union. In this view our existing super "nations:" the United States, the U.S.S.R., China, and India are the forerunners to the emerging supranational systems. The fact that they came into being through revolution and force rather than voluntary collaboration marks a difference in the method of international organizational change but certainly not in its direction or ultimate goals.

Stages of Integration

International integration is a long-term process. Like that of the nation-state before it, the evolution of the supranational communities will proceed through a continuum in which at least six stages beyond the nation-state have been identified.

The Integration Continuum and its Major Stages

0	free-trade area	2	common market	4	political union	6
separate nation-states	1	customs union	3	economic union	5	integrated supranational system

The stages are:

(1) Free-Trade Area: no tariffs or nontariff restrictions between member countries; no common external tariffs or policies;

(2) Customs Union: same as free-trade area plus common external tariff and consultation on trade policy;

(3) Common Market: completely free movement of goods, capital, and people among member countries, common external tariffs, harmonization domestic policies, and coordination of international economic policies;

(4)) Economic Union: same as the common market plus common currency, integrated domestic policies, and a common international economic policy;

(5) Political Union (united states): complete unification of monetary, fiscal, social, and foreign policies; supranational system has in fact replaced the nation-state as the source of sovereignty and security.

(6) Integrated Supranational System: in addition to stage 5, educational and cultural norms are harmonized.

Using this continuum allows us to define integration not only as an enlargement of an existing supranational business system by accepting new members into it, but also as the movement along the continuum from a lower to any higher stage of integration. Thus, both the development of the Latin American Free Trade Association (LAFTA) into a customs union and the entry of Great Britain into the European Economic Community (EEC) would be examples of integration. Similarly, a regression to a lower stage of integration or an exit of one or more members out of a supranational business system constitutes disintegration as we use the terms in this study.

Integration and disintegration may be simultaneous processes: some supranational systems may be formed or expanded from the dissolution of others. For example, the expansion of European Economic Community by the entry of Great Britain leads at the same time to the scrapping of the European Free Trade Association. In Asia and Africa, where currently several integration plans vie for implementation, future integration will inevitably force many of these to disintegrate.

Implications

The consequences of international integration are many and far-reaching. Although their specific characteristics can only be revealed by the history of the future, several implications are already clear.

—The integrated supranational systems replace small national economies with multifold larger world-regional communities.

—The supranational economies create demands for products and technologies that are neither feasible nor workable in segmented national markets.

—Large-scale production and large-scale marketing offer inherent superiorities in the integrated environment.

Cultural and ethnic pluralism of the supranational systems generate both diversity and dynamics to a degree much higher than any typical nation-state economy has traditionally encountered.

—Growth in size and complexity of organizations and institutions will necessarily result from the integration.

—New skills and refined techniques for solving business problems will be a primary prerequisite for successful operations.

—Money and capital markets must sooner or later be completely aligned with the multicountry integrated economies; currency convertability within each supranational system, and ultimately a single system-wide monetary unit are, therefore, realistic long-term expectations.

—The integration of national units into greater markets implies increased growth opportunities for the individual firm; this in turn invites keener competition and requires more aggressive strategies of growth than what has been customary in most countries.

—Since political integration must inevitably follow, though not immediately or completely, the role of national governments will tend to change toward being a socio-cultural agency as the economic, technological, and military defense functions are gradually transferred to the supranational organs.

Since it is the statesmen of the nation-states who preside over the process of international integration, one should not expect that the transfer of power to supranational organs will be either swift or uncontested. Nor will it be a matter of ideology. The decisive forces are economic and social processes that have outgrown the nation-state system.

Although the concept is new, supranational systems as such are not. The United States of America, the Union of Soviet Socialist Republics, the Chinese Peoples' Republic, and India all qualify as supranational systems. The fact that they have so far considered themselves (for lack of a more appropriate model) to be nation-states in no way changes their integrated supranational character. One might say that they become supranational systems without knowing it or seeking it. They were products of particular historic accidents rather than preconceived plans that characterize the present integration movement. Furthermore, it is the existence of these supernations and their power that has spurred the vastly weaker *real* nation-states to seek safety in various integrated supranational arrangements.

31

International Integration in Europe

The decade after World War II marked a turning point in European political ideology. Until then the inviolable and overriding maxim had been nationalist separatism—a concept of nationhood based on chauvinistic prejudice and arrogant feelings of superiority. The common aspirations were to seek absolute sovereignty and to increase the country's independence from others through policies aimed at self-sufficiency and subordination of the interests or independence of others. Interdependence was to be avoided and minimized.

Since the war the trend has turned. Nationalist separation, though still in evidence, was superseded by internationalist Pan-Europeanism as the central ideological maxim. *Rapprochement,* based on international cooperation and the mutual interests that followed, released what have become self-sustaining forces for a closer and closer commercial and industrial interdependence of European nations. The principle of supranationality emerged as the conceptual vehicle for and the political objective of the new ideology. Under supranationality, sovereign nations are bound by decisions made by agencies which are independent of national control.

The reasons for the decline of nationalism and the rise of supranationalism go back to the ultraprotectionist obliteration of international economic relations during the interwar period, especially to the depression-ridden Thirties, when trade and currency restrictions, bilateral connivances, and other forms of international discrimination and blackmail perverted trade and investments by substituting nationalist political criteria for economic ones. This period of international disintegration brought the nations to World War II. The cataclysmic devastation of the war not only ruined the nationalistic structure of the interwar system but also laid bare the irrationality of its ideological base.

Postwar Conditions

The initial impetus for international economic integration came from the disintegration of European business relations; in the war this disintegration had reached its ultimate stage—total paralysis. The breakdown of international trade and payments was not only a matter of ill will and poor organizational arrangements but even more fundamentally an expression of the deterioration of productive incapacities that the disintegration culminating in the war had caused. In this respect there were no victors, only the vanquished; all European participants in the conflict suffered unimaginable destruction of life and property. The situation in its essentials is outlined below.

Infrastructure

Roads, bridges, canals, terminals, and other transportation facilities had been bombed out or worn out during the war. Public utilities, fuel, and energy resources had been misused and abused often to the point of extinction. In brief, all that the economist calls social capital had been depleted through abnormal use, enemy action, and nonreplacement.

Industrial base

Manufacturing centers, factories, and mills had been the prime targets of all belligerents. Accordingly, physical destruction of the manufacturing capacity had been extremely high. The facilities, machinery, and equipment that had survived the war were, to a very great extent, run down, outmoded, and inefficient because of overuse, insufficient maintenance, and nonreplacement during the war. Much of what survived had been designed for military production and had scarcely any use in the civilian setting. The change from military to civilian production was further hampered by the disrepair of the infrastructure and the lack of labor forces. As a result, productive capacity was in general weak and was inadequate to meet even current needs, not to mention aspirations to compensate for long-time deprivations during the war.

Agriculture

European agricultural capacity, too, had suffered serious damages. In part, there had been diversion of resources and supplies to military use, and, in part, the resources had been overexploited. Lack of fertilizer and conservation practices had drained the land of its fertility and left the soil unprotected against erosion and decay. Yet the impending famine at the close of the war demanded a continued effort to maximize food production, in the short run, from all available agricultural resources and necessitated postponement of any attempt to restore capacity to its normal potential. This restoration was thus often not a long-run proposition.

Human resources

Casualties during the war had been heaviest among people between 15 and 65 years, and had been especially heavy in the 18-to-40 bracket. In both groups, more men had been killed than women. A study of the population pyramids for the immediate postwar years shows that the war caused serious avulsions in the productive age groups in all belligerent countries. The pyramids also reflect another demographic consequence of the war, namely, the sudden rise in fertility which resulted in a baby boom. Thus, the war had caused two simultaneous changes in the population structure. It had reduced the number of people in the productive age group and thereby the total labor resources, and it had increased the number of people in the nonproductive or subproductive age bracket.

Both trends were further aggravated by the fact that great numbers of invalids had to be deducted from the already depleted labor potential and added to the nonproductive portion. The practical consequence of the disproportionate ratio of productive to nonproductive elements of the population was an abnormally low ability of the society to meet its total needs. Dismal as the numerical picture was, it actually understated the severity of the problem. Many young people who had survived the war knew no other vocation than war. Others were in need of retraining and practice before being usable in their prewar employment. The low level of civilian skill compounded the shortage of productive manpower and contributed to the difficulties of converting the European economy to peacetime economic conditions in the European countries.

Foreign trade

As already indicated, international trade relations had deteriorated as the result of bilateralism and discriminatory practices to the point of intolerance at the outbreak of the war. During the war normal trade ceased completely, as all international transactions were subjected to strict governmental control or were placed under the jurisdiction of state trading agencies; that is, foreign trade was, in fact, nationalized. Postwar normalization of trade, therefore, required not only the lifting of the rationing and price controls imposed during the war but also, to a very large degree, the rebuilding of a trading organization, including overseas connections. With productive capacities in shambles—less than half of European import requirements were covered by exports—and foreign exchange unavailable, the rebuilding of a normal trading organization had very little appeal to private enterprise and de facto nationalization was prolonged despite most governments' willingness to denationalize trade.

Realignments

Obviously the European economy was in catastrophic condition. How was it to avoid disaster? How could it survive? These were the overriding questions. The search for answers soon revealed the contradiction of the wartime alliance between the Western democracies and the totalitarian U.S.S.R. It also revealed that, despite the incredible hostility and bitterness displayed in the war, the European peoples had retained the inherent strength and integrity to rise above vengeance and to unite their efforts for the benefit of all. As a result, the political forces in Europe were realigned, although the wartime alliances remained as legal encumbrances. The new alignment may be roughly described in three factions: the European countries, the U.S.S.R., and the United States.

Pan-Europeanism

In Europe itself a sense of continental solidarity replaced the prewar nationalism, and various organizations whose main mission was Pan-Europeanism in one or another interpretation emerged. The Pan-European movement captured the imagination of the younger generation, particularly the politically alert student population, which supplied it the vitality and dynamism necessary for any concrete actions among the recent adversaries in a total war. Only youthful idealism could dare to contravene the deeply derisive sentiments of the families and friends of war fatalities of only weeks or months before and to resort to rational reasoning at a time of grave emotional crisis.

Since attitudes and beliefs do not lend themselves to any simple measurement or identification, the rise of Pan-Europeanism has generally received inadequate attention in comparison with the various legal arrangements, which are much more amenable to counting and recording and, as such, abound in the literature on European integration. Having participated in international student activities in Europe, both before and after the war, this writer must attribute to the change from nationalism to Europeanism an importance greater than that given any other factor in postwar European relations. Without it much of the rest would have been doomed in advance.

Communist aggression

In the Soviet Union's design, postwar Europe was projected as an addendum to the communist orbit. The political disorganization and economic debility provided ideal conditions for subverting democratic institutions and substituting communist control. This plan was notoriously successful. The Iron Curtain moved swiftly westward, enveloping Eastern European countries, one by one, from the Baltic to the Balkans. The republics of Estonia, Latvia, and Lithuania were completely incorporated into the Soviet Union and lost any vestige of independence. Poland, Czechoslovakia, Hungary, Bulgaria, Rumania, and Albania were converted into satellite states which, for outward appearance, retained their separate identities but internally were subjugated to the monolithic and unicentral totalitarianism of the U.S.S.R. Eastern Finland and a part of Poland were annexed to Russia, and a communist regime was set up in the Soviet occupation zone of Germany. In other countries, too, communist activism thrust forward unmistakably. Constitutional elements in Greece had to fight a savage war against Soviet-armed guerrillas. Political instability in France and Italy undermined public confidence in democratic processes, and communist political activities showed vigor throughout Europe. Although communist aggression, constituting a common threat, added a new dimension to Pan-European unity, it is highly unlikely that, if left to its own devices, any part of the continent could have survived as a democratic nation. Undisputable proof for this conjecture can never be provided, as another external interest, that of the United States, set out to stop the Soviet advance.

The U.S. reaction

Because of the friendly image held of the Soviet Union during the war, the authorities in the United States were slow to react to the communist cold-war offensive. However, as the Soviets continued to reject all proposals to negotiate the restoration of self-determination in the Eastern European countries and its arrogant opposition threatened to bring to a complete standstill any international efforts to achieve peace, the United States was forced to go through an agonizing reappraisal of its position vis-à-vis the Soviet Union.

In Europe, the U.S. diagnosis called for a dual remedy: a tougher political stand to halt the Soviet offensive, and economic recovery to alleviate the economic despondency and social chaos on which totalitarian ideologies thrive. As described above, the European economy was in a most serious crisis. The only conceivable way to save it from collapse was through a massive injection of capital to rebuild the industrial base and to repair the damage to its infrastructure and agricultural production. This conviction was translated into the European Recovery Program, popularly known as the Marshall Plan.

The essence of the Marshall Plan was to allocate $11.4 billion[1] of U.S. public funds as economic aid to the European countries. Its effective duration was planned for the four-year period of 1948–52. To make sure that these funds would not be diverted to serve any nationalistic or paramilitary ends (possible resurgence of German militarism was still taken seriously) and that effective contribution was made to the integration of the different European economies, the Marshall Plan was tendered subject to the qualification that concrete organizational arrangements be made by the potential recipients of the funds which would dispel the U.S. reservations.

The European answer to this demand was the convention creating the

1 This is the total spent during the period of the Marshall Plan—April 1948 through December 1951; the allocation for the first year was $5 billion.

Organization for European Economic Cooperation (OEEC); the convention was signed in Paris in April 1948. Its signatories included Austria, Belgium, Denmark, France, Greece, Ireland, Iceland, Italy, Luxembourg, Norway, the Netherlands, Portugal, the United Kingdom, Sweden, Switzerland, Turkey, and the Western Occupation Zones of Germany (signed by the commanders-in-chief).

Forerunners to the Common Market

Although the immediate purpose of the OEEC was a temporary one—to administer the Marshall Plan funds for its four years—the organization was visualized by many, including the U.S. government, as the main vehicle of European economic integration and as the nucleus for an ultimate political unification of the continent. In certain respects the OEEC did, in the beginning at least, justify these sanguine expectations.[2] Besides serving as the general coordination and administration agency of "a joint recovery program"—the Marshall Plan—the OEEC embarked upon three ambitious programs.

One was aimed at restoring monetary stability and convertibility and at providing international clearinghouse services as a means of financing foreign trade until the international money and capital markets had recovered. For this purpose, a subsidiary organization, the European Payments Union (EPU), was formed. It was eminently successful and put itself out of business by achieving its ultimate objectives in 1959.

The second program was designed to raise the efficiency and productivity of European business enterprise. It, too, was assigned to a subsidiary organization: the European Productivity Agency (EPA). Although the EPA's achievements are more difficult to measure than those of the EPU, it was instrumental in updating and disseminating managerial technology and modern business administration practices through numerous programs, consultant teams, and publicity; the research and literature which the EPA underwrote in the areas of productivity remain the largest single contribution in this field. The EPA was absorbed by the Organization for Economic Cooperation and Development, which succeeded the OEEC in 1961.

The OEEC's third area was commercial policy, primarily trade liberalization. Here it produced impressive quantities of oratory and a printed *Code of Liberalization*,[3] but when it came to translating the words to deeds, progress was blocked by polemics and political maneuvering among its members. At the risk of oversimplifying, the lack of agreement can be attributed

[2] The hopes that the OEEC would ultimately succeed together with Parkinson's law accounted for the continuation of the organization for seven years longer than initially planned—namely, until 1961.

[3] Organization for European Economic Cooperation, *Code of Liberalization* (*Code de la libération*), August 1959.

to two competing views regrading the concrete actions which were to serve the economic interests of Europe best. Although many other quarrels took place among OEEC members, they concerned minor disagreements or temporary issues. The two fundamentally different positions have persisted to date. One school advocated global free trade as the objective to be pursued but exhibited caution in introducing toward that end any measures which might have threatened the historical trade relations. Theirs was a rather doctrinaire free-trade position based on conventional economic notions. The dominant country in this group was the United Kingdom, which emerged as the main proponent of the global-traditionalist view.

Another group of countries argued that any global free-trade scheme was beyond the powers of the OEEC to achieve and that, although it might serve as an abstract ambition to be pursued in the very long run, in the shorter run it should be subordinate to some concrete measures designed specifically to deal with the existing European crisis. Having less stake in historic arrangements, these countries felt no inhibitions in breaking with the past and in proposing radically new approaches to the problem. Its action-orientation and progressive approach made this group the prime movers in the European integration movement. France emerged as the principal spokesman of this school of thought, initially because it was the only large nation in the group which had been on the "right" side during the war. Later, the position came to be viewed as a proprietary right by some French leaders, headed by de Gaulle, a fact which has greatly complicated European relations.

Since the two factions could not be reconciled within the framework of the OEEC, the activist group went ahead on its own. In May 1950, the Schuman Plan[4] was announced by the French Ministry of Foreign Affairs. It proposed that the coal and steel production of France and Germany be pooled to form "common bases for economic development as a first step in the federation of Europe." A supranational high authority was to be created to govern the pooled industries. The plan was, in its own words, "open to the participation of the other countries of Europe," and its proponents hoped that all European countries would support the plan and that coal and steel production could be fused into a continent-wide industrial complex which would be exempt from all national and international restraints.

Nothing similar had ever before been attempted. Not even a theoretical model or a mythological novel had envisioned international mergers of entire industries by voluntary action. As a result, reception of the Schuman Plan was mixed. For many economists, particularly for the orthodox, it caused serious trepidations as something entirely inadmissible; for nationalists it brought fears of abdication and subversion of sovereignty. British spokesmen charged that the plan was likely to strengthen the cartel practices of French and German industries, and, as such, it was a step in the wrong direction. Despite the consternations, the Schuman Plan gained the support of six

[4] Named for Robert Schuman, French foreign minister at that time.

countries which, after a year of intensive negotiations, agreed on a detailed program which was formalized in the Treaty Establishing the Coal and Steel Community (ECSC). The treaty was signed at Paris in April 1951. Besides France, the signatories included Belgium, Germany, Italy, Luxembourg, and the Netherlands. Although all other European countries were invited to join the first supranational community, none accepted.

The ECSC was variously rated as a mere institutional oddity to a revolutionary breakthrough in the field of political economy. This is not the place to explore its philosophical merits. But it is by now a historic fact that the ECSC was the beginning of international economic integration under supranational institutions and policies as distinguished from the theoretical economic concept of free trade and convertibility. Whatever merits the Schuman Plan had when it was proposed may be debated, but in retrospect it did, indeed, establish "common bases for economic development" for its participant nations. Whether by design or by default, it served, in fact, as a critical experiment—the pilot operation for all the other international integration schemes.

The Treaty of Rome

As the futile bickering over economic and commercial policies in the OEEC continued with no prospect for accord, the six member countries seized on the success of the ECSC and began active planning for an enlargement of the supranational integration program. This posed a serious threat to the traditionalist forces, and a rival proposal was put forth under British sponsorship. This plan called for the creation of a *free-trade area,* in which there would be a gradual elimination of tariffs and quotas on imports and exports of manufactured products among European countries on a reciprocal basis, but nothing else. For the six this was not enough. They were resolved to strive for more tangible goals. Intensive consultation and negotiations culminated in the signing of the Treaty of Rome, establishing the European Economic Community (EEC). Although all European countries had been offered to participate in the drafting of the Rome Treaty and to join the EEC as charter members by signing it, none did. Hence, the EEC was left with the same membership as the ECSC— namely, Belgium, France, Germany, Italy, Luxembourg, and the Netherlands. Since subsequent events have distorted the original relationships among the different European countries, it is relevant to remember that General Charles de Gaulle was in political retirement at that time and had nothing to do with the structure or design of the EEC. This is not to disclaim his subsequent influence on EEC policies and behavior, but only to give the General his rightful, uninflated share in these events and, more importantly, to avoid the gross distortions of facts which personality-centered journalistic myths have propagated.

The general aim of the European Economic Community, as stated in Article 2 of the Rome Treaty, is "to promote throughout the Community a harmonious development of economic activities, a continuous and balanced expansion, an increased stability, an accelerated raising of the standards of living and closer relations among its member states." To promote these aims the Treaty embodies a complete plan which affects all aspects and types of business enterprise. The plan rests on the premise that international integration depends on the mobility of goods, capital, people, and enterprises. And, accordingly, the primary objectives of the plan are to create conditions conducive to this mobility by harmonizing environmental constraints and by neutralizing external influences upon business activity within the Community. Table 31-1 shows the basic design of the plan.

TABLE 31-1

Basic Integration Scheme of the Rome Treaty

(1) Free movement of goods	
To be obtained through	
1.1 Trade liberalization	successive elimination of tariffs, quotas, turnover taxes, excise duties, and all other forms of restrictions on the movements of goods among member states
1.2 Common agricultural policy	common prices, subsidies and support programs, stockpiling and carry-forward arrangements, standards for importation and exportation, unified market organization for agricultural commodities
1.3 Common transport policy	unification of freight rates and harmonization of shipping practices and regulatory standards of rail, highway, and inland water carriers; regulation of air and ocean transportation on Community-wide basis also if deemed advisable
(2) Free movement of capital	
To be obtained through	
2.1 Convertibility of currencies	progressive abolition of all exchange restrictions and discriminatory treatment of capital transfers among member states based on nationality or place of residence
2.2 National-treatment principle	opening the domestic capital market and credit system for Community-wide investment and credit transactions on a nondiscriminatory basis
2.3 Monetary cooperation	consultations among central banks of member countries regarding rediscount rates, reserve requirements, open-market policies, and major monetary changes

(3) Free movement of labor	
To be obtained through	
3.1 Right to resettle	abolition of any discrimination based on nationality regarding employment, remuneration, and working conditions; right to move about freely in all member states, to actively seek employment, and to take up residence in the country of employment
3.2 Common social policy	equalization of remuneration for equal work in all member countries, establishment of common units of measurement for work performance and compensation; close collaboration among member governments regarding social legislation and policies including employment, labor laws, vocational training, social security, pensions, industrial safety and hygiene, laws relating to trade unions, collective bargaining, and general social welfare
(4) Free movement of enterprise	
To be obtained through	
4.1 Freedom of establishment	right to engage in and carry on business activities, to acquire real property, to set up and manage enterprises, agencies, branches, or subsidiaries in any member country under the same conditions as its own nationals; abolition of any obstacles—legal or administrative—to the freedom of establishment by all member governments
4.2 Freedom of service	progressive removal of restrictions affecting the industrial, commercial, artistic, and professional services supplied for remuneration by residents of other member states; right to relocate service personnel and facilities; liberalization of banking, insurance, and transport services according to common policies
(5) Harmonization of internal conditions	
To be achieved through	
5.1 Common rules of competition	prohibition of restrictive business practices harmful to the consumer, including collusive price fixing; monopolistic limitation of production, markets, technical development, or investment; dividing markets or supplies; stifling competition through dominant bargaining strength, contractual arrangements, or any other means; requirement that companies operating in the EEC register all agreements covering more than one country

5.2 Common rules of aid	any state aid to business which distorts competition is incompatible with EEC; aid of social character is permissible (to consumers, to disaster areas, and to depressed areas); aid to business may be approved by EEC authorities if intended to promote economic development of underdeveloped regions, to promote projects of common interest, or to remedy serious disturbances
5.3 Approximation of laws	EEC institutions issue directives for alignment of laws and governmental regulations which affect business enterprise in the Community
(6) Unification of external relations	
To be obtained through	
6.1 Common custom tariff	internal integrative links are protected by a uniform tariff system applying to all imports from nonmember countries; no national tariff schedule different from the common tariff is permissible
6.2 Common commercial policy	foreign economic relations are structured in terms of Community-wide interests and executed in close collaboration with its supranational institutions; in tariff and trade matters the member countries act as a supranational body

Timetable

In its own terms the Treaty was to be implemented during a transition period of 12 to 15 years. Since it went in effect in 1958 the European Community should be completed by no later than 1973. The transition period was necessary to give the different industries and companies affected by the international merger time to adjust to the changing environment and to avoid unnecessary dislocations and maladjustments in the member countries. To this point the program has progressed far more rapidly than originally anticipated, and, barring any political confrontation among its members, the plan should easily meet its target date.

Organization and administration

The Rome Treaty is unique in that it does not leave the administration of the Treaty to the regular national organs as ordinary treaties do. Customarily the administration of a treaty is handled by the foreign ministry or some existing governmental department. The Rome Treaty creates its own administrative machinery, very much like the U.S. federal government, which is beyond the control of any member country's national government. There are four main organs in this supranational government:

A. The Common Market Commission: This is the executive branch for the Rome Treaty administration, consisting of 13 commissioners who serve as heads of departments similar to the U.S. Cabinet: foreign affairs, agriculture, labor, and so forth. The president of the Commission is the chief executive of the European Community. Originally there were separate executive boards for the other Community treaties, such as the European Coal and Steel Community and the European Atomic Energy Community. Later, both the ECSC and Euratom were merged into the EEC and subjected administratively to the Rome Treaty organization. The merger converted the Common Market Commission into the Commission of European Community, which is the single executive branch of the Rome Treaty as well as the other two treaties. The merger marked also a change of name from European Economic Community (EEC) to simply European Community (EC).

The Commission is a supranational body, not to be confused with an international body. What is the difference? In an international body there is representation of the different nations involved. Each member is a delegate representing the interests of his own nation-state. If the French interests and the Dutch interests conflict, then either one dominates and the other suffers, or there is a compromise. This is not the case with the Commission of European Community. Since it is not an international body but a supranational body, the commissioners and the commission staff are not delegates of their native countries but executives of the EC, whose duties and powers derive from the Treaty of Rome. Their allegiance is not to their home countries or the constitutions of their countries; their allegiance is to the Treaty of Rome.

The Commission is the most vital organ of the Community. It is charged not only with carrying out the legislative acts of the Council and the Parliament, but also with initiating policies and programs which in its judgment are necessary to attain the goals of the Rome Treaty. In developing policy proposals, the Commission is aided by a series of consultative committees, each representing an important segment or function of European society.

There are also two organs in the legislative branch of the EC government:

B. The European Parliament: Similar to the Congress of the United States, the powers of the European Parliament are not the same. At this point in time the European Parliament is a consultative rather than a legislative body; that is, it can recommend but not legislate. Therefore, the actions of the European Parliament do not have a binding power on the Commission or on other EC organs. Despite this limitation, the Parliament carries a tremendous amount of prestige, and, as a result, its recommendations amount to legislation in fact though not in theory. When it passes a resolution or submits a recommendation, all organs and officials of the EC listen very carefully and try to comply with what the Parliament proposes.

The membership in the European Parliament comes from the respective national parliaments of the member states. If the Community is enlarged to ten members, the size of the Parliament will increase from 142 to 208 members, divided as follows:

Germany	36
Italy	36
France	36
United Kingdom	36
Belgium	14
Netherlands	14
Denmark	10
Ireland	3
Luxembourg	2

It is in a sense an international body since it consists of members of different national parliaments, meeting at Strasbourg. Yet as a body, the Parliament is supposed to make rules and issue statements about the Common Market, so in this sense, it is supranational; perhaps, therefore, it should be called a hybrid.

C. The Council of Ministers: The ultimate power to legislate is left to this body. It is an international body, since each minister represents his own country: the French minister at the table represents the French government, not the Common Market, the German minister the German government, and so forth. Each member country has one representative whom the government sends to be its spokesman, and the Council is the body that passes on new policy matters. It legislates on new matters that are not part of the Treaty or that require new legislative action. Here the nation-state still holds complete control: it has final say on what goes and what does not as far as any new legislation is concerned.

We must, however, clearly distinguish between the Commission and the Council. The Commission is the administrative body that runs the show, that comes up with initiatives, with plans, with programs, with task forces, and so on. It also drafts the new policy proposals when necessary. The Council only approves or disapproves what the Commission proposes.

When member states' vital interests are at stake, it is Community practice to proceed only by unanimity, which gives each member veto power. In those cases where a qualified majority is provided for in the Treaty, the votes of the members of the Council have the following weighting:

Germany	10
Italy	10
France	10
United Kingdom	10
Belgium	5
Netherlands	5
Denmark	3
Ireland	10
Luxembourg	6

Decisions are approved only if 43 votes are cast in favor by at least 6 members. In those cases in which a simple majority is provided for, the majority is, of course, 6 out of the 10 states.

D. The Court of Justice: The judicial branch of the Community's government is the Court of Justice. All disputes arising from the implementation of the Rome Treaty are referred to the Court of Justice for adjudication and cannot be litigated by national courts. This not only gives the Community a judicial authority for testing the legality of its policies and actions within the constitutional framework of the Rome Treaty but also keeps the national courts from encumbering the Community with divergent interpretations and biases stemming from the narrow self-interest of individual countries.

The popular belief that the Court is inaccessible to nongovernment litigants is unfounded. Private companies and individuals are permitted to bring proceedings directly to the court if the Rome Treaty or Community regulations are concerned. This direct access is particularly useful to multinational firms in combating narrowly chauvinistic restrictions of the member states.

Monetary Union

The Rome Treaty contained no concrete provisions for a common currency and central bank. These matters were considered politically too sensitive at that time. People in all countries seem to have a great emotional investment in their own monetary unit. However, it was always understood that sooner or later a complete monetary union will be required if the objective of a supranational economy is to be fully realized.

Now this subject is intensely debated. A plan for transition toward monetary union was put forth in the so called Werner Committee Report. It proposed that these steps be taken toward monetary union: tax and capital market harmonization; economic and monetary co-operation through regular meetings between finance ministers and central bankers; alignment of the introduction of national budgets; and that the size and method of financing the budget be controlled by the EEC.

The committee further proposed that there be each year three conferences of the finance ministers for purposes of harmonizing their budgets; two central bankers' meetings a year on monetary co-ordination; and an attempt to narrow the bands of fluctuation in the exchange rates. The committee was hopeful that there would be a government conference by the end of 1973 to amend the Treaty of Rome, creating the new institutions necessary to enable monetary union to take place by 1980.

In 1971 the Council of Ministers passed a resolution on achieving monetary union by stages during a ten-year period. It will

> form an individual monetary unit within the international system, characterized by the total and irreversible convertibility of currencies, the elimination of

> fluctuation margins of rates of exchange and the irrevocable fixing of parity rates—all of which are indispensable conditions for the creation of a single currency...[5]

Nothing has been said so far as to the nature of the common monetary unit.

There are two monetary innovations now being used in the EEC. One is the *Agricultural Unit of Account.* Rather than price agricultural products in terms of one currency or another, they are denominated by 'units of account'. The unit itself is pegged to a specific amount of gold, in grams, so that its value will not change. It is a method of maintaining a constant price throughout the Common Market.

The other innovation is probably the more appealing as a possible forerunner of a European currency. It is the *European Monetary Unit,* or EMU. The EMU is based on Common Market Bonds, floated by the EEC. It is available in denominations as small as the equivalent of U.S. $100.00. It has been hailed as a "Milestone along the road to common currency—and a common economy—that the EEC members are pledged to achieve."[6] It may be purchased and redeemed in any member-country currencies. The price is pegged at the parity of the currencies on the date of purchase.

It is doubtful that a real monetary union, not to mention a common currency, is possible before the now-separate banking systems of member countries have become closely integrated. Especially crucial would be the integration, both operationally and organizationally, of the central banks. No amount of consultation and joint meetings can provide a substitute for an actual European Reserve System. Until these structural prerequisites have been met, monetary cooperation but not monetary union is all that one can hope for.

[5] Quoted from the Council's Resolution, point 4.
[6] "New Signs Point to Monetary Union", *Business Week,* Nov. 28, 1970, p. 28.

32

The Impact of International Integration on European Business

Internal Effects

Integration of the six countries has profoundly changed business enterprise and its environment in the Community. Instead of six small markets there is now one large market of nearly 190 million people with incomes and living standards among the very highest in the world. Admission of four new members will further enlarge the union. The absorption capacity of this market far exceeds all others outside the United States. It has effectively removed the limitations which the small national markets imposed on many industries.

Company size

On the production level the scale is no longer restricted by the limited ability of any one country to consume but can be increased many times if mass production raises productivity and reduces costs. Since the advantages of mass production vary from industry to industry, the gains from integration are more pronounced for some than for others. However, all industries are affected quite significantly, partly because most European companies were small not only for economic but also for a variety of historical and institutional reasons and could, therefore, gain from an increase in size, and partly because new production technologies such as automation and computerization have been pushing the production-cost curve further and further to the left, making it necessary to increase the production scale accordingly to enable a plant to enjoy optimal costs.

Figure 32-1 provides a graphic explanation of changed outlook in the cost-output relationship caused by integration. Companies in the fields where production techniques have remained stable have benefited as shown in Part A by sliding down the cost curve from the national cost level, which was dictated by the limited absorption of the national market prior to integration, and by adjusting their output as near to the optimal per-unit cost as competition and other market forces have permitted. For companies in the fields where mechanization and automation have replaced labor with capital-intensive systems and facilities, the opportunities for cost reduction have been twofold, as shown in Part B: by sliding down the curve as in A, and by shifting from the

FIGURE 32-1

Impact of Integration on Production Costs

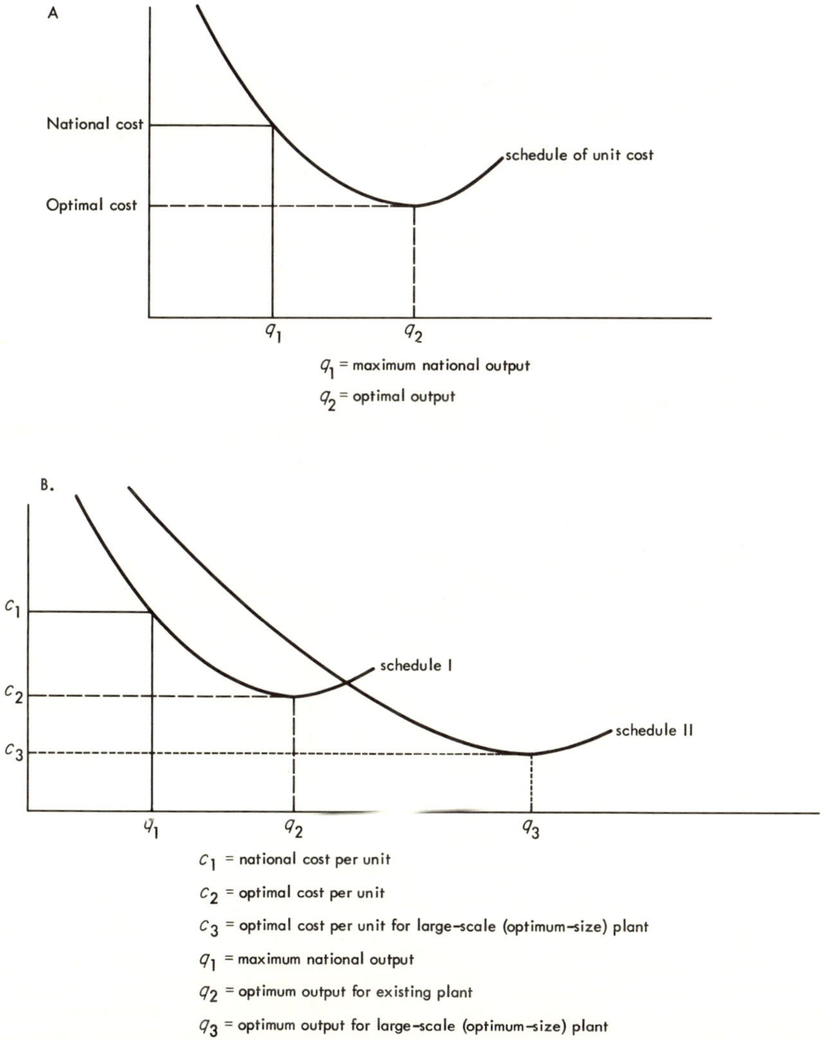

old to the new production technology as illustrated by the right-hand curve and by reducing production cost all the way to the new optimum. It is hard to imagine any industry which has been completely immune to new techniques. To a greater or lesser degree, therefore, all productive sectors have been affected by the integration process. That all companies have not exhibited equal ability to adjust to the changed conditions is a fact that needs no documentation. There have been casualties and glittering successes. And the process continues. In some industries productive assets age quickly and rejuvenation of plant occurs after relatively short intervals; in others the life is longer not only because of the large initial investments involved but often also because the production cycle itself has a long duration. For example, in the aerospace field many products (aircraft, missiles, boosters, etc.) require ten or more years of engineering, prototyping, and manufacturing before the final product is completed. Five- to ten-year cycles are not uncommon in other science-based industries. This means that the full impact of the integration on production cost has not as yet had time to run its full course. It could be argued that it has only begun. New investments in industrial capacity have outrun all predictions and have persisted at annual rates ranging between 8 and 12 percent, despite equally persistent projections by economists of a leveling off and eventual downturn. What has made the forecasts consistently wrong has been the failure to account for the dynamic pressure for increased scales of production; the integration process has generated this pressure. Ultimately the conversion from the national to the Community pattern will be completed and the forecasters vindicated.

Meanwhile the expansion of scale is being sought through modernization and new plant capacity, and more recently through a rash of corporate mergers and cooperative industrial ventures. Thousands of firms are reported to have pooled their resources under a variety of legal arrangements.[1] Company size has become the *dernier cri* in European executive jargon and is likely to remain so for the foreseeable future. Not only production costs but also such things as large cash flows, procurement advantages, research and development capabilities, and marketing strength preoccupy European industrialists as reflected in their recent statements and convention programs.

Competition

The mergers do not violate the Rome Treaty so long as the common rules of competition are not broken. In reference to this, EC Commissioner Von der Groeben, who is in charge of anticartel matters, had this to say in 1965: "The coming European market and increasing trade and competition with the rest of the world require corresponding growth on the part of many European enterprises internally by expansion and externally by association. For some commodities we can see not only the beginning of a single European market but even of its development into a world market. Present economic

[1] Cf. "Mergers Are There to Stay," *Business Abroad,* XC, No. 23 (November 15, 1965), 11.

structures in Europe are in many cases not yet adapted to this twofold re-orientation of the world economy. Mergers are consequently to be welcomed where they are economically necessary."

Unlike the U.S. antitrust laws, the EEC regulations do not equate large size with sinful behavior and no specific limitation is placed on company size per se. Rather the test for legality is the effect which a merger has upon the production and distribution of goods. If a merger contributes to rationalization and efficiency of business operations, it is legal; if not, or if it obstructs the freedom of action or choice of consumers or suppliers, it is illegal. The same interpretation has been adapted to most other aspects of cooperation among business firms. The Commission has pointed out, however, that the more dominant a company becomes in its field, the greater the assumption that any further mergers will constitute an abuse of the anticartel rules. Also, the officials take a more critical view of collusive marketing practices than of cooperation in other fields of business.

Labor cost

Despite increased mobility, manpower has become increasingly more costly as integration has progressed. This increase is primarily due to the high level of investment and business activity which have caused an extended overemployment of the labor reserves in the Community. The resultant scarcity of labor has escalated the wage level and greatly increased the bargaining position of trade unions, whose demands for pensions and other fringe benefits have become a major share of business budgets. In general the rise in wages has outstripped the productivity gains and made labor relatively more expensive than other productive inputs. Thus, the cost of labor has counteracted and in many industries more than neutralized the gains from increases in the scale of operation.

Prices

On the distribution level the integrated mass market has caused equally fundamental changes in business conditions. These changes come from three sources: tariff reduction, transportation rationalization, and large-scale marketing organizations. The removal of intra-Community tariffs, both visible and invisible, has enabled industry to cut its prices on exports to other Community countries. The more efficient companies, which previously had been constrained by the other member countries' tariff barriers, were thus released to expand beyond their traditional markets. The increased sales volume, besides permitting fuller utilization of existing capacity, has encouraged new investment in plant and organizational expansion, often further reducing costs and prices.

To these gains must be added increased competition. In industries where capacity reacts quickly to market forces, the combination of tariff cuts, lower production costs, and keener competition brought dramatic price reductions before labor costs reversed the trend. By the end of 1962, for example, consumer prices in Paris department stores showed reductions like these from the 1958 level:[2] Italian raincoat, from a dollar equivalent of 22 to 8; Dutch blouse, from 5 to 2.50; German camera, from 73 to 50; and French vacuum cleaner, from 46 to 22. Similar evidence of lower prices and increased competition could be found in all Community countries. In an era when consumer prices everywhere had moved only in the upward direction, price declines of such magnitude confounded even the radical supporters of the integration scheme.

Transportation cost

A contributing factor to marketing efficiency has been the gradual unification of the transportation systems of the member countries. Although progress in this field has been slower than in tariffs and trade, alignment of freight rates and union practices and elimination of phantom reloading charges and fees assessed on nondomestic carriers at the boundary have greatly simplified physical distribution and reduced both the cost and time of shipping. There are currently in progress programs for a physical integration of the six national transportation systems through coordination of new highway and railroad construction, especially the development of Community-wide arterials and through common objectives and standards for airport and harbor facilities.

The cardinal principle of transportation economics is an inverse relationship between distance and cost; the longer the haul, the lower the cost per mile for any given unit of cargo. The decline in cost comes primarily from the uninterrupted utilization of capital equipment and from a lower ratio of loading and terminal charges for longer hauls. Before integration the freight rates were based in each country upon the relatively short distances, which required correspondingly high freight rates. In that context, international shipments which extended over long distances were penalized by being subjected to the same short-haul freight rates as domestic cargo. For example, a freight movement from Amsterdam to Genoa was conceived as consisting of four different national shipments rather than as one uninterrupted haul. And accordingly each national segment—the Dutch, the Belgian, the French, and the Italian—applied its local rates. The emergence of an integrated rate structure helps to remove this burden of short-haul rates for long-haul cargo movements. The consequent lowering of the cost of transportation will continue to expand the markets for individual companies and their competitors until the slow and tedious process of unification of the rates has been completed and a supranational freight structure substituted for the national ones.

Marketing

Professionally managed, large-scale marketing institutions were few in pre-EEC Europe. Those which existed were limited to major metropolitan centers. The marketing revolution which the United States experienced in

[2] Cf. "Progress Report," *The Exchange,* XXIV, No. 1 (January 1963), 1.

the 1920's and 1930's had bypassed Europe. The concepts of mass merchandising, rapid inventory turnover, low per-unit markups, self-service, and coordinated promotion strategies were generally unknown or neglected. Much of the retailing and wholesaling structure had resisted any change for generations. It was in many respects utterly inadequate for meeting the requirements of mass production and further expansion of industrial activity, which the Rome plan engendered. Family-based fragmentation of retail establishments, some of which had remained unchanged for four or five generations, and tradition-determined marketing channels and pricing practices had acquired a social acceptance which had repelled economic rationality.

Although the pressure for modernization had already mounted to irresistible proportions, integration provided the final thrust for a massive overhaul of the distributive system. Parenthetically it might be observed at this point that the proponents and planners of the Common Market had failed to grasp the need for an efficient marketing system and made no specific provision to bring it about.

Although belated, the marketing revolution is now a reality but not an accomplished fact. The hard shell of traditionalism, which so long has circumscribed the European distribution system, is being forced to open wider and wider to make room for modern approaches, methods, and organizations. Many new developments have changed significantly both the institutional structure and the operational philosophy of marketing activity. But what the precise nature of these developments will be will be a subject for debate for some time to come. The common assumption that they will trace the tracks of the U.S. marketing development is not borne out by experience, and there is no logical basis for the assumption. The conditions for the European marketing revolution are quite different from those that were responsible for the American one. First, the leaders of European marketing have access to an extensive body of marketing knowledge accumulated in this country. This enables them to move faster, plan better, and make fewer mistakes. Second, the social climate and especially the ultimate consumers are significantly different from their American counterparts. A study conducted under the sponsorship of the American Management Association draws these conclusions:

> The European consumer...has deep-rooted traditions and displays a degree of distrust toward new equipment and techniques. He does not respond too easily to those favorite terms of Madison Avenue—*new, better,* and *bigger*—in fact, one might state unequivocally that he prefers the *old* and *trusted.* The typical European doesn't want to be first with the new Cadillac in his neighborhood....
>
> Another "notable" characteristic is the European's general distrust of the written word.... He neither believes all that is said to him nor trusts the press and radio altogether. In short, he is skeptical by nature, and his skepticism has built into him a sort of outwardly cynical attitude toward big projects and ideas.
>
> Highly important, the European is not accustomed to saturation advertising; he even resents it. He doesn't like to be pushed—he is "from Missouri"... in that he must be convinced.

He has good social ethics. There is less delinquency in Europe than anywhere else in the world. The European is honest; he is an excellent credit risk and will always pay his debts—at least individually!

The European cares nothing about *belonging.* He likes to do things in his own way; "keeping up with the Joneses" is a meaningless phrase.... This is true from Holland to Sicily. Unlike the U.S., where people operate through organizations of all sorts, there are scarcely any comparable groupings in the Common Market countries. The largest organized group is that of the *veterans.* ...Also influential are the *intellectuals,* for it must be said—and this is important—that Europe respects and even worships them.... Another powerful group is *labor.* But in European countries...the workers' community is isolated from the rest of the population and is moved by a strong class antagonism.

What, generally speaking, is the European's motivation? For one thing, he will usually prefer security to profit increase. This attitude has been encouraged by the fantastic development of government-sponsored social security agencies which give the worker full protection against all health and other risks. Equally significant...is the craving for *ownership.* The European gets a greater satisfaction from having than from using the goods he buys.

What about woman's place? True, she is not so powerful in Europe as in the U.S., but her position is different; she exerts her influence in a softer way, mostly in domestic affairs. She does not control the wealth of the country, and there are very few career women.

The last European characteristic that ought to be mentioned is the insistence on ample leisure that so impresses the visiting American. The long break for the midday meal is common all over Europe. The same thing is true about vacations: They, too, are leisurely. In France, for example, the legal vacation period is now three weeks. This same attitude toward leisure also affects the number of national holidays.... On the average, they add 7 to 10 days per year to the workers' free time (compared to the U.S.). That these consumer characteristics must have a reaction on the structure, strategies, and policies of marketing seems hard to contravene.[3]

Changes in progress

The long period of continuous prosperity which the EEC countries have enjoyed has set in motion some basic changes in the European market. First, the fear of unemployment as a block to consumer spending is disappearing, and the consumer's time perspective is shrinking; his traditional inclination to hold money and defer purchases is being replaced by a preference for current purchases and deferred payments. Development of social-insurance programs which shift the responsibility for future emergencies from the individual to the government is accelerating this trend. The practice of *hire-purchase,* the European name for installment credit, has become a generally accepted means of bridging the gap between the future and the present.

Second, income disparities between the rich and the poor are diminishing; lower incomes are raised by social-security and welfare programs, and the high incomes are held back by high, progressive taxes. This has not converted the EC into a classless society like that in the United States; people are still peasants, workers, bourgeoisie, intellectuals, or nobles. But these distinctions are becoming less sharp and their economic impact less significant.

[3] American Management Association, *The European Common Market,* Report No. 18 (New York, 1958), pp. 86–88.

With the income pyramid broadening out in the middle, class distinctions are not transmitted to the market place to the same degree as in the past, and consumption breaks its traditional pattern.

Third, mass production compounds the trend toward economic coalescence of the social strata. Its influence comes from the supply side. As the per-unit cost of manufacturing declines with increasing scale and more efficient technology, the price difference between mass-produced and custom-made, especially hand-made, products widens. The differential induces the higher social classes to abandon their traditional reliance on custom-made exclusivity and to accept standard manufactures instead. This is already apparent not only in consumer durables such as appliances and sporting equipment but also more and more in house furnishings, foods, and even wearing apparel.

The coalescence of the classes gives the European market a greater depth than it has ever possessed, permitting a manufacturer to penetrate with his product several or even all the social strata of the population. The vertical growth of the market will continue. Class consciousness is receding grudgingly and will not completely disappear so soon. But as a prime factor in consumer demand it is shifting to a middle-class value system that is developing from the economic advantages of large-scale production and marketing. And, as a consequence, the horizontal growth of the international integration is reinforced by a vertical growth that in addition to affecting the size also affects the structure of the market.

External Impact

The creation of the European Economic Community started a new chapter in international economic relations. The totality of its impact will be known only at a future date. For the time being the EC remains a prime source of international dynamics, and as such it has a profound effect upon world commerce in general and on the economic relations of the industrial world in particular. In this chapter we will discuss the EC's role in Europe. Its impact on the United States, Latin America, and the Afro-Asian countries will be analyzed in subsequent chapters.

For continuity it is necessary to revert back at this point to the cleavage between the British-led libertarians, who advocated general trade liberalization as the cure of all international ills, and the French-led dirigists, who forced the pace of integration and economic growth on a supranational level as a deliberate policy. The creation of the EEC transposed the cleavage from an ideological to an institutional plane, where debate and diplomatic machinations no longer sufficed to control the situation. The libertarian opposition, therefore, was compelled to react in a concrete way to the Rome Treaty to prevent any further erosion of its own international position. However, they had no clear answer to the problem confronting them. And while a better formula was sought, a delaying action was fought on the propaganda front, where the

EEC was portrayed as a divisive force destined to undermine the best interests of the other European countries, the United States, and the unassociated developing nations. The anti-EEC propaganda drew its main vigor from economists and statesmen, some world-famous, who considered the EEC a utopian folly which had no chance of success. But when, instead of withering away, the EEC started to progress rapidly, something more tangible was needed.

The Stockholm Convention

After a series of conferences an international *Convention establishing the European Free Trade Association,* popularly known as EFTA, was signed at Stockholm in January 1960 by Austria, Denmark, Great Britain, Norway, Portugal, Sweden, and Switzerland. It entered into force in May of the same year.

The stated objective of the Stockholm plan is to promote "a substantial expansion of economic activity, full employment, increased productivity and the rational use of resources, financial stability and continuous improvement in living standards" (Article 2). All these and some subsidiary objectives are to be achieved through what amounts to the one provision of substance in the Convention, namely, liberalization of trade in manufactured goods among the seven member countries. The liberalization procedure and the time table match those of the Rome Treaty. There is no common external tariff nor any alignment of social, agricultural, and economic policies.

Since each country has different external tariffs, the gradual elimination of the internal barriers creates artificial incentives for importers to divert their shipments to the member country with the lowest tariff on the particular product involved and from there to redistribute it duty free within the EFTA zone. To prevent such diversion, the Stockholm Convention requires that a certificate of origin be issued for all shipments moving from one EFTA country to another to supply the customs authorities with official evidence on whether the product was produced within EFTA and, as such, is entitled to free entry or whether it was not and, thus, is subject to tariff. Products that contain ingredients imported from nonmember countries in combination with domestic ingredients are to move duty free if more than 50 percent of their value was created internally; otherwise they must bear the full burden of the tariff.

Although this plan seems simple, in reality the movement of goods among EFTA countries must be subjected to strict certification and customs inspection, and complete liberalization of the movement of trade is out of the question. Also, so long as the external tariffs are not unified, the Stockholm plan has a built-in incentive for its own corruption; the tariff differences act as a lure for the unscrupulous to profit from subverting the origin-certification requirement. In concept, then, the EFTA scheme is a self-contradiction which cannot endure in the long run. Its critics argue that being operational on economic grounds never was its primary purpose; rather, it was designed as a collective device for supranational bargaining with the EEC countries.

EFTA–EC Relations

Shortly after the formation of EFTA, Great Britain filed for membership in the EC. Its application was conditional on the EC's argument to admit to membership all other EFTA countries if any of them desired. This show of EFTA solidarity was interpreted by the other side as a political pressure tactic and further contributed to continental, particularly French, suspicions and distrust of British intentions.

At home, too, the British government was faced with political fears and dissentions. The opposition Labor Party denounced the application as a threat to the nation's working class and vowed to fight it through Parliamentary as well as electorate processes. For the British public, membership in the EC seemed to be an either/or choice between their Commonwealth together with all the glory, power, and historic ties that it represented, and the Continent, from which their country had always remained aloof. Since these were primarily political fears, they required political answers. The government's strategy was: (a) to demand significant concessions from the EC—something that seriously imperiled the success of the ensuing negotiations—and (b) to imply that the real issue was greater than an economic union: it was *European leadership*. This touched an open nerve in the French body politic. Like Britain, France had lost an empire after World War II and was groping for new outlets for its frustrated national pride. Hence, both countries suffered from the same affliction and both reached for the same medicine: leadership in Europe. A clash was inevitable. It came when, after months of intrigue-ridden negotiations, President de Gaulle personally administered the *coupe de grace* by vetoing the British application.

British efforts to join the Common Market were renewed in 1967. But again political bickering, nationalistic prejudice, and beggar-your-neighbor philosophies paralyzed the negotiations. But these failures had not been in vain. They had served not only as outlets of overheated national frustrations both in Britain and France, but also as testing grounds for the tenacity and resolution of each side.

Thus, the third application for British membership in the EC could be launched in an entirely different atmosphere. This time the application was quickly accepted by the EC and subsequently ratified by the British Parliament. Similar applications by Denmark and Ireland were also accepted by the EC. All three were officially admitted as new EC members in January 1973.

The Enlarged European Community

With its four new members the EC will form an economic giant big enough to challenge the U.S. Although smaller in terms of GNP, the enlarged EC's external trade will be considerably larger and so will be its members' monetary reserves. Also, in key international bodies such as the IMF, GATT, and U.N., the combined voting power of the EC countries dwarfs that of the U.S.

The prospect of having to negotiate with an outside entity more powerful than itself is forcing American officials and businessmen to rethink their international strategies and methods. The main areas of uneasiness vary with the economic sector.

For the U.S. industrialist the enlarged EC is a two-edged sword: while it creates new opportunities for direct investments, there is fear that it will spawn mammoth European corporations whose competitive power may rewrite the pecking orders not only in the European sphere but also in other world markets, including the U.S. itself. Up until the present legal and tax problems combined with nationalistic narrow-mindedness of business itself have inhibited progress in forming EC-wide firms. As these inhibitions are overcome, the number of European multinational companies is, indeed, likely to increase.

In the agricultural trade the U.S. and the EC have long feuded over the relative blackness of pots and kettles: each labeling the other protectionist while maintaining that its own protectionist practices are for the common good. The reports of American grain and other products subject to the EC's variable import levy have undoubtedly suffered during the last decade. But the loss has been more than offset by increases in exports of agricultural products not subject to the variable levy (livestock feed, soybean products, etc.). Since the relative share of animal products in the European consumer diet is predicted to continue increasing, the need to import oil cake and soybean feeds can be expected to increase even more rapidly in the future.

For the U.S. banking industry the potentially most critical unknown is the EC's new plan for complete monetary union. Through successive stages of narrowing the allowable band of exchange rate fluctuations the member country currencies are to be brought into a fixed alignment with rates completely frozen. At that point there will be a common money in substance though not in form. Since every EC currency will then offer identical risks and fluctuations to nonmember countries, their separate identities will have only bookkeeping relevance. The world money market equations will be solved in terms of the EC currency amalgam rather than its individual components.

To solidify the amalgam, intracommunity transfers and capital accounts will be denominated in a common *unit of account,* which will serve as a semi-formal, yet very real, EC-wide monetary unit until such distant time when a formal common currency can take its place. This will depend on how rapidly the nationalistic symbolism of separate currencies will lose its political sensitivity, which at this writing remains prohibitively potent.

But whether a fixed exchange-rate amalgam, a common unit of account, or a fully formalized monetary unit, the emergence of a common EC currency is certain to weaken the dollar hegemony which was already shaken by the 1971 devaluation. By providing a new medium of payment, backed by a mammouth economy and available in sufficient volume to meet any conceivable need including reserve requirements, the EC currency will create for the first time since World War II a real alternative for the dollar in international finance. No national currency has so far enjoyed the capacity to provide such an alternative. International banking practice also would change. Right now completely geared to the dollar, a broader and more flexible method would be a necessary corollary to a common EC currency.

Mutual Advantages

Beneath the surface of rivalry, the U.S. and the EC are inescapably committed to common interests and obligations. Both need and aspire to a world of peace and stability, economic growth especially in the underdeveloped countries, financial liquidity, and liberalization of trade, travel, and investments. Only jointly can the U.S. and the EC, along with Japan, keep the world moving toward these goals at any visible speed. They share, therefore, the responsibility to shape the monetary and trade policies which are necessary for an efficient and equitable international economy. A selfish bickering and pursuit of national advantage at the others' expense are clearly contrary to these common interests and responsibilities.

West European Free Trade Zone

Affiliation of Denmark, Great Britain, and Norway with EC was tantamount to the disintegration of EFTA. The few remaining members, all small countries, lacked the size and diversity requisite for continuing as a viable supranational system. The Stockholm Convention had become an empty shell.

Rather than reverting back to the pre-EFTA situation, which would have required that national trade barriers be re-erected, these countries opted for a free trade connection to EC. And, in July 1972, the Treaty of Brussels was signed creating a European free trade zone for manufactured goods. Except for Spain (whose government has been anathema for its neighbors), all West-European countries belong to the zone. The Brussels Treaty excludes agriculture and there are no provisions for broader economic or political union.

33

International Integration in Latin America

Initially international integration in Latin America took two parallel forms: the Latin American Free Trade Association, popularly known as LAFTA, and the Central American Program of Economic Integration, generally called the Central American Common Market. Both these programs took their initial conceptual and organizational ideas from the European integration movement and have been subsequently inspired by the achievements of the EEC. But they are not mere imitations of the European programs. The real impetus for closer economic cooperation among the Latin American countries has come from the very grave economic problems that have plagued the continent.

Subsequently two additional integration plans were adopted: the Andean Group and the Latin American Common Market.

The two original schemes are quite different from each other. Constitutionally, one is loosely defined, slow, and indecisive; the other is more tightly organized, is more resolute, and was progressing rapidly. Until the "football war" between Honduras and El Salvador threatened to tear it apart. The incident resulted from a referee's ruling at a match of the national soccer teams of the two countries in 1969. In size, too, the two stand in sharp contrast; one spans a continent, and the other is confined to five small republics. It is necessary, therefore, to examine each plan separately before their potential can be analyzed from a business point of view.

The Latin American Free Trade Association: LAFTA

The blueprint for economic integration of the South American continent is provided by the Treaty of Montevideo, which was signed in February 1960 by Argentina, Brazil, Chile, Mexico, Paraguay, Peru, and Uruguay. Colombia and Ecuador signed toward the end of 1961, and Bolivia joined the plan later.

Objectives of the Montevideo Treaty

Although the ultimate aim of LAFTA is the establishment of a South American common market patterned after the Rome plan, the Treaty of Montevideo has much more limited objectives, which can be classified as short-term, intermediate, and long-term goals.

Under the short-term objectives the Treaty is concerned with (a) the expansion of present markets and trade, and (b) the gradual elimination of barriers to intra-South American trade. Under the intermediate objectives, the Treaty calls for (a) maximum utilization of available production factors; (b) more effective coordination of the development programs of the different production sectors; and (c) special measures in favor of countries with relatively less advanced economies. Under the long-term objectives, the Treaty seeks (a) to achieve progressive complementarity and integration of the national economies, and (b) to create gradually the conditions necessary for a complete economic community among the signatory countries.

The short-term objectives are clearly defined and detailed in the Treaty. The intermediate objectives, such as the joint development, the allocation of resources, and the industrialization program, can be considered no more than skeletons, the flesh for which has to be supplied through future negotiations. The long-term objectives of the Treaty are no firmer commitments than joint resolutions of good intentions and expressions of hope conditioned by the progress and the achievement of the short-term and intermediate goals. A peculiar feature of the entire Treaty is that every step is left open to further negotiation and revision.

Provisions of the Treaty

The contracting parties (member countries) are required to eliminate with respect to "substantially all of their reciprocal trade" the duties, charges, and other restrictions on imports originating in the territory of any other contracting party (Article 3). The elimination of duties and other restrictions will be achieved by means of periodic negotiations. The member countries will draw up (1) national schedules, specifying annual concessions which each country is to grant the others, and (2) a common schedule, listing products upon which all the LAFTA countries agree to eliminate restrictions within a period of 12 years (Article 4). Each country is committed to grant annual reductions in duties on goods appearing on their national schedules of not less than 8 percent of the weighted average of duties applicable to third (nonmember) countries.

The common schedule or list consists of products on which all the member countries have agreed to eliminate duties and restrictions. It is negotiated every three years, at which time the weighted average of the duties and charges applicable to the goods in the schedule are to be reduced as follows: 25 percent after the first three years, 50 percent after six years, 75 percent after nine years, and substantially all after 12 years (Articles 5–10).[1] The concessions granted on products in the national schedules can be revoked through the annual negotiations; those granted on the common schedule are irrevocable.

The members of LAFTA are free to determine each year the products on which they want to make reductions as well as the magnitudes of the reduction. The only stipulation is that the total liberalization meet the prescribed minimums. Thus the logical move for a member country to make is to concentrate its tariff reductions on products which do not compete with domestic industry in the early years. The tariff reduction affecting the highly protected domestic industries could be put off until the latter part of the 12-year period.

The fact that a free-trade area is the form of integration provided under the Treaty means that existing national tariffs against third countries are maintained, and there is no requirement to establish a common external tariff. The Treaty does, however, recognize the need for reconciling import and export regimes, as well as the treatment accorded to goods, services, and capital coming from outside the area. Provision is also made for "progressively closer coordination of industrialization policies," and the negotiation of "mutual agreements on complementarity by industrial sectors."

The Treaty provides special treatment for agriculture and for the less developed member countries. The participating countries are to coordinate their agricultural development and trade policies in an effort to expand their mutual trade in agricultural products.

With respect to the less developed countries (Bolivia and Paraguay) obligations to reduce tariffs and other restrictions may be implemented "under more favorable conditions specially agreed upon." Moreover, such countries may adopt special measures to protect their domestic industries, whether for balance-of-payments reasons or as a part of a temporary program to encourage economic development. In addition, arrangements are to be made for financial and technical assistance to promote the expansion of productive activities in the less developed countries, particularly the processing of their own raw materials.

In sum, therefore, one can say that the signatories to the LAFTA Treaty seek to create gradually, over a period of 12 years, a free-trade zone where goods produced in any signatory country are traded anywhere within the zone,

[1] Miguel Wionczek, *The Latin American Free Trade Association,* International Conciliation, No. 551 (New York: Carnegie Endowment for International Peace, January 1965), pp. 19–20.

free of institutional restrictions and each country maintains its own tariff structure with respect to countries outside the zone.

The Treaty provides a number of escape clauses which are significant. The contracting parties may impose provisional nondiscriminatory restrictions on imports originating in the area if such imports have serious repercussions on productive activities of vital importance to the economy (Article 23). They may also impose restrictions to correct an overall unfavorable balance of payments (Article 24). Furthermore, agriculture is accorded special treatment. Imports of agricultural products may be limited to the amounts needed to meet a deficit in domestic production and to amounts required to equalize the price of imported and domestic production (Article 28). Normal supplies of agricultural goods are to be made available to consumers without disrupting regular productive activities (Article 27). The less developed countries of the region are also accorded special treatment. They may reduce duties on imports from within the LAFTA zone on more favorable terms than the other countries, may adopt restrictive measures to correct a balance-of-payments deficit, and may take appropriate restrictive measures to protect domestic output of products of vital importance to economic development (Article 32). In other words, the Treaty virtually excludes agricultural products except to the extent that members voluntarily choose to include them and allows the countries to suspend the provisions in case of injury to home industries or balance-of-payments deficits.

The Treaty also distinguishes between commodities produced and traded at present within the zone and commodities which are not traded at present within the zone, either because they are not produced yet or because they are produced only for domestic consumption. The LAFTA signatories are committed to negotiate only on commodities (except agricultural commodities) which are currently traded. They are, however, urged to include as many goods as possible which enter inter-Latin American trade after the Treaty becomes effective (Article 14).[2]

Central to the Treaty are the principles of *reciprocity* and *complementarity*. According to the reciprocity principle, each country will negotiate concessions on import restrictions with the expectation that concessions given and received will result in a more or less equal expansion of that country's imports and exports with the area as a whole. The underlying purpose of the reciprocity principle is to avoid situations where increased zonal trade will give rise to increased balance-of-payments deficits and where a country would receive benefits from increased export trade at the expense of the industrialization programs of other members.[3] The complementarity principle refers to efforts to promote balanced economic growth for the zone as a whole. It recognizes that many countries cannot widen the industrial base within the

2 Theodore A. Sumberg, "Free-Trade Zone in Latin America," *Inter-American Economic Affairs,* XIV, No 1 (Summer 1960), 56.

3 Raymond F. Mikesell, "The Movement toward Regional Trading Groups in Latin America," in *Latin American Issues,* ed. A. O. Hirschman (New York: Twentieth Century Fund, Inc., 1961), p. 139.

confines of national markets. Hence, industrialization requires broader, supranational markets and specialization and complementarity within Latin America with respect to various industries. This complementarity is envisioned to occur by means of planning and negotiation rather than by means of market forces. It is hoped that the various countries will specialize in the production of various finished products and intermediate goods, selling them in the entire LAFTA zone.

One notes here a priority on cooperation and planned expansion of trade and national output and a de-emphasis on competition. There is a deep concern for the coordination of industrialization policies of the various LAFTA countries, for the promotion and protection of their industries, and little mention of the role of competition in promoting efficiency.

Administrative structure

The Treaty also creates two administrative organs—the Conference of the Contracting Parties and the Standing Executive Committee. The Conference is the supreme organ of the Association and is charged with implementing the Montevideo Treaty—laying down rules of procedure, promoting negotiations, appointing the professional staff, and making other administrative policy decisions. It is composed of delegations from each of the contracting countries; each delegation has one vote. The Conference may make decisions only if two-thirds of the contracting parties are present and no negative votes are cast.

The delegations making up the Conference are representatives of their governments and are subject to control by the latter. They are not delegates to a supranational body acting independently of their governments, as are the EEC delegates to the European Parliament. Therefore, to the extent that governments are subject to the pressures of special interest groups, so will the Conference delegates be subject to these pressures; and decisions made or not made by the Conference will be very much the result of pressure politics of the member countries.

Also, the requirement that decisions may be made only if two-thirds of the contracting parties are present and if no negative vote is cast makes decision making very difficult, especially for large changes. Any one country holds veto power over the entire Conference.

There is no machinery whatsoever for the enforcement of LAFTA provisions or decisions. The EEC provides for an International Court of Justice, which decides cases and enforces the provisions of the Rome Treaty; members are bound by the decision of the Court. There is no court or any other judicial review board in the LAFTA Treaty which would bind the signatories to abiding by the LAFTA commitments. Hence, adherence is, in essence, voluntary.

The Standing Executive Committee, located in Montevideo, is the permanent operating organ of LAFTA. It is responsible for supervising the implementation of the provisions of the present Treaty and handles all "housekeeping chores" of the organization; it has no policy making powers.

The Central American Program of Economic Integration (The Central American Common Market)

In December 1960, the General Treaty on Central American Economic Integration, the basic instrument of the Central American Common Market, was signed in Managua, Nicaragua. This treaty includes five countries, and it comprehends the main points of all the various treaties, conventions, and protocols which preceded it.

Key provisions

The General Treaty of Central American Economic Integration provides for the immediate elimination of duties and charges on 20 commodity groups, for free internal trade, and for a common external tariff to be achieved in ten years. Subsequent to the signing of the Treaty, plans were laid to accelerate its implementation—the deadline for completely free trade and a uniform tariff was moved up to 1966.[4]

The Treaty also provides for certain nondiscriminatory practices. The signatories are committed not to grant tariff concessions to countries outside the Union on imported goods which are produced within the Union. Duties may be levied on commodities imported from within the Union only if the goods are subject to internal taxation; the duty may not exceed the amount of the internal tax. Also, countries may not sell within the Union at a price lower than the domestic price of the goods (antidumping or price nondiscrimination), and direct or indirect export subsidies are forbidden. The Treaty provides for the construction and maintenance of communication and transportation facilities and for the standardization of rates charged for their services; for nondiscriminatory treatment of capital investments made by nationals of any country within the Union; and for industrial integration of the several economies.

In sum, therefore, the signatories to these two Central American treaties aim at creating something between a customs union and a common market: All goods produced within the Union may be traded within the Union free of institutional restrictions, and the countries as a group maintain a common tariff on goods originating outside the Union. Also, there are plans for partial planning on a supranational level plus mobility of some productive factors. The countries have gone beyond a customs union but have not provided for the full mobility of resources required for a bona fide common market.

The governing institutions

The general administration of the Central American Program of Economic Integration, the official name of the Central American Common Market, is to be carried out by three bodies: the Central American Economic Council, the Executive Council, and the Permanent Secretariat.

[4] William R. Gigax, "The Central American Common Market," *Inter-American Economic Affairs,* XVI, No. 2 (Autumn 1962), 60–61.

The Central American Economic Council is the governing body for the coordination of the economic policy of the contracting states. It is composed of the ministers of economic affairs of the five countries.

The Executive Council acts as the steering committee of the Economic Council. Its function is to implement the General Treaty in conformity with the basic principles established by the Economic Council. This body is composed of one titular official or delegate and one alternate appointed by each of the contracting parties. Resolutions are adopted by majority vote. The Permanent Secretariat handles all operational business of the CACM.

Basic Economic Problems of Latin America

These economic integration schemes in Latin America should be regarded as a response to certain economic difficulties which have plagued the Latin American economies for decades. The most important considerations are (1) balance-of-payments difficulties, and (2) an inadequate rate of industrialization and development. The architects of these schemes hope that development can be accelerated and balance-of-payments difficulties alleviated through the economic integration of the participating countries.

International Payments

Latin American countries face both cyclical and secular balance-of-payments problems; that is, they have experienced great instability in their export earnings, and they have had great difficulties in achieving secular growth of exports in value terms.

The instability in export earnings is a consequence of the commodities which Latin America exports. These countries are primarily producers of food and raw materials (primary products), which comprise a very large percentage of their exports. For example, in 1962, food, agricultural materials, and minerals and metals constituted 90.6 percent of the total value of Latin American exports.[5] Furthermore, many of the countries are heavily dependent upon one or two commodities for export earnings. For example, exports of coffee and bananas account for about 80 percent of Central America's export earnings.[6] Crude oil accounts for about 90 percent of Venezuela's export earnings, and coffee accounts for about 80 percent of Colombia's exports.[7]

[5] Computed from the *United Nations Statistical Yearbook* (New York: United Nations, 1963), Table 160, "World Trade by Commodity Classes and Regions."

[6] Gigax, "The Central American Common Market," p. 61.

[7] John P. Powelson, *Latin America: Today's Economic and Social Revolution* (New York: McGraw-Hill Book Company, 1965), p. 147.

Primary products' earnings fluctuate widely as a consequence of violent shifts in supply or demand or both. Raw materials experience very great fluctuations in demand because of business-cycle developments in the industrialized countries, which are the principal buyers of Latin American exports. In periods of recession, demand for raw materials falls greatly, causing large fluctuations in prices and export earnings. Also, there are fluctuations in supply caused by vagaries of the weather on crops. Demand for food tends to be quite stable, but supply tends to be unstable because of the effects of the weather.

There are also serious limitations on the amount that export earnings from primary products can be increased. Primary products tend to have low-price and low-income elasticities of demand, so that increased output will result in both lower prices and lower revenues. The income elasticity of food products has been estimated to be 0.25 for the United States[8] because of the high living standards and the near saturation of demand for food. Also, demand for raw materials tends to be price and income inelastic due to the declining economic importance of raw materials relative to total input and output in the U.S. economy. Raw-materials consumption increases at a lower rate than gross national product. This reduction in the relative importance of raw materials is due to increased efficiency in their use and to the introduction of synthetic substitutes. Therefore, if Latin American countries wish to stabilize and increase their export earnings, they must diversify their exports in favor of commodities which possess greater stability of demand and supply and have higher price and income elasticities.

Economic Growth

The rate of economic development (defined as growth of per capita product) is regarded as too low by Latin American policy makers. Although living standards in Latin America are on the average higher than those in Africa and Asia, they are still low relative to the Western industrialized countries.

Not only is per capita income quite low in Latin America, but the rate of population growth is extremely high, requiring high rates of economic growth in order to prevent per capita income from falling. Population growth for Latin America as a whole averaged 2.5 percent per year for the decade 1951–60, and it is expected to accelerate in the 1960's. Again there is substantial variety of rates among countries, with population in Costa Rica growing at 3.6 percent and that of Paraguay growing at 1.5 percent.[9]

[8] T. W. Schultz, "Economic Prospects of Primary Products" in *Economic Development for Latin America,* H. S. Ellis and H. C. Wallich (New York: The Macmillan Company, 1962), p. 315.

[9] Computed from data in United Nations, Economic Commission for Latin America, *Economic Bulletin for Latin America.*

Certainly if the people of Latin America are to enjoy a higher standard of living in the near future, income must grow very rapidly, substantially in excess of the rate of population growth, which will probably rise to about 3 percent. Or, to state the problem in another way, rapid population growth makes it imperative that Latin American income increase rapidly so that living standards may improve rather than deteriorate.

One of the factors limiting the growth of national product has been the limited export earnings of these countries. Since Latin American countries are for the most part primary producers and production is heavily concentrated on a few products, they have a very high propensity to import. Imports are required both for diversifying consumption and as inputs for diversifying production. When income grows, import demand grows without a commensurate growth of exports (due to low price and income elasticities of foreign demand), so that these countries quickly find themselves suffering from falling terms of trade and balance-of-payments deficits.

In an effort to overcome this export limitation on national income growth, Latin American countries have, historically, adopted policies of import substitution. They have erected tariff and other barriers against imports and have tried to develop their own industries behind protective walls. They have encountered serious difficulties and limitations in carrying out these policies because of limited domestic markets (due to low incomes and small populations).

As a consequence, most of their industries are uneconomic and high cost. They continually encounter supply bottlenecks when they cannot obtain needed imported inputs, and the small size of the market makes them operate on a scale far too small for low-cost, efficient output. Also, policies of import substitution have not resulted in decreased vulnerability to the vicissitudes of foreign trade. Formerly, vulnerability was directed more toward consumption goods; when export earnings fell, these countries were unable to purchase the consumer goods they needed. Now this vulnerability is directed more at supply; when export earnings fall, these countries cannot purchase the intermediate goods required as inputs for their industries, so that production must be curtailed and firms must operate far below their capacities.

The Latin American economic-integration schemes were designed to assist these countries in overcoming their export and domestic-market barriers to growth. In fact, the schemes are regarded as "engines of growth and development." Domestic markets are frequently too small to allow an industrial firm to operate at minimum-cost capacity. The integration agreements will open up the markets of a number of countries to that firm. Furthermore, since these countries cannot produce at sufficiently low cost to be competitive with the industrialized countries, they will promote exports among themselves rather than with third parties. Also, so that they can be less dependent upon imported intermediate goods, they contemplate specializing among themselves. One country, for example, could produce tires, another certain automobile parts, and another steel, and another could assemble the finished product.

Effects of International Integration

Opinion is widely divided among economists regarding the potential of the Latin American integration arrangements. Roughly, the opinions can be classified into two groups—one group feels that there is little potential in the arrangements, and the other feels that the potential is very great. There is very little opinion between the two poles.

Pro-integration argument

Those who see great potential in the integration schemes see them as engines of growth and development. They recognize that the major obstacle to industrialization in Latin America is the absence of a sufficiently large market which would allow manufacturing industries to operate at a high-level, low-cost capacity. Because of the limitations of the national markets, many industries never become established and others are unable to expand. The markets are limited by the smallness of the nation's population and the low purchasing power of its inhabitants. Also, the industries which do exist are low-volume, high-cost operations which cannot compete in export markets. If firms were able to produce for the entire Latin American area and not just for their national markets, some industries which formerly were uneconomic would become economic and others could expand to a more efficient level of output. Also, the various countries could specialize and cooperate in the development of various branches of industry, thereby expanding the flow of imports and exports among them while maintaining their trade with the outside world. In this way, they expect to reduce not only the countries' vulnerability to the vicissitudes of international trade but also their dependence on the export of primary products, increasing their export earnings at the same time.

Once the industries have been established in Latin America, they are expected to eventually become sufficiently efficient to meet world competition. In this way, Latin countries could increase their exports to non-Latin areas as well as to the Latin area itself. Also, by selling in a supranational market, these countries could overcome some of their market imitations to industrialization, thus speeding up industrialization and development.

Anti-integration argument

Those who see little potential in the arrangements point to various provisions of the treaties and to the structures of the Latin American economies. At present only about 10–12 percent of Latin American imports consist of goods originating in other Latin American countries, and about 60 percent of that trade is conducted between Brazil and Argentina. The commodities which are traded within Latin America are overwhelmingly agricultural—in 1965, for example, 45 percent of inter-Latin American trade was composed of foodstuffs, 17 percent was agricultural raw materials, 4 percent was mineral raw materials, 25 percent was fuels, and a scant 3 percent was in manufactured goods.[10] Comparing these figures with those of 1950 and 1955, one can hardly detect any change. When one considers that Latin American countries export primary products and import mostly manufactured goods, he cannot escape the conclusion that at present the Latin American economies are not very complementary—that is, for the most part they do not export the goods which other Latin American countries wish to import. Hence the economic possibilities for increased trade are seriously limited.

Also, there are a number of provisions in the LAFTA Treaty which are either contradictory to the principle of trade liberalization or allow the countries involved to avoid their commitments. Of particular importance is the provision which deals with agriculture. Agricultural commodities are exempted from the Treaty; however, since these countries are overwhelmingly producers and exporters of agricultural goods, exemption of these goods from the free-trade provisions exempts most of the economy from trade liberalization.

The distinction between goods presently traded and those not presently traded and the commitment to free trade only on the former are also serious obstacles to the liberalization of zonal trade. Since production in most of these countries is heavily concentrated on a very few products and even fewer are exported, economic diversification may still result in foreign trade in only a few commodities.

Also, the numerous escape clauses may prevent the provisions of the treaty from being implemented. The Treaty allows countries to erect barriers to trade if increased interzonal trade causes serious harm to industries vital to the development of the economy. They can also erect barriers to correct a balance-of-payments deficit. When one considers that capitalists in Latin America are accustomed to heavy protection and that many of the existing industries there are uneconomic and viable only behind heavy protective walls, it seems likely that the escape clauses will be invoked.

Some of the more doctrinaire critics speculate that LAFTA will be more trade diverting than trade creating. In general, a country will gain if integration arrangements create trade where none existed before and will lose if it diverts trade from low-cost to high-cost sources. Since many Latin American industrial undertakings are high-cost operations, it is feared that the free-trade zones will result in the member countries buying more from high-cost producers within the zone and less from low-cost producers outside the zone.[11]

[10] United Nations, Economic Commission for Latin America, *Economic Survey of Latin America,* 1965 (New York, 1967), pp. 46–77.

[11] To this might be added that to become efficient, in the sense of being competitive in the world market, the new industries need even longer production runs because of automation and other technological changes which keep pushing back the optimum size of the modern manufacturing units.

Much of this difference in opinion about the potential of Latin American integration schemes comes (1) from whether the writers are considering long-run or short-run time periods; (2) from the expectations they have for the success of Latin American industrialization policies; and (3) from their expectations of balance-of-payments developments.

Those who are skeptical look at current Latin American problems. They make no allowance for structural change of the Latin American economy through industrial growth. Furthermore, they recognize foreign trade as the sole remedy for the problem. On both accounts they are more wrong than right. It is not the mechanistic rearrangement of existing productive capabilities that is the main essence of international integration but the creation of opportunities for industrial growth and diversification. To judge a dynamic process from a purely static perspective can hardly yield realistic results.

Those who are optimistic rightly look to the long-term prospects of trade possibilities while the countries are developing and the structures of the economies are being altered. Much will depend on the parties. If the governments invoke the escape clauses to the extent that the treaties are rendered virtually nonoperative, serious difficulties with balance of payments and development policies will, of course, persist as before. If these clauses do not become serious hindrances and the treaties are implemented judiciously, the movement will gain strength from its own motion.

The success of the Latin American integration arrangements is critically linked to the success of general economic development. If these countries are successful with their development efforts, they will not be so hesitant to participate in extended foreign trade; but if their policies are not successful and their industries do not prove viable in international markets, then these countries may again retreat behind protective walls, and the integration schemes will be suppressed.[12] Balance-of-payments developments are another critical factor for the success of these schemes. If export markets (mainly in the industrialized countries) contract or do not adequately expand, these countries will experience balance-of-payments deficits. To correct these deficits, they are likely to cut down on imports by erecting barriers to trade, thus defeating the integration plans.

On the other hand, if development and integration plans go well, the various countries will be more willing to grant concessions far beyond the ones stipulated in the treaties by including agricultural goods and new goods in their negotiations; such actions will make the goals of the integration treaties much more viable.

In a very real sense this is a circular situation where success breeds success and failure feeds on failure—a highly interdependent condition where suc-

[12] A politically sensitive point is that LAFTA can appear to be a scheme in favor of the more industrialized countries whose production efficiency is greater than that of the others. Internally, too, there is the question of relative efficiency. LAFTA can be viewed as being in favor of the low-cost, large producers but against the high-cost, smaller firms, which in all Latin countries constitute the vast majority. If the latter resort to political action, another coup d'état may be its Latin expression.

cessful development and favorable balances of payments will enhance the chances for success, and successful integration efforts will accelerate development. Successful economic policies in Latin Ameria are heavily dependent on high export earnings in their traditional markets (the industrialized countries). If export markets collapse because of recessions, it is most unlikely that Latin America can achieve its objectives. Perhaps the most important aid that the industrial countries can extend to Latin America is to maintain cyclically stable, secularly growing purchases of their export products.

All writers on the subject seem to agree that the Latin American area faces numerous difficulties in expanding trade. Transport facilities are lacking; adequate financial provisions do not exist; and negotiations are made on a product-by-product basis. The LAFTA Treaty does not provide for the development of transport and financial facilities—these matters will have to be dealt with in separate arrangements. However, the Central American treaties do provide for the building of transport facilities. Negotiations on a product-by-product basis are very difficult and frequently leave the countries hopelessly quibbling over how many tons of paper and how many glasses to allow in. They do not negotiate on broad categories of commodities as the EEC countries and now also the United States do.

Diversion of imports

One potentially serious problem which LAFTA faces is how to deal with imported goods coming into its area which may be re-exported to other countries within the area. Whenever one has a free-trade area and the various countries within the zone have greatly varying tariff structures, there is an incentive for exporters from outside the zone to sell their goods in the countries where tariff rates are lowest and then to re-export them to the high-tariff countries. If this possibility is not eliminated through administrative controls, the tariff rate of the lowest tariff country for any one commodity becomes the effective rate for the entire free-trade area.

The EFTA countries have dealt with this problem by requiring certificates of origin for all goods traded within the EFTA zone. Goods from outside the zone which are re-exported from one member country to another are subject to a duty equal to the difference in duties between the two countries. This procedure has resulted in a tremendous amount of "red tape," and one wonders whether, with all this administrative work, trade can in any meaningful way be called "free."

Apparently the signatories to the LAFTA Treaty have not anticipated this re-export problem, for there is no provision for it and there is no mention of it in the literature. The latter would suggest that the problem has not yet manifested itself because the countries to date have done so little with respect to freeing their trade. However, there is a great potential for this problem to arise. The Latin American countries have very different tariff structures as well as very different tariff levels. This means that in the event of free trade within the region, it would be very profitable to divert goods to low-tariff countries and to re-export them to high-tariff countries. If measures are taken to prevent this re-export trade (by the use of certificates of origin or some other similar device), administration becomes extremely cumbersome and the opportunities for corruption abound.

The Andean Subregional Group

The Andean Group was formed in late 1968 by a group of five countries along the west coast of South America: Bolivia, Chile, Colombia, Ecuador, and Peru. The thinking behind Andean integration was that, as LAFTA progress had bogged down due to the difficulty of achieving agreement between countries of such diverse economic strength and varying degrees of industrialization, the Andean countries, being small and having more in common, could more easily agree among themselves. As they discovered, it still was not easy.

There is, however, very significant economic variation between the individual countries of the group, and this divergence is a primary cause of difficulty in the negotiations.

> A major obstacle to a successful economic union is that policies that would bring about the most rapid gains in real economic growth for the Andean Group as a unit could also result in an unequal distribution of benefits among member countries. None of the participating countries wants to let another country receive more of the benefits from integration than it does. Consequently, the countries have been bargaining with each other in an attempt to achieve a balance between growth and equitable distribution of gains among the countries.[13]

This problem seems to be common to all Latin integration attempts.

Recently, there has been a strong surge of nationalism through Chile, Boliva, and Peru with the nationalization of natural resource-based industries and some other critical activities. The question arises as to what effect these political events will have on Latin integration, particularly as economic integration has been interpreted in some circles as an effective means of keeping communism out of an area. It is unlikely that the increased nationalistic awareness will retard integration. The value of joint economic action among these countries is becoming more self-evident with time. If anything, some of the long overdue social and agrarian reforms may speed integration significantly, as one of the present hindrances is the pressure to maintain the status quo for many powerful "traditional establishment" vested interests.

[13] William H. Bolin, "How South America is Moving Ahead with the Andean Common Market," *Business Abroad,* September 1969, pp. 13–14.

A New Thrust Forward

Disillusioned with the progress achieved and in a concerted effort to consolidate the Alliance for Progress programs with Latin American integration movement, the presidents of the Americans met at Punta del Este, Uruguay, in the spring of 1967 to draw up the diplomatic instruments necessary for the establishment of a Latin American Common Market. The conference succeeded in producing the necessary declaration and obtaining the pledge from President Lyndon B. Johnson for U.S. foreign aid to help finance the project.

The common market would include both the LAFTA and the CACM countries and would be open to other Latin American nations. A series of preparatory measures dealing with infrastructure, foreign trade, agriculture, education, science, and health are to be taken before 1970, when the common market program will go into effect. It is scheduled to be completed by 1985.[14]

From the U.S. standpoint, the consolidation of the two integration programs and the Alliance for Progress is considered desirable, as it will promote closer working relations between the United States and its Latin American neighbors and require a deeper commitment on the part of Latin American leaders to economic development of the area. Nothing yet indicates whether the two trouble-ridden programs can be revitalized and upgraded by the proposed common market scheme. The chances are considerably less than good for an early success.

[14] *Reunión de Jefes de Estados Americanos* (Washington, D.C.: Union Panamericana, 1967), pp. 62–67.

34

International Integration in Africa, Asia, and the Pacific

Africa is a vast amalgam of diverse peoples, terrains, and resources. The continent has been subjected to a wide variety of influences; colonialism on the part of several cultures has been a salient factor in African history. With resources that are at once diverse and rich, Africa suffers from awesome underdevelopment that is only accentuated by the comparison to the wealthy European countries. Africa is thus a fertile bed of emotions and ideologies. There is a tremendous desire to emulate Western civilization's successes through economic progress; there is equally powerful strong commitment to preserve the African individuality. Can both these ideals be attained? Are modern industrial civilization and the aboriginal cultures of Africa congruent or conflicting? These are the most fundamental questions which form a common focus for the otherwise diverse nationalities and policies of African peoples.

African Nationalism

A most pervasive political force in contemporary Africa is nationalism. It is encountered everywhere and it affects all institutions, particularly international business enterprises. At the time when nationalism in the western world is in decline, if not in demise, the strong emphasis on nationalistic attitudes in Africa may seem strangely at odds with western views. African leaders, however, see in strong nationalistic awareness of the native people a rational means for important ends.

Internally, it is a means of nation-building, of overcoming a lack of national identification among the general public. As such, nationalism is (a) to supply the counterforce to tribalism which still divides the loyalties of many Africans, and (b) to give meaning to the irrational way in which African independence was parceled out. The borders of most African countries mark nothing else than the way that the colonial holdings of European countries were divided in pre-independence days. There is scarcely any ethnic, cultural, or economic rationality to these borders.

Externally, nationalism means to eradicate colonialism from Africa; that is, to remove the dominant influence of industrial nations and to inspire indigenous leadership and initiative. This is a costly ambition. Its price includes the loss of technology, capital, and trade, which is the essence of the neo-colonial linkage. International integration among African states is believed to provide a superior alternative to this linkage.

Need for Integration

The importance to African nations of international integration derives not only from the basic economic factors, but also from political and social considerations which cannot be easily separate from each other. The basic motive on the economic level comes from the realization that for all but a few of the larger African countries, modernization renders at least some form of international co-operation inescapable due to the small size of domestic economics.

Africa's political geography is conspicuous with its large number of small independent countries. (See map on p. 538). Nearly all of these emerged from the collapse of colonialism after World War II. Their large subjugation to foreign rule with economic exploitation and social mistreatment has left lasting scars in the continent's consciousness. Abolition of the remaining colonial influence and the prevention of its reoccurence are, therefore, absolute requirements for any viable politics in African countries. This is a precarious requirement, for the point at which constructive international cooperation ends and undue foreign influence starts is not readily ascertained. Chauvinistic extremism against any non-African influence has already led to an international isolation of certain African countries. Hopefully, these are exceptions rather than indications of continental trends.

Pan-African Integration

Integration in Africa has been developing along two main lines: Pan-African schemes which encompass the entire continent, and regional plans which are limited to a few neighboring nations.

The Organization for African Unity (OAU) represents the main Pan-African integration effort. It was created in 1963 by the treaty of Addis Ababa which was ratified by 39 African countries. The purposes of the OAU as defined in Article II of its Charter are: (1) to promote unity and solidarity of the African States, (2) to coordinate and intensify their cooperation and efforts to achieve a better life for the peoples of Africa, (3) to defend their sovereignty, their territorial integrity, and independence, (4) to eradicate all forms of colonialism from Africa, and (5) to promote international cooperation, having due regard for the Charter of the United Nations and the Universal Declaration of Human Rights.[1]

With regard to the implementation of these goals the Charter provides that Member States shall coordinate and harmonize their general policies, especially in the following fields: (1) political and diplomatic cooperation; (2) economic cooperation, including transportation and communication; (3) education and cultural cooperation; (4) health, sanitation, and nutritional cooperation; (5) scientific and technical cooperation; and (6) cooperation for defense and security. The Charter also specifies a policy of nonalignment with any other bloc.

A valuable by-product of this cooperation was the creation of the African Development Bank. However, in other respects the OAU has little to show. It suffers in that there are no specific timetables for achieving the goals which are set forth in its Charter. In fact, a realistic appraisal of the operations of the OAU since its inception would show that progress toward its goals has been almost negligible. The only tangible results of the Organization have been the creation of study groups and of further meetings in order to discuss more concrete proposals for the future. The Organization has succeeded, however, in presenting a somewhat unified voice for Africa in the world forum.

Regional integration in Africa has been substantially more successful on the regional level. Indeed, regional economic cooperation has existed for some time in Africa. For example, the French colonies in French West Africa and French Equatorial Africa had close links in trade, finance, and common services during the colonial era. When these colonies became independent states in 1959, they continued their economic cooperation in the form of the West African Customs Union. Later this organization broke apart due to disagreements on import duties and indirect taxation. Two new organizations resulted. One is called *Entente* (Conseil de l'Entente) with four members: the Ivory Coast, Niger, Dahomey and Upper Volta. Its goal is primarily the coordination of external policy and is based to a great extent on the personal confidence of the heads of state. What appears most critical is the growing disparity of wealth between the Ivory Coast and its fellow members. Recently, the Ivory Coast has actually been supplying foreign aid to the other states. The other organization is called Central African Economic and Customs Union (Union Douaniere et Economique de l'Afrique Central). It is made up of the Congo (Brazzaville), Central African Republic, Chad, Gabon, and Cameroon. The organization advocates the elimination of all trade barriers,

[1] *Treaties and International Agreements Registered or Filed With the Secretariat of the United Nations* (New York, 1964), 479, p. 72.

procedures for the equitable distribution of industrial projects, coordination of development programs, and a common customs tariff. The organization calls for a secretariat and the sharing of tax revenue and has the added feature of the monetary union common to most ex-French colonial countries. The group has a common central bank—the Banque Central des Etats de l'Afrique Equatoriale et du Cameroun. France provides funding for the bank and is leadingly active in its management.

An executive committee was set up to supervise and coordinate the plan, and up to now it has enjoyed moderate success.

A unique device called a solidarity fund was formed through a pooling of 20 percent of all customs receipts of the member nations, and is used for purposes of poverty relief. Through this integration plan, the Central African Republic and Chad have been able to vastly reduce their transportation costs, in that they have been able to utilize the transportation facilities of those nations that do have ocean ports.

Sharing benefits "equally and fairly" has been the main problem for the group. For example, the location of an oil refinery and the distribution of its profits caused heated debates and serious diplomatic confrontation among its member countries.

The broadest organization of French Africa, which has been the strongest exponent of integration, is the Afro-Malagasy Co-Operation Organization (Organisation Commune Africaine et Malgashe), formed in 1965 by former French colonies. Its objectives include: the harmonization of customs regulations; establishment of an African common market; agreement on taxation; regulation of insurance and other costs involved in trade; stabilization fund for steadying prices; standardization of investment codes; and suppression of subversion in the African states.

Although weak in formal structure, there have been positive results, especially in agriculture through the establishing of a common market in sugar and unified dealings with the International Coffee Agreement. Future plans include two multinational insurance companies, a joint shipping company, and mutual consultation on planning. They have also established a permanent African committee on higher education, with offices in each of the member nations.

The East African Economic Community, also known as the E.A.C.M., is composed of three former British colonies: Kenya, Tanzania, and Uganda. As early as 1927, these three nations, then British colonies, were joined together in various economic enterprises. This occurred because the British found it much easier to govern efficiently if they consolidated currencies, customs, postal and telecommunications systems, harbors, railways, and a joint development bank.

In 1961 the earlier governing structures were replaced by the East African Service Organization. This group has continued earlier programs and has also worked out plans to free restrictions on capital movement and to establish a common external tariff.

Problems have arisen for this integration scheme because each member was eager to keep new heavy industries in its own country, as well as most of the benefits. In 1965, Tanzania started its own currency, Kenya reacted by refusing to allocate industrial facilities, and the ensuing crisis threatened to break up the E.A.C.M. The three members met in Uganda and were able to work out a new agreement in production distribution, the allocation of new industries, and new trade quotas. This averted a breakup, and seems to show that this scheme is determined to succeed.

Trade disparity does exist among the members because Kenya is more industrialized and exports almost all the industrial goods to the other two. Kenya is also the only member able to maintain a positive balance of trade. Despite these disparities the members seem determined to make the plan work.

In *Southern Africa* there exists a customs union and a de facto currency union between the Republic of South Africa and the smaller states of Lesotho, Botswana, and Swaziland. The movement of labor from the lesser developed states to the more industrially advanced South Africa is permitted under these agreements. Aside from these factors, however, there is little desire among the nations involved to achieve any closer form of economic integration.

The Arab States

North Africa and the Mideast provide a contrast to many of the characteristics of sub-Saharan Africa; in other respects, however, similarities of resource endowment, historical parallels, and foreign relations tend to blur the differences of geography and religion.

The North African and Mideastern unity attempts have revolved principally around the *Arab League*. Begun in 1945, it is designed to strengthen the ties between Arab states, to coordinate Arab policies, to direct those policies to a common good, and to preserve their independence. The League has been highly political in nature but has helped to pave the way also for economic unity.

The Arab Common Market is the League's chief economic achievement and is composed of most of the Arab nations in North Africa and the Middle East. Its original purpose was to obtain complete Arab economic union patterned after the Rome Treaty. There was to be freedom of movement of both capital and persons, free exchange of domestic and foreign goods and products, freedom of residence and work as well as transport and transit, and freedom of establishment and rights of ownership. No timetable for accomplishing these goals was set, however.

Another economic offshoot from the Arab League is the *Maghreb* group of Morocco, Algeria, Tunisia, and Libya. Maghreb has historically connected a geographic region; the emergence of Tunisia and Morocco in 1956 as independent states transformed the region into a political force that culminated in Algerian independence in 1962.

Both these related integration plans suffer from the fact that the Arab economies are not only noncomplementary but, due to their dependence on petroleum, are also inevitably linked with the main oil-consuming countries in the industrial West. In addition, rapid population growth has not been offset by a corresponding increase in economic output. There is a great disparity in wealth distribution, with a few very wealthy persons and a mass of people living barely at subsistence level. Political problems have arisen through the turmoil of carrying on a prolonged crusade against Israel.

In the implementation of any "sharing" plan, one of the prime stumbling blocks is the unwillingness of those monarchal states (kingdoms) to give up their resources to the betterment of the "democratic" states. The kings' attitude is to give priority to their personal wealth and power, thereby raising serious doubts about any early achievement of an economic union.

Integrative and Disintegrative Forces

There are both internal and external forces which bear upon the integration of African states. While it is extremely difficult to weigh the relative impact of each of the forces upon integration efforts so that one can measure the degree of success or failure of integration in Africa, it is still useful to present the major factors and the reasons why they are significant.

The internal forces that are working for integration among the independent states in Africa include (1) a consciousness on the part of Africa's leaders that the relatively small size of many African nations, their uneven resource endowments, the small size of their markets, and the distortions in the pattern of economic activity inherited from the colonial period seriously inhibit attempts at development purely on the national scale, and that cooperation might lead to a widening of the horizon of such development, (2) political considerations which take the form of a desire to present a collective African front in matters affecting the continent as a whole, (3) a strong desire to alter the heavy metropolitan-colonial orientation in the cooperative ventures of the colonial period and to replace it with increased cooperation among African nations themselves, (4) the inclusion of "timetables" to allow the countries involved to make the necessary adjustments that integration efforts entail, (5) common monetary systems and provision for certain common services (transportation and communication). To a large degree these factors exist as holdovers from colonial days when currencies were tied to the "mother country" and common services were provided to reduce costs for the colonial power, and (6) common economic policies exist between many of the former colonial possessions in that their economies had been geared to the needs of the colonial power, and that now in independence the nations find similar needs to set up viable national economies and cooperative efforts with similar nations.

External forces that are working toward integration in Africa can be presented in three main points. These are (1) the United Nations Development Decade 1960–70, which sought to create the preliminary background to foster economic cooperation in Africa, (2) steps by the Economic Commission for Africa, in particular, the setting up of the African Development Bank, which serve as the foundations on which the superstructure of African cooperation is to be built, and (3) experiences of the European Economic Community, which have demonstrated both the desirability and feasability of integration among nations.

Examination of the factors working against integration in Africa reveals that these, too, may be divided into internal and external considerations. The internal forces which are working against integration are (1) extreme nationalism, which may turn any development efforts inward due to a desire to create a national consciousness before proceeding to a multinational basis, and (2) tribalism, which forms a significant factor in the internal political and social developments of many African states. The Biafran secession from Nigeria and the assassination of Tom Mboye in Kenya are vivid examples of the importance of tribalism upon the internal actions of the African nations.

Forces of a primarily external nature which are hampering integration efforts are (1) African state public investment programs are heavily dependent on foreign grants, loans, technical expertise, and personnel. Estimates of this dependence runs anywhere from 40 to 60 percent. Therefore, any change in foreign attitude toward conditions in Africa will seriously affect African development. (2) Existing foreign economic commitments may cause serious difficulty for negotiating new integration efforts among African states. The EC Associated States is an example of this sort of foreign commitment. (3) Balance of payments problems may cause difficulties for nations desiring to align themselves in an economic integration effort. (4) Weak treaties for integration which allow for too many loopholes and not enough concrete steps for action will inevitably cause delays into integration efforts. (5) The benefits achieved from integration may in the initial stages be small quantitatively and undramatic qualitatively so as to fail to sustain both the interest and the efforts of all participating states.

The African nations face several problems other than the forces which work against integration efforts. Specifically, these problems deal with the structure of the African economy and the resource base from which integration efforts must evolve. It is obvious that the continental and particularly the regional integration efforts must recognize the problems and deal with them effectively if they are to succeed in any meaningful manner.

General problems faced in Africa are:

1. *Poverty.* The continent as a whole is very poor. Total African income in 1966 was $41 billion for a population of 320 million people. This is approximately $130 per capita. If one excludes the republic of South Africa from these computations, the figure for income becomes $29 billion for a popula-

tion of 300 million. Per capita income then falls to $97.[2] It should be noted that these figures include subsistence production—that is, agricultural production produced for consumption within the household and not for sale in the market.

2. *Agrarian output.* African market economies are concentrated on primary production—mainly of agrarian products—for export. One-third of Africa's total output is exported. Industrial production in all of Africa accounts for only 2 percent of the world total.

3. *Intra-African Trade.* Trade between the African nations is very small considering its importance in any economic integration effort. In 1964 intra-African trade was estimated to be $588 million, which was 7 percent of exports, while in 1961 the figure was $470 million, which was 9 percent of exports.[3] The declining percentage figure for intra-African trade is accounted for by the increased exports of petroleum, iron ore, and diamonds, which are of little significance in intra-African trade.

4. *Monetary diversities.* Aside from the common monetary bases which are found on a few regional bases as holdovers from the colonial era, there is much monetary diversity in Africa. Currently there are 25 different currency areas in Africa, many of which have strong links with a world trading currency—notably the franc or pound sterling. At present the African franc and sterling currencies are not freely interchangeable with each other. This factor will cause difficulties in any efforts to achieve anything more than integration on a small regional basis.

5. *Infrastructure.* A final area for consideration which may in fact pose the biggest hurdle to economic integration is the infrastructure of the nations themselves. In order to facilitate the coordinated development of the common market goal on even a regional basis, the nations of Africa must seek to coordinate development plans in the public sector with regard to health, education, power, highways, railways, water development, and the like. This has not been done in the past and it is only now that a common concern for these areas is being developed.

Looking at the integration efforts that have developed in Africa and also looking at the problems facing the continent in general and the problems facing the integration efforts in particular, one must conclude that economic integration in the sense of the United States model or even the EEC model will evolve very slowly, if at all. The problems that must be overcome are immense compared to those that the developed nations had to face. In all likelihood the African nations will not approach the scale of the present EEC progress by 1985 or even the year 2000. But it is important to note that the seeds of economic integration have been sown in Africa and that the desire is there among the leaders of Africa to make that seed grow into something tangible that will benefit the people of Africa.

When one looks at the staggering birth rate in Africa and also the appalling mortality rate and the extremely low income that most Africans

[2] *United Nations Statistical Yearbook 1967,* 19th ed., (New York, 1968).

[3] *A Survey of Economic Conditions in Africa 1960–1964,* (New York, 1968).

must subsist on, the problems facing integration efforts in Africa seem overwhelming. It becomes apparent that the African nations will for some time be dependent on foreign aid, cooperation, and financial and technical involvement. Organizations such as the EC Association will continue for an indeterminate period as Africa is forced to look to the outside world for immediate and meaningful benefits from cooperation to solve the massive problems of the continent.

Time alone will reveal the future of economic integration in Africa, but as has been proved to be the case with political regroupings, time may not be on Africa's side. However, even if the far-reaching schemes for regional economic integration may not at present be widely negotiable, important economic gains may still be derived from the initiation of more limited forms of cooperation for the joint promotion of selected regional projects, or even from the establishment of preferential trade groupings falling short of a common market. These beginnings may subsequently provide the foundation for more profitable cooperation later. To achieve and maintain even the more limited forms of cooperation will pose a challenge of great proportions for the leaders of Africa.

Appendix

Map of Africa and Near East with Basic Political Divisions

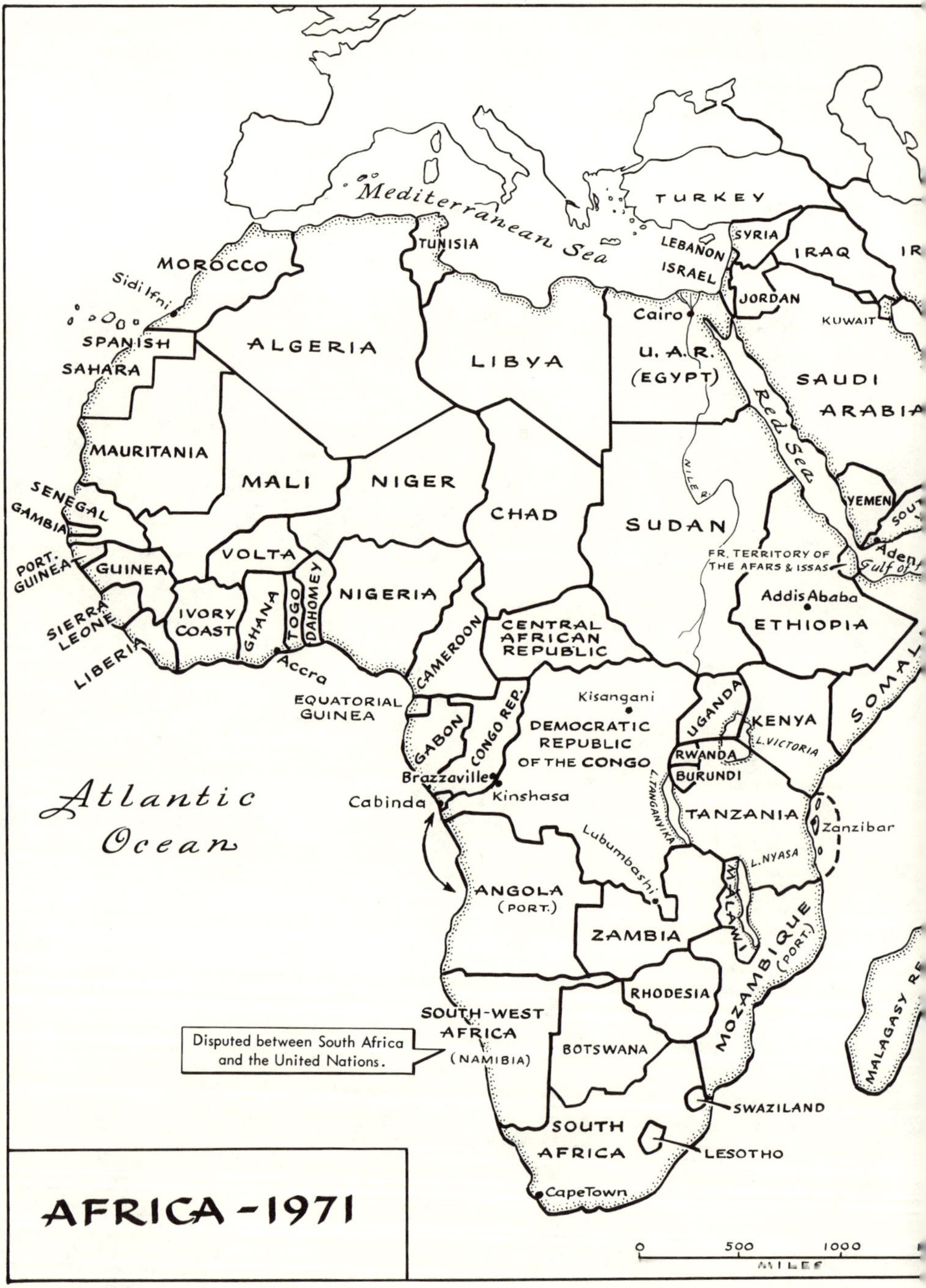

African and Near Eastern Nations Membership in ( )

ALGERIA	(A, E, F)	MALI	(A, B, K)
ANGOLA	(J)	MAURITANIA	(A, B, K)
BOTSWANA	(A, H)	MAURITIUS	(A)
BURUNDI	(A, K)	MOROCCO	(A, E, F)
CAMEROON	(A, K, L)	MOZAMBIQUE	(J)
CENTRAL AFR. REP.	(A, D, K, L)	NIGER	(A, B, C, K, L)
CHAD	(A, D, K, L)	NIGERIA	(A)
CONGO (BRAZ.)	(A, D, K, L)	RHODESIA	(I)
CONGO (KINSHASA)	(A, D, K, L)	RWANDA	(A, K, L)
DAHOMEY	(A, B, C, K, L)	SAUDI ARABIA	(F)
ETHIOPIA	(A)	SENEGAL	(A, B, K, L)
GABON	(A, D, K, L)	SIERRA LEONE	(A)
GAMBIA	(A)	SOMALIA	(A, K)
GHANA	(A)	SOUTH AFRICA (REP. OF)	(H)
GUINEA	(A)	SOUTHERN YEMEN	(F)
IRAQ	(F)	SUDAN	(A)
IVORY COAST	(A, B, C, K, L)	SWAZILAND	(H)
JORDAN	(F)	SYRIAN ARAB REPUBLIC	(F)
KENYA	(A, G)	TANZANIA	(A, G)
KUWAIT	(F)	TOGO	(A, C, K, L)
LEBANON	(F)	TUNISIA	(A, E, F)
LESOTHO	(A, H)	UGANDA	(A, G)
LIBERIA	(A)	UNITED ARAB REPUBLIC	(A, F)
LIBYA	(A, E, F)	UPPER VOLTA	(A, B, C, K, L)
MALAGASY REPUBLIC	(A, K, L)	YEMEN	(F)
MALAWI	(A, I)	ZAMBIA	(A, I)

Economic Integration Organizations

A. ORGANIZATION OF AFRICAN UNITY (OAU)
B. WEST AFRICAN CUSTOMS UNION (UDEAU)
C. ENTENTE
D. EQUATORIAL CUSTOMS UNION (UDEAC)
E. MAGHREB
F. ARAB LEAGUE (ARAB COMMON MARKET)
G. EAST AFRICAN ECONOMIC COMMUNITY
H. SOUTH AFRICAN CUSTOMS UNION
I. FEDERATION OF RHODESIA & NYASALAND (DEFUNCT)
J. PORTUGUESE CUSTOMS UNION
K. THE ASSOCIATED AFRICAN & MALAGASY STATES (EEC ASSOCIATION)
L. AFRO-MALAGASY CO-OPERATION ORGANIZATION

Asia

Forerunners to present-day Asian integration are the world's two most populous countries: China and India. Each with its own subcontinent combines many diverse peoples, cultures, languages, and earlier states into a massive integrated economic system. Although their relatively low level of economic development does not permit them to rival the United States or the U.S.S.R.—the other two accomplished common markets—in terms of GNP they have no internal barriers of the kind which the current international integration movements seek to abolish.

During two decades of self-imposed isolation China has concentrated on completing and consolidating the internal integration of its mammoth commonwealth. Its recent overtures to start to reopen trade relations with the West indicate that a satisfactory level of internal cohesion has been achieved.

In the rest of Asia, international integration is still in formative stages. Although no fully operational plan yet exists, a number of plans, agreements, and organizations have been established to promote regional cooperation and integration. The more important ones include: the Association of South-East Asia (ASA), the maphilindo (RCD), the Pacific Free Trade Area plan (PAFTA), the Ministerial Conference for Economic Development of South-East Asia, the Conference of South-East Asia on Development under the auspices of Japan, and the Association of South-East Asian Nations (ASEAN). In addition, business and industry groups from five Pacific Rim countries (Australia, Canada, Japan, New Zealand and the United States) have formed the Pacific Basin Economic Cooperation Organization for the purpose of providing private enterprise an international institution in overall economic development of the Pacific Basin.

All these organizations which came into being in the 1960's reflect an increasing recognition of the need for international integration in Asia. Their program, however, has been retarded due to lack of any organic relationship among the different organizations. None has the ability to go it alone without adequate political support or financial means.

To provide a comprehensive organizational framework the *Asian and Pacific Council* (ASPAC) was formed. Its members include Australia, New Zealand, Korea, Japan, Taiwan, Malaysia, South Vietnam, Thailand, and the Philippines with a total population of about 250 million. Other countries of the region may join if they wish. Burma, Indonesia, Singapore, Cambodia, and Laos have indicated interest to negotiate for eventual membership.

A major purpose of ASPAC is to work toward an Asian common market. Preparatory studies and negotiations both on government and nongovernment levels for this end are in progress. The fact that the membership includes both advanced and primitive countries greatly complicates the matter.

In a detailed study of complementarity, special country bias, and intensity in trade flows between advanced western Pacific countries and selected developing countries in Asia and the Pacific Professor Drysdale reaches this conclusion:

> "The nature of intensity, complementarity, and special country bias in trade flows among advanced western Pacific nations suggests that policies designed to promote closer integration, especially between Japan on the one hand and Australia and New Zealand on the other, might prove beneficial. In the second place, linked by high complementarity in exports and imports with Japan, and considerable special country bias with both Australia and Japan, the developing countries in the Asian-Pacific regions are relatively much more important to the trade of these two countries than they are to the world at large.

> . . . Thus, there is a strong case for coupling any policy initiative by advanced western Pacific nations with the extension or adoption of trade policies specially designed to accommodate the needs of developing countries in the Asian-Pacific region.[4]

The need for special provisions to deal with the less developed member countries is perhaps the most difficult to meet. Their preponderant dependency on Japan as a market for their raw materials and as a source for their manufactured goods conjurs up political fears of colonialist domination and pits them against one another in competition for a better position in the Japanese trade. That is to say, no horizontal division of trade would result among the developing countries, while a vertical trade division with Japan as the pivot would continue. The situation is similar with direct foreign investments. Most Asian developing countries have investment incentive programs to attract capital. In their zeal to outdo the neighbors they not only compete but tend to overconcede.

Because of these problems a lower degree of collaboration than full integration seems feasible for the immediate future. A customs union rather than an economic community is all we can reasonably expect at the present stage in the Asian and Pacific region.

[4] Peter Drysdale, "Japan, Australia, New Zealand: The Prospect for Western Pacific Economic Integration," *The Economic Record,* Vol. 45 (September, 1969), pp. 327–29.

35

Theoretical Issues of International Integration

International integration represents an intention to permanently reorganize relations, first, among the participant countries, and, second, between the integrating group and the outside world. As such, it is a long-term proposition. Short-term effects, either positive or negative, can therefore have but temporary relevance. The real test of any integration scheme requires a long-term, dynamic perspective. This chapter is devoted to such a test.

Basic Premise

International economic integration rests on the premise that there are economies of scale which cannot be exhausted within the limits of national business systems as autonomous economic entities—economies which can be achieved only in a larger sphere such as the European Economic Community, the Latin American Free Trade Association, or some similar scheme. The prime purpose of international integration, then, is to increase the size of the economy or the business system enough to release the latent economies of scale. This would mean that the productive efficiency of the integrated business system would rise to a higher level than the respective efficiencies of the member countries as independent entities.

Consequently, any long-term test of the effects of international integration must be formulated in terms of the theoretical proposition that there is a definite relationship between the size of a business system and its efficiency. Is there such a relationship? And, if so, what are the characteristics and ramifications of it? Answers to these and similar questions can be given only when the meaning of both of the variables is clearly understood.

Efficiency

To define the precise meaning of economic efficiency is less simple than it appears. A number of yardsticks could be used, but each would render a different result. For example, either the consumption or production of goods and services might be used but with different results. If production is used, the additional question intrudes: To what should total production be related to make it meaningful? To total population to get per capita figures? To the labor force to express the productivity of the productive age groups of the society? Or to those actively engaged in producing to show the efficiency of the actual participants in the production process? But would any or all in combination be synonymous with the efficiency of the business system as a whole? How about the value of leisure? How about the differences in working conditions, differences among industries, among countries, among cities, among occupations, etc.? An additional shortcoming in using production per person is that it measures efficiency as a function of labor time; the unit of measurement is the time people spend at work. But how different would the results be if efficiency were measured by the ratio of product to the inputs of services of all productive agencies and resources? And is this not the more inclusive and, therefore, more appropriate measure of overall efficiency?

This list of questions is by no means exhaustive. But it points up the necessity of adopting a compromise criterion which could be used as a standard point of reference. No such criterion has so far been agreed upon. Indeed, most writers on the topic indulge in the comfort of free and unlimited choice of undefined terms.

In the opinion of this author, the overall efficiency of a business system is best defined as the quantity of goods and services which it provides per head of the society. For particular purposes, however, this general measure can be supplemented by the product of an hour's or a year's work.

Size of the economy

The terms *economy* and *business system* are usually used to distinguish one country from others. Thus there must be some dimensions which are common to both a nation and its economy. The size of a nation is expressed in either geographical area or number of people. Although both population and area have relevancy to the concept of national economy, neither gauges the essential aspects of the productive system as such.

The most generally acceptable measure of the economy is the gross national product, at least in concept, since it endeavors to embrace all goods and services produced during a given interval. In actual use the GNP is much less satisfactory than it is as a concept. As pointed out in other connections, the GNP figures do not lend themselves to meaningful international comparisons; they are particularly misleading for countries where much of the production is distributed without any recordable market transactions; these do not show up in the GNP data.

Another way to think of the economy is as a market. But a market for what? The size of the market for goods differs from the size of the market for the factors of production. Density of population, existence and location of natural resources, and the institutional framework all bear upon the size of the market, each reflecting a different dimension of the size of the economy.

Aspects of Integration

It should be evident from the foregoing that no simple explanation of the relationship between the size and the efficiency of the economy is possible. Instead of any direct link one must search for a multitude of links, each of a different kind. These four seem particularly significant for reasons which the ensuing discussion will reveal: production cost and the size of production units, economic organization, foreign trade, and the cost of government.

Cost of Production

Economies of scale and mass production are a basic axiom in economic theory. The central point of this axiom is that as the size of a production unit—a firm—grows, specialization of equipment and skills develops, thus increasing efficiency and decreasing costs. However, economic theory has nothing to say about the cost-size relationship of the economy as a whole. International integration has posed the question: Is the cost-size axiom valid for the entire business system? Does the economy as a whole have an average cost curve with an optimum like that which the firm is postulated to have? If it does, then there must also be an optimum size for an economy—one which determines whether a particular international integration scheme will have positive or negative effects on the society.

Anti-integration argument

No agreement, not to mention proof, exists on this vital question. And instead of moving toward a consensus, the economists, often under the pressure of political action, have become divided even on the basic axiom of the economies of scale for a firm. What for a long time have been accepted as self-evident truths have now been challenged by opponents to international economic integration as pure speculations. A well-known spokesman for this point of view, Professor John Jewks of Britain, has accumulated extensive statistical data to show that more than half of world manufacturing output is produced by small factories employing fewer than 500 people, and that in even the highly industrial countries the average factory accounts for less than 1 percent of total manufacturing output.[1] This is to prove that large enterprises do not dominate world production, that there are ample opportunities for small factories and small countries, and that international integration is not justified in terms of production cost.

This deduction does not seem tenable on closer analysis. First, statistical evidence of this type is open to a number of qualifications. Second, even if correct, the average figures are misleading, for there are certain industries where large-scale operation is a rule which has some special importance in the sense that the country is critically dependent upon their presence and that they are destined to expand most rapidly and to engender growth in other sectors.

Pro-integration argument

The argument for large-scale economy and thus for integration is based on the following reasoning:

(a) The larger the country, the larger the economy; and the larger the economy, the larger the aggregate market.
(b) The larger the aggregate market, the larger the size of the firms.
(c) The larger the firms, the lower the unit cost of production.

This argument presupposes first that an increase in the size of the country leads to an increase in the size of the market; second, that an increase in the size of the market must lead to an increase in the size of the production unit and that at this point the classical axiom of specialization and efficiency applies. It is difficult to agree that all these relationships will hold in all cases. For example, there is little positive evidence that the size of the firm parallels the size of the nation; some large countries have only small firms and some small countries do have some large firms. But if allowance is made for the level of industrial development, there seems to be a rather good correlation between the reasoning and reality. This may be explained in part by the fact that a large country enjoys increasing returns which arise from the indivisibilities (various administrative, economic, and political overheads) which it can utilize better, and in part from the windfall advantages occurring when the market and the economy grow. This would suggest that at least an analogy exists between the optimum of a firm and the optimum of the economy.

Economic Organization

The size of the firm may be expressed in terms of the number of people employed, of the value of output, of the total sales, or of the total assets. Each of these is a measure of a different dimension. Yet none or even all in com-

[1] According to Jewks's computation, it is less than $\frac{1}{100}$ of 1 percent.

bination truly reflect the size of the production unit as such. This is true because the statistical data are based upon a legalistic rather than an economic concept. Methods of business organization long ago outgrew the conceptual apparatus of economics. A business enterprise no longer complies to the assumptions of being a single legal entity, operating a single factory, producing a single product, and distributing it in a single market. In fact, one single entity may control several factories and any factory may produce a number of products. Such diversification opens a gap between the unit of technical efficiency and the unit of managerial control. One enterprise may organize itself in the form of several corporate bodies bound together by ownership, contractual arrangements, and common management.

The discrepancies between the size of the production unit and the size of the legal entity tend to be the greatest in large companies because of their complex structures which often include scores of subsidiaries on one or more levels of subordination. Although it is true that in small countries the market limits the size of a production unit such as a factory, it does not limit the size of the company, which can grow through branching into different lines. However, a specialized firm can grow in a country only if it becomes international. Thus, the size of the country imposes at least two significant constraints upon an enterprise: it delimits the size of the technical production unit; and it requires large companies to either diversify or to become multinational.

The diversified large firm will remain subject to the first constraint, its technical production units being limited by the size of the market. But it could gain through a wider distribution of administrative overhead and especially through its relative power over transactions with other firms, which in small countries would generally have to be smaller by necessity. Thus a diversified large firm in a small country possesses a strategic power position in that it buys mostly from smaller and weaker companies and sells mostly to smaller and weaker companies. Since such a situation is conducive neither to effective competition nor to optimal allocation of resources, it can be argued that small countries with very few large diversified companies lack the internal competitive balance necessary for efficiency and innovation.

That leaves the companies which chose the other alternative of expanding beyond the boundaries of a small country. For a multinational company the domestic segment shrinks to a fractional part of its overall size, and its objectives and strategies are refocused from the national to the international perspective. The company cannot permit itself to be dominated by the considerations or conditions of any single country but must have plant and policies appropriate to its total position. The main rivals of a multinational company are other multinational companies rather than the national firms in any of the various countries in its operational orbit. Therefore, the behavior of the multinational firm may or may not conform to the requirements of effective competition in any particular country. It will compete if competition is consistent with its overall strategy and expectations regarding the reactions of its multinational rivals. But it will refuse to lower itself to compete in one particular country if that would jeopardize its other markets by provoking retaliatory actions or by disrupting orderly development of its corporate goals.

When international cartels develop, their effect is likely to be greater on the small countries because (a) if there is only one producing company, the cartel will allocate the entire national market to it and permit no outside competition; and (b) if there are a few producing companies, they may be fused by the cartel to produce a single-enterprise country. Also, there is a built-in inclination for small economies to develop cartels. The preliminary to any international cartel is a national cartel. In a larger country the members of the domestic industry are more numerous and have much greater difficulty reaching an agreement; even when they do, the agreement tends to be unstable and vulnerable to diverse reactions to new situations. In a small country the internal framework is already cartelistic as far as any large company is concerned. All that is needed is to come to terms with the external competitors.

Consequently, the organizational characteristics of business enterprise in reference to competition and cartels are quite different in small economies than in large ones. Effective competition, diversity, and change are more likely to be associated with the latter than the former. Technological progress and international adjustment are more probable in large economies (a) because of the possibility of escaping from restrictions by vested interests, (b) because of the greater variety of resources in which to invest, and (c) because there are more opportunities for marketing outside the established channels of conventional practice.

In sum, the organizational aspects of a small country tend to be even more constrictive than the technological aspects. Technologically an economy is suboptimal if its markets cannot absorb the output of the most efficient plant in a particular industry; and it is optimal if its markets are large enough to provide adequate outlets for such a plant. Organizationally, the economy is suboptimal if it lacks the necessary number of competitors to spur efficiency and to compel the construction of the technically most efficient facilities. In other words, an economy large enough to absorb the output of at least one optimum-sized plant may still be too small to provide the incentive for its construction. This means that the technically optimum size of an economy is much smaller than the organizationally optimum size, the technical optimum being a necessary but insufficient precondition for the organizational optimum.

International Trade

Can international trade offset smallness?

It has been stressed elsewhere in this book that the theoretical notion that international trade can have the same effect as domestic trade has been proven fallacious by experience, mainly because efficient production in the modern world is often mass production with highly mechanized and automated plants. Mass-production facilities, to be justified, require mass markets—markets which are not only large but also reasonably homogeneous and stable over time. Export markets can seldom meet these requirements. They are subject to sudden political interference, to monetary restrictions, and to constantly changing local conditions, all of which make rational forecasting, planning, and stable operation highly precarious. Mass production, therefore, is seriously constrained if the internal market is too small to absorb most of the output.

A large economy possesses some clear advantages over its smaller counterparts from the foreign-trade standpoint. Because of the size of its internal consumption, it can absorb the bulk of its production at home and thus be less sensitive to foreign influences. For the same reason it can fully utilize the economies of scale. And, its size and influence enable it to be dominant in international transactions.

Are these advantages accessible to small economies? The last two certainly are not. A small nation may be dominant over still weaker ones, especially if it holds a monopoly position or if its own products are highly in demand. But it clearly cannot possess any significant influence upon larger economies. The same can be said about international fluctuations. A small economy depends on foreign countries both for sales and supplies and is thus inseparably tied to the international markets. If it tried to insulate itself against world economic fluctuations, it would have to curtail its exports, which provide the only means for achieving an optimum scale of production and for procuring the necessary imports.

From the international-trade standpoint, then, a small nation gains significantly from merging its economy with others through international integration. Conventional trade liberalization measures such as attempted under the GATT program cannot produce the same advantage for smaller nations. But will this argument still hold after the small nations have combined into large integrated entities which equal or exceed in size the present giants such as the United States? Probably not. However, a more conclusive answer must wait for the integration movement to run its course.

The Cost of Government

It is probably true that the cost of government in any economy varies with the type or system of government that a country has. But given any particular system, the cost of government depends in a variety of ways on the size of the economy. In internal affairs, both a small and a large nation need more or less similar central institutions for the legislative, executive, and judicial functions. But on regional and local levels they differ. In a large nation, where the central institutions of government are farther removed from the individual communities, industries, and citizens, the need for various subinstitutions and agencies is also greater. But not in proportion to the size. As in business, certain functions can still be performed centrally regardless of the size with little or no change in cost.

For the cost of social services the available data are inconclusive. Both educational and health services, however, tend to be more expensive in the small than in the large countries. However, a more decisive factor than the size is the density of the population. Low-density areas may require suboptimal hospitals and schools and thus lead to higher operating costs. This point holds only for governmental services where mass production economies exist. They include housing, electrical power, social insurance, judicial and legal services, and public safety. In others mass-production economies are negligible in a technical sense but may be very significant in a human sense. This is true for the professional and educational services whose practitioners' qualifications and proficiency depend to a high degree upon participation in the intellectual life of their respective specialties. A small country may lack the opportunities for such participation. Often a professional in a small country must spend much effort to become multilingual to be able to communicate with his peers in larger countries. Thus again the weight of the argument tips the scales against the small economy. On a per capita basis its government seems more costly if the same services are rendered.

In foreign affairs the disadvantage is even greater. The need for a diplomatic service is determined no less by the number of contacts with the outside world than by the size of the country itself or by the international problems that may arise. It needs the same number of embassies and consulates as a large one. As was mentioned above, a small country is more dependent on foreign markets and sources of supply. This is true not only for business enterprise but also for social, political, and military needs. A small country is more internationally exposed; that is, it has a longer frontier per capita. For all these reasons, a small nation must spend a higher percentage of its income, both aggregate and per capita, on international relations.

Conclusion

On all four accounts—technological efficiency, organizational optimality, international trade, and cost of government services—international integration offers significant theoretical advantages to small nations. Although in certain areas the advantages are offset to various degrees by disadvantages, there is little doubt that without integration small economies are deprived of optimal production and effective competition, that internal stability and progress are precariously dependent upon the vicissitudes of international markets and foreign political actions, and that governmental and professional services are restrained more than in a larger integrated economy.

How large the integrated entities should become and if there is a size beyond which further expansion of the integrated group of countries will lead to negative results remain unknown. It seems quite clear, however, that the average total cost behaves not too differently from the costs of a firm in that it declines with the increase of the economy. Whether the curve will have a general optimum and whether it will then start rising are currently unanswerable questions. Until the answers have been found, there is no theoretical foundation for determining how big or how little an integration scheme should be or how many countries make an optimal unit.

Static (Short-run) Effects of Integration

In textbook economics international integration is usually discussed in a static framework; that is, the focus is placed on the immediate, short-term effects analyzed from the narrow perspective of trade liberalization. Furthermore, the analysis is predicated upon a series of highly unrealistic assumptions, among which the following are the most important: that the products of different countries are uniform and can be freely substituted in all respects (fungible goods); that the institutional framework in all countries allows free and unhampered competition, i.e., that there are no rigidities such as public policies or social legislation which interfere with optimum allocation or resources and manpower; and that this shift of demand from one source to another will not cause a change in the cost of production. That all of these represent highly untenable propositions needs hardly to be emphasized.

As the two previous chapters have shown, international integration is an almost all-inclusive concept. International trade represents but one aspect, and not even the most important aspect of it. Any endeavors to explain the effects and meaning of integration in terms of the theory of trade, therefore, suffer from very considerable limitations. But since this approach has been given a rather inflated significance, let us briefly summarize its main points.

The Textbook Version

In the absence of tariffs, the prices of a given commodity at the points of production can only vary by the differences in transportation charges with respect to any market. That is, the sum of the costs of production and of distribution for all producers must be equal for a given product in a given market. It was demonstrated in Chapter 6 that when any country imposes a tariff on imports, two effects will immediately be noted. First, the production of the affected commodities will shift from lower cost foreign facilities to higher cost domestic facilities. Second, consumer demand will shift in such a way that fewer of the commodities and more of their close substitutes will be desired. These two effects presume some degree of elasticity in consumer demand for the commodities and some excess capacity in the production facilities of the country imposing the tariff. Both productive efficiency and consumer satisfaction will decrease when tariffs are imposed.

The establishment of a free-trade area can produce both positive and negative production effects, as noted above. Production of a given commodity will shift from higher cost domestic facilities to lower cost member-country facilities (positive effect); however, production of some other commodity could shift to more expensive member facilities from cheaper, nonmember facilities (negative effect). Certain demand and price shifts will also result, but for the present these will be ignored. It should also be noted that economies of scale, imperfect competition, and the costs of transportation will dampen these effects.

If a customs union is created between two countries, the following five cases involving trade creation and trade diversion can be distinguished. It is assumed that economies of scale, imperfect competition, and transportation cost do not exist. A one-commodity situation is examined.

(1) Both participating countries produce the commodity prior to the formation of the union. The union will create trade because the less efficient country will cease production and import its needs from the more efficient producer.

(2) Both countries produce the goods prior to the union, but the most efficient producer is a foreign country. Here, trade creation will result as in the above case, but the situation is not so efficient as universal free trade since, in that case, neither member country would produce the good.

(3) Only one member country produces the good, and it is a cheaper source than any foreign country. In this case, neither trade creation nor trade diversion occurs under the union.

(4) One member country produces the commodity under the protection of its tariffs, while the other member country imports it from a third country which is the least cost producer. The establishment of the customs union could shift the nonproducer's imports from the more efficient foreign producer to the less efficient member producer if the export price of the two countries differs by less than the important duty charged by the foreign producer. If the duty is less than the price differential, there will be no diversion.

(5) Neither member country produces the commodity. No change will take place after the formation of the union, as both countries will continue to import from the lowest cost foreign producer.

Tariffs and trade restrictions are impediments to efficient production and resource allocation. As such they tend to decrease international economic efficiency in the hope of benefiting the levying country by increasing its employment of resources and decreasing its dependence upon foreign states. The universal free-trade situation, the absence of all trade barriers, then, is the theoretical optimum from the standpoint of efficiency. It follows that customs unions which shift the aggregate production from higher to lower cost producers (trade creation) are beneficial because they bring the allocation system closer to the optimum while customs unions which shift aggregate production from lower to higher cost producers (trade diversion) are detrimental because the allocation system less closely approximates the universal free-trade situation. But even a trade-diverting customs union may become beneficial in the long run as its internal development is likely to change the preunion cost and efficiency factors. Thus, the reader is again cautioned against an uncritical acceptance of the simplistic models of the static theory of integration.

VII

Environmental Dynamics: Modernization of Developing Areas

Two-thirds of the world population live in countries which have yet to enter the 20th century; many have yet to reach the 19th. These underdeveloped countries are seeking industrial development but have not achieved such preconditions for it as an acquisitive psychology, technical capacity, and stable government.

36

The Economic Environment

Land, labor, capital, and management are the necessary factors for productive activity in any area. In the underdeveloped countries their characteristics, roles, and interdependencies create peculiar conditions and place different requirements on management than they do in the industrially advanced countries. As will be shown in this and the following four chapters, the availability of raw materials, manpower, capital, and executive talent is closely related to the pattern of land use and social organization. The availability of natural resources is often a function of the infrastructure, especially the transportation facilities. The size of the industrial labor force depends on the degree to which the people are tied to the land and on the degree to which agricultural production can support the urban population. Capital availability for industrial investments is correlated to capital requirements in the agricultural sector; diversion of capital to industry meets strong resistance if the food supply is insufficient. Management talent available to industry depends on ideological values, education, and even on land use patterns. As industrialization progresses, an awareness of the role of industry and management in the economy develops, and with it the whole system of values, preferences, and availabilities changes.

Employment Structure

The logical place to begin an investigation of the economic structures of a country is in an analysis of the activities which support the society or which provide the people with their livelihood. To factually demonstrate the contrasts between developing and developed countries the data for three countries of each type are juxtaposed in Figure 36-1. One pair represents large countries, one medium countries, and one small countries. They were chosen from 17 other pairs studied, any of which could have been used, as they all showed the same contrasts. The various productive activities are grouped into four structurally different economic classifications. Primary activity consists of agriculture and other extractive industries (mining, logging, fishing, oil production, etc.); secondary activity embraces manufacturing, processing, and construction industries; tertiary activity includes wholesale and retail trade, transportation, and communication industries; the service sector consists of government personnel, professional people, and miscellaneous consumer services. Whether the service group should be combined with the tertiary one or presented as a separate element is debatable. In economic literature both are often lumped under the tertiary designation.

FIGURE 36-1

Employment by Activity in Developed and Underdeveloped Countries, Percent

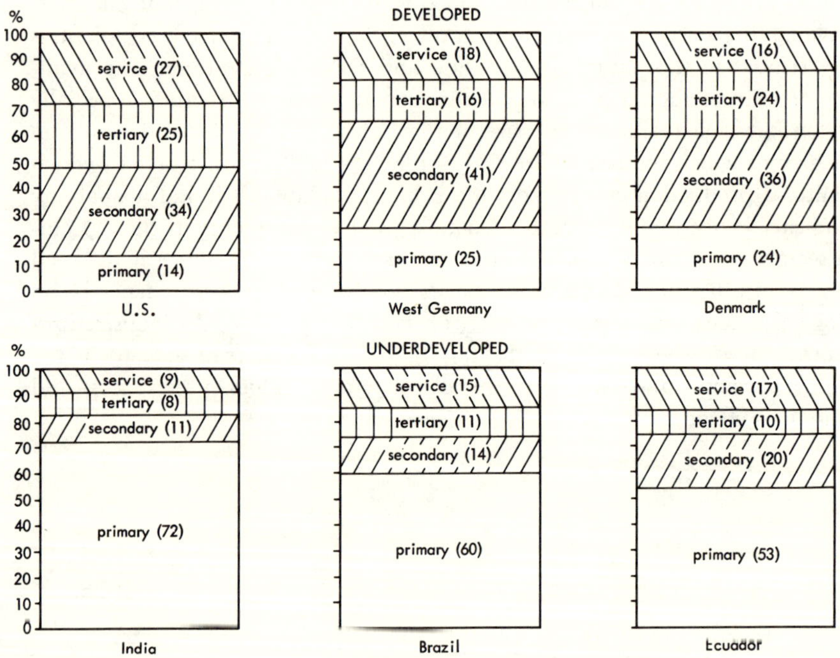

The chart forcefully reveals the structural differences in the economic environment of business in the developed and underdeveloped countries. In the former, industrial activities dominate—accounting for a third or more of total employment—followed by the trade and service group, and leaving extractive industries the smallest segment. In the underdeveloped countries everything is overshadowed by primary industries, on which over half the total population depends. Tertiary and service activities come second, with approximately 20 to 25 percent of the total, while industrial employment represents the smallest space, with 10 to 20 percent.

A statistical breakdown of the primary segment shows that agriculture accounts for eight- to nine-tenths of it in the great majority of developing countries. Consequently, the employment pattern of these countries rests firmly on land resources. To understand the foundations of the economic structure and the opportunities which it might hold for industrial and commercial enterprise, one must first understand both the inertia and the logic of land utilization. The remainder of this chapter analyzes this subject and shows its impact on different business activities.

Land Use and Natural-Resource Allocation

When dealing with land and the allocation of natural resources in underdeveloped countries, it is necessary to examine two major factors: the contribution which land makes to total national production, and the level of productivity of the land or the effectiveness with which land resources are employed.

With regard to the first factor, the data on employment in Figure 36-1 are reinforced by figures on national product. Although differing in degree, these figures (Table 36-1) reveal the same basic pattern as the employment discussed above. Namely, the proportion of gross national product which comes from agriculture and raw materials is much higher for developing countries than for developed ones; the proportion of GNP from the service sectors is comparable to that of the industrial nations; and the proportion from manufacturing is generally much lower.

Generally, during the development process, the industrial sector of a country develops first in the consumer-goods areas: food processing, textiles, and other nondurables. These industries are more labor intensive than the capital-goods industries and require less initial capital. There is also a developed market for these goods in the relatively densely populated urban areas. Also, consumer-goods industries have growth potential because import substitution can take place; thus, growth of these industries is not held back by the rate of growth of demand but can exceed it as long as there is opportunity to substitute for imports. The development of the capital-goods industries comes at a later stage when there is a high enough savings rate for sufficient

TABLE 36-1

Gross National Product by Economic Sector, 1960–64

	Percentage of Gross National Product				
Country	*Agriculture & Livestock*	*Mining & Petroleum*	*Manufac-turing*	*Con-struction*	*Service & Other*
Germany	6.2	3.1	42.2	6.7	41.8
Central America	34.1	1.1	13.4	4.5	46.8
Argentina	18.4	1.2	20.0	4.3	56.1
Brazil	28.2		25.8		app. 40.0
Chile	9.4	4.7	23.6	3.8	58.5
Colombia	32.9	3.4	18.1	3.3	42.3
Ecuador	35.8	2.4	15.9	3.7	42.2
Paraguay	36.8	nil	16.6	2.3	44.3
Burma	43.2	1.5	10.3	2.7	42.3
Thailand	37.8	nil	12.1	5.7	44.4
Indonesia	60.0	5.0			
Greece	30.0	1.2	20.0	5.8	44.0
Yugoslavia	24.8	36.7		6.5	32.0
United Arab Republic	31.2	21.3		4.0	43.5
Nigeria	58.0	1.0	5.0	7.0	29.0

Source: U.S. Dept. of Commerce, *Overseas Business Reports* (Washington, D.C.: U.S. Government Printing Office. 1960–64), for countries named.

outlays of capital and a large enough market for these heavy goods in other industries to warrant their production.

Thus, for most of the developing countries, a large proportion of the gross national product comes from agricultural and raw-materials production, and to the extent that industry exists, it is generally in the area of light consumer goods. This means that a large part of the GNP must be derived directly from the land of the country—from production of agricultural commodities and livestock, from the mining of minerals or drilling of oil, or from the processing of foodstuffs and textile fibers.

Another general characteristic of the underdeveloped countries is that they specialize in the production of one or two commodities. Such production is generally labor intensive and uses a large portion of the land in the production process. In Colombia, for example, over 30 percent of the agricultural land is used for coffee.[1] These agricultural or mineral commodities are ones in which these countries have a comparative advantage either because of low labor costs and large reserves (in the case of minerals and oil) or because a certain amount of potentially productive land is well suited to a particular crop (in the case of agricultural commodities).

The productive activities in these countries become centered around the

[1] U.S. Dept. of Commerce, "Basic Data on the Economy of Colombia," in *Overseas Business Report OBR 64–35* (Washington, D.C.: U.S. Government Printing Office, April 1964), p. 8.

single specialties to a very high degree, and the countries derive most of their export income from these few goods.[2] Diversification in exports comes only at later stages of development. For example, over 70 percent of Bolivia's exports are in tin, and over 70 percent of Colombia's exports are in coffee. Petroleum accounts for over 93 percent of Venezuela's exports and over 85 percent of Iran's exports; and cocoa beans make up over 65 percent of Ghana's exports. On the other hand, for Mexico and Argentina, which are more developed, the percentages for any single commodity are less than one-quarter of the total. Thus, for the underdeveloped countries, the land itself is the basis for the economy and its use pattern is of major importance.

Barriers to Land Use

Despite the fact that land is of such decisive importance to these countries, the majority of them utilize no more than one-quarter of their land area for agriculture, and in some cases, the percentage is very much less than this. The United States and Germany, on the other hand, utilize about half their land area for agriculture.

The reason for this low percentage of use is twofold. First, a number of *natural barriers* limit the amount of land which may be productively used. In some cases, access to the land is inhibited. In Latin America, for example, the Andes definitely limit access to the interior portions of the countries on the west coast. Also, a great amount of the northern and eastern part of South America is covered by dense forests and jungles, which defy exploration of the area. The land itself is sometimes very rich in mineral reserves and is productive, yet it cannot be reached. Such is the case with Brazil, whose interior is said to hold one of the richest reserves of iron ore in the world. And similar conditions prevail in several of the Asian and African countries as well. For many, settlement of the land does not include the interior sections, which are often the richest in natural resources.

In other cases, natural barriers to land use stem simply from the unproductive nature of the land itself. Where deserts and mountain ranges exist, it is impossible to make the land agriculturally productive. (Irrigation projects are possible, but the expense is prohibitive for a country with a very limited amount of capital.) Such is the case with the United Arab Republic. Although agriculture is the mainstay of the economy, it is limited to approximately 6 million acres in the Nile valley and the Nile delta, where the water supply is adequate. Thus, the U.A.R. can use only about $2\frac{1}{2}$ percent of its land for agriculture.

But barriers to productive land use in the underdeveloped countries are not limited to natural ones. There is a second type which involves the amount of *capital* which these countries have available for developing the land. It is impossible to use land productively if there are no roads and transportation equipment to move the labor force, equipment, and commodities to and from

[2] United Nations Statistical Office, *Yearbook of International Trade Statistics, 1962* (New York, 1963), data under countries listed.

the site of production. Furthermore, production itself cannot take place if farming and mining machinery are not available. The basic lack of capital is probably the major reason for the low percentage of land in use in the developing countries. Thus, it is typically not the lack of land, as a great amount of land remains idle, but the physical and economic access to land which currently prevents full utilization of this resource.

Land Productivity

Along with this inability to use large proportions of available land, the underdeveloped countries face problems with respect to the land that is in use, especially agricultural land. The productivity of land used for agricultural purposes is generally much lower for most commodities than it is in the developed nations. As shown in Table 36-2, crop yields in grains and cereals in Latin America, the Middle and Far East, and Africa rarely exceed half to two-thirds of what they are in North America. And in most cases they run far below one-half. For potatoes, yields range from less than one-third to just over one-half, and for cotton, from about 20 percent to about 80 percent of the yields in North America. Thus, with less land available, the underdeveloped countries make less productive use of the land which they do use.

TABLE 36-2

Crop Yields 1962-63

	Yield—100 kg Per Hectare						
Crop	*World*	*North America*	*Latin America*	*Middle East*	*Far East*	*Africa*	*Oceania*
Wheat	12.6	15.9	14.0	10.2	9.3	7.3	12.7
Rye	12.2	12.9	6.1	10.3	6.0	1.1	4.2
Barley	15.4	18.3	10.0	10.3	11.8	6.9	11.6
Oats	14.5	16.6	10.8	10.9	11.2	2.0	9.6
Maize	20.7	40.4	11.8	17.8	10.0	10.5	22.2
Millet & sorghum	7.2	27.7	13.1	10.7	4.8	—	16.6
Rice, paddy	19.9	41.7	18.4	29.6	16.9	13.4	40.0
Potatoes	107.1	209.4	61.3	111.5	96.7	65.6	156.0
Sweet potatoes & yams	73.0	97.0	70.0	185.0	102.0	—	—
Cotton	3.3	5.1	3.1	4.3	1.5	1.2	—

Source: Statistics Division, Food and Agricultural Organization of the United Nations, *Production Yearbook, Volume 17, 1963* (New York, 1963), Table 12A: "Summary of Major Crops, by Region," p. 36.

These low yields are due, in part, to the limited extent to which modern farming methods and equipment are utilized in these countries. Table 36-3 shows that nine-tenths of the tractors used in the world for agriculture are located in Europe and North America. Europe and North America also use approximately 75 percent of the nitrogenous fertilizers, over 75 percent of the

TABLE 36-3

Means of Production

Region	*Number of Tractors Used in Agriculture, 1962*	*Consumption of Commercial Nitrogenous Fertilizers, 1962–63*	*Consumption of Commerical Phosphate Fertilizers, 1962–63*	*Consumption of Commerical Potash Fertilizers, 1962–63*
			(1000 Metric Tons)	
Europe	4,070,000	4920	4830	4880
North America	5,273,000	3540	2930	2300
Latin America	423,000	370	330	210
Middle East	91,000	330	140	20
Far East	84,000	1750	780	690
Africa	209,000	170	250	100
Oceania	358,000	50	890	90

Source: Statistics Division, Food and Agricultural Organization of the United Nations, *Production Yearbook, Volume 17, 1963* (New York, 1963), Tables 100–127: "Use of Fertilizers, Tractors, and Pesticides."

phosphate fertilizers, and over 85 percent of the commercial potash fertilizers in the world. Yet these two areas contain only 18.5 percent of the total agricultural land area.

Character of holdings

The low yields are also due in part to the nature of the land holdings in the underdeveloped areas. The vast majority of the rural population of these countries owns either no land at all or only tiny holdings of a few hectares. Their family incomes are near subsistence level, which constrains their ability to modernize traditional production methods. Their practices date back for centuries, and their implements are equally antiquated. The holdings themselves are generally so small that efficient economies of scale could not be reached even with newer tools. Greece, for example, has approximately 1 million farmsteads, with an agricultural population of approximately 4½ million. Eighty-five percent of these farmsteads are under 5 hectares in size, and these tend to be subdivided through inheritance. In Yugoslavia, 90 percent of the total farm area is in private holdings, nearly all limited to 10 hectares. In Thailand, the majority of farms range from 3 to 5 hectares. For Brazil, about 45 percent of the farms are less than 10 hectares and another 15 percent range from 10 to 100 hectares. The estimates for Latin America in general are that almost three-quarters of the farms are 20 hectares or less in size.

Tenure

A number of countries, those of Latin America in particular, face another problem regarding land holdings—land tenure. Recent estimates for Latin America show that almost 65 percent of the land is controlled by only 1.5

percent of the total number of farms. And all of these are over 1000 hectares in size. In Bolivia the extent of holdings is even greater, with 6 percent of the farms, all over 1000 hectares, controlling 92 percent of the land. For Venezuela, in 1956, 1.6 percent of the farms controlled almost three-quarters of the farmland.[3]

Generally, for historical reasons, the land of these large farms is the better land of the country. Absentee ownership is a common phenomenon, and labor for the farms is supplied by the *colono* system. According to this system, cash payment is not the general form of compensation for work; rather, the worker becomes a tenant farmer on a small parcel of land and, in return for this, he must work a certain amount of time on the large estate. The tenant farmer is economically discouraged from improving the land on which he works, for he will receive insignificant benefit from any increased production; the absentee owner neither knows nor cares, for his primary interests lie elsewhere.

Implications for Business

The results of such a farming system are that there is little concern for the productivity of the farm and land use in general. This raises three important issues for business: the cost of developing industrial projects, the supply of raw materials, and the size of markets.

Industrial projects

No industry can develop in isolation from other productive sectors of the society; it must rely on a structural base which includes a supply of raw materials and capital goods as well as energy sources and transportation facilities. If these do not exist, the enterprise must develop them itself or withdraw from the venture.

To a certain extent, the structural base can be supplied through the importation of capital, but this source is limited by the ability of these countries to export and secure foreign aid. And typically this ability is far short of what is needed for a fully developed industrial sector since the developing countries rely heavily on the exportation of agricultural goods and mineral products for capital imports. These exports are produced either at low levels, in the case of agricultural goods, or, in the case of minerals, at levels far below potential because insufficient capital within the country makes it impossible to fully exploit high-quality reserves. And, in many cases, the mineral reserves of a country have been partially ignored because of the concentration on one or two major agricultural crops.

Diversification is possible only to the extent that such concentration can be relaxed, or, in other words, to the extent that import capacity can be obtained through some means other than the production of one or two goods.

[3] Albert O. Hirschman, ed., *Latin American Issues* (New York: Twentieth Century Fund, 1961), pp. 165, 177, 187. U.S. Dept. of Commerce, *Overseas Business Report, OBR 61 75,* "Basic Data on the Economy of Brazil" (Washington, D.C.: U.S. Government Printing Office, June 1964), p. 8.

Raw materials

Because the patterns of land use for the underdeveloped countries are characterized by low-yield production and low-level exploitation of the variety of resources, there is neither a well developed domestic source of supply for raw materials nor a high capacity to import raw materials or capital. Furthermore, even at low levels, the import capacity is unreliable, as it fluctuates with the prices on the world market, which for agricultural and primary goods vary widely and almost without pattern from year to year. It must also be remembered that most of the industry in these countries is of the light, consumer-goods type and not of the capital-goods variety. Such industries can supply neither capital equipment nor a variety of basically processed goods for an industrial enterprise. Thus, the costs of developing an industry in these countries may involve not only the cost of setting up production facilities but also the cost of overcoming the present pattern of natural-resource allocation and use. This pattern is such that only the few primary commodities receive the greatest attention.

Markets

The third major issue for business is the need for a market for the goods once they are produced. The pattern of land use in the underdeveloped countries limits the domestic market for manufactured goods in two ways. As stated above, agricultural production in these countries is based upon labor rather than capital-intensive production methods. The land is often tilled as it has been for centuries, without much use of machinery and other industrial devices, such as soil additives, for increasing productivity. Thus the demand for heavy machinery for agriculture as well as for capital goods of all types is low. A significant demand for capital goods cannot develop before a country can supply its fundamental requirements for foodstuffs and textiles from indigenous sources and can utilize savings and exports for capital investments.

Up to the point of self-sufficiency, the lighter consumer industries can grow faster than demand because of the opportunity for import substitution. Investment needs in these industries are lower than those for capital-goods industries, and, with the general shortage of capital in these countries, it is in this sector that most investment takes place. Therefore, with regard to industry, the patterns of land use in the underdeveloped countries have affected both the supply and the demand considerations of industrial enterprises, limiting the supply of raw materials and capital equipment and limiting the markets for heavy goods once they have been produced.

Effect of Land Use on Labor Force

An urban, industrial population can exist only to the extent that the agricultural population can produce food beyond its own needs. What import capacity exists in the developing countries goes mostly for manufactured imports and not for food. With farms of small size employing traditional, outdated agricultural methods, the question of food supply for the cities becomes a critical one. And it becomes even more critical when one examines the high proportion of the population in the agricultural sector in most of these countries—from 50 to 80 percent. These people operate farm enterprises with a high degree of "disguised unemployment," that is, with a number of people living on the farms who do not add to the productivity of the farm's operation. Thus, much of whatever output there is is consumed right on the farms and some of it is consumed by individuals whose contribution to production is negligible. Whatever is left over serves as the food supply for the urban population.

Further complications arise when one also accounts for the generally high rates of population growth in the underdeveloped countries. As most of the population lives in the agricultural sector, the absolute increases in this sector will be greater, making it more and more difficult to supply the urban population with food.

The mobility of the labor force is also related to land-use patterns. As the land has not been used productively for agriculture, the levels of per capita income for agriculture have always been very low absolutely and considerably lower relative to industrial per capita incomes. The people have, to a considerable degree, been tied to the land for their livelihood. And the nature of the farm holding has further tightened this tie. Most of the farms are run by families, with little desire on the part of the members to break kinship ties and move away from the farmstead. But, as the developing countries progress, several significant pressures increase rural-to-urban labor migrations. Rural population pressure becomes a "push" factor. The higher salaries and the excitement of urban life contribute a "pull" factor to the migration. Agriculture can keep a farmer, but it offers no inducement to his educated children.

Effect of Land Use on Financial Resources

Land-use patterns in the underdeveloped countries determine the patterns of investment and the distribution of public and private funds to the various sectors of the economy. Nearly all underdeveloped countries have national development programs which establish priorities and channel funds received from government revenues and grants of aid to certain projects in different economic sectors. These programs often recognize that the needs of the country involve outlays of capital funds in all sectors of the economy. The division of these limited funds is based in part on the need to make available land more productive and inaccessible land available for productive use. In Ghana, for example, the government has been following an extensive plan to apply modern technology and methods to agriculture. (Almost 70 percent of the export income of Ghana comes from agricultural goods.) The Mexican government has channeled part of its investment into irrigation and reclamation projects in the north and, at the same time, has emphasized diversification in agricultural production and exports. Programs for developing railways and roads have been designed to increase accessibility to the more remote areas and to aid in the exploitation of resources in many of these nations.

The amount of funds needed for such development programs often depends on land-use patterns. Where certain agricultural and mining methods have been used for generations, it is difficult to introduce modern techniques. And where one or two crops traditionally provide the mainstay of employment and income, it is necessary to overcome prejudices against different crops before they can actually be produced. Much delay, effort, and waste can occur before new crops and new methods are understood and established.

Because of the restrictions, land-reform projects are generally expensive. It is necessary to establish a reform program acceptable enough to receive support from the population as a whole. In the administration of the project, funds must be used to pay original landowners for their land and to pay civil servants for their work as the plan is being carried out. In Latin America, the payment for the land is usually divided (in varying proportions) between cash and government bonds. But these bonds often mature before the new owners can pay the government for their holdings. The governments must fill the gap with funds from other sources. Also, there is often an initial drop in output after a land-reform program has been introduced, and several years are required before the previous productivity level is reached. Land reform, like any social reform, unbalances the economy for a period of time, and there is no way of compensating for it before the new methods have become effectively adopted.

Absolute poverty

The common denominator for the otherwise diverse peoples of the developing nations is a low per capita income which severely restricts an individual's ability to satisfy his material needs. Often the situation for the large masses of population is further aggravated by a lopsided income distribution which allows a small minority of the rich to claim a large share of the national product. But even if a more equitable distribution were achieved much of the population of the so-called third world still have little chance to rise above the physical subsistence level, that is, to have the means for food, clothing, and housing in sufficient quantities to meet man's minimum biological needs. These people are poor in the absolute sense. Poverty here does not mean being worse off than someone else or being unable to follow one's own pursuit of happiness—doing his own thing—but rather being able to sustain life, to exist at all.

In the slums of the industrial countries poverty ordinarily means something quite different; there, poverty is more a matter of difference between aspiration and achievement than of living on the margin of biological subsistence—it is a relative poverty. Some people have less than others, but since their wishes and desires—shaped by the standards of their more affluent compatriots—are not similarly constructed, there is a gap between what they can afford and what they and many others perceive as necessary for humanly acceptable standards of life. The poverty line in the United States, for example, has been defined roughly as about $3700 per year for a family of four. Contrasted with the $100 per capita annual income in the poorer developing countries this looks mighty plush. Contrary to his own perception, an American poor would be regarded as rich in much of Africa, Asia, and Latin America. This is not to say that the problem of poverty in the United States does not exist. It is, however, a problem of quite different character from the poverty experienced in the developing countries.

The destitution of the homeless millions in India, the tribesmen of Africa, or the peasant populations in almost any underdeveloped country has no equivalent in the industrial world. For absolute poverty there is an unmistakable, absolute, solution: higher real income.[4]

Why the developing countries have never been able to rise above the absolute poverty level, not to mention reaching the threshhold of prosperity, is graphically explained by the vicious circle of poverty. As elaborated by the late Professor Ragnar Nurkse, the self-perpetuating system of economic causation can be depicted in the following diagram in which the arrows show the cause-effect relationship:

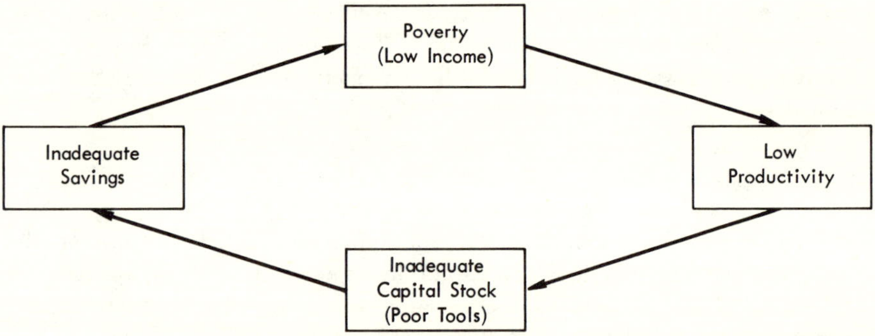

To improve their lot, these people must somehow break this circle. That they realize this and have come to regard it not only as an economic imperative but as a political and ideological maxim is a fact that no government, old or new, autocratic or democratic, can any longer ignore. Indeed, the tide of political awakening that in the last generation has swept away what seemed invincible colonial empires (British, French, Dutch, Belgian, etc.) gained much of its immense force from the rising expectations that greater contact with the outside world has brought to those peoples.

THE URGE TO INDUSTRIALIZE. The same contact has helped to point also to what the underdeveloped world has now accepted as the only answer to this problem—industrial development. The faith in industrialization is so

4 The advanced country poverty problem probably has no solution short of an equalization of income distribution, for the reason that the richer these countries get and the richer their peers get, the more the levels of aspiration of the low-income people increase; hence, the perception of poverty may even increase.

deep-rooted and profound that it is often looked upon not only as the basic economic objective but also as a political ideology; in some places it has become a fanatic devotion.

The urge to industrialize, to grow in economic strength and political stature, is the force which unites the underdeveloped world and propels it to mobilize its energies on a global scale as happened recently at the World Trade and Development Conferences and similar joint efforts. One need not become a prophet to predict that these have been but the first global manifestation of the potential power which the brotherhood-in-poverty and unity in goals and aspirations are placing in the hands of the underdeveloped countries, despite their differences in many other respects.

The fact that the governments of the underdeveloped countries are irrevocably committed to industrialization at all costs does not mean that they possess the capacity to bring it about or that they go about it intelligently. But they are not standing still; they are not only hoping, but acting. Discontent to wait until what, in the West, is considered "normal economic progress" runs its course, they are determined to force the pace and to shorten this process. This, they believe, can be accomplished by artificial insemination and spawning of industrial development on a crash program basis by government initiative and action. Inspirations for such beliefs come in great measure from the Soviet Union, partly as example and, more importantly, as propaganda expounding the slogan of rapid results by communist methods.

Income Structure

Nearly all available measures of income, either national or personal, for the developing nations are based upon United Nations statistics, which are derived from questionnaires filled out by the different governments. When one contemplates the difficulties encountered by professional economists and income accountants in defining and measuring national products of the United States or Canada, it becomes apparent that the income data for developing areas can be only rough approximations.

Table 36-4 shows all the countries broken down by continent and by gross national product per capita; the continental divisions are arranged horizontally, the GNP classes, vertically. Most of the countries in class I ($0–$99) are African and Asian, with Bolivia, Falkland, and Oceania except Australia and New Zealand constituting the small remainder. The alarmingly high figure of 49.7 percent of the world's population lies in this first class. The second class ($100–$299) includes most of the rest of Asia and the Middle East, Africa, and roughly two-thirds of the population of Latin America—in all 17.1 percent of the world population. The third class ($300–$599), with 18 percent of the world population, includes the Republic of South Africa, the U.S.S.R., the more backward European countries, and the more developed countries of Asia, the Middle East, and Latin America. The fourth class

TABLE 36-4

Per Capita GNP, World Totals by Region

	I *$0–$99*	*II* *$100–$299*	*III* *$300–$599*	*IV* *$600–$1199*	*V* *$1200+*
	Africa	Africa	Africa	Africa	Africa
	Angola Cameroun Cen. African Republic Chad Congo Dahomey Gabon Kenya Liberia Libya Malagasy Republic Mali Mozambique Niger Nigeria Sierra Leone Somalia Sudan Tanganyika Republic of Togo Uganda Upper Volta	Algeria Ghana Mauritania Morocco Federation of Rhodesia & Nyasaland Tunisia	Republic of S. Africa	—	—
Pop. (000,000) :	153	40	18	—	—
GNP/capita :	$75	$155	$397	—	—
	Asia & Middle East	Asia & Middle East	Asia & M.E.	Asia & M.E.	Asia & M.E.
	Afghanistan Bhutan Brunei Burma China India Mongolia Muscat & Omen Nepal Pakistan Sarawak Thailand S. Vietnam Yemen	Aden Bahrein Ceylon Hong Kong Indonesia Iran Iraq Jordan Macao Philippines S. Korea Taiwan Turkey U.A.R. (Egypt)	Cyprus Japan Lebanon Malaya Singapore	Israel	Kuwait Qatar

TABLE 36-4 (Cont.)

Pop. (000,000): GNP/capita:	226 $72	241 $155	101 $313	6.7 $1066	.25 $2722
	Oceania New Hebrides Territory of New Guinea Samoa	Oceania —	Oceania —	Oceania —	Oceania Australia N. Zealand
Pop. (000,000): GNP/capita:	2.8 $45				12.9 $1315
	America Bolivia Falkland Greenland	America Brazil, Br. Guiana, Colombia, Dom. Republic, Ecuador, El Salvador, Fr. Guiana, Guatemala, Haiti, Honduras, Martinique, Mexico, Nicaragua, Paraguay, Peru, Surinam, Virgin Is., W. Indies	America Argentina Canal Zone Chile Costa Rica Cuba Panama Puerto Rico Uruguay	America Venezuela	America U.S. Canada
Pop. (000,000): GNP/capita:	3.3 $99	138 $257	43.5 $447	6.7 $1066	198 $2521
World totals Pop., per cent: GNP/capita:	 49.7 $73	 17.1 $198	 18 $489	 7.5 $971	 7.7 2387

($600–$1,199), containing 6.7 percent of the world population, consists almost entirely of the more advanced Western European countries, with only Venezuela and Israel from the rest of the world. The fifth class ($1200+) is composed of the United States and Canada; Australia and New Zealand; Luxembourg, Sweden, and Switzerland; and Kuwait and Qatar, two Middle East sheikdoms whose economies depend almost entirely upon the exporting of oil and thus they can scarcely be considered developed. This last class amounts to only 7.7 percent of the world population.

Although the low average per capita GNP of underdeveloped areas is common knowledge, the sheer population bulk and the number of countries which lie within the first three classes are striking. If consistent data were available on disposable income and were substituted here for GNP, one would observe a considerable shift downward from classes II and III. It is estimated that disposable income as a percentage of gross domestic product varies between 60 percent and 82 percent in underdeveloped countries with an arithmetic mean of approximately 75 percent.[5]

Many authorities suggest that because of inequitable taxation and inequitable distribution of land and capital, the distribution of income in the developing countries, where large groups of the population have no reserves, is far more unequal than in the advanced countries. Also, it is expected that after the primary distribution of income is made to the factors of production, there is a considerable percentage redistribution toward the holders of land, liquid assets, and reproducible capital in the developing countries—a significantly larger shift than occurs in the developed countries.[6]

An analysis of family income data shows that two-thirds of the families belonging to the poorest categories receive barely a third of total available income. In the upper group, the top 20 percent of families receive between 50 and 60 percent of total income. To emphasize the inequality of income distribution, 5 percent of the wealthiest families take between 22 and 40 percent of total income. These are averages for the developing countries as a group. There is some disparity between countries but not much.

A comment needs to be added pertaining to the middle income groups. If we leave out the first and fifth quintiles, we find that the middle three quintiles accrue less than half of total income—varying from 36 to 45 percent.

Several important implications can be made from this smallness of intermediate income classes.

First, the wider inequality in income structure is associated with a much lower average income per capita. This leads to a far more serious impact on material and psychological misery than in the more advanced countries. Also, positive savings are possible only at much higher relative income levels. Thus, the concentration of savings is even more restricted to the top of the income pyramid. Some savings may be possible in the fourth quintile in advanced

[5] Simon Kuznets, "Quantitative Aspects of the Economic Growth of Nations; I.V. Distribution of National Income by Factor Shares," *Economic Development and Cultural Change,* VII (April 1959), 95–96.

[6] Kuznets, "Quantitative Aspects of the Economic Growth of Nations," p. 6.

countries while only the top 3 to 5 percent can save in developing countries.

Second, the unequal income structure stabilized with the low rate of growth of income per capita. The countries of Latin America, Africa, and Asia have had growth rates far lower than in the developed countries during their earlier phases of growth. The lack of much hope for a significantly perceptible rise in the level of real income has permeated the economic climate of the developing countries and reduced hope of any near term shifts in industrial structure.

Third, it is quite possible that income inequality has not narrowed in the developing countries within recent years. The cumulative effect of a concentration of past savings that formed the pattern of older developing countries does not seem to be repeating itself in the younger developing countries. Factors such as dramatic increases in birth rates in conjunction with declining death rates threaten to widen the income inequality. It is at this point that political factors often have the upper hand. The stresses set up by extreme income pressures may lead to political and social reforms and sometimes to war.

There is a danger in attempting to predict the future progress of the underdeveloped countries based on the analogy that the unequal income distributions in Western Europe that led to accumulated savings and basic capital formation can be repeated in the presently developing countries. Different tax structures, inadequate governmental agencies, and differing philosophies regarding reinvestment of profits back into the economic system may mean that the government is unable to serve as the basic agent in capital formation and economic growth.

What is needed is a much better knowledge of the trends of income distribution and the factors that determine the structure. This structuring of economic dynamics must be generated over a considerable time span. Any compression of the observation time leads to overgeneralizations, extrapolations of trends, and lack of regard for the economic and social structure of technological changes.

Technical Distortions in International Income Comparisons

Even assuming consistent national-income accounting methods and definitions, several factors make statistical comparisons between the developing and the developed countries less meaningful than those between two developed countries.

Exchange-rate disparity

The use of foreign exchange rates for converting local currencies into U.S. dollars understates the true income of a low-income country. The purpose of comparing incomes is to see the relative amounts of goods and services which different countries produce or consume or both per year. Goods and services produced within a low-income country are typical cheaper, relative to the same goods and services produced in the United States, than those which enter foreign trade. Thus production for consumption within the economy tends to be undervalued in terms of U.S. dollars or for that matter in terms of any other industrial country's currency. This distortion is greater for countries in the lowest income groups and gets progressively smaller as one approaches the economic level of the country whose currency is used as a yardstick. The distortion occurs because most inputs which make up the final value of the national product cost less in an underdeveloped country than in an industrial country. An accurate comparison, therefore, would require that the prices in the developing country be marked up to the U.S. level and the quantities of goods and services which make up its GNP be multiplied by these new prices. This process would produce a much higher GNP value, which is a more accurate indicator of the real GNP than the unadjusted value, that is, the GNP computed at indigenous prices. Needless to add, this method presents quite insurmountable problems for most users of international income figures. As a substitute for it, some economists have suggested that the exchange-rate disparities be compensated for by multiplying the GNP figures for underdeveloped countries by the following correction coefficients:

Countries	*Coefficient*
Class I (under $100)	3.0
Class II ($100–$299)	2.5
Class III ($300–$599)	2.0
Class IV ($600–$1199)	1.5
Class V (over $1200)	no correction

Although only a rough conversion, this method is believed to give a more accurate measure of real income than unadjusted data. Table 36-5 shows the differences which such corrections produce in the basic income structure of the world. Instead of 49.7 percent of the world population with a per capita GNP of under $100 per year, the figure drops to 0.4 percent, although those

TABLE 36-5

World Income Distribution—1960

	Money GNP		*"Real" GNP*	
Countries with GNP Per Capita	*Percent of World Population*	*Percent of GNP*	*Percent of World Population*	*Percent of GNP*
I (under $100)	49.7	16	0.4	0.1
II ($100–$299)	17.1	13	60	16
III ($300–$599)	18	26	9	6
IV ($600–$1199)	7.5	17	15	22
V ($1200+)	7.7	28	16	55

Source: Everett Hagen, "Some Facts about Income Levels and Economic Growth," *Review of Economics and Statistics,* XLII, No. 1 (February 1960); and P. N. Rosenstein-Rodan, "International Aid for Underdeveloped Countries," *Review of Economics and Statistics,* XLIII, No. 2 (May 1961).

in class II rise from 17.1 percent to 60 percent. Correspondingly, those in class V rise from 7.7 percent to 16 percent of the total world population. Thus income distribution is not so radically skewed as actual dollar data lead one to believe.

Nonmarket income

Another factor which leads to the understatement of national income in developing countries is the prevalence of barter. National-income accounting as now practiced is limited to monetary activities valued at market prices. In the developing areas, vast amounts of informal, noninstitutionalized trading take place for which no records are kept and which, therefore, remains unaccounted for in national income and produce accounts. Particularly in rural but also in urban areas all members of the family take part in some type of trade or barter activity. Much of barter takes place in either used merchandise or agricultural commodities. Statisticians tend to concentrate upon the activities of heads of households, ignoring the activities of the rest of the family. But because of the lack of occupational specialization, much more of this labor-intensive activity takes place than official data reflect—activity which substantially contributes to the material well-being of those living in those countries.

Another labor-intensive activity of importance in a backward economy is breaking of bulk. This distribution activity amounts to selling or trading extremely small (by American standards) quantities of merchandise from a standard size; units of ten matches from a box and teacups of salt from a 2-kilo bag are examples. The function of these part-time distribution intermediaries is undeniably important in their context, but again the difficulties of measurement are obvious. As official statistics of tertiary activity rise, the actual figure (in terms of both labor and sales volume) falls since activities like those above are taken over by more efficient middlemen.[7] Although many countries, for example Brazil and India, attempt to estimate the amount of agricultural commodities consumed by growers, these figures are invariably understatements or very conservative estimates.

The Duopolistic Problem

The economies of many developing countries are typically *dual economies*; that is, they have backward sectors in partial contact with far more advanced sectors. The concept of a dual economy may serve as a useful frame of reference, for it accounts for the heterogeneous nature of the developing nations.

[7] Peter T. Baver and B. S. Yamey, "Problems of Classifying Economic Activity in Underdeveloped Areas," in *Underdeveloped Areas—A Book of Readings and Research,* ed. Lyle W. Shannon (New York: Harper & Row, Publishers, Inc., 1957), p. 140.

The two sectors of a typical underdeveloped country have been called the *contact-points* and the *hinterland*. The contact-points are the commercial centers, ports, and other areas where there has been extended exposure to Western influence, where a substantial number of foreigners reside as government or business representatives, and where an economic mentality distinctly orientated toward Western practice has arisen. The agricultural sector, the hinterland, has been isolated from modern influences. The result is a surprisingly well-defined dichotomy. The cleavage concerns more than cultural differences—although these are great. Economic organization, technology, and financing are also greatly affected.

The historical origins of duopoly need some explanation. It is a result of colonial rule and the economic imperialism of the colonial powers. Most colonialists sought to maximize their company's profits. The most advantageous manner to do it was by exploiting the cheap labor and exporting the raw materials needed by their home countries. Local entrepreneurship was not fostered, and railways were constructed in order to gain easier access to the raw materials usually located in the rural areas.

During the "imperialistic" period most of the underdeveloped nations showed rising overall GNP figures. However, most of the gains went to elements at the contact-point. "The export sector became an island of development, but the rest of the economy made little advance, and the export sector remained surrounded by subsistence conditions and inferior methods of production."[8]

One might have expected an increase of exports to induce further investments, and through the multiplier-accelerator principle the entire economy might have developed. This did not occur, and some answers to why it did not are provided by Meier and Baldwin:[9]

(1) The returns of the export trade usually went to the foreign enclave. These people used the export earnings not for diversified investment but to satisfy their need for imported "nonproductive" goods or else to invest in the narrow export sector. Much of their capital was returned to their home country.

(2) The prices paid to indigenous labor were the result of a market which was perfectly competitive on the supply side but monopolistic on the demand side—that is, on the side of the foreigners. Therefore, it was possible to keep wages at a subsistence level. As consumers, the indigenous populations faced the same foreigners, who now took the role of oligopolists; the price of imports was high, and it was difficult for the indigenous population to finance a development program.

8 G. M. Meier and R. E. Baldwin, *Economic Development* (New York: John Wiley & Sons, Inc., 1957), p. 326.

9 The discussion here follows closely the analysis of Meier and Baldwin, *Economic Development,* pp. 328–32.

37

Population and Human-Resource Problems

World population has quite suddenly entered a period of vast expansion. After relative stability and a slow but steady increase during antiquity and the Middle Ages, it reached a turning point soon after the start of the Industrial Revolution. From an estimated 750 million in 1775 the number of people has risen to more than 3 billion. As prophesied by Thomas Malthus soon after the upturn, the progression has been more geometric than arithmetic. A second upturn was registered during World War II. And it now appears that by the year 2000 world population will range between 6 billion and 7 billion; thus, within the next generation, the growth will exceed that of all history to date.

The population explosion, as this sudden expansion has been aptly named, is centered on the underdeveloped parts of the world. Table 37-1 gives projections prepared by the U.N. Secretariat by geographic area. Using the median estimate as the base, the population of the underdeveloped countries, including communist China, will exceed 5 billion and that of the developed countries, including the U.S.S.R. and its European satellites, will be less than 1.3 billion by the year 2000, giving a percentage distribution of 80 to 20. As Figure 37-1 shows, the numerical disparity will become greater as the curve for the underdeveloped countries continues to bend at a sharper angle than that for the industrial world.

The statistical determinants of population growth are *birth* and *death rates,* which show the number of births and deaths per thousand. One represents the inflow and the other the outflow. As long as they remain constant

TABLE 37-1

World Population Distribution, Millions

	1965	*Forecasts for the Year 2000*		
Continent	*Population*	*High*	*Medium*	*Low*
Africa	310	864	768	384
North America	292	376	312	294
Latin America	165	686	592	532
Asia*	1825	3779	3458	3103
Europe*	444	563	527	491
Oceania	18	35	32	28
U.S.S.R.	231	402	353	316
World	3285	6994	6130	5449

* Exclusive of U.S.S.R.
Source: United Nations, *Population Studies.*

FIGURE 37-1

Population Trends in Developed and Developing Countries

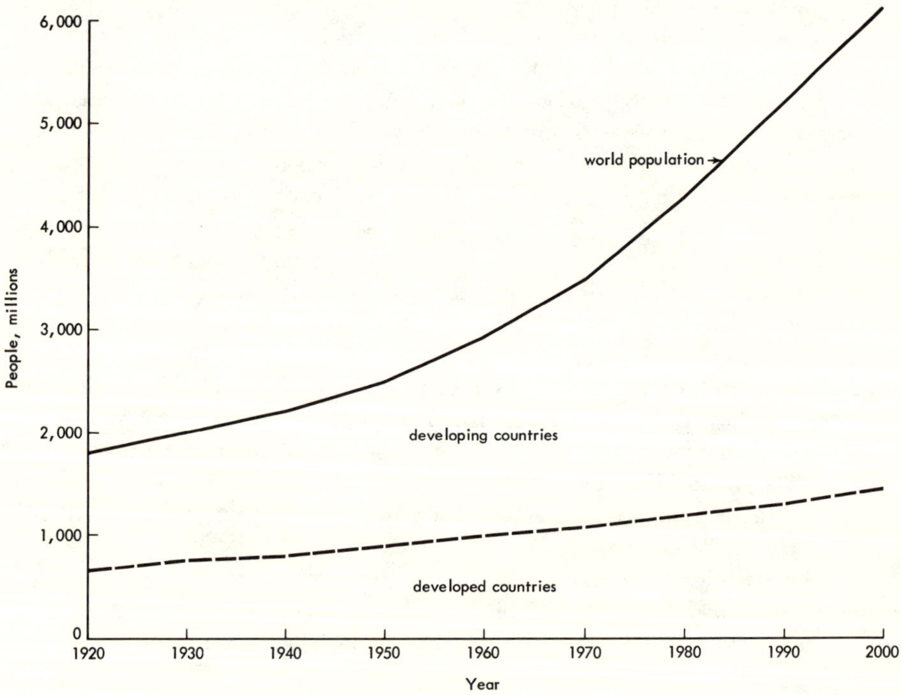

TABLE 37-2

Population Growth Rates (Exclusive of Immigration)

Continent and Country	*Birth Rate*	*Death Rate*	*Growth Rate*
Africa			
Ghana	52.4	20.9	31.5
Morocco	31.1	12.0	19.1
Egypt	42.4	17.8	24.6
Zanzibar	17.3	6.7	10.6
North America			
Canada	27.9	8.1	19.8
Costa Rica	38.7	9.0	29.7
Guatemala	49.2	17.2	32.0
United States	24.1	9.4	14.7
Puerto Rico	31.6	6.8	24.8
South America			
Brazil	43.0	20.6	22.4
Chile	35.5	12.1	23.4
Colombia	43.8	12.6	31.2
Peru	31.2	6.3	24.9
Asia			
Burma	36.0	21.4	14.6
Ceylon	35.5	9.7	25.8
Republic of China	41.2	7.2	34.0
Japan	18.0	7.5	10.5
Philippines	20.2	7.7	12.5
Ryukyus	26.0	4.4	21.6
Thailand	37.4	9.8	27.6
South Viet Nam	33.9	7.1	26.8
Europe			
France	18.3	11.2	7.1
W. Germany	17.6	10.8	6.8
Greece	19.3	7.3	12.0
United Kingdom	16.5	11.6	4.9
Oceania			
Australia	22.6	8.9	13.7
New Zealand	26.7	8.9	18.8
Fiji	40.3	7.0	33.3
American Samoa	37.5	6.8	30.7

Source: *Statistical Papers Series A,* XII, No. 3 (New York: Department of Economic and Social Affairs United Nations, 1960), Table VII.

or move parallel, the population remains stable. But, when the birth rate increases or the death rate decreases relative to the other, population will grow. Table 37-2 presents a breakdown of the relevant rates for 29 countries for which reliable statistics are available.

The high growth rate of the underdeveloped areas has resulted primarily from a radical reduction of the death rate while the birth rate has either remained constant or even increased. Why do these divergent tendencies exist?

Death Rate

The death rate has decreased suddenly in the underdeveloped world because of modern methods and means of controlling epidemics, famines, and wars. Smallpox, plague, and malaria alone used to kill countless millions in the primitive societies, where hygienic standards and physical resistance were low. Medical advances and international campaigns to stamp out epidemics have vastly changed the situation in recent years. The political unification of territories and international policies for peace have greatly reduced local wars and intertribal vendettas, which in the past were a constant source of genocidal annihilation of peoples.

Birth Rate

The birth rate does not adjust to the lower mortality rate primarily because of social and religious attitudes. For the uneducated masses large families not only symbolize virility, strength, and social importance but also provide a system of collective economic security: the larger the family, the better one's chances in illness, misfortune, and old age.

Many specific factors combine to perpetuate the high birth rate. First, people marry young, increasing the society's fertility. Late marriage can rarely be made popular in underdeveloped societies. In Communist China, a birth-control campaign was directed against early marriage on the grounds of immaturity, unhappiness, and the need for study and work.[1] That this argument was ineffective can be seen by the collapse of the plan a few years after it was launched. The argument now has shifted to the health of young wives, the proper care of children, and the rest and relaxation of young husbands.[2] In nontotalitarian countries such efforts are even more difficult and have met with no recognizable success to date.

Second, the status of women discourages family limitation. The traditional role of the female as child bearer and caretaker of offspring encourages a high birth rate. The woman confined to a domestic position is obligated to fulfill her function as a mother. This particular obstacle to family planning may be diminishing as developing countries grant increased freedom to women.

Third, children are needed in agrarian societies for two reasons: (a) Children are productive agents. At some point they enter the labor force and contribute to family income. This is of special significance in intensive agriculture, where the number of children working may determine the productivity of a family's plot of land. (b) Children are potential sources of security in the parents' old age. This factor will be less important as institutions other than the family (possibly the village or the state) provide more extensively for the aged.

Fourth, in developing countries the extended family system predominates.

1 "Family Planning in China," *The Economist*, Aug. 25, 1962, p. 705.
2 "Family Planning in China," p. 705.

The presence of multiple generations in a household permits early marriage and makes it possible for adolescents to undertake the role of parents while they are still socially immature since the main responsibility in the household will not rest on them. As a result, two methods of birth control, postponement of marriage and nonmarriage, are unlikely to develop in such family-oriented societies.

Fifth, religion tends to reinforce high birth rates. Dogmas associating childbirth with Divine Providence and glorifying children and the poor frustrate efforts for birth control and undermine the logic of family planning. Peasant inertia, apathy, and reluctance to change have similar effects.

Sixth, the problem of communication remains to be solved. There is ignorance about the purpose of birth control, the means to effect it, and its consequences to the individual, the children, and the family as a whole. Illiteracy handicaps information programs. In addition, people are often not aware of lowered death rates and the consequent diminished need for children for a relatively long time. As a result, the population pressures in developing countries not only are certain to continue but also in all likelihood will be aggravated in the future. National policies, both economic and social, will by necessity be focused on these pressures.

Population Policy

All surviving societies have had institutions for marriage, procreation, and child care which were powerful enough to keep the birth rate in excess of a high death rate. The growth of population has been viewed as the source of prosperity and power. Only the contemporary crisis has compelled reconsideration of these deeply ingrained values. Their popular acceptance, however, has hardly been affected. Despite the decline of death rates for more than a century, the incentives for high birth rate have continued largely unchanged, except the industrial countries whose children have become less productive and more expensive. In the agrarian countries fertility has remained high though the need for many children no longer is evident.

If excessive population is to be prevented some restraint must be imposed upon the freedom to have children. This would inevitably involve external regulations of family life. Here logic and reason crash against society's long-held reward-and-punishment systems, values, and sentiments. Rightists and leftists alike abhor any notion of demoting familial autonomy. And no legislation directly regulating family life can reasonably be expected in any foreseeable future. However, much could be accomplished by indirect means if a population policy with clear and unambiguous objectives were formulated.

A relatively simple way to reduce fertility would be to discontinue economic subsidization of large families at the expense of childless couples and single persons. Governments could eliminate tax allowances for children, equalize tax rates for single and married people, eliminate scholarships and housing allowances for married students, provide free abortion clinics, distribute contraceptives freely, reduce paid maternity leaves for women, allocate public housing on criteria other than family size, raise fees for marriage licenses, and reverse other traditional policies which encourage childbearing.

Additional measures, going beyond mere neutralization of the existing economic advantages of large families would be: governmentally rewarded sterilization programs, child taxes, and educational programs showing that unrestrained procreation is harmful for both the family and society.

Family planning as now advocated cannot meet this challenge. First, the oft-repeated aim of the family planning movement is to enable the couples to have the number of children they desire. The size of the family and spacing of children are considered basic human rights with which no outsider should interfere.

Thus family planning and national population policy are two very different subjects. The family planning by each separate couple aims to satisfy their specific wishes; it cannot meet any given national population objective any more than an individual's personal plan would achieve a desired level of the national income.

Second, the family planners have seen the problem from a narrow perspective. Namely, they see the main problem as the acceptance of contraceptive devices, or the discovery of a device which would be readily accepted. The basic question that a citizen may not wish to use any contraceptives is left aside. No compulsion is contemplated, only voluntary participation. This makes family planning politically acceptable and, at the same time, ineffective for population control. Without basic socioeconomic changes, painful as they may be, population control on a national level seems unattainable. To have population control, the focal point of policy must be shifted from the family to the society: the state, the nation, and ultimately the world. And as in other societal spheres from highway traffic to monopolistic collusion, regulation requires legal sanctions to be effective.

A population policy must cover not only childbirth but also migrations, age and sex compositions, geographic distribution, familial status, and socioeconomic implications of a target population size. Thus, coordinated regulation of all these areas is needed. Such regulation can come to pass only if the political leaderships cease evading the real issues and start exerting governmental authority in this critical field. To do so, it would have to come to grips with cultural taboos, religious dogma, family-centered sociology (promotion and glorification of family life and activities over nonfamily activities), the status of women, and the welfare economics which subsidizes large families. So far the politicians in no country have proven even remotely adequate for the task.

Return to Natural Calamity Theory

The lack of progress in population policy has disillusioned the scientific community to the point where social and political processes are written off as ineffectual and the grim prospect of natural calamities as an inevitable outcome is predicted. This view is eloquently expressed by Dr. Ray, the head of the Pacific Science Center in a recent interview:

"The world's most important problem, its greatest potential for destruction? Runaway population increase. Our own sense of security is false, because we think that the increase-rate of population is falling, or can be brought under control. It is, in the United States and Western Europe, but not in other parts of the world. If we continue on the course of the last 2000 years, that is, to allow human reproduction to be a matter of individual choice or happenstance, in 100 years—a mere blink of the eye in biologic history—mankind is doomed.

"Unless we change drastically, in 100 years Earth's population of about four billion will have increased to 25 billion. And I don't believe we are going to be able to find a rational agreeable way to do anything about it. I believe that some natural force will step in, epidemic or disaster, to reduce the human population on this planet.

"We're the only animal that has the opportunity to learn from experience. It will be a shame if we are unable to outwit this inevitability. For world population, I don't see a solution, but I hope that some society survives. But how could we have an oasis of tolerable living conditions and adequate food in a teeming world? There's no placid acceptance of starvation on total scale. Those that have not destroy those who have.

"The only answer for this nation is cessation of its efforts to support the rest of the world. Let nature take its course. Worst of all is the rushing in to save starving populations whose unfortunate lot it has been to suffer such irreparable brain damage from severe malnutrition that its children never can be normal. No matter how desperately appealing are the pictures of pitiful pot-bellied Biafran children, the unkindest thing we can do is to strive to maintain life when the mind has been severely affected.

"Humane? I'm not sure that it is humane to condemn a child to dreadful suffering to ten years of age when without our interference his life might have terminated in infancy. The misguided sympathy and desire to save those poor people—for what: There can be no happiness in their lives, there is not the slightest possibility of it. And worst of all is the burden upon a healthy population to support them in miserable half-life. We just can't do it.

"The Declaration of Independence to the contrary, men are not created equal. Politically perhaps, but not genetically. We come in all variations and combinations of genes. Work with some mammals has indicated that where there has been severe malnutrition, the next two or three generations, even when adequately nourished, will show the effects mentally and physically. Again, save them—for what? For the appeasement of our own guilt feelings?

"There is no obvious or clear answer to supporting with food or housing or medical care or education or anything else the probable population in 100 years. It is impossible.

"It must be recognized that this is so. The quality of life everywhere must deteriorate. When that happens, what is the obvious outcome? Strife. Rioting. A berserk world. Break-down of all public services including simple sanitation. Then the stage is set for disease on a scale unknown since the Middle Ages.

"Re-evaluating Christian attitudes toward human life is going to be extremely hard to do. Medical science currently is devoted to the prolongation of life under any circumstances, by any means. A sad example was President Eisenhower, kept alive beyond his natural span by every unnatural means at the command of modern medicine. We really fear death, will not allow ourselves to accept death as an inevitable part of life.

"We even pretend that we do not have to age! This is ridiculous, foolish beyond words. It's time to take a good, hard, long look at ourselves, our society our troubled world, and say, 'It can't go on without some real changes. Now what do we want? Do we want human society to survive? Is it important?'

"By 1975, 85 per cent of the people of the world will live in Africa and Asia. Can the remaining 15 per cent take care of them? I'm sorry, dreadfully sorry, but there just won't be enough to go around. World famine not only is possible, we're on collision course with it.

"We no longer can talk of unearned 'rights.' We'll have to get back to working for 'rights' to adequate food, housing, education, opportunity, a place in the sun—and not everybody is going to make the grade. I don't see this obsession with the lowest strata of humanity, against all natural biologic experience. We must accept that life is unfair.

"I think it would be lovely and beautiful to believe that if you removed all the cares from human beings—the concern for housing, food, care of children, clothing, education of young, medical needs—that they would enter upon a euphoric period of creative accomplishment. We've had enough evidence to show that as people are able to enjoy leisure, only the exceptional person becomes more creative or uses his time in useful ways. Or even is happy with it."[3]

Effects of Population Pressures on Business

The consequences of rapid population growth vary according to national circumstances. For the economically advanced countries, growth may mean greater markets and an expanding economy. For the nonindustrial, developing countries, the effects typically are the opposite. The analysis on the succeeding pages reveals the general ill effects of overpopulation and the stakes which business enterprise has in population planning and demographic policies in the underdeveloped countries.

Productive and Nonproductive Population

A study of the populations pyramids in Figures 37-2 through 37-5 shows that the age structure differs significantly in the two developing areas, Brazil and Malaya, from that in the two advanced countries, the United States and Sweden. For the former the pyramids rest on a wide base, which is indicative of a high birth rate, and are characterized by concave sides, as mortality also is comparatively high. For the latter the pyramids take a beehive shape with a relatively narrow base and convex sides, which reflect longevity and low mortality.

Figure 37-6, in which aggregate figures of the underdeveloped and developed sections of the world are portrayed, proves that these are not exceptional cases. The diagram shows that the proportion of nonproductive age groups in the society is much higher in the underdeveloped areas than in the developed ones—a fundamental reason for the low national products and the widespread poverty in underdeveloped countries. The adverse numerical ratio tells but a part of the story. The productive person in an underdeveloped country must in general not only produce for a greater number of the non-

[3] Quoted by permission from *Northwest Today,* Seattle Post-Intelligencer, October 19, 1969, pp. 10–11.

FIGURE 37-2

Malaysia, Population by Age and Sex

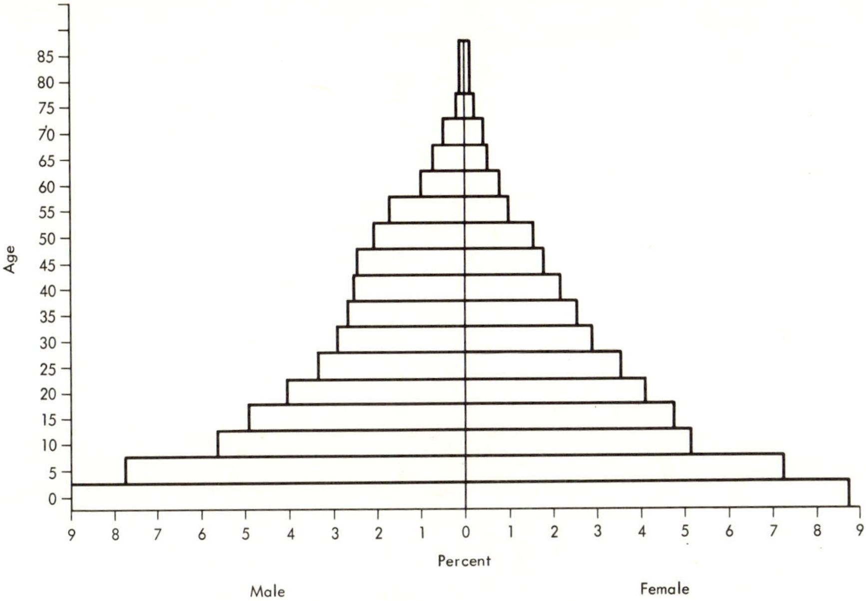

FIGURE 37-3

Brazil, Population by Age and Sex

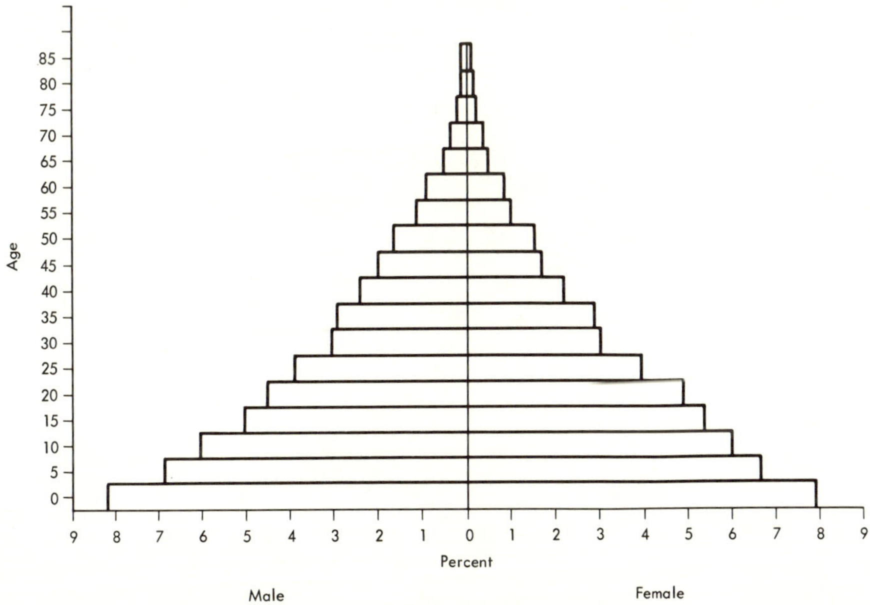

FIGURE 37-4

United States, Population by Age and Sex

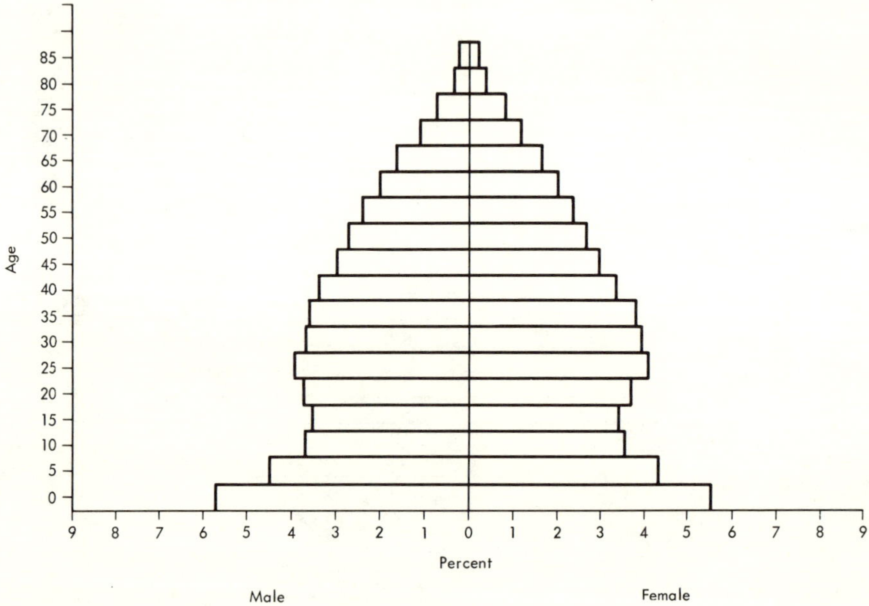

FIGURE 37-5

Sweden, Population by Age and Sex

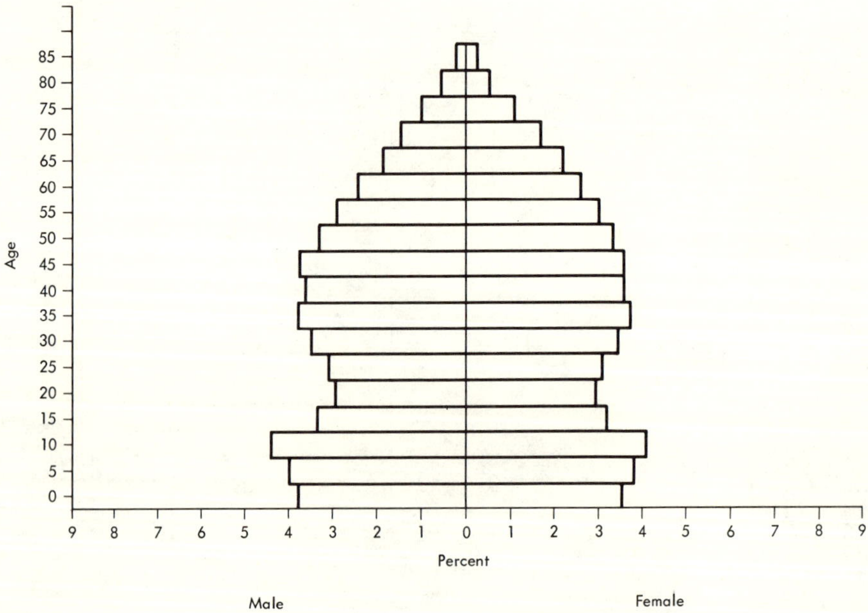

FIGURE 37-6

World Population Distribution

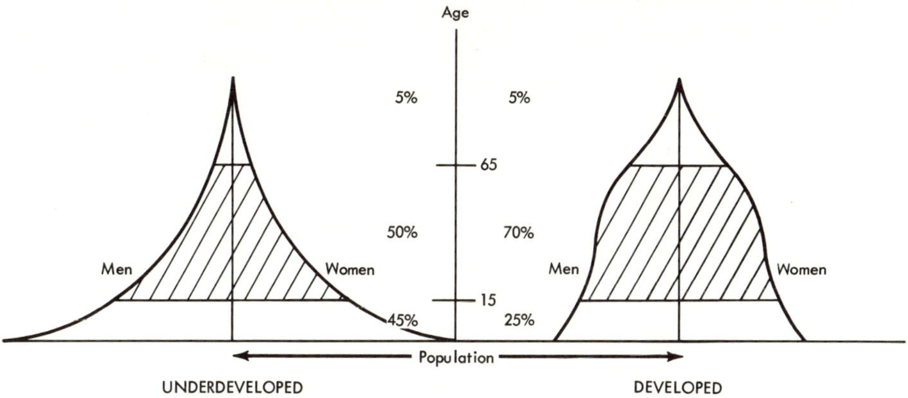

productive youth and aged than does a productive person in an industrial country but also do it with less capital, technology, education, and fewer tools.

The current population explosion is contributing to the disproportion between productive and nonproductive segments of the population since the reduction of the death rate has been caused primarily by success in curbing the incidence of infant mortality. Consequently, population growth is taking place mostly in the broad base of nonproductive young people while the available work force remains the same as before. It might be reasoned that this problem is temporary and will correct itself once the first generation of the infants raised with new medical care has reached maturity. Demographers generally discount this argument for two reasons. First, children who will marry and reproduce before reaching productive maturity will cause at least a serious delay before the productive cycle can catch up with the reproductive one; and second, the poverty, squalor, and hunger which characterize life in the developing countries will prohibit an average life span comparable with that in the industrialized world. In other words, those who manage to reach the productive years cannot be counted to live as long as those in the advanced countries.

For business the consequences of unfavorable age distributions are far reaching. The domestic market, because of the broad nonproductive base, is interested chiefly in meeting subsistence needs. The production and marketing of consumer goods is limited because of the overriding demand for food and clothing. The production of goods is further lessened by the shortage of mature workers. A large proportion of the population is below labor age, and, of those old enough, the vast majority must be employed in meeting subsistence needs. The demands of the nonproductive populace for basic food commodities and raw materials for clothing and housing lessen the availability of products for export trade and capital formation.

Although the analysis of the problems stemming from the peculiar age distribution of the developing countries is irrefutable on logical grounds, some influential men at national and international levels are attempting to contradict it for *dogmatic* reasons. The following statement made by Bernardo Colombo of the Holy See, during a U.N. conference, provides a poignant example:

> In countries where human physical force still plays a role, the fact that the average age of the active population is relatively low is a very positive element for their development. For this and similar reasons, it seems to me that any opinion that speaks of an unfavorable age structure under these conditions, where the population is largely young, should be reconsidered, if not reversed.[4]

Food Production at the Expense of Industry

To feed their exploding populations the developing nations have two available means: to increase the efficiency of their agricultural resources through chemical fertilizers, insect sprays, hybrid research, and better farm implements; or to make more complete use of agricultural products by such means as direct consumption of grains, transforming indigestible crops like soybeans into digestible products, and changing peoples' dietary habits.

Each of these methods is costly in terms of both capital and human resources. And each generally means the sacrifice of domestic industry and commerce. Urgently needed industrialization will be further delayed by agricultural demands for capital. The existing domestic firms will have more limited markets, as consumers spend greater amounts for food, with less for consumer items, and as government taxation (needed to supply capital for agricultural investment) depletes the spending money of the populace. Foreign commerce may diminish as agricultural investment makes exportable raw materials less available, and, as food materials which once were exported become comparatively rare because of population pressures, the country's ability to import is impaired.

The common-sense response to these negative aspects is that business and industry do not really lose as long as the investment capital stays in the country —the increased farm income will be circulated in the economy and eventually enter all parts of the economy. Two points invalidate this argument. First, increased efficiency of production and more efficient use of products can bring gains to business only indirectly, over a long period of time, and with the intervening loss of possibly increased food consumption without savings and investment.[5] Second, a rise in per capita output in an economy dominated by subsistence agriculture does not necessarily lead to an increase in marketable food surplus, on which the urban and nonagricultural population usually depends. Unless farm prices fall and make it necessary for the farmer to increase his sales in order to make the same income, he may choose to retain

[4] United Nations, *Report on the U.N. Conference on the Application of Science and Technology for the Benefit of Less Developed Areas,* V (New York, 1963), 43.

[5] The average income elasticity for food is between 0.7 and 0.8 in the developing countries of Asia and the Far East.

increased output for his own consumption rather than pursue a higher cash income for which he may have little use in part because of the scarcity of goods and in part because of his habitually constrained standards of consumption.

Effect on Foreign Trade and Investment

Population pressure in developing countries has two primary effects on foreign trade and direct investment activities: it lessens the economic capability for both import and export trade; and it discourages foreign business investment in the country.

An explosive population rate usually lowers sales by foreign exporters to a developing country. The squeeze on domestic capital permits less money to go into purchases from abroad. An exception to this is the necessity of importing basic food requirements. Opportunity for exporting by foreign firms is limited until the developing economy has been able to get a step ahead of its population, leaving some capital for foreign purchases. Only when this is possible is it valid to argue that an expanding population increases the market potential.

Foreign firms importing from the developing country are similarly affected by rapid population growth in part because the output of exportable commodities would be different if fertility trends were different and in part because of different tendencies for the domestic consumption of exportable commodities.[6]

A reduction of fertility both increases the supply of foreign exchange and makes it easier to use this supply for purchases of capital goods. The output of exportable commodities would be increased by reduced fertility because the total supply of the development capital would be greater and because the share devoted to export industries would be larger.[7] The total supply would be increased because of more savings and tax receipts available and because of a higher fraction of such funds used productively. More capital for export industries results since certain commodities, such as food, have a demand relatively responsive to the number of consumers. With lowered fertility, the capital normally channeled into increasing the production of these goods for the additional population could be used to increase the output in export commodities.

Population pressure discourages investment from foreign business firms for two reasons. First, exploding birth rates frequently lead to economic and social instability, which can result in financial collapse, market deterioration, or government intervention in business through either regulation or nationalization.

Second, the countries in the early stages of development can absorb

[6] Ansley J. Coale, *Population Growth and Economic Development in Low Income Countries* (Princeton, New Jersey: Princeton University Press, 1958), p. 309.

[7] Coale, *Population Growth and Economic Development in Low Income Countries,* p. 310.

relatively few direct investments.[8] The capacity to do this depends on such factors as the existence of skilled labor, competent administrators, and markets, and of basic transportation, communication, and power facilities. None of these essential characteristics are found in the swelling numbers of infants and children who are the mainspring of the population pressure in developing countries. And, where the skills do exist, the need to duplicate existing facilities to keep pace with the population increase prevents the basic industries from reaching a level of development that can be utilized by foreign business investors. Until the domestic economy is ahead of the population and the capacity of the country to absorb capital is increased, the bulk of foreign investment will have to come from benevolent governments or through the help of international financial institutions designed for such purposes. We discuss this topic further in a subsequent chapter.

Developing and Upgrading the Labor Supply

The growth of manufacturing and other business activities, especially export trade with advanced industrialized nations, requires technical training and education beyond the elementary stage. Literacy alone, bench mark though it is, does not suffice. School records reveal that the crucial weakness in the developing countries is secondary education. To make people employable by business and industry, or for that matter by government, as clerks, technicians, foremen, or junior executives of various kinds, they must have passed the secondary level. Unfortunately secondary education is too often neglected in the developing countries in favor of elementary and university education. In Africa, for example, it is estimated that the proportion of persons who have received secondary education varies between one-third and one-fifth of the number of existing jobs with needs for such education.[9]

Statistical data on education usually overstate the educational progress made in the developing countries, especially in regard to literacy and to primary education. The illiteracy figures are generally compiled by each country during a population census, and the measurements used vary widely. In many countries the ability to read and write one's own name constitutes literacy.[10] The value of such a literacy test to industrial productivity is questionable. In most developing countries functional literacy is probably much lower than is shown in official statistics. The United Nations is working toward a standard definition of literacy to provide a worldwide standard. Under this

[8] United Nations Department of Economic and Social Affairs, *The Capital Development Needs of the Less Developed Countries* (New York, 1962), p. 6.

[9] Alan Curle, *Educational Strategy for Developing Societies* (London: Tavisstock Publications, 1963), p. 87.

[10] Hilda Hertz Golden, "Literacy and Social Change in Underdeveloped Countries," in *Underdeveloped Areas—A Book of Readings and Research,* ed. Lyle W. Shannon (New York: Harper & Row Publishers, Inc., 1957), p. 109.

definition "a person is literate who can with understanding both read and write a short simple statement on his everyday life."[11] Even this seems modest in light of business realities. Although the value of literacy in traditional, handicraft-agrarian cultures may be limited, for industrial enterprise and modern agricultural production it is imperative. Golden points out the "importance of the dissemination of literacy and education in the transformation of peasant-agriculture nations into urban-industrial nations." She indicates the strong interdependence of literacy and economic advancement and shows how their growth must proceed hand in hand.[12]

With the exception of some urban institutions, the level of instruction is generally low in schools of underdeveloped countries. Teachers lack adequate preparation and are usually overburdened with large classes. Although some countries such as India have issued governmental decrees limiting class size to a specified figure, such rules have had little practical effect. The subject matter taught in the primary schools is of great importance. Traditional education in colonial schools was modeled after its European counterpart. Even the independent nations of Latin America patterned their schools after those of Europe, primarily those of France. The curricula of the schools have emphasized basic intellectual skills and have often included European history and languages with little attention to the local culture. Many classes have been taught in the language of the colonial power. The result of this system of education has been an accumulation of unrelated and often, to the learner, irrelevant or unimportant facts quickly forgotten after the examination: a skill in reading which enables the student to recite aloud to the instructor but does not allow him to understand the words he reads; a general ignorance of methods for improving agriculture; a preparation for a higher education which very few are able to attain; a knowledge out of context and useless in the environment in which the individual must live. In short, it is an education void of domestic culture and all of its practical aspects. This form of education is still dominant in many developing areas of the world today.

Although most countries have compulsory education, the regulations are not well enforced in practice. The economic level of the population, especially in rural areas, is the primary obstacle. Children are required to work in order to contribute their share to the family income. Diseases and malnutrition keep enrollment and attendance down. To people on subsistence income, food is more important than education.

The attitudes of the population toward education is another obstacle to school attendance. Uneducated parents rarely see any benefit in learning to read and write. The children themselves may take a negative attitude if the education does not lead to foreseeable and desirable goals. Colonial and traditional schools have presented an image of hard work and vigorous discipline which discourages many. The fear of schools and the necessity of foresaking

[11] United Nations Educational, Scientific, and Cultural Organization, *Manual of Educational Statistics* (Paris, 1961), p. 234.

[12] Golden, "Literacy and Social Change in Underdeveloped Countries," p. 113.

present satisfactions for uncertain benefits in the future result in a negative attitude toward school of any kind. Even if all other factors were favorable, very few countries could afford to provide the teachers, schools, and books for mass education.

A problem seldom confronted by Western educators is that presented by the variety of languages found in the countries of Asia and Africa. Margaret Mead suggests, "...that a basic condition of successful literacy—on any large scale—is that it should be attained in the mother tongue."[13] This condition makes education even more difficult and expensive. Again, this is a problem of allocation of scarce resources, and the returns to education, although great, are slow in coming. The necessity of mass education to economic development is obvious; the means to attain it are not.

Secondary education

The secondary school enrollment ratios are more meaningful than those for the primary school, as they represent individuals who will remain literate. The state of secondary education in underdeveloped countries has been described as follows:

> The main feature of secondary education right up to the present time is its claim to be the education of an elite chosen, first, on the basis of its social position, and secondly on the strength of a special type of intelligence suited to meet the criteria of a verbal and exclusively intellectual education.[14]

The ability to attend secondary school is limited much more than the ability to attend primary school by the economic position of the individual. When a young man reaches the age for secondary school, he is generally expected to contribute a considerable share to the family income or to be already economically independent. In some cultures a potential student may also be blocked from enrollment by social position. In rural areas, secondary schools are even less accessible than the primary ones since distance and transport facilities become the ruling factors.

The quality of secondary education in underdeveloped areas is often high. These schools are essentially aimed at preparing the student for higher education, and the standards are quite rigorous. However, here again one finds a lack of relevance to everyday life in the subject matter. Those who do not finish secondary school or who do not go on to a university are trained to do little else than clerk and keep books. Technical, agricultural, and forestry training are typically conspicuous by their absence from the secondary educational programs of developing countries. The objective of the secondary schools is to teach an individual to appreciate literature and culture but not to prepare him for an active participation in the productive processes of his society.

[13] Margaret Mead, "Professional Problems of Education in Dependent Countries," in *Underdeveloped Areas,* ed. Lyle W. Shannon, p. 345.

[14] United Nations Educational, Scientific, and Cultural Organization, *The Primary School Curriculum,* Monographs on Education No. II (Paris, 1961), pp. 238–39.

Higher education

Higher education in underdeveloped countries is provided only for a select few. Although, as with primary and secondary education, the schools are often "free," it is only the very wealthy who can afford to attend.

It is also true that higher education is very expensive to the state, resulting in an insufficient number of institutions and teachers. Entrance requirements are set very high to balance the number of students. These conditions can be expected to improve with economic development and perhaps can be tolerated for the present. The basic difficulty, however, is an antiquated university structure unable to cope with modern needs. A student who wants to study chemistry must take a full engineering or pharmacology curriculum; or, if he is interested in biology, he must enroll in the medical program. Designed to train the nineteenth-century professions, such a university is ill-suited for educating psychologists, political scientists, or technicians for such modern fields as automatic computation, aerospace, or electronics. Hence, those who do receive higher education are often trained for nonproductive professions or find little opportunity for applying their skills.

> Although the systems of professional and higher education are being re-examined in almost all underdeveloped countries, there is still too great an emphasis on literary-historical and narrowly legal training.[15]

On the other hand there are individuals who obtain a highly specialized, technical, or scientific education and cannot find jobs in which to apply their knowledge because a backward society may not have advanced enough to need particular specialists. Persons receiving their education at an American or European university are very often confronted by this situation and, ironically, are compelled to leave their native lands to find employment in their technical specialty.

Another serious deficiency of universities in underdeveloped countries is their relative lack of training in *business administration* and organization. This problem is being felt more all the time as these countries strive for economic development. The initial phases of the process—building an infrastructure of roads, communications, power railroads, etc.—generally require a large, efficient government bureaucracy. Industry depends on specialized managers. These countries, therefore, must continue to depend on foreign administrators to run their business until they develop indigenous skills for management and motivate talented individuals to acquire managerial training.

Negative Implications

The population problem in underdeveloped countries is interlaced with social, political, and economic issues. It is fraught with dogma and beset by

[15] B. F. Hoselitz, "The Recruitment of White-Collar Workers in Underdeveloped Countries," in *Underdeveloped Areas,* ed. Lyle W. Shannon (New York: Harper & Row, Publishers, Inc., 1957), p. 188.

counterclaims from nutritionists, agronomists, political realists, and social idealists. Its implications to business are mainly adverse. They can be summarized as follows:

(1) Rapid population growth causes an expansion of the broad base of unproductive young people.

(2) This expansion increases the emphasis on food production—at the expense of business and industry—and channels capital and workers to agriculture in order to feed the expanding population.

(3) The quality of the labor force suffers as the country is pressed to provide education, food, clothing, and housing for additional millions.

(4) To keep up with population growth, governments may be forced to appropriate for basic consumption needs resources which otherwise could go for investment in industry and in the infrastructure.

(5) Increased family size lessens the possibility for individuals as well as for government bodies to accumulate the capital for expanding business and industrial activity. Large family size permits little saving and weakens the tax base of the nation.

(6) Insufficient capital limits imports; and increased domestic demand lessens potential exports.

(7) Social instability and inability to absorb foreign capital discourage investment by the firms of industrialized countries.

This list of the negative consequences of rapid population expansion obviously cannot be applied in its entirety or to the same degree in all developing countries. Business and industry in some countries expand regardless of growth rates. The presence of valuable resources attracts domestic and foreign development. And the availability of land, as in some South American nations, may counter the negative aspects of rapid growth.

The predictions of ill effects must be applied selectively, and they will vary in degree in different developing countries. No hard and fixed rules relate population to business development, but the trends are significant. The indications are that business and industry will find great contrasts and paradoxical conditions for a long time to come in an underdeveloped country. Predictions of an early solution to the population problems are unsupported to date; the situation will require intelligent analysis and socially responsible action not only from governments but also from business enterprise.

38

Industrial Manpower

The underdeveloped countries present business with a paradoxical labor situation: a high rate of unemployment and a critical shortage of employable workers. The paradox derives primarily from the growth and structure of the population and secondarily from the scarcity and the misdirection of educational programs to develop the talents necessary for industrial employment.

Unemployment and Underemployment

The high population growth rates, as indicated earlier, have led to a population structure in which the under-25 group constitutes the largest percentage of the population. A striking example of the population structure in some countries was indicated in a report which stated, "At least 40 percent of the total population in the countries studied [Burma, Ceylon, Hong Kong, India, Pakistan, Singapore, and Thailand] consisted of persons under 15 years of age."[1] In this situation, "the demand for new jobs may increase more rapidly than the growth of the population."[2] High birth rates in underdeveloped coun-

[1] International Labour Office, "Employment Prospects of Children and Young People in Asia," *International Labour Review,* LXXXVIII, No. 6 (December 1963), 565.

[2] International Labour Office, *Employment Objectives in Economic Development: Report of a Meeting of Experts,* Studies and Reports, New Series, No. 62 (Geneva 1961), p. 26.

tries mean that every year the number of persons reaching working age is much larger than it was the year before.[3]

The environments of the traditional agrarian sectors of many of the underdeveloped countries, particularly in Asia, also contribute to the increase in unemployment. The available arable land in these countries is already being cultivated to such an extent that the increase in population can no longer be supported by the village communities, and these people must, therefore, move to urban areas in search of employment. If the young people of working age remain on the land, they just swell the ranks of the underemployed because the intensity with which the land is already being cultivated will not permit further productive employment.

To a modest but increasing degree, the "tide of rising expectations" in underdeveloped countries is another lure; young people go to the cities in search of more income with which they hope to acquire a higher standard of living. After moving to the cities they compound the already acute unemployment problem, as they usually lack the skills and education to qualify for a job.

Skilled Labor

In direct contrast to the underemployment and unemployment which are usually prevalent in underdeveloped countries, skilled labor is often in critically short supply.[4] Some specific examples can be cited. In Iran the shortage of skilled workers in industry was estimated in 1963 to be 27,000 whereas the schools and training facilities were graduating only about 2300 skilled workers per year. In Egypt skilled-worker requirements for the period 1959–64 were estimated to be 67,000, but training was negligible.

Thus, the industrial sectors of most of the underdeveloped countries could absorb some of the unemployed and underemployed labor if they had the requisite skills for employment. It has been noted previously that a substantial percentage of the population in underdeveloped countries is semiliterate. Literacy is a basic condition if wage earners are to perform anything more than unskilled, manual labor. The inability to read or write with full comprehension is an enormous handicap since in almost any kind of skilled labor the ability to read blueprints or instructions of various kinds is required.

Another major aspect of the unemployment problem is that even if unemployed labor had the required skills, industry could absorb only a limited number of them. The number of workers engaged in mining and manufacturing increases only slightly. Even in the industrializing countries industrial employment is barely keeping pace with population growth. Countries which have economic development plans estimate only relatively small gains in employment through industrialization. For example, the percentage of estimated employment to be generated by industrial development over varying lengths of time,

[3] International Labour Office, "Employment Objectives in Economic Development," *International Labour Review,* LXXXIV (November 1961), pp. 394–95.

[4] United Nations, Department of Economic and Social Affairs, *Report on the World Social Situation,* E/CN.5/346/Rev. 1 (New York, 1961), p. 13.

usually five years, was only about 12 percent in India, 10 percent in Pakistan, 20 percent in the Philippines, and 18 percent in Ceylon.[5] The experiences of some countries indicate the same trend. In Greece, although the output of manufacturing industries rose 50 percent between 1952 and 1957, industrial employment did not rise at all; the quantum index of manufacturing industries increased by 50 percent in Egypt between 1947 and 1954, but employment actually declined by 5 percent; and between 1950 and 1957 in Israel the output of industry nearly doubled, but employment increased by only 50 percent.[6]

Thus, the industrial sectors of the underdeveloped countries are employing capital-intensive techniques imported from the developed countries. Although they have a critical need for skilled labor and technicians, they cannot utilize all their unemployed and underemployed people. Even if industrialization progressed rapidly, demand for new manpower would not necessarily grow at the same rate, as new and more mechanized machines and equipment would be used and management would have to learn to utilize labor more effectively. Thus, it is not unlikely that the labor input required for any given quantity of production will decline.

Labor Unrest in Underdeveloped Countries

Labor unrest is typical of underdeveloped countries because of the disintegration of the traditional social structure which industrialization and modernization bring about. All workers pass through a transitional phase before they are converted from peasant farmers to industrial laborers.

The process of decline and transition of an indigenous culture is slow. It began in most areas with the arrival of the first explorer, missionary, or trader and has been going on for 300 years with increasing exposure to Western culture. Every attempt by an entrepreneur to influence the behavior of his personnel is, almost by definition, aimed at cultural change. Its result, in terms of motivation or any other goal, must be interpreted in a varied and complex framework.

In newly developing areas the most significant cultural differences separating management from the labor force are frequently nothing more than the differing sources from which the two groups derive their basic social, economic, and emotional security. Each group expects the other to behave as if it shared the same perception of the proper source of this security, and it is frustrated to the extent that this is not so.

Management must recognize this difference, not only to satisfy its workers, but also to comprehend the cultural aspects of the relearning and readjustment processes which must be completed before any industry-oriented labor force

[5] International Labour Office, *Employment Objectives in Economic Development*, p. 42.

[6] International Labour Office, *Employment Objectives in Economic Development*, p. 43.

can emerge. To achieve labor commitment, management ultimately must provide the native labor force with a substitute for their traditional sources of security. Teaching new skills and assisting physical adaptation to a new habitat are helpful but only as a start. The roots of the problem go much deeper and require positive demonstrations and continuous reassurance that the industrial enterprise will offer the individual and his family security comparable to that offered by the traditional structure. Communications and reappraisal are crucial to the achievement of this reassurance and to its continued reinforcement as the commitment grows. No simple formulas solve these problems. Even history is of little value since the developing areas are undergoing industrialization in a world quite different from that in which the high-income countries were industrialized. Only an enlightened pragmatism, based on a continuous study of social forces and structured to the necessities and resources of the day, can provide guidance for dealing effectively with the human element in the industrial setting of the developing countries.

Labor and Politics

The repeated association of deliberate economic development and extreme nationalism is not accidental. Nationalism presents an essential, nonrational unifying force that may ease and rationalize the hardship of personal change. The importance of this commitment increases as rapid economic transition undermines various intermediate social structures that shared or even captured loyalties in the preindustrial social system.[7] The fully committed industrial worker, in whatever occupation, will become involved in political associations —unions, occupational groups, or even residential groups. The type of organization may vary from the formal party to the spontaneous street mob. Either extreme provides an agency of leverage and protest, which may have direct consequences for the social system or only the indirect effect of draining off dissident energies.

Industrialization and Government

Although production organizations typical of industrialism are by no means absent in a nonindustrial context, they are not likely to dominate the particular societies now on the eve of industrialization. Of the four major nonindustrial production organizations—familial, custodial, contractual, and voluntary—the latter two are closest to industrial requirements. Voluntary organizations, however, generally do not exist in societies with centralized government and settled agriculture, and thus they cannot be considered as possible models for industrial motivation.[8] Contractual organizations, on the other hand, depend in part on the presence of a centralized government.

[7] David A. Apter, *The Gold Coast in Transition* (Princeton, New Jersey: Princeton University Press, 1955), pp. 322–23.

[8] Stanley H. Udy, Jr., *Preindustrial Forms of Organized Work* (New Haven, Connecticut: Human Relations Area File Press, 1959), p. 9.

Centralized government, however, does not in itself involve any mechanisms directly conductive to contractual forms. In contrast, it provides a direct basis for custodial organizations through consolidated control over resources.

Under the typical conditions of settled agriculture and centralized government, custodial relationships are more likely to develop than are contractual ones. Where they dominate, custodial forms are generalized to all situations and groups, regardless of their technical suitability. Inasmuch as they involve social recruitment, ascription, and diffuseness, they are in direct opposition to the principles and objectives of industrial management and, for that matter, to economic development as such.

In addition, the center of this latent opposition to industrialism seems to lie in the political system, either directly or as reflected through social stratification. At the same time, centralized government is necessary for the ultimate development of contractual forms and is certainly essential to industrialism. It is thus not surprising that many newly developing areas that are in fact developing successfully are characterized by political unrest as well as labor unrest. At a given point of development a choice may have to be made between assured political stability and effective industrialization measures. If the industrialization measures undermine the political structure too severely, the industrialization effort may collapse. The shift from custodial to contractual bases of organization thus emerges as a crucial test for newly developing areas.

Authority in the Industry

That the discipline of industrial employment is different from that of agriculture and that adjustment to the new discipline is difficult for the recruit to industry have often been observed. Primitive peoples can readily learn industrial skills; their real problem lies in adjusting to *industrial discipline.* The pace of agricultural employment depends on the season and the weather conditions, and much of the planning of work procedures is left to the individual or to the group. Industrial employment is machine paced, the method of work is prescribed by the industrial engineer, and the employee must put in a full day and week. Timetables, routines, and standard procedures must be followed. And tardiness, absenteeism, turnover, and unwillingness to accept initiative and responsibility become labor problems.

On the other hand, the effect on the worker of adjusting to the tempo of industry is often overstated. What is thought to be maladjustment may be passive insubordination in protest against low wages, poor working conditions, and especially poor supervision.[9]

Industrial unrest in developing areas, as in industrialized nations, may result from disputes over the terms of employment. However, industrialization creates new forms of *employment relations* that disturb the values of the older culture. The traditional superior and subordinate positions usually found in underdeveloped areas are based on autocratic, benevolent paternalism, which

[9] A. M. Malik, *Labor Problems and Policy in Pakistan* (Karachi: Pakistan Labor Publications, 1954), p. 14.

is not readily adapted to factory situations. The function of management, the relations between employer and employee, and the status of the employee must be reexamined in this context. These issues cannot always be disentangled from the general environment of limited commitment to the labor force, divided loyalties, urban slums, nationalism, and racial discrimination.[10]

The forms of authority common to preindustrial labor are frequently more extreme than those in the factory. The plantation majordomo and the feudal landlord are more distant from the worker than is the unit foreman, and the scope and degree of their authority is greater partly as a consequence of this distance. The legitimacy of authority is not so clear to the newly recruited factory worker as it is to the preindustrial worker.

The transition is from a system of authority that is both general and personal to one that is both specific and impersonal. This shift affects the worker's ability to understand the orders received. A premium is placed on understanding the language in a specific manner, which involves simultaneously conceding the legitimacy of its source. When the manager is a member of an alien culture—i.e., when he is imported from an industrial society—the language problems become particularly acute. For even in industrial societies managers of factories have inherited and thus enjoy some of the moral sanctions applied to their occupational ancestors—the owner-entrepreneurs of early industrialism. However, in industrializing societies managers should no longer affirm their "God-given" rights, but they and many others may still think in these terms, though perhaps in a less religious vein. In any case, the task of bridging the gap between a trained and committed labor force and one that is neither—of socializing newly recruited factory workers to the "proper" authority—is usually assigned to the authority system itself.

The assumption is that the lack of labor-force commitment can be compensated for by an increase in the amount of authority allocated to managers.[11] What then is the solution? Some maintain that traditional authority and sanctions should be maintained in the factory, at least during the initial period of industrialization. This is believed to reduce significantly barriers to commitment.[12]

The apparent success of Japanese industries in easily gaining high levels of labor-force commitment is attributed to the maintenance of the *status quo ante* with regard to authority.[13] However, the high positive value placed on the continuity of the authority structures has some roots in cultural relativism. It seduces some observers into apologizing for the establishment of sweatshops in newly developed areas. The rejection of the *status quo ante,* although incom-

10 Malik, *Labor Problems and Policy in Pakistan,* p. 14.

11 Wilbert E. Moore and Arnold S. Feldman (eds.), *Labor Commitment and Social Change in Development Areas* (New York: Social Science Research Council, 1960), p. 37.

12 Horace Belshaw, "Industry and Agrarian Reform," *Far Eastern Survey,* XVI (July 2, 1947), 153–56; Willbert E. Moore, *Industrialization and Labor* (Ithaca: Cornell University Press, 1951), pp. 142–47.

13 Marion J. Levy, Jr., "Some Social Obstacles to 'Capital Formation in Underdeveloped Areas,'" in *Capital Formation and Economic Growth,* ed. Moses Abramovitz (Princeton, New Jersey: Princeton University Press, 1955), pp. 441–501.

plete and frequently naïve, can be one of the strongest forces for economic development in many preindustrial societies. And, rejection of the previous working conditions is one of the motivations for accepting factory employment.[14]

This discussion of authority in industry is less than consistent if not confusing. But so is the subject itself. Anybody with personal experience with industrial problems in the underdeveloped world will find the contradictory tendencies a true reflection of the reality. The problem is a vital one for any enterprise expanding into the developing world.

Unions

Compared with labor organizations of the developed countries, the unions of the developing countries represent an economically weaker but politically more explosive force. To understand this force, one must understand the circumstances that condition union activity as well as the character and scope of the unions themselves.

Generally, unionism in developing countries is a house divided against itself. Rudimentary education and lack of experience in industrial labor-management problems diffuse the efforts of the workers to express their protests and to realize hopes. In spite of the rapid growth of unions, effective unionism is rare. The greatest obstacle is the apathy of workers. Unemployment, underemployment, and an irregular labor supply often make the collection of union dues impossible and seriously undermine the union's economic position.

A multitude of small, independent unions view the business world from a feudalistic perspective. They form many rival federations, based on political affiliation, social ideology, or religious beliefs, which resist amalgamation into integrated labor movements. Union leaders are usually outsiders—middle-class intellectuals with doctrinaire philosophies, usually nationalist or Communist—who lay greater stress on political issues than on the practical problems of wages, working conditions, and productivity. As a result, most of the unions are tied to some political party and put its interests first. Another type of union leadership comes from the opportunist who capitalizes on the workers' predicament and discontent by extorting employers and seeking political office for personal gain.

Collective bargaining is in its infancy in most developing countries. Workers do not understand it, and union leaders prefer to practice politics. Although most developing nations encourage union growth, nearly all restrict collective bargaining by limiting the right to strike, enacting comprehensive labor codes, and providing for compulsory arbitration or labor courts. In summary, the labor unions of developing countries are characterized by small size, financial weakness, reliance on outside leadership, interunion rivalry,

[14] Moore and Feldman, *Labor Commitment and Social Change in Developing Areas*, p. 39.

absence of national unions, inadequate use of the methods of trade unions, and inability to rely upon the organized strength of workers.

Industrial Wages

To be effective in wage bargaining, unions must be able to exert enough power to compel recognition and fair dealings from management. Theoretically, a perfect balance of power between a union and management should exist. In the industrial countries unions have generally acquired the strength to bargain with management and often have even become the dominant party because of labor legislation and labor-oriented public policies.

In the developing countries unions seldom possess the power to bargain effectively. As indicated above their financial resources are seriously limited. In addition, they are vulnerable to political action and economic recession. As a minority group, industrial workers find their interests sacrificed when they conflict with those of the nonindustrial majority. The impact of an economic downturn is felt with the greatest force in the industrial sector, yet the industrial worker is less able to cope with unemployment than are agricultural families.

Lacking the strength and experience for effective bargaining, unions in the developing countries resort to disruptive tactics such as riots and demonstrations designed more often to get favorable legislation enacted than tc influence the outcome of any particular wage settlement or of some other problem. Many union leaders still believe that the function of a union is to "hurt" the employers, no matter what the circumstances. This attitude is a relic of the struggle for independence, when civil disobedience was regarded as the appropriate attitude.[15]

Whether unions and other occupational groups are strongly or weakly political is partially a function of the existence of alternative means of political expression and influence. Perhaps this is why overwhelming importance is attached to trade-union activities by the political parties in those countries—a reflection of the importance of the labor movement and its capacity to influence social life.

The effectiveness of wages and salaries as incentives for productivity depends to a substantial degree on the employee's assessment of the nonfinancial rewards and penalties connected with his job. The newly recruited worker may gain or lose social status,[16] an important nonfinancial consideration. Any system of social stratification (unequal rewards for social performance), even a complex multidimensional one, raises questions of equity since it rests on the differential functional importance of positions and on the differential talent of persons.[17] Existing systems tend to transform inequality

[15] Wagiono Ismangil, *The Nature and Role of Labor Movements in Developing Countries,* 299 Research Paper (Berkeley, California: University of California, School of Business Administration, 1963), p. 66.

[16] Moore, *Industrialization and Labor,* pp. 21–44 and 99–102.

[17] Kingsley Davis and W. Moore, "Some Principles of Stratification," *American Sociological Review,* X (April 1945), 242–49.

of position into inequality of opportunity.[18] Thus commitment to a system of reward based on merit and of mobility consistent with talent and training may still inspire the employee in a developing country to attempt to alter the system as well as his place in it.

Government Interference

In underdeveloped countries where collective bargaining exists, such as Pakistan, Argentina, and Chile, the governments generally control the outcome. In 1966, for instance, the government of Chile limited wage increases to 50 percent of the previous year's price rise. The developing nation's government is likely to suppress wage increases, as wage determination is very closely tied to growth potentialities. The government judges most wage agreements by their effect upon the entire economy, as does the government of an advanced country, but it generally has more direct power than the government of an advanced country to suppress wage hikes or to decree increases.

When capital formation is at stake, the government probably would not support union worker demands for higher wages. However, governments of developing nations are not unchecked in suppressing wages; for example, efforts by the Argentinian government to freeze wages in 1959 endangered the regime of President Arturo Frondizi.

In Turkey, the government is one of the three groups of employers. Little attention is paid to training or to incentive programs, and, consequently, turnover of personnel is high. The Turkish labor code sets standards for working hours, workers' health and safety, etc., for all classes of employers. Arbitration courts in the provinces hear cases of wage disputes. Made up of workers, these boards are so slow that, although most cases are decided in favor of the worker, very few benefits accrue to workers in general. Decisions are ultimately subject to government policy. Many areas have minimum wage laws, but few are enforced. Minimum wages vary widely in different industries, even at comparable skill levels. Government policy in Turkey suppresses unions, largely because of pressure from powerful private business interests.

Training of Union Cadres

Through the efforts of the International Labor Organization of the United Nations and the International Conference of Trade Unions, programs are now under way to develop indigenous cadres for labor unions in the developing countries. Training centers are in operation on three continents, and others are being planned.[19] Their objective is to establish comprehensive programs in all developing countries. Peculiarly enough, a very sizable fraction of the best trainees have been absorbed into government and management

[18] M. T. Tumin, "Some Principles of Stratification," *American Sociological Review*, XVIII (August 1953), 387–94.

[19] A. Zack, *Labor Training in Developing Countries* (New York: Frederick A. Praeger, Inc., 1964), p. 18.

positions. It is unlikely, therefore, that union leadership will undergo rapid improvement.

Worker Participation

The trade unions may play a very important part in improving productive efficiency within the industry. If the workers take interest in their work, they may suggest from their experience many practical ways of minimizing waste of raw materials, improving the distribution of the work load, and making minor technical readjustments. In Russia, the Stakhanov movement, which contributed very much to the successes of Soviet planning in the mid Thirties, was to a great extent nothing but a method of mobilizing the workers to find ways of increasing productivity and to reduce costs through better division of work and minor technical innovations.[20] But workers must be encouraged to offer such suggestions and must be assured that these will be given proper consideration. Joint production committees, work councils, etc., are valuable means of associating the workers with improvement in productive efficiency. The trade unions, as the natural leaders of the workers, may make such instruments of workers' participation really effective.[21]

However, wages are generally low where labor is inefficient and where there is a labor surplus. Many factories in developing areas employ more labor than necessary. The prices of locally produced goods are relatively high because of insufficient capital equipment, poorly organized manufacturing processes, and lack of a mass market. To create markets for export and to compete with imported goods, industrial processes must be made more efficient. Only in this way can there be more jobs at higher wages. But in the course of these adjustments technological unemployment occurs. Like the craftsmen and the sweatshop laborers, industrial workers protest against technological change, first, because they are already suffering from serious unemployment, and second, because increasing productivity is not reflected in higher wages. The reallocation of the labor force as a consequence of technological change is much more difficult and painful in a developing area than in one already industrially developed.

Possible Adverse Effects of Unions

Autonomous unions enjoying free collective bargaining are not an unmixed blessing. Union objectives can conflict with rapid economic development in the following ways:

(1) Union pressure for higher wages may promote managerial efficiency, but it may also discourage foreign investment and increase inflationary tendencies.[22] The problem of maintaining a reasonable balance between rising

[20] Maurice Dobb, *Soviet Economic Development Since 1917* (London: Routledge & Kegan Paul, Ltd., 1951), p. 429.

[21] S. Ghosh, *Trade Unionism in Underdeveloped Countries* (Calcutta: World Press, 1960), p. 349.

[22] International Bank, *The Economic Development of Jamaica* (Baltimore: The Johns Hopkins Press, 1952), p. 71.

wages rates and rising productivity is not automatically resolved by free collective bargaining. Programs for rapid economic development are in themselves inflationary, and free collective bargaining adds to inflation. Developing areas require foreign investment; one of the few attractions that they have to offer to foreign capital is low wages.

(2) Genuine collective bargaining must be supported by the economic power to threaten work stoppages, but developing areas cannot afford the luxury of strikes and lockouts. Mature collective bargaining may develop in the long run, but to the government financing a major program for rapid economic development, work stoppages appear to be irresponsible. As a consequence, many governments, while encouraging unionism, do not permit strikes and in effect dictate the terms of employment.[23] Although such procedures are understandable, they undermine the basis of job-oriented unionism and invite political action or even strikes against the government. The tendency for unions to become primarily political bodies is thus encouraged.

(3) Although it is understandable that unions in developing areas should be nationalistic and involved with ideological issues which may determine the form of national government, continued preoccupation with these issues to the neglect of the worker's welfare on the job can only contribute to economic and political instability.[24] The result is a political struggle for the control of unions, jurisdictional rivalries, and a close tie between collective bargaining and political issues.

(4) Although unions sponsored by governments and some socialist unions have favored technological change in the hope of benefiting the working class in the long run, no union in developing areas can command the loyalty of the workers without centering its attention on the preservation of jobs at the expense of technological change. Unless industrial expansion can be maintained at a rate that will permit absorption of the technologically displaced, which is unlikely, resistance to technological change will continue to be a major obstacle to industrialization.

Development of Industrial Manpower

An international survey of manpower by Harbison and Myers[25] reveals that, although important progress is being made in the organized, purposeful development of industrial manpower in a number of underdeveloped countries, it is often too restricted both in coverage and quality. Training in high-level industrial skills is still a relative rarity.

23 Malik, *Labor Problems and Policy in Pakistan,* p. 30; U.S. Dept. of Labor, *Labor in India* (Washington, D.C.: U.S. Government Printing Office, 1961), pp. 15–16: and U.S. Dept. of Labor, *Summary of the Labor Situation in Taiwan,* p. 10.

24 International Bank, *The Economic Development of Jamaica,* pp. 222–25; Malik, *Labor Problems and Policy in Pakistan,* pp. 6, 30, 139; United Nations, Department of Economic and Social Affairs, *Report on the World Social Situation,* p. 385.

25 Fredrick Harbison and Charles A. Myers, *Manpower and Education* (New York: McGraw-Hill Book Company, 1965).

On-the-Job Training

Formal in-service training programs are rare. And often the supervisors who are to do the training are so busy with their own tasks that they do not have the time for it.

The Asians in East Africa and the Syrians and the Lebanese in West Africa have effective on-the-job training for their own people both in the wholesale and in the retail trades, but they avoid training any of the African natives and thus they have contributed little to the further development of the natives.

In the partially developed countries, many kinds of institutions give on-the-job training, but, except in China, these institutions are given much less attention than they deserve and in many cases the potential of such training has hardly been discovered, let alone exploited. The study by Harbison and Myers indicates that some Latin American countries are stressing employer-financed programs for vocational training in industrial plants. In Colombia, for example, they have developed an outstanding program of apprenticeship training, night courses for adult workers already employed, and training of plant personnel to organize and operate their own skill-development programs within the factories.

In some of the semiadvanced countries more attention is being paid to upgrading the qualifications and improving the performance of people already employed in strategic occupations. Thus, in such countries as India and Egypt efforts have been directed toward developing management-training programs, supervisory-training courses, productivity centers, institutes of public administration for employed civil servants, etc.

On-the-job training has, in general, spread more widely among institutions in the semiadvanced countries. In several, including Algeria, Indonesia, India, Egypt, and many Latin American countries, the armed forces are used as a training ground for technical and administrative education. In some, such as Mexico, employers are held responsible for establishing and maintaining "schools" for the education of the employees and their children.

In Uganda the government advocates technical training and apprenticeships to increase the competence of the African artisan, and the government has increased the number of apprenticeships in the technical schools. Although many of the natives have done well in the training programs, generally their response to the opportunities offered them has been poor. The natives demand training but they will not sacrifice any of their current earnings, and they cannot foresee that the training will bring sufficient increases in their earnings to more than make up for what they are losing during the training period. Many of the natives who start in the training programs leave before the courses are finished. The time span of their expectations is very short.

Technical and Vocational Schools

An alternative to on-the-job apprenticeship is offered by technical and vocational schools supported either by the government or by industry. In Senegal, Guinea, and the Ivory Coast, technical and vocational training schools have a particularly important role to play. On-the-job training operates under serious handicaps, and it does not provide opportunities to learn the higher skills. The structure of this school system is similar to that used in France, where a three-year professional certificate and also a seven-year course leading to a baccalaureate are available. In addition various special-training schools cover a wide range of specialized trades. The major criticism of the technical and vocational schools is that they have no contact with the actual work situations and that the training therefore tends to be too abstract.

In Nyasaland the mission centers broke the initial ground in the technical training of the natives. The Soche Trade School opened in 1960 under government auspices with 53 trainees to provide technical training for such occupations. Training-within-industry courses dealing with job relations are conducted by the Labor Department in cooperation with several of the largest industrial organizations in the country. The progress of job-oriented programs has been hindered by the uncertainties of employers regarding future manpower requirements and operating conditions, the costs involved, and the general unavailability of training personnel.

In Argentina, Brazil, and Chile the governments have taken the first major steps in establishing technical and vocational schools to train people for jobs in industry. In Brazil an employer by law must hire a certain number of youths between the ages of 13 and 17 and send them to the government training schools while paying them a wage comparable to that received by an apprentice. Also in Brazil such major industrial organizations as Varig, the aviation and airline concern, have established their own training schools and train their own mechanics, pilots, and other operating personnel, as well as their own sales force. In Argentina, a number of companies have special training programs for their employees, but the government also has training schools. These schools are paid for by a 1 percent tax on the wage bill of every industrial employer. Most of the schools are adapted to the location and emphasize the skills needed by the industries in their respective communities. The Ministry of Education also maintains "general" industrial schools, which give a more theoretical education than do the apprentice schools that are set up regionally. In Chile relatively few training courses are found in factories. Workers who claim to have skills are given a chance to prove it, and those who want to acquire skills do so by working with an experienced operator who has probably learned his trade in the same manner. One of the most important institutions offering technical education is the Universidad Technica Santamaria, outside Valparaiso. This school was founded in 1932 as a result of a bequest by one of Chile's leading industrialists. It has about 500 students in regular daytime courses; it trains skilled workers, foremen, and engineers. Its graduates are in great demand all over Chile.

Most of the developing countries still rely on the business firm that employs the people to give them training, and that training is seldom done in a formal manner. Those countries that have developed good technical and vocational schools are reaping the benefits of them and are trying to develop more. For a company to enter a new market in a foreign country, that country must be able to offer a supply of trained, skilled workers or suffer the economic consequence of losing the investment to some neighbor that can offer the company the supply of labor which it needs. Thus, the pressure for better and more efficient education and training of industrial labor forces is building, and better programs can reasonably be expected to result from it.

39

Managerial Resources and Executive Development

The industrial progress and vigor of any society depend first on its leadership's ability to find, develop, and utilize natural, financial, and human resources effectively. Narrowly conceived as entrepreneurship in classical doctrine, this leadership in modern society is exercised by managers of business enterprise.

Managerial cadres are indispensable for modern industrial civilization and for economic growth. For countries striving to lift themselves from an agrarian—often from a nomadic—primordial society to modernity in a few decades, the problem of managerial resources is crucial.

Scarcity of Managerial Talent

Managerial talent is scarce in the developing countries. Compared with capital, labor, and natural resources, management is typically in the shortest supply. This scarcity has its historical roots in the social organization and general cultural environment, which not only lack space in the hierarchy for the managerial group but also repel it as a threat to the traditional sanctions of name and power.

As previously indicated, the school systems of the developing countries have not produced many potential industrial managers, partly because higher educational or technical institutions are too few and partly because the cultural influences have caused the existing schools, until very recently, to neglect teaching subjects helpful for entrepreneurial growth.

Accurate statistics on the number of managers are available only for a few industrial countries. Using one of these as a model, one can calculate how many managers other countries should have if they are to reach the standards of the developed countries. This analysis requires establishing a ratio for the United States, for example, between the number of managers and some other statistic that is significantly related and is reliably reported for all countries to be compared. Total management requirements can then be calculated for each country by working back from the other statistic (since the actual number of managers is unknown). The ratio used is the number of "managers"[1] to the total economically active population. The latter figure is significantly related to the number of managers and is reported by the United Nations for almost all countries. The most revealing comparisons using these data are: (1) the United States to another country in a recent year, and (2) the United States in a year when the United States approximated the other country's present development (or even in a year in the U.S. "take-off period") to the other country in the current year. However, the second comparison is not possible since the U.S. data do not cover its underdeveloped stage. Therefore, a compromise is made using the U.S. ratios for a current year and for the first year that manager statistics were available, 1900. Table 39-1 presents these ratios.

From them, one sees that Chile in 1960 would have needed 510,000 managers to equal the 1960 ratio of the United States for managers to economically active population (1 to 4.15) and 610,000 to equal the 1900 U.S. ratio (1 to 3.47).[2] Although no available data tell how many managers they really had, it is significant that only 16,896 students were enrolled in the third level of education in Chile in 1959, or about one-thirtieth of the total managerial need (and some of the students were from other South American countries). The same year, in the United States, 3,377,273 students were enrolled in higher education, or about one-fifth of the total number of managers (almost 17 million).

Although these statistics are very crude, they strongly underscore the fact that the developing countries are not presently educating the number of people needed to fill the managerial functions required by an industrial society, even

1 The number of "managers" used in calculating the ratios for the United States is the adjusted total of the three Bureau of the Census occupational classifications: "professional, technical, and kindred workers," "farmers and farm managers," and "managers, officials, and proprietors." The number was adjusted by subtracting some individual groups, e.g., actors and actresses, athletes, artists, that did not fit.

2 The revelation that there are now actually fewer managers in proportion to the economically active population than there were in 1900 is an interesting sidelight to this study. Although the preparation and reporting of data since 1900 have changed, a decrease in the ratio is constant during the whole period and does not seem to be attributable to census changes. This might indicate that the United States reached its peak manager-worker ratio at the time of its greatest percentage of industrial growth, and since then the managerial function has been declining, while services, sales, and clerical activities have increased proportionately. If this is true, the task of building a managerial pool in the developing countries is even greater than originally thought.

TABLE 39-1

Managerial Requirements

Country	*Managers Needed in 1960 to Match U.S. Ratio of Managers to Economically Active Population*		*1959 Graduates from*	
	U.S. 1960 Ratio, 1 to 4.15	*U.S. 1900 Ratio, 1 to 3.47*	*Third-Level Educational Institutions*	*Second-Level Educational Institutions*
Brazil	4,125,000	5,000,000	14,311	16,608
Chile	510,000	610,000	1183	6915
India	24,500,000	30,000,000	266,704	574,258
UAR (Egypt only)	2,000,000	2,500,000	8041	25,297
Spain	420,000	500,000	7504	19,452

Sources:

(1) The 1900 statistics for the United States are from *Historical Statistics of the United States, Colonial Times to 1957* (Washington, D.C.: Bureau of the Census, 1960), p. 74.

(2) The 1960 statistics for the United States are from *Statistical Abstract of the United States, 1961* (Washington, D.C.: Bureau of the Census), pp. 203 and 215.

(3) Economically active population statistics for the foreign countries are from the *United Nations Statistical Yearbook, 1961* (New York, 1961 and 1962).

(4) Statistics for the number of graduates are from *World Survey of Education—III* (New York: United Nations Educational, Scientific, and Cultural Organization), pp. 24, 28–29.

allowing for large statistical errors in comparison. If one considers that enrollments in the schools are primarily in literary, religious, and historical studies, the managerial outlook becomes even more pessimistic. Consequently the scarcity of management is likely to continue.

Cultivation of Managerial Resources

According to Stepanek, two assumptions explain the origin of industrial managers.[3] One assumption states that entrepreneurs are produced by their environment and not by any direct action on the part of a government agency. The second assumption states that the best managers are those individuals with an aptitude for and experience in entrepreneurship. This aspect has been succinctly explained by David C. McClelland, who sees a relationship among achievement, motivation, and entrepreneurship. Today personality exams predict entrepreneurial behavior. People who score well on these tests are faster learners, do better high school work, work harder at laboratory tasks, and do their best work when it counts for the record. People with high scores are also

3 Joseph E. Stepanek, *Managers for Small Industry* (New York: Free Press of Glencoe, Inc., 1960), p. 43.

resistant to social pressure; have experts or knowledgeable people for friends, prefer risky occupations, and enjoy greater odds. From this McClelland draws conclusions regarding the development of entrepreneur-managers. He states that if a child scores well on the test he will have a high level of entrepreneurship as an adult and rapid economic development as well. A child's score depends on his home environment. If his home environment is favorable toward business, he will do well. If it is adverse to business, he will not.[4]

Most people, including managers, in developing countries are not motivated to change. They do not enjoy taking risks. However, for those individuals who do, methods must be devised to attract their attention, and perhaps in this way the more rapid development of entrepreneurship in developing countries can be brought about. In numerous cases, government loans to individuals who lack aptitude have failed to promote entrepreneurship through training. To take one example of many, in Lashio, Burma, training of paper makers was nearly all wasted time. After much interviewing and testing of the individuals being trained, it was found that they were training for management positions only for prestige.[5]

Sources of Management Talent

Managers originate from seven background areas in developing countries: artisans, merchants, industrial families, workers in large-scale industry, people in government service, members of the armed forces, and those in other professions.

Artisans are skilled workmen and apprentices; with a little capital through savings, they can extend their markets outside their immediate neighborhoods. In favorable conditions, an artisan can expand a small enterprise into a factory. According to Stepanek, this period of growth from small artisan enterprise to factory involves approximately two generations.

Merchants have generally shown a low aptitude for becoming managers of industrial enterprise. Their interests and skills are much better suited to arbitrage and speculative transactions aimed at producing quick profits than to long-range planning and supervision of complex corporate bodies. This judgment might not hold if the merchant has had adequate education and training in business administration. But at present very few merchants are able or have the experience to discharge high-level management responsibilities. Their main contribution is in the small businesses traditional to the particular country or region.

Industrial families could be expected to be the ideal source for managerial talent in the developing countries. To a degree this is true; many outstanding executives have had their start in family business. But an even greater number of people with the same background have never come close to qualifying as executives in the true sense of the term. Too often, family-owned business

[4] David C. McClelland, "The Use of Measures of Motivation in the Study of Society," in *Motives in Fantasy, Action, and Society*, ed. John W. Atkinson (Princeton, New Jersey: D. Van Nostrand Co., Inc., 1958), p. 518.

[5] Stepanek, *Managers for Small Industry*, p. 27.

becomes an instrument for pursuing whatever the family members' interests may be. Management of the business, then, is a mere extension of family affairs and is subject to the logic, or more often the illogic, that characterizes familial ambitions and interests. Such a point of view is obviously ill suited to professional management.

Although there is relatively little large industry in the developing countries, it is rapidly becoming dominant on both the supply and the demand sides of the management market.

Bureaucracy

To date, however, the most significant source of managerial talent in the developing world has been government service. In many countries, if not in most, it is likely to remain the principal source. The incentives and motivations of people who seek government service stem from the prestige attached to white-collar jobs in general and officialdom in particular. This motivation is closely correlated to the relative scarcity of educated persons. Because of this scarcity, the government normally pays higher salaries than those paid by other employers in a developing country. Hence, the competition among seekers of government jobs is keen, and the screening, despite nepotism, is thorough by necessity. The caliber of government employees, therefore, is higher than that of most other occupational groups in the developing countries.

But equally important is the experience which government employment provides. All officials, even small ones, must make decisions. At the same time, they must learn to understand and comply with policies and directives imposed by higher authority. To fill his position properly, an official must place himself at the service of the bureaucratic hierarchy of which he is a part and synchronize his own actions to the system so as to serve the policy goals of the government. And he must do this effectively and economically. There is, thus, a close parallel between an official and an executive. The latter's efficiency is manifested in maximum profits, the former's in maximum fulfillment of the government programs. As Max Weber observed, "Bureaucracy has a rational character: it is dominated by rules, purposiveness, methods, and objectivity. Its origin and growth has had everywhere a revolutionizing effect, in a special sense; an effect which the advance of rationalism usually produces wherever it occurs."[6] It might be added that, in order to do his job effectively, an official must choose the persons and other means which are most efficient. He therefore is compelled to make use of facts, techniques, and scientific knowledge and to rely less on personal relationships and family ties. Such rational behavior is typically foreign to the value systems dominant in many developing countries. Hence, the growth of governmental bureaucracies, greatly speeded by political independence, helps alleviate the lack of managerial resources both by screening and by conditioning people for rational behavior and social action in the context of a purposeful organizational structure.

6 *Wirtschaft und Gesellschaft* (Tuebingen), II (1947), 678.

Environmental Constraints

A prerequisite for managerial development in the underdeveloped world often is a change in the existing ideas and attitudes regarding the nature and role of management. Business executives are conceived as the entrepreneurs of classical and neoclassical doctrine; historically they have become synonymous with *profit takers* lacking both interest and position in the society and its culture. As pointed out above, careers in government enjoy a unique prestige; the profit motive is replaced by the incentives of official privileges and social prestige. Therefore, the public image, or more correctly, mis-image, of managers has to change before broad-scale indigenous development of management resources can be expected.

Even if an underdeveloped nation trains a certain number of qualified managers, they will not necessarily become available for managerial employment. Because of the social stigmas, many use the training credentials to gain entry to some nonbusiness occupation. And, because of the relative discomforts of their own countries, others use their newly acquired qualifications to seek employment abroad.

The propensity to emigrate seems to be on a constant upswing among promising young people in all developing countries. Thus, the quality of indigenous management is not automatically raised by the introduction of business administration courses in the schools or by government aid for education at foreign universities. Steps must be taken to eleminate the exodus and to make opportunities in domestic business more attractive to the best talent. The austerity of a brisk industrialization policy, with its hardships and forced savings, generally aggravates this problem.

Other environmental conditions and social-structure characteristics have restricted the number of persons who have had management positions, even when they have had adequate educational background. Entrance into higher level jobs has often been controlled by family ties, by class or caste, by friendship, or even by political affiliations. This control has worked to the detriment of developing managers by restricting the range of experience accessible to persons with good potential and by placing in high positions persons with lesser abilities. Further limitations on the development of a national pool of available managerial talent have been imposed by the geographic and social immobility evidenced in many of the developing countries. People are often tied to their immediate vicinity because insufficient communications cannot tell them where better jobs are; thus management jobs are filled only from among those persons immediately available.[7] Also, custom sometimes ties people to the land even when they are otherwise free to go.[8]

[7] Howell Davis, ed., *The South American Handbook—1961* (London: Trade and Travel Publications, Ltd., 1961), p. 367. Regarding Chile: "The difficulties of archipelago, forest, and desert make communications a problem. . . . The three southern provinces can only be reached by sea or air, for there are no roads or railways to them."

[8] Davis, *The South American Handbook—1961,* p. 366: "The land worker is not a peon, but he is by tradition closely bound to his patron. He now receives a living wage, and is free to move, but custom holds him to the estate." Also, Raymond Frost, *The*

Dependence on Expatriates

In view of these obstacles, many countries remain dependent on imported American and European managerial talent. Although some regulate the employment of nonnationals, especially in the blue-collar categories, this restriction does not usually apply to managers, directors, and persons generally in charge of business undertakings. In fact, some multinational companies have been specifically asked by local authorities in developing countries not to relinquish management from their own control. This has been interpreted variously as an indication that the local interests want to be "sheltered and looked after by exogenous managers or that the local talent is nonexistent and no alternative to importation is available."[9]

Although the social and historical restraints on managerial resources are being broken by the necessity to industrialize and by the experience which industrial growth itself engenders, any improvement will be slow and tedious. First, the social processes are slow, and traditional values, deep rooted. Second, the industrialization process feeds on its own offspring by creating new managers but at the same time creating an even greater need for managers. All new enterprises represent a net addition to the demand for managerial personnel. In the same way, establishments involving larger capital investments require higher level managerial services and proportionately greater managerial capabilities than do smaller firms.

Development of Managerial Resources

Managerial resources may be upgraded for industrial management in four ways: workers may advance themselves; they may be provided with education by the community or the state; they may be trained by enterprise managers; or they may be aided by noncompany development facilities.

The first, self-education, can easily be dismissed except on a very rudimentary scale. A more constructive notion is that the community, the state, or the society should make the proper investment in advanced-education and vocational-training programs. But governments have concentrated their efforts in the technical sector, and only recently has there been serious appreciation of the fact that a basic obstacle to the growth of business and industry in developing countries is the shortage of managerial skill and know-how.

Backward Society (New York: St. Martin's Press, Inc., 1961), p. 143: "In addition there are other reasons which prevent labor from getting where it is wanted at the right time. Labor may be tied to one place by the nature of its existing occupation. When the labor force is mainly composed of peasant proprietors, they are obviously tied to the land they farm. They may also be tied by debt, by social and family relations, and by preference for a life on the land."

9 Raymond F. Mikesell, *United States Private and Government Investment Abroad* (Eugene, Oregon: University of Oregon Books, 1962), p. 94.

Accordingly, governmental apathy in the management-development area is declining and a more positive attitude is gaining strength. Concrete manifestations of the change can be found in several developing countries. For example, in India the government has established the Administrative Staff College at Hyderabad, where managers from private business, public enterprise, and civil service undergo a training course which deals in 13 weeks with decision making, organization, production control, human relations, and other subjects of business administration. Because of a lack of qualified professors, the school utilizes the syndicate method, which groups the participants so that each will bring a different background and skill (accounting, banking, production, labor relations, etc.) to the group; the learning results from the interchange and synthesis of their knowledge. The students are undersecretaries in government, second-level executives in industry, and presidents of small companies.

Some Indian universities have also introduced managerial subjects. Bombay, Calcutta, Delhi, and Madras universities have programs which include a number of business courses, most taught by practitioners. Competent instructors are extremely scarce, and practically no research is conducted in business administration. All these factors produce rather rudimentary results.

Latin American nations, too, have an insufficient number of college graduates and middle-class citizens, and few give any training in business administration. A step in the right direction is indicated by the extensive program conducted by the School of Business Administration in São Paulo, Brazil; guided by a group of professors from Michigan State University, it provides the first four-year undergraduate program and first graduate program in business administration in Brazil.[10] In Chile, some experimental programs have recently been introduced, mostly organizations of multinational companies, to develop some impetus for managerial education. What success they will have remains to be seen.

Company Development of Managers

A central problem faced by nearly all multinational corporations operating in the developing countries is the selection and training of indigenous management cadres. And a critical part of this problem facing U.S. companies with overseas subsidiaries is the extent to which Americans may be indispensable assets or unnecessary liabilities as full-time resident employees in the foreign operation. In contrast to the case in domestic operations, in overseas operations differences in citizenship cause major problems. The unity, the morale, and consequently the efficiency of an organization will suffer if it is cleft by citizenship blocs.

The citizenship question also has important implications in the economic struggle between capitalism and communism. The political acceptability, and hence the existence and influence, of private foreign investments depends to

[10] John C. Shearer, *High Level Manpower in Overseas Subsidiaries* (Princeton, New Jersey: Industrial Relations Section, Princeton University, 1960), p. 107.

some extent upon the willingness of foreign investors to develop nationals for and to promote them to high-level positions. Nationalistic developments have discredited the view that nonnationals must manage modern enterprises in underdeveloped countries. In the long run, the company that is staffed primarily by nationals has the best chance of becoming an accepted part of the society in which it functions.

Most multinational companies are taking steps to shrink the role of Americans in management overseas and to make more use of local executive talent. One key motive is to improve relations with foreign countries, especially the emerging, intensely nationalistic nations. But here is where the supply of managers capable of running a complex business operation is most sharply limited. Here, too, foreign businessmen must revise and greatly expand their present programs for the management training of nationals. In view of the lack of government assistance and of technical and business schools, the best source of high-level manpower is usually the organization itself rather than the open market.

Obstacles to Company Development

Success in nationalizing management depends upon the industrial advancement of the host environment and upon the relative participation by home offices and by subsidiaries in decision making in the critical functional areas of management.[11] It may be possible to use nationals of lesser ability if the home office makes most of the decisions, the employees are well indoctrinated, and the subsidiary is well controlled. But this is only a partial solution; the real questions are: What are the impediments to hiring nationals? And what methods can the companies use to develop a national management force?

The two main obstacles usually cited to the filling of overseas positions with nationals are the "inherent inabilities" of nationals and the scarcity of properly trained or experienced nationals.[12] The first obstacle is itself a highly tenuous proposition, and the second can be overcome with long-range planning by the international enterprise.

The inherent inabilities are these: nationals have conflicts of loyalty to the country and the company; nationals are not "company men"; that is, they lack the requisite domestic company experience; and nationals are disqualified by general national character weaknesses.[13] The conflict of loyalty is, of course, an argument of doubtful validity, and the preference of the companies for company men is of doubtful desirability. The accepted national stereotypes which some claim as character weaknesses also cannot be substantiated. Different character traits (which so many Americans consider undesirable because they are different from the "right" American traits) do not disqualify foreign nationals from responsible positions; these traits only make them more

11 H. W. Singer, *International Development: Growth and Change* (New York: McGraw-Hill Book Company, 1964), p. 71.

12 Shearer, *High Level Manpower in Overseas Subsidiaries,* p. 91.

13 Shearer, *High Level Manpower in Overseas Subsidiaries,* pp. 92–93.

valuable, as they do not lack the cultural empathy that many American businessmen abroad lack. As expounded above, the scarcity of properly trained or experienced nationals is the most potent reason for the present abundance of imported management in the overseas subsidiaries. What do, and what can, the companies do to overcome this shortage?

Recruitment

The first phase of development is recruitment. Most parent organizations properly consider American colleges the natural source of future management. Consequently, they have developed extensive, costly, and aggressive programs for contacting, appraising, and "selling" candidates, sending scores of recruiters to the colleges in the annual search for promising graduates.

The passivity of the overseas subsidiaries in this area is in marked contrast to parental aggressiveness. The present reliance on public advertisements, personal contacts, and unsolicited applications has proved insufficient to meet native managerial needs. Almost all companies exhibit an astonishing lack of imagination and action in this critical area. Most companies even fail to inform the host country colleges of their manpower needs; the few recruiting contacts that do exist between the two are generally indirect and inefficient. The need is for active, systematic, on-campus recruiting programs. Such action by American and other multinational firms might induce other employers to follow their example and thereby create a market mechanism for efficient allocation of critically scarce foreign managerial talent.

A second source of uniquely qualified nationals is those studying at universities in the United States and Western Europe. U.S. parent corporations are increasingly tapping this source by recruiting, at American colleges, foreign nationals to work in their homeland subsidiaries. These graduates, in a sense, have the ideal combination of traits; their understanding of the indigenous culture and business behavior can be integrated with an American educational background and long exposure to American ways of thinking and acting and to "peculiar" American business behavior.

The Institute of International Education, a New York organization that administers various foreign-study programs, reports that more firms than ever are using its listings of foreigners educated in the United States.[14] The companies use the files for such specialized purposes as finding a Chilean trained here in mining engineering or a Thai who has majored in marketing.

U.S. firms have generally been ineffective in developing useful selection criteria for foreign nationals. Most companies select nationals without the benefit of sound procedures or objective criteria, or they utilize selection criteria modified from those of the parent company, often putting the foreign nationals at unwarranted disadvantages.[15] The selection decision must not be based, as it often is, upon how well the recruiter feels the national will fit into the

[14] *The Wall Street Journal* (New York), March 8, 1965, p. 14.

[15] "Human Problems of U.S. Enterprise in Latin America," *Cornell Conference Report* (Ithaca, 1957), p. 28.

American-dominated firm; this procedure will not secure nationals who will be most valuable to the firm in the long run.

Managerial Training

In some multinational companies a distinction is made between "training" and "development." Training programs are planned investments to prepare local nationals, generally recent graduates, for greater technical or managerial responsibilities. These post-college programs run into problems, as college graduates of underdeveloped nations have a distaste for further formal education and an antipathy toward the manual aspects of the programs; they look upon themselves as "crown princes" having had the benefit of a more extensive and formal education.[16]

Development programs are investments in more mature, higher level nationals to groom them for very responsible positions. Training investments are often made through group programs, but investments in development are generally on an individual basis.

Training in the host country

A vicious circle is encountered in internal management development carried out without the benefit of college-trained nationals since such development is intertwined with technical training. The nationals do not have enough technical competence to enable them to be left alone on the job. Therefore, the foreign supervisor intervenes frequently on job problems, but this very bypassing and close supervision prevent the nationals from developing their own talents. Possibly management should provide more and better technical training at the management as well as at the work level to create a situation in which management from the parent company can be withdrawn from the close supervision they often provide.[17]

Management, of course, tries to make up for the nationals' deficiencies by providing more parent-company supervisors and, therefore, closer supervision—a self-defeating course. Instead they should shift men from supervision into management training, thus providing for greater operating efficiency and an accelerated program of personnel development.

Although the importance of allowing the national independent responsibility is emphasized, he cannot develop simply by being alone or through formal training programs. He can develop best through the coaching of a skillful boss, providing that this coaching is directed toward giving him greater responsibility and decision-making power.

This process can be formalized through what is coming to be known as the "counterpart system."[18] At first an expatriate executive and a local national

16 "Human Problems of U.S. Enterprise in Latin America" (1957), p. 31.

17 "Human Problems of U.S. Enterprise in Latin America" (1957), p. 33.

18 "Human Problems of U.S. Enterprise in Latin America," *Cornell Conference Report* (Ithaca, 1958), p. 64.

occupy the same formal position, with the foreigner wielding authority for his national counterpart. Later the expatriate gradually relinquishes his authority to the national and assumes an advisory role. Finally, the foreigner repatriates and leaves the national in complete charge. In these cases the timing of the counterpart-to-consultant-to-exit stages must be established to combat the tendency of the national to depend too much upon the expatriate or the tendency of the foreigner to hold on for too long.

In the training of nationals, the training of exported U.S. management must not be overlooked since they will be supervising the nationals and greatly conditioning their attitudes. Special attention must be given to exported management to make them aware of the particular social and cultural barriers they will have to face and overcome.

Training in the country of the parent company

Most companies rely heavily on the assignment of individual employees to the United States for special training within the parent company. There, training is a conscious effort to acquaint the foreign national with the economic, political, and social institutions of the United States and to "Americanize" his outlook, as foreigners are well known to resist American methods and moral standards. One company tried two nationals as general managers of one of their subsidiary operations but found that neither would accept American financial controls or test marketing methods.[19] The firm finally placed an American on the job.

A spokesman for the Singer Sewing Machine Company reported that foreign attitudes on ethical matters sometimes differ from prevalent U.S. standards. He stated, "I remember one employee in Thailand who cheated the company and was sent to jail. When he got out, he came back fully expecting to get his old job back again as if nothing had happened. He thought he had paid his debt in full."[20]

One of the most elaborate training programs involving visits to the United States is conducted by the First National City Bank, with headquarters in New York City. Two-year executive training programs modeled on the home-office programs are common. This initial training is supplemented with six months at the bank's New York offices. Another firm puts management recruits through advanced management courses at a well-known U.S. university followed by 23 months of work in this country.

This training of young nationals in the United States may result in greater difficulties in the short run, but it does promote more rapid and complete management development, and it facilitates the early identification of talent as home-office executives get to know the nationals well during their stay.

The effectiveness of training nationals in the United States is reduced by a number of problems. Many qualified nationals are ineligible because of their

[19] *The Wall Street Journal* (New York), March 8, 1965.
[20] *The Wall Street Journal* (New York), March 8, 1965, p. 1.

difficulty with the English language. Even in training in the national's home subsidiary, the national should have a command of English.

Also, few subsidiaries have operations on as large a scale as even the smallest domestic operation, so training in the United States must be modified to be appropriate and easily transferred to the subsidiary.[21] Some companies have solved this problem by sending trainees from underdeveloped nations to their smaller subsidiaries in Europe or Canada.

The nationals upon return to their home country are prone to effect a superior attitude toward their subordinates and expect to be treated with care. Also, if the training program is too long in the United States, the national might become dissatisfied with his circumstances and opportunities in his home subsidiary. And often neither the salary nor the promotional opportunities are so good for the returning national as they are for exported, parent-company management.

Structural Changes

The structure of the organization itself can have an important effect upon the development of nationals. Positions should be in line with the qualifications of the available people, with subsequent revision of duties and responsibilities to keep pace with the individual's development as he acquires experience. For example, the creation of an additional top level of supervision provides the opportunity to use less experienced people in subordinate positions but heading functional areas of responsibility.[22] This procedure permits assigning to these positions employees who still need some additional supervisory guidance to handle the full responsibility involved.

Structural changes can also stimulate the advance of nationals, particularly when the organization is expanding. If a department grows in the number of people employed and in the weight of its activities, the top jobs become even more difficult, and superiors are inclined to think that nationals do not yet have the experience or the ability to handle such responsibility.[23] At times it is possible to subdivide a department in an expanding organization, thus providing more promotion opportunities and more opportunities to take on jobs that do not have the forbidding magnitude of those in the larger department. These modified organizational structures are not, of course, permanent arrangements, but they do help in the identification phase of manpower generation. The company can more easily ascertain those in whom the firm might well invest more time and money.

Development Programs

Programs to train nationals for top management positions contain the fundamentals of management development and are usually presented through

21 B. F. Hoselitz, "The Recruitment of Management in Underdeveloped Countries," *International Social Science Bulletin,* VI, No. 3 (1954), 441.

22 "Human Problems of U.S. Enterprise in Latin America" (1958), p. 65.

23 "Human Problems of U.S. Enterprise in Latin America" (1958), p. 65.

many formal, in-company courses lasting from a few days to a few months. These programs could, to a much greater extent, contribute to the generation of national manpower resources. The present programs are not particularly concerned with the further nationalization of management but only try to arouse a great zeal for the American way of doing things whether it correctly fits the particular environment or not.[24]

Promotional Opportunities

In general, the effectiveness of these training or development programs or both is severely limited by two conditions within the overseas subsidiary itself: the domination of the upper levels of subsidiary management by Americans, and the lack of incentive for overseas American management to develop nationals.

The reliance on U.S. personnel in the less developed areas gives rise to a direct Gresham's law.[25] The poorer American manager knows that there is no equal position for him at home; his income is considerably better abroad, and his place in society commensurably higher. He is, therefore, not interested in training a replacement for himself and tends to drive out or fails to attract local personnel who could become efficient managers. This situation must be eliminated, as the success of management-development programs in these areas depends far more on the willingness and the efforts of the parent company executives than it does on any formal program.

Resignation

A problem of many overseas firms is retaining nationals after they have been trained. A firm must be prepared to make continued employment sufficiently attractive. The problem of having promising nationals leave after the company has invested in them is one of the most important in overseas operations; almost without exception firms reported losses soon after the completion of training programs of at least 25 percent of the participants.[26] This situation is partially due to the fact that promotional opportunities are blocked for the national and partially due to the fact that nationals doing similar work usually receive considerably less for their services than parent-company management in the foreign subsidiary.

The prestige of training in the United States increases the value of a local citizen to other bidders for his services. According to many overseas managers, their companies' salary programs often prevent the retention of their most valuable nationals.[27] There is also a conviction among capable nationals that in most American subsidiaries the highest posts are either reserved for Americans or, at least, the nationals are at a decided disadvantage in com-

24 Shearer, *High Level Manpower in Overseas Subsidiaries,* p. 106.
25 Mikesell, *United States Private and Governmental Investment Abroad,* p. 118.
26 Shearer, *High Level Manpower in Overseas Subsidiaries,* p. 110.
27 "Human Problems of U.S. Enterprise in Latin America" (1957), p. 33.

petition with Americans for these positions. This is especially noticeable in the financial area, where worry is expressed about giving nationals control over money, since in many underdeveloped areas payola is an accepted way of life.

Therefore, if American companies are to retain their investments in national managers, an assessment of wage and promotional structures is in order. Steps in the form of promotional opportunities and wage adjustment and security must be taken to commit these managers to their jobs.

American Nationalism

Success in training and developing local nationals for executive positions seems to be creating a new problem which neither practical management men nor theoreticians had anticipated. Multinational U.S. companies which have tried to promote a local national into a position above that held by an American expatriate executive in the same affiliate have encountered angry resistance from the American concerned. Quite often the American expatriate has been so strongly opposed to being in a position subordinate to that of a local national that he has either asked for a transfer or left the company entirely. If this had happened only in African or Asian countries, one might speculate that it was based on deep-seated racial prejudices. But the problem has become even more acute in European affiliates, in which local nationals of high competence are relatively more available for general management positions and in which only certain technical or functional executives must be brought in from the United States.

Conciliation of Conflicts

The American overseas subsidiaries (or those of any other developed nation) are engaged in a circular battle. On the one hand, they must do some "Americanizing" of their foreign management, at least in the rudiments of business technique and ethics. But on the other hand, the point at which to stop and let the national take over in the way he feels is best in his culture, lest the firm be added to the list of "ugly Americans," is hard to determine.

U.S. companies and the governments of the emerging nations must do more than they are in the field of management development. In the international sphere, the United States' International Cooperation Administration participates in management training and development activities in the underdeveloped countries. Also, the International Labor Organization is currently developing a program to provide an international center for advanced training of managers at Turin, Italy, making use of buildings and grants made available by the Italian government.[28]

Only by concerted cooperation of multinational companies, governments, and international agencies can the problem of effective management develop-

28 *Social and Labor Aspects of Economic Development* (Geneva: The International Labor Office, 1963), p. 34.

ment be solved. Governments cannot do it alone, since the multinational companies must provide opportunities in their organizational structures for native personnel. But the companies cannot adequately train all the needed management talent; governments in the underdeveloped areas must help by providing a broader base of educated manpower from which the firms can recruit and by instilling the social attitudes required for management responsibilities. Only through the development of managerial resources in the emerging nations to organize the ingredients of production and modern commerce can economic progress be more rapidly and lastingly achieved.

40

Central Planning

Central planning has become a dominant force in the underdeveloped world. The overriding problems of these societies—the inadequacy of the existing infrastructure, the slow rate of industrial growth, the low productivity of the people, the lack of technical and managerial talent, and the shortage of capital—compel governments to operate from strongly purposive platforms and to emphasize activistic approaches. Laissez-faire attitudes find little room in either the political or the economic realm. Pressures for improvement have led to two types of action: national development planning and the establishment of state enterprises. The former is visualized as the total mobilization of the resources and manpower for rapid development, and the latter, as a vehicle for the initiation and management of the production activities necessary to achieve the development goals. Private enterprise, therefore, finds itself in an environment where the public sector is proportionately large and where the opportunities, uncertainties, and rewards are tightly meshed both with the planning process and with the policies and practices of the state corporations. The effect of planning is even greater on the multinational company than on national private investors since the role assigned to foreign investors is invariably subject to separate guidelines which may be either restrictive or preferential.

Meaning of Central Planning

Planning means different things to different people. Since it was first developed in the U.S.S.R., it is often used as a synonym for the Communist system. Even the United Nations documents classify countries as private enterprise or mixed economies on the one hand and as centrally planned economies on the other. In contrast to this, some economists argue that any regulation of business by government is a form of central planning, however indirect. They would include in central planning even such measures as fiscal policy, monetary open-market operations, and wage-price guidelines.

Neither of these definitions is suitable for analytical purposes. The first one excludes all non-Communist countries, and the second confuses *central* (or national) planning with *sectoral* and functional regulation of business activity. As the adjectives "central" and "national" suggest, the pivotal point of the concept is the existence of a national center empowered to integrate all aspects of economic life into a cohesive program, the central plan, which not only supersedes any sectoral or functional plans but also is identified with the nation's economic objectives and the national interest. As such, the central plan, even if loosely knit, is vastly different from the various regulatory bodies found in most democratic countries; these operate more or less independently in their respective sectors (maritime commission, power commission, trade commission, communications commission, etc.). Such agencies do have an effect on the business environment, but they do not produce a plan as such; indeed, their actions are often mutually incongruous.

In this book planning means central initiation and coordination of economic activity without regard for the political system involved. The central plan integrates information, objectives, forecasts, and directives regarding production, distribution, consumption, and capital formation, for a slated period, usually several years.

Planning Models

Although central planning must necessarily reflect the peculiarities of the country where it is practiced, and, as far as specifics are concerned, each plan is different from all others, in concept and design there are but two basic models: the Soviet and the French. The former began in the late 1920's and serves as the basic blueprint for the entire Communist world. Its basic functions and processes were described in Chapter 2. The latter is of postwar origin. Met initially with considerable skepticism outside France, it now overshadows the Soviet model in both the developing and developed countries and has aroused considerable interest, if not imitation, even in the Communist orbit.

French Planning. In actual practice most underdeveloped countries combine the Soviet and the French planning principles in random ways. In most countries the original approach was to imitate the compulsion system of the Soviet Union. But in the 1960's the French approach has been emphasized and therefore deserves further elaboration.

Using input-output tables and national economic accounts, the central planning authority, in collaboration with representatives of business, agriculture, and labor on Modernization Commissions,[1] draws up an agreed plan for the future development of the economy. Unlike the Soviet Gosplan, the French central plan is only "indicative," not "imperative." But, it is much more than a forecast because all sectors of the economy are committed to it through their participation in its preparation and through the public attention which the plan commands. Although the French plan lacks Soviet-type directive and it is prepared only at the industry level, not covering individual private firms, it coordinates the production and investment programs of the different branches of the economy, increases the quality and flow of information, eliminates dislocations, and promises a balanced market for individual firms.

Company managements still make their own decisions, but they do so with knowledge, provided by the plan, about the intentions of the rest of the economy and about the government's credit, tax, and price policies. Much of the success of the French plan is attributed to the so-called *announcement effect.* If the managers of private enterprises are convinced that the government is determined to execute the the programs and actions required of it in the public sector, and, hence, that there is a good chance that the development goals can be achieved, then the plan for the private sector not only represents what is required of private enterprises but also reveals the opportunities for expansion in various industries. In effect, it becomes a matter of self-interest on the part of businessmen to increase productive capacity in line with the opportunities outlined in the plan.

Figure 40-1 illustrates the processes of French planning. Objectives are determined on the basis of systematic studies of various industries and regions, and these are synthesized under various growth assumptions. Parallel to this, a process of consultation is carried out with committees of general competence (such as the Economic and Social Council) and with specialized committees (such as the Modernization Commissions); this consultation is followed by the process of decision making, in which the legislative and executive agencies of the government participate.

France, at present, is in its Fifth Plan covering a total period of 20 years. Planning began with the decision of the provisional government, presided over by General de Gaulle, to initiate a "modernization and equipment plan" and to put in charge a new government agency, the *Commissariat Général du Plan.* The First Plan, the reconstruction or Monnet Plan, was less sophisticated than later efforts as a piece of econometrics but was, by virtue of the very ample powers of intervention in the economy which the authorities then had, a plan in a much more rigorous sense than were those that followed. The Second Plan covered the four years 1954–57; the Third, the years 1958–61; the Fourth, 1962–65; and the Fifth Plan began in 1966.

[1] In France itself, the planning apparatus consists of 27 Modernization Commissions of 30 to 50 persons each. The members are representatives of the following groups: high-level civil servants; producers (heads of private or nationalized enterprises and farmers); leaders of business associations; trade unionists; and university economists and other independent experts.

FIGURE 40-1A

Stages of the Fourth Plan (1962–65)

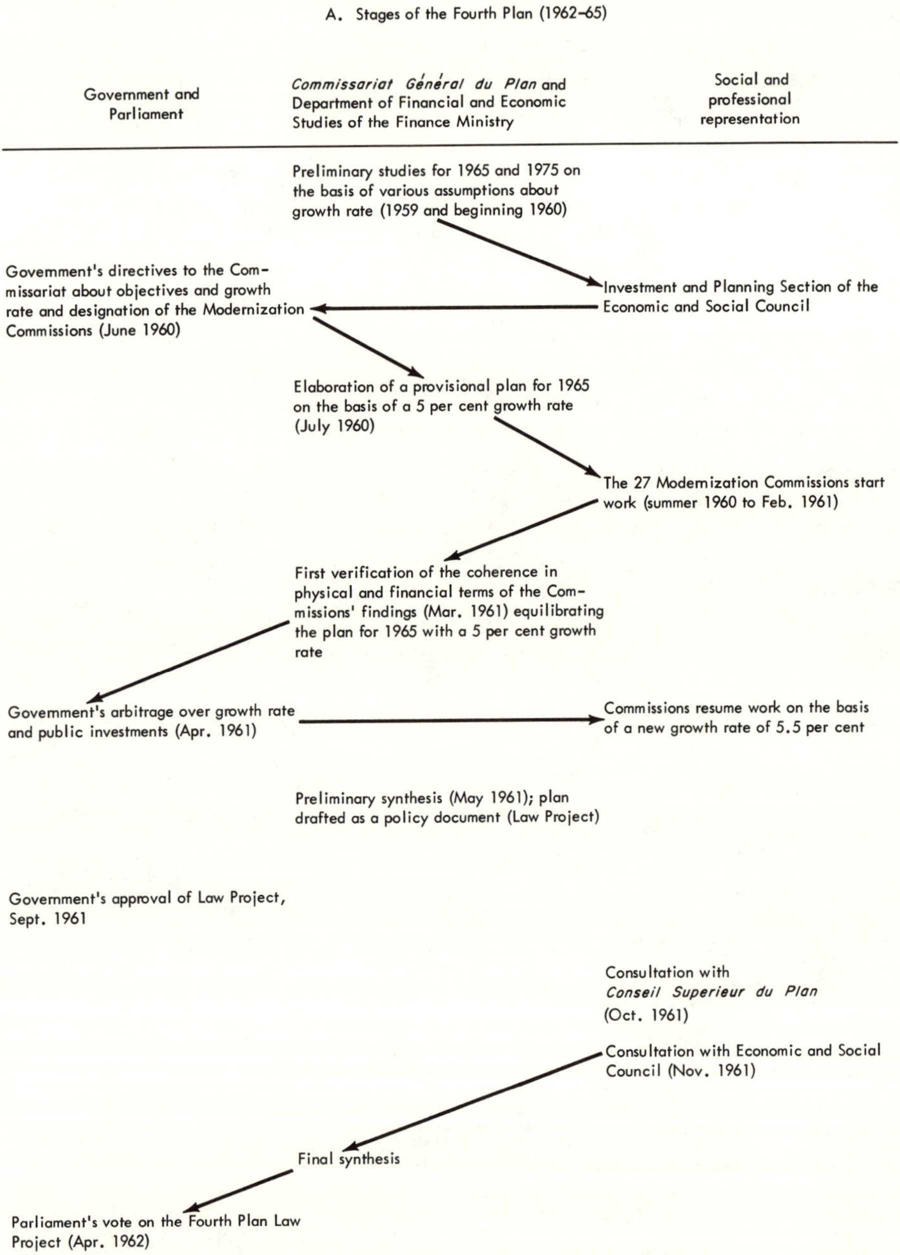

Source: *The French Planning Commission.*

FIGURE 40-1B

Calendar of the Preparation of the Fifth Plan

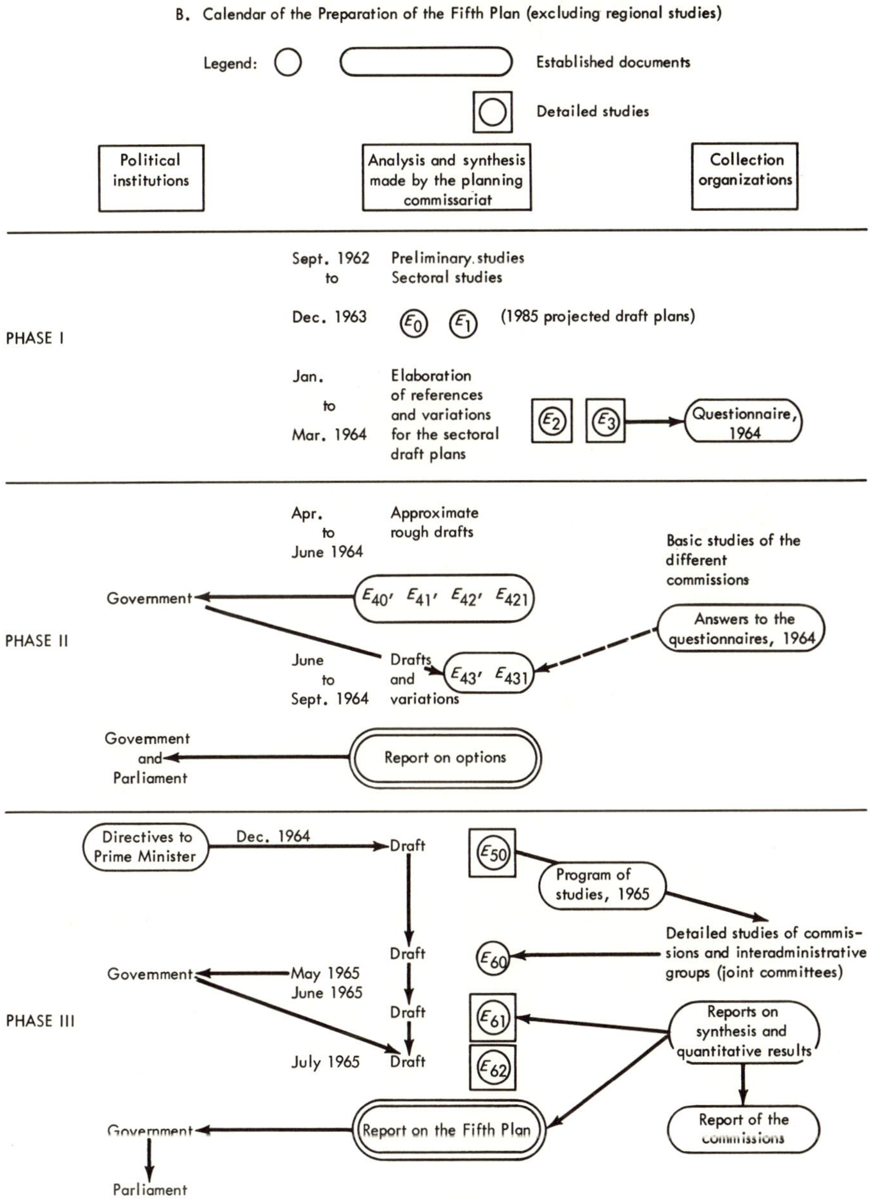

Source: *The French Planning Commission.*

It was the post-Monnet plans, particularly the Fourth Plan, which set the tone for the special type of "soft" planning in which the French have led. In its own wording the Fourth Plan is described as "a framework of investment programs for the period 1962–65 and an instrument for orienting economic expansion and social progress."

Extent of Central Planning

The urge for economic progress is universal in the underdeveloped world. In Asia all countries now have development plans; in Latin America, where the Alliance for Progress has encouraged planning, the same is true; in Africa the lone exception is Ruanda-Urundi. A comprehensive study conducted by Albert Waterston, a planning expert for the World Bank, reveals that over 100 countries practice central planning of some sort.[2]

In the numerous development plans a wide variety of approaches is evident. Omitting the case of an economy entirely directed by the state, as in the communist countries, the intervention of the government to implement development plans may proceed on three different fronts essential for multinational firms: the use of policy instruments, especially commercial, fiscal, and monetary policies; direct controls, such as quotas, price controls, and exchange licenses; and governmental investment and operation. The last alternative is most likely in areas where private enterprise is believed to be uninterested in or incapable of achieving the goals of the plan. In most cases all aspects of planning are encountered, but the proportions vary with the particular government's political orientation and approach to its economic problems.

The Planning Leaders. India and Pakistan stand out in Asia in terms of their commitment to development planning and in the scope and quality of the national effort to solve economic development problems. In these countries, aggregate plans are formulated with relatively sophisticated techniques. They try to link aggregate plans to sectoral and project breakdowns and to emphasize action programs. Although Indian economic planning has the reputation of being the most experienced, sophisticated, and comprehensive in the non-communist, underdeveloped world, it certainly has not solved many of the country's problems. However, it is important from the standpoint of the multinational firm to understand the size and complexity of the Pakistan and Indian plans and the strong government support for them. A growing flexibility in the planning approach used by these two countries will give more direct emphasis to promotion of the private sector as a major vehicle of growth.[3]

The Small Effective Planners. The planning in Malaysia and China (Taiwan) does not compare with that in India or Pakistan in com-

2 *Development Planning: Lessons of Experience* (Baltimore: Johns Hopkins Press, 1965).

3 Douglas S. Paauw, *Development Planning in Asia* (Washington, D.C.: National Planning Association, May 1965).

prehensiveness, sophistication, and national support. However, these countries have shown promise in their development planning, which uses private enterprise as the vehicle for economic growth and development. Generally the government will stimulate the growth of the private sector by providing overhead capital, financial stability, and technical guidance, particularly for the benefit of lagging sectors in the economy.

In both Taiwan and Malaysia, planning began by tackling problems at the lower level and by emphasizing the rural agricultural sector; then gradual progress was made toward establishing an aggregate planning framework. This bottom-to-top approach made the problems of coordination between aggregate and lower level planning less severe than they are in most other Asian countries, where the top-to-bottom approach is used.

A third example of the planning operations a multinational firm must deal with is illustrated by the Philippines and Thailand. In both these countries the actual plan is an academic venture with very little impact on decision making or action. The Philippines have produced several plans, none of which has been taken seriously or strongly implemented. Thailand is a newcomer to the field. Private enterprise has accounted for a substantial part of investment activity, while public-sector activity has concentrated on providing investment in social overhead facilities; but even this public expenditure has been more a result of ministerial activity than of the central plan.[4]

The failure of the plans in these countries to adapt to the basically private-enterprise nature of the economies appears to be a major factor in preventing planning from obtaining widespread governmental and popular support. This development has major implications for the possible operations of multinational firms because it means it is important for the companies to be more aware of the operations of various ministry programs than of the operations of the central planning agency.

Unlike the approach in the Philippines and Thailand, the doctrinaire, nationalist approach in Ceylon, Burma, and Indonesia has made the central plans an overpowering consideration for all international enterprises. The development plans in these countries have had an unusually high political component, which the government has manipulated for various experimental purposes as well as for exercising almost complete control over foreign-owned businesses.

Effects of Central Planning on Multinational Management

Table 40-1 summarizes a recent survey of international businessmen in 67 countries.[5] The results of this survey are more interesting for what they do

[4] Paauw, *Development Planning in Asia,* p. 11.

[5] Millard H. Pryor, Jr., "Planning in a Worldwide Business," *Harvard Business Review,* XLIII, No. 1 (January–February 1965), 136.

TABLE 40-1

National Planning Organizations

	Middle East and Africa	*Latin America*	*Europe*	*Far East*	*Total, All Areas*
A. How active?					
Countries with active national planning organizations	12	11	12	9	44
Countries with no national planning organizations	2	6	5	3	16
Countries whose policy is unknown	6	1	0	0	7
Total responses	20	18	17	12	67
B. How useful?					
National plans very useful in planning local operations	0	0	2	1	3
National plans of some use in planning local operations	3	2	3	7	15
National plans of no use in planning local operations	9	9	7	1	26
Total responses	12	11	12	9	44

not show than for what they do, at least in a direct sense. The businessmen surveyed, mostly Americans, believed that only two-thirds of the countries where they operated had central planning. This reveals a serious lack of knowledge, since the actual proportion was much higher. Since the executives are unaware that central plans exist, they obviously cannot find them useful in any way for company planning. The more important question is why such a shocking discrepancy between the businessmen's awareness and the actual facts exists.

One explanation is that many governments which have planning bodies have failed to grant them any effective powers and that, therefore, they have very little practical influence on the economic life of the country. Another explanation degrades the value of the plans to international executives by asserting that the plans are so designed as to be of no assistance to business managers. However, even the apologists recognize that these explanations are less than convincing. The author of the survey goes on to note that it is becoming more and more imperative for multinational companies to take into consideration the national plans of a country regarding plant location and the determination of what goods to produce. This conclusion is expressed by the following quotation:

> In spite of the limited amount of influence which national planning has had on international business activities in the past, the success of France and other European countries in utilizing this technique, coupled with the proliferation of new planning groups, suggests that the concept will gain more and more

> acceptance and that, in the near future, national plans will become a significant factor in developing international business strategy.[6]

This prediction has not yet become a reality, not because the plans are insignificant or lacking in practical value but because management has been slow to grasp the meaning and implications of central planning. Part of this failure to adapt is apparently attributable to a doctrinaire opposition to governmental regulation of business and to general and national planning in particular.

Adaptation of Business Planning to National Planning

Since central planning is interpreted and implemented in different ways by different countries, the prerequisite for any intelligent utilization of the plan by business firms is an accurate assessment of a particular government's commitment to the plan. Equally basic is a clear understanding of the planning machinery, including the actual powers of the different agencies concerned, since the plan has quite different implications if official organs exist for its vigorous enforcement than if they do not.

In addition, it is important for a firm to consider the following specific aspects of the plan:

(1) the overall objective
(2) the breakdown between public and private investment
(3) the sector priority considerations
(4) the project priority considerations
(5) the performance criterion for operating companies

The overall objectives of a country's plan

A company first has to be aware of the overall objectives of a country's plan. Broadly speaking, an emphasis on increasing national income together with concrete estimates of the proposed increase are to be found in all central plans. However, the expansion of employment opportunities is almost an equally important objective in many plans, notably those of Ceylon, India, and Pakistan. Ceylon has a detailed plan in terms of employment; quantitative estimates of the increase in the labor force in various sectors are one of the guiding considerations in arriving at the planned investment outlay and its distribution. The objective of achieving balance in international payments in some of the plans means that companies that will invest in, or set up, import-replacement or export industries will be looked upon with greater favor. In the Ceylonese plan, for example, high priority is given to the need for import-saving production and for expansion of exports, particularly in agriculture. China (Taiwan) stresses increases in exports to meet the import requirements of development programs.

[6] Pryor, "Planning in a Worldwide Business," pp. 136–37.

Breakdown between public and private investment

A second item that multinational companies have to consider when studying central plans is the breakdown between the public and the private sector. Since state enterprise will be the subject of the next chapter, the discussion here will be limited to the private sector in central plans using the Economic Commission for Asia and the Far East (ECAFE) countries as examples.

In the Asian countries considered, the private sector is responsible for a large share of investment outlay for industrial development. Table 40-2 shows the share of the private sector in the planned investment of previous development plans. As the table indicates, the role of the private sector in industrial development has been a dominant one in Pakistan and the Philippines, whereas the public sector has been more important in Ceylon, China (Taiwan), and India.

The actual plans do not, generally, greatly restrict the fields of endeavor for private enterprise. However, actual practice may create restrictions despite the plan. In the ten-year plan of Ceylon, although no general restriction is placed upon industries in which the private sector is not allowed to operate, a rather comprehensive list of industries, including fisheries and petroleum refining, has been reserved for the public sector in actual practice. The cardinal principle in the second five-year plan of Pakistan is that there should be no complete reservation of industries for the public sector, except defense industries. However, the government participates directly in those enterprises essential for overall development where private capital is not forthcoming.

In the three-year program of the Philippines, the basic policy provides that efforts to bring about economic development must be undertaken primarily by the private sector, with the government limiting itself to (a) projects which the private sector is unwilling or unable to undertake because of huge initial

TABLE 40-2

Share of Private Sector in Planned Investment

Country	*Plan*	*Percentage of Private Sector in Industrial Investment*	*Total Investment*
Ceylon	Ten-year plan	27	34
China (Taiwan)	Second four-year plan	43	38
Malaysia	Second five-year plan	not available	57
India	Second five-year plan	42	39
	Third five-year plan	43	39
Pakistan	First five-year plan	not available	36
	Second five-year plan	71	39
Philippines	Three-year program	77	69

Source: United Nations, ECAFE, *Formulating Industrial Development Programmes,* Development Programming Techniques, Series No. 2 (Bangkok, 1961), pp. 115ff.

capital outlays; (b) social overhead, including public works and utilities; (c) education, research and surveys, industrial assistance, and public health; and (d) all other services necessary for the development of the private sector. Under the current program, the state is also required to encourage private investment in what are considered to be strategic areas of industrial development, particularly the textile, pulp-and-paper, cement, glass, agricultural tools, and food-processing industries,

Sector-priority considerations

The third level of central planning that affects multinational management is the sector-priority considerations. The following are typical priority criteria that companies will have to weigh their plans against:

(1) industries having a large foreign exchange benefit coefficient[7]

(2) producer-goods industries which reduce the import component of future development expenditure

(3) industries using indigenous raw materials

(4) consumer-goods industries meeting essential needs

(5) industries making the largest net contribution to national income per unit of investment

This list merely represents the multiplicity of factors taken into consideration in fixing priorities. Determination of the order of priority requires the weighing of these various factors; this has not generally been done quantitatively except in the Philippines. Also, certain core projects like iron and steel in India and fertilizers in Pakistan are retained irrespective of foreign exchange costs.

In China (Taiwan) decisions on the priority of an industrial project are largely influenced by the extent of the market. A project is established when its product is urgently needed in sufficiently large quantities or when the product can be manufactured with indigenous materials or with by-products of industries.

In Pakistan, the Planning Commission carried out studies on the comparative foreign exchange benefits and the social profitability of various industries. Having thus established the comparative eligibility of industries, it gave emphasis to various projects according to a number of factors, the main ones being the importance of the product to the national economy, the potential demand for it, and the export possibilities. A noteworthy feature of the foreign exchange benefit calculation in Pakistan has been the subtraction of the potential foreign exchange lost because of the nonexport of the domestic raw materials from the total foreign exchange earned or saved in each case. This calculation could be extremely important to a company planning an investment in, for example, textile manufacturing and wanting permission and tax aid or incentives from the government. If Pakistan were an exporter of

[7] As used here the foreign exchange benefit coefficient is defined as the ratio of foreign exchange benefit to foreign exchange cost of a project.

cotton and a heavy importer of finished textiles, which caused a drain on the country's foreign exchange, a textile industry would seem ideal and thus, supposedly, would gain rapid approval. Yet, when the balance is made, it may well be that the loss from the formerly exported cotton is more than the gain in finished textiles, especially if the new industry is inefficient and turns out high-priced, low-quality goods. In this case a multinational firm could find its proposal turned down.

Project-priority consideration

Once the eligibility of industries is determined on the basis of sectoral priorities, the next step is project selection and combination on the basis of feasibility with respect to resources, particularly foreign exchange and technical manpower. The problem of priorities in project selection, besides the fact that they are subject to general industrial priorities, requires supplementary criteria with respect to scale and choice of technology drawn up in light of employment targets and resource availability.

This requirement could mean that the multinational companies may not be able to set up the size plant they desire; or, if a company wanted to move into some market that was expanding rapidly, the priority could be given to some other company that had come in previously with a small, uneconomical plant but that had been promised the right to expand as the market grew.

The possibility of a conflict between the technology a multinational firm may wish to use and the employment goals of a central plan also exists. The conflict may be between the objectives of maximum output and saving on one hand and of providing maximum employment on the other. Some countries attempt to achieve a balance between them. In Pakistan, labor-intensive methods are favored in the production of consumer goods by assigning an important role to the development of small-scale and cottage industries while capital-intensive projects are accepted in other areas.

Operating criteria once established

Once a multinational firm has been successful in dealing with a country and its central planning operations and has established an enterprise within the country, a new field of government-company relations comes into operation. However, a company that has been aware of a country's objectives and levels of plans as outlined above should be in a position to maintain a successful working relationship with the government and its economic planners.

The criteria that a government will use in judging whether a company, once established, is yielding the expected benefits from the negotiation and planning stages are much the same as those a company had to be aware of in the beginning. The criteria will vary somewhat from country to country, especially regarding the priority they are given, but they will include, in general, the following items:

(1) Is the firm providing steady or increasing employment at a satisfactory level?

(2) Is the foreign exchange benefit working out as calculated?

(3) Is the firm training nationals for high-level positions or eventual takeover or both?

(4) Are the tax benefits to the government as much as expected?

(5) Has the new enterprise disrupted or helped other industries, price levels, etc.?

(6) Have the concessions granted the firm, such as tariff protection, helped the country or the economy as a whole?

A multinational firm will have to live with such scrutiny far beyond the initial negotiation stages.

Finally, will a multinational firm that goes into an unplanned sector of the economy rather than into a planned private sector be faced with measuring up to the criteria mentioned above? In general, the scrutiny of the unplanned sector probably will not be so great, but conditions vary from country to country. However, whether a firm is in a planned or an unplanned sector, an awareness of a country's economic development plan should be part of management's knowledge.

Being in a country's planned sector could very well have advantages that offset additional restrictions. Since most countries plan those sectors that are considered most vital, a company in this area may find that the government is much more willing to grant it tariff concessions, foreign exchange allocations, favorable tax treatment, or other privileges.

41

State Enterprise

State enterprise seems to be a universal corollary to central planning. Throughout the underdeveloped world government-owned industrial and financial enterprises have emerged shortly after the implementation of a plan. In the initial stages the state acquires some of the enterprises through nationalization of pre-existing private firms, but later they are started by public investment in new ventures. Also, in the early stages state acquisitions and investments have been rather erratic and incoherent, but in a few years, usually in a decade or so, the public sector consolidates itself into a well-defined pattern.

Most new nations are now close to this consolidation stage. In what direction, or perhaps at what rate of speed, they will proceed from there on remains to be seen. The limited cases available suggest that the future course will be more predictable and more geared to specific and realistic objectives than in the past; therefore, the powers of the public sector will be more likely to increase than to decrease. Whether or not this power will be used is a different question, although it probably will.

Factors Favoring State Enterprise

It would be fallacious to attribute the rise of state enterprise solely to central planning. Government has always been a major factor in economic development. Even in the heyday of laissez faire in the mid nineteenth century, government policy established the framework of the legal, administrative, and monetary institutions that, by protecting private property and facilitating capital accumulation, created the prerequisities for economic development through private enterprise in the new economies.

One of the chief factors in the establishment and the expansion of state enterprise in underdeveloped countries has been the argument that if the public sector does not undertake the venture, it will not be done because there is a lack of availability or willingness on the part of private capital. Even in Western countries the government has not hesitated to intervene during periods when a particularly rapid economic expansion was required and could not be achieved by private enterprise. In France and in the United Kingdom following World War II, such intervention implied not only government direction of economic development, in particular through public investment, but also the placing of major industries under public operations, as in the case of the coal and steel industries in Great Britain. Even in the United States during World War II, the government, to foster development of industries such as synthetic rubber, aluminum, and atomic energy, particularly vital to the defense effort, erected new plants at its own expense, to be operated by major private concerns.

Economic development and modernization of the social structure imply for all the underdeveloped countries irrespective of their views on the role of the government in the economy a substantial increase in investment by the public sector. In some fields, such as transportation, investment may be imperative for economic development. In other fields, such as social welfare, health, and general education, investment, even if its impact on economic development is likely to be less direct, may still be demanded by the population. It is therefore understandable that in developing countries the share of the public sector in total capital formation is relatively high and generally substantially larger than its share in gross domestic product.

Different perspective

In the underdeveloped countries the choice between development through private enterprise or through a government-controlled enterprise must be seen in a different perspective than it is in the West. The main difference is that in most underdeveloped countries economic development is only a part—even though a most important part—of the process of transformation and modernization of the whole society. In the West the transformation was a slow, evolutionary process lasting several centuries. In the underdeveloped countries of today transformation is so urgent that the economic and social changes assume by necessity a revolutionary character.

The approach to the division of the public and private sectors varies widely in different countries, but several categories can be attempted. In the first group of countries the major objective is to achieve the necessary transformation without destroying what is considered essential and of permanent value in the traditional civilization. Changes in economic and social structure are considered necessary only if they are essential for facilitating development or for eliminating flagrant economic or social injustice, such as absentee land ownership. In these countries the process of modernization is intended to be pursued in harmony with the basic tendencies of the people and without imposing great hardships on them. It involves only a minimum of coercion and seeks to gain by persuasion and education the approval and active participation of the people.

Such a system is not hostile in principle to private property and free enterprise. There is, however, in some countries a residue of suspicion from the recent and still well remembered past, when private enterprise was connected with colonialist and monopolistic exploitation. The view is therefore generally held in these countries that private enterprise should be strictly supervised in the public interest to avoid antisocial excesses and that it should be allowed limited participation in or be excluded from certain fields of particular importance, such as armaments manufacture and public utilities. In some other countries the emphasis is put on speed of development, mainly to obtain economic or military power, and, as a result, public enterprise is favored because the government can keep more direct control over the activities.

A more lenient attitude toward private enterprise is held in countries where less emphasis is put on social and cultural transformation and where groups actively participating in large-scale private enterprise have retained positions of influence and power.

In his analysis of the role of the state in economic growth, Alexander Eckstein[1] hypothesized the conditions under which the state will play a greater or lesser role in the process of economic growth. This hypothesis, which appears to hold up well when checked against actual experience, states that the tendency for massive state intervention and initiative in the process of industrialization will be greater when the following conditions are true:

(1) a greater range of ends and a higher level of attainment are sought;
(2) a shorter time limit is set for the attainment of the ends; that is, a more rapid rate of economic growth is desired;
(3) a more unfavorable factor and resource endowment is present;
(4) a greater institutional barrier to economic change and industrialization exists; and
(5) the economy is more backward in relative terms.

Factors That Limit the Size of State Enterprise

In contrast to the preceding list a number of factors have a negative effect on the expansion of state enterprise among underdeveloped countries. According to A. H. Hanson, the strongest opposition to public enterprise usually comes from those sections of the community which, for self-interest, are hostile or indifferent to economic development itself.[2] In most countries,

[1] "Individualism and the Role of the State in Economic Growth," in *Comparative Economic Systems,* ed. Morris Bornstein (Homewood, Illinois: Richard D. Irwin, Inc., 1965), pp. 419–26.

[2] *Public Enterprise and Economic Development* (London; Routledge & Kegan Paul, Ltd., 1959), p. 183.

the most important of such groups is the *landowning aristocracy.* Economic development inevitably disrupts the traditional rural structure, which is the source of the landowners' wealth. It creates new expectations among the peasantry, raises the price of agricultural labor, and stimulates the demand for land reform. "His suspicion of public enterprise, therefore, expresses his personal fear of the economic development which it exists to promote. Similar considerations affect the attitudes of money lenders, speculators, and indeed all those sections of the community which thrive by battening upon the economic weaknesses of poverty-stricken, agrarian society."[3]

An even wider base of opposition to state enterprise may be provoked by the government's efforts to accumulate the resources necessary for the creation of public enterprises. A comparatively high level of taxation may be introduced that would bear the heaviest on the upper wealthy classes. Hanson comes to this conclusion:

> For all the above reasons, even the most obviously necessary kinds of public enterprise have sometimes to make their way amid the unfavorable gestures and hostile maneuverings of the wealthy. Upon the social status, political attitudes, far-sightedness, and intelligence of this section of the community, therefore, will partly depend both the extent of public enterprise and the quality of its organization.[4]

To this must be added the loan of skilled manpower and especially technical and managerial personnel. From a purely economic standpoint the manpower problem is the most serious of all, and the future expansion of the public sector in many countries will depend upon the solution to it.

Scope of the Public Sector in Underdeveloped Countries

No clear-cut measure of the size of the public sector exists, so no accurate intercountry comparisons or trends over periods of time can be ascertained. Several possible methods of measurement can be attempted, but first a common definition of the public sector is needed. Regrettably, the definitions are not standardized. The coverage of the public sector in terms of administrative authorities—the central, the state, and the local governments—or in terms of the inclusion or exclusion of pubilc enterprises falling within the scope of each of these authorities varies from country to country. Even the ownership of state enterprises extends from the wholly state-owned and state-operated enterprises to the substantially privately owned and privately operated activities. These difficulties are compounded by nonuniformity in the definitions or in the methods of computation of the national accounts and by the varying degree of reliability of the basic data from which these accounts are prepared. In view of the difficulties caution must be exercised in using public finance data for intercountry comparisons.

[3] Hanson, *Public Enterprise and Economic Development,* p. 186.
[4] Hanson, *Public Enterprise and Economic Development,* p. 186.

TABLE 41-1

Percentage Distribution of Public Investment in Selected Underdeveloped Countries, 1950–59

	Social Overhead Capital			*Directly Productive Activities*				
	Transportation and Communication	*Energy*	*Total*	*Industry and Construction*	*Agriculture*	*Total*	*Health and Education*	*Other*
Latin America								
Argentina	42	21	63	13	44	17	8	12
Colombia	69	5	74	14	11	15	4	7
Mexico	38	—	38	34	14	48	14	—
Venezuela	37	1	38	31	13	44	—	18
Africa								
Ghana	36	5	41	27	5	32	21	6
Nigeria	48	9	57	17	—	17	8	18
Sudan	29	9	38	11	15	26	22	14
Asia								
Burma	30	15	45	32	15	47	5	3
Ceylon	22	8	30	16	35	51	11	8
India	32	8	40	13	29	42	16	2
Philippines	40	—	40	9	22	31	15	14
Thailand	43	8	51	13	19	32	12	5

Source: United Nations, Department of Economic and Social Affairs, *World Economic Survey* (New York, 1959), p. 85.

Measurements Used

Table 41-1 shows that the priorities used in the development plans of most underdeveloped countries result in an allocation of a very large share of the total investment to such social-overhead facilities as transportation, communications, and power. The low share spent for directly productive activities reflects that industry and agriculture are enterprises often left primarily for private enterprise.

The average figure of Table 41-1 can be somewhat misleading, however. In India, for example, the share of public investment in industry amounted to less than 5 percent during the first five-year plan of 1951–56, but it increased to 19 percent during the second plan, with most of the investment concentrated in heavy capital goods such as iron and steel and machine construction. For the third five-year plan (1961–66) the share of public investment in large-scale industry increased to 24.2 percent.

As an indicator of how large the government share is in the expenditure on total gross domestic product and gross capital formation Table 41-2 compares selected years and developed and underdeveloped countries. The share in the underdeveloped countries in expenditure on gross domestic product runs less than that in the developed countries, but the share in gross capital formation is usually higher.

TABLE 41-2

Government Share in Expenditure on Gross Domestic Product and Gross Capital Formation, Percent of Total

	Share in Expenditure on GDP		*Share in Gross Capital Formation*	
	1959	*1963*	*1959*	*1963*
Developed countries				
Canada	24	24	28	29
United Kingdom	26	27	40	40
United States	24	26	16	17
Underdeveloped countries				
Ceylon	22	n.a.	45	n.a.
China (Taiwan)	21	18	36	24
India	11	n.a.	74	n.a.
Philippines	10	11	25	15

n.a.—not available in the needed form
Source: *United Nations Year Book of National Accounts Statistics, 1964* (New York, 1965).

Latin American Enterprise

A special study made of the ownership of productive enterprise in Latin America gives an unusual amount of data about the breakdown between the

TABLE 41-3

Ownership of Productive Enterprise in Latin America for the 30 Largest Businesses, Percent

Argentina	*Top 10*	*Top 20*	*Top 29**
Government	84.5	67.9	61.3
Private	10.7	20.4	20.5
Foreign private	4.8	11.7	18.2
Brazil	*Top 10*	*Top 20*	*Top 32*
Government	71.8	68.2	59.1
Private	10.5	16.5	20.0
Foreign private	11.4	15.3	20.9
Colombia	*Top 10*	*Top 20*	*Top 32*
Government	69.4	58.9	54.1
Private	29.6	36.3	39.1
Foreign private	0.0	44.0	6.1
Chile			
Including copper and nitrate exporters	*Top 10*	*Top 20*	*Top 30*
Government	48.7	46.4	43.2
Private	0.0	7.6	10.6
Foreign private	51.3	46.0	46.2
Excluding copper and nitrate exporters	*Top 10*	*Top 20*	*Top 30*
Government	75.9	68.3	63.3
Private	5.6	14.7	18.0
Foreign private	18.5	17.0	18.7
Mexico	*Top 10*	*Top 20*	*Top 30*
Government	100.0	88.5	82.2
Private	0.0	8.7	13.9
Foreign private	0.0	2.8	3.9

Statistics for Six countries Combined	*Top 10*		*Top 20*		*Top 30*	
	A†	B‡	A	B	A	B
Government	78.2	82.7	68.1	71.7	62.4	65.8
Private	10.5	11.5	18.1	19.3	21.2	22.4
Foreign private	11.3	5.8	13.8	9.0	16.4	11.8

* Reliable information on next largest firm not available.

† List A includes Chilean copper and nitrate exporters.

‡ List B excludes Chilean copper and nitrate exporters.

public and private sector in the six Latin American countries with the highest national incomes.[5] Table 41-3 shows the results of this survey.

Lists were compiled of the 30 largest business enterprises in each of Brazil, Mexico, Argentina, Venezuela, Colombia, and Chile. The lists were restricted to 30 since "these enterprises appeared to exercise such a predominant influence on economic life." They constitute the key group of "big business" in several Latin American countries. With notable exceptions, particularly in the case of Mexico, virtually every industrial enterprise below this level is privately owned.[6]

Several procedures were followed in compiling the lists and making statistical calculations. The size of the firms was determined by capital and reserves or, as in the case of a few wholly state-owned enterprises, by approximate equivalents of capital and reserves. Statistics on the firms represent accountings on January 1, 1963. In some cases since that time notable changes have occurred, especially with the new copper law in Chile giving the government a greater stare of ownership in the mines. However, the tables do give a good relative reading on the various sizes of the different sectors. Wherever availability of data permitted, all branches of business activity were included —industry, finance, commerce, mining, and utilities. Because of the special position of copper and nitrates in the Chilean economy, two lists were compiled for that country, one including all investments and the other excluding copper and nitrate exporters.

As the table shows, government ownership is highest in Mexico and lowest in Chile (including copper and nitrate exporters) and Colombia. Latin American private ownership is highest in Colombia and lowest in Mexico. Excluding petroleum investments in Colombia and Venezuela, foreign private ownership is highest in Chile and lowest in Mexico and Venezuela.

The last section of Table 41-3 presents unweighted means of ownership ratios for the six countries. Although these figures are useful for general comparison, averages of this nature often lead to oversimplification—huge foreign investments in Chilean copper averaged with preponderant state investments in Mexico obviously results in statistical injustice to both countries. However, the study is a very useful attempt to quantify the size of the public and private sectors in underdeveloped countries.[7]

5 Frank Brandenburg, *The Development of Latin American Private Enterprise* (Washington, D.C.: National Planning Association, May 1964).

6 Brandenburg, *The Development of Latin American Private Enterprise,* p. 51.

7 As a comparison, in 1962 the Soviet Union had over 200,000 state enterprises, more than 100,000 construction sites, over 2900 state repair and service stations, 7500 state farms, and about 45,000 collective farms. The state owned a network of railways over 124,000 kilometers long, 251,000 kilometers of motor roads, airlines and planes, hundreds of thousands of state warehouses and trading establishments (which accounted for 70 percent of all retail trade), and also a wide network of cultural and educational establishments (including 739 universities and colleges and 3329 secondary technical schools), banks, foreign trade organizations, and scientific institutions. State property accounted for about 90 percent of all the production facilities of the country and for 94 percent of the total industrial output. From I. A. Yevenko, *Planning in the USSR* (Moscow: Foreign Languages Publishing House, 1962), p. 11.

Organizational Characteristics

Although in detail the organizational forms of state enterprises vary, in concept they fall into four types.

Departmental Management. This is the traditional form in both developed and underdeveloped countries. It is financed by annual appropriations from the government treasury and pays its revenues to the treasury. It is run by civil servants and is subject to the government budget. It maximizes government control and minimizes flexibility.

The Public Corporation. This form provides room for a degree of enterprise and initiative on the part of management. It is free from parliament accounting, auditing, and appropriating and from civil-service recommendations. Its management, especially on the operating level, behaves very much like that of a private firm.

The State Company. This is an enterprise established under the ordinary company law of the country in which the government has a controlling interest through its ownership of all or some of the shares.

The Operating Contract or Managing Agency. The government enters into a contract with an established private company for management of a public enterprise and agrees to reimburse the contractor for all costs incurred. The contractor is given full authority in management and receives a fixed fee.

Differences between public and private enterprises

In public enterprises there are generally more layers of policy formation, as one can see by comparing the respective hierarchies of control. In large private enterprise, the base of the hierarchy is the management group, consisting of a number of officers with specific executive responsibilities, perhaps under the leadership of a general manager. They take orders from a board of directors, which may or may not allocate functional duties to its various members. The board is responsible to the shareholders, who have an opportunity to change the composition of the board.

In public enterprise, there is a similar hierarchy up to the board level. Immediately above comes the minister, whose functions are similar to those of the shareholders only to the extent that he appoints, dismisses, and criticizes the members of the board. Apart from the fact that he can do things more effectively than an assembly of shareholders, he is more continuously concerned with policy formation, being able to give orders to the board in general or specific terms at any time.

The function of a shareholders meeting, to the extent that there is any analogy to it in public enterprise, is carried out by the legislature, whose members have been loosely described as representatives of the shareholders in the state enterprise. Shareholders are thus the electorate. Thus, where a private enterprise has a three-level hierarchy, a public enterprise has a four- or five-layer one.

The subject of management practices raises the question of the applicability of the traditional and the modern theories of management to the underdeveloped countries. Some authors feel that the old concepts of line and staff and span of control while becoming outdated in the modern developed countries might be relevant in many lesser developed countries' public enterprise. They feel the simpler and cruder approach which was employed in earlier U.S. business history may still be relevant to underdeveloped countries.

The Performance of State Enterprise

For a multinational firm operating in an underdeveloped country knowledge of the guidelines or criteria under which the state enterprises operate is equally as important as knowledge of the extent of the public sector. A publicly owned industry can arrange its prices and services so as to use resources and capital efficiently (in an economic sense). It may try to promote economic growth or to push ahead with fruitful innovations. It may, wisely or unwisely, provide higher wages for its workers or lower prices of its outputs in the hope of promoting economic welfare. It may even try to ease the impact of its decisions when they might harm a particular region. All these actions will affect the operations of multinational firms operating in these countries whether they are using the services of a state enterprise, operating in joint venture with one, or competing against one.

Numerous possible criteria measure the success of public enterprises. The problem is compounded when there is disagreement on what level the firm should be rated; these levels range from its own internal efficiency to broad social judgments. Three approaches can be taken based on different views of what state enterprises should be doing. Each deserves separate comment.

Commercial Guidelines

The so-called *commercial guidelines* concept for the operation of state enterprise is concerned solely with the internal efficiency and profit motivation of the venture. If a state enterprise operates in a purely competitive market, defined as one where there are many buyers and sellers but none with the power to control or influence the market and where everyone is well informed of market conditions, the state enterprise's price and operating level would be fixed automatically by supply and demand and it would behave *commercially*. However, this situation rarely presents itself since pure competitors are not often taken under public ownership (though they are quite frequently subsidized).

The problem of a state enterprise acting as a commercial firm becomes complicated because many public firms are in a monopoly position in their markets. In a monopoly the demand curve slopes downward and results in a marginal revenue curve which is different from average revenue. Since each additional unit sold reduces the price on all the others, the marginal revenue to be gained from any increment of production is less than its price. The profit-motivated commercial firm will look at marginal revenues and marginal costs in setting output and will produce at the point of greatest profit, that is, where marginal revenue equals marginal cost. This would be point A or output Q_1, in Figure 41–1. However, when a state monopoly in an underdeveloped country is dealing with a scarce item, the government is often more concerned with the maximization of physical output than of *value output.* In this case the government would require the enterprise to operate at point B or output Q_2. Under such conditions, a commercial criterion for the state enterprise could not apply.

Socialism by Price Guidance

A second criterion for the guidance of state enterprise is called *socialism by price guidance,* which has also been misnamed *marginal cost pricing.*[8] Unlike true marginal cost pricing this criterion does not equate marginal cost to marginal revenue to determine the price and the output; instead output is expanded until marginal cost equals average cost. For example, in Figure

FIGURE 41-1

Cost-Revenue Relationships for a Monopolistic State Enterprise

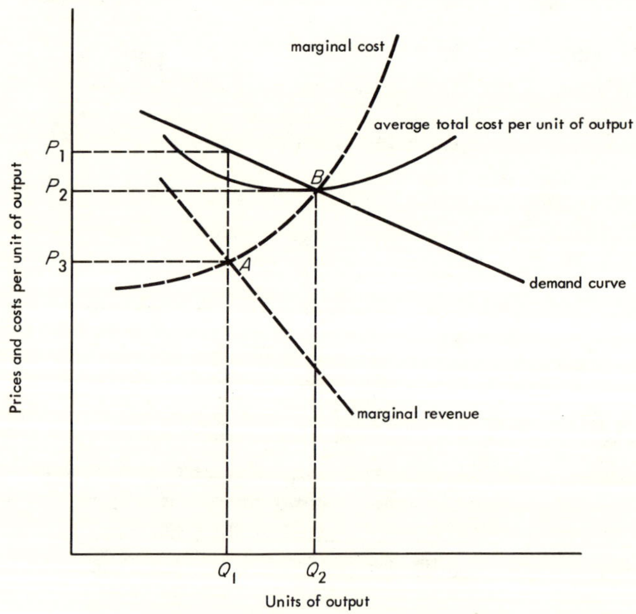

[8] William J. Baumol, *Economic Theory and Operations Analysis* (Englewood Cliffs, New Jersey: Prentice-Hall, Inc., 1961), p. 257.

41–2 a private firm would figure its marginal cost price at point *A*, produce output Q_1, and sell at price P_1; but a state enterprise using so-called *marginal cost pricing* would be forced to produce at output Q_2 and sell at price P_2, a situation where the marginal cost would equal the price. Or under the same principle, if the situation were such that the limitation of inputs retricted the state enterprise to an output of Q_1, the government, under socialism by price guidance, would through price controls force the public firm to sell at price P_3, where marginal cost equals marginal revenue rather than P_1. The marginal cost, not demand, would be the determining factor in the price.

There are severe defects in using this guideline for the administration of a state enterprise. First, if the government fixes the price below the demand, a rationing or quota system will also have to be brought into existence. Second, if an enterprise is in a situation where there are economies of scale and costs are declining, as in Figure 41–2, the state enterprise will incur a deficit for each unit sold under this operating criteria, requiring subsidization by the treasury. Third, marginal costs are difficult to define and to measure in monopolistic state enterprise, and even when they are properly measured the question remains whether short-run or long-run marginal costs should be used.

FIGURE 41-2

Possible Outputs and Prices for a State Enterprise

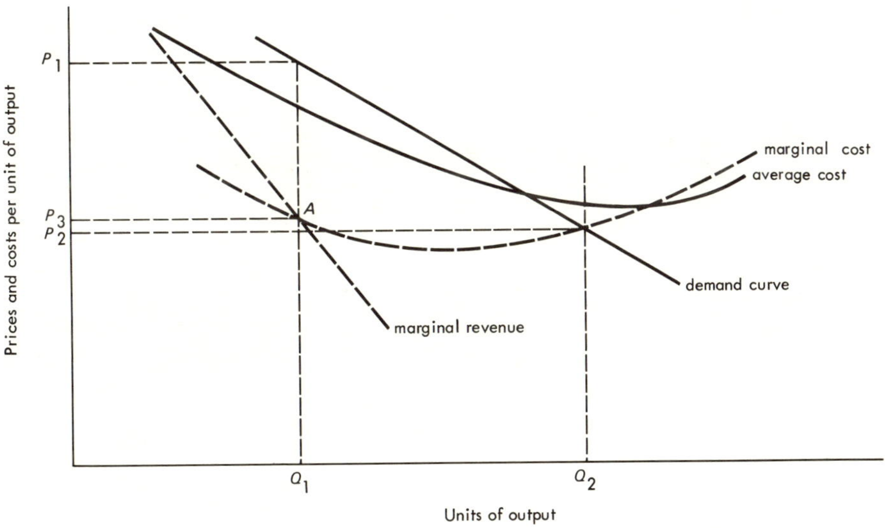

Pure Social Orientation

A state enterprise can also be operated strictly on a *social-orientation* basis, where it becomes an adjunct of public finance. The difference between this criterion and those described above is that no attempt is made to have prices on marginal costs; the venture is run strictly for what output it can provide. Many state enterprises are thus undertaken in areas that the government considers vital to the public interest, and the revenues and costs involved are wholly subordinate to the objectives of some social optimum. Professor V. V. Ramanadham points out that in India prices of public enterprises can, and often do, serve a different function from that of prices in the private sector by including elements of taxation and subsidization.[9] He found that subsidy elements were quite prevalent in the Indian public sector, meaning that the output of the public enterprises was often sold at less than cost. He found in conclusion that "the public sector, in the aggregate, is characterized by elements of heavy subsidization rather than taxation, the total net revenues being inadequate even for the payment of interest charges on capital employed."[10]

Effects of State Enterprise on the Operations of Multinational Firms

The structure of state enterprises and the public sector is of vital importance to the operations of multinational firms in underdeveloped countries. The effects of the public sector can range from a drastic curtailment of a multinational firm's operations if the sector the company is in is nationalized to an expansion of the opportunities of a company's operations if the state enterprise provides a needed service.

Investment

Therefore the public sector can largely determine the pattern and volume of private investment either through controls and restrictions or through encouragement and incentives. For example, where public investments are largely of an infrastructure character, e.g., transport, power, and urban utilities, they are an essential precondition for private investments which require transport, power, etc. Another illustration of the interaction of the public sector and the operations of a multinational firm can be given. Suppose a firm wished to develop the potential of cattle raising in an underdeveloped country through a meat-packing plant. Nobody proposes state farms or state ownership of cattle; nobody proposes state factories for meat canning; and nobody proposes state trading in cattle or meat. Therefore, at first sight, this does not seem to have much to do with the public sector. However, an examination of the situation shows the essential role of the public sector. If the cattle are diseased and must be inoculated to eliminate the disease, who is going to train the veterinarians and send them out to the villages? Who is going to provide the serum? Who is going to persuade the farmers that cattle can be an economic asset and that a few healthy cattle are better than a large herd of diseased cattle? If cattle are a status symbol, who is going to provide

[9] "Tax and Subsidy Elements in Public Enterprise Prices," *The Review of Economics and Statistics,* XLVI, No. 4 (November 1964), 396.

[10] Ramanadham, "Tax and Subsidy Elements in Public Enterprise Prices," p. 395.

alternative symbols of social status or better forms of investment such as savings banks? Improvements in cattle raising may mean new grazing grounds, which may require land reform. Who will undertake the necessary measures? Cattle grazing may require government action on conservation and soil erosion. Cattle raising and meat-packing will be useless without transport facilities—roads, railways, port facilities, etc. Finally, the exportation of the meat products may depend on trade agreements with neighboring countries.

The example of India

The relationship between the public and the private sectors in India is a good illustration of the effects that government undertakings can have on multinational firms. Although India is by no means a typical country, it does stress public ownership and public-sector activities strongly but at the same time considers a contribution from the private sector essential.

The pattern in India can be examined from two different angles, both of importance to multinational firms. By looking first at some of the laws that affect the actions of private enterprise and then by reviewing the reasons for the organization of certain activities in the public sector, the effects on the operations of multinational firms can be better understood. The first five-year plan in India (and the three that have been formulated since) recognized "that the private sector is capable of making an important contribution to the development of the economy if it accepts new obligations to the people."[11] The "obligations to the people" were rather definite in their effects on some industries. For example, the Industries (Development and Regulation) Act of 1951 set up a schedule for 37 industries including certain important consumer goods, capital goods, and producer goods industries; and industries producing fuel, equipment for generation, transmission, and distribution of electrical energy, fertilizers, heavy chemicals, automobiles, arms and ammunitions, miscellaneous implements, and precision instruments. After setting up the schedule the Act prescribed the following procedure:

(1) All the existing industrial undertakings in the scheduled industries had to be registered within a prescribed period.

(2) No new industrial unit could be established or substantial extension to existing plants made without a license from the central government.

(3) The government was given power to order an investigation in respect to any scheduled industry or undertaking if, in its opinion, there was an unjustifiable fall in the volume of production or a marked deterioration in quality, or an increase in price for which there was no justification.

(4) If any industry or undertaking did not carry out the directions issued after such an investigation, the government could take over its management.[12]

The Act further provided for levying a tax on goods manufactured in any scheduled industry to cover the expenses of maintaining administrative,

[11] Ajit K. Dasgupta, Amitava Sen, and Jati K. Singupta, *Planning and the Plan* (Calcutta: Post-graduate Book Mart, 1961), p. 86.

[12] Dasgupta, Sen, and Singupta, *Planning and the Plan,* p. 86.

technical, and managerial staff in the government Development Councils, for promoting scientific and industrial research pertaining to the industry, for improving the design and quality of the products of the industry, and for providing facilities for the training of technicians and labor in the industry.

The role of private enterprise and multinational firms was further defined in a 1956 Industrial Policy Resolution. To define the role of the state, industries were classified in three categories. The first category of 17 industries, including air transport, life insurance, and steel, is the exclusive responsibility of the state. The second category of 12 industries, including telephone industries and shipyards, is progressively state owned; the state generally takes the initiative in establishing new undertakings, but private enterprise is expected to supplement these efforts. The third category includes all the remaining industries; their development is undertaken ordinarily through the initiative and enterprise of the private sector, although the state may start any industry even in this category. The following is the role of the organized private sector in respect to these three categories:

(1) To establish new units in already approved undertakings and to expand the existing privately owned units or to cooperate with the state in establishing new units for industries scheduled in the first category. In appropriate cases privately owned units may also be permitted to produce an item in this category for meeting their own requirement or as a by-product;
(2) To develop either on its own initiative or with state participation the field of second-category industries; and
(3) To successfully implement the industrial programs as formulated in the successive five-year plans.[13]

Thus, the many effects of state enterprise on the operations of multinational firms range from a minimum of insuring that the operations fit into the framework of the social and economic policy of the state to a maximum of fixing the price of output, demanding a certain quality of output, approving expansion plans, all the way to taking over the industry.

The second area where India provides some insights into the effects a multinational firm might expect from the public sector in a country where it is operating is the nationalization of industries. Again, India does not necessarily provide a typical situation. The susceptibility to nationalization in any particular country would have to be weighed against the economic and social conditions in the country. However, India gives some rationale for nationalization in a country that is not nationalizing only to drive out private business or foreigners.

The particular reasons for taking over certain activities can be enumerated as follows:[14]

[13] Dasgupta, Sen, and Singupta, *Planning and the Plan,* p. 89.

[14] V. V. Ramanadham, *The Control of Public Enterprise in India* (New York: Asia Publishing House, 1964), pp. 19–21.

(1) Air Transport

At the time of nationalization the following points were emphasized:

(a) The air services in the private sector were uneconomical because of the nonrational character of the industry as a whole.

(b) Progress through the acquisition of new equipment was doubtful under private enterprise, although it was considered urgently necessary in the national interest.

(c) The air services were to be developed as a public utility not working with profit as the main motive.

(2) Life Insurance

The following special reasons were given for nationalization:

(a) Life insurance was not conducted with the required degree of efficiency and responsibility in the private sector, by and large; for example, inordinate delays occurred in the settlement of claims.

(b) Investment malpractices developed, causing the undesirable concentration of financial power in a few quarters and endangering the policyholders' interest.

(c) Funds could be made available, after nationalization, for developmental activities in the government's programs.

(3) Road Transport

Among the reasons for its nationalization were the following:

(a) The development of an efficient, adequate, economical, and properly coordinated system of road transport was necessary.

(b) Road services had to be coordinated with railway services.

(c) Transport services had to be provided in unremunerative areas or routes.

(d) Surpluses accumulated would benefit the public excheques.

(4) Warehousing

The only reason for organizing warehousing in the public sector was to establish a network of storage and warehouse facilities as an aid in the improvement of agriculture marketing.

From the above it can be seen that nationalization of an industry can come in a wide variety of enterprises. However, in each case there was an apparent feeling on the part of the government that the public could not be properly served by private enterprise or that the function was so vital to the nation that direct government control was necessary. Multinational firms operating in areas of potential nationalization will have to be acutely aware of such things as standards of service and rates of growth that governments deem desirable for the welfare of their populations or for the security of the government itself.

How successful has India been in its combination of the public and private sectors, and has the government action limited private ventures? In some cases the Indian experience has been hailed as a real success.

> The complementary relationship between the public and private sectors has been clearly demonstrated in the case of India. In India, public ownership and public-sector activities are strongly stressed in the plan. About two-thirds of all planned investment is public investment. At first it was wrongly feared that this situation might lead to an atrophy of the private sector—that it would wither away in the shadow of the powerful public sector. But nothing of the sort happened. Quite the contrary, when the conviction spread that the government was willing and able to implement the targets of the five-year plan, people began to think in terms of an expanding economy and expanding markets. The result was a burst of private investment in all directors.[15]

However, there are indications that the operations of the private sector, particularly foreign private investment, have been often hindered by government actions and undertakings. The aid given to India in 1966 by the ten-nation Aid India Consortium, following the devaluation of the rupee, was accompanied by urging from the U.S. government and other creditors "to unravel at least some of the tangle of official red tape that is stifling private business."[16]

It thus appears that state enterprise and attempts at combining the sectors by underdeveloped countries will always contain some elements of restrictions on private ventures; multinational firms will have to learn to live with this situation.

[15] H. W. Singer, *International Development: Growth and Changes* (New York: McGraw-Hill Book Company, 1964), p. 155.

[16] "International Outlook," *Business Week,* June 25, 1966, p. 142.

42

International Economic Relations

Being committed to rapid modernization, the developing countries are heavily dependent on the external world. The means of industrialization—machines, technology, and management—as well as the means of sociopolitical growth—civil service, informed electorate, infrastructure—and a great many other capabilities which control the pace of progress all require foreign inputs. A massive demand for imports and a heavy burden of international payments thus are characteristic of the international economic relations of the developing countries. And as both a corollary and a constraint, the inabilities to export, to attract foreign investments, to acquire aid, and to borrow from abroad determine both the scale and the tempo of the modernization process.

Trade Position

How the foreign trade of the developing countries has fared in comparison with that of the industrial world can be seen from Figures 42–1 and 42–2. On both export and import sides it lags far behind; and, the developing countries' share in the world total instead of increasing has been shrinking. What has caused this diminishing share? This question can best be answered by looking at exports and imports separately.

Exports

The exports of most developing countries consist of a few primary products. Coffee, tin, petroleum, bananas, copra, jute, sugar, wool, or some other raw material usually heads the list. In some countries, like Brazil, Colombia,

FIGURE 42-1

Export Trends

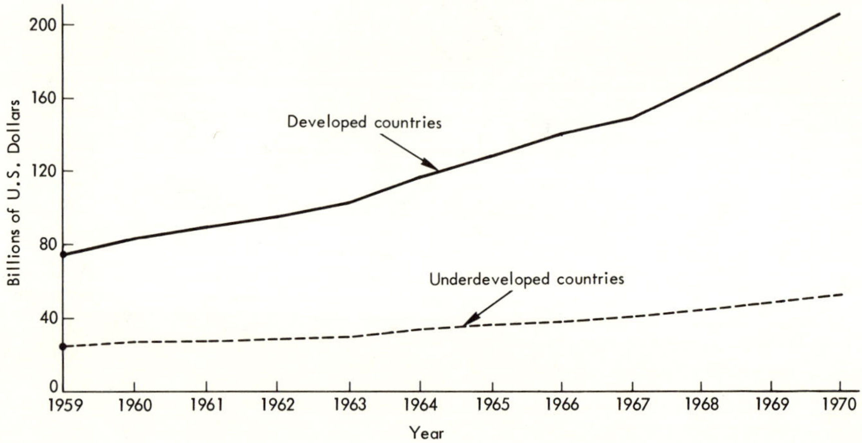

FIGURE 42-2

Import Trends

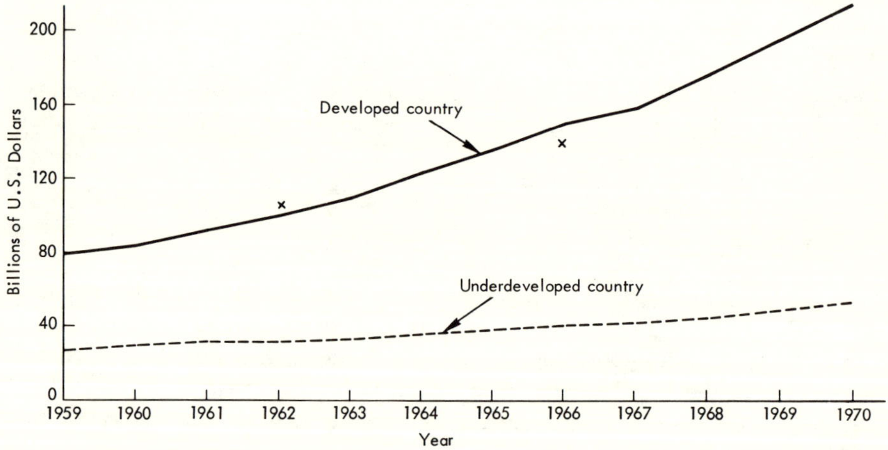

or Venezuela, the principal product accounts for more than two-thirds of the total. But even where no single product dominates, the typical export mix of a developing country is limited to a few commodities, primarily crude materials.

With this fact in mind, the following factors, which contribute to the adverse trends in the trade of the devolping country, can be identified:

(1) Much of the increase in world exports in the last two decades has occurred in products not produced by the developing countries, that is, manufactured consumer goods, capital equipment, and the like. This means that they have not been competitive where demand has been strongest.

(2) The prices received by the developing countries for their exports have lagged behind prices received for exports by the developed countries. Again, this is primarily because developing countries concentrate their exports in low-value commodities for which demand is relatively inelastic. As incomes rise or prices decline, the consumption of such products does not increase.

(3) Price fluctuations, at least in the short run, have contributed to instability of earnings from exports and, depending upon the period measured, also depress absolute levels of export earnings in the developing countries.

(4) The increasing use of synthetics and substitutes has reduced export earnings in the developing countries. In fact, one of the main threats to export earnings in recent years has come from the competition of synthetics to raw agricultural materials, such as cotton, wool, jute, hard fibers, and rubber. With the exception of petroleum, and other minerals, almost all products exported by the developing countries have been affected adversely by synthetics and substitutes. Even in the case of petroleum and minerals, technology has, in many instances, reduced consumption in unit if not in absolute quantities. For example, it now takes less tin to make a tin can than it once did.

(5) Tariffs and import quotas imposed by the developed countries either to protect internal industry or for other reasons have also reduced the export earnings of developing countries in both primary products and manufactures (principally textiles). In terms of their impact on the ability of the developing countries to compete in the export market for manufactures once they begin conversion from purely agricultural economies, these impediments are exceedingly detrimental to long-term earning potential.

(6) The developed countries themselves provide considerable competition to the developing countries in products that are the specialty of the latter. This situation further reduces the opportunity of the developing countries to increase their export earnings.

In summary, all of the foregoing adverse factors have, in varying degrees and at different times, depressed the export earnings of the developing countries. The gross impact of these adverse factors becomes even more apparent when one realizes that exports provide developing countries with 25 percent of their national income compared with a world average of 10 percent.

Imports

Most of the developing countries are highly dependent upon imports for the acquisition of goods and services leading to domestic capital formation for economic development. In fact, imported capital goods have generally contributed 30 to 40 percent of the funds devoted to domestic investment programs. To the extent imports are constrained by inadequate earnings from exports, financing for economic growth must be obtained from other countries in the form of foreign aid or long-term loans.

Terms of Trade

The terms of trade (the ratio of export prices to import prices) have generally worsened for the developing countries. Since the products which they export have declined in value compared with the products which they must import, a larger quantity of exports is required to maintain any given import volume. This requirement is often hard to fulfill. On the supply side the resources for further expansion of production may be limited or the entrepreneurship and capital may be lacking. On the demand side, the world market may be near to saturation and any attempts to increase the supply may depress prices and fail to improve the export earnings. Moreover, the demand for the products imported by the developing countries is generally less price elastic and more income elastic than the demand for their exports. Increased prices of imported capital goods are thus readily accepted, and the pressure to import more manufactured consumer goods accompanies any rise in discretionary income. The situation is further aggravated by the fact that the supply of the primary export commodities of the underdeveloped countries responds readily to price increases but resists any adaptation to price decreases. In the farm and plantation sectors the upward elasticity is explained by the incentive which a higher price provides for putting new land in cultivation or for shifting it from domestic possibly noncash-crop production to export commodities. Conversely, the downward stickiness of supply stems from the inability of the producers to discontinue production after a price decline, as the resources invested in the plantation often have no alternative short-run use. Also, the drop of export prices reduces the producers' total income, and to counteract this tendency producers are often eager to increase output. Thus, a reverse (negative) elasticity relationship between price and supply may exist for the tropical agricultural commodities.

In the mining sector the picture is different. Demand fluctuates widely in response to business conditions in the industrial countries. Because of the accelerator principle, the magnitude of these fluctuations often surpasses the variations in industrial activity. Since the output cannot adjust itself to the constantly shifting market, prices tend to follow the demand fluctuations. The stickiness of the supply is again more serious in the case of falling prices than rising prices, mostly because social legislation does not permit layoffs of workers or discontinuations of production except when approved by the government.

Global Perspective

From a worldwide perspective the foregoing suggests since 1950 (1) an increasing share of world trade by developed countries, (2) an increasing share of world trade between developed countries, (3) a decreasing share of world trade by underdeveloped countries, and (4) a decreasing share of world trade between underdeveloped countries and developed countries.

Trade does take place between the developed and developing countries largely because of the traditional exchange of manufactures for raw commodities. About 80 percent of the trade flow from developed to underdeveloped countries consists of manufactured products, and nearly 90 percent, of the counterflow of mineral and agricultural commodities.

International Commodity Agreements

A controversial solution to the export problem of the developing countries is offered by international commodity agreements, which have been a major world trade issue for more than a decade. The international commodity agreements are intergovernmental control devices designed to regulate the supply of a product on the world market. Their objectives are twofold: to stabilize world prices of the commodity, and to guarantee the exporting nations an acceptable export income.

To achieve both objectives an international commodity agreement must establish a mechanism for supporting and maintaining prices at higher levels. The importing countries are expected to agree to such an arrangement to sustain the growth potentials of developing nations, the principal exporters of primary commodities. There are three basic type of commodity agreements.

THE BUFFER-STOCK OPERATION. This arrangement attempts to remove surpluses from the market and return them to the market when shortages occur. In this way, prices, consumption, and production are stabilized. It provides for an institutional mechanism which buys whenever price is abnormally low and sells whenever price is abnormally high. The high and low ranges are set by the parties to the commodity agreement.

This control device has definite limitations in that the funds required to finance the buffer stock are substantial and the operating policies difficult to establish. In the case of the International Tin Agreement, which uses this device, the size of the fund has proved to be a serious problem. Efficient management has a definite effect, also. The commodity involved must be storable and nonperishable for lengthy periods.

MULTILATERAL PRICE AGREEMENTS. This type is based on an obligation accepted by exporting countries to sell certain guaranteed quantities of the commodity at prices not exceeding a certain maximum figure. Conversely, the importing countries prescribe quantities at a certain minimum price. Thus the exporters are assured both a minimum volume of exports and a minimum price. The advantage of this scheme is that the market price can fluctuate freely between these administered limits while excessive fluctuations are stopped. Its disadvantages are (1) problems of administration; (2) practically all importing and exporting countries must participate or the agreement will fail; and (3) it is applicable on commodities with limited quality differences only.

THE QUOTA SCHEMES. The third control scheme limits the quantities of the commodity which any producing country can enter into world trade, i.e., which any country can export. If an internal surplus occurs, the government of the country involved is obliged to intervene in its national market to prevent any leakage to the world market beyond the agreed-upon quota. If demand for the commodity is inelastic, this scheme can maintain prices at high levels, but only for short periods. When it is extended over longer periods, difficulties arise because individual producer countries, attracted by higher prices, may refuse to join on the premise that it is more profitable to enjoy unlimited volume, or they may find the leakage of domestic surpluses to the world market uncontrollable. The greater the differential between the internal and the maintained world price, the greater the inducement to the domestic supply to escape. On the demand side, the user nations are encouraged by the artificially high prices to develop synthetics and seek other substitutes for the commodity. A further disadvantage to the producing countries themselves is that by limiting the individual producers and creating a high price, fewer efficient high-cost producers are subsidized at the expense of low-cost producers, who need the volume to operate successfully. Thus, the seed for future problems is planted, and the deterioration of the terms of trade is set in motion.

The international control schemes have been applied to wheat, sugar, tin, and coffee. For several others the efforts have failed, primarily because of the conflicts of interest between the export and import countries and a lack of unanimity among the different producer countries themselves.

The UNCTAD Conference

The United Nations Conference on Trade and Development was the first in-depth review of the workings of the world trading system since the Havana Conference of 1947 which gave birth to the GATT framework for world trade. The initial UNCTAD Conference, which was held in Geneva from March to June 1964, concerned itself primarily with the widening "trade gap" between the industrial and the developing countries, and also with the general dissatisfaction of the poorer countries with the existing GATT framework for world trade.

The Conference was convened at the request of the lesser-developed countries (LDC's). This request was prompted by two main considerations—(1) that the GATT primarily functions in the interest of the industrial states and gives too little attention to the particular situation and problems of the LDC's, and (2) that, partly as a consequence of this inadequacy of the GATT, international trade and world commercial policy have, since the end of World

War II, apparently moved in such a way as to deprive LDC's of their just share in world economic growth.

The UNCTAD Conference pointed out that unless new mechanisms were brought into play, the developing countries would experience a protracted external imbalance in their trade, due to the inequality between the slow expansion in exports of their primary commodities and the rapid growth of their demand for imported manufactures. It has become apparent that this growing "trade gap" is the major hurdle in the struggle to achieve the UN Development Decade's five-percent annual growth rate for developing nations.

This failure by the LDC's to participate fully in the growth of world trade has been a severe disappointment to them. It has come at a time when the developing nations have placed a greater emphasis on accelerated economic growth than at any previous time in their histories. Economic growth for these capital-hungry and frequently food-deficient countries would normally require an expansion of imports. The deliberations also identified some of the specific factors at work principally in the economies of the industrially advanced countries which tended to reinforce the more general factors inhibiting the expansion of exports of developing countries. In the developed market economies, with which the developing countries conducted over two-thirds of their trade, such factors included price support programs, customs duties and taxes, and fiscal charges imposed on consumption of tropical products, export subsidies on commodities of interest to developing nations, and high levels of tariffs imposed on processed products as compared with those applied to such products when exported in their natural form.

Factors and underlying considerations for the recommendations of the Conference were inspired by the belief that the development of equitable and mutually advantageous trade could promote higher standards of living, full employment, and rapid economic progress in all countries of the world. In this regard some lines of advance in respect of trade in primary products and manufactures and of trade between developing countries were indicated. More specifically, in respect of trade in primary commodities, there was a need for a deliberate effort on the part of all industrialized countries to remedy the adverse tendencies resulting from the dependence of the developing countries on primary commodity trade. The comprehensive action suggested in the conference report included international commodity arrangements as well as an accelerated removal of existing obstacles and the forestalling of the creation of new obstacles to commodity trade.

It was noted by the Conference that several of the developing countries had a heavy dependence on foreign-earnings from the export of minerals and fuels, and it was recommended that the developed countries should effectively reduce and/or eliminate barriers and discrimination against the trade and consumption of these products, particularly internal taxation, with a view to increasing the real income of the developing nations from these exports. The Conference also recommended action to provide the developing countries producing minerals and fuels with an appreciable increase in the revenues which accrue to them as a result of the export of these natural resources.

The UNCTAD Conference's Committee on Commodities was in favor of international commodity agreements as a corrective measure, where these were desirable. All members agreed, however, that the entire international community should make a concerted effort to expand and stabilize international commodity trade, either by the conclusion of agreements or by means of other types of arrangements, according to circumstances. The Committee listed those commodities giving cause for immediate concern as cocoa, sugar, and coffee, and those requiring close attention as copper, cotton, iron ore, lead and zinc, rice, rubber, tea, tobacco, and vegetable oils.

UNCTAD was made a permanent organization of the United Nations in order that there would be a constant review of the implementation of the recommendations of the Final Act of the Conference and also so that there would be a world forum from which the needs of the developing countries could be brought to the world's attention.

The purposes of the new U.N. organ are: (1) to promote international trade, especially with a view towards speeding economic development, particularly trade between countries with different stages of economic development, between developing countries, and between countries with different systems of economic and social organization, (2) to formulate principles and policies on international trade and related problems of economic development, (3) to initiate action, where appropriate, for the negotiation and adoption of multilateral legal instruments in the field of trade, and (4) to act as a center for harmonizing the trade and related development policies of governments and regional economic groupings. These purposes were taken largely from the original recommendations of the UNCTAD Conference in Geneva.

The Conference signified two new developments. The first is that there is a great importance attached to the fact that the Conference did occur. A global conference, convened under United Nations auspices, at which "trade and development" matters are up for discussion within the avowed context of "underdeveloped nations versus developed nations" is a landmark of high order, especially in terms of the standards which existed in pre-UNCTAD days.

The second implication of UNCTAD is that it revealed that a "united front" among underdeveloped nations is possible, at least when some major matters are at stake. The cohesion was remarkable, especially when one considers that the developed nations, on their part, were unable to retain a fully consistent posture throughout.

It is important to realize, however, that even if the UNCTAD "solutions" to the commodities problem prove successful, the problems of the LDC's in regard to trade and economic development will not necessarily disappear. The real hope of the developing nations is to begin to build a more diversified economic base and to move from the traditional "one crop dependence." This will require diversified commodity production, a certain level of manufactures and semimanufactures, and attraction of capital investments from the developed nations. It is important that all nations recognize their responsibilities in this regard.

Foreign Investments

Portfolio Investments

Investment in stocks and bonds issued by developing countries is a negligible factor in the flow of long-term capital to such countries. In fact, there has been virtually a complete cessation of such investment in the United States since 1931 with the exception of a few loans made by large commercial banks and insurance companies. Conversely, prior to the stock market crash in 1929, stocks and bonds of some developing countries were traded freely in capital markets and were even held by small investors.

Some of the reasons for this trend are:

(1) A general distrust in the United States of foreign bonds, with many selling at substantial discounts. Much of this attitude is attributable to a history of defaulted interest and principal payments.

(2) The governments of developing countries have traditionally insisted upon rates of interest so low that there is limited appeal to prospective investors.

(3) International political tension, based partly upon differences in worldwide ideologies and also upon internal instability within the developing countries, has retarded interest in portfolio investment.

Thus, portfolio investment can be discounted as a significant source of funds for the developing countries.

Direct Investments

In terms of the total world flow, developing countries receive modest amounts of capital from the private sector of the developed countries. However, this flow does not even begin to meet the need for funds to finance long-term economic growth. Direct investments in petroleum and other natural resources, which make up a substantial portion of the foreign investments accounted for in the statistics, are important only for a few developing countries.

Many suggestions and recommendations have been advanced to increase the flow of funds from the private sector of the developed countries to the poorer nations. For example, it is stated that developing countries must make internal investments in social overhead such as schools and housing as well as in transportation and power to attract investment.[1] Other inducements such as tax concessions, profit guarantees, accelerated write-off privileges, and exemptions from duties on equipment and materials are used by some to attract foreign capital.

Another inducement has been by way of bilateral agreements in which

[1] Joseph Grunwald, "Why Not Invest in Latin America?" *Harvard Business Review*, XLI, No. 6 (November–December 1963), 126.

the country of origin and the country of destination agree to a mutually acceptable code of behavior in respect to direct investment. Such agreements are designed to protect investors against unilateral actions on the part of the government of the developing country such as outright expropriation, forced convertibility of repatriated profits at "pegged" rates of exchange, and nationalization of profits. In fact, the United States has over 30 such agreements with developing countries, and other developed countries are following suit.[2]

These measures are directed principally toward improving the economic climate for investment in the developing countries. Given the profit motivation of private enterprise, this approach seems well calculated. However, it does not take cognizance of factors such as worldwide ideological differences and political instability, which are only partially influenced by economics. And what is perhaps most important is the slowness with which Western business has been adapting itself to the conditions of the developing countries.

Economic Aid as a Source of Foreign Exchange

The flow of funds from the public sector of the developed Western countries has been the principal source of long-term capital for the economic growth of the developing countries.

Table 42–1 shows the distribution by source of both public and private capital imported by the developing countries.

The growth in the flow from the U.S. public sector has begun to level off. Also, the form of the flow from the public sector has changed in a way disadvantageous to the developing countries—namely, through the tying of loans. Furthermore, evidence suggests that the United States is unlikely to increase its absolute contribution in the near future. And the other developed Western countries, except possibly in the case of former colonial affiliations, are unlikely to increase their contributions.

In recent years, the United States has increasingly tied its foreign aid to the developing countries to the purchase of products manufactured in this country. The purpose of this measure is to offset a chronic deficit in the U.S. balance of payments. The disadvantages to the developing countries of aid tied to the purchase of products in the United States are readily apparent:

(1) There is a good possibility that some of the products purchased in the United States will be more expensive than comparable products purchased elsewhere.

(2) If this is true the developing country will have to supplement the aid with other funds to finance an equivalent quantity of goods or be content with purchasing smaller quantities.

2 United Nations, *World Economic Survey 1965. Part I, The Financing of Economic Development* (New York, 1966), p. 58.

TABLE 42-1

Flow of Aid from Developed Countries[1] (1960 and 1968)

Country	*Total Official and Private Resources*		*Official Resources*		*Development Assistance*		*Private Capital Flow*	
	1960	*1968*	*1960*	*1968*	*1960*	*1968*	*1960*	*1968*
Belgium	182.2*	243.0	101.0*	93.0	101.0	88.0	81.2	150.0
France	1,325.1	1,482.9	848.3	855.2	847.3	855.2	476.8	627.7
Netherlands	238.6	276.1	35.3	134.4	35.3	134.4	203.3	141.7
Portugal	(36.9)	48.1	36.9	34.8	36.9	34.8	—	13.3
United Kingdom	880.8	769.3	407.0	428.3	407.0	428.3	473.8	341.0
Italy**	298.3	550.4	105.1*	149.5	90.9	165.2	192.9*	400.9
Germany**	628.2	1,663.4	351.9	595.1	237.4	553.7	276.3	1,068.3
Japan**	246.1	1,049.3	143.5	808.8	105.1	355.2	102.6	240.5
Austria	5.7	73.7	.1	27.9	0.1	22.8	5.8	45.8
Denmark	37.9*	73.7	5.5	28.7	5.3	28.7	32.4*	45.0
Norway	10.2	57.7	10.1	23.1	5.2	25.5	.1	34.6
Sweden	46.6	128.8	6.7	71.4	6.7	71.4	39.9	57.4
Switz.	156.8	241.8	3.5	18.9	3.5	18.9	153.3	222.9
United States	3,818.2	5,809.0	2,776.0	3,605.0	2,702.0	3,314.0	1,042.2	2,204.0

[1] Includes both bilateral and multilateral aid. In thousands of U.S. dollars.
* Considerably higher than the year before or the year after.
** Official aid includes reparation payments.
Source: O.E.C.D., *Development Assistance Efforts and Policies of the Members of the D.A.C.*, 1969, pp. 296–99.

Colonial Tradition

Great Britain, France, Belgium, Portugal, and the Netherlands began aid activities as a result of having been colonial powers. Today, their aid still goes primarily to their ex-colonies.

While all of these countries talk about spreading their bilateral aid to more countries, only the French have made any kind of an attempt to broaden its aid. About 15 percent of all French aid now goes to countries which were not ex-French colonies. This is considerably higher than the percentage of bilateral aid from the other ex-colonial powers to countries where there are no historical ties.

As recipients of aid, the ex-colonies have several advantages. They are given more kinds of aid. In particular, receiving debt-servicing aid is a big advantage extended exclusively to these countries. They receive a high percentage of their aid in grant form or as "soft" loans. They are also given special trading advantages either through the British Commonwealth or through the EC. They also enjoy direct communication with their aid source through large administrative organizations which are designed to insure good communications. There are also the intangible advantages that accrue to a

TABLE 42-2

Flow of Resources Related to GNP and National Income

Country	Total Official and Private Resources GNP		Total Official and Private Resources NY		Official Resources GNP		Development Assistance GNP		Private Capital Flows GNP	
	1960	*1698*	*1960*	*1968*	*1960*	*1968*	*1960*	*1968*	*1960*	*1968*
Belgium	1.59	1.17	1.98	1.46	.88	.45	.88	.42	.71	.72
France	2.15	1.17	2.81	1.55	1.38	.68	1.38	.68	.78	.50
Netherlands	2.11	1.09	2.56	1.49	.31	.53	.31	.53	1.79	.56
Portugal	1.46	.94	1.66	1.09	1.46	.68	1.45	.68	–.	.26
United Kingdom	1.22	.75	1.50	.79	.56	.42	.56	.42	.65	.33
Italy	.88	.73	1.11	.96	.31	.20	.27	.22	.57	.53
Germany	.88	1.26	1.14	1.65	.49	.45	.33	.42	.39	.81
Japan	.57	.74	.69	.94	.33	.57	.24	.25	.24	.17
Austria	.09	.65	.12	.87	.–	.24	.–	.20	.09	.40
Denmark	.64	.59	.79	.70	.09	.23	.09	.23	.54	.36
Norway	.23	.64	.30	.85	.22	.26	.11	.28	.–	.38
Sweden	.36	.50	.46	.70	.05	.28	.05	.28	.31	.22
Switzerland	1.83	1.41	2.16	1.70	.04	.11	.04	.11	1.79	1.30
United States	.75	.66	.92	.81	.54	.41	.53	.38	.20	.25

Source: O.E.C.D., *Development Assistance Efforts and Policies of the Members of the D.A.C.*, 1969, pp. 306–8.

country when it knows it has some specific party it can turn to for financial assistance as well as other types of special assistance such as planning assistance.

The other developing countries do not share in these advantages. They are more likely to receive loans, must become more self-reliant if they are to survive, and they have a harder time communicating their needs to those countries which could help them if sympathetic to their problems.

Aid Programs

There are also major differences between the aid programs of these countries. The most obvious example is in the emphasis of the individual aid programs. France, for example, tends to emphasize the exportation of the French culture in her aid program. Portugal, on the other hand, tends to emphasize keeping control of her colonies while the British emphasize the need for self-reliance and the building of a viable economy in the areas where she gives her aid.

Germany, Japan, and Italy began their foreign aid programs as a result of reparations payments. For Germany and Japan, there was also the desire to become accepted members of the world community. Foreign aid was used to help achieve this goal.

There are major differences between the aid programs of the ex-colonial countries and those of Germany, Italy, and Japan. The reparations-paying countries have fewer forms of aid than the ex-colonial powers, but they give it to a broader range of countries. This statement needs to be modified to take into account the increasing concentration of Japanese aid in Asia. The reparations-paying countries have been heavy contributors to multilateral agencies. Germany, for example, is the second largest contributor, in absolute terms, to multilateral agencies. Only the United States contributes more.

Denmark, Sweden, and Norway are the newest countries in Europe to begin major aid programs. Being small countries, with limited resources, they have placed most of their funds in multilateral air organizations. What bilateral aid they do give is in the form of technical assistance. Each country assists in an area where it has special competence. For example, Denmark gives agricultural aid and Sweden gives health and family-planning assistance.

Other countries have smaller aid programs. Among those located in Europe are Spain, Switzerland, and Austria.

Communist Aid

Aid from the communist countries was about one-sixth of that provided by the developed Western countries during the 1955–65 period. Nearly 60 percent of the total was allocated to four countries: Afghanistan, India, Indonesia, and the United Arab Republic. The concentration of aid to strategically situated countries with weak or volatile governments underscores the political motivation of communist aid. Moreover, the emphasis on prestige projects that command worldwide attention (sports stadiums, main streets, a dam on the Nile) is obviously aimed at exploiting the propaganda value associated with such projects.

In fact, all things considered, the dollar value of the economic assistance from the communist countries is suspect. First, a full picture of such economic assistance must be pieced together from many sources by scanning newspapers and journals, monitoring radio broadcasts, reviewing government reports, and, occasionally, by noting official communiques issued by the contracting parties. In most instances, the details of the credit agreement are unclear or incomplete.

Even if a financial sum is assigned to the loan and is determined to be reasonably accurate, a second problem arises in converting the amount, which may be expressed in rubles, rupees, or some other monetary unit, to a dollar value for purposes of comparison. For example, rupees are converted into dollars at the official rate of exchange of the International Monetary Fund. But the dollar is a fully convertible currency, whereas the rupee has limited convertibility. Therefore, a dollar loan might be considered more valuable than a loan made in rupees. That is, even after conversion at the IMF rate, the rupee loan would still be overvalued.

This situation applies equally to the case of a ruble loan that, for purposes of statistical comparison, is converted to dollars at the official Soviet exchange rate. The evidence suggests that the Soviet exchange rate overvalues the ruble with regard to its purchasing power in terms of the U.S. dollar. Thus, loans made in rubles and converted to dollars at the arbitrary Soviet exchange rate are overvalued in terms of the U.S. dollar, and a comparison of such loans with those made by the developed Western countries can be grossly misleading.

The dual problem of sketchy and unauthenticated information regarding the details of credits extended by the communist countries and the statistical impurities likely to result from conversion of the foreign monetary value of such loans to dollar amounts for comparative purposes creates a "credibility gap" of sizable proportions.

External Debt

The inflow of borrowed funds to the developing countries has roughly quadrupled during the 1960–70 decade. In geographic distribution, South Asia and the Middle East have experienced a particularly rapid rise in the external debt (sixfold), and Latin America and Africa have registered comparatively modest increases. However, serious consideration is being given by high U. S. officials to methods of facilitating and stimulating both aid and lending to the Latin American countries.

The reason for this trend is twofold: the inability to export enough to earn the foreign exchange needed to pay for imports, and the inadequacy of indigenous capital markets to supply the funds required for economic and social development. Which of these two is more important is a matter of interpretation. Both are fundamental.

Whether the rapid growth of external debt will turn out to be a blessing or a curse for the developing countries remains to be seen. The potential danger lies in the increasing burden of fixed obligations created by the interest and amortization, commonly called the *debt service requirements,* which place a continuous drain on both the income and the foreign exchange reserves of these countries.

Debt-servicing capacity of developing countries is the relationship between export earnings and debt-service requirements. It therefore makes the implicit assumption that the long-term capital borrowed abroad has already been converted to productive uses and is making a positive contribution to export earnings. As discussed above, this may or may not be the case.

Whether the rapid growth of external debt will turn out to be a blessing or a curse for the developing countries remains to be seen. The potential danger lies in the increasing burden of fixed obligations created by the interest and amortization, commonly called the *debt-service requirements,* which place a continuous drain on both the income and the foreign exchange reserves of these countries.

Debt-servicing capacity is the relationship between export earnings and debt-service requirements. It therefore makes the implicit assumption that the long-term capital borrowed abroad has already been converted to productive uses and is making a positive contribution to export earnings. This may or may not be the case.

U.N. data indicate that the average annual increase in debt service is outstripping the average annual rise in export earnings with the result that reserve balances are being drawn down to debt-service requirements. This is an additional drain on reserve balances, which are also being reduced to cover the cost of imports not financed by earnings from exports. This condition will persist until the long-term capital borrowed from abroad is converted to uses that will cover the cost of debt-service requirements and produce export earnings in excess of expenditures on imports.

Unfortunately, the developing countries most vulnerable to this condition are those with the highest proportion of short-term debt, the highest ratio of service charges to export receipts, the lowest ratios of external liquidity to import expenditures, and the highest degree of export concentration in one or two primary commodities.

Summary

The total flow of external long-term capital—from earnings on exports, direct private foreign investment, and from the public sector of the developed countries, either bilaterally or through the multilateral agencies—is unlikely to increase in the near future. The assumed level flow of external long-term capital presupposes a continuing hardship on the developing countries because the level of debt service tends to rise faster than the level of new capital transfers. The result is a steady decline in the net amount of long-term capital available for economic development. Moreover, if the long-term funds are not converted to productive uses, the debt-service obligation must be met from reserve balances or by a reduction in short-term imports, either of which is anathema to most developing countries.

The developing countries are, therefore, confronted with a true dilemma. They need more external long-term capital for economic growth; but the evidence suggests that they do not presently have the capacity to take on increased quantities of new debt, at least on terms currently available.

Perhaps the developed countries can do more to ease the debt-service burden of the developing countries. Suggestions include measures such as moratorium, consolidation, rescheduling, and refinancing. In such cases, what has usually been involved is the spreading over time of previously incurred obligations to reduce their impact on the developing country's external balance.

With regard to the terms of long-term capital available to developing countries, numerous agencies will provide funds for well-planned projects over extended maturities at attractive rates of interest. In fact, since the advent of the International Development Association in 1960, the trend has been toward easier terms, both bilaterally and through the multilateral agencies.

In the final analysis, however, the resolution of the present dilemma rests with the developing countries themselves. They must utilize the long-term external funds presently available to them in a manner that will produce more export earnings or import substitutes, thereby not only meeting the mounting total of debt-service requirements but also making a steadily growing contribution to a rising standard of living. To accomplish this they must create the conditions necessary for an efficient allocation of resources and higher productivity. Whether this can be done without freedom of enterprise and an active participation of private capital will remain the focal issue.

Bibliography

Part I

Bishop, William W., Jr., ed., *International Law Cases and Materials* (2nd ed.). Boston: Little, Brown & Co., 1962.

Bloomfield, Lincoln P., "Law, Politics, and International Disputes," in *International Conciliation. The Carnegie Endowment for International Peace.* New York: The Carnegie Endowment, January 1958.

Carlston, Kenneth S., *Law and Organization in World Society.* Urbana, Illinois: University of Illinois Press, 1962.

Friedmann, Wolfgang, *The Changing Structure of International Law.* New York: Columbia University Press, 1964.

Hudson, Manley O., *Cases and Other Materials on International Law.* St. Paul, Minnesota: West Publishing Co., 1929.

Judicial and Statutory Definitions of Words and Phrases. St. Paul, Minnesota: West Publishing Co., 1904.

Katz, Milton and Kingman Brewster, Jr., *The Law of International Transactions and Relations, Cases and Materials.* Brooklyn: Foundation Press, Inc., 1960.

Krause, Walter, and John Mathis, *International Economics and Business: Selected Readings.* Boston: Houghton Mifflin Company, 1968, p. 444.

Loucks, William N., *Comparative Economic Systems.* New York: Harper & Row, Publishers, Inc., 1965.

Nehrt, Truitt and Virgil Wright, *International Business Research: Past, Present, and Future.* Bloomington: Indiana University, 1970.

Pratt, Edward Ewing, *Modern International Commerce.* Boston: Allyn and Bacon, Inc., 1956.

Salera, Virgil, *Multinational Business.* Boston: Houghton Mifflin Company, 1969.

Shaw, C., ed., *Legal Problems in International Trade and Investment.* Dobbs Ferry, New York: Oceana Publications, Inc., 1962.

Surrey, Walter Sterling, ed., *A Lawyer's Guide to International Business Transactions.* Philadelphia: Joint Committee on Continuing Legal Education of the American Law Institute and The American Bar Association, 1963.

Taylor, George E. and Ben Cashman, *The New United Nations.* Washington, D.C.: American Enterprise Institute for Public Policy Research, 1965.

Terpstra, Vern, *International Business Course Descriptions.* Ann Arbor: University of Michigan, 1970.

Zenoff, David B., *International Business Management.* New York: The Macmillan Company, 1971.

Part II

Aitkin, T., Jr., *Foreign Policy for American Business.* Harper & Row, Publishers, Inc., 1962.

Allen, K. G. D. and J. E. Ely, *International Trade Statistics.* New York: John Wiley & Sons, Inc., 1953.

Bach, George Leland, *Economics: An Introduction to Analysis and Policy* (6th ed.). Englewood Cliffs, New Jersey: Prentice-Hall, Inc., 1968.

Bauer, Raymond A., I. di Sola Poll, and Lewis Dexter, *American Business and Public Policy: The Politics of Foreign Trade.* New York: Atherton Press, 1963.

Cohen, Benjamin J., *American Foreign Economic Policy.* New York: Harper & Row, Publishers, 1968.

East-West Trade, A Common Policy for the West, a statement on National Policy by the Research and Policy Committee for Economic Development, May 1970.

Eesti NSV Teaduste Akadeemia Majanduse Instituut, *Eesti NSV Majanduslikud Sidemed NSV Liidu Rahvamajanduse Süsteemis.* Tallinn: Kirjastus Eesti Raamat, 1965 (Economic Institute of The Academy of Sciences, Estonian S.S.R.).

Ellsworth, P. T., *The International Economy* (3rd ed.). New York: The Macmillan Company, 1964.

Fforde, J. S., *International Trade in Managerial Skills.* Oxford: Basil, Blackwood and Mott, 1957.

Gates, T. R. and F. Linden, *Costs and Competition: American Experience Abroad.* New York: National Industrial Conference Board, 1961.

Grub, P. and K. Holbik, *American-East European Trade.* The National Press, 1969.

Haberler, G., *A Survey of International Trade Theory.* Special Papers in International Economics, No. 1. Princeton, New Jersey: Princeton University Press, 1961.

Johnson, Harry G., *Harmonization of National Economic Policies Under Free Trade.* Toronto: University of Toronto Press, 1968, pp. 71–84.

Kolde, E. J., "Eesti Rahva Vabadus Maailma Uhiskondliku Arengu Taustal." *Tulimuld,* XXI, No. 3, (1970), 122–30.

———, "International Trade Policy at the Crossroads." *The Korean Business Journal* III, No. 1, March 1969, 92 ff.

Mathur, P. N., "Gains in Economic Growth from International Trade—A Theoretical Explanation of Leontief's Paradox." *Kyklos,* XVI, No. 4 (1963), 609–25.

Meade, J. E., "The Theory of International Economic Policy," vol. 2 of *Trade and Welfare.* London: Oxford University Press, 1955.

Metzler, L., "The Theory of International Trade," in *Survey of Contemporary Economics,* I, ed. Howard S. Ellis. Homewood, Illinois: Richard D. Irwin, Inc., 1948.

Ohlin, Bertil, *Utrikeshandel och Handels politik.* Stockholm: Bokförlaget Natur och Kultur, 1943.

Sumberg, Theodore A., "Free-Trade Zone in Latin America," *Inter-American Economic Affairs,* XIV, No. 1 (Summer 1960), 51–64.

———, *The Tariff History of the United States* (6th ed.). New York: G.P. Putnam's Sons, 1914.

Taussig, Frank William, *Selected Readings in International Trade and Tariff Problems.* Boston: Ginn & Company, 1921.

Travis, W.F., "International Trade Theory and the Trade Expansion Act of 1962," *Daedalus, LXXXXI* (Summer 1962), 527–42.

Vernon, Raymond, *Manager in the International Economy.* Prentice-Hall, Inc., 1968.

Wilczynski, Jozef, *The Economics and Politics of East-West Trade,* New York: Frederick A. Praeger, Inc., 1969.

Part III

Adams, Walter, *The Brain Drain,* New York, The Macmillan Company, 1968.

Axelrod, Robert, *Conflict of Interests.* Chicago: Markham Publishing Company, 1970.

Baker, Palmer, "European Taxation of Foreign Source Income," in *Taxes and International Business, a Symposium.* New York: National Association of Manufacturers, November 1964.

Balderston, F. E., "Models of Multiple Branch Organization," *California Management Review,* IV, No. 3 (Spring 1962), 4–12.

Ballon, Robert J., *Joint Ventures and Japan*. New York: Charles E. Tuttle Co., 1967.

Behrman, Jack N., *National Interests and the Multinational Enterprise*. Englewood Cliffs, New Jersey: Prentice-Hall, Inc., 1970.

———, *Some Patterns in the Rise of the Multinational Enterprise*. Chapel Hill: University of North Carolina, 1968.

———, *U.S. International Business and Governments*. New York: McGraw-Hill, 1971.

Brewster, Kingman, Jr., *Anti-Trust and American Business Abroad*. New York: McGraw-Hill Book Company, 1958.

Chandler, A.D., *Strategy and Structure*. Cambridge, Massachusetts: The M.I.T. Press, 1962.

Donner, F. G., "World Wide Corporations in a Modern Economy," *Canadian Chartered Accountant*, LXXXII, No. 1 (January 1963), 34–38.

El Sherbini, Abel Aziz, "The Quandary of Foreign Manufacturing Affiliates in Less-Developed Countries," *California Management Review*, VII, No. 3 (Spring 1965), 7–14.

Ewing, John S. and Frank Meissner, eds., *International Business Management: Readings and Cases*. Belmont, California: Wadsworth Publishing Co., Inc., 1964.

Farmer, Richard N., *International Management*. Belmont, California: Dickenson Publishing Co., 1968.

Farmer, Richard N. and Barry M. Richman, *International Business, An Operational Theory*. Homewood, Illinois: Richard D. Irwin, Inc., 1966.

Fayerweather, John, *Management of International Operations*. New York: McGraw-Hill Book Company, 1960.

Friedmann, Wolfgang C. and George Kalmanoff, *Joint International Business Ventures*. New York: Columbia University Press, 1961.

Gabriel, Peter P., *The International Transfer of Corporate Skills: Management Contracts in Less Developed Countries*, Boston: Harvard University, 1967.

Gordon, Nathan, "The Role of Tax Treaties," in *Taxes and International Business, a Symposium*. New York: National Association of Manufacturers, 1962.

Haire, M. and others, "Cultural Patterns in the Role of the Manager," *Industrial Relations*, II, No. 2 (February 1963), 95–118.

Hall, Edward T. and W. F. White, "Intercultural Communications: A Guide to Men of Action," *Human Organization*, XIX, No. 1 (Spring 1960).

Harbison, Frederick C. and Charles E. Myers, *Management in the Industrial World*. New York: McGraw-Hill Book Company, 1959.

Hellmann, Rainer (translated by Peter Ruof), *The Challenge to U.S. Dominance of the International Corporation*. New York: Dunellen, 1970.

Hirshleifer, Jack, "On the Economics of Transfer Pricing," *The Journal of Business*, XXIX, No. 3 (July 1956), 172–84.

Hodgson, Raphael and Michael Mickaelis, "Planning for Profit in World

Business," *Harvard Business Review,* XXXX, No. 2 (March–April 1962), 60–79.

Hodgson, Raphael and Hugo E. R. Uyterhoevens, "Analyzing Foreign Opportunities," *Harvard Business Review,* XXXX, No. 2 (March–April 1962), 60–79.

Homans G. C., *The Human Group.* New York: Harcourt, Brace & World, Inc., 1950.

Khusro, E., "An Investigation of Liquidity Preference," *Yorkshire Bulletin of Economics and Social Research,* IV, No. 1 (January 1952), 1–20.

Kircher, D. P., "Now the Transnational Enterprise," *Harvard Business Review,* XLII, No. 2 (March–April 1964), 6–11.

Kolde, E. J., "Administrative Structure of International Business with Special Reference to Foreign-Based Affiliates," *University of Washington Business Review,* XXII, No. 3 (February 1963), 38–50.

———, "Business Enterprise in a Global Context." *California Management Review.* Summer 1966, pp. 31–48.

———, "Culture Context of Multinational Organization." Seattle: University of Washington, 1971.

———, *International Business Enterprise.* Englewood Cliffs, New Jersey: Prentice-Hall, Inc., 1968.

———, "Les Fonctions des sociétés affiliées domiciliées à l'étranger dans la structure administrative d'une entreprise commerciale internationale," *Revue Economique et Sociale* (December 1962).

———, "Organization and Management of Overseas Affiliates in a Multinational Firm," *The Fifth Anniversary Review.* Graduate School of Business Administration, Seoul National University, 1971.

———, "Strategy—The Firm and International Business Policy," in *Proceedings of NUBAC Conference.* Vancouver, Canada: University of British Columbia, October 1964.

———, *Working Papers on the Organization and Behavior of the Multinational Firm.* Seattle: Graduate School of Business Administration, University of Washington, 1972.

Kolde, E. J., and Richard E. Hill. "Conceptual and Normative Aspects of International Management," *Academy of Management Journal,* X, No. 2 (June 1967), 119–28.

Learned, E. P., F. J. Aguilar, and R. C. K. Valtz, *European Problems in General Management.* Homewood, Illinois: Richard D. Irwin, Inc., 1963.

Lewis, R. and R. Stewart, *The Managers: A New Examination of the English, German and American Executive.* New York: Mentor Press, 1961.

Linfield, Seymour L., "Looking Around: Overseas Operations," *Harvard Business Review.* XXXVIII, No. 5 (September–October 1960), 41–50.

Litvak, I. A. and C. J. Maule, "Conflict Resolution and Extraterritoriality," *The Journal of Conflict Resolution,* September 1969.

Lovell, E. B., *Managing Foreign Base Corporations.* New York: National Industrial Conference Board, 1963.

Loyd, P. J., *International Trade Problems of Small Nations,* Durham, N.C.: Duke University Press, 1968.

McCreary, E. A., "Those American Managers Don't Impress Europe," *Fortune,* LXX, No. 6 (December 1964), 138–39.

McMurray, Robert, "Where Out-of-Pocket Costs Make the Best Transfer Price," *N.A.A. Bulletin,* XXXXII, No. 12 (August 1961), 33–34.

Meek, Marcellus R., "Intercorporate Pricing in Foreign Operations," in *Marquette University Institute on Taxation.* Milwaukee, 1962.

Mikesell, R. F., ed., *U.S. Private and Government Investment Abroad.* Eugene, Oregon: University of Oregon Books, 1962.

Mock, Edmond J., "Financing Overseas Subsidiaries and Evaluating Their Earnings," *Business Topics,* XII, No. 3 (Summer 1964), 31–37.

"Multinational Companies," *Business Week,* No. 1755 (April 20, 1963), 62–68.

National Industrial Conference Board, Inc., *Managing Foreign-Base Corporations.* New York, 1963.

O'Connell, D. J., and J. L. Benson, "Sourcing Abroad for Domestic Profit," *Harvard Business Review,* XXXXI No. 2 (March–April 1963), 87–94.

Patinkin, Don, "Multiple-Plant Firms, Cartels, and Imperfect Competition," *The Quarterly Journal of Economics,* LXI, No. 2 (February 1947), 173–205.

Peloubet, Maurice, "European Experience with Value-Added Taxation," in *Tax Institute of America.* Princeton, New Jersey, October 1963.

Pizer, S. and F. Cutler, "U.S. Trade with Foreign Affiliates of U.S. Firms," *Survey of Current Business,* XXXXIV, No. 12 (December 1964), 20–26.

Richman, Peggy, *Taxation of Foreign Investment Income and Economic Analysis.* Baltimore: Johns Hopkins Press, 1963.

Robinson, Richard D., *International Business Policy.* New York: Holt, Rinehart & Winston, 1964.

Rolfe, Sidney E., *The International Corporation.* Istanbul: The International Chamber of Commerce, 1969.

Root, Franklin, "U.S. Business Abroad and the Political Risk," *MSU Business Topics.* Winter 1968, pp. 73–79.

Rose, S., "The Rewarding Strategies of Multinationalism," *Fortune,* September 15, 1968.

Servan-Schreiber, J.-J., *The American Challenge,* New York: Atheneum, 1968.

Skinner, C. W., "Management of International Production," *Harvard Business Review,* XXXXII, No. 5 (September–October 1964), 125–36.

Steiner, George Albert, *Multinational Corporate Planning,* New York: Macmillan 1966.

Task Force on the Structure of Canadian Industry, *Foreign Ownership and the Structure of Canadian Industry,* Privy Council Office, Ottawa, 1968.

Vernon, R., "Saints and Sinners in Foreign Investment," *Harvard Business Review,* XLI, No. 3 (May-June 1963), 146–61.

Weintrants, Leon, *International Manpower Development.* New York: Frederick A. Praeger, Inc., 1969.

Yoshino, M.Y. "Administrative Attitudes and Relationships in a Foreign Culture," *MSU Business Topics.* Winter 1968.

Part IV

Aufricht, Hans, *The International Monetary Fund.* New York: Frederick A. Praeger, Inc., 1964.

Badger, D. G., "The Balance-of-Payments: A Tool of Economic Analysis," *International Monetary Fund Staff Papers.* Washington, D.C., September 1961.

Balassa, Bela, ed., *Changing Patterns in Foreign Trade and Payments.* New York: W. W. Norton & Company, Inc., 1964.

Bernstein, E. M., "Strategic Factors in Balance of Payments Adjustment," *International Monetary Fund Staff Papers.* Washington, D.C., August 1956.

Bloomfield, A. I., "Short-Term Capital Movements Under the Pre-1914 Gold Standard," *Princeton Studies in International Finance,* No. 11, Princeton, New Jersey: International Finance Section, Department of Economics, Princeton University, 1963.

Crump, N., *The A B C of the Foreign Exchange Market.* London: Macmillan & Co., Ltd., 1963.

Dufay, Gunter, *The Eurobond Market.* Seattle: Graduate School of Business Administration, University of Washington, 1969.

Evitt, H. E., *A Manual of Foreign Exchange* (4th ed.). London: Sir Isaac Pitman & Sons, Ltd., 1955.

Export and Import Procedures. New York: Morgan Guaranty Trust Co., July 1962.

Friedman, Milton, "The Case for Flexible Exchange Rates," in *Essays in Positive Economics.* Chicago: University of Chicago Press, 1953.

Gustav, Cassel, *Money and Foreign Exchange After 1914.* New York: The Macmillan Company, 1922.

Haberler, Gottfried, "The Market for Foreign Exchange and the Stability of the Balance of Payments." *Kylos,* III, No. 3 (1949), 193–218.

Hawtrey, H. G., *The Gold Standard in Theory and Practice* (5th ed.). London: Longmans, Green & Company, Ltd., 1947.

Henning, Charles, *International Finance.* New York: Harper & Row, Publishers, Inc., 1958.

International Monetary Arrangements: The Problem of Choice, Report on the Deliberations of an International Study Group of 32 Economists. Princeton, New Jersey: International Finance Section, Princeton University, 1964.

International Monetary Fund, *Annual Reports 1963, 1964, 1965.* Washington, D.C.

———, *Articles of Agreement: United Nations Monetary and Financial Conference, Bretton Woods, New Hampshire.* Washington, D.C.: U.S. Dept. of the Treasury, 1964.

———, *Balance of Payments Manual* (3rd ed.). Washington, D.C., 1961.

———, *International Reserves and Liquidity.* Washington, D.C., 1958.

Kindleberger, C. P., *International Economics* (4th ed.). Homewood, Illinois: Richard D. Irwin, Inc., 1968.

Kindleberger, Charles P., "Measuring Equilibrium in the Balance of Payments," *Journal of Political Economy,* November/December 1969.

Klopstock, Fred H., "Impact of Euromarkets on the United States Balance of Payments," *Law and Contemporary Problems,* Winter 1969.

Laffer, Arthur B., "The U.S. Balance of Payments—A Financial Center View,"

Lederer, Walter, "Measuring the Balance of Payments," in *Factors Affecting the U.S. Balance of Payments,* 87th Cong. 2nd sess., Joint Economic Committee. Washington, D.C.: U.S. Government Printing Office, 1962.

Machlup, Fritz, "Three Concepts of the Balance of Payments and the So-Called Dollar Shortage," *Economic Journal,* LX, No. 237 (March 1950), 46–68.

National Industrial Conference Board, *Obstacles and Incentives to Private Foreign Investment 1967–68,* New York, 1969.

Nehrt, Lee C., *International Finance for Multinational Business.* Scranton, Pennsylvania: International Textbook, 1967.

Nurkse, R., "Conditions of International Monetary Equilibrium," in *Readings in the Theory of International Trade,* eds. H.S. Ellis and L.A. Metzler. Homewood, Illinois: Richard D. Irwin, Inc., 1949.

Orcutt, Guy, "Measurement of Price Elasticities in International Trade," *Review of Economics and Statistics,* XXXII, No. 2 (May 1950), 117–32.

Sammons, R. J., "Some Balance-of-Payments Pitfalls: Comment," *American Economic Review,* XLI, No. 5 (December 1951), 938–39.

Scammell, W. M., *International Monetary Policy.* New York: St. Martin's Press, Inc., 1957.

Scott, Ira O., *European Capital Markets,* Office of the Comptroller of the Currency, 1968.

Southard, F. A., *Foreign Exchange Practice and Policy.* New York: McGraw-Hill Book Company, 1940.

Stein, Jerome L., "The Nature and Efficiency of the Foreign Exchange Market," in *Essays in International Finance. Princeton,* New Jersey: Princeton University Press, October 1962.

U.S. Dept. of Commerce, *The Balance of Payments of the U.S. 1949–51.* Washington, D.C.: U.S. Government Printing Office, 1952.

Vernon, Raymond, *Manager in the International Economy.* Englewood Cliffs: Prentice-Hall, Inc., 1968.

Wasserman, J. M., L. W. Hultman, and L. Zsoldos, *International Finance.* New York: Simmons-Boardman Publishing Corp., 1963.

Yeager, L. B., "A Rehabilitation of Purchasing Power Parity Theory," *Journal of Political Economy,* LXVI, No. 6 (December 1958), 516–30.

Zenoff, David B. and Jack Zwick, *International Financial Management.* Englewood Cliffs: Prentice-Hall, Inc., 1969.

Part V

American Marketing Association, *Marketing Definitions.* Chicago, 1960.

Brink, E. L. and W. T. Kelley, *The Management of Promotion.* Englewood Cliffs, New Jersey: Prentice-Hall, Inc., 1963.

Bryson, G. D., *American Management Abroad.* New York: Harper & Row, Publishers, Inc., 1961.

Clemens, Eli W., "Price Discrimination and the Multiple-Product Firm," in *Readings in Industrial Organization and Public Policy,* ed. The American Economic Association. Homewood, Illinois: Richard D. Irwin, Inc., 1958.

Cracco, Etienne, *International Business—1970. A Selection of Current Readings,* East Lansing: Michigan State University, 1970.

Due, John F., *Intermediate Economic Analysis* (3rd ed.). Homewood, Illinois: Richard D. Irwin, Inc., 1956.

Eastman, J. K., *Graphical Economics.* Chicago: Quadrangle Books, 1960.

Edgett, R. H., "Strategy—Development of International Markets," in *Proceedings of NUBAC Conference.* Vancouver, Canada: University of British Columbia, October 1964.

Emori, Morihisa, *The Japanese Trading Company,* Tokyo: Mitsubishi Shoji Kaisha, 1968.

Howard, J. A., *Marketing Management.* Homewood, Illinois: Richard D. Irwin, Inc., 1963.

Lavidge, R. J. and G. A. Steiner, "A Model for Predictive Measurements of Advertising Effectiveness," *Journal of Marketing,* XXV, No. 6 (October 1961), 59–62.

McCarthy, E. J., *Basic Marketing: A Managerial Approach.* Homewood, Illinois: Richard D. Irwin, Inc., 1964.

Mauer, William A. and Thomas H. Naylor, "Monopolistic-Monopsonistic Competition: The Multi-Product, Multi-Factor Firm," *The Southern Economic Journal,* XXXI, No. 1 (July 1964), 38–43.

Roseborough, H., "Some Sociological Dimensions of Consumer Spending," *Canadian Journal of Economics and Political Science,* XXVI, No. 3 (August 1960), 452–64.

Ryan, W. J. L., *Price Theory.* London: Macmillan & Co., Ltd., 1962.

Shillinglaw, Gordon, *Cost Accounting: Analysis and Control.* Homewood, Illinois: Richard D. Irwin, Inc., 1961.

Stanley, Alexander O., *Handbook of International Marketing.* New York: McGraw-Hill Book Company, 1963.

Watson, Donald Stevenson, *Price Theory and Its Uses.* Boston: Houghton Mifflin Company, 1963.

Westfield, Fred M., "Marginal Analysis, Multi-Plant Firms, Business Practice: An Example," *The Quarterly Journal of Economics,* XIX, No. 2 (May 1955), 256–68.

Part VI

Balassa, Bela, *The Theory of Economic Integration.* Homewood, Illinois: Richard D. Irwin, Inc., 1961.

Bienen, Henry, "An Ideology for Africa," *Foreign Affairs,* April 1969, p. 545 ff.

Calman, John, ed., *The Common Market.* Belfast: Anthony Blond, 1967, pp. 9–29, 64–74.

Clark, Colin, *The Common Market and British Trade.* New York: Frederick A. Praeger, Inc., 1962.

Cochrane, James D., "U.S. Attitudes Toward Central American Integration," *Inter-American Economic Affairs,* XVIII, No. 2 (Autumn 1964), 73–92.

Coppock, John O., *North Atlantic Policy—The Agriculture Gap.* New York: Twentieth Century Fund, Inc., 1963.

Davis, Lance E., Jonathan R. T. Hughes, and Duncan M. McDougall, *American Economic History.* Homewood, Illinois: Richard D. Irwin, Inc., 1961.

Dell, S., *Trade Blocs and Common Markets.* New York: Alfred A. Knopf, Inc., 1963.

Diebold, William, Jr., *The Schuman Plan.* New York: Frederick A. Praeger, Inc., 1959.

Doski, Richard S., "The Montevideo Treaty and New Trade," *Inter-American Economic Affairs,* XIV, No. 3 (Winter 1960), 117–20.

Ebres, R., *L'Integration Economique Internationale.* Paris: Presses Universitaires de France, 1966.

European Economic Community, *Treaty Establishing the European Economic Community* (English language edition). Brussels, 1957.

European Free Trade Association, *Convention Establishing the European Free Trade Association.* London: H.M. Stationery Office, 1960.

Farag, Attiat, "The Latin American Free Trade Area," *Inter-American Economic Affairs,* XVII, No. 1 (Summer 1963), 73–84.

Frank, Isaiah, *The European Common Market: An Analysis of Commercial Policy.* New York: Frederick A. Praeger, Inc., 1961.

Graduate Institute of International Studies, *The European Free Trade Association And The Crisis of European Integration.* London: Michael Joseph, Ltd., 1968.

Green, R. H. and K. G. V. Krishna, *Economic Cooperation in Africa: Retrospect and Prospect.* Nairobi: Oxford University Press, 1967.

Griffin, Keith B., "The Potential Benefits of Latin American Integration," *Inter-American Economic Affairs,* XVII, No. 4 (Spring 1964), 3–20.

Hirschman, A. O., ed., *Latin American Issues, Essays and Comments.* New York: Twentieth Century Fund, Inc., 1961.

Humphrey, D. D., *The United States and The Common Market.* New York: Frederick A. Praeger, Inc., 1963.

Kelley, W. B., ed., *Studies in United States Commercial Policy.* Chapel Hill, North Carolina: The University of North Carolina Press, 1963.

Kenen, Peter B., *International Economics.* Englewood Cliffs, New Jersey: Prentice-Hall, Inc., 1964.

Kolde, Endel J., "Transformation of International Business Relations," in *World Trade and the Citizen,* pp. 3–16. Vancouver: University of British Columbia, 1967.

Kojima, Kiyoshi (editor), *Pacific Trade and Development,* Paper No. 9, The Japan Economic Research Center, Tokyo, 1968.

Letiche, J. M., "Reciprocal Trade Agreements in the World Economy," *American Economic Review,* XLVIII, No. 5 (December 1958), 954–66.

Lopez del Carril, Nelson J., *Integración Latinomericana y Derecho Comunitaro.* Buenos Aires: Abeledo-Perrot, 1967.

Maritano, Nino, *A Latin American Economic Community.* Notre Dame, Indiana: University of Notre Dame Press, 1970.

Moulin, Leo, ed., *L'Europe de Demain et Ses Responsables.* Bruges: College d'Europe, 1967.

Pincus, Joseph, *The Central American Common Market.* Washington, D.C.: Agency for International Development, U.S. Dept. of State, 1962.

Robson, Peter, *Economic Integration in Africa.* Evanston: Northwestern University Press, 1968.

Ruiz Gracia, Enrique, *Europa de los Europeos O Europa de los Americanos.* Madrid: Ediciones Cid, 1966.

Solomon, A. M., "The Economic Integration of Latin America," *The Department of State Bulletin* (October 23, 1967).

United Nations, Economic Commission for Latin America, *The Latin American Common Market.* New York, 1959.

———, *Report of the Central American Economic Co-operation Committee.* New York, 1957–58 and 1958–59.

———, "The Montevideo Treaty," *Inter-American Economic Affairs,* XIV No. 2 (Autumn 1960), 19–28.

Urquidi, Victor L., *Challenge of Development in Latin America.* New York: Frederick A. Praeger, Inc., 1964.

———, *Free Trade and Economic Integration in Latin America.* Berkeley: University of California Press, 1964.

Varga, Eugene, "Theoretical Problems of the Economies of the Common Market," *Problems of Economics* (October 1962).

Wionczek, Miguel S., *Latin American Free Trade Association,* International Conciliation, No. 551. New York, January 1965.

Part VII

Agarwals, Amar N., *Education for Business in a Developing Society.* East Lansing: Michigan State University, 1969.

Agency for International Development, *Gross National Product, Growth Rates and Trend Data,* Washington: U.S. Govt. Printing Office, 1970.

Alexander, Robert J., *Labor Relations in Argentina, Brazil and Chile.* New York: McGraw-Hill Book Company, 1962.

Alpert, Paul, *Economic Development.* New York: Free Press of Glencoe, Inc., 1963.

Apter, David E., *The Gold Coast in Transition.* Princeton, New Jersey: Princeton University Press, 1955.

Apter, D. E., *The Politics of Modernization.* Chicago: University of Chicago Press, 1965.

Baran, Paul A., *The Political Economy of Growth.* New York: Monthly Review Press, 1962.

Barnard, Chester, *The Function of the Executive.* Cambridge, Massachusetts: Harvard University Press, 1938.

Batten, J. D. and Dale H. Stouder, "Compensation & Job Evaluation," *Personnel Journal,* XLIV, No. 11 (December 1965), 609–12.

Bauer, P. T. and B. Yamey, *The Economics of Underdeveloped Countries.* Chicago: University of Chicago Press, 1957.

Baumol, William J., *Economic Theory and Operations Analysis.* Englewood Cliffs, New Jersey: Prentice-Hall, Inc., 1963.

Belshaw, Horace, "Industry and Agrarian Reform," *Far Eastern Survey,* XVI, No. 13 (July 1947), 153–56.

Benham, F. and H. A. Holley, *A Short Introduction to the Economy of Latin America.* London: Oxford University Press, 1960.

Black, Eugene R., "Poorer Countries Meet Population Growth," *The Commercial and Financial Chronicle* CXLIII, No. 6060 (June 1961), 14.

Blass, Walter P., "Economic Planning, European Style," *Harvard Business Review,* XLI, No. 5 (September–October 1963), 109–20.

Boeke, J. H., *Economics and Economic Policy of Dual Societies.* New York: Institute of Pacific Relations, 1953.

Bornstein, Morris, *Comparative Economic Systems.* Homewood, Illinois: Richard D. Irwin, Inc., 1965.

Clawson, Marion, ed., *Natural Resources and International Development.* Baltimore: Johns Hopkins Press, 1964.

Committee on Science and Public Policy, *The Growth of World Population.* Washington, D.C.: National Academy of Sciences, 1963.

Cooke, Morris, *Brazil on the March.* New York: McGraw-Hill Book Company, 1964.

Cowan, C. D., *The Economic Development of Southeast Asia.* London: George Allen & Unwin, 1964.

Curle, Alan, *Educational Strategy for Developing Societies.* London: Tavistock Publications, 1963.

Dasgupta, Ajit Kumar, Anitava Sen, and Jati Kumar Sengupta, *Planning and the Plans.* Calcutta: The Post-Graduate Book Mart, 1961.

Davis, Kingsley and Wilbert E. Moore, "Some Principles of Stratification," *American Sociological Review,* X, No. 2 (April 1945), 242–49.

Dobb, Maurice Herbert, *Soviet Economic Development Since 1917.* New York: International Publishers, 1948.

Edwin, M. Martin, *Development Assistance,* Organization for Economic Cooperation and Development, December, 1969.

Elkins, Walter, *Migrants and Proletarians.* London: Oxford University Press, 1960.

Enke, Stephen, *Economics for Development.* Englewood Cliffs, New Jersey: Prentice-Hall, Inc., 1963.

"Family Planning in China," *The Economist,* CIV (August 25, 1962), 705–6.

Food and Agricultural Organization of the United Nations, *Production Yearbook, Volume 17, 1963.* Rome, 1964.

Francis, Roy G., *The Population Ahead.* Minneapolis: University of Minnesota Press, 1958.

Friedmann, John and Alonso Niellian, *Regional Development and Planning.* Cambridge, Massachusetts: The M.I.T. Press, 1964.

Froehlich, W., "Land Tenure," in *Industrialization and Social Stability: Experience and Prospects in Asia.* Milwaukee: Marquette University Press, 1961.

Frost, Raymond, *The Backward Society.* New York: St. Martin's Press, Inc., 1961.

Galbraith, J. K., *Economic Development.* Cambridge: Harvard University Press, 1967.

Galenson, Walter, ed., *Labor and Economic Development.* New York: John Wiley & Sons, Inc., 1959.

———, ed., *Labor in Developing Economies.* Los Angeles: University of California Press, 1962.

Geiger, Theodore and Winsfred Armstrong, *The Development of African Private Enterprise.* Washington, D.C.: National Planning Association, March 1964.

Gerschenkron, A., *Economic Backwardness and Historical Perspective,* Cambridge: Harvard University Press, 1962.

Ginzberg, Eli, *Human Resources.* New York: Simon and Schuster, Inc., 1958.

Gordon, Lincoln, "Private Enterprise and International Development," *Harvard Business Review,* XXXVIII, No. 4 (July-August 1960). 134–38.

Hackett, J. and A. M. Hackett, *Economic Planning in France.* Boston: Harvard University Press, 1963.

Hanson, A. H., *Public Enterprise and Economic Development.* London: Routledge & Kegan Paul, Ltd., 1965.

Hanson, Simon G., *Economic Development in Latin America.* Washington, D.C.: The Inter-American Affairs Press, 1961.

Harbison, F. E. and C. A. Myers, *Education, Manpower and Economic Growth.* New York: McGraw-Hill Book Company, 1964.

Hennessy, Josselyn, Vera Lutz, and Giuseppe Scimone, *Economic 'Miracles.'* London: The Institute of Economic Affairs, 1964.

Hertzler, J. O., *The Crisis in World Population.* Lincoln, Nebraska: University of Nebraska Press, 1956.

Hickman, Bert G., ed., *Quantitative Planning of Economic Policy.* Washington, D.C.: The Brookings Institution, 1965.

Hirschman, Albert O., ed., *Latin American Issues.* New York: Twentieth Century Fund, Inc., 1961.

———, *The Strategy of Economic Development.* New Haven, Connecticut: Yale University Press, 1958.

"Human Resources and Economic Development," *Monthly Labor Review,* LXXXVI, No. 3 (March 1963), 262–67.

Huynh Thi Kieu-Dung, "Manpower Planning in Economic Development," 299 Research Paper, University of California, Berkeley, California, 1964.

International Labour Office, *Africa Labour Survey,* Studies and Reports. Geneva, 1958.

———, *Bulletin of Labor Statistics.* Geneva, annually beginning in 1965.

———, *Employment Objectives in Economic Development: Report of a Meeting of Experts,* Studies and Reports, New Series, No. 62. Geneva, 1961.

———, "Employment Prospects of Children and Young People in Asia," *International Labour Review,* LXXXVIII, No. 6 (December 1963), 564–95.

———, Fifth Asia Regional Conference of the I.L.O., "Labour and Human Resources Factors in Economic Development of Asia," *International Labour Review,* LXXXVII, No. 4 (April 1963), 293–314.

———, "The Population and Labour Force in Asia, 1950–80," *International Labour Review,* LXXXVI, No. 4 (October 1962), 348–68.

———, *Report of the Director General,* International Labor Conference, Sessions 37 and 39. Geneva, 1954 and 1966.

———, *Vocational Training in Latin America,* Studies and Reports, New Series, No. 28. Geneva, 1951.

———, *Why Labour Leaves the Land,* Studies and Reports, New Series, No. 59. Geneva, 1960.

———, *Yearbook of Labour Statistics, 1963.* Geneva, 1963.

———, *Yearbook of Labour Statistics, 1964,* 24th Issue, Geneva, 1964.

———, "Youth Employment and Vocational Training Schemes in the Developing Countries," *International Labour Review,* LXXXVI, No. 3 (September 1962), 209–34.

International Planned Parenthood Federation, *The Case for Planned Parenthood.* New York, 1965.

Ismangil, Wagiono, "The Nature and Role of Labor Movements in Developing Countries," 299 Research Paper, University of California, Berkeley, California, 1963.

Jacoby, Neil H., *The Progress of Peoples: Toward a Theory and Policy of Development with External Aid,* A Center Ocassional Paper, Santa Barbara: The Center for the Study of Democratic Institutions, June 1969.

Kapp, William K., "Economic Development, National Planning and Public Administration," *Kyklos,* VIII, No. 2 (1960) 172–204.

Kawashima, Takeyoshi, "A Summary and Analysis of the Familial Structure of Japanese Society," in *Japanese Character and Culture.* Tucson, Arizona: University of Arizona Press, 1962.

Kelly, W. B., ed., *Studies in United States Commercial Policy.,* Chapel Hill, North Carolina: The University of North Carolina Press, 1963.

Krause, Walter, *International Economics.* Boston: Houghton Mifflin Company, 1965.

Lanham, Elizabeth, *Administration of Wages and Salaries.* New York: Harper & Row, Publishers, Inc., 1963.

Leibenstein, Harvey, *Economic Backwardness and Economic Growth.* New York: John Wiley & Sons, Inc., 1957.

Levy, Marion J., Jr., "Some Social Obstacles to 'Capital Formation in Underdeveloped Areas' " in *Capital Formation and Economic Growth,* Moses Abramovitz, ed. Princeton, New Jersey: Princeton University Press, 1955.

Lodge, George C., *Spearheads of Democracy: Labor in the Developing Countries.* New York: Harper & Row, Publishers, Inc., 1962.

Malik, A. M., *Labor Problems and Policy in Pakistan.* Karachi: Pakistan Labor Publications, 1954.

Mason, Edward S., "The Planning of Development," *Scientific American* CCIX, No. 3 (September 1963), 235–44.

Meier, Gerald M., *Leading Issues in Development Economics.* New York: Oxford University Press, Inc., 1964.

Meier, Gerald M. and R. Baldwin, *Economic Development.* New York: John Wiley & Sons, Inc., 1957.

Moore, Wilbert E., *Industrialization and Labor.* Ithaca: Cornell University Press, 1951.

Müller, Kurt, *The Foreign Aid Programs of the Soviet Bloc and Communist China.* New York: Walker, 1967.

Myint, Hla, *The Economics of the Developing Countries.* New York: Frederick A. Praeger, Inc., 1964.

———, *Economic Theory and Underdeveloped Countries.* London: Oxford University Press, 1971.

Nurkse, Ragnar, *The Problems of Capital Formation in Underdeveloped Countries.* Oxford: Basil Blackwell, 1955.

Okun, B. and R. W. Richardson, eds., *Studies in Economic Development.* New York: Holt, Rinehart & Winston, Inc., 1962.

Organization of American States, *Economic Survey of Latin America, 1962.* Baltimore: Johns Hopkins Press, 1964.

Outflow of Trained Personnel From Developing Countries, United Nations, November 5, 1968.

Paauw, Douglas S., *Development Planning in Asia.* Washington, D.C.: National Planning Association, May 1965.

"People—Not Population," *The Economist.* CCXII (September 1964), 892–93.

Peterson, William, *Population.* New York: The Macmillan Company, 1962.

"Population Boom Would Ease Latin American Woes," *Burroughs Clearing House,* XLIV, No. 1 (October 1964), 77–80.

Piquet, Howard S., *Aid, Trade and the Tariff.* New York: Thomas Y. Crowell Company, 1953.

Powelson, John P., *Latin America: Today's Economic and Social Revolution.* New York: McGraw-Hill Book Company, 1964.

Prybyla, Jan S. and Harry G. Shafer, *From Underdevelopment to Affluence, Western, Soviet, and Chinese Views,* New York: Appleton-Century-Crofts, 1968.

Ramanadham, V. V., *The Finances of Public Enterprises.* New York: Asia Publishing House, 1963.

Research Committee on Foreign Aid, A symposium, a survey and appraisal by Indian Economic Center, 1968.

Robinson, R. D., *International Business Policy.* New York: Holt, Rinehart & Winston, Inc., 1964.

Schultz, Theodore W., "Economic Prospects of Primary Products," in *Economic Development for Latin America.* London: Macmillan & Co., Ltd., 1962.

Shannon, Lyle W., *Underdeveloped Areas—A Book of Readings and Research.* New York: Harper & Row, Publishers, Inc., 1957.

Sherbini, A. A., "Marketing in the Industrialization of Underdeveloped Countries," *Journal of Marketing,* XXIX, No. 1 (January 1965), 28-32.

Singer, H. W., *International Development: Growth and Change.* New York: McGraw-Hill Book Company 1964.

Stern, R. M., "International Compensation for Fluctuations in Commodity Trade," *Quarterly Journal of Economics,* LXXVII, No. 2 (May 1963), 258–73.

Szezepanik, E. F., *Symposium on Economic and Social Problems in the Far East.* Hong Kong University Press, 1962.

Taylor, George W. and Frank C. Pierson, *New Concepts in Wage Determination.* New York: McGraw-Hill Book Company, 1957.

Thompson, Warren S., *Population and Progress in the Far East.* Chicago: University of Chicago Press, 1959.

Tinbergen, Jan, *Central Planning.* New Haven, Connecticut: Yale University Press, 1964.

Tumin, Melvin T., "Some Principles of Stratification: A Critical Analysis," *American Sociological Review,* XVIII, No. 4 (August 1953), 387–93.

Udy, Stanley H., Jr., *Preindustrial Forms of Organized Work.* New Haven, Connecticut: Human Relations Area File Press, 1959.

UNCTAD Review of International Trade and Development, United Nations: New York, 1969.

United Nations, *Economic Bulletin for Asia and the Far East.* New York, June 1959 and September 1961.

———, *Formulating Industrial Development Programmes,* Development Programming Techniques Series No. 2. Bangkok, 1961.

———, *Planning for Economic Development.* New York, 1963.

U.N. Department of Economic and Social Affairs, *The Capital Development Needs of the Less Developed Countries.* New York, 1962.

———, *Domestic Financing of Economic Development.* New York, 1950.

———, *Patterns of Industrial Growth, 1938–58.* New York, 1960.

———, *Population Report for 1 July 1960.* Statistical Papers. New York, 1960.

———, *Report on the World Social Situation.* New York, 1961.

U.N. Economic Commission for Asia and the Far East, *Economic Survey of Asia and the Far East 1960.* Bangkok, 1960.

———, *World Economic Survey, 1962. II: Current Economic Developments.* New York, 1963.

U.N. Educational, Scientific, and Cultural Organization, *Facts and Figures.* New York, 1960.

U.N. Statistical Office, *Statistical Yearbook, 1963,* 15th Issue, New York, 1964.

———, *Yearbook of International Trade Statistics, 1962.* New York, 1964.

Urquidi, Victor L., *The Challenge of Development in Latin America.* New York: Frederick A. Praeger, Inc., 1962.

———, *Free Trade and Economic Integration in Latin America.* Berkeley: University of California Press, 1964.

U.S. Foreign Assistance In the 1970's: A New Approach, Report to the President from the Task Force on International Development, March 4, 1970.

Watanabe, S., "The Brain Drain From Developing to Developed Countries," *International Labor Review,* April, 1969.

Waterston, Albert, *Development Planning: Lessons of Experience.* Baltimore: Johns Hopkins Press, 1965.

———, "A Hard Look at Development Planning," *Finance and Development* (June 1965).

Wharton, Clifton R. "The Green Revolution: Cornucopia or Pandora's Box?" *Foreign Affairs,* April, 1969, p. 464 ff.

Yavenko, I., *Planning in the U.S.S.R.* Moscow: Foreign Languages Publishing House, 1962.

Zack, Arnold, *Labor Training in Developing Countries.* New York: Frederick A. Praeger, Inc., 1964.

Indexes

Indexes

Author Index

E

F

G

H

I

J

K

L

M

P

R

S

Subject Index

M

N

Nation-state concept, 77-79, 483

U

V

W

Z